The Reform Era in Russia (1855–1881) witnessed the emancipation of the serfs, economic and social change, the reform of all imperial institutions, and the growth of national identity among Russians and the Empire's expanding Jewish population. Consequently, the "Jewish Question" became one of the most hotly debated topics in Russia. Attitudes toward the Jews which evolved during this period persisted up to the Revolution and beyond. This book, based on exhaustive archival research of materials published during the period, studies the interplay of public opinion and official policy. The author examines the attitudes of all sectors of Russian educated society toward the Jews. He also explores how a new group, the Russian Jewish intelligentsia, sought to define a modern Jewish identity in the midst of a multi-ethnic Empire.

IMPERIAL RUSSIA'S JEWISH QUESTION, 1855–1881

Cambridge Russian, Soviet and Post-Soviet Studies

Series list continues on page 535

IMPERIAL RUSSIA'S JEWISH QUESTION, 1855–1881

JOHN DOYLE KLIER

Elizabeth and Sidney Corob Reader
in Modern Jewish History

University College London

CAMBRIDGE
UNIVERSITY PRESS

Published by the Press Syndicate of the University of Cambridge
The Pitt Building, Trumpington Street, Cambridge CB2 1RP
40 West 20th Street, New York, NY 10011–4211, USA
10 Stamford Road, Oakleigh, Melbourne 3166, Australia

First published 1995

Printed in Great Britain at the University Press, Cambridge

A catalogue record for this book is available from the British Library

Library of Congress cataloguing in publication data

Klier, John.
Imperial Russia's Jewish Question / John Doyle Klier.
   p.   cm. – (Cambridge Russian, Soviet and post-Soviet studies : 96)
Includes bibliographical references.
ISBN 0 521 46035 2
1. Jews – Russia – History – 19th century.
2. Russia – Ethnic relations.
3. Russia – History – Alexander II, 1855–1881.
I. Title. II. Series.
DS135.R9K534 1995
947.004924 – dc20   94–9145   CIP

ISBN 0 521 46035 2 hardback

CE

Contents

Acknowledgments

This book, the product of twenty years of research and writing, neatly encapsulates my entire academic career. It is a pleasure at last to be able to thank the many individuals and institutions who assisted its completion.

I began this work in my first academic post at Fort Hays State University in Hays, Kansas. The Department of History, the School of Arts, and the Graduate School at Fort Hays were consistently supportive of this project, providing release time, research materials, and travel funds. Fort Hays also granted me two leaves of absence and a sabbatical, which I spent as an Honorary Visiting Fellow at the School of Slavonic and East European Studies, University of London.

In 1977–8 and 1981–2 I participated in the Young Faculty Exchange between the US and the USSR, sponsored by the International Research and Exchanges Board. My first stay in the USSR was also supported by a Fulbright-Hayes Fellowship. This was a time when it was impossible openly to conduct research on Jewish topics in the USSR, and I was forced to work under a cover topic – "the growth and development of the Russian periodical press." Most of my research was conducted in the friendly surroundings of the Newspaper Reading Room of the Library of the Academy of Sciences (BAN) of the USSR, before the tragic fire in that institution. I read journals at the Saltykov-Shchedrin State Public Library in Leningrad, now renamed the Russian National Library. (Hopefully the time is not far distant when the the word "Public" will be restored to its title – it will always be "The Publichka" to me.) I also worked at the Lenin Library in Moscow.

Fort Hays supported a summer research visit to YIVO Institute for Jewish Research in New York. I spent a number of very pleasant summers participating in the Summer Research Laboratory at my Alma Mater, the University of Illinois, Urbana-Champaign. I also received a grant from the Kennan Institute for Advanced Russian Studies of The Woodrow Wilson Center in Washington, DC, to do research in the Library of Congress. The National Endowment for the Humanities sponsored my participation in a summer seminar at the University of Pennsylvania, directed by Professor Alfred Rieber.

I left Fort Hays in 1989 to take up a position in the Department of Hebrew and Jewish Studies at University College London, generously endowed by Sidney and Elizabeth Corob. Mid-voyage I spent a term at the Annenberg Institute for Judaic and Middle Eastern Studies in Philadelphia, Pennsylvania. The excellent facilities and supportive staff enabled me to complete a first draft of this book. University College London also generously assisted my research through the Office of the Dean of the Faculty of Arts, and the Institute of Jewish Studies, under its chairman Dr. Manfred Altman. I have also made research trips to the Russian Federation supported by the British Academy and the British Council.

In the waning days of the Soviet Union I was at last able to do extensive archival research on a Jewish theme. In 1991 I spent two months in Kiev through an exchange between the Canadian Institute of Ukrainian Studies of the University of Alberta and the Institute of History of the Ukrainian Academy of Sciences. I would like to thank Dr. Heorhii Kasianov, Dr. Tatiana Arseenko and Irina Sergeeva for their assistance. I am especially grateful for help which I received from personnel at the State Historical Archive of Ukraine. I have also been able to work at the Central State Historical Archives (TsGIA), now the Russian State Historical Archive in St. Petersburg, and at the Central State Archive of the October Revolution (TsGAOR), in Moscow, now metamorphised into the State Archive of the Russian Federation (GARF). I am deeply grateful to the many archivists and librarians who made this work possible. I also acknowledge bibliographical assistance from Dr. Genrich Deych and Valerii Gessen.

I wish to thank the British Library, the New York Public Library, and the university libraries of Illinois, California-Berkeley, Harvard, Yale, Columbia and Helsinki, Finland.

I would like to thank Tim Aspden for preparing the maps for this volume, and Ian Chapman for his lost weekend which produced the chart on page 224. I am especially grateful for the patience of my copy-editor at Cambridge University Press, Sheila Kane.

The manuscript of this study at times ballooned to over a thousand pages, so I am especially grateful to those who were willing to read all or part of it, and to recommend cuts and revision. These stout-hearted readers included Robert B. Luehrs, Jonathan Frankel, David Saunders, Hans Rogger and Benjamin Nathans. Their long suffering was exceeded only by the secretaries who typed variants of this work over the years, including Gloria Pfannenstiel, Mrs. Katie Edwards, and Mrs. Leah Chapman. Perhaps the greatest pleasure to emerge from the opening of the closed society in Eastern Europe has been the opportunity to discuss and debate aspects of this work with native scholars. I had especially fruitful discussions with Dr. Viktor Kelner, Dr. Aleksandr Lokshin, and Viktoriia Khiterer. I especially thank Professor Ralph T. Fisher for his help, support and encouragement over very many years.

Pity the spouse and children of historians forced to suffer the curse of "The Book," which drains away energy and time from family life. Sebastian and Sophia, perhaps because they are such keen readers themselves, were always sympathetic to these demands, while providing a welcome distraction from them. This book is dedicated to my wife Helen, not only for her patience and valuable editorial advice, but for forcing me to keep always in mind the reader's most important question: "What's the point?"

To Helen
for love in a cold climate

Preface

The goal of this study is to explore the genesis and development of public opinion on the Jewish Question in the Russian Empire between 1855 and 1881. Simply put, what did interested parties understand by the expression "the Jewish Question," and how did they propose to resolve it? In turn, what impact did public opinion have on the Jewish policies of imperial Russia during the Reform Era?

How is it even possible to speak of "public opinion" in the middle of the nineteenth century in the Russian Empire? At the beginning of the reign of Alexander II in 1855, there were twenty illiterates for every Russian who could read. The absolute total of literates was no more than 800,000 in an empire of approximately 68 million persons, and even then the majority were unsophisticated town and country readers, satisfied with devotional literature and the adventure yarns characteristic of the so-called *lubochnaia* literature.[1] As late as 1897, only 21 percent of the population claimed to be literate. At the outset of the Reform Era, the voice of public opinion was conveyed by literary monthlies with a total circulation of no more than 30,000 subscribers, and 67 general interest newspapers selling about 65,000 issues. Even the most popular newspapers failed to sell more than 10,000 copies throughout the 1860s.[2] In 1856, there were 49 public libraries, serving perhaps 10–15,000 patrons. In 1868, a grand total of 568 bookshops provided for the entire Empire.[3] If the days of the "censorship terror" of Tsar Nicholas I – when, it was said, there were more censors than books published – were waning, the censorship bureaucracy was still in place.

The identity of these readers is crucial, for numbered among them was the small elite of educated persons known as *obshchestvo*, or "society." This melange of landowners great and small, professionals, intellectuals and even bureaucrats was precisely the element which the reform-minded government sought to enlist in the process of change. As the state pursued the perilous tasks of emancipating the peasantry and creating new public institutions, it invited society to collaborate with the government in identifying the evils of the day, and seeking solutions, a phenomenon known as glasnost. While the common people, the *narod*, were not consulted, this never prevented society from speaking in their name. Public opinion – in the sense of the attitudes of "society" – existed, was courted by the Tsar and his ministers, and its judgments were frequently taken to heart.[4]

This was demonstrably the case for the so-called Jewish Question. Heretofore discussion of the status of the Jewish population was a state monopoly. A censorship regulation dating to the time of Nicholas I specifically forbade the press to venture opinions on the civil status of the Jews. While the Jewish Question was thus *terra incognita* for society at the start of the Reform Era, by the time of Tsar Alexander II's assassination in 1881 it had become a major topic for public debate. No periodical, especially in the Pale of Settlement where most Jews resided, could plausibly avoid discussing it. All ideologies developed by post-emancipation society were constrained to declare a position on the Jews. It should be stressed that these positions did not follow neat ideological lines. This was due in part to the roles envisioned for the Jews in the complex economic and political strategies which the government devised for the imperial borderlands, but it also derived specifically from conscious government initiatives to place the Jewish Question on the public agenda.

Examples appeared at the very beginning of the Reform Era. Queried in 1858 on the possibility of permitting a press polemic on the status of the Jews in Russia, censorship officials welcomed a public debate "which will provide a new occasion for elucidating the matter, and which may assist the government to attain the goal of bringing the Jewish people closer to the other inhabitants of the Empire."[5] A newly formed commission, the Commission for the Organization of Jewish Life in the Empire, noted in 1872 how much it relied for information upon material which had appeared in both the Jewish and Russian periodical press.[6]

As in the capital, so in the provinces. In 1864 the Governor-General of Kiev, Podolia and Volynia provinces reported to the Ministry of Internal Affairs that he was using the local newspaper, *Kievlianin*, published with a state subsidy, to conduct a public debate on the vital question of the state Jewish school system.[7] In 1868, the Governor-General of the Northwest Region authorized a special commission to discuss the Jewish Question, taking care to have the event fully publicized in the official *Vilenskii vestnik*. In response to the anti-Jewish pogroms which coincided with the end of the Reform Era, Minister of Internal Affairs N. P. Ignatiev convoked a commission in every province of the Pale, to query society on the proper response to the Jewish Question. This process reached its logical conclusion in the revolutionary year 1905 when a meeting of the Committee of Ministers resolved that "the government can satisfactorally resolve the Jewish Question only if, in the course of its work, it pays attention to the views of the Russian population on this subject and, consequently, bases this or that measure on the firm foundation of public opinion."[8]

As this study will demonstrate, these sentiments were not mere rhetoric: public opinion and official policy enjoyed a truly symbiotic relationship throughout the Reform Era. Government initiatives, such as the relaxation of the Pale for some categories of Jews, set an agenda for Russian publicists. Press debates, such as the polemic regarding the activities of the Jewish kahal, helped to shape official attitudes toward the Jews. (Indeed, bureaucrats themselves did not shy away from contributing to press polemics on the subject.) The archives of imperial Russia are filled with press clippings relating to various aspects of the Jewish Question, not infrequently leading to official action.[9] The press spoke as the representative of society (and in the name of the *narod*), and the government listened.

The methodology of this study is straightforward: I have attempted to read all contemporary materials published in Russian relating to the Jewish Question. These materials fall into three main categories – the periodical press, books and pamphlets, and official documentation, both published and archival.

In the first category, I have conducted a detailed examination of the runs of approximately 200 periodical publications which appeared between 1855 and 1881. Most of these titles are newspapers. The public discussion of the Jewish Question corresponded to the period in which the newspaper began, slowly but surely, to displace the literary monthlies, the so-called "thick journals," as the carriers of public opinion. Early in the Reform Era, polemics on the Jews appeared almost equally in thick journals and newspapers, but the balance soon shifted almost entirely to the latter. Able to react quickly to events, bolstered by the creation of a network of local correspondents and the emergence of news services, free of the need to present an in-depth picture, newspapers were well positioned to deal with the bits of life that comprised the complicated mosaic of the Jewish Question. In addition, a number of Russia's most prominent publishers, such as

A. A. Kraevskii, M. N. Katkov and A. S. Suvorin, took a special interest in the Jewish Question. Major publications of the two capitals, *Golos, Sanktpeterburgskie vedomosti, Novoe vremia* and *Moskovskie vedomosti,* at one time or another made the Jewish Question their special preserve.

The Jewish Question in the Russian Empire was preeminently a question of the non-Russian borderlands – Ukraine, Belorussia, the Baltic provinces and Novorossiia – and the Kingdom of Poland. These were areas that witnessed the growth of a vigorous provincial press. The economic and social life of the region spawned such periodicals as *Odesskii vestnik* and *Novorossiiskii telegraf,* while the special political objectives of the government, especially the program of Russification, produced *Kievlianin, Vilenskii vestnik* and *Varshavskii dnevnik.* All of these newspapers played prominent roles in debates on the Jews.

Besides the giants of the press, this study also considers ephemeral and uninfluential publications. These papers were the detritus of Russian journalism, vanishing without epitaph or lament. They were pitched to the lowest common denominator of the reading public. It is just such newspapers, however, which provide insights into the commonplace, everyday local attitudes and concerns, such as never made their way into the columns of their more elevated contemporaries in the capitals. If nothing else, they were closer to the *narod,* especially in the towns, than more sophisticated and expensive publications.

Almost all of the publications reviewed here were published legally in the Russian Empire. There were a few exceptions, most notably the dissident Alexander Herzen's celebrated *Kolokol,* published in London, and the clandestine socialist press of the 1870s and 1880s. Their illegal character is significant, because they may be used as exemplars of what the Russian press might have looked like without censorship. A survey of their contents, in fact, suggests that the censorship made little qualitative difference to the range of issues explored in the press.

There were numerous books and pamplets published in Russia on aspects of the Jewish Question. With a few exceptions, such as the idiosyncratic productions of the renegade Polish priest Ippolit Liutostanskii, they failed to have the same impact as materials published in the periodical press. The surest criterion of the success of a book lay in the extent to which it was reviewed, discussed and plagiarized by the periodical press. A surprisingly large number of books were actually newspaper series republished in book or pamphlet form. The most influential and contentious book published on the Jews in nineteenth-century Russia, Iakov Brafman's *Book of the Kahal,* began its existence as a series of articles in the provincial *Vilenskii vestnik.*

The imperial government was diligent in publishing the huge mass of documentation generated by official commissions on the Jewish Question, if only for in-house use. The codification of Russian law, the *Polnoe sobranie zakonov*, frequently included the background to the promulgation of laws and decrees, offering valuable insights into the minds of policy makers.[10] In recent years, previously closed archives have been opened for the study of the Jewish Question. I have conducted research in the major archival collections of Kiev, Leningrad/St Petersburg and Moscow.

My work in the archives of the Chief Board of Press Affairs, responsible for press censorship, in St. Petersburg, led to my conclusion, more fully developed elsewhere, that the censor was an occasional hindrance to a full and open discussion of the Jewish Question, but ultimately was unable to prevent a full public debate.[11] This point is illustrated by reference to the guide to literature on the Jews and the Jewish Question published in 1892, *Sistematicheskii ukazatel' literatury o evreiakh*, without which I could not even have attempted this project. The *Ukazatel'* lists 9,579 main entries, with numerous sub-divisions. (My own research suggests that there is a third again as much material which was omitted from the *Ukazatel'*.) The articles cited ran the gamut from "proofs" that Jews engaged in ritual murder, to articulate calls for the complete civil and political emancipation of the Jews. Governmental policies were not exempt from rebuke. Virtually the only off-limits topics were works of Jewish prosyletism (the one area where the Russian Orthodox Church displayed an active interest in the Jews during this period), and open calls for violence against Jews, although contemporary Jewish publicists reckoned that virulent criticism of Jewish social and economic life had the same effect as outright incitement to violence. There was little that could be said about the Jewish Question that the Russian press did not say. There was much that appeared in the press which the Russian government took into consideration.

This study is divided into three parts. Part 1 deals with the onset of the Era of the Great Reforms, when the Russian state implemented a policy of glasnost, whereby society was invited to discuss a whole range of pressing social and economic issues, including the Jewish Question. Until the early 1860s the resultant discussions of the Jewish Question had an abstract and arcane quality. They featured philosophical debates over the national character of the Jews, and the mutual expression of good intentions by Jewish and gentile spokesmen. A specific group of Jewish activists, whom I describe as the

"Russian Jewish intelligentsia," emerged. They engaged the attention, sympathy and support of Russian society for their stated intention to draw the traditionalist Jewish community into the modern world. A vague consensus developed that Jews were to pursue rapprochement and "merger" with Russian society, itself grown more tolerant and accepting.

This public discussion occurred against the background of the first hesitant reform of the restricted legal position of the Jews. Reform was originally designed to exploit the mental and economic resources of the Jews for the needs of the state, but it also served as a symbolic pledge that the Jews too would share in the fruits of the Great Reforms.

Part 2 explores the process whereby the Jewish Question moved from the theoretical to the practical plane. While Jewish reform was carried out in time-honored fashion within the closed circle of the Russian bureaucracy, Russian society used the opportunity to develop its own concrete views and assumptions about the Jews. Upon occasion, this "public opinion" served to shape and influence governmental actions. Indeed, on the level of the provincial administration, officials at times welcomed or even solicited public consultation with knowledgeable elements of society, Jew and gentile.

This process occurred amidst the first major crisis of the Reform Era – the failure of the Empire's Polish policies, and the Polish uprising of 1863. This crisis brought the national question firmly to the fore, and focused attention on the imperial borderlands, where Jews were a significant minority, and an integral part of the existing socioeconomic system. Post-emancipation economic change, and debates over the various strategies of Russification, brought a greater urgency to debates surrounding the Jewish Question.

Part 3 examines the decade of the 1870s, when the Great Reforms were completed and fully implemented. The Empire began to suffer the pains of incipient modernization. The stresses of rapid social and economic change began to blight the naive optimism of the early Reform Era. This spirit of disenchantment was especially pronounced in the case of the Jewish Question. The role played by the Jews in the modernizing economy was consistently viewed in a negative light. The claims of the Russian Jewish intelligentsia to be successfully leading the processes of rapprochement and merger were sharply challenged. If, at the start of the decade, Judeophobia became an important component of Russian liberal thought, by the end of the decade it served as one of the anchors of the new ideology of Russian conservatism. This period of stress and disillusionment particularly lent itself to the gestation of more occult and demonic forms of anti-Jewish prejudice, home-grown and borrowed from abroad.

Even before the pogroms of 1881, in short, the Jewish Question, which cut across so many different areas of the life of the Empire, emerged as one of the most insistent issues to appear in the pages of the Russian press.

Transliteration from Russian follows a modified Library of Congress system. Soft and hard signs are omitted in the text, but included in the notes. The orthographical reforms of 1918 are followed. The one exception is the ubiquitous word *kahal*, which is rendered in its more familiar Polish form. The transliteration of Yiddish follows Uriel Weinrich's system in his *Modern English–Yiddish/Yiddish–English Dictionary* (New York, 1968). Transliteration of Hebrew follows a modified version of the system of the *Encyclopedia Judaica* (Jerusalem, 1971).

Place names reflect Russian imperial usage (i.e., Vilna rather than Wilno or Vilnius), except for locations in the Kingdom of Poland, which are rendered in Polish. Ukrainian personal names are initially given in their Russian and Ukrainian forms. English versions are given for familar Russian names or terms (i.e., Alexander II and Ignatiev, not Aleksandr and Ignat'ev). Jewish personal names are usually rendered in their Russian forms. Western and Polish names are generally given in their original, not Russianized forms, save for those who had a fully "Russian" career.

All internal Russian dates are given according to the unreformed Julian calendar in use in nineteenth-century Russia, which was then twelve days behind the western Gregorian calendar. Events in the Kingdom of Poland are double dated. In the case of ambiguity, dates are designated OS (Old Style) or NS (New Style).

Archival citations follow Soviet categories and employ the following abbreviations: *fond* (f.), *opis'* (op.), *delo* (d.) or *edinitsa khraneniia* (ed. khr.) and *list* (l./ll.). Obverse pages are designated as (o).

A few words are necessary about the terminology employed in this book. I uniformly characterize Russian attitudes toward the Jews as either Judeophobia or Judeophilia, two admittedly clumsy terms, but those used by contemporaries. I have been scrupulous in avoiding the terms Antisemitism or antisemitic when dealing with Russian attitudes. These terms were of German provenance, and were first used by Russians to refer to foreign phenomena. Judeophobia and Antisemitism were not synonyms in the period under discussion.

A central concern of this study is to define the Russian terms *sliianie/sblizhenie* and to show how their casual and imprecise use by publicists had important repercussions in the on-going debate over the Jewish Question. They are either translated as merger/rapprochement, or used in the original.

A full list of abbreviations used in this work precedes the endnotes.

Areas reserved for Jewish residence within the Russian empire in 1855

Introduction

Count P. D. Kiselev, decorated hero of the Napoleonic Wars, lawgiver for the Romanian principalities, reformer of the Russian state peasantry and Minister of State Domains, was not a man accustomed to failure. But early in 1856 he was forced to admit defeat to his new sovereign Alexander II. In 1840 he had been appointed chairman of a "Committee for the Transformation of the Jews" (KOME).[1] Now, sixteen years later, he wrote to inform the Tsar that the Committee's mission of promoting integration of the Jews into Russian life had failed. Kiselev explained to the Tsar that the task of merging the Jews with the rest of the population "is hampered by various restrictions enacted on a provisional basis containing contradictions and restrictions."[2]

Kiselev, hardly the first Russian bureaucrat to make this admission, was a link in a long tradition. Virtually once a decade after 1772 Russian administrators paused to ponder the failure of their dealings with the Jews. Kiselev's own committee had been appointed in 1840 out of dissatisfaction with the results of a new law code promulgated for the Jews in 1835. This code was a response to criticisms made by earlier committees in 1823 and 1812 of the first comprehensive Russian code for the Jews, the Statute of 1804. The twenty years preceding the promulgation of the 1804 Statute also witnessed many twists and turns in Russia's Jewish policies.

While officials might differ on how to resolve the Jewish Question, there was general agreement as to its nature. A consensus had developed steadily since the incorporation of a substantial Jewish population into the Russian Empire in the course of the three partitions of Poland in 1772, 1793 and 1795. This consensus was an amalgam of vague national and religious prejudices, the pragmatic policies of officials on the scene, and a copious borrowing of fashionable western theory and practice. Russian bureaucrats agreed that Jewish settlement

1

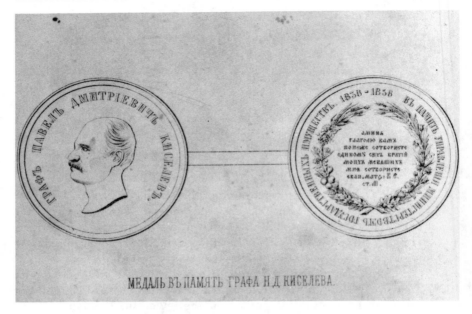

1 Memorial commemorating Count P. D. Kiselev

constituted a problem in the form of a generalized threat to the good order of the Empire and the prosperity of its inhabitants. This problem was encapsulated in two words, "fanaticism" and "exploitation."

Of the two, fanaticism took priority, because exploitation flowed logically from it. The Jews, it was said, considered themselves a chosen people, superior to all the nations among whom they dwelt. They loathed the non-Jew, and kept themselves isolated and apart from gentile society. Jews felt no loyalty to the place of their birth, to their fellow subjects, or to the monarchs who ruled over them. Their alienation, firmly buttressed by religious teachings, easily led to extremes, including outrages such as the ritual murder of non-Jews. Fanaticism determined the economic pursuits of the Jews, all based on forms of exploitation. The Jews disdained physical labor as something best left to Christians. They sought an easy life, at the expense of their gentile neighbors, especially the peasantry. Clustered in trade and commerce, the Jews were an unproductive, parasitical class. National well-being mandated that the population be protected from them, and that the Jews themselves be "rendered harmless."[3]

The chief contribution of the reign of Nicholas I to this consensus was to clarify its ideological underpinning. In the past, the malevolence of the Jews was attributed, in a vague way, to their religious beliefs. Now, under Western influences, especially the tradition tied to the German writer Johann Eisenmenger, commentators placed blame specifically on the Talmud. Reform of the Jews, rendering them harmless, was intimately linked to the repression or attenuation of talmudic beliefs.[4]

The first innovation of the Nicholine period was the introduction of obligatory military service for Jewish townsmen, voiding an exemption which they had enjoyed in Russia since the reign of Catherine II. Instead of rallying to the colors, however, many Jews shirked military service, which encouraged the government to adopt ever more ruthless methods of conscription. Jewish draft evasion was more than understandable. No Russian subject sought with any eagerness a service term which lasted twenty-five years in the early part of Nicholas' reign and was notorious for its brutality. In addition, the Russian government authorized the communal leadership to apportion the draft of recruits, and the *kahalniki* often resorted to the recruitment of young boys, who became the so-called *cantonists*. Military personnel worked hard to convert these young recruits to Christianity, making military service virtually synonymous with apostasy, and creating a notorious chapter in Jewish martyrology. The demands of the state on the communal leadership pitted it against the community as a whole, discredited the leaders' moral authority, and shattered the illusion of Jewish unity as a bulwark against the outside world.[5]

In 1835 the government published a new law code for the Jews, refining the statute of 1804. The Pale of Jewish Settlement, those areas of the Empire where Jews were required to reside, was precisely delineated. Jews were given equal access to elections for the institutions of local self-government, thus rectifying an important omission of the Statute of 1804. (This largesse was largely a consequence of the abolition of most forms of local administrative autonomy in the aftermath of the Polish Revolt of 1831 rather than a concession to the Jews. Shortly thereafter, numerical restrictions were placed on the rights of Jews to participate in local government.)[6] Restrictions were placed on the age at which Jews might marry, a reflection of Austrian and Prussian practices designed to restrict the fecundity of the Jewish population. A final distinctive touch was the creation of the office of "Jewish expert" (*uchenyi evrei*), to assist the local authorities in their dealings with the Jewish community.[7]

The code of 1835 actually left intact many of the features of the Statute of 1804, especially those which attempted to attract the Jews to agriculture and other "productive" livelihoods. It also retained an open invitation to Jews to enroll in any state educational institution. Pious Jews ignored this invitation, confirming the belief that they rejected any opportunity to enter the broader framework of Russian life.

Writing to the Governor-General of Kiev in 1841, Kiselev explained how, despite the government's best efforts, the Jews maintained their separate existence. He detailed the institutions and phenomena which assisted this process, beginning with education. Every young boy was tutored by an ignorant, superstitious and fanatical teacher (*melamed*). They inculcated in their charges intolerance toward the adherents of all other religions. The second obstacle to the unity of Jew and Christian was the autonomous Jewish community, or *kahal*, possessing administrative, judicial and economic powers which allowed it to tyrannize over the individual Jew. The third element was a separate Jewish tax system, the so-called "basket tax" (*korobochnyi nalog*), an impost levied on kosher meat. This independent source of income, Kiselev complained, allowed the kahal to operate outside official oversight and control. Finally, the cultural alienation of the Jews was manifested by a distinctive style of dress, exemplified by sidelocks for men and shaved heads and wigs for women. Jewish traditional costume derived from the fashions of medieval Poland, but was given religious sanction by tradition. It now made Jews repulsive and contemptible in gentile eyes.[8]

Beginning in 1844 the government promulgated new legislation for the Jews, based on the Kiselev Committee's diagnosis of the factors which retarded the integration of the Jews into Russian society. Some of these regulations, such as fines for wearing traditional garb, were vexsome, but incidental to the essence of Jewish life.[9] Three other legal initiatives, on the other hand, threatened the wholesale transformation of Jewish life.

The first was an attempt to make productive workers out of the Jews. In the past this objective was pursued by schemes for the forced resettlement of Jews. The Kiselev Committee proposed a new procedure. All Jews were to be sorted into one of two categories, "useful" (*poleznyi*) and "useless" (*bezpoleznyi*). The first category included Jewish merchants, tradesmen who were formally enrolled in a craft guild, farmers, and Jewish "townspeople" (*meshchane*) who despite being registered in the census as urban dwellers, actually lived in the countryside where they pursued a "settled way of life" and owned some real estate. "Useless" Jews were those who did not satisfy these criteria. Typically they were the rural Jewish "townspeople" who eked out a miserable existence as inn-keepers or employees on large estates. They were given five years to qualify for the "useful" category. At the end of five years all Jews were to be removed from the countryside except those enrolled in a craft guild (*tsekh*). (Thus, apparently, even "useful" meshchane would be forced to resettle.) After resettlement those Jews who were still classed as useless were to bear a higher rate of military recruitment. Draftees from the "useless" category would serve an abbreviated ten-year term in the auxiliary forces, and be expected to learn a trade in the army which they could ply upon their demobilization. In this way, the project's drafters nonchalantly declared, the government would advantageously resolve the fate of 1,100,000 human beings.[10]

Not all Russian bureaucrats shared such blithe confidence. On leave in London, the Governor-General of Novorossiia, M. S. Vorontsov, sent a scathing critique of the project to the Kiselev Committee on 16 October 1843. He condemned the use of the term "useless" for human beings, and denied that this was a legitimate characterization of the economic activities of the Jews. The only effect of the Vorontsov critique was to induce the Committee to rename the category of "useless" to "not pursuing productive work."[11] In fact, the resettlement never took place because the assortment (*razbor*) which was supposed to precede it was never implemented, due to logistical problems. The outbreak of the Crimean War in 1854 finished the project. In Dubnow's felicitous phrase, the war in the Crimea distracted the government from its own "war against the Jews."[12]

An equally curious fate befell the government's second major reform, the abolition of the kahal, decreed on 19 December 1844. The kahal was the surviving remnant of Jewish autonomous communal government in medieval Poland. All Jews in a given area were members of the Jewish community (*evreiskoe obshchestvo*), which was governed by a small executive body, whose members were called *kahalniki*. These community elders exercised complete control over internal taxation. This was a major instrument of social control since the community bore collective responsibility for all state obligations, including taxes and military recruitment, which the elders were able to allocate as they saw fit. The kahal also oversaw internal order, and the administration of justice. The new law abolished the kahal as an executive body, and placed the Jews under control of the rural or urban police administration, as appropriate. For purposes of taxation, however, all Jews were theoretically subordinated to the nearest city or town.

As Michael Stanislawski aptly comments, "it is difficult to assess exactly what this law was intended to do."[13] The new mechanism which the government devised to replace the kahal bore a striking resemblance to the old. The community was still under collective responsibility, charged with apportioning its taxes and responsibilities. The new officials, called collectors (*sborshchiki*), who were to be elected, corresponded almost exactly to the old kahalniki. The law left in place the rabbinical court, the *bet din*, as the effective administrator of criminal and civil law for the Jewish community.[14] Russian legislation did not even dispense with the distinct system of Jewish taxation, the taxes on kosher meat and the tax on sabbath candles. Both were retained, but brought more overtly under state control.[15]

Classification and resettlement, the abolition of the kahal, and restrictions on dress, were all essentially negative, coercive measures. In response to local initiatives by maskilim, and at the urging of the Minister of Education, S. S. Uvarov, the Kiselev Committee also authorized a strikingly positive step in the struggle against "fanaticism": creation of a full-blown state school system for the Jews.

The Jews of the Russian Empire were hardly uneducated, of course. Virtually every Jewish boy had been through a course of religious studies under the direction of private teachers, the *melamdim*, in schools known as *hadarim*. This was precisely the kind of instruction which reformers hoped to extirpate, however. It was here, they believed, that young Jews were inculcated with religious superstitions and hatred for Gentiles, the so-called *goyim*. The struggle with fanaticism had to begin by replacing the traditional *heder* with a more progressive system, following the educational models of the Berlin Haskalah, the Jewish enlightenment movement. The decision to create such a system was expedited by the fact that the government required the Jews themselves to pay for it. This was in part why the existing system of Jewish taxation, which the Kiselev Committee had excoriated, was retained.

Count Uvarov made a great show of soliciting the help and support of the leading lights of world Jewry, such as Sir Moses Montefiore, the English–Jewish philanthropist, and Adolphe Crémieux, the French–Jewish statesman, in support of the project. To implement the scheme in Russia, he invited the director of a "progressive" Jewish school in Riga, the Bavarian native Dr. Max Lilienthal, as well as any other foreign Jews willing to participate.[16] The public rationale given for the creation of the system was that the Jews had not heeded the government's invitation to enter public schools, and so the state was providing them with another option.[17] In a secret instruction, however, Uvarov explained that "the goal of the education of the Jews consists in their rapprochement with the Christian population and the eradication of the prejudices inspired by the study of the Talmud."[18]

The project envisioned the creation of a system of primary, secondary and advanced schools. Besides creating the new school system, the ukaz of 1844 also mandated the registration of all *hadarim* and yeshivot (advanced schools for the study of the Talmud) and the certification of all *melamdim*. The latter were given twenty years to acquire fluency in the Russian language. The project envisioned the gradual elimination of the private school system, as more and more state schools were created.

Anomalies abounded in the curriculum. Although a major purpose of the schools was to wean the Jews away from the Talmud, Uvarov feared that Jews would boycott the system if it was stripped of Talmudic studies. Thus study of the Talmud, albeit under strict governmental supervision, was included in the curriculum. Initially all schools were under the direction of Christian overseers, so this concession did little to allay the fears of the Jewish community that the schools had a conversionary intent.

Practical difficulties soon arose. There was no significant pool of "progressive" teachers in Russia that the government could call upon to staff the schools until the rabbinical schools began to produce graduates. Suitable textbooks and reading materials were not available in the Russian language. Consequently the schools were given a germanic character. The ukaz of 1844 which created the system provided for the recruitment of teachers abroad, in Germany. Educational texts were based on the work of German authors. As the ultimate product of necessity, "Jewish" subjects were taught in German.

The new school system was not a quantitative success. An object of criticism for traditionalists and reformers alike, it was continually modified over the next three decades. Jewish parents were especially reluctant to entrust their sons to schools directed by insensitive Christian bureaucrats. When pressured by the government to produce students, the Jewish community used the schools as a dumping ground for students of the local Talmud-Tora, the communal charity school for orphans and the poor. This did nothing to enhance the prestige of the schools. By way of contrast, in the first years of the educational reform, when the government attempted a census of Jewish students in private schools, it counted 69,464 students in over

5,000 institutions. In 1855, official records showed 3,363 students in the various institutions of the state system.[19]

The government introduced one final reform in conjunction with the educational changes. The Russian government counted on the cooperation of the Russian Orthodox clergy in maintaining social order. Since it equated the Jewish rabbi with the Orthodox priest, it is not surprising that the government sought to utilize the rabbinate. The ukaz of 1835 drew together responsibilities that had been allocated to the rabbinate since 1804 and attempted to turn rabbis into something resembling government officials. They were made responsible for keeping the vital statistics of the community. In addition rabbis were expected "to direct the Jews to the observance of their moral obligations, to obedience to the general laws of the state, and to the established authorities." A formal system of triennial election was instituted. The government strengthened the public prestige of the rabbinate at every turn, even exempting its members from military service. But how might the government enlist the help of the rabbinate in its struggle against fanaticism, when the social authority which the rabbi enjoyed in the community was a reflection of his prestige as a talmudic scholar? Consequently, in most communities a dual rabbinate soon evolved. The official, "crown" or "state" rabbi was the ostensible leader of the community. In fact, his sole qualification was his ability to read and write Russian. Alongside him a talmudic scholar continued to direct the religious needs of the community as before.

A solution to this problem, the government hoped, was to use the rabbinical schools to create a new class of "enlightened" rabbis. Freed from their customary fanaticism, and offered preference and advance, these new model rabbis could be expected to support the policies of the government. Official hopes were soon disabused, as experience demonstrated the futility of expecting the graduates of the state rabbinical schools to be elected to the communal post. A four year course in general studies did not make them masters of the Talmud, and their perceived arrogance and self-confidence deterred the traditionalist majority of most communities from giving them even the figurehead post. Within a decade of founding the state rabbinical schools, the government realized that only direct state intervention could ensure the election of graduates to the post of state rabbi. Such electees were not true communal leaders, but "crown rabbis," government bureaucrats who found themselves totally isolated within the community which they sought to enlighten and to lead.[20]

One additional set of allies was recruited to the government's side.

In 1843 governors-general were authorized to appoint Jewish "inspectors" – progressive Jews who were to exercise a positive moral influence over the Jewish community. This led to the creation, in 1850, of the post of "Jewish Expert," officials attached to the chancellery of governor-generalships located in the Pale. Jewish Experts, a motley assortment of devout and renegade Jews, became an important source of first-hand information for the local authorities. In addition, such individuals frequently served as defenders of the Jewish population from unfair accusations.[21]

As this general survey suggests, the thirty-year reign of Nicholas I was distinguished by a program of social engineering designed to change the face of the Empire's Jews. It was a population that was growing. Figures from the Ministry of Internal Affairs in 1849 placed the Jewish population living in the Pale of Settlement (excluding Finland and the Kingdom of Poland) at 1,041,000 out of a total population in the Pale of 16,697,000.[22] The statistics of the tax census (*reviziia*) of 1857, whose totals are incomplete for three provinces within the Pale, list a total of 539,466 male Jews within the Pale, and a total of 563,970 of both sexes in the Kingdom of Poland. The Jews thus constituted approximately 2.5 percent of the empire-wide population of 68 million people.[23]

The Statute of 1835 definitively established the boundaries of the Pale of Settlement. Jews were permitted to settle freely in the provinces of Grodno, Vilna, Podolia, Minsk, Ekaterinoslav, and in the regions of Bessarabia and Belostok. Residence in other provinces was somewhat circumscribed. Jews could live freely in Kiev province, with the exception of the city of Kiev itself (where they were confined to two districts); in Kherson province, except for the port of Nikolaev; in the Tauride, excluding the naval base at Sevastopol; in Mogilev and Vitebsk provinces, excepting peasant villages; in Chernigov and Poltava provinces except for cossack villages; Kurland province was open only to Jews who had lived there before the last census, and a similar restriction applied to Riga and Shlok, the only areas in Lifland province where Jews were permitted to reside.[24] An anti-smuggling initiative of 1843 produced a ban on new settlement of Jews in villages within 50 versts (33 miles) of the Empire's western frontier.[25] The Kingdom of Poland was never considered part of the Pale. Before 1863, a variety of special restrictions still prevailed for the Jews of the Kingdom. After 1863 they were granted a form of civil emancipation.[26] Russian policy makers never succeeded in their desire to devise a uniform code of laws for the Jews of the Kingdom of Poland and the Empire.

At this juncture the regulations of the Pale, encompassing thousands of square miles of settled and unsettled territory, could hardly be considered a crippling restriction. The Pale spread over prosperous areas, and contained the important fairs and trade routes of western Russia. Novorossiia in particular was a major growth area, filled with economic opportunities which attracted many Jewish settlers. At its heart was the port of Odessa, fast becoming the fourth city of the Empire and a major economic and cultural center for Russian Jewry. The economic crisis which was to afflict the Jews in the second half of the nineteenth century was the result, not merely of legal restrictions, but of a changing economic scene. Especially ruinous for Jews was the destruction of the old patriarchal economy of which they were an integral part.

Additionally, the walls of the Pale were not insurmountable. Temporary sojourns to the interior of up to six weeks were permitted for the settlement of legal or commercial affairs. Merchants of the first and second guilds were permitted to visit the capitals of St. Petersburg and Moscow, internal ports, and the major fairs, such as the famous one at Nizhnii Novgorod. A shortage of craftsmen in the interior encouraged Jews to travel there illegally, and there is a voluminous literature testifying to a clandestine Jewish presence in the interior.[27]

The Jews of the Russian Empire did not display cultural unity. In the Caucasus lived exotic Krimchaks and "Mountain Jews," little distinguished from their Turkic neighbors. The Jewish sect of the Karaites, centered in Lutsk in Volynia, Troki in Lithuania, and in the Crimea, enjoyed a privileged legal position because of their ability to convince the Russian government that they rejected the Talmud. The majority of Russian Jewry were Ashkenazim, taking their traditions and culture from the great medieval centers of France and Germany. There were no substantial settlements of Sephardim, whose culture was linked to Iberia. The Russian community was divided between the Hasidim, followers of a populist religious movement originating in Eastern Europe in the 18th century which centered on a *tzaddik*, a charismatic religious leader, and the so-called Mitnaggedim ("Opponents"), who espoused a non-hasidic, traditional form of Judaism. Despite the enmity the two groups often displayed toward one another, their doctrines were in essential conformity with the fundamental tenets of traditional Judaism. The Hasidim were more mystical and ecstatic in their worship, but both groups shared a common regard for talmudic authority and a traditional style of life. The Mitnaggedim were numerous in Lithuania and the northwest, while the major Hasidic centers were in the Ukraine and the southwest. As a rule, Hasidism was considered especially fanatical, backward and obscurantist by Russian officials. The Haskalah, or Jewish enlightenment movement, did not make meaningful inroads into Russia before 1825. Only toward the end of Nicholas' reign could the Haskalah be properly described as a movement, with a substantial number of adherents. Even then they numbered in the thousands amidst the traditionalist millions.

As Nicholas' reign drew to a close, one thing was clear. The government's war against fanaticism had been very much a private one. Jewish settlement remained on the frontiers of the Russian Empire, far removed from the capitals or the Russian heartland. Work on the Jewish Question was a monopoly of Russian bureaucrats, exemplified by the efforts of Kiselev's committee. For the average educated Russian, Jews were unknown aliens. While the attitude of Russian society to the Jews might waver between apathy, antipathy or sympathy, the basis for all attitudes remained the same – a naive ignorance.

PART 1

The era of the Great Reforms

Jews intruded on the thoughts of Russian officials at the end of Nicholas I's reign only as a source of cannon fodder to fuel the disastrous Crimean campaign. Plans to sort the Jews into categories according to their productivity evaporated under the pressures of wartime, giving way to ever more punitive demands from the recruiting officer. The new Tsar, Alexander II, sought to continue his father's war, but it was increasingly apparent that Russia was exhausted. Nor was there further blood to be squeezed from the Jewish stone. The Jewish committee headed by Kiselev (the KOME) recognized this reality even before the death of Nicholas I in 1855, making cautious hints to the Tsar that the rate of Jewish conscription was too high.[1] Thus the Committee was sympathetic when, on 9 April 1855, twenty merchants and Honored Citizens explained in a petition to the government that there were simply not enough people in the Jewish population to satisfy the official quotas. Productive elements were being drained out of the community even as the Jews continued to be accused of avoiding the draft. The petitioners asked for simple mercy: take Jewish recruits at the same rate as the rest of the population. The justice of this appeal was affirmed by the Governor-General of the Baltic Provinces, Prince A. A. Suvorov, and the Governor-General of the Northwestern Provinces, I. G. Bibikov. The latter warned that Jewish communities would soon be unable to meet their financial obligations to the state.[2] The Kiselev Committee took its cue to propose the relaxation of rules for conscripting under-age recruits and community leaders, as well as for ending the drafting of passport-less Jews. It took some time for these changes to work their way through the bureaucratic machine but, on 26 August 1856, the worst abuses of the old Nicholine system, especially the cantonist system, were changed.[3]

Russia's humiliation in the Crimean War focused the mind of Alexander II and his advisors on the need for internal reform. The

13

2 Tsar Alexander II

most significant consequence was the emancipation of the enserfed Russian peasantry. Exactly the same logic that applied to peasant emancipation was used to justify the relaxation of the legal disabilities of the Jews. Action in both cases grew from a clear recognition that the system in place was no longer functioning properly, or even adequately. On 30 March 1856, in his celebrated speech to a gathering of the Moscow gentry, Alexander noted that "the existing order of rule over living souls cannot remain unchanged. It is better to abolish serfdom from above than to await the day when it will begin to abolish itself from below."[4] Historians differ as to whether security, military or economic considerations were decisive in convincing the Tsar that change must come, but there can be no doubt that the resolution and personal determination he displayed in this one matter grew from recognition of the failure of the old regime.[5]

Early in 1856 the KOME considered the failure of the policies of the previous twenty years to merge the Jews with the rest of the population. Out of these deliberations grew a memoir which Kiselev submitted to the Tsar on 14 March 1856. Kiselev identified eleven points which retarded merger. The government had failed to exercise satisfactory oversight and control of matters pertaining to the Jewish faith, thus losing the struggle against fanaticism. The government inconsistently pursued the goal of progressive education for the Jews. Moreover, noted Kiselev, education was of little practical benefit to Jews, since even those who obtained an advanced degree were denied the opportunity to enter state service, virtually the only employment for an educated individual. Jews were obstructed from participating with Christians on equal terms in municipal self-government. A whole series of enactments denied the Jews equality in residence, the exercise of property rights, and the pursuit of trade, commerce and crafts. Separate recruitment systems existed for Christians and Jews. The entire corpus of Russian legislation on the Jews was rife with contradictions and anomalies. In short, Kiselev provided the Tsar with a bill of indictment of a failed system.[6]

On 31 March 1856, one day after his speech to the Moscow gentry, Alexander followed the lead of Kiselev's report and ordered the KOME to conduct a comprehensive review of Russian legislation applicable to the Jews in pursuit of the general goal of "the merger (*sliianie*) of this nation with the native population, insofar as the moral condition of the Jews will permit it."[7] All the significant reforms of Jewish life in the next decade were progeny of this command.

The shape of peasant reform – and indeed, even the economic justification for emancipation – grew from doctrines of economic liberalism assimilated into Russian thought since the beginning of the century when the government sponsored a Russian translation of Adam Smith's *The Wealth of Nations*. The Russian Free Economic Society had sponsored an essay contest in 1814 on the topic of the superiority of free over forced labor. These doctrines were used to justify the emancipation of the serfs, albeit without land, in the Baltic provinces in the reign of Alexander I. By the 1840s, liberal economic theory had become part of the intellectual baggage of virtually all educated Russians. Not unexpectedly, liberal theorizing dominated the public debate on peasant emancipation which the government permitted briefly in 1858–9.

Debate on the Jewish Question was restricted to the inner workings of the Russian administration before 1857, and here economic theory also echoed loudly. The Pale of Settlement, which restricted the free movement of goods and services, was an obvious target for liberal

3 Prince I. I. Vasilchikov

criticism. The discussion of officials on the possibility of relaxing Jewish disabilities had obvious analogues with the simultaneous debate on peasant emancipation. In June of 1856, in response to the Tsar's request for an examination of obstacles to the merger of Jews, S. S. Lanskoi, the Minister for Internal Affairs, questioned the governors-general and the governors of the provinces of the Pale on the impact of restrictions on the economic life of the Jews. He received a number of revealing responses.[8]

The three provinces of Kiev, Podolia and Volynia, governed by Prince I. I. Vasilchikov, had high concentrations of Jews. Vasilchikov reported that the towns of the region were choked with Jewish master-craftsmen, reduced to idleness because of intense competition. They remained unemployed or were forced to resort to chicanery to survive. This problem could easily be solved by opening the interior Russian provinces to certified Jewish craftsmen. Skilled individuals would move to areas where there was currently a shortage, and the communities of the Pale, now plagued by tax arrears, would be freed from an unproductive burden. The prescient Vasilchikov touched on political considerations which soon become of more interest to the central administration: the dispersal of idle Jews would deny a fertile field to Polish revolutionary propaganda.[9]

At the other end of the bureaucratic scale came a memorandum from a humble scrivener, I. K. Kozakovskii of Grodno province. Kozakovskii complained that the chief elements of official policy toward the Jews, the spread of education, the destruction of their prejudices and the protection of Christians from their exploitation, were all weakened by the overcrowding of Jews in the Pale. The unity imposed by the Pale enabled them to escape supervision and the force of official edicts. The Jewish masses remained bound by talmudic prejudices and routine while an atypical Jew who acquired a secular education was crushed by communal persecution. In the realm of daily life, overcrowding prevented Jews from earning an honest living. Instead, their economic pursuits harmed the general interests of the state and the well-being of the local population.

To illustrate his contentions, Kozakovskii offered a description of a typical small district town in the Pale. Its population might include thirty to forty tailors, ten to twenty furriers, twenty to thirty cobblers, fifty or more agents and go-betweens (*faktors*), and hundreds of petty tradesmen. There could be no question of most of them earning a decent or honest living.

> The impossibility of fulfilling the decrees of the government gives them the opportunity not to fulfill them: they trade in contraband, alcoholic beverages, stolen horses, and pursue all manner of fraud, sucking the vital juices from the hapless population. The close mutual ties between them, their concentration in one place, paralyzes all efforts of the local administration to destroy their lawlessness.[10]

The obvious answer, according to Kozakovskii, was to allow Jews to live throughout the Empire. Jews settled in the midst of a gentile population would find it extremely difficult to hide census evidence upon which taxes and obligations were based. The notorious poverty of the Jewish community, expressed in tax arrears, would be abolished by giving resourceful Jews more scope for their enterprise. Basic commodities, such as a sheepskin coat, cost twice as much in the Great Russian provinces as in the Pale because of the monopolistic practices of Russian merchants. An influx of new merchants would bring down consumer prices. Skilled craftsmen were also in short supply in the interior, Kozakovskii reminded his readers, as anyone who attempted to find a locksmith in Penza during the local fair could attest. A tailor in the interior charged 5 to 10 rubles for a task for which a Jew in the Pale received 2 to 4 rubles. This was why the cost of living was so high in the interior. Jewish distillers worked for wages below those of Christians, and even the lowly agent saved his customers much time and energy. Nor would the obvious economic benefits flowing from the Jews possibly be offset by their negative moral influence. The 700,000 Jews in the Pale would be only a drop in the vast Russian ocean. As his trump card, Kozakovskii turned to the example of European states. "Political economy warns against the dangers of restrictions, and the experiences of many European states – Spain, Portugal, France, England, Germany, Holland – show the harm that comes from restricting the rights of Jews and the advantages which come from extending them."[11]

Foreign models were also on the mind of the Governor-General of Novorossiia and Bessarabia, Count A. G. Stroganov, when he wrote to Lanskoi on 22 January 1858 regarding plans to place the Jews in categories. The example of Western Europe demonstrated the impossibility of changing Jewish beliefs by coercion. Instead, medieval European states succeeded only in reducing the Jews to complete degradation. No sooner were Jews given a modicum of rights, however, than they quickly became useful members of society. After receiving partial emancipation in Germany in 1812, Jews served willingly in the national armies. At the present time in Western Europe

> the Jews are not satisfied with successes on the stock exchange alone, but study foreign languages, heretofore assumed to be contrary to their religion, fill up the universities, have notable success in literature, science and art, clearly demonstrating that if the Jews had never seemed capable of such undertakings, the fault lay in their socially debased position, and not in the shortcomings of their nature.

Russia herself could only benefit from the skill of the Jews in petty trade. "They not only pursue it in towns, but transport various objects to the countryside which are necessary for the domestic life of the peasants, a great benefit for people living far from the towns." Stroganov rejected the counter-argument that the Jews might exert a harmful moral influence where they settled, for there was no possibility of a half million Jews corrupting 65 million Russians. Indeed, the moral level of the Jews was not as low as many assumed: they were a sober and industrious people, who merely needed more scope for their undertakings. "Therefore, allowing Jews to live in all parts of the Empire and to enjoy equal rights with Russians ... not only corresponds to the law of justice, but will be advantageous to our national economy while at the same time, no doubt, weakening the religious fanaticism of the Jews."[12] As striking as were these sentiments from the provinces was the fact that Lanskoi fully concurred with them.[13]

Such emancipationist sentiments continually reappeared throughout the early reform era. An 1861 report to the KOME (headed by Count D. N. Bludov since 1856, when Kiselev was appointed ambassador to Paris), Lanskoi and the Minister of Education E. P. Kovalevskii recommended the relaxation of the Pale. The two ministers attributed the "abnormal relationships" between the peasants and the Jews to the irregularities created by the Pale.[14] In 1862 A. Sivers, the governor of Kharkov province, submitted a wide ranging memorandum on the Jews condemning the Pale in strictly economic terms. Outside the Pale was a monopoly of all groups against the Jews. Inside the Pale there was a monopoly of the Jews against everyone else. Monopolies brought nothing but harm: there was an improper correlation between supply and demand, an absence of competition, a burdensome increase in costs, the enrichment of one class at the expense of another, the stifling of credit, and the general atrophy of trade and commerce. The only group that actually opposed the abolition of the Pale, Sivers claimed, was the Russian merchantry which used the Pale to maintain its monopoly position.[15]

Similar sentiments were expressed in 1863 by the Minister of Finance, M. Kh. Reitern. He attributed the moral decline of the Jews, which so concerned the government, to their inability to make an honorable, decent living. He predicted that an improvement in the Jews' material condition would be reflected in educational aspirations and moral development. The Jews, he noted, constituted from 10 to 12 percent of the population in some provinces, and they were almost exclusively engaged in trade and commerce. A ratio of 1:10 between middlemen and producers was simply too high. The Jews were impoverished, while the local population was entirely driven out of the field of trade. The Russian interior, meanwhile, especially its agricultural regions, suffered from an underdeveloped commerce, and would benefit from an influx of competition, capital and enterprise. Predicting an increase in tax revenues, a decline in smuggling, the revitalization of commerce, and greater prosperity for the village population in the Pale, Reitern advocated opening the interior to Jews who were actively engaged in trade, commerce, and crafts.[16]

Given such community of thought on the desirability of change, why was reform of the Pale so long delayed and so incomplete? The answer to this question offers additional affinities with the process of peasant emancipation.

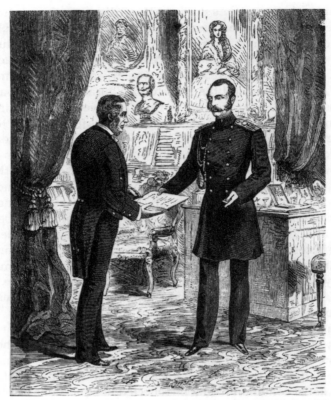

4 Tsar Alexander II and S. S. Lanskoi prepare the decree liberating
the Russian serfs

The emancipation decree of 19 February 1861, five years in the
making, was bewilderingly complex. In part this was a reflection of the
geographical diversity of the Russian Empire, but an important component was the desire to safeguard the welfare of the peasant community. The framers of the legislation were deeply distrustful of the "dark
people" they were about to emancipate. They were dubious of the
individual peasant's ability to maintain his domestic economy and pay
his taxes. Especially feared was the rise of a large landless rural
population comprising peasant debtors who had lost their farmsteads.
As a safeguard, the emancipation settlement allotted land to peasants
not as individuals, but as members of the peasant community (*obshchina*). This legal entity was responsible for the payment of taxes and
obligations through a system of collective responsibility (*krugovaia*

poruka). The peasant community also administered justice at the local level and regulated entrance and egress from the community. The great concern of the reformers was that the peasants would drink away their land at the village tavern and decline into an idle rural proletariat.[17] As the same bureaucrats who had overseen the drafting and implementation of the emancipation decree turned to the question of Jewish reform, it suddenly occurred to them what the nationality of that predatory village tavernkeeper might be. As a precaution they included in the emancipation decree a provision that land occupied by peasants under temporarily obligated status could not be sold to Jews prior to a final division of the land.

The twin stereotypes of the drunken, naive peasant and the crafty, enterprising Jew, fanatical in his hatred of Christians, was to bedevil all efforts of the Russian government to grant to Jews their full share of the Great Reforms. For example, on 6 October 1860, the Governor-General of the Northwest, V. I. Nazimov, submitted a lengthy report to the capital on the need to reform the position of the Jews. (Nazimov was the Tsar's trusted collaborator, whose manipulation of gentry proposals for limited peasant reform produced the "Nazimov Rescript," which provided the backbone for the subsequent emancipation process.) As a basic principle, he rejected wholesale emancipation for the Jews. Given their present condition, he warned, such a concession would only reinforce parasitism and middleman activities, and be widely regarded as a reward for bad conduct.[18]

In 1862 the new Governor-General of Novorossiia and Bessarabia, P. E. Kotsebu, offered his impressions of the correct way of resolving the Jewish Question. Like his predecessor Stroganov, he proposed the elimination of the Pale, but gradually and cautiously. At first, he argued, Jews should be permitted to settle, conduct trade and obtain land only in the urban areas of the Empire. "Permission for the Jews to settle in the villages and the countryside," he warned, "would place them in direct contact with our agricultural population, which in its present material and moral condition would be more likely to fall victim to the speculative activities of the Jews than to derive benefit from close relations with them."[19]

This was certainly the opinion of Alexander II, who was deeply distrustful of the Jews and prone to place a brake on the emancipationist enthusiasms of some officials. His approval for minor relaxations in the Nicholine legal system was always given grudgingly. When the KOME rejected Count Stroganov's proposal for expeditious emancipation of the Jews in 1858, the Tsar noted on the minutes of the meeting, "I quite agree." He was equally unenthusiastic about subsequent proposals.[20] It was the Tsar who authorized the KOME to tie reforms to the moral level of the Jews, and he had a relatively low estimate of where this level lay. Consequently, despite several well-argued proposals, comprehensive abolition of the Pale never took place. The closest the regime came was the law of 28 June 1865. Significantly, it retained the old idea of categorizing the Jews, by devising groups of "good" Jews who could leave the Pale. The drafters of this legislation themselves admitted that "recognizing the need to proceed with changes to a long-established order, it should be accomplished with caution and gradually, especially in the present case where it might mean the rapid flood into the interior of a long-alien element."[21]

Just as Alexander II attempted to involve the gentry in the emancipation of their peasants, so too was the elite of the Jewish community involved in the torturous process of ameliorating restrictions on the Jews. Throughout the reign of Alexander II merchants played an important leadership role in the Jewish community, continuing an old Jewish tradition of the use of *shtadlanim*, or high-level intermediaries.[22] In the early nineteenth century the typical *shtadlan* was a military contractor; thereafter they came from the milieu of the *otkupchiki*, Jews whose wealth was made in leasing the immensely profitable tax farms of the state liquor monopoly. The most famous example was that of Evzel (Iosif) Gavrilovich Gintsburg, and his son Goratsii (Horace). The senior Gintsburg, originally from Kamenets-Podolsk, made his fortune as a tax farmer, and founded a famous banking house in St. Petersburg.[23] The House of Gintsburg was very well connected in official circles, and played a prominent role in state banking operations and railroad finance. There were other Jews of equal fame, such as the railway magnate S. S. Poliakov, but none devoted themselves as assiduously to the interests of the Jewish community in Russia as the Gintsburg Circle.

Merchants like Gintsburg, even though religiously observant, were cosmopolitan and at ease in the upper reaches of the government. Given their vested interests, they were often consulted on pending legislation. Well aware of what was happening in the ministries, they often volunteered their services and advice. Despite the rise of other claimants, Gintsburg and his friends and business associates in Petersburg became the quintessential mediators between the state and the Jewish community until the first decade of the twentieth century.[24]

It was the merchant elite who responded to the government's reevaluation of Jewish rights, and helped to supply impetus to the

5 Baron G. O. Gintsburg

process by their intervention. Thus, in 1856, the Riga Honored Citizen Moisei Brainin, on his own authority, petitioned the Tsar to allow *all* Jews to settle throughout Russia. When the KOME began to reassess the legal rights of Jews, this petition was given serious consideration.[25] Getting wind of these discussions, and aware that the government was still toying with the old project of categorizing the Jews, a group of St. Petersburg first guild merchants, with Gintsburg at their head, sent a petition to the government in June of the same year.

> Should the government differentiate by the extension of rights between those who have failed to distinguish themselves by their

attitude, usefulness and industry, and the young generation who
have been educated by and in the spirit of the government, as well as
the upper levels of the merchantry who have for many years developed the economic life of the region, and the conscientious craftsmen
who earn their bread by the sweat of their brow, then all the Jews,
seeing in these select few the focus of the government's justice and
good will and the exemplar of what it wishes to be done, will happily
aspire to the ends indicated by the government ... We request that
the Benevolent Monarch welcome us, and deign, *separating the wheat
from the chaff*, to encourage our good and commendable activities by
granting moderate privileges to those of us who are deserving and
enlightened.[26]

The petitioners went on to specify that these rights should go to
Honored Citizens, merchants of the first and second guild, soldiers
with an honorable discharge, and artisans who could produce special
commendations of merit.

A number of Jewish historians, especially S. M. Dubnow, viewed this
request with disgust. Dubnow observed that the petition

reflects the humiliating attitude of men who were standing on the
boundary line between slavery and freedom, whose cast of mind has
been formed under the regime of oppression and caprice. Pointing to
the example of the West where bestowal of equal rights had contributed to the success of Jewish assimilation, the St. Petersburg petitioners were not even courageous enough to demand equal rights as
the price of assimilation, and professed, perhaps from diplomatic
considerations, to content themselves with miserable crumbs and
privileges for "the best among us." They failed to realize the mean-
ness of their suggestion to divide a nation into best and worst, into
those worthy of a human existence and those unworthy of it.[27]

Whatever the moral honesty of the merchants' petition, it was an
accurate reflection of the limits of the possible in the 1850s. Simultaneously with this petition the Jewish Committee was rejecting Brainin's
prior request to the Tsar that all categories be allowed to settle
throughout Russia. The residence rights of first guild merchants were
expanded only after agonizing debate and soul-searching within the
government, all the more striking because officials recognized that
only 108 candidates were eligible. As it was, the final bureaucratic
justification of greater merchant rights closely followed the wording
of the Gintsburg petition.[28] Even after first guild merchants received
the right to reside outside the Pale (16 March 1859), the Gintsburg
Circle continued to appeal for similar rights for other categories such
as gymnasium graduates and, in particular, for artisans. A petition

on behalf of the latter group, submitted in July of 1862 and including a list of eighty separate restrictions on the Jews in and out of the Pale, prodded the government along the path which led to the opening of the Pale to artisans in 1865 and to army veterans in 1867.[29] Given the mood of the government, an approach characterized by gradualness and differentiation was probably the most efficacious. Members of the well-informed Gintsburg Circle were aware of continuing discussions within the government on some system of dividing the Jews into categories and tailored their requests along these lines.[30]

The 1862 petition which proposed gymnasium graduates as recipients of legal largesse demonstrates another feature of the merchant outlook: an acceptance of the government's emphasis on education as a decisive factor for the resolution of the Jewish Question. The merchants ignored the anti-talmudic thrust of official educational policy while falling in squarely with calls for "merger" (*sliianie*). The merchants interpreted this to mean acquisition of Russian language and a more secular outlook, both to be obtained in Russian schools. In September of 1858, twelve prominent Jewish merchants, with Baron Gintsburg at their head, urged greater rights for Jews with a higher education. This petition helped to inspire the law of 4 May 1859 which made secular education mandatory for the children of first guild merchants – more a desideratum than a realistic objective – and, more importantly, required that within ten years all teachers in state or private Jewish schools must have a school diploma.[31] Finally, the merchants' concern with education as a conduit for citizenship led to the formation in 1863 of the Society for the Spread of Enlightenment among the Jews of Russia (OPE), whose operations were never far removed from public debates on the Jewish Question.

The merchants were not professional educators, nor were they renowned for their erudition, be it talmudic or secular. As a consequence, in their relations with the government they were forced to collaborate with a second group of would-be reformers, the Russian Jewish intelligentsia.

The term "Russian Jewish intelligentsia" is customarily employed as a catch-all category for any group of Jews who adhered to values at variance with the ideological consensus of the traditionalist Jewish community in Eastern Europe. It frequently serves as a synonym for "maskilim." Closer examination suggests that this usage is too broad. In particular, it obscures the ideological differentiation taking place within Russian Jewry throughout the nineteenth century. Therefore, it is imperative to create an ideological spectrum of Jews which better reflects this differentiation.[32]

At one extreme were a group best described as the "Old Maskilim." They were the pioneers of Haskalah in Russia, men like Isaac Ber Levinson (Levinsohn), author of the maskilic manifesto *Te'udah beyisrael*; Bazilius Stern, the celebrated Odessa schoolmaster; or the lowly third guild merchant, Kofka Grosman, who dreamed in the 1830s of establishing a progressive Jewish school in Uman, that nest of Hasidism.[33] They may stand for the whole band of lone wolves, "freethinkers," and autodidacts, who took up the banner of Mendelssohn. The acceptance – with its implied protection – which they received from the Russian state, and the state Jewish school system which they helped to inspire, made possible a second generation of maskilim.

These "Young Maskilim" were the graduates of the state Jewish schools, and especially the state rabbinic institutes at Vilna and Zhitomir. They were the cadres of school teachers and state rabbis with which the Russian state proposed to fight the "religious fanaticism" of the Jewish masses. Imbued with the arrogance of youth, reinforced by a sense of mission, and scornful of many of the traditions and practices of the community, they clashed with those they hoped to save. Many young rabbis were elected to their posts through governmental coercion, and they were under continual threat of not being reselected at the triennial elections required by law. The community itself trusted them to do little more than keep the communal record books, and even these were supposed to be "cooked" in order to reduce the demands of the state recruiting officer. The Young Maskilim shared the traditional maskilic confidence in the good intentions of enlightened rulers toward the Jews, and the ability of the state to work progressive change. Consequently, they continually importuned the Russian authorities with plans to reform and improve the Jews. When the opportunity presented itself, they shared their ideas with Russian society.

A third group is most deserving of the sobriquet "Russian Jewish intelligentsia," and the term will be restricted to them alone in the course of this study. They too were invariably the products of the state Jewish school system, and they often remained dependent upon the system created by Nicholas I for employment as teachers or Jewish Experts. Unlike the Old and Young Maskilim, however, they were more perceptive in recognizing the shortcomings and inadequacies of mainstream Haskalah. They lacked the faith of the passive maskilim that the internal eradication of "fanaticism" by the Jews themselves would lead directly and rather mechanically to some form of emancipation. Rather, they campaigned overtly for Jewish emancipation as a basic human right which did not need to be earned. They neglected significant features of the Haskalah schema, such as the civilizing power of the study of Biblical Hebrew. For them the customary Haskalah emphasis on the use of the vernacular became a virtual passion for Russian as an emblem and pledge of citizenship. While the Maskilim, Old and Young, were inwardly directed in their efforts at reform – albeit willing to call upon the Russian state for support – members of the Russian Jewish intelligentsia considered themselves part of Russian society, entitled and obligated to participate in public debate, an attitude fostered by the atmosphere of the Reform Era.

The Russian Jewish intelligentsia early on confronted the challenge of defining a Jewish identity – and identifying a role for Judaism – in modern Russian society. This search was complicated by the fact that the development of Russian national identity was itself in a state of flux, exemplified by the struggle between the Slavophiles and the Westernizers. How could one define a "Russian Jew" when there was, as yet, no satisfactory definition of a "Russian" (*russkii*) within the context of the multi-national (*rossiiskii*) Empire? As a further complication, other peoples of the Empire, especially the Poles and Ukrainians, who lived alongside Jews in the western provinces, were also engaged in a search for national identity.

The debates surrounding this definitional quest of the Russian Jewish intelligentsia were often arcane, conducted by a miniscule part of the Jewish population, and completely beyond the ken of the traditionalist majority. They were conducted almost entirely in Russian before a Russian audience, which was frequently invited to serve as a participant or referee. These obscure debates are worth chronicling, however, because they played a vital role in shaping Russian society's assumptions about the Jews, especially educated and "enlightened" Jews, and the broader Jewish Question.

Another group of Jewish intellectuals may be termed the "Total Assimilationists." This group included an elite which had attended Russian universities, and who pursued careers in the wider circles of imperial society. Typically, they ignored their ties to the Jewish community and its problems. (This was the category of Jew who so often "returned" to the community in the aftermath of the crisis of the pogroms of 1881–2.) A negligible percentage of Total Assimilationists converted to Christianity in order to advance their careers. (The most famous of these apostates, Daniel Khvolson, was said to have answered the query as to whether he had converted out of conviction with the quip: "Yes, out of the conviction that it was better to be a professor in St. Petersburg than a *melamed* in Shnipishok.")[34] The attitude of the Total Assimilationists was neatly expressed in a petition submitted to Count Kisilev in 1856 by thirty-four students at the Medical-Surgical Academy. They sought modification of a secret instruction of Tsar Nicholas I which restricted the admission of Jews to state service, despite guarantees contained in the Jewish Statute of 1804.

> Not daring to judge the reason for such a restriction [they explained], we dare only to pray our Fatherland not to confuse us, who have been educated in its spirit and under its eyes, from the mass of our unhappy race. It was not the Talmud which we studied, and it is not to Palestine that we belong any longer, but to Holy Russia ... From all our soul we thank the government for giving us the highest good – education. But our people judge education by its actual utility; the eyes of all our young generation are upon us, who first scorned its prejudices.[35]

Like all paradigms, this differentiation of the Jewish community cannot be considered hard and fast. Individuals frequently slip back and forth between categories. Consider the case of Lev Levanda. He began as a typical Young Maskil, served as a Jewish Expert for his entire life, and offered maskilic critiques of traditional Judaism in both his publicistic and literary works. Yet he also sought to establish himself as a Russian writer, while using his works to sharply criticize the regime's refusal to grant full equal right to the Jews. He ended his life as a moderate Zionist. Judah Leib Gordon was an equally complex figure. He kept to his maskilic ideals with admirable tenacity, at great emotional cost after the pogroms of 1881 and the rise of Zionism. He too was a litterateur, but restricted himself largely to Hebrew. His credentials as a member of the Russian Jewish intelligentsia are equally strong, however, given his employment as the secretary of the OPE and his battle for Jewish civil rights. More complex still was the career of the convert Daniel Khvolson, who never lost a sense of Jewish identity. He earned a living as a Hebraist, and was an important figure in defending Russian Jewry from the Blood Libel. Despite equally convincing credentials as a Total Assimilationist and a Russian Jewish Intelligent, he was also a leading sponsor of one of the most Mendelssohnian initiatives of Russian Jewry: an attempt to publish an edition of the Hebrew Bible in Russian translation. Each of these individuals fits, at a certain stage in their careers, into one of the categories established above, but only with difficulty can they be forced to remain there. This will help to explain why Russian society had its own difficulties in defining those "enlightened Jews" who claimed to be its ideological allies in the struggle against Jewish fanaticism. In any event, these categories may serve as a frame of reference and a starting point.

Even if Russian society had been able to ignore the importunities of the Jews themselves, the actions of the government underlined the seriousness of the Jewish Question. A steady stream of new legislation was promulgated between 1856 and 1865. The initial measures were made in the context of the post-Crimean War relaxation of military discipline. Jewish recruitment was equalized, and the various abuses which had crept into it were voided. The Jewish cantonist system was abolished, in line with the ending of the parallel system which existed for the children of Christian soldiers.

As the reform era began to develop in earnest, the legal position of the Jews was addressed in a consistent and focused way. Two principles emerged. The first was the retention of the Nicholine doctrine of categorizing the Jews. However, the emphasis was now placed more on rewarding "good" Jews than punishing "bad" Jews. The second principle was gradualism, succinctly voiced by the KOME, on 17 February 1859, when it rejected Count Stroganov's call for the full and immediate equalization of Jewish rights: "the equalization of the Jews in rights with the native population cannot be carried out other than gradually, by means of disseminating among them true enlightenment, by changing their internal life, and by directing them toward useful pursuits."[36] This rubric was confirmed by the Tsar.

The regime contented itself with granting the basic right of settlement throughout the Empire to select groups, "the best among us," as the Jewish merchants had put it. On 16 March 1859 a decree permitted the hundred or so members of the first merchant guild, if they had been enrolled for at least two years, to settle outside the Pale, with their immediate families and a number of servants and agents. Jews who had been first guild merchants for ten years were allowed to settle outside the Pale on a permanent basis, and this right could be passed on to their heirs. The Jewish first guild merchant thus became a sort of hereditary Jewish nobility. In 1861 the merchantry was joined by another tiny minority – Jews who had received a university degree. These graduates were permitted to live anywhere, and to enter any branch of state service.[37]

The comparison of these privileged categories of Jews with Russia's own hereditary nobility is not a facetious one. As wealthy Jewish merchants began to appear inside and outside the Pale the question of landownership arose, applicable to land that was in the hands of the gentry. While the Russian government relentlessly pursued schemes for Jewish agricultural colonization, it rejected the efforts of individual wealthy Jews to purchase land. The official objection before emancipation was that Jews might buy gentry land which had peasants settled upon it. Jews would then "own" Christian souls, a state of affairs which could not be accepted by a Christian state with an established church. This precise point was made in the emancipation decree which forbade Jews to seize gentry land in default of mortgages.[38] A parallel statute specifically forbade the sale of noble-owned land to Jews.[39]

Within a year conditions began to change, and the government's intentions along with them. The "temporary obligated status" of the peasants, during which they were still under the authority of the nobleman who owned the estate, began to expire in some areas. Landowners found themselves short of capital and occasionally unable to attract their former serfs to work on their estates. Credit institutions did not exist which might have enabled the peasant to buy even small amounts of private land. In the Pale, Jews were a group unique for their possession of significant liquid capital. When, in 1862, a group of Jewish first guild merchants in the Ukraine petitioned the government to allow them to buy land, their request was granted with the proviso that no temporarily obligated peasants live on the land in question.[40]

The civil service, ownership of land, medals for outstanding performance in school: these were the dreams of a small elite. For the average Jew, the resident of the so-called "Jewish ant-heap," it was more scope that was needed. Piecemeal rights slowly began to trickle down to them as well. Residence restrictions within the Pale were relaxed and Jews were permitted greater residence rights in such restricted cities as Nikolaev, Sevastopol and Kiev, all of which were important trade or commercial centers.[41] On 3 June 1862 Jewish veterans from the guards' battalions were permitted to reside in St. Petersburg, where they had been stationed. (Alexander II blocked a wider grant to all army veterans.)[42]

On 28 June 1865, after almost ten years of debate, foot-dragging and red tape, the regime promulgated what should have been the most significant law for Jews of the reform era, a Jewish equivalent of the emancipation decree for the peasants. The new law permitted Jewish mechanics, distillers, brewers, master-craftsmen and craftsmen to leave the Pale.[43] These categories did not encompass the entire Jewish population, but they were generous compared with what had gone before. Instead of producing the flood of Jews into the interior which the framers of the new law had feared, the new law produced only a trickle. What went wrong?

Contemporaries advanced numerous explanations for the failure of the law of 28 June to set the Jewish masses in the Pale into motion, and they will be discussed below. Suffice it to say here that the law was born out of time. By 1865 the law, so long in coming, no longer reflected the clear objectives of the state. The Jews had always been seen as fanatical and ignorant, dedicated to harming Christians. But they had also been seen as wretched and downtrodden, too weak to carry out on a grand scale the teachings of the Talmud. The Polish uprising of 1863 directed the attention of Russians to the borderlands – the Ukraine, Lithuania and Belorussia – as an area where the struggle for superiority between Polish and Russian culture must be waged. These borderlands were coterminous with the Pale and its hundreds of thousands of Jews. Faced with the task of Russification, Russian bureaucrats began to see the Jewish Question in quite a different light from that which illumined their policies before 1865.

1   Moshkas and Ioshkas

Before 1858 the Jewish Question was not a topic for public debate in the Russian Empire. In general the tsarist regime did not welcome advice or criticism from society regarding its actions. In the case of the Jews, moreover, a specific regulation prevented it. A secret censorship rule dating from the 1840s forbade journalists to espouse the cause of civil rights for the Jews. Such appeals, the censor explained, demonstrated a lack of confidence that the government would show its benevolence toward the Jews in its own way.[1] Official materials appeared upon occasion, largely in the publications of the Ministries of Education (MNP) and Internal Affairs (MVD). The MVD *Journal* carried a number of descriptive articles, which offered tendentious surveys of the religious beliefs of various Jewish groups in the Russian Empire. These works were mainly an indictment of the fanaticism of rabbinic Jewry.[2] *Belles-lettres* offered the reader literary creations which were either fantastic, exotic or crude stereotypes, none of which gave the Russian reader a realistic view of Jews or Judaism.[3] The situation changed early in the Reform Era when the internal governmental monologue was suddenly transformed into a dialogue. Changing circumstances permitted journalism to explore the Jewish Question and pass judgment on the state's seventy-five year old experiment with the Jews.

Discussion of the Jewish Question benefited from the general relaxation of the censorship which characterized the Reform Era. One of the first acts of the new government was to abolish the notorious Committee of 2 April 1848 that had presided over the "censorship terror" which followed in the wake of the revolutionary outburst of 1848. The censorship mechanism itself was in flux until the government finally introduced a new set of regulations in 1865 which abolished pre-censorship of periodical literature in the two capitals.[4]

Besides the general relaxation of censorship the government also permitted the discussion of previously forbidden social issues in the hope of enlisting public cooperation and support, especially toward the forthcoming peasant reform. Since the government was itself exploring the situation of the Jews, it is not surprising that a parallel discussion surfaced in the newly liberated press. On 16 January 1858 the government permitted the discussion of the peasant question (i.e., the emancipation of the serfs) in the press, subject to certain guidelines.[5] Soon the editor of the Petersburg *Russkii invalid*, P. S. Lebedev, requested the censor to permit publication of articles calling for civil rights for Jews on an equal basis with all other subjects. This provoked a debate within the censorship as to how this request should be handled. It was decided that articles of this nature could be published, but that they would require specific permission from the central censorship office on each occasion.[6]

The experience of the government with discussion of the Jewish Question mirrored that of the Peasant Question: public discussion and debate, once permitted in any form, proved very difficult to control.[7] The Jewish Question, with its religious, political, social and economic ramifications, was too broad to permit effective oversight. Writers could indirectly call for equality for Jews by questioning the premises – fanaticism and economic exploitation – upon which Jewish disabilities were based. Critical evaluations of the economic consequences of the Pale of Settlement implied its dissolution. Philosophical reevaluations of Judaism, and especially the nature of the Talmud, challenged the government's justification for shielding the Christian peasantry from Jewish malfeasance.

Despite the efforts of the government to impose uniform standards upon the censorship through the oversight of the Chief Department of Press Affairs in Petersburg, the personality of individual censors could make a great difference in what was or was not published. Before 1863, press censorship was largely the responsibility of the Ministry of Education. Local censorship boards in the major cities throughout the Empire were under the authority of the director (*popechitel*) of the corresponding educational district. Local boards did not always carry out their functions to the satisfaction of the center. The classic case was that of N. I. Pirogov, who served as administrator of the Odessa educational district from 1857 to 1858, when he was transferred to Kiev in what was widely seen as punishment for his actions in Odessa. Pirogov continually complained to the capital about censorship norms, and his slackness toward his subordinates in the Odessa censorship committee was the despair of the Governor-General, Count

УНИВЕРСИТЕТЪ.
БЫВШИЙ РИШЕЛЬЕВСКИЙ ЛИЦЕЙ.

6 The Richelieu Lyceum in Odessa

A. Stroganov.[8] Just these circumstances enabled a publication under control of the Governor-General's own office, *Odesskii vestnik*, to play a leading role in debates on social issues in 1858. Even in areas where censors were more scrupulous than Pirogov, however, there was still room for honest disagreement. Censors, often men of letters themselves, did not always err on the side of caution. This was the background to the first public debates on the Jewish Question, in Odessa.

The man most responsible for the *annus mirabilis* of *Odesskii vestnik*, when that normally staid provincial publication was on the cutting edge of debate on the leading issues of the day, was N. I. Pirogov (1810–81).[9] Pirogov was a physician by training and became a national hero for his organization of medical services during the Crimean War. He was also a pedagogical theorist, and a man of such progressive views that he was always an anomaly in the Russian bureaucracy, especially in the provinces. Late in 1857, Pirogov, then director of the Odessa educational district, persuaded the Governor-General, Count Stroganov, to transfer publication of the official paper *Odesskii vestnik* from his office to an editorial board staffed by teachers at the local Richelieu Lyceum. The council appointed two professors, A. Bogdanovskii and A. I. Georgievskii, to serve as editors. Under their guidance, and with Pirogov's active support, the paper published a wide range of innovative articles on local and national issues. The paper's continual espousal of a progressive point of view was expedited by

Pirogov's loose direction of the local censorship. The results alarmed Count Stroganov and the Chief Office of Press Affairs in the capital, and at the end of the year editorial control was returned to the office of the Governor-General.[10]

It is not surprising that the first significant article of the reform era on the Jewish Question appeared in *Odesskii vestnik* or that its author was the local Jewish litterateur and publicist O. A. Rabinovich. Osip Rabinovich was born in 1817 in the village of Kobeliakakh, Poltava province. His father was a liquor tax farmer who, apparently under the influence of contacts from his business, gave his son an unusually broad secular education (although religious instruction was not neglected). In 1840 Rabinovich entered the medical school of Kharkov University, but was soon forced to leave because of the failure of his father's business. He sought employment in Odessa, and by 1848 found financial security as a highly regarded notary public. In the cosmopolitan community of Odessa, Rabinovich was encouraged to pursue his literary aspirations as a poet and publicist.[11]

Articles on the Jews were rare in the Russian periodical press in the 1840s, and articles about Jews by Jews were rarer still. Thus Rabinovich created a mild sensation locally when he published in No. 34 of *Odesskii vestnik* for 1847 his first publicist piece, "The New Jewish Synagogue in Odessa." The furore was especially strong among the Jewish community, for Rabinovich's article was a paean to the city's new choral synagogue, where services were conducted in the reformed German fashion.[12] Exactly a year later Rabinovich followed his initial effort with an article in No. 34 of *Odesskii vestnik* for 1848 entitled "Upon the Occasion of a Good Word." Rabinovich praised an article on European Jewry which had appeared in the Petersburg weekly *Illiustratsiia*.[13] What a joy it was, Rabinovich exclaimed, to find an article in the Russian press which did not accuse the Jews of perfidy, greed, parasitism and fanaticism, but treated them in a humane and balanced way. While the Russian government itself, he claimed, actively sought the betterment of Jewish life and "does not deny us the precious name of true sons of Russia," Russian writers as a whole used their position to blacken, mock and humiliate the Jews. In closing, Rabinovich offered an insight into his own frame of mind at this time. Why did the Jews refuse to reply to the slanders of Russian writers, especially when there was an increasing number of educated Jews who were able to intercede for their coreligionists in print? "If they have been silent, it is only because they judge themselves unworthy to stir up quarrels over absurd fantasies, and they hope that this will all

7 O. A. Rabinovich

end with the approach of an epoch in Russian literature when well-intentioned and truth-seeking writers will throw off prejudice and try to look at the Jewish people objectively."[14]

By 1858 Rabinovich clearly decided that the new epoch had arrived. He published in *Odesskii vestnik* (10:25/I/1858) the article "Concerning Moshkas and Ioshkas."[15] The article, written in naive style, was an appeal to the Jewish masses to recover their dignity and self-esteem lost under Polish rule. Rabinovich explained that in medieval Poland the Jews became economically dependent upon the Polish petty nobility, the *szlachta*. Eager to retain their favor, Jews debased themselves and played the fool before their employers. They answered to diminutives and nicknames just like those which the Poles gave their pets and favorite horses. Since the "Pan" enjoyed pulling the Jew's sidelocks, he grew them longer. Even the dress so beloved of Jewish traditionalists was no more than the costume of medieval Poland, and as such another symbol of the Jews' degradation.

Rabinovich's admonition mirrored the maskilic call to the Jews to "be a man on the street," and as such was nothing new, except for its appearance in a Russian newspaper intended for a broader audience. At the same time, Rabinovich's description of the disabilities imposed upon the Jews by Old Poland sounded a contemporary ring for the attentive reader.

> You were happy to have special quarters and special streets: you were happy that you were named Mairoki and Moshka; you were very happy not to have to furnish soldiers nor to be responsible for municipal government ... But subsequently, things appeared differently; you could not leave your special quarters; you wished to bear arms but couldn't; you wished to hold office, but they were closed to you; you cried out that you were named Moisei or Moses, Ber or Bernhard, but they still called you Moshka or Berka.

In due course, as editor of the Russian Jewish newspaper *Rassvet*, Rabinovich would call more overtly for an extension of Jewish rights, but "Concerning Moshkas and Ioshkas" served as a preliminary attempt to draw public attention to the plight of the Jews. Rabinovich's effort was strikingly successful.

Odesskii vestnik (25:4/III/1858) soon carried a response from A. Dumashevskii, himself a Jew, who later became a frequent commentator on the Jewish Question. A university graduate, he pursued a civil service career, most notably as editor–publisher from 1872 to 1875 of *Sudebnyi vestnik*, published by the Ministry of Justice. While recognizing Rabinovich's good intentions, Dumashevskii rejected both his methods and his goals. Dumashevskii was especially critical of what he believed was Rabinovich's oversimplification of the diversity within the Jewish community. This community might best be divided into three camps, he explained to his readers. At one extreme were the conservative "Old Believers" who treasured every petty belief and custom of their ancestors, including their ancient Polish nicknames. They were an embalmed mummy, unresponsive to outside stimuli who "being born blind do not know that they are blind." At the opposite pole were the Jewish progressives, among whom Dumashevskii clearly numbered himself, who were free from all prejudices and venerated only the laws of truth and necessity. Caught in between these two extremes was a third group, the superficially enlightened. These Jews affected Western garb, displayed a veneer of civilization, and styled themselves as Abram Markovich or Naum Moiseevich, as Rabinovich advised. Unfortunately, they rejected faith along with superstition, and became no better than "man–beasts" devoid of a moral anchor. Thus lay the fruitlessness of Rabinovich's call for Jewish self-respect. The traditionalists to whom he was primarily speaking were the group least likely to heed him, and the example of the superficially enlightened demonstrated that a mere change of name accomplished nothing.

Dumashevskii conceded that Rabinovich was concerned with more than the grammatical form of names, and that he recognized the "profound moral-political sense which is preserved under the plastic form." All the more reason why it was wrong to waste attention upon external, accidental qualities and ignore the real prerequisite for Russian Jewry, "the spread of sacred truth."

This latter prescription reveals Dumashevskii as an archetypical representative of the Russian Jewish intelligentsia whose ideas appeared more and more frequently in the columns of Russian newspapers. Often men of high educational achievement themselves, they sought to establish their own bona fides with the government by shepherding the Jewish masses toward reform and self-improvement. Although they sought to lead by example, they were hardly in a position to do so. As matters stood in 1858, a highly educated Jew was an outsider, fully accepted by neither the Jewish nor gentile world.

Dumashevskii's censure of Rabinovich for wasting his energy on non-essentials is revealing. The general nostrum which he proposed, "the spread of sacred truth," was vague theory, lacking even the symbolism of Rabinovich's proposal. Unlike Rabinovich, he spoke about the masses, not to them, and his criticisms lacked the sympathy of Rabinovich for the downtrodden Jew. His audience was Russian society alone. He tried to prove himself by accepting completely the official critique of Jewish fanaticism as well as the attendant educational prescriptions. Against all the evidence, publicists like Dumashevskii confidently assured the Russian public that education was making headway among some Jews, and that it would quickly and reliably resolve the Jewish Question. As proof and surety, they offered themselves, as though an individual with a university degree was anything other than an anomaly in either Jewish or Russian society. Yet framers of Russian public opinion were initially pleased to listen to the voices of men like Dumashevskii expressing sentiments which they longed to hear from all Jews.

Rabinovich's article received a less critical reception from non-Jewish St. Petersburg. A *feuilleton* surveying contemporary literature which appeared in *Russkii invalid* (39:19/II/1858) singled out Rabinovich's article for special praise: "Honor and praise to the worthy

representative of the Jewish nation. Grant full success to his goals."
The *feuilletonist* in turn attacked the most common prejudices voiced
against the Jews by Russian society. The military could find no fault
with the Jews, he argued, since they served honorably in the Crimean
campaign, sacrificing their lives alongside Russians at the siege of
Sevastopol. A set of parallel obligations now fell on both Jew and
gentile. Let the Jews follow Rabinovich's advice and regain their
dignity. As for Russian society:

> We will be worthy of our age if we reject the wretched habit of
> permitting into Russian history things which expose the Jews to
> shame and mockery; rather, we recall the reasons which led them to
> such a state; we will not forget the aptitude of the Jews for science, art
> and knowledge and, giving them a place amongst us, we will use
> their energy, resourcefulness and cleverness as a new means of
> satisfying the needs of society, which grow every day.

Such sentiments established *Russkii invalid* as the Jews' foremost
defender in the capital press, and initiated a brief vogue of Judeophilia
in a number of prestigious publications.

Typical of the blossoming relationship between the press and the
Jews was a lengthy *feuilleton* by Rabinovich which was published in
Russkii invalid (83:17/IV/1858) entitled "An Antiquated View in the
Light of Day." Rabinovich replied to a theatrical review of the play
"Manikhim-ben-Izrail" published in the conservative *Severnaia pchela*
(14:18/I/1858).[16] The anonymous author objected to the play's sympathetic portrayal of medieval Jews surrounded by a barbaric Christian
community. The Jewish characters were uniformly virtuous save for a
renegade convert to Christianity. To the critic this all rang false: the
Jews, on the basis of their moral teaching of "an eye for an eye," could
not be other than enemies of their Christian persecutors. The playwright was faulted for imputing to his Jewish characters such Christian virtues as humaneness, forgiveness and toleration.

The reply of Rabinovich practiced what he had preached in "Concerning Moshkas and Ioshkas," by forcefully asserting Jewish self-
worth. He dismissed the *Severnaia pchela* reviewer as atavistic in his
struggles against the new tolerant spirit of the age. The reviewer
condemned the Jews for shortcomings such as money-grubbing and a
desire for revenge, which were imposed and reinforced by a thousand
years of persecution. Rabinovich countered that for the Jews

> our sacred duty should be to escape from shortcomings through the
> common aspiration of humanity for self-improvement; our first obli-
> gation should be to avoid hiding them or giving them mild names;

but this does not deprive us of the right to be proud of our nationality, of our origins which are older than classical times, our great destiny in the fate of nations, which we enlightened through our recognition of the Divinity ...

Such an assertion of Jewish national pride was not the usual staple of Russian journalism, but Rabinovich did not stop there. He refuted his rival's claim that Jews had a moral obligation to hate Christians. This argument demonstrated his ignorance of Jews, their religion and their traditions. "A Jew not only can but even should be virtuous just like a Christian for a very simple reason: Christianity sprang from Judaism." The injunction to "love thy neighbor as thyself," Rabinovich announced, was first enunciated by synagogue leaders who sought to apply the teaching of the Scriptures to practical life. There were a thousand places in the Talmud which advocated ignoring insults, doing good to one's enemy, and treating all living things well. The Talmud specifically said that good people of every nation will inherit heaven, and it never made the claim that there is no salvation outside Judaism. Ancient Judaism, like Christianity, had Divine Revelation at its foundation and consequently the basic virtues of the two religions were identical.

Rabinovich's riposte to *Severnaia pchela* demonstrated how effectively an articulate publicist might deal with attacks based on religious prejudice. The debate was one based largely on abstractions, an approach that worked well in the climate of vague liberalism which characterized the Reform Era. At the same time, Rabinovich went far beyond the efforts of "enlightened" Jews like Dumashevskii who were satisfied to ignore or disavow the Talmud. Rabinovich cited it casually, without apology, for the positive moral teachings which it contained. He was not prepared to acknowledge the official doctrine that the Talmud was a font of fanaticism whose influence had to be combatted at every turn. This refusal was a logical corollary of Rabinovich's declared respect for Jewish nationalism and tradition. In any event, while his articles were significant for their priority, they were only preliminary skirmishes before the grand debate on Jewish rights.

The article which more than any other attracted widespread attention to the Jews was another product of *Odesskii vestnik*, "The Odessa Talmud Tora" (26:6/III/1858), from the pen of N. I. Pirogov himself. Pirogov described his recent visit to the Odessa Jewish community Talmud-Tora, a charity primary school for orphans and the children of the poor. He found the conduct of the school in sharp contrast to that of the typical Jewish *heder*, which was invariably crowded with dirty

8 N. I. Pirogov

and underfed "Moshkas and Hershkas" chanting their lessons in a Yiddish sing-song. In little more than a year the Odessa Talmud-Tora had been transformed by its new director, Dr. Goldblium. Students were neatly and cleanly dressed, properly nourished and educated in "pure German" rather than Yiddish.

Pirogov marvelled at the mutability of the human character which made such a dramatic transformation possible. His pleasure was diminished by a melancholy fact: during the months in which the reform of the Talmud-Tora moved forward, not a step had been taken by the city's Christian population to improve the unsatisfactory state of its own schools. Pirogov explained this striking contrast by pointing to a virtue which the Jews of Odessa possessed and which Christians apparently lacked – conviction. Judaism made education a sacred religious duty, and Jews faithfully fulfilled this dictate. Whatever the merits or demerits of Jewish schools – and they were not all reformed

Talmud-Torahs – Jewish children attended them in large numbers. Christians, although they might believe that "God is the Word," lacked the proper conviction to translate this belief into reality with the same enthusiasm displayed by the Jews. Holding up the Jews as an example, Pirogov urged Christians to support education with more than lip-service.

"I know that many people will take offense at these parallels," Pirogov admitted in the course of his article. In this he was more than a little prophetic. The article triggered a flurry of activity within the Chief Department of Press Affairs, with officials great and small defending or condemning Pirogov.[17]

In public, Pirogov was challenged by N. B. Gersevanov's article, "The Jewish School in Odessa," which appeared in the prestigious *Sanktpeterburgskie vedomosti* (8:15/IV/1858). Gersevanov was no mean opponent. He was a native of Odessa who had been educated at the Richelieu Lyceum and traveled extensively abroad. He pursued a military career, rising to the rank of major-general. He was heavily decorated in the Crimean War. He won his journalistic spurs, contributing articles on literature and various public issues to *Syn Otechestva, Otechestvennye zapiski, Odesskii vestnik* and *Severnaia pchela*. He was subsequently an articulate opponent of peasant emancipation, peppering the Editing Commission which was preparing the reform with critical memoranda.[18]

Gersevanov's journalistic consideration of the Jewish Question merits special attention as one of the first efforts to frame Russian Judeophobia according to secular, "scientific" principles developed in the West. He declared his intention to eschew religious considerations. His specific objection lay in Pirogov's claim that the Jewish school, and by implication the Jews themselves, had been transformed in one year. This was impossible, asserted Gersevanov, because no people in the world displayed more tenacity in preserving their national character than the Jews. One could examine their history for 1,000 years and see the survival of their ancient traits, especially their violent and warlike disposition.

Pressed by critics, Gersevanov expanded his contentions and revealed his sources in two lengthy articles which he published in *Severnaia pchela* (63/64:21/23/III/1859). Gersevanov's chosen opponent was not so much Pirogov as Rabinovich. He disputed Rabinovich's claim that Jews who followed the dictates of their religion not only could but *should* be virtuous like Christians. In theory, said Gersevanov, this might be true, but in reality people often failed to do what their religion commanded. Nations, like individuals, acted on the basis of their national character, a composite of temperament and descent (*proiskhozhdenie*). Citing the authority of the French ethnographer Moreau de Jonnès, Gersevanov assigned the Christian nations, by temperament, to the Indo-German race (*plemia*) which dwelt in Europe; the Jews belonged to the Semitic race which inhabited Asia. Gersevanov attributed a descent and temperament to each race, making it appear that they were found in de Jonnès' work, although in actual fact they were not. The Semites ("The East") were descended, after the biblical flood, from Noah's son Shem. Their temperament was chloric and erotic, their national characteristics were hard-heartedness, hot-temperedness and voluptuousness. The Indo-Germans ("The West") were descended from Japheth. Their temperament was lymphatic and sanguine, their national characteristics were kind-heartedness and humanitarianism. From the East came the rule of force, represented by Cyrus, Mohammed, Chengis Khan and Timulane; from the West arose the rule of law, represented by Pericles, Joseph II and Catherine the Great. The history of relations between East and West was the struggle between barbarism and enlightenment.

The qualities of the Jews fully reflected their origins, according to Gersevanov. He cited Moreau de Jonnès in support:

> There is to be seen in the Jewish race, throughout the time of their existence as a distinctive nation, all the features of the Arab race: a broad and lively mind, a strong inclination toward imitation, and together with this a persistent, almost instinctive attachment to ancient customs; a spirit of observation and calculation to a very high degree; a violent and unquiet character, never satisfied by their fate; bravery in war; unusual persistence in the most hopeless situations in war; finally, bilious and turbulent passions, so that in their chronicles, more than those of any other nation, are to be met at every step rebellions, plots, mass condemnation of whole societies, including children, leading to the most inhumane punishments.[19]

As evidence of the Asiatic qualities of the Jews, Gersevanov pointed to their distinctive characteristics of polygamy, human sacrifice and false prophets. Their warlike temperament explained why the Jews were unable to live in peace with their neighbors or to defend their own independence since when there was no external enemy they fell to fighting one another.

All the vices of the East were contrasted with the virtues of the West in Gersevanov's schema. He was forced to pretend that early Russian history was characterized by peace and political tranquillity, conveniently forgetting the violence of Russia under the Mongols or the civil wars of the appanage period. Assuming such a temperament for Russians, Gersevanov then portrayed Jews and Russians as antipathies, for whom coexistence was impossible.

Despite the scientific patina of his arguments, Gersevanov reverted to the standard European litany of complaints against the Jews. They could not be good citizens because they considered themselves temporary sojourners in the land. They despised their neighbors and exploited them through deceitful trade and commerce. The Jews excelled as spies, smugglers, inn-keepers and counterfeiters. All nations hated the Jews because the cement of Jewish nationalism was hatred toward all other peoples.

In principle Gersevanov believed in the remediability of the Jews, albeit in the distant future. In Europe, he admitted, the Jews had received civil rights and become good citizens, but only because their long residence there had weaned them away from eastern influences. A similar transformation was impossible in Russia because the Jews were more sly and sophisticated than the simple Russian. As matters now stood, the admission of the Jews into the Russian interior would threaten disaster for the good and trustworthy peasant. A time might come when the Jews could be given greater rights in Russia, but it was not imminent just because Jews called themselves Moses and Iosif and a few youngsters in a Talmud-Tora had been taught to wash and groom themselves.

The solution, claimed Gersevanov, was best suggested by Dumashevskii's critique of Rabinovich: moral education and intermarriage with Europeans. Dumashevskii had not in fact recommended intermarriage, but it fitted Gersevanov's theorizing well for it was a quasi-racial solution. Ironically, a racial solution of this kind corresponded neatly to a "theological" one: mixed marriages between Jews and Russian Orthodox were illegal in Russia. Jewish partners would have to convert to Christianity, thus ending their status as Jews at a stroke, for Russian law recognized "Jew" only as a religious confession.

Gersevanov's provocative articles drew numerous responses. Despite their diversity, the replies all shared one common thread, a rejection of Gersevanov's racialist methodology. Dumashevskii quickly disavowed his self-proclaimed ally. Writing in *Odesskii vestnik* (51:8/V/1858) he dismissed Gersevanov's argument as rooted in religious bigotry due to its denial of sympathy between Christian and Jew.

A more forceful defense of the Jews was offered by L. I. Mandelshtam in *Sanktpeterburgskie vedomosti* (102:14/V/1858). He disputed the claim that the Jews were unable to mature and develop because of their strong national attachment, an argument which confused national loyalties and the maintenance of incidental properties such as habits, fashion and prejudices. Accidental characteristics could be abandoned without difficulty. Nationality (*narodnost'*) was something else. Nationality comprised a people's history, law, literature, unity and religion, and was quite properly preserved by a nation as the source of its strength. The Jews could be proud of their particular history, which enjoyed an antiquity older than any save India and China. Jewish law was as complex and developed as the Justinian Code. Jewish literature encompassed all fields of human learning, and much of European knowledge was based on rabbinical works. For Jews, religion could not be divorced from a feeling of national unity.

Mandelshtam raised the question which was to bedevil the debate on the Jewish Question. What were the constituent elements of Jewish nationality? Which of these elements were essential or valuable? What might Jews be expected to abandon in order to integrate themselves into Russian society? Mandelshtam presented these issues in embryo, but he was already asserting that Jewish nationality was something that the Jews would retain. He did not offer specifics as to what this entailed.

The Jewish critic A. Passover offered another perspective in *Moskovskie vedomosti* (90:17/IV/1859), at that time a prestigious liberal paper edited by V. F. Korsh. Gersevanov's muddle of unrelated materials and strings of French quotations, joked Passover, resembled Gogol's *Diary of a Madman*. (Passover was undoubtedly aware that Gersevanov fancied himself a gifted critic of Gogol.) More to the point, he faulted Gersevanov for discussing the Jews without reference to religion. This was an inappropriate omission when studying any national group but especially the Jews whose entire existence was suffused by religious principles. Moreover, religion could not be separated from national character; religion was its surest expression. Consider Gersevanov's use of the racialist argument. He attributed all vices to the Semites and all virtues to the Indo-Germans, including the Slavs. Yet the "Eastern institutions" which he ascribed to the Jews could be called Eastern only by one who was totally ignorant of the early Russian chronicles which offered numerous examples of polygamy and human sacrifice among the Russians in the tenth century. It was a religious system, Christianity, which drew them away from such abominations. Religion not only expressed national character but was capable of changing it.

Passover did not reject racialist concepts or deny that Semites and Indo-Germans might display important differences. What he condemned was Gersevanov's attempt to make these distinctions an unbridgeable chasm separating the two races, and denying any sympathy between Russians and Jews as a way of denying equal rights to the latter. Passover envisioned racial differences as complementary, in a manner which recalled Herder rather than Gobineau.[20] It was the Semites who produced the great religious concepts found in the Old and New Testaments, and which were so fruitfully developed by the Indo-Germans. "Indo-Germans provided the soil, the Semites provided the seed." Consequently, there was no fundamental divide between Russians and Jews. His biological model rejected the political implications of Gersevanov's thought.

Another anonymous rebuttal appeared in the thick journal *Russkii vestnik* (22:/VIII/1859) by Ia. R—T, entitled "Are the Jews Fit for Military Service?" The author pointed to the service of Jewish officers and enlisted men in the armies of all the European Great Powers. What had transformed the proverbially weak and cowardly European Jews into valiant and courageous troops were the free conditions of life and a recognition of their moral worth by the peoples among whom they lived. "The Jews, persecuted and trampled in the mud, whether by Polish pans, Turks, the Orthodox or Catholics, cannot be defended [as a consequence of their] being treated like dogs. But this Jew, at the first whiff of freedom, at the first indication of his human dignity, is reborn and considers himself a citizen, ready for every civil sacrifice, ready to give his blood and his life for those who consider him a free man." This author found the racialist approach not worth refutation, although Gersevanov attributed the ferocity and courage of the Jews to their Eastern blood.

The appearance of the article in *Russkii vestnik* reveals that the debate on the national character of the Jews was passing from the columns of the periodical press into the pages of the thick journals, at this time still the ultimate intellectual arbiters on social issues. Among this elite, a special role was played by the journal *Sovremennik*, edited by the poet and publicist N. A. Nekrasov. The publication was a leader in the emancipation movement and served as a breeding ground for the "revolutionary-democratic ideology" represented by such collaborators as N. G. Chernyshevskii and N. A. Dobroliubov.[21] Therefore the comments of *Sovremennik*, contained in its "Contemporary Survey" (69: 1858), carried special weight. With the debate well under way, the anonymous author, who declared himself a resident of the Pale, could pass critical judgment on the arguments of both sides.

Like virtually all other observers, the author rejected the racialist approach, as well as Gersevanov's attempt to disentangle religion from the Jews' national character. It was not instinct which shaped the Jews but history, a history expressed in the religious beliefs of the Jews. Religion was the basis of their moral and intellectual life and the underlying foundation for all their civil institutions. The authors supported Mandelshtam's contention that religion was the key to the national unity of the Jews. Gersevanov was correct in his identification of the Jews' resistance to change, but he had incorrectly located it in the vague concept of national character rather than religion. This resistance to change cast doubt on Pirogov's observations about the Odessa Talmud-Tora. While the external form of this religious school might well have changed, its essence must remain the same, because that essence was tied to religion. Without changing the religious concepts of the Jews – something that obviously could not be done in ten months – it was impossible to change the conditions of Jewish education.

Clearly religion was a vital consideration, so the view which the *Sovremennik* critic took is of the utmost importance. He reduced the essence of Judaism to a faith in the coming of a Messiah and to adherence to the Mosaic Law. These religious concepts had survived through centuries of persecution, but they had been warped and distorted as a consequence. They now gave rise to a number of serious faults: opposition to the spread of a Christian concept of citizenship among the Jews, a propensity toward usury and theft in their dealings with Christians, and their self-abasement before the strong and arrogance toward the weak. The author stressed that these were the fruits of persecution and expressed sympathy for the Jews' predicament. Best of all, the process was a reversible one. Wherever civilization had progressed to such a point as to give the Jews civil rights, their status and character both improved. Where they were persecuted, their moral character declined still further. Even the Russian situation gave some cause for hope. Within the Pale, the author had seen Jews act with charity toward poor Christians which was a demonstration of a growing closeness of Jew and gentile in Russian society. Pirogov was to be thanked for pointing out another symptom, the Jewish passion for education.

Despite this positive close, the article is a good example of the ambivalence which infused "progressive" Russian approaches to the

Jewish Question. The author was clearly sympathetic to the Jews and their historical travails, and he accepted that the grant of civil rights to the Jews improved their character. Yet he never suggested that the Jews of Russia be given such rights. Nor can the censorship be blamed for this omission: Gersevanov's first article had stipulated that all the fuss was eventually about equal rights. Nor had *Sovremennik* achieved its fame through editorial caution. There remained the problem of the depraved moral character of the Jews which had been shaped over a thousand years. There might be hopeful signs – Jewish charity, the yearning for education – but the author disputed Pirogov's claim that young Jews had been reborn through ten months of schooling. He thus offered a circular argument. The Jews could not be allowed out of the Pale because they were usurers and cheats. The Jews would not cease to be usurers and cheats until they were given civil rights. Perhaps the author approved of the government policy of gradualism, but he never said so. Even if gradualism was the answer, the author's professed belief in the steadfastness of the Jews in their religion, and his recognition of the degenerate state of their beliefs, ensured that moral reform of any type must be painfully slow.

Where should potential reformers begin? What specific elements of Judaism required change? The author identified the essentials of Judaism as a belief in the messiah and adherence to the Mosaic Law. Since the belief in the coming of the messiah kept the Jews from becoming good citizens of the states in which they dwelt, it must be abandoned. Reducing the essence of Judaism to messianism and Mosaic Law thus produced a demand for changes more sweeping than those inspired by the governmental critique of Judaism, which laid all the blame on the Talmud, not the "primordial" beliefs of the Jews.

Maintaining its support for an emancipatory resolution of the Jewish Question, *Russkii invalid* opened its pages to L. I. Mandelshtam (58:15/III/1959) to reply to the *Sovremennik* article. Mandelshtam cut to the heart of the matter on Jewish disabilities. If the government recognized the necessity of restricting the activities of the Jews in order to serve a higher social good, the Jews could and would accept it. The fear among the Jews, however, was that the government did not correctly understand what it was doing in restricting Jewish rights. Restrictions were in error if they were based upon the assumption that the Jews stood at a lower level of civilization than the rest of the population. Historically the Jews had made numerous contributions to world civilization, especially in the development of law. Contemporary Jews maintained an elaborate social welfare system for the members of the community. If there were fewer examples of Jews helping poor Christians, it was because the gentile population was better off as a whole than the Jewish. Judaism nonetheless made charity to all men incumbent upon all Jews. The Jews were avid in their pursuit of education with the consequence that they were the first people in Europe to boast of universal literacy. Answering the claim that the Jews were apathetic to the government's educational efforts, Mandelshtam pointed out that the Jews had paid out nearly 3 million rubles in state taxes since 1843 for the upkeep of the state Jewish school system.

The chief reason why the Jews were made to look so bad, complained Mandelshtam, was that they were held to a completely different standard from the rest of the population. "Non-Jews demand from all Jews without exception a standard of education which is attained only by the highest circles of society, while at the same time educated Jews are not given those civil rights which the very lowest sort of other people possess." The Jews, alone in the world, were not allowed to have a rabble. What Moshka and Ioshka did was attributed to all Jews, while the crimes of Stepan or Ivan were their own individual business.

Despite such treatment, Jews had historically demonstrated a willingness to adopt the clothes, customs, language and style of life of the peoples among whom they lived. This was emphasized by the tendency of the great thinkers of Judaism to write in the vernacular wherever they lived: Josephus Flavius in Greek, Maimonides in Arabic, Spinoza in Latin, Disraeli in English, Heine in German. Despite Gersevanov's racialist claims, the Jews easily assimilated the national characteristics of their neighbors. French Jews were flippant, English Jews were dryly devout, German Jews were pedants, and Polish and Turkish Jews were superstitious.

The commonality of the Jews and the other peoples of the Russian Empire was also demonstrated by history. The Jews, far from being aliens, had long shared the life and history of Russia. Jews lived in the Crimea before there was a Russian state. Georgian families like the Golitsyns and Bagrations testified to their Jewish origins. Before Vladimir accepted Christianity the southern steppe was ruled by the Jewish Khazars. Russia was obligated to the Jews for the Bible, which was the very bulwark of the Russian throne. Indeed, Mandelshtam declared confidently, all Russian Jews shared with Russians one tsar, one learning, and one hope in the future.

Reform was the subject of many pens, but there was disagreement as to whether it would require ten months, ten years or ten centuries.

Mandelshtam promised Russian society that if it would give the Jews the opportunity, they were prepared internally. Granted equality, teamsters with teamsters, craftsmen with craftsmen, merchants with merchants, Jews would prove equal in charity, morality, humanitarianism and pursuit of education. Here was a direct challenge to the more pessimistic programs of Gersevanov and *Sovremennik*.

The discussion of the Jewish Question in 1858 suggested that the epoch of sympathy and objectivity toward the Jews foreseen by Osip Rabinovich had arrived. Jewish litterateurs, led by Rabinovich himself, rushed to greet the new era. A majority of the articles which appeared in the press in 1858 on the Jewish Question came from Jewish pens. A growing number of publications acquired the services of a "house Jew" who specialized in discussion of the Jewish Question. Aside from calls for national self-improvement and civil equality, however, Jewish writers did not necessarily display a set of common assumptions or even a common approach. Their initial efforts suggested what was to come, a vigorous debate on the nature and future of the Jews as a national-religious group.

Alongside Jewish publicists appeared non-Jewish writers, often individuals who claimed first-hand knowledge of the Jews and wished to apply correctives to public assumptions, be they hostile or friendly toward the Jews. The debate quickly acquired a theoretical character, evolving into complex assessments of the national character of the Jews. Gersevanov's articles, with their overt racialist perspective, however abstruse, were an anomaly, a surprisingly up-to-date sample of pseudo-scientific Judeophobia. Racial Antisemitism was not influential in Western Europe at this time, and it is not surprising that it found little response among Russian writers inclined to follow the Western lead. Gersevanov was also an exception in his claims that the Jews could not remain as Jews – for intermarriage would have stripped their racial identity – and be good citizens. All other observers at this time concurred that the Jews could be improved, although they differed sharply as to the time required. There was also a tendency, even from those who professed sympathy to the Jews, to accept that in the mass they were in a depraved and fallen state, however this decadence might be explained.

A survey of this first Russian debate on the Jewish Question suggests one final observation. The participants quickly focused on the essential question of civil rights for Jews. The Russian censorship, in this as in other regards, proved quite unable to control the public debate on the Jewish Question once it slipped the censor's leash.

2   The *Illiustratsiia* Affair of 1858

Illiustratsiia, edited in St. Petersburg from 1858 to 1861 by V. R. Zotov, was a journalistic cross-breed, a newspaper with the pretensions of a thick journal. It was filled with illustrations, often of travel narratives, and at the hefty subscription price of 14 rubles per annum was clearly intended for a prosperous audience. The centerpiece of the publication was Zotov's pseudonymous column "Diary of an Acquaintance," in which he surveyed the issues of the day.

A native of the Pale of Settlement himself, Zotov was disgusted with the vogue of sympathy toward the Jews in the press in 1858. In his "Diary" (25:26/VI/1858) Zotov offered a corrective. He focused on the foreign activities of the Russian Jewish magnate Evzel Gavrilovich Gintsburg. Gintsburg had recently given an opulent ball in Paris, and the French press had written it up, together with fulsome testimonials to Gintsburg. Speaking of "Mr. N" (Gintsburg), one French correspondent praised the social position, based on his generosity, which he had achieved in Russia at a time when most Russian Jews lacked civil equality. Zotov belittled the philanthropy of Mr. N, and hinted darkly at the origins of the family wealth. (The Gintsburg fortune originally derived from the profits of liquor tax-farming.)

Given the Judeophile mood in the capital, sharpened by Gersevanov's recent attacks on the Jewish national character, even such a casual peccadillo did not pass unnoticed. Once more *Russkii invalid* took the lead. An anonymous *feuilletonist* (168:3/VIII/1858) defended the "God-forsaken and persecuted tribe," arguing that they should receive full civil rights (and showing again how quickly the censor's restraints on calls for equal rights for Jews broke down). The author observed that *Odesskii vestnik* was filled with reports of Mr. N's charitable exertions, most recently in the form of aid to sixty impoverished families. Informed commentators confirmed the economic benefits of the Jews' commercial adroitness. Where Jews were given equal rights they quickly became useful and loyal citizens. England provided a contemporary illustration. A scion of the Rothschild family, Baron Lionel de Rothschild, had just been seated in the House of Commons.[1] The author appealed to Russian society to view the Jews as equals, rather than as despised "Yids" (*Zhidy*).[2]

Rising to the challenge, Zotov devoted his next "Diary" (35:4/IX/ 1858) to a lengthy attack upon *Russkii invalid*'s defense of the "West-Russian Yids."[3] He dismissed examples of Jewish virtue and utility. Mr. N's contribution to the poor was a shabby imitation of the assistance which Russian millionaires had given to destitute families during the Crimean War. Zotov assailed Gintsburg's "worship of the golden calf" which had enabled him to enlarge an initial capital of 1,000 rubles into 10 million in two years. As for Baron Rothschild, another Jewish millionaire, his election was not "the triumph of truth over superstition," as claimed by *Russkii invalid*, but rather the victory of "gold over civilization."

The most interesting and contentious part of Zotov's column was his examination of the origins and significance of the word "*zhid*," whose use *Russkii invalid* had rejected. As Rabinovich's "About Moshkas and Ioshkas" had already revealed, names meant something in status-conscious Russian society. Indeed, more than linguistics underlay Zotov's analysis of the word, for he used it as a starting point for an extensive critique of the failings and shortcomings of the Jews.

There was nothing improper in using the word "Yid" to describe Jews, argued Zotov. Other terms, such as *evrei*, which Zotov derived from *Evera*, or Israelite (*Izrail'tiane*), derived from Izrail or "Godsee-ing" Jacob, were rooted in a particular time and place and would be anachronistic in contemporary Russia. To use them would be the equivalent of calling Russians "Slavs," Italians "Romans," Swedes "Scandinavians," and Frenchmen "Gauls." What did modern Yids have in common with the ancient Israelites? Certainly not the language or alphabet, and neither the religious rites nor the religious beliefs of the theocratic Israelite state. If one sought vestiges of the ancient Israelites, the place to look was the modern Karaites. Zotov belabored the Jews by praising this Jewish sect. He followed the erroneous belief – fostered by Karaite spokesmen – that the adherents of the sect had left Palestine before the crucifixion of Christ. Karaites followed a religious system that was closer to that of Christians, he claimed, and had no special aversion to the followers of Christ.

A number of phenomena made the Jews different from the Karaites.

Divided by schisms, by conflict with the hostile Sadducees, by the fanaticism of the adherents of the Cabala and other obscure symbolic works like the Mishna and Tosefot, they finally lost their nationality to the yoke of Roman despotism and became, together with the heathens, the enemies of Christ; under the name of *Iudei* they were driven beyond the limits of the Roman Empire and came into Europe with their irritating character, greed, physical degeneration and filthiness, the inevitable stamp of an age-old slavery.

In Germany they acquired the gibberish which they still spoke in everyday life. Each nation that came in contact with them adopted a phonetic version of the name, Iudeus, which the Jews called themselves. Thus they were called *Jude, Giudeo, Jew, Żyd, Zhid.*

If there was nothing inherently negative in the name "Yid," why did negative connotations now cling to it? The humiliation of the Jews sprang not from their name, Zotov explained, but from their conduct. They were hated because their espousal of the Talmud made them hostile to civilization. As proof Zotov offered his readers two talmudic citations: "the world was created for the Jews alone, but nothing was created for Christians, not rewards, not even punishments"; and "all other nations are unclean nations, hostile to God; Jews are not to have kindred relations with them, they are to guard against food or drink from them; Jews may without sin break their word to non-believers ... may rob them, oppress them, enslave them."

Zotov broke no new ground in using talmudic quotations to discredit the Jews, and hostility to the Talmud had been an inspiration for state policies toward the Jews as early as the reign of Nicholas I. Zotov was, however, the first Russian author to employ the Talmud in public debate. Gersevanov, for example, mentioned the Talmud in passing but displayed no acquaintance with the lush tradition of anti-Talmudism in Western Europe. Zotov saw the Talmud as pernicious because its tenets were translated directly into action by the "West Russian Talmudists," a sarcastic euphemism which he substituted for "Yids." Examples abounded to show that Jews considered all Christians to be *goyim* who could be cheated and abused without moral scruple. In the villages of the Pale, Jews were coarse and unenlightened inn-keepers and factors, opportunistic intermediaries between the Polish nobility and the peasants. Jewish rumor-mongering embroiled the landowners in squabbles with one another, while the Jewish tavern-keeper encouraged drunkenness among the peasants. In wartime Jews bowed and scraped before both sides in their eagerness to make a profit. Urban Jews were no better. They were "swindlers, usurers, who survive by greed, cunning and a piece of herring, so as to increase their capital and to catch undetected a golden fish in troubled waters." Zotov chose his favorite target, Mr. N, as the archetype of such rascals. Only after he had amassed a fortune did Mr. N become concerned with appearances or status. Rich Jews, with a veneer of refinement, were the ones who no longer wished to be called "Yid."

The obvious conclusion from Zotov's observations was that the Jewish Question could not be solved by the grant of equal rights, for too great a gulf separated Jew and gentile. Efforts to promote civilization among the Jews through the special state Jewish school system had been a conspicuous failure. It was well and good to speak in general terms about equality, but publicists needed to see the West Russian Talmudists at work. Live among the Jews for a year, Zotov advised, and one would recognize the impossibility of their assimilation into Christian society. There were good reasons for keeping the Jews in restricted areas and for circumscribing their occupational rights. The Jews, sunk in superstition and Talmudism, had to be left alone. Only enlightenment, morality and the development of humane feelings – distant prospects indeed – could lead to assimilation. "Enlightenment alone makes people equal."

Russian Jewish intellectuals, able to count on the sympathetic encouragement of the nation's most respected publications, saw Zotov's tirade as a provocation to which they hastened to reply. *Odesskii vestnik* published the rebuttals of two writers, Faddei Berezkin (117:18/X/1858) and P. Liakub (139:11/XII/1858). Both authors offered cursory defenses of the Talmud and also rebutted Zotov's romanticisation of the moral superiority of the Karaites. Typically, they both stressed the role that educated, enlightened Jews were already playing in Russian society. The most noteworthy responses appeared in two prestigious publications in Moscow and St. Petersburg, *Russkii vestnik* and *Atenei*.

Russkii vestnik was an enormously successful thick journal, with 5,700 paid subscribers in 1862. Under the able leadership of M. N. Katkov, at that time a leader of Russian liberalism, the journal advocated a program of moderate, liberal reform. Among contributors was I. Chatskin, an Odessa Jew who came to Moscow after eight years of service in the Odessa educational system. In the "Contemporary Chronicle" section of *Russkii vestnik* (17: September 1858, 133–44) he published an article "*Illiustratsiia* and the Question of the Extension of Jewish Civil Rights." Zotov's subsequent attack on Chatskin, and the scandal which it precipitated, have obscured the actual content of this article, so it is worth considering for the insights it provided on the willingness of Russian Jewish publicists to make concessions to public opinion. It also stands as the self-portrait of Russian Jewry, both traditionalist and enlightened, which at least some members of the Russian Jewish intelligentsia sought to convey to the Russian public.

Chatskin couched his motive for responding to Zotov in the rhetoric of the day: he felt compelled to answer "a conscious deviation from the commitment to progress." *Illiustratsiia* took one man, Mr. N, and made him the exemplar of the entire race, a dishonest tactic which would be immediately rejected if employed against Frenchmen, Germans or Russians. Worse still was *Illiustratsiia's* attack on civil rights. Unable to argue against greater rights for enlightened individuals, the publication was forced to pretend that there were no enlightened Jews in Russia. Chatskin devoted most of his article to demonstrating the fallaciousness of this argument. He did not deny the fallen state of the West Russian Yids, for he himself spoke frequently of their "moral degeneracy." Zotov, he complained, failed to recognize the reasons for this degeneracy and, more importantly, neglected the abundant exceptions which Chatskin could observe in his own home town. He offered a paean to Odessa Jewry: they possessed a beautiful synagogue in which religious worship was becoming ever more refined. Ignoring the Talmud-centered education of West Russian Jewry, Odessa Jews studied in the state primary schools and passed on to the gymnasium. Odessa boasted Jewish doctors, philologists and writers. Because of Odessa's identification with enlightenment, Jewish traditionalists viewed it as Gehenna, and imagined the city surrounded by a yawning, fiery pit.

This last statement is revealing. In emphasizing the merits of Odessa Jewry, a very small percentage of the Empire's total Jewish population, Chatskin did not deny Zotov's hostile characterization of the vast majority of the Jewish population. In fact Chatskin specifically conceded the existence of "persistent fanaticism" amongst Russian Jewry. This fanaticism took the form of a reluctance to coexist with Christians, a willingness to fleece the peasants in the villages at every opportunity, and a preoccupation with money-grubbing in the towns.

What was the source of this "persistent fanaticism"? Not, as Zotov claimed, the Talmud. Chatskin denied that the Talmud deserved either the denunciation or panegyrics which had been heaped upon it by friends and foes. The contents of the Talmud hardly mattered. They were complex and could only be understood in their historical context.

The average "West Russian Talmudist" was hardly capable of such intellectual endeavors. As a consequence the Talmud was nothing more than "a drop in the ocean of those conditions which account for the moral degeneracy of Russian Jewry and encourages them in their alienation from and hostility to Christians." In the context of Russia's recent tradition of hostility to the Talmud these sentiments might be considered praising with faint damns, and they left unresolved the fundamental question of *why* West Russian Jewry was so degenerate. Defenders of the Jews traditionally pointed to the centuries of persecution, but Chatskin chose to ignore the issue. He pressed home the claim that Zotov was dishonestly selective in his survey of Jews and his denial that they could safely be given civil rights. Thus Zotov overpraised the Karaites, while any visitor to Odessa could testify to their isolated life and alien ideas. *Illiustratsiia* railed against England because experience there demonstrated that Jews could be good citizens. What the English had really done was to banish those prejudices which still motivated *Illiustratsiia*'s author, prejudices which in the past produced St. Bartholomew's Night and the horrors of the Spanish Inquisition. Zotov conclusively revealed his medieval fanaticism by rummaging through ancient history in order to justify the use of the name Yid. Had the author forgotten, Chatskin remonstrated, that in Russia "Yid" had become synonymous with petty tradesmen and usurers?

Chatskin's article reflected the mood among some acculturated Jews that "the best among us" be given equal rights – the path that the Russian government was then following. Russia would not be endangered by granting equal rights to the West Russian Yids, Chatskin assured Zotov, for "the humble Polish Jew, burdened by fanaticism and greed, will not tumble straight from his tavern into a vice-governorship." Contending that enlightenment should be the criterion for civil rights, Chatskin also introduced a new, universal precept. It was not enlightenment which makes all people equal, as Zotov claimed, but the very fact of their being human (*chelovech'nost'*). This may have been only a rhetorical flourish, however, since Chatskin did not develop it. What the reader was likely to take away from the article was the impression that Zotov was a fanatic, but that so were the West Russian Yids. The difference between them was that Zotov, as an educated man, had no excuse to offer for his fanaticism. He deserved scorn, not the pity that was appropriate for the unenlightened Yids.

Atenei, edited by E. F. Korsh, counted the most prominent members of the nascent Russian liberal movement among its contributors, as well as such celebrated authors as Saltykov-Shchedrin, Goncharov and

Turgenev. Nonetheless, it had a scholastic quality which discouraged a wider readership, and it failed to survive beyond 1859. The rebuttal to *Illiustratsiia* which it published by M. Gorvits (5: IX–X/1858, 421–39) was typical of its more academic approach. Gorvits did not feel obliged, as had Chatskin, to concede too much to prevailing prejudices. Rather, he demolished Zotov's forays into Jewish linguistics and history. The Jews had never called themselves anything but *bene Izrael* and their country *erez Izrael*. Zotov's attribution of a pre-Christian genesis to the Karaites was simply ludicrous: specialists knew that they emerged from a schism among Jews in the Arab Caliphate around AD 750. Far from rejecting any authority save the Bible, the Karaites had their authorities and codes which corresponded directly to the Talmud. Not that the Talmud was the diabolical book assumed by Christian fanatics in the Middle Ages. Unlike Chatskin, Gorvits defended the integrity of the Talmud and Cabala as well. They were the legitimate and brilliant offspring of Greek and medieval philosophy.

Zotov assumed an eternal hatred between Jew and Christian. Gorvits followed the liberal formulas of Western Europe and attributed Jewish misanthropy to the systematic persecution of their religion by Christian Europe. Faults which the Jews had acquired in the course of centuries, moreover, were quickly remedied. Zotov called for the Jews to display an interest in civilization. "One has to be blind or a fanatical enemy of everything Jewish to deny their aspirations to become enlightened and to serve as useful citizens of their native country." Gorvits compared the Jews to the modern Greeks, whose natural character had been flawed by the corrosive influence of Turkish domination. A parallel fate had befallen the Jews. "Does the author really hope to correct these faults by an article which reopens old wounds? No, this is not love, but an attack upon a people who deserve the respect of other nations."

It was Zotov's turn to pick up the gauntlet. Chatskin was seen as an easy mark, and *Illiustratsiia* addressed him in a Diary entry entitled *"Russkii vestnik* and the Question of a Proper Tone for Journalistic Opinions" (42:23/X/1858). As the title indicates, Zotov was more concerned with Chatskin's tone than his arguments. Why all the talk of the Inquisition and bonfires in the squares of Madrid, he queried, when Chatskin was apparently in agreement with the Diary's facts?

> We believe that although he speaks Jewish, he speaks Russian quite badly and pretentiously. He calls us Turks and plantation owners because we sent forth an article in which we mentioned openly the

shortcomings of the most unenlightened part of the Jews, the West Russian Jews. Chatskin agrees with our claims: that the Karaites are better than West Russian Jewry, that early instruction in the Talmud is unhealthy, that West Russian Jews are stubborn in their fanaticism, that in the villages they fleece the peasant and in the towns they are money-grubbers. If all this is true, then what is the matter with Mr. Chatskin?

As for the claim that simply being human, rather than adherence to enlightened values made people equal, the term "human" was so elastic as to be meaningless. "I can pity a poor, uneducated Yid who robs my pocket but I cannot consider him an equal merely because he is a man." Zotov closed with the hope that Chatskin would be able to read his response, since it was written in Russian. In short, he considered him superficially educated, a rival who was unworthy of serious rebuttal and one who could be dismissed with wit and ridicule.

Gorvits' refutation was a more serious matter, as Zotov himself admitted when he dealt with it in the next issue of *Illiustratsiia* (43:30/ X/1858). He recapitulated his theories about the ancient Jews and the Karaites and again attacked the Talmud. If there was any merit to the argument that the faults of the Jews were the consequence of Christian persecution, it could not hold for Russia where the Jews had been treated "like guests" since the partitions of Poland. The Jews had borne neither serfdom nor lifetime military service. Schools were built for them. Yet the West Russian Talmudists wanted more rights while still retaining the Talmud and looking down on the goyim. Having said this, Zotov professed not to disdain the entire Jewish race, but only its evildoers.

The matter might well have ended here amidst the esoterica of linguistics and ancient history but for Zotov's inability to resist one final jab. In reviewing the history of the dispute, Zotov noted that his article in No. 35 had brought forth opposition from Judeophiles, "without any doubt the agents of the well-known N, who obviously does not spare gold for the praise of his name and there thus appeared in print two Jewish litterateurs, a certain Reb-Chatskin and a Reb-Gorvits." A subsequent issue added insult to injury by publishing a series of "West Russian Sketches" which presented extremely negative descriptions of the local Yids, who were "the chief minions and champions of peasant abasement and ignorance" (44:6/XI/1858).[4]

The genesis of the "Literary Protest" of 1858 is somewhat obscure, complicated by the fact that a number of periodicals published their own version of the Protest, and signatories of one version were often included in another. The first newspaper to carry a protest was the liberal *Sanktpeterburgskie vedomosti* (258:25/XI/1858). The editors correctly noted that the dispute arose from the *Illiustratsiia* Diary of 26 June, which had attacked Mr. N and spoken rudely about the Jews in the western provinces. They explained that Chatskin and Gorvits had been more interested in defending all Jews than preserving the honor of Mr. N. *Illiustratsiia* had responded by branding the two publicists as agents of Mr. N, and had called them "Reb." The editors continued:

> Such outbursts fail in countries where the reading public possesses a tact which is able to recognize base motives disguised as personal loyalty, and where public opinion punishes with deserved shame people who permit themselves such libels. Always and everywhere literature is obligated to reject unsubstantiated insinuations against one's honor and good name. We do not know Messrs. Chatskin and Gorvits personally, and have no ties to them. But recognizing the high calling of literature, we consider it an obligation to protest against such an abuse of the printed word by a periodical which allows itself to become a weapon of personal insult.

The Protest bore eleven signatures, those of K. Kavelin, V. Spasovich, V. Bezobrazov, A. Galakhov, F. Dmitriev, N. Chernyshevskii, P. Annenkov, Ivan Turgenev, I. Ogrizko, N. Tikonravov and A. Kraevskii.[5] This version was reprinted in *Moskovskie vedomosti* (143:27/XI/1858) and *Severnaia pchela* (262:27/XI/1858).

Chatskin's article had appeared in *Russkii vestnik* whose argumentative editor, Mikhail Katkov, was sympathetic to the Jews throughout his long career, and so the Moscow thick journal played a major role in the protest. In the journal's "Contemporary Chronicle" (18:XI/1858, 125–9) N. F. Pavlov attacked the tactics of *Illiustratsiia*. He summarized the debate, clearly siding with Chatskin and Gorvits. Who is closer to the Christian spirit, he asked, Jews who defended their race, or a Christian who attacked these victims of circumstance, and slandered human nature itself by asserting that the Jews were irremediable. The base motives of *Illiustratsiia* were clearly demonstrated by the magazine's determination to call the Jews Yids. Equally insulting was the technique of putting the term "Reb" in front of the names of Chatskin and Gorvits in an effort to lower their standing in the eyes of the Russian public, forgetting that "the Jews are as guilty of being Jews as the Russians are guilty of being Russians." Pavlov also rejected as slander Zotov's claim that Chatskin and Gorvits were nothing more than hirelings of the plutocratic Mr. N.

The same issue of *Russkii vestnik* carried a short letter from Chatskin to *Illiustratsiia* which the latter had declined to print. Chatskin rejected as slanderous the charge that he was an agent of Mr. N and appealed in his defense to the court of public opinion. At no time did Chatskin himself indicate that his objections involved *Illiustratsiia*'s treatment of the Jewish Question – he was concerned with his good name.

Appended to Pavlov's article and Chatskin's letter was a piece entitled "The Conduct of *Illiustratsiia* and a Protest," which was to become the best known form of the Literary Protest. It announced that an outrage had been committed against the Russian reading public which could not be tolerated by any honorable person. The June article of *Illiustratsiia* was summarized and condemned for exciting the indignation of both Christians and Jews. Consequently, the public was offered the following Protest:

> In the interests of truth and good, literature should enjoy as much freedom as possible to defend or reject opinions. The fuller and more dispassionate is openness (glasnost), the better for literature and for life. Any published declaration has a special responsibility before society, and the greater its importance, the more it carries the character of a moral deed.
>
> *Illiustratsiia* has not simply distorted the opinion of its opponents, to which they could answer either with literary exposure or contempt.
>
> *Illiustratsiia* permitted itself to touch on the moral character of Messrs. Gorvits and Chatskin, and to infringe upon that which constitutes the highest good for every honorable human being.
>
> *Illiustratsiia* has permitted itself not simply an unsubstantiated charge, not simply an unworthy allusion, which can burst forth in the heat of an argument from a person who is either fanatical in his opinions or not sufficiently developed in his moral relationships.
>
> *Illiustratsiia* has permitted itself a slander, the more scandalous and insolent in that there did not exist the slightest pretext for it, even in the eyes of such people who do not understand any other motive save dishonorable cupidity and bribery.
>
> In the persons of Messrs. Gorvits and Chatskin all society is insulted, all Russian literature. No honorable person can remain apathetic to such disgraceful behavior, and all Russian literature should as one man indignantly protest against it.
>
> Such a general protest will best satisfy the honor of the insulted individuals and be the very best demonstration of the health of that social milieu, which by its own free act will defeat and sweep aside any unworthy act.
>
> Let this protest serve as an example and a warning for the future and let it forever safeguard our literature from similar events.

This version was signed by forty-eight people, including a cross section of well-known writers, publishers, and even a few censors. The editor promised to publish the names of new signatories in the next issue.

The next issue of the "Contemporary Chronicle" of *Russkii vestnik* (18:XI/1858, 245–7) offered an expanded list of ninety-nine signatures which included major and minor litterateurs of the two capitals. Two additional letters were published that are of special interest. The first was from Ivan Turgenev who expressed his hope that such escapades as those of *Illiustratsiia* would be forever deterred by the impact of the Literary Protest.

A second letter, written by P. Kulish, was signed by a group of Ukrainian intellectuals including N. Kostomarov and T. Shevchenko. The letter briefly reviewed Jewish history, especially the terrible persecutions visited upon them.

> In this fashion Christians, ardent in their faith and with heartfelt determination to turn the Children of Israel to the light, instead turned them away from the true path, and made nonsense of the evangelical word ... The Jews, restrained everywhere by the laws themselves, unwillingly turned to slyness and trickery, of necessity giving religious sanction to every unpunished evil which they could inflict upon Christians.

A new moment had now arrived, Kulish declared. All recognized the futility of religious persecution, and the spread of civic equality to the Jews "is sufficient to cleanse Jewish nationalism from all that is hostile to non-believers." Kulish detected a number of what appeared to be Ukrainian names on the original Protest, but none specifically tied to the emergent Ukrainian national movement. He now joined the Protest in the name of the movement, speaking for

> that nation which more than the Great Russians or Poles suffers from the Jews and expresses its hatred of the Jews by claiming many thousands of bloody victims. This nation is unable to escape the evil which is encompassed not by the Jews but in the religious and civil institutions of Poland. They thus revenge themselves on the Jews with a single-minded feeling of righteousness which is even celebrated in their poetical songs.

In the future, Jewish writers recalled with longing this "forgotten epoch" of civility toward the Jews. But nostalgia occasionally blurred and romanticized this moment. There were many motives that prompted these signatures and letters, and not all of them had much to do with the Jews. The historian S. M. Gintsburg observed that the protest did not even mention the Jewish Question and did not specify that the Protest involved a pair of *Jewish* writers.[6] Still, none of the versions of the protest appeared in a vacuum: all offered lengthy summaries of the articles, including the offending materials from *Illiustratsiia*. Signatories were well aware that the dispute centered on the Jewish Question and the insulted honor of two Jewish writers. The entire event could thus be seen, as Gintsburg says, as "consciousness of the unity of Russian and Jewish society."[7] Yet in recognizing this moment as the high point in Russian–Jewish relations during the Reform Era, important qualifications must be voiced. The ideological diversity of the signatories makes the list suspect. Liberals sat cheek by jowl with Slavophiles and "Revolutionary-Democrats," a strong indication that substantial political issues were not involved. Disagreement lurked close to the surface. *Sovremennik*'s celebrated critic N. A. Dobroliubov refused to sign the Protest, and chided the participation of Nekrasov and Chernyshevskii as inappropriate, given the participation of liberals and reactionaries.[8] In private, Count D. N. Bludov, Kiselev's successor as chairman of the Jewish Committee, characterized the Protest as "ridiculous" (*nelepnyi*).[9] The Protest, in short, was a general statement in support of "progress" in society as a whole and of decorum in arguments between literary gentlemen, and was tied to the resolution of the Jewish Question only in the most indirect way. A number of the signatories, such as I. S. Aksakov, soon emerged as leading Judeophobes, while A. Kraevskii's *Golos* became the preeminent Judeophobe newspaper of the 1860s and 1870s.

Consider the assumption of the protestors that it was an insult to call Chatskin and Gorvits "Reb." Reb was the form of address for adult males in the traditionalist community. Zotov used the term not just to indicate that Gorvits and Chatskin were Jews – he had already specified that – but to emphasize their ties to the "West Russian Talmudists," especially the Hasidim who represented the archetype of the "ignorant Yids." The implication, apparently accepted by the signatories, was that it was a personal insult to call an educated Jew a Hasid (i.e., to link him with the Jewish masses).

Most of the signatories of the Protest were Russians with little practical experience of the Jews in the western provinces, and who recoiled from the realities of the Jewish world when they finally encountered it. One of the signatories of the Protest, S. S. Gromyka, had been attacked exactly a month before the Protest for disparaging remarks on the Jews which he published in *Sovremennik*.[10] Writing in

Otechestvennye zapiski (9:IX/1858), the Jewish critic Ia. Rozenblat took Gromyka to task for a travel narrative of the western provinces in which he offered a portrait of Jewish life in a district town. The account depicted dirty streets swarming with Jews bustling about in a desperate struggle for money. Gromyka frequently used the term "Yid" for the Jews, and Rozenblat did not dispute this, conceding that it might be acceptable language in an area with a strong German influence, where the operative term was "Jude." What amazed Rozenblat was that Gromyka also used the insulting diminutive "Zhidka" ("Little Yid") which could have no linguistic justification except as a patronizing insult.

The response of all concerned is interesting for the light it sheds on the literary climate on the very eve of the Protest. Gromyka defended himself in *Russkii vestnik* (17:IX/1858, 90–5) where he was a regular correspondent. He explained that he had intended no hostility to the Jews but had sought to show how they had been ground down and degraded by the unique local conditions of the Ukraine. He blamed the editors of *Sovremennik*: if they had not spread his article out over two issues and had not edited it so sharply, his true meaning would have been clear. (*Sovremennik's* editors replied in kind. They denied that they had distorted Gromyka's meaning and claimed to have replaced "Zhidka" with "Evrei" on several occasions [10:X/1858, 609–11].) Even if Gromyka ascribed the degradation of the Jews to outside factors, his article nonetheless painted them in the very darkest of colors.

A remarkably similar course was followed by another signer of the Protest, I. K. Babst, who in 1859 published a travel account of Belorussia and the western provinces "teeming with filth and Yids."[11] Babst carefully explained that the Jew was a product of centuries of persecution which had reduced him to a degraded position from which he could escape only through money. This explained the determination of the Jews to enrich themselves through fair means or foul. Only when the Jew was given equal rights with Christians would he recognize the sinfulness of employing dishonest means against Christians, and only then would he abandon the morality of an eye for an eye. Until that moment, reality remained in the form of the physically repulsive Jew who dominated every field of trade, who engaged in massive smuggling, and who held the helpless peasant completely in his thrall while he fed on and destroyed all the resources of the region.

> The poverty and oppression of the peasants, the capriciousness and lordly laziness of the landowners, the absence of commercial sense in

> the remaining classes, the bribe-taking of the administration which is always on the side of the wealthy – taken together this works toward the complete domination of Jewish capital in the West and the Belorussian areas. Jammed and concentrated into these localities alone, the Jews concentrate all their activities here and meet no opposition. All the population is in the hands of the Jews – this is true, but what is one to do without them? The Jewish cattle-dealer, the Jewish leaseholder, squeezes all the juice from the people – this is true, but how can one get around without the Jews?[12]

The Jews were thus a necessary evil, whose harmfulness would be attenuated only through the economic and moral regeneration of western Russia – a transformation which was not soon to occur.

A different set of problems lay in the letter of P. Kulish and the Ukrainian nationalists. This letter has properly been described as a "political declaration," designed to reconcile the historically inimical Ukrainian and Jewish people, with a view to recruiting the latter for the Ukrainian national movement, which Kulish and his associates represented.[13] Kulish called for equal rights as the only way to cleanse Jewish nationalism from its hostility to the Christian world. Unfortunately, until such equality was attained, the Jews would retain their fanatical hatred of non-Jews, a situation which neither a well-ordered state nor the Ukrainian population could be expected to tolerate. Kulish's gesture of reconciliation anticipated a corresponding response from the Jews, not just toward the signatories of the Protest as individuals, but in acceptance of their role as the collective representative of emergent Ukrainian nationalism.

The Jews to which this appeal was directed were intellectuals who were oriented toward Russian culture, not toward a Ukrainian nationalism struggling to be born. The terms of Jewish–Ukrainian rapprochement, as defined by Kulish, were a recipe for disillusionment and disaster, as events quickly showed. Within a few years Jewish intellectuals were asked to make an overt choice between Russification and Ukrainization. The choice by most Jewish intellectuals of the former could not please Ukraineophiles.[14]

Kulish and his associates were driven by serious and high-minded ideals, but the same could not be said for the self-serving protesters who emerged from the conservative camp. The involvement in the Protest of *Severnaia pchela*, itself not shy in printing Judeophobe articles, had an especially comical air about it. By the end of November, Zotov recognized the seriousness of the campaign against him and made a pathetic effort to clear his name (and perhaps to save his periodical). When *Sanktpeterburgskie vedomosti* refused to print his letter of defense he sent it to *Severnaia pchela* which did publish it (266:2/XII/1858). Zotov complained that as far as libel was concerned, it was Chatskin who had called *him* a fanatic and an inquisitor. If offense had been given by the author of the "Diary of an Acquaintance" then he, Zotov, could only regret it and explain that it was unintentional. He was only an editor, after all. "As regards me personally, including the *feuilleton* of my associate, I really did not see in that phrase which serves as the point of the accusation that meaning which they attribute to it, and thus passed it without attention." This was a disingenuous defense, since Zotov himself was apparently the author of the "Diary." Since the column had been published under a pseudonym, this provided a face-saving escape.

Severnaia pchela replied, full of righteousness, in an article entitled "A Protest Against the Answer of Mr. Vladimir Zotov" (272:10/XII/1858). This particular protest was signed by "all the permanent staff of *Severnaia pchela*" and was directed against Zotov's "literary tricks." It was dishonorable, claimed this protest, for a responsible editor to blame a coworker, especially when the point at issue was not a slip but a personal insult and slander. Zotov had claimed in his defense that nobody acquainted with his literary career could believe that he was capable of a premeditated libel. Experience demonstrated otherwise, asserted the *Severnaia pchela* writers, and the axe which they had to grind came slowly into view. To confirm Zotov's past history of reprehensible conduct, they recalled a recent squabble between *Illiustratsiia* and *Severnaia pchela* which culminated in an announcement by Zotov that he was disavowing all the praise which he had heaped on the editor of *Severnaia pchela*, N. I. Grech, upon the occasion of his literary jubilee.

This particular sub-plot of the main Literary Protest demonstrates the mixed motives of the participants. *Severnaia pchela* had justly earned the status of doyen of the Russian "reptile press," and the honor of N. I. Grech, the character assassin of Alexander Pushkin and loyal servitor of the secret police of the Third Section was long past saving. Grech's coeditor, moreover, was Faddei Bulgarin, whose authorship of the novel *Ivan Vyzhigin* established him as the grand old man of Russian literary Judeophobia. It would be hard to detect any sympathy for the Jews, or indeed any mention of them in this exchange. The *Illiustratsiia* Affair was about many things, and not always about the Jews. The afterglow of this happy moment for Russia's Jews often obscured the painful reality.[15]

3   Defining terms

The year 1858 proved to be the first and last year of widespread Judeophilia in Russia. To be sure, sympathy for the Jews continued to be a staple for several influential newspapers and journals in the capitals. *Moskovskie vedomosti* and *Russkii vestnik* opened their pages to opponents of N. B. Gersevanov's racialist articles. *Russkii vestnik*, in its June, 1859 issue, published O. A. Rabinovich's short work "The Penalty Recruit" (*Shtrafnoi*). The story recounted the misfortunes of a Jewish community leader under Nicholas I who was drafted into the army when the community's taxes fell into arrears. The story was well received by the critics, and Rabinovich acquired additional prestige at home and abroad when soon afterwards the government formally ended this practice and allowed past victims to return home from the army. Although the government measure had been under discussion for some time, Rabinovich's story was popularly credited with bringing an end to the abuse.[1]

An equally positive phenomenon, from the Jewish perspective, was the spread of sympathetic sentiments from the capitals to provincial centers besides Odessa. The summer of 1859 witnessed the birth of *Kievskii telegraf* in Kiev, a paper of liberal orientation edited by N. Chernyshev. In its very first issue the paper began a lengthy series which applauded the movement of the Jews toward civil emancipation in the West and expressed the hope that civil rights would be extended to the Jews of the Russian Empire.[2]

Another convert to the cause was *Vilenskii vestnik*, which early in 1859 began to call for the gradual extension of civil rights to the Jews and the abolition of the Pale of Settlement.[3] The comments of *Vilenskii vestnik* held special significance because it was an official publication and thus more authoritative than private periodicals. Moreover, the sympathetic stance of *Vilenskii vestnik* was attributed by some commentators to the influence of the Governor-General of the Lithuanian provinces, V. I. Nazimov. Nazimov was not just another faceless bureaucrat. He was close to the Emperor and, as the author of the "Nazimov Rescript", was intimately involved in launching the official campaign to free the Russian peasantry from serfdom. This connection offers yet another parallel between the emancipation of the peasants and the Jews in the Reform Era.

These dramatic bright spots stood out all the more starkly against a darkening background. The consensus which had produced the Literary Protest was gone, never to return. The influential *Severnaia pchela*, with its close ties to the central administration and its own self-serving version of the Literary Protest notwithstanding, continued a tradition of hostility toward the Jews by publishing Gersevanov's articles. The newly founded *Domashnaia beseda dlia narodnogo chteniia*, a reactionary publication intended for a popular audience, published a vicious attack on the Jews, characterizing them as "a race outcast by God" (6:7/II; 14:4/IV/1859). Such a crude appeal to religious intolerance clearly ran counter to the spirit of the day, but no Russian allies appeared in defense of the Jews. Jewish writers, apparently considering the paper unworthy of their attention, also failed to respond.

Just as Judeophilia began to spread to the provinces, so too did a reaction against it. Writing in *Vitebskie gubernskie vedomosti*, the official publication of the administration of Vitebsk province, Mikhailo Serebriakov expressed skepticism that sympathy toward the Jews could be found among those who actually had to live in their midst. Serebriakov condemned the destructiveness of the Jewish tavernkeeper and tradesmen, and recommended that the Jews "be reconciled to nature" and engage in agriculture. He singled out the Jewish intelligentsia for special opprobrium. They muddled the reality of the Jewish Question through their "sweet words" and their tactics of condemning any opponent as a religious fanatic. Instead of seeking a meaningful resolution to the problems raised by the economic activity of Jews, they dreamed only of bureaucratic posts for themselves, claiming them as a reward for their educational attainments. Serebriakov was unimpressed.

> Jewish writers suppose that goodness of heart and nobility of character can be acquired by the study of printed books, whereas goodness and nobility are actually racial, national characteristics which pass in the blood of a race from generation to generation ... And if the character of a certain race is changed through circumstances, then it is changed gradually in the entire mass and through the passage of time, not suddenly. The expression of the Jewish face differs sharply

from the physiognomy of the European ... By the same principle, the Jew cannot change his moral character just through a university education. (14–15:4–11/IV/1859)

These arguments, echoing Gersevanov's racialism, appeared in an obscure provincial organ and were ignored outside the provinces. They nonetheless manifested a hostility which was in the air and were soon embraced by more articulate and prominent spokesmen.

The most unsettling loss for the Jewish intelligentsia in 1859 was the perceived defection of an old friend and ally, *Odesskii vestnik*. I. Sosis argues that with the departure of editors drawn from Pirogov's circle the tone of the newspaper "radically changed."[4] In fact, while *Odesskii vestnik* ceased to work enthusiastically in the Judeophile camp, it did not become actively hostile. Articles appeared which were critical of rabbinic Judaism, but they came from the pens of Karaite spokesmen intent on defending their community from attack. The article which Sosis portrays as signaling the paper's radical change was a *feuilleton* entitled "A Few Words on the Social Position of the Jews" (16:10/II/ 1859) but it was considerably more ambiguous than he suggests. True, the author pointed to the solidarity of the Jews throughout Europe and argued that most of the economic activity of Russian Jewry was unproductive. At the same time he emphasized that he did not reproach the Jews for these phenomena, but sought to explain how they had been shaped by historical circumstances. He lamented that the Jews remained a *terra incognita* for most Russians and asked "how can they merge (*slit'sia*) not just in an external sense, but truly, without misunderstanding and reservations, when we do not know one another in any way?" The author called upon the Jewish intelligentsia to inform society about the Jews' customs, internal life, beliefs and history – in short, a full history of the Jews from the fall of Jerusalem to the present "with all the glories of Jewish civilization." "Only they [the Jewish intelligentsia] can give the Jewish nation the right of entry into the common family of Christian nations, for only through humane feelings can they be merged (*slivat'sia*) and intermingled (*rodnit'sia*)." *Odesskii vestnik* carried articles refuting both this *feuilleton* (26:7/III/ 1859) and the hostile attack on the Jewish intelligentsia which had appeared in *Vitebskie gubernskie vedomosti* (73:7/VII/1859) thus suggesting at least residual sympathy for the Jews.

Of much greater concern to Jews was the treatment by *Odesskii vestnik* of the pogrom, or anti-Jewish riot, which broke out in Odessa in April of 1859. Scuffles and fights were an Odessa tradition over the Easter holidays. During the week-long celebration of the most sacred of Greek Orthodox religious holidays religious feeling ran high. The dramatic climax of the Easter service, a procession of the celebrant and the congregation around the church, attracted curious on-lookers and provided ample opportunity for real or imagined insults of the Christian faithful by Jews. A less spiritual aspect of the celebration was the notorious rowdyism and drunkenness of the common people. A more sinister element lay in the frequent proximity of Orthodox Easter to the Jewish feast of Passover. The European folk tradition which attributed to Jews the necessity of kidnapping and ritually murdering a Christian child in order to use its blood in the unleavened bread of Passover surfaced from time to time in Eastern Europe.

Geography too served to inflame passions. The Greek and Jewish quarters were close to one another, and many Jews lived in the vicinity of the Greek Orthodox Church which was the spiritual center of the local Greek population. Greek merchants had played an important role in the economic development of the Odessa port, but by mid-century Jews increasingly displaced Greeks from their pre-eminent economic position.[5] Economic rivalry was added to national and religious prejudices and antipathies. Small wonder that the Easter celebration in Odessa sometimes got out of hand.[6]

The Odessa pogrom of 1859 was a relatively mild one. A fight outside the Greek Orthodox Church triggered an outbreak of violence and looting. There was only one fatality – a poor Jewish street peddlar who was beaten to death when he accidentally encountered the rioting mob – but significant damage was done to Jewish homes. From the point of view of the Odessa Jewish community the response of the local press, and especially an article in Odesskii vestnik (42:21/IV/1859), was most unsatisfactory. Worse, the St. Petersburg newspaper Russkii dnevnik reprinted the offending piece while refusing space to a corrective article submitted by O. A. Rabinovich. Rabinovich complained to friends that Odesskii vestnik had been bribed by Greeks, who were the main perpetrators of the outrage, and had placed all the blame on Russians.[7] Russkii vestnik carried an article which made a similar charge, characterizing the report of Odesskii vestnik as "a slur against the Russian national character" both because it charged Russians rather than Greeks and because it de-emphasized the significance of the pogrom, dismissing it as a "fight" (drakh) (5: Book 1, May 1859, 50–8). The concern of Jewish spokesmen was not merely for accuracy. It was imperative to shift blame from Russians to Greeks in order to retain the illusion of Russo-Jewish amity created by the Illiustratsiia Affair.

Odesskii vestnik did finally offer a corrective of sorts by reprinting the pogrom article of *Russkii vestnik* which stressed the guilt of the Greeks. This was cold comfort for Odessa's Jewish intelligentsia. The pogrom itself was a sobering experience after the giddy hopes of the previous year. It was akin, on a minor scale, to the great disillusionment of Odessa Jewry after a more serious pogrom in 1871. Unsettling too was the apathy of the Russian press which, as a whole, paid very little attention to the incident. Press apathy rekindled a Jewish aspiration which had lain dormant for the previous three years: the desire for a Russian–Jewish publication which could give the Jews both a permanent voice in the burgeoning world of Russian journalism and a platform for the proponents of change within the Jewish community itself.

Although the idea of a Russian-language Jewish newspaper had fascinated maskilim in Russia for decades, only in 1856 were concrete steps taken in that direction. Historians differ as to the precise source of the initial approach. Some have given credit to N. I. Pirogov, the director of the Odessa educational district. Reportedly, Pirogov suggested the idea to O. A. Rabinovich and a local merchant named Joachim Tarnopol.[8] Other accounts attribute the initiative to Rabinovich and Tarnopol alone.[9] Whoever first generated the idea is ultimately unimportant: Pirogov, Rabinovich and Tarnopol were the eager midwives who made the birth of the newspaper possible.

On 23 December 1856 Rabinovich and Tarnopol submitted a formal request to Pirogov for permission to publish a Russian–Jewish newspaper.[10] Pirogov at once obtained the enthusiastic approval of Governor-General Count A. Stroganov – who saw it as a valuable vehicle for merger – and sought approval from the Minister of Education, A. S. Norov, on 4 January 1857.[11] Pirogov envisioned three objectives for the proposed newspaper: it would acquaint the Jews with the Russian language, spread confidence among them of measures undertaken by the government on their behalf, and counter rumors circulated by Jewish fanatics against the educational policies of the government. Pirogov stressed the efficacy of such a paper for destroying the prejudices of the Jews and promoting their rapprochement (*sblizhenie*) with the non-Jewish population.[12]

Despite the intervention of Stroganov on the project's behalf it was rejected by the Jewish Committee in St. Petersburg, now headed by Count D. N. Bludov. The committee members were reluctant to permit the discussion of religious matters in Russian and the Rabinovich–Tarnopol petition included on its agenda a desire to spread "true religiosity" among the Jews through citations from the Scriptures. The committee proposed instead that the would-be editors be given permission to publish a newspaper in Yiddish or Hebrew.[13] The committee's counter-proposal was declined by Rabinovich and Tarnopol: publication of a periodical in a "Jewish" language was anathema to them. In a letter to Pirogov dated 12 June 1858 they reminded their sponsor that the chief point of the undertaking was to spread the use of Russian among the Jews.[14]

Matters did not rest there. Pirogov reapplied for permission, again unsuccessfully, to the new Minister of Education E. P. Kovalevskii. In a letter to Lev Levanda, Rabinovich explained that he was rewriting the proposal with a view to resubmitting it.[15] In the summer of 1859 when Kovalevskii was in Odessa, the two prospective editors met with him. Tarnopol submitted a lengthy memorandum on the Jewish Question, published ten years later as *An Attempt at the Contemporary Reform of the Jews*, which included a section on the need for a Russian-language Jewish newspaper. The decisive moment finally came when Rabinovich and Tarnopol informed the Jewish Committee that they were willing to exclude religious matters from the purview of their program. Approval followed swiftly on 22 October 1859.[16]

Rabinovich and Tarnopol, with Pirogov's blessing, were now free to pursue their aspirations for Russian Jewry. Merely reading their proposals, to say nothing of the bureaucratic language that enveloped the Jewish Question before the Reform Era, does not provide a clear and unambiguous statement of what these aspirations entailed. Much of the disillusionment and charges of bad faith subsequently exchanged between the Russian Jewish intelligentsia and Russian publicists derived from this precise point, a consistent failure to devise a common program or even to agree upon common terms. For example, Pirogov's petition to the Ministry of Education spoke of a Jewish newspaper as a medium for the promotion of *sblizhenie* between Jews and gentiles. This word is usually translated into English as rapprochement, with its sense of promoting cordial relations. While obvious that Pirogov, Rabinovich and Tarnopol had far more in mind than merely the promotion of Russian–Jewish amity, it is more difficult to determine how they agreed among themselves. High-sounding phrases obscured two problems that were at the very heart of the Jewish Question in Russia: what did the Russians demand from the Jews? What were the Jews prepared to offer?

Various words were employed by Jews and gentiles in the 1860s to describe the hoped-for fate of the Jews in Russia. They included emancipation (*emansipatsiia*), Europeanization (*evropeizatsiia*), assimilation (*assimiliatsiia*), Russification (*obrusenie*), unification (*soedinenie*). At first glance such words have precise meanings, but not in a Russian context. Particularly troubling were words borrowed from Western European usage, such as emancipation and assimilation. The experience of Europe defined "Jewish emancipation" as the acquisition by Jews of civil and political equality with the rest of the population.[17] A precisely analogous process was difficult to visualize for Russia, with its remnants of a semi-feudal system of estates, themselves very ambiguously defined.[18] Jews might be equalized with one or another social group, or disabilities specific to the Jews might be removed, but no one legal act could "emancipate" all Russian Jewry.[19] The usual Russian word for the process of releasing a social group from disabilities – for example, the enserfed peasant population – was not "emancipation" but "liberation" (*osvobozhdenie*). Nobody in Russia ever spoke of the "liberation" of the Jews. The term "assimilation" was even more rarely used at this time and was equally obscure. It had entered the Russian language as a medical term, describing biological processes like the digestion of food.[20] The term "Russification" did not yet manifest the strong ideological associations – above all, anti-Polish – which it would acquire after 1863, and it was a term infrequently used in reference to the Jews before the Polish uprising.

The two words which were most consistently used in the first half of the nineteenth century and during the early Reform Era were *sblizhenie* (with its verbal cognates *sblizhat'sia/sblizit'sia*) and *sliianie* (and its cognate *slit'sia*). Modern translators usually render these words into English as "rapprochement" and "assimilation" respectively. In the case of *sblizhenie*, the use of an English cognate of a French noun to render a vague, if etymologically related Russian noun, is not very helpful. To equate *sliianie* with "assimilation," as it is used in modern definitions, is simply incorrect for this period.[21]

An appeal to Vladimir Dal, Russia's great lexicographer, does not resolve the problem. His dictionary entry for *sblizit'sia* offers illustrations suggesting the passage of time, the movement of two sides to meet one another, and "they got acquainted and became close, they made friends," thus implying an evolution from acquaintance to friendship.[22] The entry for *slit'* provides connotations of the flowing together of liquids, while illustrations offered for *slit'sia* suggest the imprecise blending of colors, the flowing together of two rivers, or confused and cloudy perception.[23] Clearly these terms were in a state of flux and it is small wonder that their meanings were frequently misunderstood by contemporaries. An accurate understanding of what these words meant at any particular time can be achieved only by examining them in context.

The first Russian legislators and reformers to deal with the Jews after the first partition of Poland in 1772 encountered them as an alien component interspersed among a population that was Slavic and Christian but not necessarily Russian and Orthodox. Officials were preoccupied with the regularization of the legal status of the Jews and the normalization of their social and economic relationships with their neighbors. Even in the West, systematic toleration, to say nothing of emancipation, had barely begun. Russian legislators attempted to rationalize a legal system that treated the Jews as members of one or another estate (*soslovie*) such as merchants or townsmen, and also as members of a distinct Jewish community for whom special enactments existed.

Russian Jewry as a whole was no more interested in integration into a stratum of Russian society than were average Russians. The traditional Jewish leadership repeatedly petitioned the government to preserve the system of autonomous communal government which Russia had inherited from the Polish state. The first exception to this rule – emanating from a private individual rather than the communal leadership – was also the first to toy with the terms under discussion.

Ieguda Leib-ben Noakh (Nevakhovich) was an early representative of the Berlin Haskalah in the Russian Empire. He was the first Jewish author to appeal in Russian to Russian public opinion on behalf of the Jews. In 1803, inspired by the activities of a committee which Tsar Alexander I appointed to draft a new legal code for the Jews, Nevakhovich published a small book, *The Lament of the Daughter of the Jews*.[24] Essentially an appeal for enlightened Russian society to extend toleration and protection to the Jews, the work bemoaned the Jews' status as outcasts: "At the very moment when the hearts of all European peoples draw together (*mezhdu soboiu sblizilis'*); when they have already flowed together (*uzhe slilis' v edino*), the Jewish people still see themselves despised."[25] Such phrases were typical of Enlightenment sentimentality, and reveal that when the terms were first used together, it was in a context of general humanitarianism.

In contrast to Nevakhovich's generalities, the bureaucrats of Nicholas I used the terms in reference to specific legislative acts. As the Jewish Reform Committee of 1840, chaired by P. Kiselev, began its work, it presented to the Tsar a list of principles and objectives. Alert to the dangers of the Talmud, the memoir indicted it as the source of Jewish superstition and fanaticism, the cause of their isolation from civil society, and the chief obstacle to their joining it (*soedinenie*). The religious beliefs engendered by the Talmud encouraged the Jews to view their sojourn in other states as temporary captivity, and had created a massive body of religious rites to strengthen these feelings of alienation. Religious belief found expression in Jewish communal institutions like the *heder*, the autonomous system of Jewish self-government, the kahal, and its related system of internal taxes, as well as the Jews' repulsive and contemptible medieval dress.[26]

If these were phenomena which precluded rapprochement, then clearly their abolition would facilitate the process. That is exactly what Kiselev's committee proposed to do with its abolition of the kahal, closer regulation of taxation, creation of a state Jewish school system, and restrictions on the wearing of traditional dress.

Enraptured by the changes in Western Jewry presumably wrought by the Haskalah, the Russian government attached paramount importance to the role of education. The committee memoir admitted that the purpose of the school reform was "more moral than educational." Besides weakening the role of the Talmud as the foundation of Jewish nationality (*natsional'nost'*), schooling should also promote the knowledge of Russian history and language since "nothing unifies an individual people (*plemia*) with the dominant nationality like the spread of information about its history and literature."[27] Minister of Education S. S. Uvarov echoed these sentiments on 13 December 1844 when he explained that "the goal of educating the Jews consists in their gradual rapprochement (*sblizhenie*) with the Christian population, and the eradication of superstitious and harmful prejudices instilled by the study of the Talmud."[28] Uvarov's statement is more precise than that of the Kiselev Committee's: he implied that rapprochement, which here referred to the acquisition of Russian culture and the eradication of talmudic influence, comprised two separate processes.[29]

This terminology percolated into the Jewish educational bureaucracy as well. In October 1851 Rabbi G. Lerner spoke at the opening of a state Jewish school. In the Russian translation of the speech – ironically, the original was given in Yiddish – the rabbi was quoted as praising the Tsar's wish "to bring us together (*sblizit'*), for our own good, with the other educated peoples who are subject to him" (*Podolskie gubernskie vedomosti*, 42:20/XI/1851).

By the end of Nicholas' reign, rapprochement had become the common term of bureaucratic reformers and officials. For the Kiselev Committee the term was open-ended, implying the reduction of talmudic influence and the loss of specific aspects of Jewish administration, culture and taxation, as well as the acquisition of Russian cultural trappings, especially Russian history and language. The usage by Uvarov made a more specific dichotomy between the negative (loss of Jewishness) and the positive (acquisition of Russianness). For Rabbi Lerner, rapprochement implied education, in this case the watered-down talmudic curriculum of the state Jewish schools, and presumably the German language in which they were largely taught.

There is one additional feature of Nicholine rapprochement which must be stressed. It was a one-sided process, a reworking and trans-formation of the Jews through the direction and will of an outside agency, the Russian state. The role of "society," be it Jewish or gentile, was ignored. The two ingredients of rapprochement were rude lumps of clay, or two primary colors, awaiting the hand of the artist.

In the Reform Era the term "merger" (*sliianie*) gradually came into use, but it did not carry the connotation of assimilation which it possesses in contemporary Russian.[30] Thus, when Kiselev wrote to Alexander II in 1856 to lament the failure of the reforms which had been generated by his committee, he characterized the unsuccessful objective as "merger." Alexander used the same term when ordering a review of the existing legislation with the goal of promoting the merger of Jews and Christians.[31]

The term reappears with regularity. In a report to the Ministry of Education on 22 January 1858 Count A. Stroganov observed that the extension of civil rights to the Jews would conform to justice, strengthen the economy, and weaken the religious fanaticism of the Jews. "By this path the West has moved forward to the attainment of the lofty goal of the merger (*sliianie*) of Jews with Christians, a goal tied closely with the divine truths of Christianity."[32]

On 25 October 1858 Minister of Internal Affairs S. S. Lanskoi wrote to the Jewish Committee that

> the merger or, to put it more precisely, the rapprochement of the Jewish people with the native population in education, occupation and the like ... can be attained only by the equalization of the Jews in rights with the other inhabitants of the Empire and therefore special enactments of any sort for them, excepting those treating of religion, and assorted restrictions and limitations, must be seen as absolute obstacles to their rapprochement with the rest of the population and virtually the one and only cause of the wretched condition in which they are still found among us.[33]

These citations demonstrate that while rapprochement and merger had become virtual synonyms, in contrast to modern Russian usage, to move from merger to rapprochement was to proceed from the general to the specific. Both these high officials, representing the extreme liberal position on the topic, saw the processes of rapprochement/ merger as intimately tied up with the extension of equal rights to the Jews. Yet even for liberals a religious element persisted. Stroganov saw merger as weakening the religious fanaticism of the Jews, a point reinforced by his appeal to merger as a goal tied to the objectives of Christianity. Lanskoi, in extending full rights to the Jews, sought the retention of rules which protected the integrity of Russian Orthodoxy. While neither man advocated conversion of the Jews to Christianity, it was nevertheless plain that a good deal of cultural baggage would have to be jettisoned before Jews could enter into merger on Christian terms. At the very least Judaism would remain a religious creed operating under special controls within the Christian state, to defend the latter from Jewish fanaticism.

Hidden among the comments of Stroganov and Lanskoi are the first hints that the processes of rapprochement/merger might involve society as a whole and even demand the active and conscious participation of Christian and Jew. As Jewish publicists and their Judeophile allies began to appear in the press, they had to confront the problem of rapprochement/merger, and to define and incorporate the terminology. Journalistic discussion of the possibilities and goals of a prospective Jewish newspaper – spurred by the knowledge that the authorities were contemplating permission for one – were an open invitation for the crystallization of these concepts. The way was led by two veterans who had already won their spurs as literary activists, Arnold Dumashevskii and Joachim Tarnopol.

Arnold Borisovich Dumashevskii had already appeared in print with his rejoinder to Rabinovich's "About Moshkas and Ioshkas" when he published "Do the Jews Need a Newspaper at the Present Time, and in What Language should It Be Published?" in *Russkii invalid* (75:5/IV/1859). Dumashevskii's theme, in an article filled with all the good will and vagaries typical of the Russian Jewish intelligentsia, was that "the public word is the chief tool for the rapprochement of peoples and their merging into the one unending 'I' of humanity." Dumashevskii argued that the Jews in particular were in need of a public forum. Their religious mission completed, their political independence lost, the Jews were scattered about the world. Victimized by persecution, they had developed in isolation, alienated from other peoples.

Like many Jewish intellectuals, and most Russians, Dumashevskii was willing to admit that the Jews had faults, a "wounded morality," expressed in their distinctiveness and isolated national life. But he did not exaggerate these phenomena. As in his earlier reply to Rabinovich, he specifically rejected the common Russian indictment of the Talmud. He restricted himself to a lament that "ancient truths often seem outside the scope of present concerns." Dumashevskii complained that Russians misunderstood the Jews because they viewed them through the murk of ignorance and superstition. A principal role for a Russian Jewish newspaper would therefore be to inform the general public about the nature of Jewish society, enabling it to see that "our principles are different but our aspirations are the same."

A Russian–Jewish newspaper must serve a dual purpose, external and internal. The external role would be to serve as a mediator between Jews and gentiles, informing the latter about Jewish life. The internal role would be to assist in the "Europeanization" of the Jews. From context, Dumashevskii saw Europeanization as informing Jews about the external gentile world in order to make them more appreciative of its spiritual values. A Jew grown more tolerant would lose his narrow national coloration with its stamp of exclusivity. Dumashevskii's call for the Jews to become more humane in their view of gentile society was a far cry from the bureaucratic demand for the elimination of Jewish fanaticism, the rejection of the Talmud, the abandonment of Jewish national institutions and the realignment of Jewish economic life. Rather, Dumashevskii viewed rapprochement/merger as processes arising from greater communication and understanding between Christian and Jew.

This goal was a major preoccupation of Dumashevskii's own life. After a difficult childhood during which he worked as a porter and a clerk, he was rescued from military recruitment by N. I. Pirogov. Dumashevskii attended St. Petersburg University and was groomed to join the Faculty of Civil Law but his refusal to convert to Christianity ended any thought of an academic career. Instead he joined the Ministry of Justice but here too his career was stunted and he left in 1871 to edit *Sudebnyi vestnik*. Dumashevskii provides a classic example of an educated Jew trapped between the tradition-bound Jewish community and a gentile world still too intolerant to accept him as an unconverted Jew. Dumashevskii voiced his dilemma eloquently in an article which he published in *Odesskii vestnik* (145:30/XII/1858):

> Society shouts at him [the educated Jew] from its side: "Stop! You (*ty*) aren't one of our citizens and we don't accept you into our midst; a university education might give you the rights of Honored Citizen[34]

but not those of a citizen. Stay with your Moshas and Berks: live with them and among them; there is no place for you among us!" The defeated hero returns to his former community only to be told: "Among us live Berks, Ioskis and Moskas; you are Moses or Moisei; there is no place for you among us, stay with your own."

Dumashevskii's frustration was reaffirmed at his death in 1887, when educational restrictions were being implemented for Jews. His will left a bequest of 36,000 rubles to the University of St. Petersburg to use for student stipends to be awarded irrespective of religion. He specified that the donor must be identified as "Dumashevskii, a Jew."[35]

These considerations shaped Dumashevskii's prescription for a Jewish newspaper. It was to be in Russian. Yiddish, or "jargon" as it was called, lacked prestige in the eyes of educated Jews and was incapable of expressing abstract concepts. Hebrew was an obsolete, dead language which was unfit for contemporary use. The Jewish masses might not yet understand Russian, but the existence of a paper in that language written for and about them would be a powerful goad for them to learn.

A newspaper in Russian would also make possible the collaboration of Russians. This was absolutely essential because the transformation of the Jews mandated friendly relations and cooperative activity between Russians and the most enlightened members of Jewish society. The Russian Jewish intelligentsia, represented by men like Dumashevskii, were willing to begin the joint task.

> The enlightened part of Jewish society has a sacred obligation to act upon the other members of their society to promote rapprochement between peoples, to help them cast away their distinctiveness and to appear in a true light, in order to acquaint the rest of the world with their nation and to demonstrate that the Jews are worthy of their new calling in the midst of other nations.

Joachim (Ioakhim Isaakovich) Tarnopol was a familiar name in the realm of Russian Jewish letters. He published a well-received book on Odessa Jewry in 1855, *Notices historiques et charactéristiques sur les Israélites d'Odessa*, and was a moving force in the effort to secure permission to publish *Rassvet*. He briefly served as coeditor of the new publication. Tarnopol published a number of additional articles exploring aspects of Jewish life in Russia, and his memorandum on the subject, which he submitted to Minister of Education Kovalevskii in 1859, was subsequently published in book form.[36]

Tarnopol proclaimed rapprochement to be the overriding objective

for contemporary Jewry and he used the term over and over. Tarnopol's conception of rapprochement was shaped by his understanding
of Judaism and Jewry. He rejected the concept of the Jews as a separate
nationality:

> Don't we have to join some nation or nationality? We can't survive as
> an independent people, and we don't want to. Our nostalgia for a
> better, more blissful time, for which we are frequently reproached,
> contains nothing blameworthy or unpatriotic. Our expectations are
> restricted only to a wish for true and genuine peace between us and
> other nations, and for an improved social position.[37]

If the Jews were not an independent nationality, then what were
they? Tarnopol defined Jewry (*Iudeistvo*) as a religious corporation
with foundations rooted in the Old Testament and tradition. Jewry
combined the religious collective (the synagogue) and the secular
community (*obshchestvo*). Jewry's present goal must be the religious
and moral education of its adherents based on "a reasonable correlation of religious principles and civil obligations." Tarnopol's characterization reflected the fashionable Western formulation that the
Jews were members of a religious confession, not a nationality, and he
paraphrased the maskilic injunction to be "a Jew in the synagogue and
a man on the street."[38] Curiously, while rejecting a claim to Jewish
communal autonomy based on national grounds, Tarnopol justified it
on the basis of the communal aspects of Jewry, tying it to his plan for
communal reform and reorganization.

Russian Jewry, argued Tarnopol, was badly in need of a "consistory," based on foreign models. It should be composed of a
government-appointed (Jewish) bureaucracy which would oversee
the administration of Jewish communities, protect and regulate order
in the synagogue, train rabbis, oversee educational and charitable
institutions and direct the moral development of the masses. In short,
Tarnopol's consistory would serve as mediator between the state and
individual Jewish communities.

It is apparent from Tarnopol's description of the function of the
consistory that the Jewish community would retain many of the social
institutions which it already possessed. These included entities such as
the traditional Jewish school system, the Talmud-Tora, and the extensive network of charitable and social brotherhoods. To finance the
consistory and the agencies which it was to oversee there would be
some form of communal taxation.[39] Tarnopol's project thus envisioned
the survival of institutions which Russian bureaucrats saw as the
bulwark of Jewish separatism. His principal innovation was his pro-

posal for a consistory, staffed by like-minded devotees of the Russian Haskalah, which would provide the necessary "firm, moral and enlightened support" necessary for the benighted Jewish masses.

Like Dumashevskii, Tarnopol admitted the deficiencies of the masses while attributing them to external forces. There was nothing inherently negative in Judaism: it rested upon a universal humanitarianism and love of neighbor. Christian intolerance and fanaticism had forced a self-centered isolation upon the Jews and prevented the development of civic responsibility. In those places where the true ideals of Christian justice appeared, Jews immediately displayed the positive side of their religion and became good, conscientious citizens.[40]

Where then was reform to begin? Russian critics started with the debased religious beliefs of the Jews exemplified by the Talmud and its presumed anti-Christian, anti-social ethos. Tarnopol defended the Talmud from this indictment. He denied the Talmud's role in the evolution of rites which set the Jews apart; these defects were the consequence of external circumstances. The Jews themselves had the power themselves to eliminate their flaws when circumstances changed. The Talmud did not, as so often charged, substitute superstition for essential religious belief. At the heart of Judaism remained the injunction to love one's neighbor. The Talmud did not degrade women by making study an obligation for men alone. The Talmud did not preach hatred and intolerance toward Christians. Finally, the Talmud did not mandate trade and commerce for the Jews to enable them to exploit Christians. The Jews' professions were a consequence of historical necessity over which they had no control.[41]

The key to the one-sided development of Jewish intellectual life, explained Tarnopol, was not the study of the Talmud itself, but the study of the Talmud in isolation and to the exclusion of all else. A properly reformed curriculum for Jewish scholars should include scriptural exegesis, utilizing the best talmudic commentaries, the history of the Jews and their literature, logic, a philosophical-critical examination of Jewish liturgy and rites, theology, hermetics and homiletics.[42]

This curriculum was not to serve for the average Jew, of course, but for a new generation of reformed rabbis. The transformation of the rabbinate was of critical importance for Tarnopol, because in his program the rabbi was to take the lead in introducing reform. Due for exclusion were the petty rituals and customs which the Jews had developed under the impact of persecution, as well as archaic fashions

preserved from medieval Poland. There must be reform of the synagogue service such as abolishing the auction of seats and the honor of
being called to the Torah (aliyah).[43] Any Jew acquainted with Odessa's
New Synagogue knew precisely what Tarnopol meant by service
reform: elimination of boisterous individual prayer, considered
unseemly by Western reformers, and the introduction of accompanied
choral singing.[44] Tarnopol also envisioned rabbinic sermons in
Russian.

Since Tarnopol's memorandum was an appeal for permission to
publish a Russian language newspaper, he stressed the need to spread
the Russian language among the Jews and the efficacy of the proposed
paper for promoting rapprochement. The new newspaper could serve
as the mediator between the Jews and the outside world and the
sponsor of social self-improvement until the appearance of the consistory and the training of a new generation of enlightened rabbis.

Tarnopol characterized the reform measures which he advocated as
a process of "internal self-emancipation" which would make the Jews
worthy of external emancipation.[45] "Self-emancipation," which would
lead to the gradual improvement of the moral and civic relations of the
Jews, was only a preliminary step to prepare for the "cornerstone" of
reform: the removal of all laws restricting the Jews and granting to
them full civil rights.[46]

Tarnopol specified that reformers must tread carefully lest overzeal-
ous advocacy of trivial changes in custom or ritual alienate the conservative masses from the more important goals of fundamental
cultural reform.[47] While Russian should be used in the new reform-
minded periodical, reformers should not neglect additional periodicals
in the more widely used languages of the Jewish community. The
editorial objective of a prospective Hebrew newspaper, intended for
the rabbinic milieu, could be to demonstrate the compatibility of
rabbinic Judaism with secular science. The Jews should also retain
Hebrew as a memorial and a tool for worship, although not for secular
purposes. A Yiddish newspaper should strive to offer the masses a
satirical view of their faults and foibles. In both cases the use of these
non-Russian languages would be temporary.[48]

Despite his own rhetoric, it would be misleading to over-emphasize
Tarnopol's status as a gradualist. He clearly saw self-emancipation and
external emancipation as processes which coexisted and were already
well under way. In a letter to Archives Israélites he noted Alexander II's
general commitment to policies of reform and described the emancipation of Russian Jews as a logical corollary to the emancipation of the

Russian serfs (a group, incidentally, which had done nothing to "earn" emancipation).[49] Most significantly, the entire tone of Tarnopol's writing, especially his exposition of the sources of the grinding poverty of the Jewish masses, suggested the urgent necessity of an extension of Jewish rights.

Dumashevskii and Tarnopol tackled the problem of rapprochement/ merger head on, and even a superficial summary of their views reveals how far apart they were from Russians who were using exactly the same terminology. Both men saw the key to these processes in learning Russian, elimination of cultural phenomena like traditional fashions, and greater communication and concourse between Jews and gentiles, especially between the Russian Jewish intelligentsia and the enlightened Russians who rallied to the side of insulted Jewry in 1858. Just as significant as the changes in language and style of life which they were willing to make were changes which they refused to make. The Talmud could not be repudiated because there was nothing in it which was worthy of repudiation. For Tarnopol the exclusive world of Jewish schools, charitable organizations and communal taxes were all to be retained as an essential part of the emancipated Jewish community. This was clearly not what Russians had in mind when they spoke of rapprochement and merger. (Nor was Tarnopol in any way an unrepresentative or isolated voice among educated Russian Jews.)

Ultimately there could be no consensus within Russian Jewry on the definition of Jews and Judaism because the Jews themselves were in the midst of a transformation about whose end result there was no agreement. The mass of Russian Jewry was still remarkably untouched by the Haskalah – to say nothing of the German Reform Movement – or by the myriad phenomena associated with modernization. Notwithstanding invidious comparisons customarily made by Russian reformers between Jews east and west, Western Jewry itself had yet to devise a coherent and generally accepted model of a modern Jewish community which might serve Russian Jewry as a beacon and a guide.

Russian and Jewish publicists alike were hard pressed to find a common starting point which reached beyond expressions of a vague humanitarianism. If they chose to view the Jews as a nationality, of what did their nationhood consist? The Jews of the Russian Empire preserved a national culture encompassing special languages, customs and dress. Could Jewish national identity persist if any of these features were lost? Russian Jews preserved their political identity as an exiled people with a complex matrix of relations with non-Jews who themselves were not always independent or nationally conscious. What was to happen to the Jews as national awareness began to grow among their neighbors?

To view the Jews as a religious community offered no escape. What was the essence of Judaism, without which it could not exist? Some commentators in both East and West chose to see in the alleged "simple Deism" of the Mosaic Law the essence of the Jewish religious spirit. What of the Talmud, or the mystical strains associated with the Cabala? What was to stay and what was to go? And who was to decide? Choosing to view the Jews as either a nationality or a religious community, left another question in place. Did Jews retain a historical mission, religious or secular, in the modern world? Christian commentators, however reluctantly, generally accepted the religious mission of the Jews, while seeing it as fulfilled in the Christian era. Dumashevskii, for example, noted vaguely that the religious mission of the Jews was complete, even while he held to his faith at considerable personal sacrifice. Tarnopol noted obliquely that Russian Jewry should take on the "great task of religious mediation between East and West."[50] Such casual considerations of Jewish messianism implied that it was not integral to the system of either man. Nevertheless, this echo of messianism remained to further complicate the search for a role for Jews and Judaism in the modern world.

4 *Rassvet* and the future of Judaism

Given the excitement and optimism which attended the negotiations to publish *Rassvet*, the actual appearance of the first issue on 27 May 1860 under the motto "And God said: 'Let there be light'!" was almost anti-climactic. The newspaper plunged into controversy with the very first number, and coeditor Joachim Tarnopol left in disillusionment by the twentieth issue. A combination of factors led O. A. Rabinovich to close the newspaper after only one year. A successor, called *Sion*, also lasted only a year. Despite its abbreviated existence, *Rassvet* was a significant voice for Jews – or more specifically, for the Russian Jewish intelligentsia – before the Russian public. In particular the paper participated in the continuing debate to define the concept of rapprochement (*sblizhenie*), since virtually all contributors to the paper proclaimed it as their ultimate goal.[1] In the course of this debate the term "merger" (*sliianie*) also gained popularity, and began to acquire distinct and separate connotations.

In the pages of *Rassvet*, Russians and Jews alike accepted rapprochement as a mutual activity: Jews and gentiles should work to develop normal relations with one another, to create what Jacob Katz calls a "neutral society" where religious belief is not a consideration.[2] *Rassvet* therefore took on a dual role as it operated within two parallel but distinct societies. As Tarnopol had envisioned in his memoir to Kovalevskii, the newspaper was to work internally as a critic of the shortcomings and prejudices of the Jews, and externally to refute groundless accusations and prejudices abounding in Christian society.[3] According to L. O. Levanda, an advisor on Jewish affairs to the Russian bureaucracy, novelist, publicist and Rabinovich's eager collaborator in the work of *Rassvet*, a two-tiered set of objectives was formally worked out. Levanda would oversee the "Jewish role," combatting the superstition, routine and fanaticism of Jewish life, while encouraging education and enlightenment. This would be the Jews'

9 L. O. Levanda

own contribution to the process of rapprochement. Rabinovich would take over the "Russian role" of the paper, which consisted of informing the Russian public about the true nature of Jewish life, culture and belief, as well as arguing for the regularization of Jewish life in Russia.[4] Regularization, it soon became apparent, meant the elimination of legal disabilities of all kinds, and the exposure of petty acts of discrimination and prejudice directed against Jews by Russian society. The gentile community was to respond by recognizing and eliminating these legal and social obstacles to rapprochement. This program, which looked so appealing as a theoretical construct, encountered immediate practical difficulties.

A raucous scandal grew out of Lev Levanda's anonymous article, "A Few Words About the Jews of Western Russia," which appeared in the first number. Levanda presented a grim picture of the economic destitution of the Jews in Minsk province and its social consequences. Women were driven outside the household to work, thus weakening the family. Intense poverty encouraged parasitism, fraud and criminality. Private charity magnified the problem rather than solving it. In this bleak world of Minsk Jewry, the Talmud alone gave meaning to life, but Levanda faulted the overemphasis on talmudic study as doing nothing to relieve the social crisis.

Compared to other forays against the Jews in the Russian press, such as that of *Illiustratsiia*, Levanda's article offered nothing new. His comments were drawn from the standard repertoire of the Russian Haskalah. What enraged so many of Levanda's Jewish readers was precisely the point that this piece appeared in a *Jewish* newspaper. It was seen as playing into the hands of the enemies of the Jews, as nothing less than informing to the gentile authorities.[5] Subscribers wrote to Rabinovich instructing him to "send no more copies." Tarnopol, despite calling for exposure of the bad side of Jewry, believed that articles of this sort were harmful rather than helpful to the Jews, and he moved to disassociate himself from his journalistic off-spring. He apparently took no further role in the operation of the paper, and his departure from the coeditorship was announced in the twentieth issue (7/X/1860). Tarnopol soon lent his name to attacks upon *Rassvet* for "blackening the name of Israel," especially those which appeared in the Hebrew-language periodical *Ha-Magid*, published in Lutsk, but intended for an audience in the Russian Empire.[6]

Rabinovich encountered a different set of obstacles to his efforts to carry out the "Russian role" of *Rassvet*. They came from the censorship authorities and the office of the hitherto supportive Governor-General. Censorship harassment has sometimes been seen as the chief cause of Rabinovich's decision to close *Rassvet*. Evidence is found throughout his correspondence. "The censorship here suffocates me in the most inhuman manner," he wrote in November of 1860. "One must have the strength of Hercules to fight with this monster."[7] Writing to Levanda in April of 1860 he asked: "What can I tell you about the censorship? An eternal battle, not for life but to the death."[8] In a letter to the St. Petersburg Jewish activist Leon Rozental in October 1860 Rabinovich threatened to close *Rassvet* if the Chief Office for Press Affairs (the central censorship office) did not uphold his appeal against a ban by the Odessa censor on an editorial calling for the abolition of the Pale of Settlement.[9]

It would be a mistake, however, to give unguarded credence to these eloquent laments, which were the stock in trade of any self-respecting editor dependent upon the caprices of the Russian censorship. Rabinovich was well aware of what he was in for as an activist editor: he and Tarnopol had been required to sign a statement before they began publication acknowledging that they were aware of the

Nicholine-era prohibition on calls for equal rights for Jews. Rabinovich is probably closer to the truth in the continuation of his letter to Levanda, quoted above. "My co-workers and I on the editorial board got used to these ugly battles and adopted a new strategy: in every issue we threw in something for the censor's consumption with the intention of obliquely making our point or of saving the essential thing, and for the most part we won this battle. From this you can see that the censorship was far from being the principal cause for the demise of *Rassvet*."[10]

An attentive reading of *Rassvet* reveals that the editors did indeed often win the battle despite disappointments such as the rejection of the appeal to the Chief Office for Press Affairs. An editorial forthrightly condemned the residence restrictions of the Pale, as well as the tax and passport system for alleged Jewish "idleness" (14:26/VIII/1860). Another editorial attacked residence restrictions on Jews with a university degree for rendering meaningless any aspiration for higher education (18:23/IX/1860). The theme of the section entitled "Review of Foreign Jewish Journalism," which appeared in every issue, was the benefit which foreign governments received from their emancipated Jewish citizens. The persistence with which *Rassvet* called for an improvement in the legal situation of the Jews, in fact, led to a serious discussion in 1861 in high government circles about the need to take *Rassvet* more forcibly in hand.[11] Rabinovich and his associates had no reason to be ashamed of their role as advocates of Jewish interests.

If the censor failed to kill *Rassvet*, neither did another frequently cited cause, financial difficulties arising from the small number of subscribers. *Rassvet* never had more than 640 subscribers. Rabinovich had set 800 as the break-even point. True, Rabinovich did complain to Rozental about the financial sacrifices he was forced to make, but this was while discussing a plan to place the paper on a firm financial foundation. Rabinovich refused to consider financial rescue plans which surfaced immediately after he announced his decision to close *Rassvet*.

Of more consequence appears to have been harassment which Rabinovich suffered from Governor-General A. Stroganov after *Rassvet* published several articles on the fate of Tsipka Mendak, a young Jewish girl allegedly kidnapped and forcibly baptized in Lithuania. The case created a sensation, especially when the authorities in Lithuania denied the substance of *Rassvet*'s report. Rabinovich was called into Stroganov's office and given a humiliating dressing-down during which Stroganov declared: "If something appears in your paper that does not please me, or if it should bore me while I read it, or if I just feel like it, or perhaps if my stomach aches, I will close your paper down immediately."[12] Given Stroganov's oft-demonstrated sympathy toward the Jews, his behavior toward Rabinovich has been characterized as strange. Strange perhaps in the context of official attitudes toward the Jews, but certainly not in the context of Russian bureaucratic attitudes, which dreaded scandal like the plague. *Rassvet*'s original story was widely reprinted in Russia and abroad in the prestigious Belgian *Le Nord*, ironically a newpaper funded by the Russian government as a public relations tool.[13] This led to a full investigation by the Governor-Generalship of the Northwest, and to denials of the veracity of the *Rassvet* articles by *Severnaia pchela* and *Vilenskii vestnik*. It is entirely possible that Stroganov himself was criticized for the scandal provoked by a newspaper under the supervision of his office, perhaps recalling his disastrous loss of control of *Odesskii vestnik* in 1858. Under these circumstances Stroganov's discontent is understandable although his conduct was distressingly similar to that of bureaucrats depicted in the works of Saltykov-Shchedrin.

Iulii Gessen suggests that Stroganov's displeasure may have been a reflection of the central administration's annoyance at *Rassvet*'s continued advocacy of equal rights in defiance of official policy. This displeasure, conveyed to Stroganov, may have provided the impetus for Rabinovich's humiliation and his decision to close *Rassvet*.[14] This conjecture is not supported by the available evidence. Stroganov did not after all close *Rassvet*. When new editors petitioned to take over the franchise for a Russian–Jewish paper in Odessa, Stroganov supported their application.[15] Six months later the Third Section, the political police in the capital, investigated Rabinovich on suspicion of contacts with the *émigré* dissident Alexander Herzen. Stroganov's office gave Rabinovich a clean bill of health.[16]

Rabinovich's decision to close *Rassvet* may appear an overreaction to someone who did not have to endure his humiliation in Stroganov's office, but the incident obviously made a deep impression upon him. He felt that his freedom of action was too much restrained by the gastronomic criteria set forth by the Governor-General. Writing to Levanda, he complained that the only options left to him were to "mill the wind" (i.e., to publish nothing but anodyne articles) or to explore the dark side of Jewry while remaining silent as the Jewish people were tortured. The ground rules which Rabinovich had laid down for the process of mutual rapprochement were not being met.

Rassvet devoted much space to the Jewish problem, serving as a preeminent forum for a multitude of voices. Most, if not all of the paper's editorials were written by Rabinovich himself, but as he noted editorially (16:10/VI/1860): "Our paper is not the organ of any party, and never will be." Divergent opinions were given full scope, especially those which joined in a lively debate over the essence of Judaism, the fate of the Jews, and the true nature of rapprochement. *Rassvet's* correspondents participated in a discussion that had been initiated by Christians even before the paper appeared, inspired by the publication in Germany of several classics of the *Wissenschaft des Judentums*.[17] *Kievskii Telegraf* began the debate with the publication of a five-article series entitled "Prejudice Against the Jews."[18]

The anonymous author defended the Jews from the prejudices which lingered in Russian society, especially toward educated Jews. Society must sympathize with the maskilim, he argued, for only through them could enlightenment spread to the Jewish masses. Not that the masses were without their own virtues. The Jews were sober, and a drunken Jew was as rare a sight as a sober peasant woman. The Jews were industrious, and when they cheated, it was because of their fallen state. They did not display the hypocrisy which characterized the systematic dishonesty of Christian merchants. Jews were willing to take risks in the marketplace, and they brought valuable credit to the areas where they traded. The European experience demonstrated that the Jews were not cowards, as was so often claimed, but were ready to fight and die for a true fatherland.

The Jews were not without their faults. Centuries of persecution had left a negative imprint upon them, exemplified by the debasement of their national character and traditions. Their national decline was reflected in a willingness to accept degradation, a loss of aesthetic sense which led them to tolerate the filth and squalor of the ghetto, their miserliness and self-abasement. Worst of all was the Jews' ingrained indifference to higher interests which led them to eschew social activity, to restrict their worldly horizons to the fulfillment of empty rites and to make no effort to rise from their debased state.

The Christian author's willingness to accept the inherent nobility of the Jewish national character was an echo of his sources, the writings of men like Jost and Graetz who were endeavoring to recapture the glories as well as the tragedies of the Jewish past. The author also displayed an objective attitude toward the Talmud. He characterized it as a religious-scientific encyclopedia, a demonstration of the inner moral strength of the Jews which had enabled them to survive as a people, although he faulted contemporary talmudic study for falling into the opposite extremes of mysticism and literal-mindedness.

In subsequent articles the author described the Jewish renaissance which flowered when the Jews received a modicum of religious toleration. Jewry promptly produced men of genius, ranging from Spinoza to Moses Mendelssohn, whose work was extensively summarized. Judaism had now begun to adapt itself to the demands of the modern world. This was a necessity, because before the Jews could receive equality from the modern state, they had to undergo self-emancipation, reflected in the abandonment of senseless rites. Religious reform required a scientific basis and the contemporary "science of Judaism" was making that available. The sources of Judaism were being thoroughly investigated and reformers, like Abraham Geiger, were openly proclaiming the mutability of ritual law. A battle now raged between historical-conservatives and reformer-progressives within Judaism. Given the decentralized aspect of Jewry, and the lack of an acknowledged spiritual leader within Judaism, a general agreement was impossible. Nonetheless, numerous German–Jewish communities had begun to restructure themselves unilaterally, as at Frankfurt in 1842. The spirit of Reform Judaism had begun to penetrate Jewish society and, proclaimed the author, this could only have positive consequences for the state in which they lived.

This article can be viewed as an appropriate gentile contribution to the process of rapprochement, making well-informed use of materials generated by Jewish society itself. Yet not even the optimistic author pretended that the successes of European Reform Judaism could be swiftly duplicated in Eastern Europe, where Polish Jewry represented a mighty barrier against reform. The article was an invitation from a well-intentioned segment of Russian society to the Jews to follow the European lead but with the understanding that this would be a lengthy process and that emancipation by the state was contingent upon self-emancipation by the Jewish community.

The effort of the provincial *Kievskii telegraf* was soon seconded by the respected St. Petersburg thick journal *Russkoe slovo*. The March 1860 issue carried a long article entitled "A Sketch of the Contemporary History of Judaism," dedicated to O. A. Rabinovich, and authored by A. Georgievskii, a teacher at the Richelieu Lyceum, the coeditor of *Odesskii vestnik* during its *annus mirabilis*, and the most prominent Christian contributor to *Rassvet* as the author of the "Survey of Foreign Jewish Journalism."[19] The latter column allowed Georgievskii to elucidate the ideas he first advanced in his *Russkoe slovo* article, and they are treated here as all of a piece.

Georgievskii, like Pirogov and the *Kievskii telegraf* author before him, praised the ability of Judaism to evolve and adapt itself to the modern world through its inherent vitality and creativity. The Talmud, for example, had been a positive force for the preservation of Jewish national consciousness. If abuses had arisen – "alien growths" on Judaism – it was the consequence of persecution and intolerance. Alien growths would be removed as Jews, under the impact of modern civilization, turned back to the biblical sources which constituted the true essence of Judaism. Judaism continually demonstrated its ability to respond rapidly to change. The small measure of religious toleration given the Jews of Prussia at once produced a genius in the person of Moses Mendelssohn and helped spread his school of enlightened thought. This was a process which worked two ways. The self-reform of German Jewry led the state to extend their political rights. "In this way the civil emancipation of the Jews in Germany proceeded in line with their own regeneration, and was a result of their triumph over prejudices, both their own and those of Christian society."

The virtue of the process which Georgievskii discerned in Western Europe – and which he saw as the inevitable consequence of the progressive development of European society – was that it would bring about the rapprochement of Jews with Christian society. What did this process, which Georgievskii also referred to as "assimilation," entail? The Jews of France served as a model:

> all the Jews of France have mastered the French language, they eagerly grow closer to the rest of the population and cease to differ from them in any respect, they engage in useful activities and vitalize the French national industry with their enterprise, knowledge and capital, they willingly remain in the military beyond the term of mandatory service ... they occupy the highest and most honorable positions in both the state and society.

Emancipation and rapprochement alone were not sufficient for Georgievskii. In his *Russkoe slovo* article he stressed the need for a concomitant religious reform of Judaism, and noted with approval that contemporary Jewry was engaged in just such a reform. Georgievskii was not in favor of a process of merger which would rob the Jews of Judaism, stripping away moral foundations along with alien growths. The consequence of this phenomenon would be either religious indifference, such as was detectable among the first emancipated German and French Jews, or mere religious formalism. Georgievskii rejected the third alternative: conversion to Christianity. He spoke with disapproval of David Friedlander's celebrated offer to Pastor Teller in 1799 of a qualified conversion of members of the Berlin Jewish community. He saw it as a recommendation of the German Reform-verein that none of its members had converted to Christianity.[20]

Fortunately, Judaism demonstrated itself to be very accessible to religious reform, the more so when reform grew organically instead of being forced by outside agencies, such as Napoleon's famous Grand Sanhedrin of 1807. Georgievskii was less precise as to the exact direction which reform should pursue. He clearly sympathized with German Reform Judaism – the framework of his article was a review of a book by the German reform leader S. Stern – but he also presented an objective account of critics of Reform Judaism such as Samson Raphael Hirsch. He implied that ultimately the Jews must pursue reform wherever it led so that they might adapt themselves properly to the modern world. To achieve this end, every Jewish community must continue to exercise religious autonomy and seek its own path to reform.

Georgievskii's concern for the moral integrity of Judaism, and its very survival, is all the more fascinating to find in a Russian publicist because he joined it to a concern for the survivial of Jewish nationality, a concern particularly evident in his column for *Rassvet*. Despite its title, Georgievskii's "Survey of Foreign Jewish Journalism" was actually a survey of the status of Jewish communities throughout the world and their progress toward emancipation and full participation in the national life of their respective states. The year covered by Georgievskii's column was filled with many dramatic events in the history of modern Jewry, including the foundation of the Alliance Israélite Universelle in Paris, and the creation of new Jewish entities such as the British Board of Guardians and the Board of Delegates of American Israelites. Some European commentators decried these institutions as contrary to the spirit of integration. Georgievskii disagreed. National entities like the Alliance were a normal and laudable outgrowth of Jewish national feeling, an emotion which had not and should not be lost through the processes of emancipation, merger, or reform.

Georgievskii defined Jewish nationality (*natsional'nost'*) as "one religion, one holy tongue, one great past, a common distinguishing feature and physiognomy, a national character and set of customs fixed by religious prescriptions, and a strong 'mutual sympathy'." Having identified the Jews as a distinct nationality, Georgievskii rejoiced in their continued survival. "As they enter closer relations with other peoples, the Jews fortunately do not cease to be Jews, but preserve all their essential particularities: only under such conditions can they be independent, distinctive actors in a common civilization" (*Rassvet* 52:19/V/1861). Separate, distinctly Jewish activities, such as reform of worship, improvement of traditional schooling, reorganization of community services, and the scientific study of Judaism were, ironically, best carried out in nations where the Jews were completely emancipated and closer to their neighbors in morals, customs, language and general education. Under these conditions Jewish nationality was "purified and perfected, as in a crucible."

Georgievskii desired the survival of the Jewish national character, tied to a reformed Judaism, because he envisioned a continuing world mission for the Jews. They brought fresh resources of physical and moral energy to modern European civilization. In the religious sphere Judaism had a vital role to play as "the champion (*pobornik*) of freedom of thought even in the religious sphere where it is usually given little scope." The contemporary reform of Judaism, freeing it from the burden of ritual law, demonstrated how a religion could satisfy the spiritual requirements of its followers while not clashing with the real demands of life.

It may be too much to see in Georgievskii's articles a covert critique of Russian Orthodoxy, which displayed few of the virtues which he ascribed to Judaism. On the other hand, throughout his distinguished career in state service, Georgievskii displayed a particular interest in questions of moral regeneration. It is nonetheless surprising that his comments passed the censor, especially given the irritation expressed by the censorship the previous year at the comparatively tame comments of Pirogov on the Odessa Talmud-Tora.

If the censor was nodding, others clearly understood Georgievskii's arguments. The liberal newspaper *Nashe vremia* published an extensive examination of the Jewish Question, using Georgievskii's *Russkoe slovo* articles as a starting point. Using the same factual information as Georgievskii, the author, P. Shchabalskii, arrived at very different conclusions. Shchabalskii decried the continued existence of the Jewish race (*plemia*) and of Jewish nationality. Features that Georgievskii regarded as positive, a unifying religion, a common language, style of life and set of moral concepts, and a community of interests and national institutions, Shchabalskii branded as negative because they made the Jews a *status in statu* in the Russian borderlands. The Jewish community remained protected by the charmed circle of the Talmud, which promoted superstition and rejected rationalism. Jewish nationality, in the form of a theocratic state ruled by rabbis who exercise their authority on the basis of their own reading of the Talmud, was a fossil, an anachronism in the modern state. The demise of this theocratic state, its members still dreaming of a kingdom on the banks of the Jordan, would not be lamented by any enlightened thinker.

The changes in European Jewry exemplified by the Reformverein had important implications for Russia and her large Jewish population. Shchabalskii dreamed of the merger of Russian Jewry. As reform spread eastward, Jewish nationalism would cease to exist. Jews would merge with Russians, and would be distinguished from them only by religion, a purified form of Judaism. These changes were foreshadowed in the establishment of European-style Jewish schools in Warsaw, Mitau and Odessa, in more humane treatment of Jews by Russian legislators, and by closer personal relations between Christians and Jews. The promotion of better relations was, in fact, the obligation of progressive Russian journalism. *Nashe vremia* was doing its part, and Shchabalskii expressed the hope that the new *Rassvet* would follow suit.

Shchabalskii's article, with its optimistic portrait of Jews and gentiles participating equally in the processes of reform, emancipation and integration, exemplified the full expectations of Russian liberals at this time. The Jewish masses, Mitnagdim or Hasidim were not of course consulted: they were the inert mass upon whom enlightenment would quickly work its magic. Russian maskilim, reaching a public audience for the first time, were content to encourage such beliefs. There were always exceptions, however, and as a wider forum became available with the publication of *Rassvet*, dissenting voices appeared to deny that Russian Jews could or should turn into German Reform Jews.

In two issues of *Rassvet* (9:22/VII and 10:29/VII/1860), I. S. Galbershtadt presented a stinging critique of Georgievskii's laudatory treatment of Reform Judaism. His comments are of special interest because Galbershtadt could not be called a narrow fanatic, for he was a trained attorney. He was nonetheless one of the first voices to question the right of Russian maskilim and their gentile allies to dispose in wholesale fashion of the traditional foundations of Jewish life in Eastern Europe.

Galbershtadt faulted Georgievskii's simplistic reduction of modern Jewry into two camps, represented by the reformers of the Reformverein and the Traditionalists led by S. R. Hirsch. This dichotomy ignored a third, "positive-historical approach" pioneered by Zecharia Frankel.[21]

Looking beyond the world of Jewry itself, Georgievskii's description of the march of enlightenment in Europe was far too optimistic. One need only look to the Papal States, where clerical authorities sanctioned the removal of the baptized infant Mortara from his Jewish parents, for a glaring exception.

Georgievskii likewise erred in restricting reform within Judaism only to the school of Mendelssohn and of exaggerating the importance of the Reformverein out of all proportion. Jewish tradition had always been expressed in the spirit of the times: a fundamental tenet of Judaism was that the study of the Torah could never be completed. Galbershtadt denied that the Reformverein was, as Georgievskii characterized it, "the foremost point of renovated Judaism." At best it was the voice of a few hundred individuals in the midst of millions. He rejected the central tenet of the Reformverein that "the Mosaic religion contained within itself the possibility of unending development." Such a claim struck at Divine Revelation as the basis of Judaism, reducing it to the status of an ethical system like that of Manu or Zoroaster.

Galbershtadt was especially scornful of the reformers' mistreatment of Jewish tradition (i.e., ritual law). As a non-Jew, Georgievskii had seen the "freeing of thought from the control of talmudic tradition" as natural and desirable. A devout Jew saw ritual rather as respect for the Divine.

> Strict ritual practice coexists with freedom of thought because it sanctifies the practical life of the Jew, as his practical life ought to be sanctified if he wished to be true to his tradition. Therefore, let those who emancipate themselves from ritual practice not think that they have achieved internal and external emancipation; it is a pitiful courage which rejects rites only because they are inconvenient ... No, these traditions are not growths; they are the product of the spirit and the growth of our forefathers.

This being the case, Galbershtadt expressed his sympathy for those who sought to dispose, after careful reflection, of those things which "time and circumstances have rendered superfluous," while scorning the "Don Quixotes who pray with uncovered heads" and reject ritual law merely because it was old and they were modern.

Galbershtadt did not stop at the defense of ritual law, but also heaped praise upon the *heder* where teacher and student worked together, studying from original sources. This was a thrust, not only at the Reformverein, but at the maskilic scorn for the *heder* and their defense of the state Jewish schools, which provided them with legitimacy and employment.

A reply to this dissenting voice in the chorus for rapprochement also appeared in *Rassvet* (17:16/IX/1860). The author was Emanuel Soloveichik, an Odessa physician who was destined to succeed Rabinovich as editor of the Russian Jewish newspaper. Soloveichik faulted Galbershtadt for inconsistency: he argued against the possibility of reform within Judaism, but by his admission that it was composed of essential and non-essential elements, he implied the possibility of reform. In fact, Soloveichik argued, Judaism had never ceased to develop or adapt to historical changes, or to reflect the intellectual level of any society of which it was a part. Nor was Galbershtadt's criticism of Georgievskii entirely fair. The latter had not condemned the Talmud or the *heder*, but merely pointed out how external circumstances had led to their abuse. And while Soloveichik was willing to reject strict adherence to all petty rituals, he would not reject the concept of ritual law out of hand. "I am not against the fulfillment of ritual law, even if it is senseless according to contemporary thought; I even consider it an obligation for every Jew not to insult the feelings of his fellows by scorn for rites which others consider sacred."

As this survey of a narrow debate on the essence of Judaism suggests, external consensus veiled fundamental differences of opinion among all commentators. Despite the common picture of maskilim ready to compromise important traditions of Judaism for doctrinal or pragmatic reasons, and despite their own rhetoric, some enlightened Jews were determined to retain the cultural trappings of Judaism. Georgievskii, speaking for the gentile side, was an anomaly in his sympathy for both Jewish nationalism and Judaism, although it should be remembered that his religious ideal was German Reform Judaism, a system entirely unacceptable to the mass of Russian Jews. More typical was the work of Shchabalskii who sought to reduce Judaism to the form of a religious creed, stripped of all cultural trappings.

Polemics on the nature of Judaism appeared only in the opinion columns of *Rassvet*. The "official" voice of the paper, in the form of Rabinovich's editorials, had different priorities, centering on the vexing question of rapprochement. In discussing rapprochement, Rabinovich made an assumption that was virtually unique to him: he refused to connect civil rights to the self-improvement of the Jews or to tie legal acceptance to the readiness and ability of Jews to participate in gentile society. "We do not agree with those who tie the question of our moral regeneration to the question of our emancipation. History shows that full civil rights for us never depended upon the level of our education but on the higher or lower development of people among whom we live. In this respect, our private problem depends upon the resolution of a general problem" (6:1/VII/1860). Jews should endeavor to perfect themselves, not in order to receive a reward, but as members of the common family of mankind, in pursuit of eternal perfection. Rabinovich was following an old European tradition which saw the Jews as the "barometer of civilization," but his views did not correspond to those of Tarnopol and still less to the current politics of the government in St. Petersburg.[22]

Disentangling rapprochement from emancipation was not an easy task. At times the effort brought Rabinovich perilously close to contradicting his insistence on the priority of external emancipation over internal reform, as when he used the example of the West to characterize rapprochement as the reconciliation of two hostile camps. "What is needed is toleration from one side and forgetfulness of the past on the other ... We must be freed from the various restrictions which we willingly laid upon ourselves in the course of ages, so that restrictions laid upon us from outside may fall away" (9:22/VII/1860). The role of *Rassvet* would be to serve as the point of rapprochement between Christian and Jew.

Rabinovich strove to offer practical examples of rapprochement in action. Shortly before leaving the editorship, in fact, he offered a catalogue of accomplishments by Jews on the road to rapprochement:

> They have adopted the clothes of Russians and their style of life is more and more like them; they are increasing the number of their educational institutions; increasingly they speak Russian among themselves; they engage in philanthropy; they shed their blood for their fatherland; they value state decorations as sacred things and pledge their service; they contribute to the treasury of national literature; they assist national life and amusement. (48:28/IV/1861)

If moderate ritual and religious reform are added to this list, it could become the full agenda for rapprochement as it appeared on the pages of *Rassvet* and a convenient resume of the contents of the paper for its first year.

Rabinovich was not sympathetic to the forms of Judaism which he associated with the masses. The product of a degraded society, plunged into "kopeck materialism" by its desperate struggle for survival, it lapsed further into asceticism, apathy, superstition and prejudice. To speak to the masses was to speak to "rocks and logs." It was true that an increasing number of the young generation was being attracted to the progressive spirit of the age and had begun a war with everything that was not contemporary. The result was an abnormal war between extreme destruction and extreme stagnation. Rabinovich sought a synthetic group which would espouse the golden mean in a struggle for reform (16:9/IX/1860).[23]

While Rabinovich himself avoided speaking to the "rocks and logs" in too sharp a voice, the paper viewed reform of the synagogue service with approval, and devoted much space to the question of how educated rabbis might be trained and placed at the head of traditional communities (17:16/X/1860). *Rassvet* offered extensive coverage of the dual dilemma of the state Jewish school system: the organizational inadequacies of the schools themselves and community opposition to state Jewish schools in any guise. Rabinovich took a moderate stand on the latter subject. When a correspondent recommended a policy of mandatory attendance at the state schools, Rabinovich demurred, unwilling to force reform on a reluctant society (29:9/XII/1860).

There were limits to Rabinovich's patience in matters of religion, however, and they were invariably crossed by the Hasidim. Correspondents were given free rein to depict Hasidim and their *tzaddikim* in the blackest of colors, in the time-honored tradition of the maskilim. The hostility of the maskilim was understandable: they saw the Hasidim as the most unregenerate group of "rocks and logs." Worse, the Hasidim were a continuing embarrassment to enlightened Jews, denigrating all Jewry in gentile eyes. In a letter to *Rassvet*, N. I. Pirogov, perhaps the leading Russian Judeophile, chided progressive Jews because of their inability to win over the Hasidim (27:25/XI/1860). In the next issue, Rabinovich delivered an editorial attack against Hasidism in general (28:2/XII/1860), and followed it with a denunciation of *tzaddikim* in particular (29:9/XII/1860). In a similar situation a *Rassvet* editorial responded to a published report in *Moskovskie vedomosti* in which the Governor-General of the provinces of Grodno and Kovno chided the Jews for the filth of their settlements and their slovenly garb. Rabinovich's comments would not have been out of place in the mouths of Nicholas I or Alexander II, both of whom took special aversion to traditional Jewish dress: "What is this attachment to yarmulkes, long *pe'ot* (side-locks), and uncovered necks? What is this flaunting of *taleysim* (prayer shawls) on the streets during the Sabbath? What is this appearance in slippers and caftans in broad daylight on the town squares?" (12:12/VIII/1860).

A fundamental reason for *Rassvet*'s existence was to spread Russian among the Jews, so Rabinovich examined this important ingredient of rapprochement on numerous occasions. Typical was an editorial in which he maligned the other languages of the Jews (13:19/VIII/1860).

He dismissed Yiddish as "incapable of expressing any enlightened belief." Hebrew had served the Jews in the Diaspora as "the monument of their past glory," but now it belonged to the category of dead languages. "As a sacred language it has been preserved more for sacred purposes than for common everyday life with its transitory needs." Modern Jewry everywhere was rejecting these relics of the Middle Ages for the vernacular. Russian Jews must be no exception: "Our Fatherland is Russia; therefore its language, like its air, should be ours."[24]

Rassvet devoted much attention to the entry of Jews into the wider circles of gentile society, applauding successful relationships between Christians and Jews while decrying the recrudescence of prejudice. When Jews began to donate funds for the relief of Christian victims of Druze persecution in Syria, *Rassvet* instituted a special section to list the donors. (This unsolicited participation in a purely Christian cause was of special pride to Jewish publicists. They frequently cited this moment, especially when Christian Russia was not forthcoming in times of Jewish need such as the pogroms of 1881–2.) The paper publicized an exchange of letters between Pirogov and the wealthy Odessa merchant A. M. Brodskii. In response to Pirogov's invitation to the wealthy of the Jewish community to provide stipends for poor Jewish students at St. Vladimir University in Kiev, Brodskii responded with an offer to fund stipends for a Jew *and* a Christian in order to promote a "truer and closer rapprochement" (42:10/III/1861).

More mundane events, humming with the buzz of life, were used to display the mixed successes of rapprochement. A letter from Berdichev described a charity ball to which enlightened Jews were invited, only to become involved in a scandal when one of them invited a Christian woman to dance (5:24/VI/1860). An editorial complained of the absence of any Jews on the Odessa bridge commission (8: 15/VII/1860). Christian society was scolded for a scene in a local theatre in which a young dandy insulted a "mangy Jew" who was sitting in the wrong seat (13:19/VIII/1860).

These disconcerting events were not exceptions and they prompted second thoughts by the editor. Early on Rabinovich had asked that, in pursuit of rapprochement, "Jews not hide their blemishes, and the Russian public not ignore the healthy and brilliant features of the Jewish people" (9:22/VII/1860). *Rassvet* had done its part in uncovering the blemishes, and had earned the antipathy of many in the Jewish community for its pains. Russian society failed to keep its part of the bargain. "The Jews have shown the white flag in their camp, but the other camp has not answered." True, Russian literature had taken the Jews under its protection, but there were still renegades like N. B. Gersevanov and V. I. Askochenskii, the editor of the Judeophobe *Domashniaia beseda*, who violated the fraternal mood. In their daily lives, however, most Jews could feel no change (48:21/IV/1861). Rabinovich found the landscape darkening, even as his own *Dawn* expired.

In his willingness to call for reform and to "uncover the blemishes" of Jewish life, Rabinovich drew boundary lines around the conditions of Jewish life which were truly in need of reform and those which were not. In an issue where many Jewish and gentile critics of the Jews parted company, Rabinovich refused to accept the more extreme charges of economic reformers that the Jews were guilty of "exploiting" the Christian population. Even those Russian critics deemed sympathetic to the Jews generally accepted this charge, their ultimate intentions revealed by whether he attributed this exploitation to forces external to the Jews or, rather, to some internal flaw, such as the dictates of the Talmud.

Rabinovich, whose own father was a failed tax farmer, and who himself became a businessman, was a striking exception to the rule. He was one of the first publicists, Jew or gentile, to defend the economic activity of the Jews as normal and utilitarian. A Rabinovich editorial (23:28/X/1860) offered a rare defense of petty trade as carried on by the Jews. Rabinovich faulted Russian trade legislation for its focus on the estate system. Privileges and monopolies were given to various estates, to the detriment of the national economy and the free flow of trade. The Jews excelled at using petty trade to circumvent monopolies, benefiting the national market. Rabinovich went further still when he defended the most maligned Jews of all, the inn-keeper and middleman, correctly anticipating that this defense would bring cries of rage (25:11/XI/1860). The real cause of apparent Jewish idleness, Rabinovich noted on another occasion, was the Russian legal system which prevented Jews from living throughout the Empire. Overcrowding, caused by unjust laws, was the root cause of the deformation of Jewish economic life (14:26/VIII/1860).[25] Rabinovich also defended the Jews from the oft-heard charge that they were unwilling to farm, in the course of an editorial explaining the reasons for the failure of government-sponsored Jewish agricultural colonies (27:25/XI/1860).

Equally revealing were Rabinovich's views on Jewish corporate institutions. Concealed in his rhetoric on gentile–Jewish rapprochement was his willingness to preserve, and even increase, the scope of Jewish communal institutions, as long as they were cleansed of abuses.

Rassvet carried numerous calls for the reform, but not the abolition, of the korobochka tax on kosher meat which was the principal source of revenue for the Jewish community.[26] Rabinovich went so far as to call for the creation, albeit temporarily, of a formal communal institution for the Jews of Odessa to replace the abolished kahal (15:2/IX/1860). The paper was the first to call for the creation of a "society to spread enlightenment among the Jews" with branches throughout the Pale and a central committee in St. Petersburg. Such a body was soon to come into existence.

The internal furor sparked by Levanda's "blackening of Jewry," and the concentration by many historians on the willingness of maskilim to question accepted features of traditional Judaism, has obscured the reality of *Rassvet*'s diverse stands. Gentile reformers certainly did not expect a maskilic organ to defend Jewish inn-keepers and middlemen, or to advocate new Jewish communal institutions, but only "to spread enlightenment." A closer look reveals that there was much in Judaism, as both a religion and a culture, that maskilim were not ready to abandon. The ability of publicists of all backgrounds to hide for the moment behind the rhetoric of rapprochement disguised this fact, but future realities demanded that fundamental disagreements ultimately had to be faced.[27]

5   *Sion* and the problem of nationality

After the long and arduous task of securing a Russian Jewish periodical, Jewish intellectuals were not content to see *Rassvet* fade quietly away. With Count Stroganov's approval, two Odessa doctors, Lev Pinsker and Emanuel Soloveichik, received Rabinovich's franchise. Because a St. Petersburg newspaper had already adopted the name *Rassvet*, a new name was chosen, *Sion*.

In all external respects the tie to *Rassvet* was emphasized. *Rassvet's* distinctive typeface was retained, as was its motto, "Let there be light!" and it was still subtitled "The Organ of Russian Jews." In the first number, the editors explained that this was the second year of publication, and praised Rabinovich for his past efforts. There were, nonetheless, some important internal changes. The new editors were considerably less strident in their reformist zeal. This was particularly notable in the paper's treatment of Hasidism in which it consciously sought to be more objective. Occasional criticism levied at individual Jewish communities lacked the passion of Levanda's earlier exposé of Jews in the western provinces. The "Jewish role" which *Sion* identified for itself was to enable Jews "to be sons of their time and of their nation, while still remaining Jews." This goal would be pursued in collaboration with the foremost persons (*peredovye liudi*) among the Jews who would act as cultural ambassadors to promote a correct understanding of the Jewish past and present. The editors invited contributions of a historical and historical-literary nature, which would "arouse in us a lively interest and sympathy toward our [Jewish] nationality (*natsional'nost'*), guide us toward contemporary Jewish science, make our national spiritual treasures more widely known, and provide us and all educated Russian society with a historical perspective on the peculiarities (*osobennosti*) of our contemporary life, and the character of Russian Jews."

This agenda constituted, consciously or unconsciously, an admission of failure for the bright hopes which had motivated *Rassvet*. The Jews had unveiled their flaws and received from Russian society only apathy or abuse. It was now time for the Jews to desist from self-flagellation and to assert their national worth, while waiting for Christian society to "show the white flag" of rapprochement. *Sion*, for its part, would develop something resembling a Russian version of the German *Wissenschaft des Judentums*. *Sion* thus displayed a rather academic quality, and lacked the pungency of *Rassvet*, although when events demanded, it was no less argumentative.

The change of name had been forced upon the editors, but their choice of *Sion*, an echo of the lost national homeland, proved very apt. The editors encouraged polemics over the nature and viability of Jewish national identity, which was the old struggle over rapprochement in a new guise. *Sion* was particularly alert to challenge Jewish intellectuals who wished to surrender too much of what the editors considered the essence of Jewishness.

In 1861 the then-liberal daily *Moskovskie vedomosti* published a review article (97:4/V) by R. Goldenviezer devoted to the two Jewish newspapers in Russia, *Rassvet* and Aleksandr Tsederbaum's Hebrew-German *Ha-Melits*, which began publication in Odessa in the fall of 1861.[1] Goldenviezer's assessment of the two publications revealed his assumptions about the future of the Jews. Having lost their political independence, their national territory, and their "soil," the Jews lacked "historical-political individuality," and had ceased to be a nation. Abandoning dreams of a historical mission or of political domination, Jews should pursue the common good of the nation of which they were a part and seek rapprochement with its peoples. (Goldenviezer employed rapprochement and merger as synonyms.) He compared the Jews to a plant which was transferred to alien soil and required acclimatization in order to survive. The key to this process – "in Russia we must endeavor to become Russians" – was already understood by the intelligentsia but still had to be communicated to the mass.

Goldenviezer has frequently been branded as a "radical assimilationist," a characterization given added weight by his subsequent conversion to Christianity. Nonetheless, his call for the assimilation (*osvoenie*) of the Jews displayed some qualifications, which are apparent in his review of the contents of *Rassvet* and *Ha-Melits*. Goldenviezer praised *Rassvet* for its liberal inclination and absence of prejudice and extremism. He lauded the paper's efforts to serve as the "judge of national interests." Goldenviezer savaged *Ha-Melits*. It lacked any firm editorial line, and was filled instead with self-congratulation and boasting. Filled up with translations and work plagarized from other publications, it lacked a single interesting article. Goldenviezer questioned the logic of a newspaper printed in Hebrew, supplemented by German-language articles written in Hebrew characters. Hebrew, except for the Bible, was a dead language. This was not to denigrate Hebrew, he hastened to add, because parts of the Scriptures were unsurpassed for the beauty of their language. Hebrew could offer inspiration to a contemporary Jewish poet, while religious philosophers could use it to convey elevated thoughts. Unfortunately, the artificiality of classical Hebrew vocabulary rendered it unfit to discuss everyday needs and concerns. Few Jews knew Hebrew well, and only a skilled expert could use it for daily conversation.

Goldenviezer waxed lyrical when discussing the Russian language. He urged that "Russian thought, Russian language, and Russian interests should become our thought, our language, and our interests; only then can our complete assimilation into Russian life give us the opportunity to achieve the improvement which we want in Russia." Yet his full approval of the direction of *Rassvet*, his willingness to retain Hebrew for some uses as a national language for poetry or philosophy, and his veiled call for civil rights ("our desired improvement") lends an ambivalence to his "radical assimilationist" tag.

This is even more the case with a similar article by "A Russian Jew from Berlin" which appeared in *Russkii invalid* (251:12/XI/1861). This author, who also used rapprochement and merger as synonyms, sought to explain why this process in Russia lagged behind the West. Linguistic differences between Russians and Jews were a source of mutual alienation, especially the latter's retention of an obsolete but sacred tongue. Hebrew cut the Jews off from Russian life, especially from education. Specialized Jewish education produced people who were morally upright, but not adapted to the modern world. This was demonstrated by the failure of Russian Jewry to produce a single man of genius, such as Moses Mendelssohn. Jewish intellectuals, on the other hand, were more interested in distancing themselves from the masses than in helping them. Rabinovich's *Rassvet*, he claimed, did not concern itself with moral improvement, but with condemning and blackening the name of Russian Jewry.

The author sought changes which would make his coreligionists "Russian citizens of Jewish descent." Echoing Goldenviezer he proclaimed: "Let the new generation, from the cradle, think in Russian, speak in Russian, feel Russian, and be Russian, body and soul." This goal would require the translation of the synagogue service into Russian. A progressive rabbinic leadership would be trained in new Russian rabbinic institutes, modeled after the Breslau rabbinic seminary in Silesia. Internal emancipation, he assured his readers, would rapidly lead to wider civil rights and eventually to complete civic equality.

Although he urged the Jews to become Russian in culture, it was imperative that "we should hold firmly to the faith of our fathers." Meaningless externals might be changed, but not the essence of Jewish religious beliefs. Even as Jews lost their Jewish cultural trappings, their faith must be strengthened. Thus, while Jews should study alongside gentiles in Russian public schools, they should also receive religious instruction for two or three hours a day. For this purpose a special Jewish school system should coexist with the public schools in every town, village, or shtetl. The new enlightened rabbis would oversee a curriculum encompassing religion and Hebrew.

"Radical assimilation," as characterized by these two exponents, while proclaiming the complete Russianization of the Jews, contained many qualifications. Jewish institutions, such as a religious school system, would still exist. Hebrew would remain as an object of formal study, and a link tying all Jews together. Even so, their perspective, derived from the perspective of the German Reform movement, made them unacceptable both to moderate maskilim and traditionalists, and *Sion* served as a willing forum for partisan counter-attacks. Iu. Goldendakh's attack on Goldenviezer is a striking example of the growing assertion of Jewish national identity (6:11/VIII/1861). The appearance of a new Jewish self-esteem was accompanied by a shift of language: Goldendakh was the first publicist to differentiate between rapprochement and merger. He was the first commentator to attach a pejorative connotation to the word merger, characterizing it as a negative force. (This dichotomy, anticipating the modern Russian usage, was not accepted by Goldendakh's contemporaries, another demonstration of the enduring ambiguity surrounding the terms.)

Goldendakh defended the utility of Hebrew and the Hebrew-language press. It existed in the enlightened West, where it was adapted to modern uses, being used to translate a novel by the French author Eugene Sue and a book on chess. Contra Goldenviezer, the Jewish masses did know Hebrew, and their unusually high level of literacy ensured that Hebrew could ably serve as a vehicle for the propaganda of reform.

Goldendakh disputed what the reform program should entail. He

denounced the call for the Jews to "become Russians" as an unacceptable act of merger which would strip the Jews of "their independence
and of everything tying us to our past." Advocacy of merger was even
more incongruous in an age when "nationality comprises the alpha
and omega of all political events." All right thinking Jews accepted the
need for rapprochement, but none could accept merger.

Goldendakh offered examples of his conception of rapprochement
as a positive force. He accepted Goldenviezer's analogy of the Jews as a
plant transported to alien climes and in need of acclimatization. The
plant could retain its special qualities, and still participate in the life
and conditions of the different plants which grew up around it. So too
the Jews. They could retain their national identity while still acting as
loyal citizens in different nation-states. In England, for example, the
Jews retained their distinctive benevolent institutions such as the
Board of Deputies. The Board defended the human rights of Jews
scattered all over the world while simultaneously the Jews of England
showed themselves ready to shed their blood for England. A better
example was the United States of America, "that miscellany of every
possible nationality, each retaining its religious practices, its nationality, and its customs." This is what Goldendakh envisioned for
Russian Jewry, a dual status which would permit them to retain a
national identity within a larger state structure.

The growing validation of Jewish national consciousness is strikingly apparent in a *Sion* editorial replying to the article of "Russian
Jew" in *Russkii invalid* (29:29/II/1862). The editors faulted his obsession
with the acquisition of Russian by Jews, since he ignored the practical
difficulties involved. "Russian Jew" himself had observed that Jews
began to participate in gentile society once it abandoned its old anti-
Jewish prejudices. Why then blame the Jews for the slow diffusion of
Russian culture at a time when Christian prejudices still endured?

Sion offered its own list of reasons why the Empire's Jews were slow
to speak Russian, none of them very flattering to Russians. On a daily
basis, Yiddish served the Jews as the language of a separate caste of
tradesmen within the wider society. Where economic necessity
required that Jews acquire another language, such as Ukrainian, they
easily did so. Russian culture offered nothing that Jews saw as worthy
of imitation, in contrast to German culture. There was even a "German
Party" of Jews in Russia, seeking to introduce their fellows to the
cultural riches of Germany. How could Jews become "Russian, body
and soul" when they were denied everything that would expedite that
process: they lacked the elementary right of living among Russians,

they were forbidden to hire Russian-speaking Christian servants, and the state itself prevented the translation of Jewish prayers into Russian.

Rapprochement required more than just the good intentions of the Jews themselves. *Sion* identified three prerequisites. Russian participation in the commercial life of the Empire must grow sufficiently to force knowledge of Russian out of economic necessity. The institutional network of Russian culture must expand sufficiently to justify and expedite its adoption by Jews. The author in *Russkii invalid*, for example, had advocated the common education of Russians and Jews. Where was this supposed to take place? – In the western provinces, where the Jews were restricted by law and there were no Russian schools? No school system existed for the emancipated peasantry who in any case scorned the Jews as unbelievers. Nor could Jews be expected to study in the Polish schools, where the aristocratic pans viewed them as "less than human."

The Jews of Russia were faulted for their failure to produce great men, but great thinkers were a product of the surrounding community which produced them and interacted with them. Moses Mendelssohn was able to achieve much because he was dealing with a gentile society which produced men like Kant, Lessing and Herder. Russian society had yet to produce men of this calibre. Nor had Russia fulfilled its commitment to rapprochement:

> Enlightened Russian Jews should regret no sacrifice or hardship serving the general prosperity of Russia, or the promotion of active relations between their coreligionists and the Russian people; but these hardships will be crowned with success only when all of Russian society seriously and energetically concerns itself with the removal of blockades and obstacles which obstruct the intellectual, scientific and economic welfare of Russia in general and Russian Jews in particular.

The pages of *Sion* reveal the growing self-confidence and assertiveness of Russian Jewish national awareness, even while displaying its links with the maskilic tradition. Typical was an article of Lev Gordon which was a salvo in the battle over the use of Hebrew (17:27/X/1861). Hebrew, asserted Gordon, should be the medium through which the Jewish intelligentsia – especially graduates of the state rabbinical schools such as Gordon himself – led the Jewish masses to modern civilization. It should be used, not only because it was universally understood by the Jews, but because it was a carrier of Jewish nationality. "In the interests of our religion and our nationality (*natsional'nost'*), in opposition to the growth of indifference, should we not wish to preserve the means of spiritual unity for all our brothers who are scattered around the globe?"

Not only was Hebrew a unifying bond, but its retention and use would enable Jews to contribute to Russian culture. "Russian culture does not know the riches of our Talmud and Midrash; it does not know of the existence of our great thinkers, our Maimonides, Ibn-Gabirol, Ibn-Ezra, Halevy, and countless others; it does not know our history and our fate across time and throughout the world; it does not know our poetry." The Russian Jews' knowledge of Hebrew also provided them with a vehicle to participate in the *Wissenschaft des Judentums*, the Western effort to place the study of Judaism upon contemporary scholarly foundations. In this way, Russian Jews could make a significant contribution to modern culture.

These steps toward development of a modern Jewish national identity did not occur in a vacuum. National movements were developing in other parts of the Empire, especially in the Ukraine. The resolve of the Jewish intellectuals to link their own national program with the dominant Great Russian nationality provoked conflict with the emergent Ukrainian movement. In the ensuing debate, *Sion* spoke for a Russian orientation. The conflict arose from the activities of the periodical *Osnova*, published in St. Petersburg from 1861 to 1862. *Osnova* signified for the Ukrainian national movement what *Rassvet* had represented for Russian Jews, a long-sought vehicle to pursue the national interest. As its name indicated, *Osnova*'s editors sought to provide a base for the rediscovery of the Ukrainian past and traditions which had been obscured by an overlay of Polish culture. *Osnova* published, in Russian and Ukrainian, works of popular literature and folklore, new fiction, economic and historical studies. Contributors included outstanding Ukrainian intellectuals and artists such as T. G. Shevchenko, Marko Vovchok, N. I. Kostomarov, P. A. Kulish and V. B. Antonovich [Antonovych].

At various times articles published in *Osnova* referred to the Jews of the Ukrainian provinces as "Yids" (*Zhidy*). This usage prompted an indignant letter, of a sharp and critical tone, sent anonymously to the editors by a young Jewish doctor V. O. Portugalov.[2] Portugalov announced his support for the general line of the new publication but pointed out to the editors that his young contemporaries had ceased to use the epithet "Yid" and asked them to do the same. He asked rhetorically whether they sought a return to the days of Bohdan Khmelnytsky or merely sought to boost circulation through the use of such insulting rhetoric. The editors responded by printing excerpts from Portugalov's letter, contrary to his request that it not be published, with an accompanying editorial "A Misunderstanding of the Word 'Yid'" (11: November 1861). The editors explained that no other form than Yid (in Ukrainian, *Zhyd*) existed. Its neutral nature was demonstrated through its use by Shevchenko, who had never been accused of being hostile to the Jews. Portugalov's request was seen as analogous to a Russian refusal to be called by the popular usage *Moskal*, or the rejection by the Poles of *Liakh* and the Germans of *Nemets*.

This response was somewhat disingenuous. While *Zhyd* was indeed the sole Ukrainian term, *Osnova* was published in both Ukrainian and Russian. The editors were fully aware of the word's pejorative connotations in Russian, for some of them had signed the special Ukrainian protest against *Illiustratsiia* in 1858. Nor was there any need for a public dispute, since Portugalov had specifically asked that his letter not be published. Alternatively, the editors could have defended Ukrainian usage and left it at that. Roman Serbyn argues that the editors had to reply because they believed that his claim that *Osnova* was prejudiced toward Jews was shared by other educated Jews.[3]

The editors resolved to make a public declaration. Denying that *Zhyd* on the lips of Ukrainian intellectuals had hostile intent, they admitted that, as used by the peasantry, the term *was* insulting. Jews were deeply resented by the peasantry, and with good reason.

> Up to the present day, the Jews have kept themselves apart while living among the South Russian population; they have nothing in common with our people, and do not take a single step toward rapprochement with them; on the contrary, they often act against the spirit and needs of our people. For a nation (*natsiia*), nothing can be more harmful than the existence in its midst of different nationalities (*narodnosti*) which keep off to one side and are apathetic to its fate or – still worse – endeavor to subjugate it to their power or influence.

The editors nonetheless declared their respect for the talent and ability of the Jews and invited them to contribute to the prosperity of the land and people of South Russia.

Sion offered an editorial rebuttal. No educated Jew could be unaware of the negative stereotypes conveyed by the term Yid. *Sion* was well-equipped to discuss them, having carried an erudite exploration of the philological and cultural origins of the word in its first issue.[4] Yet the editors preferred to let this particular issue pass, announcing that

> we don't see how one could require Poles to replace "Żyd" with the expression "Believers of the Old Law" (*starozakonny*) which would only signify the religious and not the ethnic (*plemennaia*) aspect of the Jews; and there is no foundation for making a similar demand of the Little Russians ... Even in Russia Yid can't always be considered insulting: the term Yid is more popular, and the term Jew (*Evrei*) is more official, and one who is accustomed from childhood to use the former expression should not be ordered to change just because it offends us.

This declaration was disingenuous indeed, for Portugalov was on firm ground when he complained that a Jew not offended by being called a Yid would probably not be insulted by anything.

Sion's editors were eager to put the linguistic argument behind them because they wished to concentrate on another charge, the complaint that Jews in the Ukraine, insofar as they had loyalty to any nationality but their own, sympathized with the Russians. They accused *Osnova* of putting the interests of the Little Russians, only a part of the population, above the interests of the state as a whole. "Desires for national exclusivity cannot be fruitful ... They are especially harmful when they seek to divide a nation which by racial origins or by common political or political-economic interests should constitute one whole." *Sion* offered the misguided Ukrainians an object lesson.

> Look at the educated Jew: he is a Jew and he considers the Jews of all other countries his brothers in faith and origin; in addition he is a Russian, or Frenchman, or Englishman, etc. and is ready to sacrifice everything to the interests of the Fatherland; he is a cosmopolitan and, when religious and political interests are not involved, all men are equally dear to him.

P. Kulish replied to this attack in an article entitled "Foremost Yids," a mocking reference to *Sion*'s earlier call for "foremost persons" to provide leadership to the Jewish masses. Kulish expressed his frustration and disillusionment. The purpose of the offending article in *Osnova*, he explained, was to voice regret that Jews in the Ukraine lived apart from Little Russians and to urge the "leading Jews" of the Ukraine to spread new civic ideas among their coreligionists in order to advance the common good. This well-intentioned suggestion had now been greeted with lies and misrepresentations on the part of *Sion*, an indication of just how far "leading Jews" were willing to go in pursuit of their narrow national ends.

> Because we do not rhapsodize over the activities of their forefathers in the Ukrainian land and don't see heavenly blessings in those things which the Jews do everywhere today, inside and outside of the

area where they are permitted to live, the foremost Jews don't beat around the bush but speak of us as proponents of the Inquisition and revivers of barbarian, feudal times.

Listening to Jews speak of patriotism, mused Kulish, reminded him of the comic scene in Gogol's *Taras Bulba*, where the Jews assured the Zaporozhian Cossacks of their loyalty. The Jews invoked "the interests of the Fatherland" so ardently as to make them apparent rivals of the Muscovite tsars in "gathering the Russian land." Far from expressing true patriotism, this verbiage was just a screen to shelter Jewish wrongdoing. The Ukrainians of *Osnova* had a right to feel betrayed by the Jews, Kulish lamented. They had been in the forefront of the Literary Protest of 1858. Kulish revealed that he personally had written the letter signed by Kostomarov, Vovchok, Nomis and Shevchenko. The sentiments of that letter had not changed, he declared, even though the Jews' true nature now revealed itself.

Kulish's admission demonstrates my earlier contention that signatories of the various literary protests were often motivated by more than concern for literary propriety. Ukrainian intellectuals defended Jews from a personal attack with the hope and expectation that Jews, or at least those in the Ukraine, would see it as a gesture inviting their participation in the Ukrainian national revival. The Jews' failure to do so, understandable in the absence of any benefits more tangible than those on offer from the Russian government, led to bitterness and recriminations.

Even worse than Jewish apathy, from the Ukrainian point of view, was their political treachery. *Sion*'s editorial was seen as an act of political informing, a denunciation of the aspirations of the Ukrainians to the imperial government. This accounts for the vitriol and bitterness which characterized the conduct of *Osnova*. These polemics were not only "the first public debate in modern times on Jewish–Ukrainian relations," but also the beginning of a long struggle between rival national aspirations in the Ukraine.[5]

If Kulish was prepared to invoke the golden year of Jewish–Christian amity in Russia, so too were the editors of *Sion*. They sought to repeat the success of 1858 with an appeal to the Russian public, using the "unparalleled abuse and baseless and dishonorable accusations" of Kulish as a pretext. Russian literature must not ignore such conduct, the editors announced, inviting Russian writers to adjudicate the dispute, assessing guilt and blame as appropriate. "The ground upon which it [Russian literature] stands is not yet so firm, the conditions among which it develops are not yet so

10 N. I. Kostomarov

auspicious, that it can remain calm in an affair of this type" (21:24/XI/
1861).

The response of the journalistic world demonstrates how much the
mood had changed from 1858. Many periodicals, such as *Moskovskie
vedomosti*, which had helped to lead the Literary Protest, declined to
comment at all. Those which joined the debate placed *Sion* in the dock
with *Osnova*. The Russian Jewish intelligentsia could no longer depend
on universal support when they engaged in polemics.

Even as Russian journalists began to adjudicate the dispute, *Osnova*
carried a far sharper thrust in its January 1862 issue from the pen of
N. I. Kostomarov entitled "To the Judeans" (*Iudeiam*) – a term he used
in a sarcastic effort to avoid giving offense. Kostomarov, a renowned
professor of history at the University of St. Petersburg, and a leading
Ukrainian patriot, was no friend of the Jews. From a historical perspective he condemned their alliance with the Poles in the ruination of
Little Russia. His assessment of the Jewish national character may be
gauged from his openly stated belief, which he published in the

Russian press, that contemporary Jewish fanatics still practiced ritual murder.[6] Kostomarov summarized the historic grievances of the Ukrainian people against the Jews. The issue was not the existence of the Jews as an alien nationality, he insisted. Germans, Frenchmen, Greeks and Tatars lived a separate existence in the Ukraine without provoking popular displeasure. Unfortunately the character of the Jews was shaped by the Old Testament which made them eternal sojourners in the land of others while they awaited their Messiah. Talmudic beliefs overwhelmed the superficially held values of humanism and cosmopolitanism about which the Jewish intellectuals boasted. It was because of these attitudes that the Jews were universally persecuted and oppressed. Yet they still managed to survive through techniques unique to them. "'Money! Most of all the Yid loves money,' echoes from unrecorded time ... This eternal Jew seized and held on to the world's weak spot, and directed the world, and the world was deceived; thinking the Jew under its heel, it does not realize that it is on the leash of the Jew."

The history of the Ukraine presented a classic example. In Western Europe, as the masses were being enserfed, a trade-commercial class managed to survive to the day that it might challenge the feudal barons, develop a distinctive civilization and promote human equality. In Poland and the Ukraine, Jews seized the economic prerogatives of the middle class. They served as the agents of the Polish pans in the exploitation of the Ukrainian peasantry. Jews lived by the dictum that "what is good for the upper classes is good for the country," and thus had to suffer the consequences when the Cossacks rose against their oppressors in 1648. Ukrainians did not hate the Jews from religious motives, argued Kostomarov. They tolerated Muslims and Catholics in their midst. They hated Jews because they were thieves, always in pursuit of their own best interests.

Despite the lessons of the tragic past, Jews maintained their fatal alliance with the pans. They were able to control trade and commerce because of the sloth of the landed gentry and the degradation of the peasantry. As the beneficiaries of the status quo, they wished to preserve it. No better example of the Jews' disdain for the common good could be found than their continued domination of the alcohol trade, an endeavor which required them to promote peasant drunkenness and irresponsibility. It was precisely this alienation of the Jews from the best interests of the Ukraine that *Osnova* had identified and asked the Jews to correct.

Instead the Jews had turned upon *Osnova*, seeking, as was their wont, the weak point through which to destroy the Ukrainian publication. The weak point which *Sion* chose was the Ukrainians' defense of their nationality.

> Won't one accustomed only to regarding Russia and Russian life with a one-sided view easily conclude that writing in the South Russian language, defending the South Russian nationality – represents an attempt to dissolve the unity of Russian life, to stir up national antipathies, and in the future perhaps to destroy the state? Doesn't writing in South Russian work against the political unity of Russia?

Kostomarov defended *Osnova* from these serious charges. The journal's publishers did not seek separation but only recognition that Russian nationality exists in two forms, the Great Russian and the Little Russian. The growth of the Russian state was based on the principle of the cooperation of peoples rather than that of unity imposed upon constituent parts. Jewish publicists, however, mouthed grand phrases about enlightenment, humanism and cosmopolitan goals even as they sought to stir up Great Russian patriotism and, if possible, the antipathy of the government, by accusing the Ukrainians of a malevolent desire to disrupt national unity.

Kostomarov, a man who had and would suffer for his Ukrainophile sympathies, correctly anticipated future travails. In the years following the Polish uprising of 1863, the imperial government placed bans on publications in Ukrainian. The Ukrainophiles themselves had to endure the hostility of the Russian press and the intimidation of the Russian government. *Sion*'s accusations were indeed politically charged.

Kostomarov declared that the Ukrainophiles claimed even less than the Jews offered to give. Ukrainophiles did not ask Jews to abandon their ancient distinctive features, but only to support the best rather than the worst interests of the region in which they lived. Despite the intimations of *Sion* about the part and the whole, what was good for the South was equally useful for Moscow, Viatka or Novgorod. Consequently, the Ukraine would welcome a new order of things in which the Jews would receive equal civil rights and free entrée into diverse economic activities. These prerogatives would have to be balanced by strong competition from Ukrainians to prevent all fields of the economy from falling under Jewish domination. If Ukrainians lost in a fair fight, so be it – the national failure would be honestly admitted. As for nationality, if the Jews preferred to side with the Great Russians, if they were too vain to wish to be Ukrainians, then let them go. The Ukraine demanded neither the national nor the religious conversion of the Jews.

Kostomarov's apparent call for the expansion of Jewish rights – and his attendant qualifications – was typical of an emergent trend of thought among liberal thinkers, and not just Ukrainophiles. In principle the Jews should be equal, but given social and economic realities, the naive lower classes had to be safeguarded from Jewish excesses, a proviso which virtually paralyzed any active espousal of Jewish rights. At the same time, Kostomarov's disdainful dismissal of Jewish participation in the Ukrainian national movement suggested that efforts to reconcile these two peoples, who had both suffered unhappy fates, had broken down almost at their inception. The interests of Russian Jewry were identified with the dominant majority, not with the politically weaker national minorities.

Kostomarov doubted that his arguments would change Russian public opinion since "the Jews are now the favorites of all contemporary, prominent Russia," and because they had attracted so many influential publications to their side. As an example he pointed to M. N. Katkov's thick journal *Russkii vestnik*, which joined the quarrel with an article in its November 1861 issue entitled "What Is the Harm of Monopoly?" The journal's summation of the *Osnova–Sion* debate sympathized with the latter, calling its arguments "intelligent, honorable and just." It praised the willingness of the Jews to sacrifice their nationality for the common good of the entire Russian state. It was important to stress, *Russkii vestnik* editorialized, that the Jews must never be compelled to abandon their national peculiarities or their religious beliefs. The most efficacious approach was to break down the barriers of civic and political inequality, for this process would inevitably be followed by the Jews' joining the people among whom they lived and abandoning their position as hostile aliens. *Russkii vestnik* contrasted the conduct of the Jews with Kulish's unacceptable slander made against the "foremost Yids" only because they opposed the Ukrainian national revival.

Russkii vestnik clearly had not abandoned its role, assumed during the Literary Protest, as one of the principal defenders of the Russian Jewish intelligentsia. The journal was also willing, in an abstract way, to accept the continued existence of Jewish national culture and Judaism as a moral–ethical system. *Russkii vestnik* assured its readers that the Jews wished to become Russians, and left it without further explanation. As a final irony, *Russkii vestnik* was surprisingly indulgent toward the Ukrainian national revival, for Katkov subsequently became one of its most bitter enemies. According to Roman Serbyn, "in playing down the political overtones of the Ukrainian national revival, Katkov was de-escalating the dispute and actually rendering the Ukrainians a service."[7] In general, before the Polish uprising of 1863, Katkov was unconcerned with the apparently harmless growth of national aspirations among any non-Russian ethnic group save the Poles.

Two other Russian periodicals, both claiming to be sympathetic to the Jews, arrived at diametrically opposed estimates of the nature of the Jewish national character. *Russkaia rech* (102:21/XII/1861) offered an apparent testimonial to the strength of the Jewish national character which had endured all attempts to wipe it from the face of the earth while simultaneously preserving its internal and external vitality. The author used this concession as a starting point for a revisionist interpretation of the Jewish national character. Through an examination of the religion, language, external and internal life of the Jews throughout history, he argued that the Jews were extremely prone to outside influences. Indeed, he depicted Judaism as virtually devoid of a truly national coloration. It had been acquired only after the loss of national independence when religion became the focus for Jewish national aspirations. Under the influence of persecution, Judaism lost its tradition of free development and acquired the immoveable form so apparent in the modern age. In all other areas, such as language, the Jews assumed the tongue of surrounding populations, be it Greek, Arabic or German. Circumstances changed them from a nation of farmers into a race of tradesmen. The Jewish character survived, not by being strong and resilient, but by being weak and pliable, like the willow that bends in the wind.

The author believed that his discovery had dramatic consequences. "Knowing the conditions through which the national character of the Jews was changed in the course of their historical life, we acquire power over this character and we may change it at will." Western Europe provided ample evidence that wherever the Jews were granted more freedom they fell under the moral and intellectual influence of the surrounding population: "a strange nation, which desires its own destruction, which aspires to a full merger with an alien nationality." The only area the Jews refused to sacrifice was their religion, "the steadfast aspect of the national life of the Jews." But even religion was susceptible to change in the course of national merger. While the future form of Judaism could not be predicted, the fruits of its development would undoubtedly be useful for the intellectual and moral life of mankind.

These assumptions allowed *Russkaia rech* to fault both *Osnova* and

Sion. The Ukrainians were to blame for refusing to take a wider view of history and failing to recognize that the Jewish national character was the product of outside conditions and influences. The desire of the editors of *Osnova* that the Jews work for the good of the South Russian land and people was appropriate and commendable. Co-operation, however, was not obtained through insults, reproaches and demands. The Jews would pursue a nation's goals only when they were fully a part of that nation. The Ukrainian nation must employ all its intellectual and moral skills to win over the Jews. With common interests and goals, the two nations could truly become one.

Sion, for its part, was faulted for ambiguity in its discussion of the process of merger. A merger did not occur between two abstractions, such as "the political whole," but between real people. Rather than offering to merge with the "abstract persons of political influence," Jews should accept the task of merging with the Ukrainian population. States were always comprised of a variety of nationalities, and the Jews had to select one or another with which to merge. In the Austrian Empire, Jews sided with one nationality, such as the Germans, not with the whole. *Russkaia rech* observed that merger was facilitated by the fact that Jewry possessed only religion as a permanent feature, and it disputed *Sion*'s suggestion that the Jews might preserve some of their national peculiarities. A suggestion of that nature, as well as *Sion*'s hostility to *Osnova* and the Ukrainians, did not represent the kind of leadership which the Jewish intellectuals should provide the Jewish masses, the author complained.

In its first issue for the New Year (1:4/I/1862) *Odesskii vestnik* presented an anonymous discussion of the *Osnova–Sion* debate. The article focused on a prior claim of *Sion* that the Jews had much to contribute to humanity as a consequence of their cosmopolitanism. *Sion*, insisting upon "Jewish cosmopolitanism," was doing its people a disservice, argued the critic. In the modern world of nation-states cosmopolitanism was little more than a political utopia which existed in contradiction to physical reality. "The contemporary cosmopolitan is a homeless vagrant who has lost fatherland and birthplace, and for whom all the ends of the earth are the same." *Sion*, through its insistence that a Jew might easily become a Russian, Frenchman, or Englishman, depending upon his place of residence, did not recognize the fundamental error that "it is impossible to be simultaneously a Russian and a German, impossible to serve truly the interests of two antipathetic nationalities?" Jewish nationality existed, just like any other, and could not be abandoned or denied.

A more extreme view appeared in the short-lived Moscow daily *Nashe vremia* (58:16/III/1862). Unlike *Russkaia rech*, which anticipated the rapid disappearance of Jewish nationality, or *Odesskii vestnik*, which admired the Jews' steadfastness, B. Landau (himself a Jew to judge by his name) denied that the Jews were a nationality at all, basing his claim on anthropological categories. Landau divided human beings (*rod*) into numerous races (*rasa*) distinguished by enduring physical features. Races were divided into ethnic groups (*plemia*) distinguished from one another by physical features and spiritual affinities. Language was the most obvious of these distinctions.

The ethnic division served as the basis for nationality, but it was supplemented by the impact of climate and soil, historical events, religion, and the activity of leading personalities. For an ethnic group to become a nation (*natsiia*) it had to grow and develop its life within a state structure and acquire a territory, a language, and a consciousness of its unity and power. Using these criteria, claimed Landau, the Jews were not a nationality, still less the harmful nationality characterized by Kostomarov, but merely an ethnic group. They lacked a common territory, a common language and any feeling of unity and power, and could hardly threaten or dominate Kostomarov's Ukraine.

The only bond which unified the Jews was religion, and this tie was significant only in states where religion still bore a civil character. In modern states like England, Jews were given civil rights and the isolationist, ritual side of their religion withered away. So might it be in Russia.

If the Jews were so weak, asked Landau, why had they failed either to merge with the Ukrainians or to be subordinated by them? The answer lay in the religious persecution which the Jews suffered at the hands of the Ukrainians. The more a religious sect was persecuted, the more doggedly it adhered to its beliefs. This had happened in the Ukraine and was the chief cause of the isolation of Ukrainian Jewry. Wherever the Jews were granted greater rights in contemporary Russia, they gradually merged. Landau thus served as guardian of the memory of Jewish pain in the Ukraine, just as Kostomarov exemplified the memory of historic Ukrainian grievances. Further, Landau's rejection of any unifying ties for the Jews beyond religion brought him very close to Western theorists who sought to reduce Jewishness to religious confession, and nothing more.

A variety of other papers also entered the fray, but none of their articles broke new ground or sparked further polemics. The December, 1862 number of *Vremia*, published by the Dostoevskii brothers, saw the debate as an object lesson on the need to avoid unproductive literary squabbles. *Russkii invalid* (II: 1862) continued its tradition of Judeophilia by chiding Kulish for the "coarse and indecent tone" of "Foremost Yids," while praising *Sion* for its "humane direction." *Syn Otchestva*, on the other hand, lamented that the quarrel revealed that "the idea of some sort of merger of social interests, of the elimination of the disunity and discord of its members, is for the moment only a dream" (II: 1861). The satirical magazine *Iskra* sided with *Sion*, offering poetical couplets to criticize *Osnova*'s fascination with the word "Yid" (VI: 1862). Even *Illiustratsiia*, now under a new editor, accused *Osnova* of going beyond the bounds of literary decency.

If the editors of *Sion* received a literary vindication of sorts in the public debate surrounding both the tactics and the arguments of *Osnova*, it was a pyrrhic victory. Setting Russian public opinion on to the Ukrainophiles, the editors of *Sion* found that they had to defend themselves as well. The paper took up this task in three lengthy articles devoted to the debate with *Osnova*. The first defended the editors' concept of cosmopolitanism (28:12/I/1862). Jewish cosmopolitanism was not to be understood as the impossible attempt to smooth out all national distinctions, but merely the ability of the Jews to be simultaneously Jews and loyal members of their respective national states. *Odesskii vestnik* had erred in attributing to *Sion* the belief that Jews might easily become Russians, Frenchmen or Englishmen. "We did not say this," protested the editors, "and could not say this: for an English Jew to resettle in Russia and become a Russian Jew would be as difficult as for an Englishman to become a Russian." *Sion* pronounced itself puzzled by the assertion that a Jew could not be a Jew and a German at the same time. Rather, said *Sion*, the point was that a Jew could more easily become a German than a Little Russian because, "the German nationality with its solid civilization had more attractive, assimilative power than the Little Russian" which lacked energy and strength of character. *Odesskii vestnik* offered two unacceptable choices because Jews neither wished to remain a distinct nationality and occupy a position subordinate to the area's dominant nationality (i.e., the Russians), nor to turn themselves into the local majority (i.e., the Ukrainians).

Having rebutted *Odesskii vestnik*'s concept of the steadfastness of the Jewish national character, *Sion* turned against the other extreme represented by *Russkaia rech* (38:23/III/1862). The author was the young A. Ia. Garkavi [Harkavy], later renowned as an Orientalist and the bibliographer of the St. Petersburg Oriental Institute. Garkavi asserted that the essential integrity of Judaism, the core of the Jewish existence, remained unchanged. Even the German Reform movement, for instance, accepted the authority of the Talmud. As far as externals were concerned, the Jews over their history had variously spoken Aramaic, Greek or Arabic, but they had never lost the use of Hebrew, and it never became a dead language. It remained an effective medium for transmission of contemporary ideas. The Jews were far from being malleable: the survival of their religion and their national tongue revealed an amazing strength of character. The Jews were now ready to participate in the national life of any country of which they were a part, but only while preserving their religious and moral interests, and their ties to Hebrew.

A general summing up of the debate, and the last definitive statement on Jewish nationalism was provided by the editorial "*Sion* and *Osnova* in the Court of Russian Journalism" (37:16/III/1862). The problem at issue was not that of merger, it asserted, for the Jews were willing to participate in the fate and culture of all of Russia. The problem was that *Osnova* demanded "Ukrainization" rather than "Russification." Even then, Jews were sympathetic to Little Russian culture. Jews spoke Ukrainian and sang Ukrainian folk songs, while educated Jews read Shevchenko. When forced to choose, however, circumstances demanded that the Jews choose Russian culture. Ukrainian barely existed as a literary language, save for the works of Shevchenko and the prose writer Kvitka. Most Ukrainian intellectuals had tired of the struggle of promoting Ukrainian and, like Gogol, turned to Russian, a more successful medium for transmission of enlightened concepts. Russian was the language of the Church, science, trade and commerce in the Empire. Russian literature showed itself far more sympathetic to the Jews than had Ukrainian literature which spoke of Yids not just when speaking in Ukrainian but also when speaking Russian.

The underlying subtext of the debate remained the same – Jewish nationalism.

> We again note that we never say that the Jews should try to preserve their peculiarities save for their religion; we only say that nobody has the right to demand of the Jews that they reject their harmless national peculiarities only because they are peculiarities and thus displeasing to him ... The question of precisely what national characteristics and how long the Jews might preserve them in the midst of the dominant local population we are careful not to answer ...

These were fine sentiments, but the editors were again begging the question of what specific changes would occur in Judaism and Jewry in the processes of rapprochement and merger.

Time ran out for *Sion* before a more definitive answer could be given. The editors unexpectedly announced toward the end of the publication year (43:27/IV/1862) that the paper was being temporarily suspended. The reason given was the paper's inability to refute baseless charges made against the Jews and Judaism by the Russian press. It might seem that this was precisely what the paper had been doing over the past year. Apparently the nationwide debate had encouraged the unwelcome attentions of the local censor. The Russian censorship, which included a religious arm, was always uncomfortable with press discussion of any religious matters, while *Sion* had not been shy in broaching them. According to the last editor, Soloveichik, the polemics with *Osnova* led the Odessa censor to reaffirm a rule, consistently circumvented by *Rassvet* and *Sion*, that all material dealing with the religious life of the Jews had to be passed by the Spiritual Censor, under the control of the Holy Synod. This effectively guaranteed that the material would never be passed and forced the editors to announce that they would seek government approval of a broader program.[8] Yehuda Slutsky offers a more prosaic explanation, pointing to the paper's financial difficulties due to the paucity of subscribers.[9] The editors apparently did not rule out a reappearance since they announced that they would wait until the end of the year before returning advance subscription money. In fact, the paper closed for good, the "franchise" eventually passing into the hands of A. Tsederbaum.

It was almost a decade before another Russian Jewish newspaper appeared on a regular basis.[10] The articles in *Sion* provided the last general forum in which Russian Jewish intellectuals could articulate a vision of Jewish national identity. It was all the more significant that this vision was obscure and contradictory. Still, its most salient and recurrent features can be noted. Most striking is the elan with which some Jews now publicly asserted their Jewishness. Fellow Jews branded as "extreme assimilationists," like Goldenviezer, were repudiated. The failure of rapprochement on the Jewish side was attributed to the weak attractive force of Russian culture, to say nothing of the alleged poverty of Ukrainian culture.

Exactly what constituted modern Jewish identity was less clearly delineated. It apparently included the retention of Hebrew as a language of study and prayer, and a visible symbol of the Jewish past. "Jewish literature," broadly defined to include the ground between the Talmud on the one hand and the works of the *Wissenschaft des Judentums* on the other, was also included. The sum total of Jewish national identity was subsumed under the vague phrase of "national peculiarities," which might be expected to survive merger, given the vaunted steadfastness of the Jews. This claim was diluted by the parallel assertion of "Jewish cosmopolitanism." The latter concept claimed a unique status for Jewish nationality: alone of nationalities, it could endure while Jews participated in the wider national life of other nationalities. Jews could become Russians while remaining Jews. Writers usually pointed to the West as an example of what they meant. Yet Russian Jewry was still far from attaining the legal equality which characterized those Jewish communities, nor did the spokesmen of Russian Jewry appear on the whole to welcome the complete de-nationalization which characterized at least part of the Western experience. The oft-repeated promise of Russian Jewish intellectuals to abandon their Jewish nationality for the greater good of the Russian state was qualified by the invocation of survivable "national peculiarities." Another striking omission from the writings of Jews in Russian was any mention of Zion itself, the Messiah, or the changing concept of messianism as a focal point for Jewish identity, themes which were fully explored in the debates encompassing Reform Judaism in the West, although this may have been a consequence of the influence of the clerical censor.[11]

Russian opinion was no more successful in finding a definition. Some periodicals, such as *Osnova* and *Odesskii vestnik*, clearly identified the Jews as one national minority among others within the Russian state, thus tying the question of Jewish nationalism to that of the other subject nationalities, most notably the Ukrainians. Others, such as *Russkaia rech*, followed Western models to proclaim the Jews as no more than a religious confession, highly susceptible to change and assimilation, even in the area of religion. Thus, after two years of polemics and serious debate, Jews and gentiles were no closer to a mutually acceptable definition of Jewishness, a failure that made it impossible to frame precise ground rules for the attainment of rapprochement or merger.

6   The religious element in Russian Judeophobia

The Christian religion, in its Greek Orthodox variant, was a defining component of Russian national consciousness. Byzantine traditions of intolerance toward heretics and unbelievers and the pressures of Muslim and non-Orthodox Christian adversaries combined to make Russian Orthodoxy antipathetic to rival faiths. The outbreak of the so-called "Judaizer Heresy" in Novgorod-Moscow in the late fifteenth century – whether or not actual Jews were involved – demonstrated and reinforced Muscovite hostility and insecurity toward Judaism as a religion.[1] The history of the expansion of Muscovy is rife with episodes of violence toward Jews and Judaism. The small Jewish communities which Russia acquired through her expansion in the late seventeenth and early eighteenth centuries were expelled from the Empire by 1742. The assumption that "the Muscovite tradition of religious Antisemitism" carried over into the post-partition period is therefore understandable. Early scholars of Russian Jewish history, such as Ilia Orshanskii and Simon Dubnov, considered this tradition a vital component in the development of modern Russia's Jewish policies.[2]

Allowing for the role that religious prejudice played in Russian actions, the religious tradition which imperial statesmen inherited was crude and unsophisticated in the extreme. For devout Russians, the Jews were first and foremost deicides, "the enemies of Christ" as Empress Elizabeth branded them in 1742. Contemporary Jews were infidels who threatened the integrity of the faith with their pernicious doctrines. Jews even menaced the physical safety of Christians in vague and ill-defined ways. These were sufficient grounds for the expulsion or persecution of Jews by the Russian state.

When the expanding Russian Empire began to acquire dominion over the Jewish population of the Polish–Lithuanian Commonwealth, it inherited the religious and social prejudices and stereotypes of local

123

Christians. These were a complex matrix of beliefs, developed from local conditions as well as under the influence of medieval and modern ideas from Western Europe. Concepts of "fanaticism" and "exploitation," soon to loom so large in the official mind, were not part of the old Russian religious tradition, but newly learned. Once acquired, they remained within the bureaucratic milieu. The few books and articles which popularized these ideas to a wider imperial audience were either published in foreign languages abroad, like the anti-talmudic work of Abbè Chiarini, or were confined to specialist publications like the *Journal* of the Ministry of Internal Affairs.

As publicists of the Reform Era turned their attention to the Jewish Question, they discovered these anti-Jewish prejudices and assumed that they were modern, based upon scholarship and empirical evidence. The crude religious bigotry of the old Russian tradition was unacceptable to public opinion. A typical response to attacks on Jews was to characterize the author as a fanatic or inquisitor. An important development in the early Reform Era, therefore, was the process by which religious prejudice acquired respectability. This was a two-sided phenomenon: either making the religious component of scholarly Judeophobia more overt, or cloaking religious arguments in the garb of secular philosophy. This transformation occurred in a relatively short period of time. A benchmark can be established by examining an initial failure of religious Judeophobia to exercise any impact on public opinion.

Domashniaia beseda dlia narodnogo chteniia was published in St. Petersburg from 1858 to 1877 under the editorship of V. I. Askochenskii. It was a weekly newspaper intended for an unsophisticated, barely literate audience, as evidenced by its short articles and large type. The newspaper reportedly had ties to the higher authorities of the Russian Orthodox Church.[3] It preached a message of patriotic chauvinism and religious piety, frequently reprinting church sermons. It displayed religious bigotry toward the Jews throughout its existence. The polemics of 1858 offered the paper an opportunity to comment on the theme of "Yids" (6:7/II/1859). Askochenskii looked askance at the entry of a Jew into the British parliament and the appointment of a French Jew as Consul-General in Algeria. While the defenders of the Jews in Russia hailed this as the triumph of religious toleration, he foresaw grim consequences. While the moral principles of modern civilization might lead inevitably to the appointment of Jews to high government positions, the laws which Jewish officials were compelled to follow derived from moral principles based on religious dogma. A European judge, for example, would consider a case of polygamy differently from a Muslim or Chinese judge and so, by implication, would a Jew.

A subsequent editorial returned to this theme, inspired by the European reaction to the Mortara Affair in Italy, by press reports of Jewish civil and political successes abroad, and by the Literary Protest (14:4/IV/1859). The paper derided claims that European civilization would have a positive effect upon Judaism and would bring the Jews into the universal human family. "What a flexible thing this civilization is! ... How little human civilization demands of the Jewish people, who willingly shouted before the indecisive Pilate, 'His blood be upon us, and upon our children.'"

Askochenskii poured scorn on the "civilized" call for freedom of conscience, noting that there were two contrary types of freedom. The first, propagated by the Evangelists, sprang from a recognition of the obligations and precepts of the higher law; the second was that preached by the serpent in the Garden of Eden, and led to willfulness and licentiousness. Those who offered freedom of conscience to Jews were following the prompting of the "father of lies and falsehoods." The authority of divine revelation, possessed only by Christians, should not be undermined by toleration based upon false human principles.

Theological concerns also colored the comments of the monthly journal *Strannik*, best described as a religious thick journal, edited by an Orthodox priest, V. V. Grechulevich, who had links to Ukrainian cultural circles. The February 1860 issue carried a long article by Professor Ivan Vasilevskii devoted to the conversion of the Jews. Although affirming the inevitability of conversion, the author characterized the Jews as "outcasts, covered with the shame of Christ-killing, and stubbornly opposed to the generosity of God." This was a typical response of the Orthodox Church to the "problem" of the Jews, in so far as ecclesiastical authorities showed any interest at all. (On the operational level, on the other hand, Orthodox authorities were always alert to the alleged threat posed to the integrity of the faith by "Judaizing" among the peasantry.)

The crude theological sentiments of *Strannik* and especially *Domashniaia beseda* were more insulting to the Jews than anything that appeared in *Illiustratsiia*, yet these articles were ignored by journalists.[4] This is understandable: theological questions were of little interest to the Russian press, more intent on sharing the latest advances of European science with its readers. Jewish authors, for their part, were well aware of the dangers of public religious debates with adherents of the established Church. It required the talents of a skillful publicist,

11 I. S. Aksakov

and a layman, I. S. Aksakov, to make the religious side of the Jewish
Question topical for Russian readers. The occasion was a decree of
27 November 1861 which offered full residence rights and admission to
all branches of the civil service to Jews with an advanced academic
degree. Only a tiny elite of the Jews were eligible, but dissenting voices
were nonetheless raised.

Ivan Sergeevich Aksakov (1823–86) was the scion of a gentry family
whose very name recalled the whole Slavophile movement.[5] Aksakov
was not a brilliant or original thinker of Slavophilism, but he was its
most important publicist and popularizer. He was a skilled journalist
whose publications completely mirrored his forceful personality and
whose prose was always pungent and argumentative. Aksakov's
publications never enjoyed high circulation, but his editorial sallies
were widely cited and challenged by his ideological rivals. Aksakov is
also significant as the figure who bridged the Slavophile and the
Panslav movements.[6]

Aksakov explored the Jewish Question throughout his journalistic career, but his discussion of the law of 27 November particularly demonstrated his unique ability to shape debate, to coin enduring catch-phrases, and to legitimize the sentiments of religious Judeophobia which were scorned by the public when purveyed by lesser men. He was also a major conduit for foreign – especially German – Judeophobia into Russia.[7]

"The expressions: 'idea of the age,' 'liberal idea,' 'humane thought' – operate in our progressive society as a sort of scarecrow to frighten the most courageous critic," he editorialized in his newspaper *Den* (19:16/II/1862). The new decree admitting Jews into the civil service was a case in point: the press, eager to hail its progressive aspect, failed to recognize that it could not be implemented without some important qualifications. For example, Russian society would not accept a Jew as Ober-Procurator of the Holy Synod, the secular governing body of the Russian Orthodox Church. In addition, there were philosophical reasons for questioning the admission of Jews into the civil service.

Russia, Aksakov reminded his readers, was a Christian country, and Christian teachings were the starting point for the moral and spiritual life of the nation. They produced a distinctive civil and social life and shaped education, science, law and social relations. Admittedly, Christian principles were an ideal toward which an imperfect society could only strive, but they nonetheless constituted the "Christian banner" around which the Russian nation rallied.

The Jews were an alien element which had entered Russia in the guise of a hungry, persecuted, and orphaned people. The Russian state, following the principle of Christian charity, granted the Jews a refuge, a livelihood and freedom to develop their internal and external life. A Christian state could do no more; specifically, it could not permit Jews to occupy positions of authority over Christians, especially when Jews continued to be guided by their own distinctive principles, their "Jewish banner." In Aksakov's schema, the Jewish banner encompassed the Law of Moses, itself a complete negation of Christian ideals. Christianity and Judaism were mutually exclusive moral systems, and a civil entity which ignored this fact was guilty of hypocrisy and mendacity.

Russian liberals, Aksakov complained, ignored the Christian–Jewish dichotomy and espoused Jewish emancipation "in the spirit of contemporary civilization." This spirit, unfortunately, presented such undesirable features as "the victory of the English over the Slavs ... the teaching of the materialists ... and the lewdness of women under communist influence." Liberals never understood that it was the nineteenth century of the *Christian* era and that one could seek the extension of Jewish rights on the basis of Christian principles, but not through negation of Christian principles. Jews themselves rejected the Christian banner when they demanded the free exercise of their religion, the maintenance of Jewish schools, and the continued study of the Talmud, although it contained teachings "counter to all the principles which lie at the basis of local, social and civil life in a Christian land."

Given Aksakov's lack of sympathy for the Jewish presence in the Russian state, his ultimate prescription for them was surprisingly generous. He was willing to remove all restrictive legislation from them and to grant them full communal autonomy, the maintenance of their own schools, and the right to trade and reside throughout the Russian Empire. These were concessions that would have an impact on far more Jews than the tiny minority with a university degree. Aksakov did not even reject Jewish participation in the civil service, with the proviso that their superiors be Christians and that they not directly administer the state.

Aksakov's liberality was rooted in Slavophile ideology itself and his own experiences in the Pale of Settlement as a young government official. Slavophilism shared a number of liberal values and Slavophiles like Aksakov defended freedom of the press, religious toleration (especially for Russia's Christian sectarians and dissenters), and sought the welfare of the newly emancipated peasantry. Aksakov did reject the European liberal conception of the secular state in favor of the Slavophile vision of Russian Orthodoxy as an essential component of a communal Russian society.

Aksakov's opinion of the Jews was also colored by his civil service career in the Pale which made him one of the best informed Russian commentators on the social and economic realities of Jewish life in the Ukraine. Although unable to escape the memory that the Jews had crucified Christ, Aksakov met decent and enlightened Jews in the Pale who made a favorable impression upon him. He had an opportunity to study the Jewish autonomous institutions that he was now willing to leave to the Jews.[8] Aksakov did not initially accept the charge of Jewish economic exploitation. He had closely observed the Jews' role in the fairs of the southern empire, and he described their activity in positive terms in a classic work which he published on the subject.[9] Aksakov was a signatory of the Literary Protest of 1858.

Aksakov's favorable evaluation of the Jews and Judaism did not long survive the polemical struggles triggered by his defection in 1862 from the liberal consensus. Nor should one discount the influence upon Aksakov of German Romantic philosophy, which underpinned the whole Slavophile movement. German Romantics of theological orientation, such as Friedrich Schleiermacher, emphasized the obsolescence of Judaism as a religious system in the modern world, and also minimized the links between Judaism and early Christianity. Aksakov offered at least an indirect echo of these sentiments.[10] Although Aksakov's journalism appeared without footnotes, his arguments revealed more than a passing acquaintance with a similar debate over the emancipation of the Jews in the "Christian state" which raged in Germany in the early 1840s.[11]

Aksakov's opinion's were always taken seriously by contemporaries, and many writers challenged what they saw as his appeal to religious intolerance. Contrast this with the total journalistic neglect of a *Domashniaia beseda* editorial which made conversion to Christianity the sole criterion for the extension of civil rights for Jews (43:27/X/1862). The leading publications of the two capitals swiftly offered rebuttals to Aksakov's article. The very first appeared in the February 1862 issue of *Vremia*. This particular article, although of undistinguished content, is of special interest because it may have been written by Fedor Dostoevskii. It warned against efforts to protect Christian society with tactics which might lead to fire and sword. While not accusing *Den* of fanaticism and religious hatred, the author faulted the paper for "the flippancy with which it turns to important questions, and the levity with which it theoretically solves them, a levity leading to vainglory, to boasting in the strength of its illogic."

Given his subsequent hostility to the Jews in his publicist work, Dostoevskii's intervention here is interesting. It is noteworthy that he attacked the style of *Den* more than its arguments. David Goldstein convincingly argues that Dostoevskii was motivated purely by strategic considerations. Dostoevskii had only recently returned to the St. Petersburg literary scene and was eager, with his new journal, to appear on the side of "progress," as defined by the influential thick journal *Sovremennik*, against the forces of conservatism and reaction. Only by decisively joining this camp could Dostoevskii reach an intelligentsia audience with his message of "native soil populism" (*pochvennichestvo*).[12] Dostoevskii had already come to the defense of *Sovremennik* against the attacks of M. N. Katkov's *Russkii vestnik*, and the Slavophile *Den* offered another easy target. As critics of Judeophilism often observed, the defense of the Jews was an easy way to "play

the liberal." The debate with *Den* in 1862 gave Dostoevskii an opportunity to do what he could not do from exile in 1858 – join a general
but vague liberal defense of the Jews. Dostoevskii's more critical observations on the Jews took more time to develop and grow.

Vremia was a struggling journal, and Dostoevskii's greatness still lay
before him. *Nashe vremia*, which entered the debate with an article and
an editorial (45:4/III/1862), was in the very thick of contemporary concerns. The paper had participated in the discussion of the Jewish
Question in 1860 as a typical liberal organ, but had since undergone a
dramatic metamorphosis. At the end of 1861 the publisher,
N. F. Pavlov, entered an agreement with P. A. Valuev, the Minister of
Internal Affairs, whereby the paper became an official publication. It
received a government subsidy and an expanded program. Its most
distinguished contributor was Boris Chicherin, the independent-
minded liberal, who used the paper to express his own views on the
role of the gentry in Russian political life.[13] With the direct consent of
the Emperor, Chicherin broke the censorship ban against mentioning
in print the name of the *émigré* dissident, Alexander Herzen, when he
published his famous "Letter to Herzen."[14] Thus, the paper was a
force to be reckoned with when it turned again to the Jewish
Question.

A *Nashe vremia* editorial looked askance at *Den*'s carping against the
law of 27 November 1861, viewing the decree as akin to the emancipation of the Russian serfs. *Den* had once stood for liberal principles, but
now abandoned them through its appeal to the religious concept of
the "Christian banner." The essence of liberalism was an emphasis
upon education and enlightenment as a vehicle for self-improvement
and change. It was cruel torture indeed to permit a person to gain
enlightenment in the university and then forbid him to put his learning into practice. Were educated Jews to be left nothing but the right
to read the Talmud?

Aksakov was too restrictive in his conception of the Christian
banner, the editorial continued, because he assumed that only converted Jews could become its partisans. Consider the educated Jew, filled
with reserves of spiritual strength, who rejected life as a middleman in
Berdichev or tradesman in St. Petersburg or Moscow.

> He is ready to stand under the Christian banner; through his know-
> ledge and convictions he already stands under it, lacking only the
> rite [of baptism]. He would take this important step except that in a
> dirty corner of Warsaw or some tiny town his mother would die of
> despair and his father go mad; in addition there is yet one tiny

obstacle, but one that is not easy to overcome; like a heavenly gift sent down to him by the God of truth and light it prevents him from renouncing the oppressed, abandoning the weak and siding with the victorious.

Nashe vremia detected a further inconsistency in Aksakov's argument. He did not want the Jews to have administrative rights, but was willing to give them full scope in trade. As directors of joint stock companies, factories and banks, they would be a far more dangerous influence upon Christians than in government service. Having made these points, the editor passed on the task of rebuttal to P. Shchebalskii, who had written the critique of Georgievskii's work which appeared in *Nashe vremia* in 1860.

Shchebalskii accused Aksakov of slandering Christianity by claiming that this religion, which hinged on the concept of love of neighbor, could offer the Jews no more than refuge and minimal toleration. Aksakov's argument that Jews rejected the Christian order of things was clearly refuted by the activity of the Mendelssohnian school of Jewish reform, which advocated that the Jews be true patriots wherever they might live, sentiments echoed in the pages of *Sion* and in the works of O. A. Rabinovich. The fear that Jews would fill up the State Council or the Senate was a comic exaggeration. The Jewish minority, primarily oriented toward trade and commerce, was no more developed mentally or morally than the Russians, and they could not hope to displace the latter from their place. It was not law which would prevent a Jewish Ober-Procurator of the Holy Synod, but public opinion. Unfortunately, public prejudices might go further, and deny to a Jew the post of Minister of Finance, no matter how talented and able he might be. For the good of the state, public opinion should be encouraged to free itself from prejudice. Aksakov, who had long advocated the unfettering of public opinion in Russia, must surely understand this. Turning to *raison d'état*, Shchebalskii reminded Aksakov that the Polish national movement was reaching out to the Jews with gestures of Polish–Jewish reconciliation. In the struggle with the Poles for the Russian borderlands, the state must not risk alienating a numerous and economically powerful group like the Jews.

Another rebuttal appeared in *Moskovskie vedomosti* (53:9/III/1862), an important paper which played a leading role in the Literary Protest and also printed Goldenviezer's article on the Jewish press. The paper, whose license to publish was leased to private individuals by Moscow University, was in a period of transition as the editorship passed from the liberal publicist V. F. Korsh to the mercurial M. N. Katkov. Thus, the rebuttal represented literally the last word of the Korsh editorship on the topic of the Jews.

The paper led with a letter from I. Zhivarev which *Den* had refused to print. Zhivarev agreed with Aksakov that Christians must act according to the dictates of Christian law but faulted his failure to understand that Christian law was underlain by the Ten Commandments, the moral basis for Judaism. There was no need to fear the participation of Jews in Christian society so long as both were guided by common religious principles.

An accompanying editorial observed that a debate on the civil service was premature at a time when most Russian Jews lacked fundamental civil rights. Russia must move cautiously in this direction. While European Jewry had been given equal rights, with successful consequences, Russian policy makers had to contend with Jewish morals and prejudices, which were in need of elevation. This proviso was the recurrent qualification which Russian liberals brought to the Jewish question.

The only Jewish reply came from "the Editor of *Sion*," not further identified. Since *Sion* had ceased publication, the rebuttal appeared in the pages of *Den* itself (33:26/V/1862) in the form of a letter to the editor. The author insightfully observed that the fashion of accusing the Jews without grounds had given way to the fashion of defending them without real conviction. Now, as the Jews began to acquire some rights, opponents in the nationalistic press accused the Jews of controlling the state through finance and public opinion. This phenomenon had already been observed in Germany, and the *Sion* editor predicted its appearance in Russia.

Aksakov's arguments revealed his faulty understanding of both religions, the editor claimed. Christianity's great accomplishment was to separate the political from the religious – "render unto Caesar the things that are Caesar's" – a linkage which in other civilizations was a source of social divisiveness. The exclusion of Jews from the civil service, was thus a strange way of affirming Christian values. Aksakov's claim that the Talmud made Jews poor citizens merely revealed how little he understood the nature and content of this work. Contemporary civilization, so praised by Aksakov, possessed a humane, universal character, not one based on narrow particularism.

By the standards of Russian journalism, one article and a few replies did not make a polemic. This reveals how little religious questions appealed to the editors of leading publications. Ever the innovator, however, Aksakov published a new article, "A Few Words About the

Talmud" by "A. Aleksandrov" (25:31/III/1862). This article changed the framework of the debate, and triggered a controversy which bubbled in the press for the better part of a year.[15] It shifted the focus of Russian Judeophobia away from the contemporary European debate over the "Christian state" toward the older tradition of religious anti-Talmudism, with a pedigree that dated to the Middle Ages.

Aleksandrov challenged the oft-heard claim that there was a moral unity between Christians and Jews because their religions shared the common basis of the Ten Commandments. This contention ignored the development of the Talmud during the subsequent 1800 years of Jewish history. A central concern of the Talmud was Jewish–gentile relations, and talmudic teachings displayed a special antipathy for Christ, his teachings and his followers. "Judaism can be understood and perceived only in the Talmud; it now carries the whole spirit of the Jewish nation; it contains all the secrets and clues of that incomprehensible and melancholy phenomenon encompassing the life and history of this nation." The Talmud, Aleksandrov explained, preached implacable hatred of the *goy* or gentile. *Goyim* were said to be descended from unclean spirits and were either denied eternal life or condemned to burn forever in Hell. Every crime which the Mosaic Law forbade could be perpetrated without guilt against *goyim*. They could be deceived, robbed or killed. A Russian translation of the Talmud would confirm these claims, Aleksandrov maintained.

Contemporary Jews, to safeguard themselves from the righteous wrath of Christians, pretended to reject these teachings. They claimed that the *goyim* of the Talmud were the idolaters of Hellenistic times, not present-day Christians. Yet, claimed Aleksandrov, the great medieval Jewish philosopher Maimonides equated Christians and *goyim*, and every resident of Poland or the Pale knew that the Jews commonly referred to their Christian neighbors as "the *goyim*." The pernicious effect of the Talmud might wane as Jews became more educated and enlightened. Until then the Talmud remained binding law for any Jew. If a Jew did not believe in the Talmud, what did he believe in? Consequently, Jews who refused to abandon the Talmud and return to the Mosaic Law, which was indeed compatible with Christian morality, could not be trusted with civil rights.

There were essential differences separating the Judeophobe perspectives of Aksakov and Aleksandrov. Aksakov rejected not only the Talmud but also the Mosaic Law, the underlying component of the Jewish banner. Aleksandrov located all harm in the Talmud, and made its abandonment the chief criterion for the extension of legal equality.

Aksakov did not oppose the grant of some civil rights even to talmudic Jews, but they were never to be more than "guests in the Russian land" unless they rejected the Jewish banner and the Mosaic Law (i.e., unless they formally converted to Christianity). Aleksandrov introduced the Russian public to the fear of "talmudic fanaticism" which had long exercised Russian bureaucrats, and inspired Nicholas I's sponsorship of Abbé Chiarini's tendentious study of the Talmud. Aleksandrov's opponents were not far off the mark when they accused him of relying more on Chiarini's synopsis than upon the Talmud itself.

While Jewish publicists generally avoided a battle with Aksakov's abstract religious arguments, they rushed into print to repudiate Aleksandrov. Weapons were close to hand, since the Talmud had been a topic of investigation in the West since the Renaissance. Moreover, the *Wissenschaft des Judentums* provided scholarly evidence for use against Talmudophobes. For example, a number of works had been written specifically to refute Chiarini. Added urgency was lent by the fact that the gentile friends of the Jews in Russia lacked the scholarly equipment or the knowledge of the sources to face the critics of the Talmud on their own ground.[16] This was, therefore, a golden opportunity for educated Jews to demonstrate both their devotion to their people and the utility of enlightenment to defend Jewish interests.

The first Jewish respondents to Aleksandrov were university graduates writing in the capital press. They all condemned Aleksandrov for his lack of a critical apparatus and his manipulation of sources. A. Rubinshtein, in the 102nd number of *Russkii invalid*, faulted his work as a tendentiously assembled linguistic hash of misunderstood Hebrew and Latin terms, buttressed by "authorities" of dubious expertise. Peter Liakub, also a university graduate, offered a scholarly critique in Dostoevskii's *Vremia* (5: V 1862), explaining the nature of the Talmud, talmudic learning and talmudic interpretation. He emphasized that "the Talmud is not the collection of one man, or even of one century, but it is the intellectual life of a hundred generations." Rejecting the assertion that the Talmud enjoined its adepts to harm Christians, Liakub recalled the praise of some gentile scholars for the Talmud as a compilation of useful scientific, religious and mystical teachings. Aleksandrov's agenda for Jewish rights was unfair in the extreme: by demanding that *all* Jews be enlightened before *any* of them could receive equal rights, he set higher moral criteria than existed for Christians. Dr. Iosif Zeiberling provided a scholarly *coup de grâce* in *Severnaia pchela* (149:3/VI/1862). (It is a token of the public interest in this question that *Severnaia pchela*, not known for its sympathy toward the Jews, actually carried Judeophile articles.) Zeiberling contended that the source for Aleksandrov's article was not the Talmud, but rather Chiarini's *Théorie du Judaïsme*, a work thoroughly discredited by Jewish scholars like Marcus Jost, Leopold Zunz and S. Klein. Chiarini's errors were compounded, Zeiberling lamented, by Aleksandrov's incorrect references to Chiarini's inaccurate talmudic citations. His article was a botched job of plagiarism, not to be taken seriously.

Rubinshtein, Liakub and Zeiberling knew enough about the Talmud to correct Aleksandrov's mistranslations, to detect citations of materials not actually in the Talmud, and to recognize erroneous numbering of tomes, all of which they did with obvious relish. Quite another form of defense came from two representatives of the new generation, the medical doctors Leon Zelenskii and Veniamin Portugalo. Their intervention is an apt demonstration of the evolving difference in outlook between the maskilim and the Russian Jewish intelligentsia. The Old Maskilim accepted Jewish tradition, properly understood, and the authority of Jewish law. True enlightenment combined Torah and secular knowledge. The Young Maskilim were less ritually observant, less steeped in rabbinic learning, and prepared to pick and choose which elements of tradition were suitable for the new age.[17] Zelenskii and Portugalo, the "grandsons" of the Old Maskilim, represented a further evolution in the direction of the Total Assimilationists. They were ignorant of the Talmud, and Jewish learning generally, and willing to abandon tradition when it was inconvenient to them or displeasing to gentiles. Even when this attitude led to conversion or wholesale rejection of the Jewish tradition, many Total Assimilationists retained strong psychological ties to the Jewish people.

Veniamin Portugalo was the archetype of this phenomonon. He was the same Portugalov who triggered the controversy over the use of "Yid" by *Osnova*. He subsequently acquired a reputation as a renegade in the Jewish community for his attacks on Jewish Orthodoxy. He condemned circumcision on medical grounds and allied himself to the reform movement "New Israel" in the 1880s. He merits a mention in S. M. Ginzburg's study of apostates in Tsarist Russia.[18]

Zelenskii and Portugalov responded to Aleksandrov in a letter to the editor of *Den* (32:19/V/1862). The authors claimed to speak "in the name of all Jewish youths" who had received a "contemporary, civilizing education." They answered Aleksandrov's rhetorical query of what Jews might believe in, if not the Talmud. Their response was suffused with the self-confidence of youth. They sarcastically thanked Aleksandrov for acquainting them with numerous works of which they had never heard. They consigned to specialists the task of ascertaining the accuracy of his citations. They could not do it, because they had never even seen the Talmud. "The new generation of the best of Jewish youth don't have the slightest understanding of the Talmud." If a qualified specialist could vouch for the accuracy of Aleksandrov's claims, they were willing to reject the entire Talmud.

This left the question of what would replace talmudic beliefs. "The basic unchangeable dogma of the Jewish faith lies in the Ten Commandments." Maimonides never cited the Talmud as a symbol of faith and Hillel argued that the entire Tora was based on the simple statement to "love thy neighbor as thyself." Zelenskii and Portugalov pledged themselves to apply the concept of "neighbor" in an enlightened and humanitarian way. While it might be true, the authors conceded, that there were some Jews among the lower classes who really did hate their fellow inhabitants, this was the product of centuries of persecution and exclusion. As such this hatred could not be remedied overnight. Release the restrictions on the Jews, however, and obscurantism would melt away. Permit the Jews to go forward, they asserted, and the Jews will go forward.

This type of response, aside from its tone of self-righteousness, was well calculated to please many gentile commentators. The authors' willingness to accept the charge that the Jewish masses, the majority of the Jewish population, were obscurantist and anti-Christian, joined to the admission that vices acquired over millennia could not be quickly eliminated, justified gradualism. Welcome too was their willingness to abandon the entire Talmud. Zelenskii and Portugalov proved to be lone wolves. Zelenskii disappeared as a defender of his coreligionists, and Portugalov became a gadfly who delighted in abusing the Jewish community. Most Jewish publicists refused to make concessions on this scale, even to receive their treasured "equal rights."

Christian correspondents of the liberal press also responded to Aleksandrov but they were at a disadvantage due to their own lack of expertise on the Talmud. (Nor was disdain for "talmudic obscurantism" confined to those who opposed civil rights for Jews.) They remedied this deficiency as had Aleksandrov, by relying on secondary sources and translations. The most extensive reply to appear in any periodical was by N. Melgunov in *Nashe vremia* (88:27/IV and 89:28/IV/ 1862) which sought to refute Aleksandrov through reference to the experiences of Europe. The Jews, a gifted and intelligent people, were swiftly able to assimilate European enlightenment. The rabbis of the *neu Tempel*, the Reform synagogues of Germany, were identical to

Protestant pastors. For such people the Talmud was no more a moral codex than the teachings of the Jesuits were the codex of all Roman Catholics. Some segments of the Talmud echoed the Christian precept of love of neighbor.

Melgunov proffered a glowing tribute to "foremost Jews," praising their elevating moral effect on the benighted majority. This was a veritable Christian influence since educated Jews

> have already become Christian in spirit, because contemporary education, rooted in Christianity, engenders the beginnings of Christian morality and love in a Jew who is cut off from his racial exclusivity. Christian truths are eternal truths ... hidden in the teachings of Moses, the Prophets, and in all Jewish literature, canonical and non-canonical. The entire, fundamental difference is that they are hidden there while they are openly revealed in Christian life, which flows into the flesh and blood of the educated person.

Furthermore, since the intellectual and spiritual fatherland of educated Jews was Germany, Jewish civil servants would carry Germanic virtues into Russian life. These would include precision in the Russian court system and local administration, as well as hostility to the characteristic Russian vice of bribery.

Opponents of the Jews looked askance at such praise, published in a newspaper which received a government subsidy. Still, the modern observer can find a worm or two in the apple of Melgunov's praise. He held Jews to a Christian standard and accepted the inferiority of Judaism, seeing its moral virtues as "hidden." The emphasis on the Germanic character of the Jews, with a spiritual homeland across the Elbe, was as dubious a virtue in the eyes of Russian nationalists as was the vaunted Jewish cosmopolitanism.

Other critics attempted to disregard the religious linkage of Christianity and Judaism as the basis for equality. I. Zhivarev, writing again in *Moskovskie vedomosti*, asserted that Judaism and Christianity were quite different religions, but this was no reason to deny Jews equal rights in a Christian state. Religious confession could not serve as a religious criterion for citizenship because there was no means of peering beyond the outward forms of religious ritual to the inner reality of a person's soul. The demands of Christianity were higher than the laws of the state and consequently were of no concern to it. Civil laws were written for human society, which was far removed from the moral perfection sought by religion. The force of civil law should encompass all human beings and it followed that Jews must be given equal rights.

Liberal commentators were not the only ones to respond to Aleksandrov. Periodicals with a religious orientation rushed to embrace and defend him. Writing in *Strannik*, Archbishop Anatoliia explained to skeptics why it was necessary that Jews be converted to Christianity (VI/VII: 1862). In their present state the Jews were guilty of multitudinous sins against Christians. There had been hopes that the Jews, given greater freedom, would deal justly with gentiles. That had not happened. "Their insatiable greed and especially the rules and lessons of the Talmud inculcate dishonesty and fanaticism from their youngest days and continually motivate them to employ the basest tricks, ruses and intrigues in order to harm Christians." His authority for this assertion was Aleksandrov.

Khristianskoe chtenie was a publication of the St. Petersburg Spiritual Academy, a Russian Orthodox seminary. In a discussion of public opinion and the Jews it lamented the speed with which society had rushed to defend the Jews. "The problem is this: the Jewish Question has a European significance; the French, Germans and English have resolved it in the most liberal fashion ... That means that we can safely play the liberal and in our own hearts feel ourselves to be a foremost individual."[19] Aleksandrov's article demonstrated the true state of affairs. What he revealed about the theoretical views of the Jews, guided by talmudic dictates, was confirmed in practice by historian N. Kostomarov's exposure of Jewish conduct in the Ukraine. The assertion that because the Jews were intelligent and able they should be admitted to the civil service failed to stand closer scrutiny. The Jesuits were also intelligent and devout, but did Russia want to use them as judges, administrators and bureaucrats? Russians would be sorely disappointed if they expected Jews to contribute anything to the well-being of their state.

Aleksandrov responded to his detractors in *Den* (34:2/VI/1862). He defended his scholarship from the accusations of Melgunov and Zhivarev and rejected their claim that, given the disputatious character of the Talmud, no single statement within it could be considered canonical. On the contrary, "if there are two conflicting opinions contained in it, *both* are considered the word of God." Jews could merely pick and choose among the most convenient interpretations. Aleksandrov challenged the claim of his opponents that the successful integration of Jews into the societies of Western Europe demonstrated the transient nature of any harmful impact which the Talmud might have. The anti-Christian impulse still lurked in every Jew. "Unfortunately, we aredeceivedbytheapparentreformamongtheJewsfrommakinganyfghjkl statement which is not complimentary to them ... Since we don't know about Judaism, we don't know how to deal with the Talmud logically."

Aleksandrov refused to let the Zelenskiis and Portugalovs escape through a mere pro forma rejection of the Talmud based on their ignorance of it. "How are we to judge educated Jews who do not struggle against the Talmud, but who try to hide it? When they profess that they are not believers, we have the right not to believe them." This response reiterated the lesson already learned by those Jews who participated in the *Osnova* controversy. Educated men who retained a Jewish identity were not given the choice of opting out of the religious debate. Still less were they allowed to dismiss the most outrageous of Judeophobe charges. The Jew who sought entry into Russian society had to certify his "enlightened" credentials by throwing mud at his national traditions and the mass of his coreligionists who still clung to them. The comprehensiveness of the repudiation which was required of him might differ with the circumstances, but it became a general ideological litmus test demanded by gentiles, Judeophiles and Judeophobes alike.

This tendency can be seen in the only important St. Petersburg newspaper, *Birzhevye vedomosti*, to carry an article in whole-hearted support of *Den* (143:19/V/1863). (This was, however, a *feuilleton* which was soon followed by a lengthy rebuttal.) The author, I. Gulak – a Ukrainian to judge by his name – condemned the article of Zelenskii and Portugalov as a clever ruse. The two Jews claimed not to have ever seen the Talmud, so how could they pretend to any expertise or authority in discussing it? They sought to ignore the central issue, the nature of the Talmud, and indulge in empty phrase-mongering. Gulak, who offered an idiosyncratic division of the Jews into "Rabbinites" and "Talmudists," was demonstrably one of the least sophisticated commentators on the Jewish Question, but his concentration on the misconduct of enlightened Jews suggests the growing force of this particular prejudice.

The debate in the capitals resounded only faintly in the provinces, and its treatment there served more to illustrate the immaturity of the provincial press than to add much substance. A glance at the local press does however reveal how the religious issue was received in the provinces of the Pale of Settlement.

Kievskii telegraf, the liberal Kiev paper which had defended the Jews in 1859 and 1860, published an article by an anonymous "Pilgrim" entitled "Concerning Yids Calling Themselves Jews" (42:7/VI/1862).

The editor announced that while he rejected the sentiments expressed in the article, he was publishing it because it revealed a "new kind of proof." In addition, publication would discomfit the rival *Kievskii kurier* which had recently invited articles attacking the editor of *Kievskii telegraf*, to be published at a rate of 6 rubles apiece. *Kievskii kurier* had nevertheless rejected Pilgrim's article, "even for a thousand rubles," because half of its subscribers were Jews.

Such journalistic high jinks hardly promised a serious exchange of views. In fact, the "new proofs" of Pilgrim were a throwback to the arguments of the religious press. The Talmud, now rejected by "learned Yids," was not the root cause for the disenfranchisement of Jews. Rather, it was the Jews' crucifixion of Christ which placed them under a divine judgment. Granting civil rights to the Jews would violate the will of God, and would be as unsuccessful as Julian the Apostate's attempt to rebuild the temple of Solomon in Jerusalem. The Jews loved to boast of their affinity with Christians through the Ten Commandments in an attempt to secure equal rights in a Christian state. Recent history did not indicate that the Ten Commandments had much real influence over them. In 1821 Jews had desecrated the body of the Patriarch of Constantinople after he had been murdered by the Turks. In 1859, an educated, well-dressed Jew defaced the cross on the Catholic Church in Odessa, and crowds of Jews stoned Christians during their religious processions. (This was Pilgrim's erroneous version of the anti-Jewish pogrom in Odessa in 1859.) A Yid in *Moskovskie vedomosti* argued for the separation of church and state only so that Jews could become the chief administrators of a secularized state. As for the claim that enlightenment made Jews honorable and good, "who asked for the crucifixion of the Savior but the learned and enlightened scribes and pharisees." Educated Yids would be of greater service if, instead of directing their wisdom to where it was neither wanted nor needed, they attacked the dirt and ignorance enclosing their brothers.

Pilgrim's diatribe drew an instant response from Christians and Jews writing in *Kievskii telegraf* and *Kievskii kurier*. M. Morgulis, for example, commenting in the latter newspaper "On Christians Calling Themselves Pilgrims," that the author's "new proofs" were merely the warmed-over theories of *Domashniaia beseda* (40:20/VI/1862). Pilgrim's hostility violated the tenets of Christian love in the name of which he claimed to speak. The ultimate contradiction was his exhortation, following his denial of civil rights for enlightened Jews, that these same educated Jews raise the level of their degraded brothers – so that they might be worthy of civil rights! In the same issue another Jew, M. Bykhovskii also appealed to Christian principles to justify equal rights for Jews. As for the Talmud, it was Pilgrim who used it to stir up fanaticism and intolerance through his mendacious interpretations. Yet another Jew, Gekhtmann, followed a similar approach in *Kievskii telegraf* (47:24/VI/1862), accusing Pilgrim of distorting the Christian message of love. This correspondent accepted the liberal vision of the secular state: human nature was too broad to be encompassed within the boundaries of religious belief. There must be equal rights for all.

While Jews were quoting Christian scripture to Pilgrim, a Christian, K. Strashkevich, returned the favor in *Kievskii telegraf* (51:8/VII/1862). He assayed the hostility which had clung to the Jews since classical times. The fault lay in the Jews' adherence to the form, rather than the spirit, of their religion. Judaism was on a lower moral plane than Christianity, but it was still sufficient to promote an honorable, moral life. The tendency of the Jews to abandon true morality, while adhering to fossilized ritual, made them hateful in gentile eyes. Let the Jews return to their pure morality as prescribed by the Old Testament and abandoned in the Talmud. Christians, far from perfect themselves, would be well-advised to seek their own pristine moral foundations. Out of such a moral return could come the true reconciliation of Christian and Jew.

The Kiev debate clearly lacked the pseudo-sophisticated content, replete with talmudic quotations, of the debate in the capitals. Crude religious arguments were answered with appeals to Christian charity. Jews readily gained admission to the columns of the Kiev press, but they were not as yet opposed by articulate Judeophobes. The aftermath of the Polish uprising of 1863 would change this situation, and produce a more elaborate and variegated discussion in the press of the Ukrainian capital. The articles in the Kiev press marked a hiatus in the religious debate whose true conclusion came two years later when Ivan Aksakov, who had remained silent in response to the Aleksandrov polemic, offered his summation in an important *Den* article entitled "What is the 'Jew' as Regards Christian Civilization?" (8/VIII/1864). By now Aksakov saw the Jewish Question in Russia as the task of "muffling the dissonance and eliminating the dissension arising from the existence of the Jewish race in Christian society." Aksakov continued to argue against the concept of a neutral society in which Christian and Jew could ignore religious differences and meet as equals. While Christians and Jews might live side by side, asserted Aksakov, and even achieve political unity, they could never create spiritual unity or encompass a common moral whole.

It was not simply a case of disbelief: there were many atheists living in Christian communities. But their atheism was personal and particular. It was not marked by zealotry and did not seek the creation of a new morality or the establishment of a new creed. The rejection by Jews of Christian society was much stronger and more active because of the close bonds which linked Judaism to Christianity. These two religions were successive stages in the spiritual development of mankind. Christianity was the crown of Judaism, the point toward which it had striven. Each of the two religions would be illogical without the existence of the other. Contemporary Jews were the embodiment of an obsolete historical period, "a congealed moment of human development, forever hostile to the subsequent stages of human development." Aksakov quoted the contention of the central Slavophile ideologue, Aleksei Khomiakov, that after the appearance of Christ the Jews were nothing more than a "living contradiction" without significance in the historical world.

Difficulties arose, Aksakov believed, because the Jews refused to accept their own anachronistic character. He argued that to accept the validity of contemporary Judaism meant to reject the validity of contemporary Christianity. "The Jews, denying Christianity and putting forth the pretensions of Judaism, deny the logic of the year 1864, the successes of human history, and they would return humanity to that level, to that moment of consciousness, in which it abided prior to the appearance of Christ on earth."

Although Aksakov expressed his arguments more elegantly than in the past, and made their links to the leading theoreticians of Slavophilism more explicit, they were merely a restatement of the "Christian banner" and the antithetical "Jewish banner," first expressed in 1862. Since their initial elaboration, however, Aksakov discovered a new object of concern in the guise of "enlightened Jews." These were individuals, like the articulate editors of *Sion*, or the young writers Portugalov and Zelenskii, who could not be equated with the "talmudic Jewish masses." They spoke and wrote Russian with ease, they had studied in Russian educational institutions, and they were far removed from the world of kosher and tref, sidelocks and caftans. They were able to state the case for Jewish emancipation with all the arguments of the European enlightenment. They had apparently abandoned both the "Jewish banner" and the Talmud. Where were they to be fitted into Aksakov's idealized Christian state?

Nowhere. Aksakov rejected their "negative and comfortable way" of ceasing to be Jews while neither rejecting Judaism nor converting to

Christianity. They were nothing but "moral and intellectual amphibians," devoid of any principles, untouched by the moral climate which, in a Christian state, worked even upon atheists. The "progressive Jew" stood outside the social and domestic principles upon which contemporary society rested. These principles constituted the atmosphere of Christian society and acted upon its members irrespective of the individual's personal attitude toward them. This article proved to be Aksakov's valedictory to the Jewish Question for almost two decades, but he was pointing the way for the evolution of a distinctly Russian Judeophobia.

Aksakov's success in shaping the debate on the Jews was obscured for the moment by the apparent rejection by Russian public opinion of religiously grounded arguments. Religious arguments made by the likes of *Domashniaia beseda* and *Strannik* were treated with a disdainful silence. There was almost universal condemnation of the Aksakov and Aleksandrov articles. Those few newspapers which printed positive assessments of the *Den* viewpoints either carried an editorial disclaimer or rapidly followed them with rebuttal articles.

At the same time there was an underlying ambivalence in the defenders of the Jews that must be stressed if the rapid transformation of Russian Judeophiles into Judeophobes which occurred in the next decade is to be explained. The motives of Dostoevskii in using *Vremia* to defend the Jews had little to do with conviction, and much to do with private goals. Strong apologies, such as that of Melgunov in *Nashe vremia*, were tainted by the assumption that educated Jews, "our Jews," were Christians in all but rite, and had lost the essence of Judaism which still permeated the Jewish masses.

The final irony was that, to a large extent, the polemics of 1862 made religious Judeophobia respectable, especially if it was presented with imagination and panache. While the fanaticism and prejudice of *Domashniaia beseda* were ignored, the arguments of both Aksakov and Aleksandrov in *Den* were taken seriously, and dignified with replies. The shock value of using religious arguments in a secular debate was gradually lost. A cliché like "the Jewish banner," which itself was based upon quasi-religious arguments encapsulated by the expression "the Christian state," began to function with a life of its own, becoming the shorthand for a whole set of Judeophobic associations which no longer required elaboration. Writers were aware of its significance just as surely as they were of the use of the word "Yid." A taboo was broken, enabling publicists to dip freely into a tradition of religious Judeophobia, tricked out in secular garb.

PART 2

The era of Russification

Would-be reformers of Russian Jewry did not have to devise their proposals in a vacuum. In Western Europe a wide range of reformist strategies had been deployed, and few commentators neglected to mention European precedents in support of their own proposals. The Russian preoccupation with Europe makes notable the virtual absence in Russian debates of any consideration of another model closer to hand, the Russian-controlled Kingdom of Poland.

Differences between Russia and Kongresowka, as the Kingdom of Poland was colloquially known, were substantial. The latter was governed by a unique system of law which dated to the creation of the Kingdom by the Congress of Vienna in 1815. There were debates over the extent to which legislation promulgated by the Napoleonic Grand Duchy of Warsaw before 1815 was still in force. Legal questions were compounded by the Russian abrogation of central features of the constitutional system of 1815 after the Polish uprising of 1831.

The status of the Jews was no clearer. Some jurists argued that a law promulgated on 17 October 1808 NS by the King of Saxony, in his role as ruler of the Grand Duchy of Warsaw, depriving the Jews of political and civil rights, was still in force. Additional disabilities on the Jews survived from the old Polish–Lithuanian Commonwealth. The medieval privilege of *de non tolerandis Judaeis*, giving municipal authorities the right to ban Jewish residence, was still claimed by over ninety towns. Jews were barred from new settlement within a zone 20 versts from the frontier, a regulation of special importance because it included almost a quarter of the territory of the Kingdom.[1] There were restrictions on house ownership by Jews. At the same time, Jews were saddled with the same obligations as Russian Jews, including military recruitment (as of 1843). It could be argued, therefore, that the distinct legal status of Jews in Poland was inferior to that of Jews in the Pale of Settlement. Consequently, no friend of the Jews pointed to

Kongresowka as worthy of imitation, while Judeophobes were never pleased with the ambiguities and inconsistencies in the laws covering Jews.

Russian public opinion was strangely apathetic to the situation of the Jews in Poland. This was perhaps part of a general ignorance of the Kingdom as a whole, for the Jewish Question was in the forefront of public issues in Kongresowka before the uprising of 1863. As early as 1857 the political economist Ludwik Wolski created a sensation by publishing statistics which purported to show a demographic explosion among Polish Jewry. Within 150 years, Wolski predicted, the Jewish population would equal the total of all other nationalities in Poland. Excited discussions of the implication of these figures filled the native and *émigré* press, and dominated subsequent discussions of the Jewish Question.[2]

Late in 1858 a journalistic polemic erupted in Warsaw that had affinities with the *Illiustratsiia* affair. *Gazeta Warszawska*, commenting on an unsuccessful concert by two visiting musicians from Moravia, attacked the absence of Jewish bourgeoisie and intelligentsia. They were accused of lacking concern for the welfare of the region. A group of Jewish intellectuals, led by Henryk Toeplitz and Ignac Natanson, submitted a protest, signed by twenty-three Jewish leaders in trade, finance, education and the arts, to the editor of *Gazeta Warszawska*, Antoni Lesznowski. Lesznowski responded by launching a successful lawsuit for libel. This so-called "Jewish War" (*Wojna żydowska*) was widely reported in the European press, including *Breslauer Zeitung*, *Le Nord*, *Observateur Belge*, *Czas* of Krakow and *Dziennik Posnanski* of Poznan.[3] The Polish language *Słowo* of St. Petersburg defended Lesznowski and was closed down by the censorship "for printing antisemitic material," according to R. F. Leslie.[4] There was surprisingly little echo in the Russian press. Alexander Herzen's *émigré Kolokol* reprinted the article against Lesznowski which had appeared in *Le Nord* (39:1/IV/1859). Only *Sanktpeterburgskie vedomosti* of the capital press devoted an article to the quarrel and as late as 1863 *Golos* treated the affair as unknown news (146:11/VI/1863). Noted only in passing in the Russian press was the appearance of a Polish–Jewish newspaper, *Jutrzenka*, published by Daniel Neufeld in Warsaw in the summer of 1861. *Sion* gave only a brief note, and never reprinted any material from its sister publication whose very name, "Dawn," linked it to *Rassvet*.

The spirit of the reform era gradually began to spread to the Kingdom. In 1856 Prince Ivan Paskevich, Nicholas I's ruthless administrator in Poland, died. Pashkevich's death triggered hopes that a more benevolent administration might be forthcoming. The Tsar unintentionally encouraged this hope by granting an amnesty to the Polish exiles of 1831 who were still languishing in Siberia. He also permitted the reopening of the Polish Medical Academy and even invited Polish landlords to participate in the public debate over peasant emancipation. Despite Alexander's warning – "Pas de rêveries, messieurs" – new organizations and institutions, such as the Agricultural Society, took on a political cast. Two distinct parties evolved. The "Whites" sought to push the Russians as far as possible in the direction of reform and political autonomy. The "Reds" actively prepared for an armed uprising in pursuit of complete national independence and social revolution. Both sides were aware of the growing significance of the Jews, especially in the urban centers, and assiduously courted them. The Jewish intelligentsia of Warsaw, led by Chief Rabbi Dov Beer Meisels, responded in kind. Jews participated openly and enthusiastically in the patriotic events and demonstrations of the troubled years 1861–2. It mattered not that the educated Jews of Warsaw were not representative of the Jewish population as a whole, which displayed no great enthusiasm for rapprochement or merger with the Poles – resolution of the Jewish Question was now high on the Polish national agenda.

The Russian authorities were well aware of the overtures being made by the Poles to the Jews and the provincial police closely monitored Polish propaganda among the Jews.[5] On 30 April/12 May 1861, Valerian Platonov, Under-Secretary of the Polish Council of State, wrote to Alexander II that, in the light of reform projects bruited about in Poland, "it would seem useful to do something for the Jews; several proposals on the subject which are before the Jewish Committee [of Count Bludov] could receive immediate implementation."[6] P. D. Kiselev, former chairman of the Jewish Committee, writing from France, and Dmitri Miliutin, the Minister of War, both proposed that the Jews be cultivated as a counterweight to the Poles.[7]

These tentative Russian initiatives were soon preempted by the efforts of Marquis Alexander Wielopolski. Wielopolski had long advocated the collaboration of Poles with Russia as the sole avenue to the restoration of Poland. This view made him a political outcast for much of his life, but a useful ally for the Russians in 1861 as they sought to stem the growing agitation in Poland. In March 1861, Wielopolski was appointed by Alexander II as both Director of Education and of State Cults. The latter post, which oversaw Jewish life, was an appropriate vehicle from which to launch the legal reform of Poland's Jews. Balanced between the Reds, the Whites and the Russian government, Wielopolski desperately sought allies for his own schemes of internal reform. The Jews appeared as a valuable component in an alliance designed to protect public order. Wielopolski saw the Jews as the core of a future Polish *tiers état*, well worth cultivating.[8] Jewish reform therefore became an integral part of his program for the Kingdom of Poland. Jews were permitted to participate in the September 1861 elections to create a system of limited local self-government. Twenty-eight Jews were elected to seats on town councils.

Wielopolski's other reforms, which included the abolition of labor services for the peasantry, failed to quell the growing unrest, and he was called to St. Petersburg in December 1861, in apparent disgrace. Instead, Wielopolski turned the situation to his own advantage. He won allies at court and ultimately persuaded Alexander to approve a broad reform program, which included the virtual emancipation of Polish Jewry. There was some opposition to this measure. Valerian Platonov warned Alexander on 10/22 November 1861 that

> Marquis Wielopolski clearly wishes and hopes to merge (*slit'*) the Jewish with the Polish population by means of the measures he intends for them, and to turn those who are actually Jews into Poles of the Mosaic Confession. I dare to suggest that such merging would be quite contrary to the interests and views of the government. The Jews, whose number exceeds 600,000, could easily be attracted to the side of the government which should not make Poles out of them, but leave them as Jews, with their religion, language and nationality (*narodnost'*) undisturbed.[9]

Despite these misgivings, reform was in the air. Within a fortnight of Platonov's letter, Alexander promulgated the decree of 27 November 1861 granting service rights to Jews with a university degree. As early as 1857 the Jewish Committee (KOME) had raised the issue of unifying the legal position of Jews in Kongresowka and the rest of the Empire.[10] The Jewish Committee was receptive to Wielopolski's program and, after making a few changes, approved it on 24 May 1862.[11] When Wielopolski returned to Poland in May 1862, Jewish emancipation traveled in his baggage. The appropriate decree was promulgated on 5 June 1862 NS.

The reform was a generous one. Jews received the clear right to own farmland and urban properties. All residence restrictions were abolished. Jews were permitted to serve as witnesses for notary purposes and their testimony was given equal status in court proceedings. Legal oaths were changed to make them more acceptable to Jews. Additional provisions sought to hasten the process of assimilation: Hebrew and Yiddish were forbidden for all legal transactions, the authorities were ordered to review legislation which restricted Jewish economic activities, and a new tax system was devised for Jews.[12]

The Wielopolski program failed in its broader political goals. When the Marquis attempted to crush the plotting of the Reds by conscripting 30,000 young men into the army, he triggered an uprising which spread throughout the country, involving Reds and Whites. The insurrection dragged on for sixteen months, spreading at times to Lithuania and the Ukraine. The symbolic end arrived on 5 August 1864 NS when the Russians hanged Romuald Traugutt, the last "dictator" of the insurgent government, along with four comrades. Wielopolski had long since departed to exile in Germany. There remained only the inevitable Russian retribution. General F. F. Berg, the new Viceroy of the Kingdom of Poland, began to systematically dismantle Wielopolski's reforms. Yet the emancipation of the Jews survived the wreckage of 1863. As Michael Ochs observes, considerations which had motivated St. Petersburg's original acceptance of Wielopolski's plans remained unchanged. The Jews could still be encouraged to promote economic growth in the region. Equally, the retention of Jewish equality was part of a "divide and rule" strategy employed by the Russians, directed against the economic interests of the rebellious Polish szlachta. Finally, reform in Poland in no way committed the Russian government to undertake similar measures in the Pale of Settlement.[13]

With the exception of Herzen's *Kolokol*, which lost its popularity with the Russian public by espousing the Polish cause, the Russian press generally ignored the transformation of the status of the Jews in the Kingdom. The reluctance of Russian Jewish publicists to raise the issue is understandable. There was no guarantee of what the final outcome of events might be, and the Jewish role was sufficiently ambiguous as to be read in different ways. On the one hand, Jewish activism on behalf of the Poles could serve as a demonstration that the Jews were capable of merging with the interests of their fellow subjects. Rabbi Meisels, for example, closed the doors of Warsaw synagogues in sympathy with a boycott declared by the Catholic Church after Russian troops forced their way into a church. He appeared at most Polish patriotic functions, side by side with the Catholic clergy, a living symbol of Polish–Jewish rapprochement. Yet it was impolitic to stress that his patriotism was *Polish* patriotism, presumably directed against the best interests of the Russian Empire. Meisels, who was moreover an Austrian subject, became even less an object of emulation when he was arrested by the Russian authorities. Similar problems arose in emphasizing the patriotic role of the Warsaw capitalist Leopold Kronenberg, a Jew by birth. He was one of the leaders of the White faction and deeply involved in the politics of the insurrection. His conversion to Christianity, moreover, was an object lesson that assimilation could easily go too far.

The treatment of Polish events by *Sion* is instructive. From the period 1 July 1861 to 27 April 1862, it carried only a handful of reports from Poland.[14] At no time did the editors of *Sion* offer any comment on the events in Poland. After 1 December, by accident or design, Poland vanished from the columns of the paper. During the same period the Russian supplement to the Hebrew-language *Ha-Karmel* was equally silent about events in Poland, although they had obvious implications for Vilna, where the paper was published. The conspiracy of silence by the Jewish press was joined by Russian Jewish publicists, who avoided any comment on Poland in the general Russian press.[15]

There was an added incentive for Jewish publicists to steer clear of Poland once the revolt spread across the borders of ethnic Poland to Lithuania and the Ukraine. These areas were considered an integral part of the Polish state by the revolutionaries, and they carried on propaganda and, eventually, military operations there. Instances of Jewish sympathy and support could be found, especially in cities with a large Polish party, such as Vilna. This created a very delicate situation. Whatever Polish patriots, dreaming of "the frontiers of 1772," might think, the Russian government considered these areas Russian by right of history, conquest and law. Consequently, anti-Russian activity here was not merely revolution against an oppressive, external power, but treason, pure and simple.

It is noteworthy that this reticence was confined to the Russian-language Jewish press. The four Hebrew-language periodicals which served the Empire, *Ha-Tsefirah* (Warsaw), *Ha-Magid* (Lyck), *Ha-Melits* (Odessa) and *Ha-Karmel* (Vilna), all provided commentary on the background and implementation of Jewish emancipation in Poland.[16] As Mark Baker demonstrates, these Polish events were significant for forcing Hebrew-language publicists to rethink their facile commitment to cosmopolitanism and to attempt a distinction between their national identity as Russians and their religious identity as Jews.[17] Understandably, given that these authors were speaking to a purely Jewish audience, the religious component of Judaism received greater attention than in articles which spoke to gentiles. As was the case with the Russian Jewish press, however, there was an on-going attempt to define a Jewish identity, and to seek an historical mission for Judaism.[18]

While the role of Jews in the insurrection might be ignored or disguised, the aftermath of the revolt brought the Jewish Question to the fore amidst debates over "Russification." While the term for russification (*obruset'*) came into common usage, there was widespread disagreement as to what the process entailed. Russifiers really agreed on only one point, hostility to Poland and Polish culture. It was harder to translate this antipathy into specific policies. In the administration itself, there was sharp infighting between officials at the center, most notably P. A. Valuev, the Minister of Internal Affairs, and those in the field, such as General M. N. Muravev, the "dictator" of the Northwest Region.[19] Rival journalists with a special interest in Russification, such as M. N. Katkov and I. S. Aksakov, offered their own conflicting prescriptions for dealing with the Poles.[20]

As envisioned for Lithuania and the Ukraine, rather than the lands of ethnic Poland, Russification signified a determination to destroy Polish economic and cultural influences. How this was to be done, and the role of other national elements in the process, was left to trial and error and the politics of the moment. Russification lacked a grand, preconceived master-plan on the local level as surely as on the national level.

The fundamental problem faced by the Russifiers of the borderlands was simple and direct: there were too many Poles and not enough Russians. Most of the landowners in the Northwest and Southwest, even after a half-century of confiscation, exile and sequestration, were ethnically or culturally Poles, brothers in spirit to the szlachta and magnates of the Kingdom. They ruled over peasants who were Ukrainians, Belorussians or Lithuanians. The masters were largely Roman Catholic, while the peasants were Greek Orthodox or Eastern-Rite Catholics. The nobility held a virtual monopoly of education, and it was carried on in the Polish language and spirit. As the largest literate group in these regions, Poles comprised a significant number of middle-level bureaucrats.

Russification took aim at all these props of Polish power. Polish was replaced by Russian in schools. The peasantry was freed from dependence upon the gentry through an emancipation edict more generous than that awarded to the peasants of the Great Russian provinces. Efforts to diminish Polish landholding included a ban on Poles selling estates to other Poles. Incentives, in the form of sequestered lands and favorable loan arrangements, were offered to Russians who entered state service in the region.

Every one of these measures, which exercised Russian public opinion at the time, involved the Jews either directly or indirectly. A system of state-run Jewish schools already existed – how might it be modified to reflect the needs of Russification? The Jews played a preponderant economic role in the borderlands. As estate agents, lease-holders, middle-men in the grain trade, distillers and tavern-keepers, Jews were an ubiquitous part of the rural economy. In 1862, in line with the government's desire to encourage investment in agriculture, Jews had even been given the right to purchase estates in the Ukraine, once the mechanics of peasant emancipation had been completed.[21] In urban areas, where Jews sometimes constituted a majority of the population, they dominated trade and handicrafts. The Jews were the middle element between peasant and landowner, and any attempt to transform the borderlands had to take them into consideration.

The period of Russification after the Polish revolt of 1863 can be considered the decisive moment for the shaping of public opinion on the Jewish Question in the Empire. The debates before 1863 had a theoretical, ephemeral quality, more concerned with abstractions like "human nature" than real, practical problems. One could sympathize with the Jews, "play the liberal," without knowing anything about them. That era had come to an end. The Jewish Question now entailed immediate, identifiable problems. Policy, active or passive, produced consequences. Recognition of the role of the Jews in the suddenly important borderlands produced a sweeping shift in attitudes toward the Jews, not so much the patriotism and chauvinism which swept Russian society as a consequence of the events in Poland.[22]

As Russian administrators began to develop the Russification program, they were of two minds regarding the Jews. Some saw the Jews as potential allies, a valuable counter-force to Polish influence. A principal advocate of this approach was Prince I. I. Vasilchikov, the Governor-General of the Southwest (Kiev, Podolia and Volynia provinces), where Polish – and Jewish – revolutionary activity was minimal. Writing to the Ministry of Internal Affairs on 25 November 1863, he advocated an easing of restrictions upon the Jews:

> In Jewry, numerous, educated, and liberated from restrictions, the government may find an oppositionary force against the tempestuous Poles. Polish nationalism, which is strong in the state not

because of numbers but because of education, the privileges of birth and chiefly because of the restrictions placed on the rights of other estates, cannot be neutralized and balanced by physical force alone ... The whole secret consists in bestowing an advantage on the other, apparently insignificant, Jewish element, which contains resources of vital strength which can be nurtured and strengthened at the expense of other forces hostile to the government.[23]

M. N. Muravev, the Governor-General of the Northwest Region (the provinces of Vilna, Grodno, Kovno and Minsk), where Jews had been somewhat more supportive of Polish plans, was less sanguine at the prospect of making allies of the Jews. Writing in his memoirs he observed that "the Jews played a double game: they feigned joy [on the occasion of Russian victories] but this was a sham because they helped the insurgents everywhere, and gave them money."[24] However much he distrusted them, Muravev still had to deal with the reality of Jewish influence in his bailiwick.

The Russian press was eager to join the debate on Russification and on the position of the Jews within the process. It was the regional press within the Pale of Settlement which first recognized the significance of the Jewish Question for Russification. Provincial organs were also quick to evolve an unsympathetic view of the Jews as a danger and obstacle to Russification rather than as potential allies, providing a good example of how innovations in Russian Judeophobia often moved from the periphery to the center. Vague good intentions toward the Jews in the two capitals clashed with the realities of life in the Pale. Hostility to the Jews was not an inevitable ingredient of a russifying program. A case in point is provided by the programs of two influential papers, *Moskovskie vedomosti* and *Sanktpeterburgskie vedomosti*. Debating the problems of Russification, they disagreed on almost every point except for the need to deal leniently with the Jews.

Moskovskie vedomosti, edited by M. N. Katkov, had taken the lead in calling for resistance to the efforts of the Poles before 1863.[25] Katkov was a partisan of the vindictive measures taken by Russifiers like General Muravev and the men who designed the peasant reform in the western provinces, N. Miliutin and V. Cherkasskii. Katkov had been involved in the Jewish Question from the first: it was his *Russkii vestnik* which helped conduct the Literary Protest. His daily, *Moskovskie vedomosti*, had commented on the Jewish Question at regular intervals, but connected Russification and the Jews only in 1864. Even then, in the idiosyncratic fashion characteristic of Katkov, the question was seen more in the context of a German than a Polish problem.

12 M. N. Katkov

Katkov began his coverage with an editorial devoted to the question of the appropriate language for the Jews in the Russian Empire to use as they abandoned Yiddish (45:28/II/1865).[26] The editorial noted with concern that many partisans of the German language had emerged among the Jews. This was understandable, the editor lamented, because Russian had not yet "entered into its rights" as the language of the Empire. The Empire's subjects were unwilling to learn a language – Russian – that did nothing to raise their self-esteem. Even the Poles, recognizing their tongue to be that of a defeated people, were teaching German to their children. Within two months, Katkov viewed the Jews in more serious terms. An editorial surveyed the chief obstacles to Russian influence in the western provinces (97:6/V/1865). Chief among them was the fact that the "Russian" (i.e., Orthodox) population was confined almost exclusively to the economically weak peasantry. Jews dominated the trade-commercial estates. Serfdom had prevented peasants from joining the middle class. After emancipation their economic progress was still blocked by the concentrated and mutually supportive Jewish population. A middle class dominated by politically neutral Jews was not beneficial for Russian interests in the region. The Poles recognized this fact, and had labored to draw the Jews to their side before the January uprising. It was now time for the Russian state to reverse the situation.

Katkov, who was deeply concerned with issues of national development, saw the situation almost entirely in economic terms. He complained that the western provinces were economically isolated from the centers of Russian industry. Russian goods were not shipped to the provinces because foreign goods were cheaper, the consequence of competition within the concentrated Jewish population. The Jews also traded extensively in contraband, a situation arising from Russia's misguided tariff policies. These problems would disappear with the construction of a railway network. Until that time, trade ties between the center and the periphery could be strengthened by allowing more Jews to settle throughout the Empire. The departure of Jews from the Pale would also expedite the emergence of a native "Russian" (i.e. Orthodox) middle class. At present the Jews maintained the religious and national isolation which centuries of persecution had forced upon them. The Russian state reinforced this system through its restrictive legislation. It was time, in the interests of all concerned, to break up this tiny Jewish world.

Katkov's insistence on mass action made him unresponsive to the limited initiatives of the government in giving greater rights to small elites within the Jewish community. Katkov implicitly rebuked the law of 27 November 1861, which expanded the residence rights of Jews with a university degree. He argued that equal rights should depend on their ability to become useful citizens, not their attainment of higher education (148:8/VII/1865). It would be a serious mistake to divide Russian Jewry into two rival camps, one of educated and religiously indifferent Jews living in the interior and exercising no influence over the masses, and the other a mass of religious zealots filling up the western provinces. Certainly Jews should be educated, but in primary schools permeated with the Russian spirit. Given these attitudes, Katkov's approval of the law of 28 June 1865, which abrogated the Pale for artisans, was predictable: he hailed it as "exactly the right path" (160:22/VII/1865).

Through 1866, Katkov aggressively advocated the need to Russify the Jews. He placed the task of transforming the Jews into good subjects squarely on the Russian side. Russians had to abandon the negative attitudes and stereotypes which they had inherited from the Poles. The tendency to treat the Jews as an isolated, exclusive group – a legacy from Old Poland – was particularly counterproductive. The Russian state was beginning to move away from the policy mistakes of the past by abolishing the abuses which lingered amidst the last traces of Jewish communal autonomy. The state was fortunate to have an ally in this effort, the young generation of educated Jews who were "ready to stand under the Russian banner" and to merge with Russians in every regard except religion. This pro-Russian orientation was exemplified by the desire of Russian Jews to publish the Old Testament in a Russian translation. "If the best people among the Jews turn their attention to the introduction of Russian into Jewish religious life, then the Jewish Question will be solved by itself" (32:12/II/1866).

Katkov condemned the government's failure to support enlightened Jews in this effort. The state was reluctant to permit the use of Russian for any heterodox religion or cult out of the fear that non-Orthodox views expressed in prayer-books or service books might influence the Russian Orthodox population. Yet the abdication of Russian from religion left the field to a dangerous new rival in the western provinces – Germany. The economic and cultural might of Germans on the frontiers of the Russian Empire appeared ever more dangerous to Katkov in the light of the Prussian victory over Austria in 1866 and the creation of a unified German state. Educated Jews, abandoning the "half-German, half-Polish jargon" (Yiddish) for European languages, were increasingly attracted to German. "If this process continues, the German will pass into the very heart of Russia and, without wielding a sword or spilling any blood, will win from Russia a substantial part of her western lands" (53:11/III/1866). The Russifiers had to recognize this new challenge, and work to mold Jewish educational institutions into centers of Russian culture and expedite the use of Russian in their religious life.[27] Great was Katkov's rejoicing when the Russian state, following his lead, permitted all religions in the Empire to use Russian in their liturgies on 25 December 1870.[28]

During the heyday of Russification, Katkov proved susceptible to influences from the provinces. He welcomed the campaign against the alleged abuses of the kahal launched by the Governor-General of the Northwest, E. T. Baranov, under the influence of Iakov Brafman (101:9/V/1867). Yet these influences never overwhelmed Katkov's fundamental albeit idiosyncratic Judeophilia, born of economic and political considerations. When the Russification campaign in the Northwest, exemplified by the local newspaper *Vilenskii vestnik*, turned hostile to the Jews, Katkov repudiated it with his characteristic vitriol: "Nobody who actively sympathizes with the Poles can do as much harm to Russian interests as all the Messrs. Koialovich, Zabelin, Rachinskii, etc., making their nest in the editorship of *Vilenskii vestnik* ... The policy of Russification is being harmed by the press which should be defending it" (175:20/VIII/1866). Kahal mania never became the obsession for Katkov as it did for his chief liberal competitor, *Golos*. Most importantly, Katkov never abandoned his confidence in the good intentions and the ultimate success of the Russian Jewish intelligentsia to purge the Jewish masses of their anti-social flaws, as did so many of his contemporaries. Katkov's attitudes were reinforced by his ties to a number of Russian Jewish financiers and his tendency to view matters, including Russification policies, through the prism of economic interests.

The liberal perspective on Russification and the Jews was exemplified by V. F. Korsh's *Sanktpeterburgskie vedomosti*, a major ideological rival of Katkov's *Moskovskie vedomosti*. The paper illustrates how the capital press came late to the subject, for *Sanktpeterburgskie vedomosti* made its most substantive comments only in 1868. The editors began the year with several items defending Jews from Judeophobe attacks by *Golos*, and then published a long article from Vilna which addressed the problems attending the Russification of the Jews in the Northwest. The author found much to criticize in Jewry, ranging from the isolation and fanaticism of the masses to the preoccupation of the intelligentsia with expanded rights for themselves. He accepted that deception and fraud were rife in the Jewish community and chided Jewish apologists for painting their coreligionists only in rosy colors. None of these flaws made the Jews unique, however. Like all the residents of the Northwest, the Jews had been demoralized and corrupted by Polish domination. There was no reason for the Russian government to accept the world as the Poles had made it. Despite the stereotype, Jews were not all exploiters and actually constituted a large proletariat in Vilna, "that Polish Catholic Moscow." Jews worked with incredible industry for two rubles a month, and survived on a crust of bread. The Jews dominated trade and commerce because the petty Polish szlachta was too proud to dirty their hands with trade. The Jews possessed great potential to serve the Russian state: "the Jewry of the Northwest represents ready material for the rise of a middle urban estate, productive and conservative, and *unquestionably loyal to the government*; in a word, a promising obstacle to the restless Polish element" (169:23/VI/1868).

The government would be foolish not to make use of this potent force, the paper editorialized, rather than just leaving Russification to chance (16:16/I/1869). The Russification of the Jews could best be promoted by abolishing restrictive legislation. Such legislation was doubly unfair. It treated 2 million people in blanket fashion, without any differentiation. At the same time restrictive laws were ineffective at controlling the true criminals who merely bribed the local police. If Jews were granted the basic human rights of choice of residence and profession, they would gravitate to the Russian interior where a surer Russification would take place, inculcating in the Jews both the Russian language and Russian morality.

Equating Russification with the abolition of the Pale of Settlement and the grant of civil rights to the Jews, *Sanktpeterburgskie vedomosti* opposed the more extreme measures developed by the Russifiers in the Northwest. It denounced the Jewish renegade publicist Iakov Brafman as a "Yid-turncoat," eager to slander his former coreligionists (169:23/VI/1868). The editor rejected artificial attempts at merging the Jews, exemplified by the Vilna Jewish Commission.[29] For *Sanktpeterburgskie vedomosti*, Russification became a virtual synonym for Jewish emancipation. Opposites touching, the conservative publication of Katkov and the liberal newspaper of Korsh arrived at identical solutions to the Jewish Question prompted by the necessities of russification.

While theoreticians in the capitals debated the doctrinal nuances of Russification, officials in the provinces began to implement real programs. At first they sought only vengeance against the Poles. This brought them in contact with the Jews, who were the commercial lubricant of the semi-feudal economy of the Russian–Polish borderlands. As Russian officials came to regard the Jews as allies of the Poles, or at least dangerous neutrals, they sought to deal with them under the rubric of Russification. Their activist policies, aiming at the rapid transformation of the Jews, failed as surely as those of their bureaucratic predecessors in the reign of Nicholas I. As provincial Russifiers sought to explain their failure, they proceeded to re-define the Jewish Question, and to elaborate it in new and ominous ways. These innovations spread from the provinces to the capitals, where they were integrated into new forms of Russian Judeophobia.

7 Russification in the Northwest

V. I. Nazimov, the Governor-General of the Northwest (the provinces of Vilna, Kovno, Grodno and Minsk), was removed from his post on 3 May 1863, after eight years of service. Although a trusted functionary of the Tsar in the emancipation of the serfs, his administration was deemed too lenient in dealing with the Polish revolutionary movement in Lithuania.[1] His replacement was General M. N. Muravev, scion of an old noble family made famous by its involvement in the Decembrist Uprising of 1825. By 1863, however, Muravev was the ruthless suppressor of revolution, "the Muravev who hangs, not the Muravev who gets hanged." Under Muravev and his successors, K. P. von Kaufman and E. T. Baranov, Russification arrived in Lithuania with a vengeance.

Muravev's first priority was the liquidation of Polish insurrectionary activity, which he achieved by the liberal application of the noose. Those who assisted the Polish movement in any way, actively or passively, were liable to some form of punishment. Russians were not exempted – those who had shown themselves indecisive or lenient were, like Nazimov, transferred out of the area. Polish landlords who were not directly implicated in the rebellion were made to suffer for the sins of others, as Muravev forced them to send an address to the Tsar expressing their loyalty, and heaped a tax of 10 percent upon those of questionable loyalty. In 1864 Muravev dismissed all school directors, inspectors and teachers of Polish nationality.[2] The peasants were the chief beneficiaries of the anti-Polish movement in Lithuania. A group of specialists from the capital expedited the peasant reform which was still being negotiated between the peasants and landlords. They produced a settlement more generous to the peasantry than that which was obtained in Great Russia. So successful was this settlement judged to be that it was extended to Belorussia and the Ukraine.[3]

All plans for the future of the Northwest had to consider the Jews. In Vilna province alone there were between 102,000 and 104,000 Jews,

13 General M. N. Muravev

roughly 11 percent of the total population. There were almost 100,000 Jews living in urban areas, making Jews 62 percent of the urban population. In Vilna itself, where Muravev's headquarters were located, Jews comprised 57 percent of the population, confirming its nickname as "the Jerusalem of Lithuania."[4] While Muravev distrusted the Jews, their conduct in 1863 was sufficiently ambiguous for them to escape massive repression. In a few instances they were even compensated for losses which they had suffered at the hands of the insurgents.[5] Hostility and suspicion toward the Jews were not uniform attitudes among the bureaucratic allies of Muravev. M. F. de Pule, the future editor of *Vilenskii vestnik*, observed in 1862 that "when we appeared in the western area with the banner of Russification, there was no more satisfactory ground for our activities, no more ardent accomplices, than educated Jews."[6]

In 1864 the Ministry of Education promulgated regulations for

The provinces of the Northwest, Belorussia and Lithuania
(including the Vilna Governor-Generalship: Vilna, Grodno, Kovno
and Minsk)

primary schools which required that the language of instruction be
that of the majority of the school age population, Polish, Russian,
Lithuanian or German. Jews were not mentioned, but Jewish intellectuals quickly responded. In the Sunday supplement of *Moskovskie
vedomosti*, the foundry of Russification theory, a Jewish correspondent
complained that the Jews were being left to the care of the "Polish
rebels" (XVII: 1865). He denied that the Jews had anything in common
with the Poles – the Germanized jargon of the masses was portrayed as
a protest against the Poles and Polish culture. The author was even
reluctant to permit Jews to study in Polish schools where Russian was
the language of instruction. Jews would be best served by a system of
separate Jewish schools in Poland. This plea was enthusiastically

seconded by much of the Hebrew press and by Warsaw's Russifying newspaper, *Varshavskii dnevnik*. Articles like these attracted the attention of Katkov, and he began to call for Jewish liturgical materials to be printed in Russian.

Lithuania already had a Russian Jewish school system which became the focus for reform proposals. Muravev silenced the debate with one swift stroke: he ordered that Jewish primary schools be converted into Russian language state public schools. The teaching of Russian largely replaced the curriculum of Jewish subjects.[7] In 1865 Muravev issued a circular demanding that Jews learn the Russian language as the surest means of promoting their rapprochement with Russia.[8] Quick to take its cue, the pedagogical council of the Vilna Rabbinical Seminary resolved to "end the eternal servitude to foreign enlightenment" and replaced German with Russian for the teaching of the Bible, morals, Jewish grammar and Jewish history.[9]

The eagerness of the teaching staff of the Seminary to anticipate Muravev's wishes is not surprising, for the institution was the predominant vehicle for the spread of Russian culture in the Northwest. The Seminary's graduates served as state rabbis in some of the major cities of the Empire, including Moscow, Grodno, Kovno, Chernigov, Brest-Litovsk, Polotsk, Elizavetgrad and Vilna itself.[10] Graduates served as teachers in the state Jewish school system and some went on to staff those bureaux in the state bureaucracy which dealt with Jews. The archetype of Jewish Russifiers, L. O. Levanda, followed this path. He attended a state Jewish primary school in Minsk and graduated from the Vilna Rabbinical Seminary with a teaching degree in 1854. After a stint as a teacher in Minsk, he was appointed as the Jewish Specialist in Vilna in 1860, a post he held until his death in 1888.

There were other sides to this variegated Jewish city. It was one of the oldest centers of the Russian Haskalah, and helped to produce the first generation of Old Maskilim. One of the first reformed synagogues in the Pale, Toharat ha-kodesh (Purification of the Sacred) was founded in Vilna in the 1840s. It was home to one of the first modern Jewish schools in the Empire, and it was to Vilna that Dr. Max Lilienthal came in 1842, seeking allies for the creation of the state Jewish school system.[11] The language and culture of the early Haskalah was not Russian, however. Adepts were likely to acquire their ideas from German texts and disseminate them in Hebrew. The Vilna maskilim produced two of the outstanding representatives of modern Hebrew literature, Mordecai Aaron Gintsburg [Ginzburg] (1796–1846) and the poet Abraham Baer Lebenzon [Lebensohn] (1794–1878).[12]

14 View of Vilna in the mid-nineteenth century

Hebrew and Russian were not the only competitors for the cultural loyalty of Lithuanian Jewry. The Polish element had made a determined effort to attract Jews to their cause. By 1861 the local Polish–Russian language newspaper, *Kurier Wilenski*, endorsed Wielopolski's Jewish reforms in the Kongresowka.[13] The excitement of these days, filled with a spirit of Polish-Jewish rapprochement in the borderlands, was chronicled in Levanda's historical novel *Hot Times* (*Goriachee vremia*), published in 1871.

There was yet another side to Jewish Vilna. It was an important bureaucratic center for the administration of Russian Jewry and as such a mecca for those seeking the few positions in government service open to Jews before 1861. Besides the rabbinical seminary, Vilna also shared, along with Kiev (and later Zhitomir) a monopoly on the printing of books in Hebrew characters. A censorship office was attached to the press, yet another source of employment. There were also positions to be had as Jewish Experts, and in the offices of the educational bureaucracy. Side by side on the benches in the antechambers of Russian officials sat converts from conviction, renegades and opportunists, as well as fervent maskilim, all determined to win a hearing for their various projects for Lithuanian Jewry.

The small coterie who willingly entered Russian offices were exceptions, far removed from the lives and aspirations of Jews with traditional loyalties. Vilna was one of the preeminent centers of rabbinic

Judaism, famed for its scholars. Vilna was the city of the "Vilna Gaon," Elijah of Vilna (1720–97), who led the struggle against Hasidism in Lithuania with his bans and writings. The stern and cerebral "Litvak" (Lithuanian) was a familiar Jewish folk-type. The Jewish masses, faithful to their traditions, had in the past survived the attention of those who wished them both good and ill, and they hoped to do so in the future. And while the maskilim quarreled before the Russian masters over the proper language for the state Jewish schools, most Lithuanian Jewish boys still attended *heder*.

Side by side with Jewish Vilna, but effectively isolated from it, was Russian Vilna, the garrison of troops and the headquarters of a succession of governors-general – Muravev, Kaufman, Baranov – all intent upon the pursuit of their own prescriptions for Russification. The Russifiers, adrift in a sea of mute peasants and surrounded by the hostile Polish szlachta, often felt themselves under siege.[14] This perception was heightened by dissident notes from St. Petersburg, where Muravev's ruthless measures were not universally approved. A. L. Potapov, whose appointment as Governor-General in 1868 effectively ended the Muravev era, had earlier been transferred out of the area due to his unwillingness to accept Muravev's policies. Muravev himself resigned in disgust in April of 1865, in part out of frustration with the Minister of Internal Affairs, P. A. Valuev. While some of the Russian press, most notably *Moskovskie vedomosti*, applauded Muravev's tactics, others scorned them – and Russian officials never responded well to public criticism. When the director of the Vilna Education District, I. Kornilov, came to chronicle the accomplishments of the Muravev era, he pointedly observed that every success had been achieved without the support of the Ministry of Education.[15]

Kornilov was no friend of the Jews, whom he described as a greater misfortune for the Russians than the Mongols.[16] His office was unreceptive to the advice of would-be allies in the task of enlightening the Jews. Still less did he accept any activity not under his direct control. He was particularly indignant at the activities of the Society for the Spread of Enlightenment Among the Jews of Russia (OPE). He was angered when he discovered that the Society was in contact with teachers and supervisors of the state Jewish schools in Odessa, without the knowledge of the director of that school district. When the OPE offered a tribute to the proprietor of a Jewish girl's school in Kishinev, Kornilov complained, "what right and authority does this St. Petersburg committee have, without the knowledge of the director of the district, to publish in its name thanks for the good condition of the

15 P. A. Valuev

school? What impertinent and harmful interference! Does this committee have in mind to become something in the nature of a Jewish
Ministry of Education?" Kornilov's disposition was not improved
when the OPE registered a complaint with the Governor-General's
office over anti-Jewish articles which had appeared in the official
Vilenskii vestnik. Equally unacceptable was the OPE's policy of sending
subscriptions to Russian periodicals directly to state Jewish schools in
the Northwest Region.[17] In the delicate matter of Russification there
were not to be "two masters in the field."

Vilna was also significant as a center for journalistic activity in the
Northwest. The city was home to an official paper, *Vilenskie gubernskie
vedomosti*, largely responsible for publishing official edicts, and a
typical representative of its undistinguished breed. More exotic was
one of the first Hebrew publications in Russia, *Ha-Karmel*, edited by the

Vilna maskil and school official S. I. Finn [Fuenn]. Although issued in an area which was a hot-bed of enthusiasm for the Hebrew language, the paper was undistinguished in style and content. Less impressive still were *Ha-Karmel*'s Russian and German supplements.[18] Nevertheless, *Ha-Karmel* represented the authentic voice of Vilna's maskilic community, and it was a conscientious defender of the Jews from public attacks. The paper failed to reach an audience beyond Lithuania, however, and even there its influence was slight.

Most important, as an example of the growing and maturing Russian provincial press, was the official newspaper *Vilenskii vestnik*, controlled at various times by either the office of the Governor-General or by the director of the educational district. As the Jewish Question became a permitted topic in the press, *Vilenskii vestnik* joined in as an interested party. Under the editorship of A. K. Kirkor the paper opened its pages to a wide range of opinion, most of it sympathetic to the Jews. Jewish authors found publication in *Vilenskii vestnik* easy and agreeable. Writing to his friend I. Zalkind, whose articles he had just successfully placed in *Vilenskii vestnik*, L. O. Levanda observed that "although a local newspaper cannot under any circumstance be our national organ, its willingness to act as one will have a favorable influence."[19]

The paper under Kirkor's editorship proved too responsive to the public mood. During the period preliminary to the Polish uprising, *Vilenskii vestnik* began to appear in Russian and Polish. This concession to "szlachta civilization" ended abruptly with the on-set of russification. Kirkor himself was replaced in 1865 by the ardent Russifier M. F. de Pule. De Pule was interested in the Jews only as a target for Russification, and the quicker this end was achieved, the better. He was a patron of Levanda's literary efforts, but continually urged him to abandon the Jewish milieu for a broader canvas. In a critique of Levanda's novel *Confessions of a Man On the Make* (*Ispoved' del'tsa*), he complained that "the novel reeks of St. Petersburg, but the life is Jewish: it's all Jews, Jews." He impressed upon Levanda that "it is time to stop being a Jewish litterateur in the Russian language."[20] Under de Pule's direction, *Vilenskii vestnik* did not devote much space to Jewish themes or concerns.

The situation changed dramatically in 1866, when A. I. Zabelin replaced de Pule as editor. One of his first editorials opened *Vilenskii vestnik* to discussions of the Jewish Question. Zabelin's justification for his decision had ominous implications for the Jews: "this is the only way to discover the most hopeful course for the improvement of the life of the Jewish race, in order to liberate the people of West Russia from the harmful influence of Jewry in the economic-political-moral life of the whole region." Zabelin announced that he was opening the paper first to the Jews, "the weaker side," in the hope that Jews would admit their faults and cease to demand rights and privileges while they ignored their civil and moral obligations (20:25/I/1866). There followed a three-part series on the Jews by Lev Levanda, initiating a flood of features about the Jews, almost uniformly hostile (20:25/I; 26:1/II and 27:3/II/1866).

The objective of Levanda, the ardent Russifier, was precise: to stress the Jews' antipathy to Poland and sympathy for Russia as a prelude to a call for greater civil rights. Levanda argued that the Poles had always been hostile to the Jews and that their antipathy was "an evil ghost haunting the Polish people." While the Poles had used the Jews for the economic benefit of the nation, in their "szlachta arrogance" they regarded them as a form of lower animal. The Jews were like a guest invited to a ball only because of the music and dancing which they could provide. To defend themselves from the Poles, the Jews had developed their medieval community, the kahal, as a *status in statu*. The kahal protected its members, but at the cost of a despotic domination over them.

Russian rule had begun a change for the better. The kahal, and its attendant abuses, had been abolished. If some discriminatory enactments still remained in Russian law, it was only because of the low cultural level of the rest of the population, whose religious fanaticism did not permit the Russians to emancipate the Jews quickly. The time for decisive action had now arrived. Instead of projects designed to move the Jews out of the Pale – a "Lithuanian Palestine" which the Jews would not trade for a land they knew only through rumors – the government must seek a resolution of the Jewish Question through the new generation. "Jewish youth, as one man, is ready to stand beneath the Russian banner, and they have already made preliminary preparations by studying the language, literature and history of Russia ... Let Jewish youth know ... that they have a fatherland in Russia, and Russian brothers, and the Jewish Question will soon cease to be a question."

A flood of hostile responses revealed the use which the editors made of Levanda. His articles provided grist for the mill of the Judeophobes, and he himself was displayed as an object lesson of the danger posed to the Russian cause by educated Jewish youth, even those who pretended to stand "under the Russian banner." A number of correspondents gave a very different picture of Polish–Jewish relations. The Jews were indeed hostile to the Poles, but this did not keep them from serving as willing tools in the destruction, through economic exploitation, of the sole "Russian" element in the area, the Orthodox peasantry. (Russian publicists always assumed the loyalty of the Lithuanian, Belorussian and Ukrainian peasantry in their struggle with Poles, Germans and Jews.) If Jews now pretended to side with the Russians, it was only because they always gravitated to the stronger party in any dispute. The Jews lacked any patriotism, due to their messianic beliefs and their obsessive self-interest. Despite the claims of Levanda, the Russian government had done too little to change the Jews, and in their present fallen state there could be no thought of giving them greater rights. Still less would rights promote the process of merging. The Jews were a race unalterably alien and apart. The only correct approach to the Jewish Question was the destruction of their economic domination of the region (40–42:22–24/III/1866).

Such sentiments were echoed in subsequent articles, and elaborated with ever more imaginative charges. A correspondent ridiculed Levanda's description of the "preliminary preparations" which young Jews made in order to be taken into the Russian family. To be a Russian, he explained, was to adopt Russian morals and the Russian world outlook – something no foreigner could ever do. Nor was it sufficient to study Russian history: "The years 1612, 1812, the Time of Troubles, all the great events of Russian history will be seen by a Jew simply as events which arouse in his soul neither particular sorrow nor joy." Indeed, for Jews it was even more impossible, for they were all cosmopolitans, devoid of a fatherland, perpetually in transit and awaiting the Messiah. Educated Jews claimed to understand the Messiah in a figurative rather than a literal sense, but experience showed that educated Jews were even more cosmopolitan. In words which recalled Aksakov's rejection of "moral amphibians," the author characterized educated Jews as a *magnum nihil*, neither Russian nor Jew, leaving one side of a river but unable to cross to the other shore. He then reversed himself to make another, contradictory charge that since Yiddish contained numerous German elements, the Jews were secret agents of German–Jewish propaganda. He supported this charge with a quote from Kornilov (99–101:12–14/V/1866).

This attack was only the first of many. A correspondent dismissed the significance of expanded Jewish enrollment in the public schools: Jews had discovered that when peasant children could do simple sums, they were harder to cheat (124:13/VI/1866). Educated Jews were branded as "Bazarovs," after the alienated Nihilist hero of Ivan Turgenev's *Fathers and Sons* (144:7/VII/1866). One reader offered the sarcastic suggestion that Russian Jewry be moved *en masse* to Central Asia where they could serve as "missionaries of Russian culture," while still remaining close to Palestine (152:16/VII/1866). When charged with being a Judeophobe, Zabelin, as a gesture of good faith, published a letter in defense of the Jews from Markus Oksman, the former rabbi of Tulchin. The effect of this gesture was nullified when Zabelin printed Oksman's letter in a special supplement, "for want of sufficient other materials" (155:20/VII/1866).

Not all these attacks came from gentile pens. Solomon Pravdin, calling himself "a Russified Jew of the Northwest," argued that the religious teachings of the Jews, exemplified by the Talmud, made the merging of Christians and Jews impossible. Yet after dissecting this problem in five separate articles, he could still offer no better solution than a government directive that all instruction in *hadarim*, Talmud-Toras and *yeshivot* must be in Russian.[21]

Another Jew, a convert to Russian Orthodoxy named Iakov Brafman, with more ambitious plans for Russian Jewry, made his literary debut with four articles published during Zabelin's editorship. The attainment of a public forum represented a personal success for Brafman, who was in Vilna on leave from his position as a teacher of Hebrew in the Minsk (Russian Orthodox) Ecclesiastical Seminary. Brafman, whose stated objective was the conversion of the Jews to Christianity, shared his special knowledge of the Jewish milieu with his readers. He explained why it was so difficult to attract Jews to Christianity or even to educate them in a progressive spirit, despite a thirty year effort by the state. Amateurs attributed the failure to religious fanaticism or talmudic teachings. In fact, revealed Brafman, the Jews were in the thrall of the tyrannical Jewish community, the kahal. Ironically, this institution, with its judges, rabbis, tax-collectors and officials, was actually kept alive by the Russian state to govern the Jews. To demonstrate the powers and tactics of the kahal leadership, Brafman offered translations of the communal record of a kahal from a provincial town at the end of the eighteenth century. His documents revealed measures taken against recalcitrants who refused to accept decisions of the *bet din*, the rabbinic court controlled by the kahal. The publication of these documents represent the genesis of Brafman's infamous work, *The Book of the Kahal* (*Kniga kagala*).

The Judeophobia of *Vilenskii vestnik* became so scandalous that the OPE in St. Petersburg, which nurtured hopes of serving as a central agency to advance the interests of Russian Jewry, sent a denunciation of Zabelin to the office of the Governor-General, along with a request that he be obliged to print a public apology. This initiative elicited great indignation from the local authorities, and the OPE also received a rebuke from the Ministry of Internal Affairs that such actions were beyond the scope of its authority.[22] Nonetheless, Zabelin was soon dismissed from his post, and replaced by de Pule on 1 November 1866.

It is not known what effect the Judeophobe activities of *Vilenskii vestnik* had on Zabelin's removal. They had generated bad publicity – it suffices to recall the attack on the editors by M. N. Katkov – and the intervention of the OPE. There were also complaints in this Roman Catholic region about Zabelin's frequent attacks upon the Catholic clergy. In any event, articles on the Jewish Question disappeared from *Vilenskii vestnik* for almost a year. Still, the fall of Zabelin was at best a pyrrhic victory. The damage had been done. Iakov Brafman and his theories attracted the attention of the local administration, especially Kornilov, and helped to shape administrative policy until the end of the decade.

By the fall of 1866 Kornilov was already praising Brafman to the Assistant Minister of Education, I. D. Delianov. He pressed K. P. von Kaufman, the Governor-General, to appoint Brafman to an official post in Vilna:

> Because of his moral independence, his independence from the kahal, his knowledge of the Jewish community, its literature and aspirations and, finally, because of his ties to the Jews, Brafman is a person who is useful and indeed, unique, indispensable ... Your Highness may wish to commission Brafman to collect kahal documents, quite unknown up to the present day, and their publication with a Russian translation, for reasons of state.[23]

Levanda, who had maintained correct relations with Brafman, heretofore a personal friend and an early patron, was outraged. He wrote to his friend Zalkind: "That arch-scoundrel whom you know very well, Iakov Aleksandrovich Brafman, using the present inclination of Russian society in our area, has arrived in Vilna in order to carry his mite to the altar of those who wish to incinerate his former coreligionists whom he loves so much that he is ready to smother them in his Iscariot embrace."[24] By the end of 1866, Levanda reported, "Brafman has apparently settled in Vilna for good, having chosen it as the operational point for his missionary activity."[25]

Under these circumstances, Zabelin's departure as editor of *Vilenskii vestnik* meant little. De Pule, after initially ignoring the Jewish Question, began to devote increasing attention to it. Early in 1867 Levanda was permitted a defense of the Jews and a general condemnation of the paper's line under the previous editor: "literary organs should not speak this way" (5:12/I/1867). Levanda stressed that Russification among the Jews was continuing apace (11:26/I/1867). Levanda also published a serialization of his novel *Samuil Gimpels* beginning in January of 1867. Two Jewish educators, O. Gurvich and A. Vol [Wohl] received space to debate the best approach to educate the Jews and spread Russian culture among them.[26] When Ivan Aksakov's new publication *Moskva* began to attack the status of Jews as a privileged group within the state, *Vilenskii vestnik* offered full coverage of the ensuing debate (83:20/VII/1867; 106:12/IX/1867). Yet de Pule was also impressed by Brafman, and published part of his on-going translation of kahal documents.

Brafman had done well for himself, and was now firmly ensconced in Vilna as censor of Jewish books. After successful meetings with high officials, his confidence and ambition blossomed. Levanda complained that "his arrogance grows with every day; his judgments about Renan, Buckle, Mendelssohn, Levinson, Jost, Graetz, and other thinkers whom he has not read nor even looked at, deserves a slap in the face."[27] As Brafman's influence grew, so did the concern of the Jewish community in Vilna, especially when rumors began to circulate that Brafman was arbitrarily changing the meaning of some of his kahal documents. A prominent local Jew, Iakov Barit, petitioned Governor-General von Kaufman to convene a special commission to examine Brafman's charges. Such a body was formed under the chairmanship of V. A. Tarasov and began deliberations on 29 July 1866. Barit and Levanda served as "Jewish Experts." Members also included Brafman, the educator A. Vol, and the Vilna state rabbi Sh. Kliachko.[28] Levanda, for one, wrote that he was attempting "to direct Brafman toward fresh waters."[29] Matters stood at a promising pass until E. T. Baranov replaced von Kaufman as Governor-General on 9 October 1866.

Baranov fell completely under Brafman's spell. On 24 August 1867, he issued a circular to the governors of the Northwest Region which completely accepted Brafman's claims about the kahal. The communiqué noted the powers of self-administration which the Jewish community exercised, and the resultant social and economic harm.

> Such a privileged position of the Jews serves only to intensify their isolation and harms rather than benefits the government. Their isolation creates many abuses and hardships for the Jews themselves since it facilitates the preservation, in secret, of the kahal institution of

the Jews which has been abolished by the government. This isolation, which placed the Jews in a position independent from Christian society, gives them [the Jews] the opportunity to abuse their relationship with Christians because every Jew is well aware that in the case [of wrongdoing] he will receive protection and defense from his communal institutions.[30]

For a Brafmanesque ailment, a Brafmanesque remedy was prescribed. To end Jewish isolation, Baranov proposed that Jews who lived in shtetlakh and peasant villages should be made participating members of the peasant *volost*, the administrative system of peasant self-government devised after emancipation. (An exception was made for the small class of Jewish merchants.) Hitherto, all Jews who lived in the countryside, except agricultural colonists, were registered as merchants (*kuptsy*) or townsmen (*meshchane*) in the nearest urban center, preserving the fiction that the Jews were fundamentally members of the urban classes. Brafman's proposal sought to tie the Jews more closely to the rural community. They would pay the same taxes, save the land tax since they would not own agricultural plots, and bear the same obligations. The Jews, bound thus by common interests to the local population, would abandon exploitation of the peasantry. "If not moral feeling, then a commonality of interests and fear of the force of the peasant commune's power will serve to bridle their passion to survive by any means, even illegal ones, at the expense of the poor peasant."[31]

The plan required a few qualifications at its very inception. In many villages and townlets, the Jews were in a majority. The merging of Christian and Jewish societies might give the latter a numerical advantage on decision making bodies. Baranov therefore specified that, in communal decisions, two-thirds of the Christian membership must participate, and at least half of them must favor the majority position.[32]

Brafman also indicted the charitable associations of the Jewish community as agents of kahal repression. Reflecting this concern, Baranov instructed the governors to assemble detailed information about the resources and operation of these institutions. He also requested a report on the size of the Jewish and Christian population in every town and shtetl, their respective holdings of real estate, the state of Jewish taxes, and the fiscal standing of each. The governors were asked to comment on the proposal for joining the two communities. (Baranov's circular expanded Brafman's influence beyond the Northwest: the Governor-General of the Southwest sought similar reports from his governors in 1868.)[33]

Baranov's initiative was unwelcome news indeed to the Jewish Experts already sitting on the Vilna Jewish Committee, to which the responses of the governors were directed. The Jewish members found themselves hard pressed to defend the Jews from a mounting indictment. Both Vol and Kliachko offered lengthy rebuttals to Brafman's attack upon Jewish brotherhoods, only to have their defenses categorically rejected by a session of the commission on 31 May 1869.[34]

The delaying tactics of the Jewish members were served by the normal tendency of the Russian bureaucracy to move slowly. Baranov proved to be the last advocate of a radical, Muravev-style solution to the complex problems of the region. On 2 March 1868 he was replaced by A. L. Potapov, an old foe of Muravev's measures. With Potapov a different spirit entered the administration, and this change was reflected in the fate of the Vilna Jewish Committee.

Potapov was certainly not ill-disposed toward Brafman, fully accepting his claims about the survival of a secret kahal. This allowed Brafman to dominate the commission and to intimidate those who disagreed with him. The new Governor-General did make one significant change in the commission's mandate. Reorganized under the chairmanship of P. N. Spasskii, it was authorized to consider the general question of increasing the civil rights of the Jewish population. Yet rumors about the work of the commission, and the role played by Brafman, continued to vex the Jews of the Northwest. In October 1868 Potapov reported to his superiors in St. Petersburg that Vilna Jews had secretly – and illegally – collected the enormous sum of 17,000 rubles in order to send representatives to the capital to undermine the work of the Vilna Commission. He ordered an investigation and the seizure of the funds.[35] Such unrest forced Potapov to take a more dramatic step. On 13 September 1869 he invited the Jewish communities of the region (enlarged to include the two Belorussian provinces of Minsk and Vitebsk) to elect deputies who would review the work of the commission. Two deputies were elected in each provincial capital. In most cases they were the religious and social leaders of their respective communities. Eli Lederhendler makes the point that the elections provided an unprecedented opportunity for maskilim and the leaders of the traditionalist community to collaborate on a matter related to the common welfare of Russian Jewry.[36] From Vilna came Iakov Bariat and Emmanuel Levin; M. Knorozovskii and Sh. Bulkovshtein were elected from Grodno; I. Levi and G. Shapiro were the choice of Kovno; Z. Minor and M. Solomonov were sent from Minsk; and the delegation was completed by L. Zeltser and B. Fogelson of Vitebsk. Levin was

16 Jewish Deputies to the Vilna Commission of 1869

actually a resident of St. Petersburg, where he served as the secretary of the OPE. He had been chosen by Vilna in order to involve the activists of the capital, in a way that recalled the old techniques of *shtadlanut*.[37] He promptly established himself as the de facto leader and spokesman for the delegation, a role which was criticized by some of his colleagues.[38] The commission's meetings with the elected deputies lasted for a week, beginning on 5 October 1869.

In some respects the Vilna Commission was an unexceptional phenomenon. The Russian government had employed committees to explore aspects of the Jewish Question for the better part of a century. It was not unusual for the government to invite Jewish participation: the so-called Rabbinical Commission had a fully Jewish membership.[39] Other government commissions had produced reports favorable to the expansion of Jewish rights. Some form of emancipation for Russian Jewry did not lack official resolutions, but political will.

On the other hand, the Vilna Commission was extraordinary on two counts. It was a local initiative, which nonetheless had implications for all the Jewry of the Empire, and it was marked by an unprecedented degree of publicity. At first, news of the commission leaked out only as rumor. Then, early in 1868, *Sovremnennyi letopis*, the Sunday supple-

ment to Katkov's *Moskovskie vedomosti*, announced the existence of the
commission and gave an overview of its efforts to promote the merger
of Christians and Jews. The methods proposed by the commission, still
bearing the marks of Baranov's circular, were attacked by the Jewish
publicist A. Landau in the liberal *Novoe vremia*. He urged the commission to publicize its activities, and to seek the views of Jews from
outside the narrow boundaries of the Russian bureaucracy (18:26/I/
1868). When Potapov formally invited organized Jewish represen-
tation in 1869, the fact was well publicized, perhaps in an effort to
discourage rumor-mongering. There followed a vigorous campaign
against the features of the Baranov proposal still under consideration
by the commission. *Birzhevye vedomosti* and *Sanktpeterburgskie vedomosti*
both carried critical reviews, and the Russian Jewish weekly *Den*
conducted a virtual press crusade against the Baranov measures.
When the Jewish delegates first met with the Russian administration in
Vilna, they were empowered to publicize fully their activities and
deliberations. The readers of *Den* were treated to an insider's account
provided by Grodno deputy M. L. Knorozovskii, as well as comments
on his reports from other deputies.[40] No Jewish committee had ever
been so well covered by Russian journalists.

The newly elected Jewish delegates entered their first session with
the Vilna Jewish Commission with some trepidation. Judeophile newspapers were already predicting disaster on the basis of their knowledge of the preliminary drafts of the commission's project, which
envisioned the complete amalgamation of Christian and Jewish communities in both towns and villages. As *Sanktpeterburgskie vedomosti*
editorialized: "It is not apparent what this committee is about –
perhaps the successful expansion of the Jewish proletariat, perhaps
the replacement of one form of serfdom with another, with collective
lords and collective slaves; but judging from the measures they have
under consideration, the last thing they have in mind is an improvement in the life of the Jews." It would be a unique solution to the
wretched poverty of the Jews, the paper observed, to restrict their
rights further, when rightlessness was the cause of their poverty
(269:30/IX/1869). On the eve of the first meeting of the Jewish delegation in Vilna, a *Sanktpeterburgskie vedomosti* editorial offered a critique of the proposal to merge communities. Merger, it noted, could
occur in one of two ways: either the assimilating element must stand at
a higher level of development than the group to be assimilated, or the
latter must be small enough to be lost in the larger mass. The prerequisite of a higher cultural level did not hold for peasants or towns-

people in the western provinces. Far from restricting the number of Jews in a way that might expedite merging, restrictive legislation concentrated them in one place. Assume that merger really could take place. What would the government have to show for its trouble? More wretched Belorussians and Lithuanians, the very groups that the government was presently trying to Russify. The plans of the Vilna Commission were a recipe for disaster (273:4/X/1869).

The editorial writers of *Birzhevye vedomosti* were equally unimpressed. They queried the logic of efforts to solve a social problem on a local level when it was national in scope. The editorial condemned the commission's plans for a year-long waiting period during which the Jews could not exercise their rights in the communities of which they would become members. The Jews would presumably still have to pay special Jewish taxes while being unable to utilize resources drawn from the funds of the new joint community. More to the point, Jews and peasants lacked a religious, social or economical basis to create a common communal life. Either the Jews would destroy the village, or the village would destroy the Jews (265:30/IX/1869).

Of these two outcomes, the latter was the more probable, the paper soon predicted. Since the village community was devoted to agriculture, where were the Jews to fit in? The project did not consider that they might become farmers because it made no mention of providing land for the Jews. It was predictable that the project would merely swell the Jewish proletariat, creating in the village a host of homeless, landless people, with no chance of finding employment. Assimilation could not be legislated, and the Vilna proposal threatened even greater alienation of Jews from Christians, and the consequent danger of physical clashes (269:4/X/1869).

The Odessa-based Jewish newspaper *Den* took a special interest in the activities of the Vilna Commission. Early in its existence, *Den* editorials took swipes at the Baranov circular and its prescription for Christian–Jewish merger. Rather than merging, claimed the paper, the Jews in the cities would fall under the influence of the Polish ruling class. Assimilation in the countryside would founder on attempts to merge two diametrically different social estates (16:29/VIII/1869). The paper diligently provided what information on the commission was available, and scored a journalistic coup of sorts with its reports from commission delegates. In one regard, the activities of the Vilna Commission, with its stated commitment to merger, raised ideological problems for *Den*. From the first the paper had presented itself as an active partisan of Russification, yet now led the public campaign against a practical step in that direction. The paper was saved from its dilemma by a favorable outcome of the deliberations in Vilna.

The deputies who met in Vilna for the first time on Sunday, 5 October 1869, had no reason to be optimistic. The moment was not a propitious one for Jewry in the Northwest: a serious crop failure in the region had reduced many Jews in Kovno province to destitution, and *Den* was filled with reports of resettlement schemes to alleviate their grinding poverty (12:1/VIII/1869). There was disagreement as to the proper way to organize, with some delegates resenting the role of the OPE secretary, Levin. Even the favorable impression conveyed by their first meeting with Governor-General Potapov was soured during a subsequent meeting with his adjutant, Prince Bagraton, which turned into a heated argument over the nature of Jewish short-comings. Certainly nothing prepared the deputies for the reception they received the following day, when deliberations began. They were offered a proposal filled with concessions, as well as the anticipated project of Baranov. At every point where the deputies raised objec-tions, the government gave way. There were four principal areas of debate: a proposal to abolish the Pale of Settlement, regulations to govern Jewish religious life, the plan for merging Jews and Christians in urban centers, and the plan to subordinate rural Jews to the peasant community.

The first proposal called for the virtual abolition of the Pale: Jews who were Russian citizens were to be permitted residence anywhere in the Empire. They were to enjoy all the prerogatives of the rest of the population, including the right to participate in local government and to acquire real estate. A minor qualification provided that Jews might not settle in a new area in such numbers that they outnumbered the native population. Faced with this generous proposal, most delegates were prepared to accept it with joy. Three delegates reasoned that they had come too far on the road to full emancipation to be satisfied with anything less now. They lobbied against the prohibition against too-large Jewish resettlement in a separate protocol.[41]

The dissident opinion is very revealing about the mood of Jewish Russifiers at the time. They were confident that, in response to the progress which Jews had made on the path to Russification, and reflecting the course of analogous events in the West, the emancipa-tion of the Jews was imminent. The central government was gradually enlarging the number of categories of Jews permitted into the interior. Indeed, the delegates learned that the decision of the Vilna Commis-sion to press for the elimination of the Pale was inspired by the belief that the Minister of Finance had submitted a similar proposal to the State Council seven years previously, and that it had received imperial confirmation in principle. The delay in execution was said to be a consequence of the need to modify existing statutes. (This rumor was, in fact, an apparent reference to the internal debate on enlarging the Pale which culminated in the law of 28 June 1865 on Jewish artisans.) Every Russian newspaper, Judeophile and Judeophobe, was calling for abolition of the Pale. There was apparently no reason to accept half-measures now. The dissenting protocol was politely received by Russian officials.

The second major consideration involved regulations for official oversight of Jewish religious life. These proposed regulations had a variegated origin. At the center was Brafman's claim that the kahal exercised its coercive power over individual Jews through the rabbinate. Rabbis had the power to adjudicate legal cases between Jews and to place recalcitrants under a ban (the *herem*). The state needed to maintain a clear watch on the internal workings of the religious leadership in order to prevent abuses.[42] There was another constituency for the proposal. Some of the members of the Vilna Commission, like L. O. Levanda, were graduates of the Vilna Rabbinical Seminary (albeit with a teaching degree). They were well aware of the difficulties faced by their fellows in securing an official position as a state rabbi, and of surviving triennial elections. Their hand could be seen in the recommendation that state rabbis be elected by the local congregation, but serve at the pleasure of the Governor-General. No religious rite was to be performed without their express approval. As one delegate complained, the state rabbis were to receive prerogatives ordinarily associated only with the higher clergy of the Roman Catholic Church, who alone had the right to bar participation in religious rites.

The delegates saw this proposal as a violation of the old Russian proverb, "don't bring your own rule to another's monastery." They found themselves in the same position as the representatives to the Napoleonic Grand Sanhedrin, forced to accept innovations in the life of Jewry without communal approbation or consultation. Initially the Vilna delegates were terrified – if they accepted this measure they could justly be attacked by their constituents for betraying the integrity of Judaism. To the delight of the delegates, therefore, when they voiced their reservations and concerns to the Governor-General, he accepted them without demur. On his own authority Potapov issued an order that Russian officials under his authority were not to interfere in Jewish religious life.[43] Without Jewish cooperation, the commission was unable to draft a complete program for official control of Jewish religious life.[44]

The third area of discussion was the question of amalgamating Christian and Jewish communities in urban areas. This was a question which was already in a state of flux since the system of municipal self-government was being reorganized. Under legislation dating to the time of Nicholas I, the rights of Jews to participate in municipal government were much restricted. Jews were forbidden to comprise more than one-third of the elected members of the municipal councils (*duma*) and a Jew could not be elected mayor. This regulation held no matter how high the proportion of Jews in a particular town. With the creation of a new system of local government, the Ministry of Finance proposed to relax these norms. The Vilna Commission resolved to go further still. The commission recommended that the rule be changed to require only a simple majority of Christians in elected posts, that Jews with secondary or higher education be allowed to hold any post in municipal government, and that Christians and Jews vote together, instead of using separate curiae.

This generous reform made a great impression on the delegates, but they still asked for more. They requested that Jews who did not meet the required educational norms still be eligible for a post if they were elected to it by a unanimous vote of their Christian neighbors. Once again, the commission's bureaucrats agreed with the delegates.[45]

This left for deliberation only the keystone of the initial project born of the efforts of Brafman and Baranov: the plan to subordinate the Jews in the countryside to the peasant community. The finished project was presented to the delegates by Brafman himself, who offered an impassioned defense of it. It provided that Jews were to be included as members of a peasant community, and all separate Jewish communal institutions were to be abolished. While the new order was gradually implemented, Jews were to be forbidden to move residence or to vote for or serve in the community administration for a period of three years, except for one Jew who would be elected as a representative to the peasant council (*skhod*).

The deputies replied to Brafman's charges and recommendations with a lengthy protocol of their own. Brafman's cornerstone, upon which all else rested, was the concept of the secret kahal. In fact, the deputies argued, there were other historical phenomena which better explained the isolation of the Jewish people. Since the fall of Jerusalem the Jews had lived among people who refused to recognize them as equals and who kept them degraded and apart. The Jews turned inward for comfort and support, a tactic made even more necessary by persecutions which the Jews had suffered since the Middle Ages. With the advent of enlightenment and progress, the causes of Jewish separatism had vanished. The only factor which still promoted Jewish solidarity was the terrible poverty which afflicted them (a clear reference to the Kovno famine). With the diminution of poverty – which the delegates argued could be accomplished through the abolition of the Pale – the last vestiges of Jewish solidarity and isolation, which Brafman had mistakenly identified with the defunct kahal, would evaporate. The project of Brafman, on the other hand, would reduce the Jews to the status of landless peasants, or *batraks*, struggling under a new form of serfdom. Such a course would run counter to the path of emancipation through education mapped out by the Tsar himself. Once again the delegates were successful, and despite the urging of Brafman, his project was rejected.[46] Instead, the commission's final report offered a vague proposal to organize communities of Jewish and Christian merchants and townspeople "and others," in which Jews would enjoy full electoral rights.[47]

Having carried all before them, the deputies determined to make one final point. While they paid lip-service to the principle of gradualism which characterized official policy toward the Jewish Question, they sought to move more rapidly. They were in advance of a group of St. Petersburg Jewish activists who had recently presented a petition to the Tsar asking that full civil rights be given to Jews with an advanced education. As they completed their deliberations, the deputies presented a letter to Potapov in which they took issue with this petition. "We must say that the Jews of this region are not in solidarity with these people in their request; the means which they recommend in their private proposal have no correlation with the magnitude of the disaster afflicting the mass of our coreligionists." The only expedient to resolve the Jewish Question was the immediate opening of all the Russian Empire for Jewish settlement. The deputies even petitioned that committees be set up to render formal assistance to such resettlement endeavors, and this was included in the final report of the commission.[48]

The readiness of Potapov to accept the recommendations of the Jewish deputies metamorphosed the project of the Vilna Commission from one filled with risks and ambiguities for the Jews into a virtual agenda for Jewish emancipation. It was a demonstration of how far the Russification campaign had evolved, shaped at least in part by the realities of the situation. There were no further legislative or administrative initiatives in the Northwest to the end of Potapov's service in 1874. Indeed, when a group of prominent Jews, including several members of the Vilna Commission, petitioned Potapov in 1872 to permit the election of Jewish deputies for consultation with state institutions, he ignored their request.[49]

The impact of the Vilna Commission was more national than local. Its protocols were forwarded to St. Petersburg where they were one of the first bodies of evidence to be considered in 1872 by the newly created Commission for the Reorganization of Jewish Life (KUBE). Ominously, the first meeting of the KUBE was more inclined to fault the Vilna Commission for failing to collect information on Jewish burial brotherhoods than to consider relaxation of the Pale.[50] Despite the defeat of his projects, Brafman's continuing influence enabled him to wreak a terrible vengence on the Jews, maskilim and traditionalists alike, who had bested him in Vilna.

Eli Lederhendler sees the activity of the Vilna Commission as important for the development of modern Jewish politics in Russia. He stresses the role played by maskilim on the commission in defending the Jewish community as an organized socioeconomic phenomenon from the unwelcome attentions of the government.[51] This contrasts with the willingness of maskilim in the past to take the side of the government against the traditional community, in such episodes as the school reform of 1844. This analysis ignores the obvious fragmentation and in-fighting that marked the delegation. There was resentment against the intrusive role of the OPE representative, Levin. A further rejection of the politics of the St. Petersburg *shtadlanim* can be seen in the delegates' rejection of their policies of gradualism and preference for the elite. Furthermore, if maskilic Russifiers like Levanda did play the role I attribute to them in framing the original project that was submitted to the delegates, then the maskilim had not yet abandoned their inclination to impose reforms on a reluctant community. On the other hand, the increased self-confidence of these Jewish spokesmen, their skill at operating within the political context of Russification, and their ability and willingness to mobilize and direct public opinion, demonstrates the Young Maskilim's evolution into an articulate Russian Jewish intelligentsia.

8   "Kiev is Russian"

"Kiev was, is and shall be Russian!" was the slogan of the Russifying newspaper *Kievlianin*, first published in 1864. The first premise was debatable, and the paper's prediction remained to be seen. The central claim for the Russianness of the region was patently untrue. Kiev was the administrative center of the governor-generalship of the South-west Region, comprising the three provinces of Kiev, Volynia and Podolia. These territories, commonly known as Right-Bank Ukraine, were acquired by Russia only at the end of the eighteenth century. The influence of its past lay heavy on the region.

The population of Right-Bank Ukraine was sharply differentiated. At one extreme were the Polish nobility, a majority of whom at the time of the partitions were impoverished *szlachta*, frequently lacking even a landholding. The nobility of the Ukraine was predominately Polish, and overwhelmingly Roman Catholic. Even after a concerted effort of the Russian government, dating from the Polish uprising of 1830, to reduce the size of the Polish noble population, this element comprised 82 percent, 85 percent and 89 percent of the nobility in Kiev, Podolia and Volynia provinces respectively.[1]

The peasantry, on the other hand, were the so-called "Little Russians," identified by a distinctive culture and language – although Russian activists were undecided as to whether Ukrainian was a separate language or a dialect of Russian. The gap between masters and serfs was reinforced by religion. The Ukrainian peasantry were overwhelmingly Russian Orthodox, especially after formal unification with the Russian Orthodox Church of about 2 million Roman Catholic Uniates in 1839.[2] Despite rhetoric about the peasant "little brothers in faith," the Russian authorities usually found it convenient to work with the Polish elites in the region for the control of the enserfed masses, at least prior to the Polish uprising of 1830.[3]

During the second Polish revolt of 1863, Russian nationalists rejected

The provinces of the Southwest, Right and Left-Bank Ukraine, the Crimea and Bessarabia (including the Kiev Governor-Generalship: Kiev, Podolia and Volynia)

this state of affairs. Mikhail Katkov in particular, raised the alarm against the agitation of the "Polish Party" in Right-Bank Ukraine. Katkov saw the struggle in the Ukraine as one of life or death to determine whether Russia or Poland was to survive as a nation. He offered an array of proposals designed to bring about the Russification of the region, focusing initially upon freeing the "Russian" (i.e. Ukrainian) peasantry from the influence of their Polish landlords.[4]

A final accounting with the Polish gentry in the Ukraine was not so simple, however. Unlike their less cautious brothers in Lithuania and Belorussia, Poles in the Ukraine had conspicuously ignored the uprising. As a consequence, there was no good legal pretext for sequestering their estates, as was done with much ruthlessness in the Western Region. The Ukraine lacked its Muravev. Instead, the Russian government relied upon new legislative initiatives to reduce the power and influence of the Poles. A wide-ranging decree of 5 March 1864, offered a variety of incentives and privileges for non-Poles to acquire land in the Western and Southwestern Regions. In addition, Poles were forbidden to sell estates to other Poles. This law sought the gradual passage of local estates into loyal hands. To expedite the process, a redesigned emancipation act was implemented, which gave the peasantry slightly larger landholdings, and brought to an immediate close the period of "temporarily obligated status" for the peasants through the appointment of imported Russian land arbitrators.[5] Even with these reforms, Russifiers recognized that eliminating Polish influence would be slow and gradual.[6] Shortages of both capital and Russians raised the question of the role of the Jews.

By any standard, the Jews were a significant force in the Southwestern Region. The three populous provinces of the governor-generalship had the largest concentration of Jews in the Empire. Jews constituted over 11 percent of the total population of Right-Bank Ukraine, making them more numerous than the Polish nobility itself.[7] While all Jews, excepting agricultural colonists, were theoretically members of the urban social estates, in reality they ran the gamut from impoverished craftsmen and tavern-keepers to emergent capitalists. Although tied to the szlachta by traditional economic relationships, the Jews were not necessarily allies of the Polish aristocracy, especially in the context of the changing economic conditions of the post-emancipation period.

Imaginative Russian officials looked to the Jews as potential allies even before the uprising of 1863 focused Russian attention on the area. The most articulate spokesman for this point of view was Prince I. I. Vasilchikov, Governor-General of the Southwestern Region from 1855 to 1862, and a consistent advocate of relaxing legal restrictions upon Russian Jews.[8] Typical was a proposal he submitted to the central administration on 25 November 1862, urging the government to utilize the considerable economic force represented by Ukrainian Jewry, not only to increase the prosperity of the region, but also to create a counterforce to Polish nationalism.[9] Vasilchikov was also instrumental in convincing the Jewish Committee to recommend to the Emperor that Jews be permitted to purchase land – specifically, noble estates – in the Southwestern and Western Regions.

Proponents of this course noted that local landowners were in straightened circumstances because Jewish capitalists refused to lend them money without real estate as collateral. Moreover, Jews might procure gentry land which had already passed to the members of other social classes. In this way, Polish land would pass under Jewish control.[10] Thus, the decree of 26 April 1862, which gave the Jews in the Southwestern and Western Regions the right to purchase gentry land, assumed that the Jews were allies of the Russian cause in the Ukraine.[11]

The Polish revolt sharpened the views of militant Russifiers, and discredited accommodationist positions. Mikhail Katkov, it will be recalled, saw the Jews as raw material for Russification (by spreading Russian among them), but never regarded them as useful in themselves. Small wonder that as early as 1863 Katkov complained to P. A. Valuev, the Minister of Internal Affairs, that noble landowners in the West and Southwest were selling their estates to Jews.[12] Katkov was usually an accurate barometer of official concerns, especially in the course of the Polish crisis, so it is not surprising that his disquiet was soon followed by restrictions on Jewish landholding.

A decree of 5 March 1864 offering incentives to any Russian subject to acquire land in the western provinces specifically excluded Poles and Jews.[13] A more stringent measure soon followed, forbidding Jews to purchase *any* gentry land in the area (and thus effectively cutting Jews off from rural landholding).[14] A year later, concerned that the Jews were circumventing these interdicts, the government forbade Jews to hold mortgages on any property purchased under the rubric of the privileges of 5 March 1864.[15] The governors of the region were uniformly hostile to any attempt to expand Jewish leaseholding in the Ukraine.[16] Vasilchikov's successors, N. N. Annenkov and A. P. Bezak, were both inspired by memories of the role of Jews in the feudal szlachta economy and by new fears that Jews might replace the szlachta as exploiters of the peasantry. Their concerns were fully shared by the Tsar. To an observation of Annenkov in 1864 that "the question of the Jews has the highest importance and deserves the special attention of the government," the Tsar noted "very true."[17] The economic activities of the Jews particularly disquieted Prince A. M. Dondukov-Korsakov, Governor-General between 1869 and 1877. Against this background of ambivalence and hostility to the Jews, the Russifying press made its appearance.

In the Northwest, existing organs like *Vilenskii vestnik* were merely turned to official needs of the moment. Elsewhere, new periodicals with the specific task of supporting the government and pursuing policies of Russification had to be created. This was the origin of such publications as the Kiev-based monthly *Vestnik iugo-zapadnoi i zapadnoi Rossii* or the official *Varshavskii dnevnik* in Warsaw. The lifelessness of these publications highlights the government's difficulty in finding the

17 V. Ia. Shulgin

requisite personnel for the unprestigious and lowly paid task of
journalism. (Indeed, this was one reason that so many Jewish intellectuals were to be found writing for the periodical press, since they
lacked other opportunities.) For this reason the Kiev Governor-
General was delighted to secure the services of Vitalii Iakovlevich
Shulgin (1822–78).

Shulgin was the scion of a Russian family in the Ukraine, where he
was reared and educated. He secured degrees from St. Vladimir University in Kiev, and embarked upon a career as an historian and a
partisan of an improved history curriculum for secondary schools. He
published articles on the history of the Ukraine in the prestigious
Russkoe slovo. Shulgin's skills as both a scholar and lecturer pointed to a
distinguished career at his alma mater, where he taught from 1850. In
1863, attempts were made to give him a chair in history at St. Vladi-

mir's, but his lack of an earned doctoral degree led several members of the history faculty to object. Although finally elected, Shulgin indignantly refused the post. Thus, in 1864, when the government was casting about for a suitable editor for a paper to pursue a Russifying line, it found Shulgin, a man of culture, ability and demonstrated literary skills, available. Shulgin agreed to undertake the task when the office of the Kiev Governor-General offered a subsidy of 6,000 rubles to the new periodical. In July of 1864, Shulgin began to edit and publish *Kievlianin*, performing his duties until his death in 1878. The paper remained under the control of his family until 1917.[18]

Shulgin has been called "the Kiev Katkov" and his paper "the Kiev *Moskovskie vedomosti*," and there were many obvious affinities.[19] Like the "Thunderer of Strastnoi Boulevard," Shulgin inveighed against "Polish intrigues" and "Little Russian separatism" in the Ukraine. And, like *Moskovskie vedomosti*, *Kievlianin* was not initially hostile to the Jews, although Judeophobia became one of its most prominent hallmarks in later years. *Kievlianin*'s treatment of the Jewish Question is especially interesting because of Shulgin's semi-official status.

It should be stressed that Shulgin was not just a paid hack, and always retained a mind, and a voice, of his own. In his initial editorial, Shulgin took note of the paper's subsidy but declared that "*Kievlianin* ceases to be the organ of the administration as soon as that administration pursues the interests of a single party rather than the interests of Russian society" (1:1/VII/1864). With this critical attitude, Shulgin did not escape difficulties with the censor. The newspaper's mix of official and independent voices made it one of the most widely read and quoted organs of the provincial press. On the Jewish Question, *Kievlianin* under Shulgin usually reflected the views of the Governor-General's office but he was also capable of marking out new and distinctive directions. A study of *Kievlianin*'s editorial positions on the Jewish Question is therefore an important model of the mutual influences of public opinion and official policy.

Shulgin the historian lamented the political role which the Jews played in the Ukraine,[20] but as befitted an editor with his background, the first dealings of *Kievlianin* with the Jewish Question involved education. The third issue carried an informational article on Jewish trade schools in the Southwest, and within a week the paper played host to a debate on ways and means of reforming the state-run Jewish school system.[21] The debate was dominated by members of the Russian Jewish intelligentsia, often employees of the Jewish school system, eager to proclaim the enthusiasm of the Jewish population for merger. The schools debate persisted into 1865, especially after the Ministry of Public Education published F. Postels' critical description of the Jewish school system.[22] At one point, Shulgin announced that he had received sufficient material to publish several issues of *Kievlianin* devoted to nothing but Jewish education (55:15/V/1865). Shulgin never lost his pedagogical interests, moreover, and long after *Kievlianin* became a leading Judeophobe organ, it still carried numerous articles on both state and private education for Jews.

This was a concern fully shared by a government in the midst of exploring how schools might spread Russification. The office of the Governor-General of the Southwest employed *Kievlianin* to conduct its own investigation of the Jewish Question in education.[23] In 1864, the Governor-General's office published a survey of past efforts to educate the Jews as a prelude to the gradual extension of their civil rights. The article reviewed disagreements within the Jewish community between orthodox and progressives as to the design and function of the Jewish school system. Since book censorship was also a responsibility of the educational authorities, the article queried what sort of books the government should authorize Jewish presses to print. The Governor-General's chancellery explained that it wished to avoid the mistakes of the past and was therefore raising the issues for debate in the press. Jews were admitted to submit their own opinions on the twin issues of Jewish educational institutions and Jewish presses to the local government, and even to write in Hebrew if they preferred. Appropriate submissions would be published in *Kievlianin* (58:12/XI/1864). This was a remarkable invitation, for the tsarist bureaucracy was not known for inviting public debate on *any* subject in the press, except under exceptional circumstances. Rarer still was an open invitation to private individuals to share their thoughts on public issues, together with a promise of publication. This in itself was an indication of how the Jewish Question was moving into the center of public debate. The invitation in its pages also reflected well on *Kievlianin*, demonstrating the close relationship between Shulgin's newspaper and the provincial administration.

The results of the invitation were not blessed with success, however. In 1867, *Kievlianin* complained that satisfactory answers from the Jews were not forthcoming. Jews addressed the issue in an "overly romantic way," demanding equality and privileges in compensation for past suffering (91:1/VIII/1867). This particular article served not only as the obituary of the information-gathering efforts of the administration, but also as an indication of *Kievlianin*'s Judeophobic reorientation.

The central task of education, as envisioned by the Russian government, was to weaken the fanaticism of the Jews, and to merge them with Russian society. It was inevitable, therefore, that Shulgin should turn from educational issues to considerations of the possibility of true and complete merger. The first editorial which Shulgin wrote on the Jewish Question struck themes to which he returned again and again (24:25/VIII/1864). Shulgin assumed that all participants in the debate over Jewish education desired to facilitate the integration (*sblizhenie*) of the Jews into Russian society. But integration must be viewed as a dual process. Externally, it meant the grant of rights to the Jews to facilitate their entry into public careers. Internally, it produced a commonality of outlook which joined together the interests and aspirations of enlightened people of every nationality within the state. Shulgin lamented that Jewish publicists pursued only external integration, seeking only equal rights, while neglecting internal measures which promoted broader integration. "It seems to us that the aim of integrating Jews with Russians has still not accomplished much if our schools annually produce some scores of enlightened Jews who, gaining various positions, disappear into our official world, while the Jewish masses remain in their secluded world, separated from Russian society by the particularities which rule their outlooks and conceptions." Certainly there was nothing unnatural in enlightened Jews seeking greater rights, but if they truly desired the national good they would acknowledge the favorable position of the Jews compared to the embittered and long-suffering Russians, "carrying on their backs the many contradictions of our life."[24] In short, Jews would have to be prepared for external integration through the process of internal integration, which Shulgin defined as spreading enlightenment and humanity among the Jewish masses. This was nothing more than the familiar official prescription that the Jews must lose their fanaticism before they were emancipated. Previous spokesmen for the Jewish community, such as Joachim Tarnopol and the members of the Gintsburg Circle, had accepted this approach. It no longer satisfied the young generation of Jewish intellectuals, the product of a Russian education, who argued that rights must be given unconditionally. This approach ensured a clash with *Kievlianin*.

Many of the "contradictions of our life," borne by the Russian peasantry, were economic. Indeed, no discussion of the Jews in the Southwest could neglect their role in the local economy, especially when this issue was muddled up with the broad question of russification. As early as 1864, Shulgin hinted at his negative perception of the contemporary role of the Jews in the Ukrainian village, although initially he partially attributed it to the effects of the Pale of Settlement (36:22/IX/1864). Ambiguity also marked the introduction which Shulgin penned for a critical series dealing with Jewish overinvolvement in petty trade which condemned Jewish domination of the rural tavern trade. Shulgin stressed that the Jews alone should not be blamed for economic malfeasance, since governmental legislation played a role in creating it (20:16/II/1865; 21:18/II/1865; 22:20/II/1865).

Shulgin was sufficiently convinced of the economic harm caused to the area by the Jews, whatever the underlying causes, and responsive enough to the concerns of the local administration, to welcome enthusiastically restrictions placed by the central government on the purchase of land in the western provinces. *Kievlianin* presented Jewish economic activity in harsher terms than before. Shulgin brushed aside liberal qualms that restrictions produced monopolies: there was already sufficient competition for land between Russians in the region, and restrictions on Jews merely abolished "monopoly for a few." There was no question as to what group would be better for agriculture, for Jews never showed any inclination for farming, and their trade in alcohol in the rural villages directly undermined agricultural prosperity. An alarming phenomenon in the post-emancipation era was that peasants, freed from Polish landlords, had fallen under the sway of the Jews, who were more dangerous because they were more economically advanced.

Political considerations ultimately overshadowed economic factors. In principle, Shulgin decried withholding civil rights from national minorities since these tactics led only to alienation and isolation, the hallmarks of the Jews after centuries of persecution. But principle was beside the point in the present instance. The ultimate consideration was the welfare of the region, which could only be served by the introduction of a Russian landholding class. It was immaterial whether restrictions rested upon Jews or some other nationality. "Political necessity demands Russian landowners here; if Germans lived here in the same numbers, in the same material condition, and in the same relationship with the Polish and peasant elements as the Jews, then in all truth, they too would suffer the restriction which has been fixed for the Jews at the present time" (86:24/VII/1865). Significantly, Shulgin had no objection to the Jews buying farmland in other provinces, such as Kherson in New Russia, nor was there any talk of restrictions on the lease of land, subsequently to become a special obsession of *Kievlianin*.

Since its inception, *Kievlianin* had offered an open door to the

Russian Jewish intelligentsia, and they replied to Shulgin's editorial in the person of M. Morgulis, a student in the law school of St. Vladimir University, and in the future an indefatigable Jewish publicist, who had already appeared in *Kievlianin* with an article on the school debate.[25] Morgulis challenged all of the assumptions of the editorial. He denied that restricting one group in a particular economic endeavor made it freer for others; it merely permitted limited competition for a monopoly. As for the charge that the Jews were inept agriculturists, Shulgin confused skill in physical labor with skill in economic management. The objects of this debate were not Jewish leaseholders or tavern-keepers, Morgulis reminded Shulgin, but Jewish capitalists seeking good investments for their money. Through proper utilization of their capital, they would encourage useful and productive peasant labor. Morgulis pointed to the example of Jewish capitalists in the sugar beet industry, where they had developed a notable expertise.

Morgulis found Shulgin's political arguments similarly unconvincing. The Ukraine was currently undergoing an agricultural crisis in the aftermath of emancipation. The peasants, embittered by the loss of land which they considered theirs, refused to provide their labor to gentry estates. The Polish gentry in their turn were reluctant to rent their land to the peasants, or sell it to Russians, whom they viewed as political enemies. Under these conditions, Russification could not move at a rapid rate.

The dilemma would be easily resolved, argued Morgulis, if the Jews were permitted – indeed encouraged – to purchase land from Polish landlords. The Poles, long used to business dealings with the Jews, would not object. Even assuming for the moment that the Jews were a neutral element in the area, it was better to have the land in their hands than in those of the hostile pans. If the Jews were politically indifferent, permission to own land would capture their loyalty. But the Jews were not neutral, claimed Morgulis, pointing to their loyalty to Russia during the recent uprising. Jewish landowning, he concluded, was the perfect expedient. It would improve agriculture through a needed influx of capital, and it would transform the Jews into true Russians and a reliable bulwark against the Poles (94:12/VIII/ 1865).

Shulgin printed a reply, dripping with anger and sarcasm, in the next number of *Kievlianin*. He not only denied Morgulis' economic and political arguments, but offered sharper attacks on the Jews than had yet appeared in *Kievlianin*. He condemned Jews as alien and anti-

Christian. The Poles were at least Slavs and Christians, and their replacement by Jews would surrender "our brothers united in blood and faith, flesh of our flesh, blood of our blood," into the hands of aliens (*inoplemenniki*) who were "enemies of Christianity in principle." One day, zemstvo institutions and reformed courts would be introduced into the western provinces, increasing the need for educated people. When the time came to staff these institutions, the peasants would either refuse to elect those alien to them in faith and nationality, with the result that semi-literates would be placed in office, or else the Jews would extend their influence over all aspects of life.

> Yes, Mr. Morgulis, your plan is very good: the Jews, to be sure, will dislodge the Polish element from western Russia sooner than we can. Nonetheless, it seems to us that we will not sin against the wishes of Russian society if we refuse the honor granted to Kiev of being the new Jerusalem, and to western Russia, the second Promised Land. History shows that Poland paid too dearly for this honor. (95:14/VIII/ 1865)[26]

This outburst broke new ground. Shulgin's ferocious rejection of the Jews, before whom even the Poles were preferable, and condemnation of Judaism as anti-Christian, implied that no amount of "internal integration" would ever suffice to merit equal rights for the Jews. This direction was not pursued for the moment. Throughout 1865, *Kievlianin* printed straightforward, if somewhat critical, surveys of Jewish culture and economic life,[27] and through the whole of 1866, not a single editorial or significant article was published on the Jewish Question. This did not mean that Shulgin had forgotten the Jews: his views were merely in a state of gestation.

It took only the exertions of Jewish publicists to bring the Jewish Question back into the columns of *Kievlianin*. Shulgin was suspicious of their motives and their intellectual honesty, prefigured in his 1865 attack on Morgulis' attempt to draw a distinction between the negative activities of Jewish tavern-keepers and factors, and the positive contribution of Jewish capitalists. Shulgin came to see tavern-keepers as an advance guard for the Jewish plutocracy. By ruining the peasants with drink, the Jewish publican delivered them into the hands of their wealthy coreligionists. What could be said of the allegedly high-minded intellectuals who defended the capitalists? Was the sharp division between fanatics and the enlightened in the Jewish community really as deep as it was said to be? These were questions to which Shulgin would return.

Meanwhile, other matters demanded Shulgin's attention, especially a recent law which permitted persons called to the colors to hire a replacement. For the Jewish community, which had been shattered by contention when Jews were made responsible for military service in 1827, the new law was a god-send. Individual communities raised thousands of rubles in order to hire Christian recruits – invariably peasants – in lieu of members of their community. The 50,000 strong Jewish community of Berdichev, for example, reportedly paid 20,000 rubles per annum for Christian substitutes, and provided no army recruits (13:28/I/1867). The situation captured *Kievlianin*'s attention, especially because of the widespread perception that trade in exemption tickets was turning into a racket controlled by Jews.

The situation prompted some editorial musings by Shulgin early in 1867. He reviewed his earlier observations on internal and external integration. Things had not changed, as Jewish publicists continued to demand rights, while ignoring the inimical and self-centered relationship of the Jewish masses toward the economic and moral well-being of the peasantry in the western provinces. The new recruit law served as a contemporary example. Shulgin had no qualms about allowing the Jews to hire substitutes for the army, because he believed that Jews made bad soldiers. The danger was that the Jews might convert the system into a trade, deceiving and misleading recruits, or charging a heavy fee for their services in securing a substitute. The sight of Jews brokering between reluctant conscripts and paid substitutes had all the attributes of Negro slavery, with the Christian peasants being the human goods, and the Jews being the tradesmen. This was nothing less than another form of Jewish exploitation.

Kievlianin launched a journalistic crusade – perhaps reflecting administrative concerns – against abuse of the recruit trade, chronicling misdeeds and conscientiously reprinting articles from other papers (nos. 29, 35, 44 for 1867). Most suggestive was an article by A. V. Gudin-Levkovich which complained that the recruit law had become a special privilege for the Jews. In Podolia province, for example, where the Jewish male population was 102,515 (of a total male population of 825,623), only four army recruits were Jews. At the same time, of the 909 hired substitutes, all were Christians taking the place of Jews. The government had always attempted to impose recruitment equitably, since it was *l'impôt du sang*, but the Jews were making a mockery of this intention. Why should the Jews enjoy this preferential treatment? (43:8/IV/1867).

Gudin-Levkovich's article was *Kievlianin*'s initial contribution to the conceptualization of the Jews as a "privileged race" within the Russian

Empire, soon to become a Judeophobic catch phrase. The slogan gained wide currency through its use in an article entitled "A Jewish Privilege," which appeared in no. 51 of *Moskovskie vedomosti* for 1867. A correspondent wrote to the paper to complain of the obstacles placed in the way of a young Jewess who desired to convert to Russian Orthodoxy. The writer had been informed (incorrectly, in fact), that she could not be baptized until six weeks after her initial declaration of intent, and then only with the permission of the Jewish community. *Moskovskie vedomosti* had been complaining for years about the inappropriate role of the Russian state in safeguarding the purity and authority of an alien religion like Judaism, through such institutions as the state rabbinate (280:20/XII/1864; 149:16/VII/1866; 101:9/V/1867). The person who most successfully popularized this phenomenon, however, was not Katkov, but Ivan Aksakov, once again playing midwife to new themes in the Judeophobic tradition.

Aksakov's *Den* had closed in 1865, due to a lack of subscribers, but in 1867 a group of Moscow merchants, eager to have a paper to argue their interests, especially the need for a protective tariff, persuaded Aksakov to resume his activities in a new paper, *Moskva*, which they financed.[28] The paper was a bitter critic of the government's russification policies, and was continually warned and suspended by the censor until closed by order of the Senate in 1868.

Moskva printed only four articles on the Jewish Question during its brief existence, and only two of these were Aksakov editorials. But as had been the case of the "Jewish banner" and Talmud articles published in *Den*, Aksakov's formulation of the Jewish Question was extremely influential, revealing again his genius for anticipating new developments in Russian Judeophobia. In a *Moskva* editorial Aksakov skillfully wove many diverse threads together. "One of the most privileged races (*plemeni*) in Russia," he wrote, "is undoubtedly the Jews in our western and southern provinces." Such a contention might seem strange, Aksakov admitted, to those who had become accustomed to thinking of the Jews as a persecuted and downtrodden minority, for whom any humane and educated person must feel special sympathy. Unfortunately, under this impression, the Russian government promulgated a whole series of special privileges for them. Now, at a time when Jews were almost equal in rights with Christians, except for residence in the Great Russian interior, they still retained the privilege of a protected, autonomous Jewish community. Almost one year after the first appearance of Brafman's first article in *Vilenskii vestnik*, and well before publication of any of his books, Aksakov attacked the Jews as a dangerous corporate entity.

> The contemporary structure of the Jews constitutes a *status in statu* in the western region, where the wisdom of the Polish kings and the Polish szlachta long ago strengthened Jewish domination. They agitate for the emancipation of the Jews. The question should be put differently – it is not a question of the emancipation of the Jews, but of the emancipation of the Russian population from the Jews, of the freeing of the Russian people in the West and partly in the South of Russia from the Jewish yoke. (84:15/VII/1867)[29]

This article, reprinted almost in its entirety in a *Kievlianin* editorial (91:1/VIII/1867), revealed to Shulgin the kahal in all its glory (although *Kievlianin* correspondents had been routinely discussing the kahal, burial societies and communal price-fixing).[30] Shulgin keenly anticipated publication of Brafman's "splendid work," while *Kievlianin* began its own investigation of Jewish privileges. The newspaper's discussion of the Jewish Question in 1868 was dominated by a lengthy and detailed study of the special Jewish tax system, especially the "Basket Tax" assessed on kosher meat, which Shulgin denounced as a special Jewish privilege and a prop of the *status in statu* (105:3/IX/; 106:5/IX and 107:7/IX/1867). As yet, however, Shulgin did not appreciate the full significance of Brafman's discoveries.

The paper continued its crusade against Jewish exploitation with an 1868 exposé of the impact of the Jewish tavern on the prosperity of the peasant village (93:6/VIII/1868). In 1869, *Kievlianin* denounced the Jews for circumventing the prohibition on ownership of land by acquiring long-term leases on estates. To justify a ban on all Jewish leaseholding in the area, *Kievlianin* explored in detail the allegedly ruinous impact of Jewish leases on the local economy.[31]

The campaign against exploitation roughly coincided with the administration of a new Governor-General in the Southwest Region, Prince A. M. Dondukov-Korsakov. A ban on Jewish leaseholding of any sort soon became a policy especially associated with his administration. It is unclear whether this concern of the new Governor-General was merely reflected by Shulgin, or whether the continuing exposé of leaseholding abuses by *Kievlianin* attracted the attention of Dondukov-Korsakov. Weight is lent to the latter supposition by the fact that Dondukov-Korsakov's predecessor, A. P. Bezak, died unexpectedly on 30 December 1868, and Dondukov-Korsakov was not at his post for more than a few weeks when the *Kievlianin* articles – obviously well-researched – began to appear.

Kievlianin continued to develop another theme, the lack of objectivity and egotism of Jewish publicists. In the past, the paper's attack had taken the form of pot-shots at Jewish spokesmen who appeared in the Russian press. In 1869, *Kievlianin* found a more substantial target in the form of the Odessa-based Russian–Jewish newspaper *Den*, provocatively subtitled "the organ of Russian Jews" and edited by a group of young Odessa Jewish intellectuals, including M. Morgulis, the object of Shulgin's wrath in 1865. The editors, schooled almost to a man in Russian educational institutions, vigorously attacked the enemies of the Jews, and stridently demanded that Jews be given equal rights without preconditions. Understandably, *Kievlianin* and *Den* were linked in polemics until *Den*'s demise in the spring of 1871. They debated the question of equal rights, the nature of the Jewish community, and the economic role of the Jews in the southwest. Each exchange sharpened Shulgin's existing animosity toward the Jewish intelligentsia.

Two weeks after the initial appearance of *Den* on 16 May 1869, Shulgin began a series of editorials devoted to the Russian–Jewish intelligentsia, in the guise of a review of Joachim Tarnopol's *An Attempt at a Contemporary Review of Reform in the Area of Judaism in Russia*. Tarnopol's work had been written a decade previously, but only received censorship clearance for publication in 1868. Tarnopol belonged to the school of publicists who advocated internal reform preparatory to the acquisition of full civil rights. His work provided a convenient stick with which to beat reformers who demanded more.

Shulgin reiterated his criticism of Jewish progressives who claimed that integration could only be achieved through expanding the rights of Jews, while introducing a new element. Modern, enlightened Jews, he claimed, were indifferent to the religious faith of their fathers. They retained only a narrow, nationalistic exclusiveness, albeit masked in religious phraseology (65:5/VI/1869; 66:7/VI/1869). In a subsequent article Shulgin asked, "Which Jews Agitate for the Jews?," while leveling criticisms against *Den*. Progressive Jews claimed to support merger or integration, but Shulgin detected a false note in the Jewish choir. "In general, these people are very liberal and humane – for themselves. They speak very well when the discussion concerns only the Jews and doesn't touch the interests of the rest of the population. But let matters concern the latter – and all this liberalism and humanity is put aside" (99:23/VIII/1869).

Then, in 1869, *The Book of the Kahal* appeared, providing a master key to explain all the Jews' sins. *Kievlianin* enthusiastically welcomed the book, devoting two lengthy lead articles to a review, while also printing reviews from other newspapers.[32] Shulgin proclaimed the significance of Brafman's discovery: "In the midst [of the Jewish people] many horrid things have been created, the obscurantism of diabolical superstition, fanaticism, while many thousands of Jewish heads are crammed with perverted conceptions; but the moral responsibility for all this muddle falls exclusively upon Jewish institutions, and on the Jewish government" (39:31/III/1870). Who, the paper asked, rushed to attack these revelations? – the Jewish intelligentsia. *Kievlianin* became the defender of the faith against Brafman's critics, airily dismissing all criticism. *Kievlianin* made an additional, devastating point: the Jewish publicists of *Rassvet, Sion* and *Den* could not have failed to know about the abuses of the kahal, so why had they never said anything about them? Was it because they were more concerned with protecting their own personal interests, by speaking patriotic lies? (104:1/IX/1870) Elsewhere, in an editorial entitled "The Strength of the Kahal," Shulgin suggested that the attacks on Brafman that were emanating from Jewish intellectuals were merely another indication of the kahal's power (94:8/VIII/1870).

Following Brafman, Shulgin united all threads of previous *Kievlianin* criticisms. Enlightened, progressive Jews never criticized the kahal because they were its agents. Brafman described the kahal as a Jewish national entity. Critics could now see that Jewish intellectuals served it through their narrow, nationalistic, particularistic interests. The following year, Shulgin closed the circle by including all Jews within the rubrics of the kahal, seeing them as united in their exploitation of the Christian population and pursuit of Jewish national interests. *Kievlianin* blamed the outbreak of the Odessa pogrom in March 1871 on the Jews themselves whose economic exploitation drove their neighbors to violent self-defense. Shulgin gave enthusiastic editorial support to the account of an Odessa correspondent.

> The chief cause of the disorders lies in the fact that the Jewish population exercises great advantages in Odessa: in their hands is a large part of the trade ... they have priority in all other fields of endeavor ... soon all the land of Bessarabia and Kherson provinces will pass under their control; everywhere there is ruin [as a result of] the Jews – doctors, grain-brokers, those who serve in virtually every office, on the railroad and in other institutions. Rich Jews use their wealth and influence to secure advantageous occupations, positions, jobs and work for their little brothers, to the detriment of Russians, be they government officials, landowners, doctors, tradesmen, craftsmen or common laborers.

If all Jews, merely by being Jews, were part of the same vast kahal, then there was nothing more to be said, and no need to strive for balance and objectivity. Thus inspired, *Kievlianin* evolved into the archetypal Judeophobic newspaper. Under Shulgin, *Kievlianin's* Judeophobia remained sophisticated, with an objective foundation. Attacks on the Jews were justified with facts and figures drawn from official sources, especially documentation concerning Jewish domination of the liquor trade, and Jewish draft-dodging after the introduction of universal military service in 1874. From this perspective, *Kievlianin* could be described as a purveyor of "principled Judeophobia," which adhered to certain rules, developed an inner consistency, and sought objective evidence for its criticism.

Yet *Kievlianin* came to illustrate the Russian proverb that "to live with wolves you must learn to howl" once the paper opened its columns to purveyors of fantastic, occult forms of European Antisemitism. Thus, in 1873, *Kievlianin* published, in four issues, "The Jewish Cemetery in Prague." While the work was clearly identified as a "legendary description," taken from the "historical novel of Sir John Redcliffe" (sic), it was the first appearance in Russia of this prototype of *The Protocols of the Elders of Zion*.[33] *Kievlianin* also reprinted K. Kozlovskii's credulous pamphlet on ritual murder, although in general Shulgin avoided this topic, even when other Judeophobic organs embraced it eagerly.[34] Likewise, *Kievlianin* found room in its review columns for such third-rate works of Judeophobia as Maior Osman-Bei's *The Conquest of the World by the Jews*.[35]

Despite *Kievlianin's* subsequent reputation as the quintessential Judeophobic newspaper, it always retained one peculiarity under Shulgin's editorship: consistent and energetic rejection of the Pale of Settlement. If this position appeared anomalous at first glance, it was based upon an assumption far from sympathetic to the Jews: since Jews were exploiters, an ulcer and yoke, as *Kievlianin* variously described them, the Ukraine should not be forced to serve as their sole dwelling place. This situation reveals the danger of superficially applying the term Judeophobic to Russian periodicals, without setting specific criteria. Assumptions hostile to the Jews, such as those held by Shulgin and *Kievlianin* could produce policy recommendations, such as the abolition of the Pale of Settlement, that were of great benefit to the Jews, and avidly advocated by Jewish spokesmen. By the same token, it was possible for liberal newspapers, which professed to be sympathetic to the Jews and their sufferings, to reject major legislative remedies for the Pale, out of concern for the economic consequences which would befall various social groups, but chiefly the peasantry.

Shulgin's opposition to the Pale developed from an amalgam of sympathy for the plight of the Jews, concern for local economic interests, and the conviction that it was the only way of resolving the Jewish Question. In 1864 Shulgin actually incurred the wrath of the local authorities – and was forced to issue an oblique apology – for criticizing police treatment of the Jews.

Kiev was technically, but not geographically, outside the Pale, and residence was restricted to the small category of Jewish first guild merchants. Even they were confined to the two undesirable districts of Libed and Plosk. Under the indulgent policies of Count Vasilchikov, thousands of Jews settled in Kiev, many of them illegally. The police were usually kept at bay by bribery, but they periodically conducted "hunts" or "round-ups" (*oblava*) and forcibly evicted Jews who lacked proper documentation.[36]

Perhaps reflecting the interests of local householders who rented accommodation to Jews, or businessmen who had dealings with them, Shulgin criticized the capriciousness and violence with which the "hunts" were conducted. Laws must be obeyed, he declared, but not in ways which disrupted the peace and economic order of the city. It was not humane to expel Jews from the city precipitously, in the dead of winter, and still less acceptable to rescind expulsion orders at the last possible minute (45:13/X/1864). In another context, Shulgin concluded a series on Hasidism with a call to reduce Jewish fanaticism by destroying the charmed circle in which Jews lived and by scattering them across the Empire (35:19/IX/1864).

Moving from the specific example of Kiev to the Pale in general, Shulgin criticized the concept of residence restrictions. "Taking care that Great Russia, which never did suffer from Jews, does not suffer from them now, we cluster them artificially in Western and Little Russia, which have in the past suffered much from them, and are still suffering at present." If the Jews were allowed to settle throughout Russia, on the other hand, they would be lost like a drop of water in the sea. This argument, which included a striking characterization of the Jews as "the last enserfed group in Russia," made use of familiar arguments which were Judeophile at heart, even though they accepted without question the assumption of Jewish exploitation. Shulgin conceded the premise, usually voiced by Russian liberals, that the flaws of the Jews were the consequence of persecution and discrimination. This assumption underlay his formula of "interior" and "exterior" emancipation, and was retained even after Shulgin accepted Brafman's kahal-centered explanation of Jewish exploitation. In 1869, even as Brafman was being given a place of honor in his columns, Shulgin editorialized that "we recognize admission of the Jews to the interior provinces of Great Russia as one of the necessary first conditions for the resolution of the Jewish Question" (113:25/IX/ 1869).

Events never budged Shulgin from this assumption. Even when *Kievlianin* was locked in polemics over the economic role of the Jews in the Ukraine with *Den*, whose editorial keystone was the abolition of the Pale, Shulgin continued to assert that in this one instance the Jewish publicists were correct (92:7/VIII/1869; 111:16/IX/1872). The Odessa pogrom of 1871 – unlike those a decade later – also failed to work a change in *Kievlianin*'s attitude. Attributing the pogrom to Jewish exploitation, Shulgin agreed with those who advocated opening the Pale as a means of preventing such social tensions (48:22/ IV/1872). In 1873, by which time *Kievlianin* was securely in the Judeo-phobe camp, articles insisted on the removal of the Pale. In that same year, as Shulgin applauded the diligence of the police at hounding out illegally resident Jews and warned against their purchase of real estate in Kiev, he still called for the abolition of the Pale (26:1/III/1873; 40:3/IV/1873). One of the last major series of editorials which Shulgin published in *Kievlianin* in 1876, a statistical overview of the Jewish population of Western Europe, was devoted to the premise that where the Jews were found less concentrated and thus less able to harm others, they lived better themselves, and state and society viewed them more positively (65:1/VI/1876; 66:3/VI/1876).

Kievlianin's opposition to the Pale survived Shulgin's death only by a few years. The outbreak of violent pogroms across the Ukraine in 1881, including Kiev, fed the fear that the dissemination of the Jews outside the Pale would lead to the spread of violence. *Kievlianin*, now under the editorship of Shulgin's protégé D. I. Pikhno – a far less sophisti-cated Judeophobe – strongly supported retention of the Pale.

The relationship between public opinion and official policy is diffi-cult to establish in any society, while imperial Russia presents special problems in tracing lines of influence. *Kievlianin*, as a semi-official newspaper with a special interest in the Jewish Question, offers an appropriate medium to explore the relationship of official policy to public opinion.

The apparent influence of *Kievlianin* on the Governor-General's office regarding Jewish land and lease-holding has already been

18 Prince A. M. Dondukov-Korsakov

considered. In the case of Governor-General Dondukov-Korsakov, much is known about his outlook on the Jewish Question from a 26 October 1872 memorandum to Tsar Alexander II.

Dondukov-Korsakov saw the Jews as virtually the most important problem confronting the government. As Hans Rogger has observed, this memorandum was something of a novelty because it examined not only the relationship of Jews to land and to those who lived on or by it, but also viewed in a new and largely negative light Jewish industrialists and manufacturers. These "productive" elements – in contrast to "unproductive" tradesmen, money-lenders and brokers – had heretofore been favored for their role in economic development.[37]

The Prince cited statistics to warn against the domination of Jewish capital in the Ukraine. There was one Jew for every seven Christians in the Governor-Generalship, yet they made up 32 percent of the urban population, 53 percent in shtetlakh, and 14 percent in peasant villages. Jews rented 819 estates, and had so many informal contracts that "it can be said that one-sixth of all estates are in their hands." In addition, Jews owned 108 sugar refineries, 500 (of 564) distilleries, 119 (of 148) breweries, 527 additional factories, 15,000 shops and 190,000 public houses, inns and taverns. They dominated trade in lumber and grain, the export business in these and other commodities, and served the government as contractors.

Dondukov-Korsakov's concerns would have been familiar to any reader of *Kievlianin*. Shortly before his appointment, the paper had warned of the overconcentration of Jews in the urban economy, where they controlled 36 percent of factories (except distilleries, where the percentage was higher), and warned that they were reaching out to control the only area of the economy heretofore closed to them – agriculture (93:6/VIII/1868). On 27 May 1872, Shulgin published the figures of Dondukov-Korsakov's memorandum, which had been submitted to the newspaper by the Governor-General's office (74:22/VI/1872).

While the press and administration appeared to share common perspectives and goals, there were a few significant differences in their use of statistics. Dondukov-Korsakov's concerns reflected a significant strand of modern Judeophobia and Antisemitism, the fear of economic domination by large Jewish capitalists. This element was virtually absent from Shulgin's world view. An 1868 editorial, "Jews and Vodka," while noting the role of Jewish capital in the local economy, was concerned only with its impact on the liquor trade and peasant drunkenness. Shulgin's use of the figures from the Governor-General's office in 1873 is even more revealing: he employed them to demonstrate that, despite the special pleading of Jewish publicists about the poverty and pauperization of the Jewish masses, the Jews actually lived well within the Pale, albeit at the expense of the Christian population. Shulgin's more traditional concerns were precisely with the "unproductive" elements in the Jewish population. While Dondukov-Korsakov warned of the power of big Jewish capital, Shulgin remained concerned with the petty Jewish tavernkeeper. At this juncture, then, official attitudes were in advance of public opinion in forging a fully modern antisemitic world-view. Nor did Shulgin personally ever catch up, since *Kievlianin* remained unconcerned with the large Jewish enterprises that alarmed other Judeophobes. Perhaps this was a reflection of Shulgin's own gentry origins, which allowed him to see the threat to the Russian land, yet left him cold to the significance of capital accumulation. Yet on other occasions Shulgin showed himself keenly interested in local development, and advocated modernizing banking and rail construction schemes. Perhaps this was the key: Shulgin was unconcerned with the creation of "Jewish" wealth, because it worked to the good of the area, and presumably was not drawn from exploitation or unproductive work.

In other areas, journalistic influence on the Governor-General was undeniable. Elaborating his alarm at Jewish domination of the Southwest, Dondukov-Korsakov observed that "the cause of every last Jew is also the cause of the world-wide Jewish kahal ... that powerful yet elusive association."[38] It is unclear only whether Dondukov-Korsakov imbibed Brafman directly from *The Book of the Kahal,* or indirectly from *Kievlianin.*

Certainly the memorandum's remedies for resolving the Jewish Question echo Shulgin's editorial line, almost chapter and verse. The partisans of the Jews desired equal rights, on abstract, theoretical grounds, from legalistic or humanitarian principles, declared the Prince. They forgot that rights go with obligations, and that only the educated part of Jewry was prepared to fulfill them. On the other hand, a proper resolution was not to be found in locking up the Jews in certain locales and by imposing greater restrictions and disabilities. Such a course would only strengthen the power of the Jews within the Pale, make them still more crowded and impoverished, and create conditions of evasion and lawlessness which no amount of regulation could control. The Jews must be permitted to settle in other parts of the Empire where they would follow a different way of life and accept different values and ideas, while totally abandoning their national identity. The kulaks, merchants and enterprising peasants of the interior would provide effective competition and make impossible the conditions of economic exploitation.[39]

The Judeophobes of the Ukraine, represented by Shulgin, *Kievlianin* and Dondukov-Korsakov, were ahead of their time. Their warnings against Jewish economic control of land and capital were challenged within the Jewish Committee in St. Petersburg.[40] Their proposals to abolish the Pale were similarly unacceptable. Only in the future did much of what they had to say, except for their opposition to the Pale, become conventional wisdom, especially when tied together by Brafman's thesis. Connections between the Governor-General's office – to say nothing of the editorial office of *Kievlianin* – and the Jewish Committees of the capital are harder to establish, given the many different influences and sources of information and prejudice brought to bear on such committees. Nonetheless, their judgments were given a respectful hearing there. *Kievlianin* established itself as an able and articulate voice of Russian Judeophobia, active in shaping a growing anti-Jewish consensus, in and out of government. While surely not Shulgin's original intention, this became one of the paper's best known journalistic roles, which it fulfilled until the revolutions of 1917.

9 "Kiev is Ukrainian"

The boast of Russifiers that "Kiev is Russian" was sustainable only by annexing to their cause the numerically preponderant peasant population, heretofore condescendingly viewed as the "Little Russians." Yet a rival claim was made to the hearts, if not to the minds, of this same population by a group known as the Ukrainophiles. The very name of this movement of nationally conscious intellectuals is revealing. It implied awareness of the Southwest as a distinct entity, Ukraine, with its own unique language, culture and historical memory. The Ukraine was never an integral part of the Polish state, they claimed, but had been a victim of Polish aggression and misgovernment. They denied that the Ukraine was a mere adjunct of "Great Russia," with a corrupted dialect of the Russian language, and a cultural level far below that of the Muscovite heartland.

The emergence of Ukrainian national consciousness presented difficulties for Russian intellectuals. It could be welcomed as a force hostile to Polish nationalist dreams of a restoration of the borders of 1772. The movement had a genuinely progressive pedigree with democratic and anti-feudal components. It was not separatist in any real sense at this time. Indeed, the strength of Poland in the Ukraine, in the form of the landowning classes and the Catholic Church, encouraged the Ukrainophiles to look to Russia, albeit to one freed of its centralizing, bureaucratic inclinations. However remote its objective threat to Russian power, Ukrainophilism had potential to evolve into a disruptive force. In the heated environment of the Polish revolt of 1863, Russifiers were reluctant to give the Ukrainophiles the benefit of a doubt.[1]

Ukrainophilism can be dated to the 1840s, when intellectual leadership in the Ukraine began to pass slowly from the aristocratic Polonized gentry into the hands of petty gentry, middle class and even peasant elements. It was the creation of Ukrainian intellectuals who had studied in the two Russian universities of the Ukraine, in Kiev and Kharkov. They were inspired by the tenets of Romanticism, from which so many of the national movements of the nineteenth century drew inspiration and strength. They also developed an altruistic concern for the Ukrainian peasantry. In 1845–6, led by N. I. Kostomarov, N. I. Gulak and V. M. Belozerskii (Bilozers'kyi), they organized the Brotherhood of Saints Cyrill and Methodius in Kiev. It included among its sympathizers Taras Shevchenko, the Ukrainian national poet, and the future Ukrainophile leader, P. A. Kulish. The society was anti-monarchist and anti-feudal, and dreamed of a free confederation of Slavic communities, including the Ukraine. This organizational phase ended abruptly when the society was betrayed to the authorities in 1847, and its members arrested, imprisoned and exiled.[2]

As was the case of many proto-nationalist movements, all the leaders of the early Ukrainophile movement could fit in one room or, in this case, in one prison. Consequently, Ukrainophilism remained in suspended animation until the late 1850s when the victims of 1847, older and wiser, were amnestied by Alexander II. Kostomarov, Kulish, Shevchenko, Belozerskii and others settled in St. Petersburg, where they regenerated the Ukrainophile movement. Eschewing the political dreams of the earlier Brotherhood, they engaged in creative and ethnographic work, designed to make Ukrainian a recognized literary language and to preserve the distinctive culture and folklore of the Ukrainian masses. These undertakings were pursued in St. Petersburg through a society called the Hromada (the Ukrainian village community), which soon inspired similarly named organizations throughout the Ukraine. These societies organized schools, published and distributed Ukrainian books and promoted Ukrainian cultural events. Ukrainian students organized a Sunday School movement, designed to increase popular literacy in the Ukrainian language. After tortuous negotiations with the central government, the St. Petersburg Ukrainian leadership secured permission to issue its own periodical. From 1861 to 1862, Belozerskii and Kulish published *Osnova* in Russian and Ukrainian. Virtually every important Ukrainian intellectual, great and small, published in *Osnova* during its brief existence.[3]

The very existence of *Osnova* created a target, and the editors found themselves involved in polemics from beginning to end. Even before its first issue appeared, the Polish newspaper *Czas* of Cracow and the French *Revue Contemporaine* denied the existence of a separate Ukrainian people or of a Ukrainian language.[4] More serious, because close to home and near the seats of power, were the criticisms of Russifiers, led by Katkov, and the Slavophiles, represented by Ivan Aksakov. Katkov, initially sympathetic to educational efforts in Ukrainian, grew into a bitter enemy of Ukrainophilism. He polemicized with *Osnova*, dismissing in 1861 the journal's claims for Ukrainian, and claiming that it was no more than a dialect, closer to Russian than *Plattdeutsch* was to *Hochdeutsch*. As the crisis in Poland degenerated into open warfare, his accusations grew malevolent. In 1863 Katkov declared that

> we know that the most fanatic Polish agitators expect that sooner or later Ukrainophilism will have a special use for their cause. Can it really be that our Ukrainophiles are unconsciously involved in the intrigue; can it really be that they will work for it, even now, at a time when the people of the Ukraine so energetically show their allegiance for our common Fatherland?[5]

Ivan Aksakov also saw the Ukrainophiles as dupes of a Polish intrigue. Their activities gave rise to fears of "separatism" in the Ukraine – a fear which Aksakov scornfully dismissed – and thus distracted Russian society from the real danger to the area, in the shape of the Poles and their pretensions.[6] The sentiments of both Katkov and Aksakov found reflection in the columns of *Kievlianin*, which was the foremost provincial adversary of Ukrainian "separatism." These denunciations bore fruit rapidly, for in 1863 the Minister of Internal Affairs, P. A. Valuev, issued an order forbidding the publication of Ukrainian books, excepting *belles-lettres*. Valuev was motivated by concern that many cheap editions of Ukrainian books were being published by persons of dubious political reliability. He claimed that most Ukrainians denied that their language was a separate one from Russian. "There is not now, nor can there be a separate Ukrainian tongue – that dialect used by the common people is Russian, corrupted by Polish influence."[7] The Ukrainian Sunday Schools were closed as well.

The actions of the Russian government slowed, but did not destroy the Ukrainophile movement. The center of cultural activity shifted to Kiev where a new generation of activists, inspired by the ideals of the Russian populist movement, clustered around the underground Kiev Stara Hromada (Old Community). Efforts were made to place the study of Ukrainian culture on scientific principles, through the establishment of a Southwestern Branch of the Imperial Geographical Society in 1873. The Society published extensive investigations of Ukrainian life, highlighted by P. P. Chubinskii's (Chubins'kyi) multi-volume examination of the ethnography of Right-Bank Ukraine and collections of popular songs and stories by V. Antonovich (V. Antonovych) and M. Dragomanov (Drahomanov).[8] In 1875, the Kiev Hromada acquired the liberal Kiev daily newspaper *Kievskii telegraf* to act as its mouthpiece. This accelerating activity once again alarmed the central government, as denunciations of "separatism" arrived in the capital from local Russifiers. In 1876, after reception of a critical report from an investigating commission, Tsar Alexander once more struck against the Ukrainophiles. The Southwestern Branch of the Imperial Geographical Society was dissolved, *Kievskii telegraf* was closed and, most importantly, a secret ukaz, the Ems Decree of 18 May 1876, prohibited the publication or importation of all Ukrainian books, and banned Ukrainian musical or theatrical performances. Prominent Ukrainian intellectuals, such as Mikhail Dragomanov at the St. Vladimir University of Kiev, were deprived of their academic posts.[9]

A survey of the vicissitudes of the Ukrainophile movement is necessary in order to understand the attitudes of nationalist Ukrainian intellectuals toward the Jewish Question, formed as they were against the backdrop of emergent Ukrainian national consciousness, the rediscovery of the Ukrainian past, and persecution at the hands of Russian officialdom and Russian public opinion.

Ukrainophile historians and ethnographers found much to admire in their past. There was the image of the "wild field," free from serfdom and social inequality, ruled by the "Sich" or brotherhood of free Cossacks. This romantic picture had a dark side, however, in the loss of Cossack freedom, first to Poland and then to Russia. Regretted too was the enslavement of the free Ukrainian people to Polish institutions, both secular and religious. As a folk song cited by Dragomanov put it:

> Would it not be better,
> Would it not be more beautiful,
> If in the Ukraine,
> There was no Jew,
> There was no Pole,
> There was no Union.[10]

In popular imagery, the Jew was an integral part of the system of exploitation imposed upon the Ukraine by the Poles. A familiar folk motif was that of the Jewish leaseholder on a Polish estate controlling the keys to the local Orthodox church, and demanding his handful of coins before baptisms, weddings or burials could take place.[11] The moment that shone most brightly in the Ukrainian national memory, the uprising of Bogdan Khmelnytsky in 1648, was simultaneously one of the blackest periods in the history of Ukrainian Jewry, who were principal victims of the wild violence unleashed by the uprising. Past

wrongs were not easily forgotten by those ready to suffer in the
present for the "good of the people." As the leaders of the
Brotherhood of Saints Cyrill and Methodius put it in their "Catechism," one of the fundamental declarations of their movement:

> Article 83. But the lords saw that the Cossack life was growing and
> that soon everybody would become Cossacks (i.e., free) and they
> forbade their slaves to enter the Cossack life and, desiring to
> slaughter the common people like cattle and so that they would have
> neither feeling nor sense, the lords began to flay their slaves, to hand
> them over to the Jews for such torment as was only worked upon the
> first Christians, to skin them alive, to boil their children, to give their
> mothers dogs to nurse.[12]

It is no wonder that when the presumed compiler of the "Catechism,"
N. Kostomarov, was exiled to the interior, to Saratov, on government
service, he was ready to believe that individual Jews were guilty of the
ritual murder of Christian children.[13]

In short, the question is not why Ukrainophiles might be hostile to
the Jews – in their own minds there was much justification for that –
but why they should go out of their way to be sympathetic to the Jews.
The celebrated episode of the Literary Protest of 1858 provides a telling
example.

The Literary Protest offered a useful opportunity to the reconstituted Ukrainophile movement, with P. A. Kulish temporarily at its
head. Its adepts had recently returned from political exile, and their
future publications were only long-postponed dreams. Simultaneously with the Protest Kulish was denied permission to publish an
Ukrainophile periodical. His circle was increasingly frustrated at the
need to "preach the resurrection of the dead and to awaken those who
are asleep."[14] It was not enough to simply second the existing Protest.
Instead it was given a Ukrainophile perspective and used to broach the
delicate topic of Ukrainian–Jewish relations. Kulish attributed the
negative characteristics of the Jews to Christian intolerance, which
employed harsh persecution in a misguided effort to attract Jews "to
the path of righteousness." In return, Jews endeavored to harm Christians in every possible way, bolstering their hatred with religious
sanctions. Only in old Poland had the corrupt religious and civil order
actually given the Jews the opportunity to revenge themselves upon
the hapless Ukrainian Christian population. The Ukrainians in turn
visited a terrible vengence upon the Jews, convinced in their hearts of
the justice of their cause.[15]

From Kulish's point of view, his letter was a generous initiative to the Jewish community, through their spokesmen in the press. The Ukrainophiles were inspired by a spirit different from that of the blood-letters of the past. They called for "unhindered education and equality of civil rights [which] can cleanse the Jewish nation of all that is hostile in it to the peoples of other faiths."

What appeared generous and enlightened to the St. Petersburg Hromada did not strike a resonant cord in the Jewish intelligentsia. While they could accept, as we have seen, the charge that the Jews engaged in exploitative activity, they could never agree that Jewish hatred of Christians was religiously sanctified. Ukrainophile respect for the "simple-hearted justice" of the Ukrainian people could hardly appease Jewish sensitivity over some of the most notorious episodes of Jewish martyrology in Eastern Europe. However sincere the initiative toward Ukrainian–Jewish reconciliation envisioned by Kulish's letter, it was totally ignored by Jewish writers.

By the time of the *Osnova–Sion* polemic, a bare three years later, much had changed. Both the Ukrainophiles and the Russified Jewish intelligentsia now had their own periodicals, and neither group could rely any longer on the automatic sympathy of most of Russian opinion. *Osnova* was forced to contend with critics who denied the very existence of a separate Ukrainian nationality and language. *Sion* was determined to emphasize Jewish national worth, rather than belabor national faults. Meanwhile, the Ukrainophile movement had made significant gains. One of the most striking was the decision of a group of young Polonized Ukrainian university students in Kiev to leave the camp of the Poles, deep in the throes of the agitation which would lead to the uprising of 1863, and side with the Ukrainian people. Led by Vladimir Antonovich (Volodymyr Antonovych), who published his celebrated "Confession" in *Osnova*, they rejected their past ties to Poland, which had made them "hated strangers, parasites and exploiters, enemies of this [Ukrainian] people."[16] Such declarations earned them the nickname of "peasant-lovers" (*khlopomany*).

Roman Serbyn has suggested that the *Osnova* group, as well as other Ukrainophiles, were hoping at this time for similar gestures from the Jewish community.[17] Such gestures were not forthcoming. Instead the Ukrainophiles received Portugalov's anonymous letter chiding *Osnova* for using the term "Yid." To a very limited extent Portugalov's letter was provocative, with its warning to the editors to avoid medieval enmity or a return to the times of Bogdan Khmelnytsky. Still, there was no need to provoke a scandal, the more so because the author balanced his attack with wishes for the success of *Osnova* and hopes for the good of the Ukraine. Portugalov himself, it will be remembered, had asked the editors to keep his letter confidential.[18] Having violated Portugalov's wishes, the editors went beyond their legitimate defense of the use of "Yid" to complain that "the Jews have nothing in common with our people, do not take one step toward rapprochement with them, and not infrequently act contrary to their interests and welfare."[19] Even then, however, the editors offered the remnants of an olive branch, promising that any energies that the Jews directed to the needs of the Ukraine and its people would be greeted with "true joy and love."[20]

Once *Sion* responded to the attack, however, the mood turned distinctly ugly. Kulish attacked the "blind national egoism" of the "leading Jews" who used words like "progress, civilization and human enlightenment" to shield their misdeeds.[21] Kostomarov's "To the Judeans," was more vitriolic and abusive still. In part his anger arose from the support that the rest of the press appeared to be giving *Sion* in the debate. This was reinforced by his frustration at the refusal of the Jewish publicists to fight fairly: instead of debate, he claimed, they accused their opponents of Ukrainian separatism, an act of political denunciation. Kostomarov introduced an important element into the anti-Jewish antipathy of the Ukrainophiles. Kulish's original letter to *Russkii vestnik* had been conscientious in blaming the negative elements in the Jewish national character upon Christian persecution and the religious-political order of Poland. Kostomarov, on the other hand, gave these faults a pre-Christian genesis. While Christians gave the scriptures a spiritual reading, Jews elaborated them to promote national alienation, the arrogance of a chosen people, lack of loyalty to any other land but Palestine, expectation of a Messiah who would give them domination over the world, and extreme self-interest, manifested in their relentless pursuit of money.[22]

The Kostomarov article in the *Osnova–Sion* polemic exemplified a recurrent phenomenon in Ukrainian–Jewish relations. An initiative, full of expressions of good faith and reconciliation, was made to the leadership of the Jewish community. In the event of their failure to respond in an acceptable way, which usually required them to acknowledge grievous charges, they themselves became a target for abuse and recrimination, which usually exceeded the charges initially made against the Jews. Even if Kostomarov ended his condemnation of the Jews with the hope that they would be granted full civil rights, his motive was the same one that impelled *Kievlianin* to espouse abolition of the Pale: the hope that the Jews would be able to pursue wider fields (i.e., to end their overconcentration in the Ukraine by emigration elsewhere).

Kulish and Kostomarov both expressed the desire to end their fruitless polemic with Jewish intellectuals even before they lost their platform with the closing of *Osnova* in September of 1862. The following year brought Valuev's crippling decree. Ukrainophiles now had greater preoccupations than the Jews. Yet the period of quiet, "organic" cultural work which dominated the next ten years did not neglect the problem. Jewish subjects figured prominently in the collections of Ukrainian folklore compiled by Antonovich and Dragomanov, published by the Southwestern Branch of the Imperial Geographical Society. The entire seventh volume of P. P. Chubinskii's detailed study of the ethnography of the southwest was devoted to the Jews and Poles (and recommended repressive measures against the Jews in order to end their domination of the marketplace).

The period after 1876 saw the Jewish Question still on the agenda. In the mid-1870s, Ukrainians began to enter the Russian populist movement in greater numbers. Some submerged themselves in the general Russian movement, but a few related the movement to the specific problems of Ukrainian life and made the Ukrainian people the center of their activities. Revolutionaries such as Sergei Podolinskii (Serhii Podolyns'kyi) published Ukrainian translations of Russian populist agitational materials in which Jews were specifically added to the list of enemies and exploiters of the people. These tactics provoked a private debate on the Jewish Question within the circle of Russian populists grouped around the newspaper *Vpered!* in Geneva.[23]

The Ukrainian socialists never developed a central leadership organization which could make definitive statements on ideology. The authority of prominent individuals was paramount. Of all Ukrainian activists and intellectuals of this period, the most respected was Mikhail Dragomanov, who went into political emigration in 1876. Given Dragomanov's intellectual stature, and the fact that he was keenly interested in the Jewish Question in the Ukraine, it is not surprising that much has been written about his attitudes toward the Jews. Many articles have pursued the sterile debate as to whether or not Dragomanov was an "Antisemite."[24] Little more than a superficial effort has been made to place Dragomanov's attitudes toward the Jews in the context of his total world view, beyond a few facile efforts to rationalize Judeophobe statements by invoking his "Cossack-Haidamak roots." An accurate understanding of Dragomanov's evolving position on the Jews over a decade is explicable only if placed in a broader context.

19 M. P. Dragomanov

By 1875, after years of education and foreign travel which included visits to "Ruthenian" (i.e., Ukrainian) communities in Austrian Galicia, the main framework of Dragomanov's thought was in place.[25] He was a Ukrainian patriot, a democrat and a socialist. The legs of this triad were mutually reinforcing. As a member of a persecuted minority, the very existence and culture of which was denied by the Russian state, Dragomanov sought to establish the validity of Ukrainian national identity, to create a just and equitable Ukrainian society in which national identity could find range and scope, and to work toward an overarching political system in which a common democracy and cultural-political autonomy would ensure the unhindered development of Ukrainian (and other) national identities.

As an historian and folklorist, Dragomanov sought to recapture the essential and distinctive elements of the Ukrainian past. He found these in the democratic spirit of the Cossack Hosts which produced not only a rough frontier equality, but also conditions for the growth of a sophisticated civilization mediating between Russia and the West. Menaced in the seventeenth century by the military might of the Ottoman Empire and Poland, with their antipathetic religious and social systems, the Cossacks had turned to Russia for protection, only to be stripped of their freedom and saddled with an inequitable social and political system. Russian overlordship did have its good side. By weakening the Cossacks, who despite their ideals of freedom always threatened to evolve into a ruling class, the Russians had made a "plebeian nation" of the Ukraine, all of whose inhabitants were in the same general social category. This social uniformity could expedite the evolution of a national community pursuing a program of ethical socialism. Given the importance which Dragomanov attached to this objective, it is understandable that he was a persistent critic of Ukrainian intellectuals who turned their backs on it, and pursued "all-Russian" goals. He saw them as nomads whose estrangement from the people nullified their abstract democratic ideals.[26]

Despite being accused of "Ukrainian separatism" throughout his life, Dragomanov did not want an independent Ukrainian state if it was only to take the form of existing centralized, multinational empires like those of Russia or Austria–Hungary. He called for the creation of a federation of national communities – not a federation of national states. Borrowing from the anarchism of Proudhon, whose fundamental principles included the complete independence of the individual and the inviolability of his rights *vis-à-vis* all governmental powers, even elected, representative ones, Dragomanov envisioned an anarcho-federalist system, in which individual and nationality alike could find true freedom. These ideas crystallized in Dragomanov's mind about the same time that he first began to write on the Jewish Question, and all that he had to say on the subject should be viewed in this context.[27]

Dragomanov always recognized the complexity of the Jewish Question. In his very first treatment of the problem he identified at least five or six constituent parts (*Kievskii telegraf*, 4:8/I/1875). At the same time, he recognized that individual questions were always subsumed into wider social problems. The question of civil rights for Jews was tied up with the broader consideration of the rights of all heterodox people, including Old Believers and Christian sectarians. The issues of Jewish fanaticism and the kahal merged into the general question of religious corporations and the subordination of individuals to religious institutions.[28] Approaching the Jewish Question from this vantage point,

Dragomanov always rejected solutions which he believed erred too much in the direction of either the general or the particular. For example, he faulted the liberal expedient of an immediate grant of full civil rights to the Jews, just as surely as he condemned any persecution of the Jews.[29] He argued that any approach to the Jewish Question must be comprehensive, in order to deal with its myriad social and economic elements. A piecemeal approach would create disequilibria, harming either the Jews or the people among whom they lived. Dragomanov consistently held to this opinion, even while the times changed. When the pogroms erupted in 1881, he criticized both the liberal expedient of extended civil rights, and the socialist solution of raising the class consciousness of the lower classes to the level where they could differentiate between the honest Jewish proletarian and the Jewish capitalist. There was nothing inherently wrong in either of these proposals, he admitted, but at a time of popular unrest, they represented useless, abstract theorizing.[30] He noted elsewhere that long and systematic educational work was necessary before rapprochement was possible between Jews and Ukrainians, the chief actors in the pogrom tragedy.[31] Dragomanov's position was both consistent and reasonable, but that did not make it popular, especially among socialist groups for whom the ideology of class struggle held all the answers. Nor was it palatable to Jewish intellectuals who viewed the recurrent pogroms in apocalyptic terms.

One of Dragomanov's Jewish collaborators on *Volnoe slovo*, Ben-Ami, attributed Dragomanov's ambivalence toward the pogroms to his reluctance to criticize his beloved Ukrainian people.[32] Part of the problem certainly lay in the fact that Dragomanov did not view the pogroms from a purely Jewish perspective but as part of a wider tradition of popular unrest, which he had long detected in the Ukrainian countryside.[33] Dragomanov could even point to a clear warning, which he had made in 1880, that there was a danger of popular violence against the Jews.[34] Neither the gift of prophecy nor an ability to take the long view were appreciated by the friends of the Jews in 1882, and his complex approach to the Jewish Question only won for Dragomanov the charge of being a Judeophobe.

Ben-Ami was quite correct to draw attention to Dragomanov's stance as a Ukrainian patriot, for this colored his thought on the Jews. Dragomanov, like Kulish and the *Osnova* circle before him, had a strong sense of the Jewish masses as an alien body in the Ukrainian land, whose leaders did nothing to remedy the situation. The phenomenon of Jewish separateness was a legacy of the past, the direct consequence of Polish and Russian rule. But old Poland was dead and buried, and so Dragomanov emphasized the Russian treatment of the Jews as a cause for contemporary Ukrainian misery. "The Jewish exploitation of the Ukrainian masses is unquestionably due to the concentration of Jews in the southwestern areas of Russia, a concentration created quite artificially by Russian legislation, guided in this case not only by narrow Great Russian considerations, but by the clear resolve to prevent the national development of a Ukrainian middle class."[35] The Jews now served as representatives of the Russian state in the despoiling of the Ukrainian peasantry, acting as agents of the treasury by leasing the state liquor monopoly.[36]

Once Jewry had been introduced into the Russian land, its unique characteristics ensured that it would endure, but as an alien presence. The Jews constituted a separate nation (*natsiia*) in the Ukraine, unified physically and psychologically by ethnic characteristics and the Yiddish language. Religion further reinforced the national exclusivity of the Jews. Since the Jews were almost without exception engaged in mercantile pursuits, they constituted a special class or *soslovie*, whose distinctive feature was its preference for non-productive activities. The Jews could justifiably be characterized as a "parasitical *soslovie*."[37]

Having explained the origins of Ukrainian Jewry in his role as a Ukrainian national historian, Dragomanov donned the garb of a socialist partisan of social justice. His analysis, however, was distorted by his preoccupation with the Ukrainian masses, who were overwhelmingly rural peasants. Non-agricultural social groups like the Jews were automatically suspect in his eyes, especially when they appeared to prosper at the expense of the peasantry. Dragomanov was hardly the discoverer of the concept of "Jewish exploitation," and his use of the concept was often vague and imprecise, perhaps as a consequence of his multiple identities as a son of the gentry, social historian, and Ukrainophile partisan of democratic socialism.

Dragomanov's writings were confused as to what constituted "productive work" (and its converse, "exploitation"), and what percentage of the Jews were so involved. In 1875 Dragomanov wrote that "the Jews represent an element which does not produce value; they can *all more or less* [italics mine] be placed into the category of merchants; there are too many of them, and their maintenance rests heavily upon the working classes."[38] From this it is difficult to ascertain whether the Jews were unproductive simply because they were engaged in mercantile activity or because there were too many of them. No more precise were the sentiments expressed in the program of

Dragomanov's Hromada in 1878 (signed by Dragomanov and others, but possibly not written by him): "the majority of the Poles, Jews, Germans, Hungarians, Muscovites and so on belong to the so-called upper classes, in reality the idle classes who live at the expense of genuinely productive elements."[39]

Confusion was worse compounded when Dragomanov addressed the problem in detail in 1882. Chubinskii's statistics for the Jewish population of the Southwest revealed a total population of 750,000 persons, divided occupationally into eight categories: (1) owners and leasers of land, factories and plants and their agents (72,000); (2) shopkeepers (100,000); (3) tavern-keepers (100,000); (4) employees in various forms of trade (48,000); (5) domestic servants (40,000); (6) rabbis, *melamdim* and school teachers (60,000); (7) craftsmen, teamsters and porters (160,000); (8) the poor (20,000). Dragomanov's own analysis of these figures was non-traditional, to say the least. He classed the first three categories as "unproductive," revealing his anti-capitalistic prejudices and disdain for non-agricultural labor. At a stroke, one-third of the Jewish population was declared parasitical. Dragomanov was less decisive about the fourth and fifth categories, pronouncing them unproductive as a whole, but including individual members who could be considered part of the working proletariat. There was no question as to the positive assessment of the productivity of category seven, although Dragomanov took the surprising step of including the religious-educational personnel of category six, asserting that, even given the moribund nature of Jewish learning, educators worked and did some good. This analysis, therefore, confirmed assertions which Dragomanov had made in the past that from one-third to two-thirds of the Jews of the Ukraine contributed nothing to the well-being of the area. Nor was this phenomenon confined to the Ukraine: for Belorussians, Romanians and Poles, "Yid" and "exploiter" were synonyms.[40] The confusion of Dragomanov's economic analysis makes it difficult to ascertain a vital point: what was the origin of Jewish exploitation? Was it something forced upon the Jews by external circumstances (as Dragomanov clearly implied in some of his writings), or inherent in Jews or Judaism, as suggested in his later writings on the Jewish Question. The picture is further complicated by another strand of Dragomanov's treatment of the Jewish Question, his examination of antithetical classes within an apparently unified Jewry. This was hardly an innovation, for Brafman had always differentiated the Jews into the exploited mass and the kahal leadership, and most socialist ideologues analyzed the Jewish

Question only from the perspective of class struggle. Dragomanov's analysis led him to conclusions that were far more unsympathetic to the Jews in general than those of either Brafman or the socialists because he depicted Jewish solidarity as a phenomenon which overrode class struggle within the Jewish community.

Dragomanov early on detected sharp class differentiation within the Jewish community. He noted that the parasitical life of the Jewish masses failed to elevate them from the direst poverty: rather, their activities served only to enrich a small number of "Jewish financial aces." In this instance, the "solidarity" of the Jews served only as a tool for the effective exploitation of poor Jews by their prosperous coreligionists. The latter did not want the equalization of Jewish rights, or even the right to live everywhere, lest they lose their channels of income, for the poor Jew who plundered the Belorussian peasant was the necessary servant of the Jewish contractor in driving down the cost of hired labor.[41] In 1880, Dragomanov reasserted this charge, contending that its Jewish victims were "often worse off than the Christian proletariat."[42] This view exonerated the mass of Jewish "parasites" from guilt for their actions, since their activities were forced upon them by economic realities and maintained by the restrictive Russian legislation which left the Jews a compact prey for kulaks of their own religion and nationality. After the pogroms began, Dragomanov's views became more critical. In 1882, speaking of the socialist equation of the Jew-kulak with the Christian-kulak, Dragomanov asserted that "the human kulakism of the kulak-Jew in the Ukraine is complicated by their Jewry – i.e., their nationality: by that tie between the kulak-Jews, which naturally flows from the ties characteristic of nationality as a biological phenomenon, strengthened even more by the nationality of religion, which gives the Jews a powerful organization for the attainment of their aims."

Dragomanov extended his criticism to include the working, productive elements in Jewry, "which feel themselves much closer to the exploiters of their own nation, and constantly dreams of passing into the ranks of the Jewish exploiters and, at the first convenient moment, passes into their ranks." Dragomanov's qualification, that this was the case of the Jews as individuals, not as a group, hardly drew the sting from his attack, especially when he offered gratuitous criticism of the Jews for their "sickening self-love, arrogance and passion for honor," or their arrogance and self-proclaimed superiority above the Ukrainian masses. He explicitly rejected this qualification by expressing wonder that both Jewish workers and the poor found more in common with Jewish capitalists than with the Ukrainian proletariat.[43]

Dragomanov's change of tone should be sought in his approach to the Jewish Question in the Ukraine. As noted above, Dragomanov's recognition of the complexity of the Jewish Question made him reluctant to offer the broad, generalized reforms so beloved of other reformers. This reluctance also sprang from Dragomanov's empathy for oppressed minorities, born of his own status as a victim of imperial caprice. His keen awareness of national distinctions made him reluctant to impose programs upon other nationalities of whom he knew little. The few concrete prescriptions which Dragomanov did timidly offer reveal the cosmopolitanism which prevented his Ukrainian nationalism from becoming too narrow and chauvinistic. According to Ben-Ami, Dragomanov's general solution was one of wholesale mixed marriage between the two peoples. Through this process the Ukrainian people would receive a large dose of intelligence (*umstvinnost'*), which would assist them to become a great, historical people, while the Jews would be eliminated as a harmful, alien power.[44] More to the point, Dragomanov repeatedly professed his ignorance of the Jews' internal world, and called upon others to take up the twin tasks of prescription and reform.[45]

Dragomanov assumed that the Jewish intelligentsia, who alone combined sufficient knowledge of the Jewish world and progressive aspirations, were the appropriate specialists for this task. Precisely here lay the conflict. Just as Ukrainian intellectuals were Dragomanov's despair for their refusal to join their talents to the national cause, so too Jewish intellectuals provoked him by their lack of leadership. In 1875, Dragomanov complained that Jewish progressives and "the so-called liberal Jewish press" would speak only of the need for complete civil rights, while ignoring all other facets of the Jewish Question. They spoke only of the oppression of Jews by Christians, and never offered any criticism of their own people, aside from the occasional swipe at the religious conservatism of the Jewish "Old Believers." What kind of leadership did these "progressives" provide, espousing Russo-Jewish rapprochement, and the Russification of the Jews, much as they had earlier sought to germanize their coreligionists by transforming Yiddish into literary German? Pursuing these objectives, they ignored the plight of the Jewish masses in the hands of the Jewish capitalists.[46]

In emigration, Dragomanov hoped that he had found the proper Jewish allies. In 1880, his press in Geneva published a brochure "From the Group of Jewish Socialists," to which he appended an afterword. The brochure advocated the use of Yiddish for propaganda purposes among the Jews, announced the foundation of a "Free Jewish Press," and emphasized that the Jewish proletariat must join hands with the Christian proletariat against the common class enemy. Dragomanov reprised his past assessment of the Jewish Question, and offered a hearty endorsement for the objectives of the brochure's authors.[47]

The objectives of the "Group of Jewish Socialists" came to nothing when its leading participants, such as Lazar Tsukerman, returned to Russia to work in the general revolutionary movement of Narodnaia Volia. Dragomanov's continued sponsorship of a socialist organization employing Yiddish was savaged in public debates by Jewish socialists such as Nikolai Zhukovskii and Lev Deich.[48] Thus, when Dragomanov reviewed the situation in 1882, he was less sympathetic. He faulted, as before, the progressives and their calls for an immediate grant of full civil rights. He believed that additional rights would only give the educated and better-off classes of the Jews a higher social position, while failing to address the needs of the Jewish masses. The intellectuals' obsession with equal rights led them to ignore the abnormal relationship of Christians and Jews in the Ukrainian village, and thus to overlook the pogrom potential there. The Jewish socialist, a more recent phenomenon, was likewise following the wrong path. The Jewish socialists, by their apathy to the initiative of the Group of Jewish Socialists, had rejected "going to the Jewish people." Instead, they turned their backs on the Jewish milieu and the Jewish masses, and disappeared into a wider, all-Russian movement.[49] In the aftermath of the pogroms, the folly and negligence of such a course was apparent. "Socialists and populists from the Jews, cut off from their people, can still less than others be tied to the non-Jewish masses, and only strengthen the all-Russian (i.e., rootless or *bezpochvennyi*) element among Russian socialists and Jews."[50] Until the Jewish intellectual leadership confronted the Jewish Question in all its ramifications, it would remain insoluble.[51]

"The Jewish Question in the Ukraine," which has been summarized above, was Dragomanov's most critical treatment of the Jews. Largely on the strength of it, he has been branded a Judeophobe or an Antisemite. Even Ben-Ami, always eager to defend his mentor, characterized it as Judeophobic, while attributing it to Dragomanov's frustration at the widespread condemnation of the Ukrainian people for the pogroms of 1881–2. In addition, the essay appeared in the *émigré Volnoe slovo*, which Shmuel Galai brands as an outright antisemitic organ. Galai particularly condemns a specially commissioned series, published while Dragomanov was unofficial editor, reporting the meeting of the International Antisemitic Congress in Dresden in 1882. These articles, he asserts, introduced "a new and distinctive note of modern racialist hatred of Jews into what may be described as 'old-fashioned' economic religious Antisemitism with nationalist-chauvinist overtones."[52] However, Dragomanov told Ben-Ami that he was not interested in German Antisemitism and did not even read the articles.[53] Dragomanov himself dismissed Antisemitism as a "clerical-conservative-monarchical phenomenon in Germany," hardly an expression of approbation.[54] It is also worthy of note that once Dragomanov became formal editor of *Volnoe slovo* with the issue of 8 January 1883, all discussion of the Jewish Question in the paper ceased.

This survey of the positions of the leading Ukrainophiles on the Jewish Question can best be concluded by accenting their affinities with the newspaper *Kievlianin*, however incongruous this pairing with an adversary whose unrelenting journalistic denunciations helped to persuade the Russian government to act against the movement in 1876. Yet both the Ukrainophiles and *Kievlianin* shared a role for a time as principled Judeophobes. Their hostility to the Jews sprang from objective phenomena – the economic and cultural roles played by the Jews in the Ukraine. Both revealed a preoccupation with quantifying the specific damage done by the Jews, perhaps in recognition that otherwise they could be accused of religious obscurantism and prejudice. Both Russifiers and Ukrainophiles began from a position of vague sympathy for the plight of the Jews and its effects upon the rest of the Ukrainian population. Both focused on the Jewish intellectual as the essential medium for reform and change, and each came to despair of them. Disillusionment spurred increasingly hostile attacks, prone to stray from objective reality into the sphere of fantastic and occult Judeophobia.

Ironically, the more "liberal" Ukrainophiles were less liberal in their recommendations for resolving the Jewish Question. *Kievlianin* desired the Russification of the Jews, and the economic welfare of the Ukraine as part of the Russian Empire as a whole. These objectives could best be secured, Shulgin and his successors believed prior to 1881, by the abolition of the Pale of Settlement, which would free the Ukraine from its costly burden of exploitation. The Jews would be scattered throughout the Empire and dispersed (and Russified) like a drop of poison in the ocean. The forceful competition of Russian kulaks would deter them from exploitation.

Ukrainophiles, on the other hand, were resolved to deal with the Jewish Question in place, in the Ukraine. They desired that the Jews be "ukrainianized," at least in the sense of being made more sympathetic toward the people among whom they lived. (Dragomanov, in his heart of hearts, apparently desired complete assimilation.) This would not be accomplished by the cowardly and unrealistic expedient of chasing the Jews from the Ukraine. For this reason, Ukrainophiles made initiatives to the Jews in 1858 and 1861. The failure of the Jews to respond in the hoped-for manner – for the mass of Jews remained economically and culturally unchanged, while Jewish intellectuals became Russified – produced bitter charges of bad faith. All the more reason, Ukrainophiles became convinced, why the Jews could not be emancipated until wider social and economic questions were satisfactorily resolved. This accounts for the seeming paradox of *de facto* emancipation espoused by anti-liberals, while partisans of liberal theories rejected emancipation.

10   Education and Russification

When Ivan Aksakov set out to catalogue ideological scarecrows such as "liberal ideas" and "humane thought" which dominated contemporary society, he made one significant omission – education. All would-be reformers of the Jews, however much they differed on the nature of the Jewish Question, were agreed that its resolution was to be found in the classroom. As O. Gurvich, overseer of a Vilna Jewish primary school observed in 1865, "education is the slogan of our age and in its embrace the mass of poor Jews find freedom from all excrescences and degradation."[1]

Reformers like Gurvich placed their hopes on the state Jewish school system. After many vicissitudes, that system, paid for by the tax on sabbath candles imposed on the Jewish community, had finally come to resemble the institution envisioned by its founders in 1847. The system was three-tiered, each level roughly equivalent to the corresponding state schools. Jewish primary schools, with a two-year curriculum, were designed to impart basic literacy. They approximated to parish elementary schools which were run by the Russian Orthodox Church for peasants and the lower strata of the urban population. The curriculum included the study of the Bible, the most important Jewish prayers, basic Hebrew and Russian grammar, and arithmetic. Some of the instruction, such as the study of Jewish prayers, was conducted in German. The government planned that Jewish primary schools be established in every community where it was possible to find the appropriate resources.

The second tier comprised Jewish secondary schools, corresponding to state district schools. Russian district schools offered a three-year terminal qualification, designed to serve the children of merchants, military officers, the gentry and artisans. Their objective was to provide personnel for local administrative and economic life. Jewish schools also offered a terminal qualification through a program of study lasting from three to five years, depending on the optional classes offered. Besides a religious curriculum, the schools taught Russian language, geography, history and draftsmanship. Optional courses included bookkeeping, geometry, mechanics, natural history, physics, chemistry and other commercial and technical courses.

The third tier, state rabbinical schools, corresponded to the Russian gymnasium (*gimnaziia*), a seven-year program for the sons of the gentry and government officials designed to prepare them for admission to the university. The Russian gymnasium was the focus of a bitter pedagogical battle between "Realists," who wanted more courses in science and mathematics, and "Classicists," who advocated a core curriculum based on the study of Latin and Greek. The gymnasia underwent changes during the early reform era, until the battle was finally won by the Classicists.[2] The two state rabbinical seminaries offered what was essentially the seven-year-long gymnasium curriculum, shorn of natural history, and supplemented by special courses for the training of rabbis and teachers. A three-year curriculum offered the first three years of the gymnasium (the so-called *progimnaziia*), followed by four years of classes equivalent to those in the Russian gymnasium. In addition a one-year pedagogical course was available for those entering the teaching profession, and a two-year course was offered for prospective rabbis. The similarity between the rabbinical seminary and the gymnasium had a significant but unintended consequence: graduates of the rabbinical seminary, their training supplemented by independent study, could qualify for university admission.

Passage to the university, while not actually forbidden, was not what the state had in mind for seminary graduates. As the system of primary and secondary state Jewish schools expanded, there was dire need of an adequate pool of teachers, especially since teachers in the traditional Jewish schools, the *melamdim*, were to be kept far away from the new schools. Officials also sought to transform the religious leaders of the Jewish community, the rabbis, into agents of the state. The culmination of this desire was an 1857 decree that graduates of the rabbinical seminaries, the secondary Jewish schools, or the equivalent Russian middle and secondary schools could be elected rabbi.[3] Of necessity, local officials usually ignored this law. Where the local authorities actually intervened to force the election of a qualified candidate it was inevitably at the cost of public order.

It is a telling commentary on the government's confidence in the maskilic personnel of the state Jewish schools that it required that

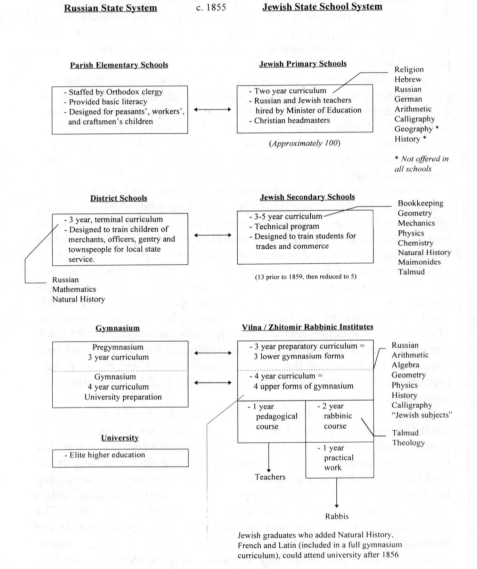

Comparison of Russian and Jewish state school systems *c.* 1855

school headmasters be Christians, as were most of the teachers of non-Jewish subjects. Even the directors of the rabbinical seminaries were Christians. The Christian overseers were bureaucrats with no knowledge or sympathy for Jewish culture. A typical assessment of the Jewish community was offered by a gentile headmaster in the peda-gogical journal *Uchitel*:

> Russians of the true Orthodox faith are obliged to see everyone as their neighbor; they make a living at heavy but honest labor, and they strive to achieve moral improvement. Judaic beliefs require rites and interpretations which admit no principles of brotherhood; they are all fanatics who live by work of the easier sort such as speculation and petty trade, giving them full scope for dishonesty and immorality. We are guided by conscience and religion in our activities, while they sleep in an unbroken dream. (17: September 1865)

The early years of the Reform Era witnessed attempts to develop and improve the state Jewish school system. In 1855 a law required that, within twenty years, none might serve as rabbi or *melamed* save graduates of the rabbinical seminaries or middle and secondary public schools.[4] In the meantime, the state attempted to extend its super-vision over *hadarim* by requiring, in 1856, local officials to grant certi-fication to any prospective *melamed*, and by making state rabbis responsible for overseeing *hadarim*.[5] The capstone law of 1857, noted above, recognized the continuing inadequacy of local resources by empowering communities to invite trained rabbis from Germany, with the permission of the Ministry of Internal Affairs.[6] (This is precisely what progressives in the Jewish community of Odessa proceeded to do, importing Dr. Shimon Aryeh Schwabacher from Lemberg.) In theory, at least, the guiding hand of the government now rested firmly upon the Jewish community, through a network of state teachers, rabbis, and Jewish Experts attached to provincial offices. Nonetheless, enduring problems forced the government to rethink its educational policies.

The schools never attracted Jews in great numbers. Despite con-siderable expenditures, and the establishment of approximately 100 institutions, fewer than 4,000 students were enrolled by 1855. This was in contrast to the traditional school system which, according to the estimates of the Kiselev Committee, numbered 5,361 institutions, 10,861 teachers and 69,464 students.[7] Yet what the state system lacked in breadth, it compensated for in depth. The schools provided a forum for the energies of the maskilim of Nicholine times, and by the early Reform Era were producing a second generation of maskilim, from whom emerged the Russian Jewish intelligentsia. Most of the Jews who appeared in print in the 1850s were either personnel or graduates of a state Jewish institution. The state schools were not only an entrée to the wider, gentile world, but also provided a path to the elite world of the Russian university. As a group, graduates were articulate and vocal, although they seldom spoke with one voice. One point upon which they all agreed, however, was the necessity for some recognition and reward from the state for their efforts.

The nature of this reward helped to define the differences between those who remained maskilim and those who constituted the Russian Jewish intelligentsia. The maskilim remained directly connected to the task of Jewish enlightenment for the masses, either as workers in the field, or advocates in the press. They expected state support, such as assistance in securing employment as teachers or rabbis. They also assumed that greater civil rights would be granted to the masses as a consequence of the spread of "enlightenment." Since the process of enlightenment was well under way – their efforts were proof of that – emancipation of some sort should come sooner rather than later.

The Russian Jewish intelligentsia came to share the view of the maskilim that the masses must be liberated. Initially, however, when the prospects for any reform in the status of the Jews were still problematical, they emphasized their position as an advanced group deserving immediate attention. They were able to communicate this view to the financial elite, represented by the Gintsburg Circle in the capital. An alliance rapidly developed between these groups. The financial "aces" had access to high officials, and a long tradition of *shtadlanut* behind them. They were able to use the educated elite's ability to frame arguments and write them in good Russian. The Jewish men of affairs already possessed numerous prerogatives, as befitted their lofty economic perch. They could point to their educated fellows as another group which satisfied official expectations of the Jews. Greater rights for educated Jews was a step forward in the ultimate objective of rights for all Jews.

The argument that the state must reward those Jews who had made important steps toward rapprochement and merger permeates petitions to the central government in the first decade of the Reform Era. The thirty-four Jewish students at the Medical-Surgical Academy in St. Petersburg who petitioned the KOME to open state service to them declared that "our people judge education by its real utility – the eyes of the whole young generation are on us, the first to scorn prejudice, overcome obstacles and hardships and to follow the generous call of the government."[8] The Gintsburg Circle in July of 1856 petitioned the government to separate the wheat from the chaff, and grant "moderate privileges to those of us who are worthy and enlightened."[9] Calls of this nature were regularly repeated, as late as 1869. By that date, however, they were decidedly out of fashion.[10] The Russian Jewish intelligentsia not only saw the resolution of the Jewish Question in the grant of civil rights to all Jews, but were confident enough to make the argument in public. At the same time, they remained dedicated to the ideal of education as a process which must accompany emancipation, and equip Jews to exercise their new prerogatives more effectively. This assumption led to recurrent debates on how best the state school system might be modified to pursue this goal.

These concerns of the Jewish world were mirrored in the Russian bureaucratic milieu. Officials serving on a committee of the Department of Internal Affairs to investigate the Jewish communal tax system, meeting between 1858 and 1863, emphasized the need to offer material inducements in order to promote Jewish education. When Alexander II visited Lithuania in 1860, Governor-General V. I. Nazimov impressed upon him the need to extend the rights of Jews who had received an education. When the new head of the Jewish Committee, Count Bludov, reported to the Tsar on the need to better the moral and material position of Jews who had differentiated themselves from the masses by wealth or education, the Tsar noted: "I completely share your view."[11] The immediate consequence of this report was the law of 27 November 1861 which granted entry into the civil service to Jews with a university degree.

The distribution of rewards to the educated highlighted problems which existed within the state Jewish school system. The minuscule enrollment hardly seemed to justify the massive expenditures, even if finance did come from Jewish pockets. Equally distressing was the persistence of the traditional educational system. Efforts to eliminate or restrict it produced only spectacular failures. An 1854 regulation requiring *melamdim* to be proficient in Russian caused their schools to disappear from view, and pursue a successful underground existence.[12] Nor was time an ally of the government: the twenty-year limit within which rabbis and *melamdim* were obligated to acquire a suitable education and language skills came and went without real change, and the government was forced to recognize the impossibility of enforcing the requirements.[13]

The institution of the state rabbinate fared no better. Only heavy-handed interference of Russian officials, and resultant public scandal, secured election of "enlightened" rabbis. Even then the communities had their revenge. They delayed or underpaid their salaries, and refused to confirm them during the triennial elections, unless they proved willing to look the other way as the community functioned in its old, "fanatical" way. The true leader of the religious community, as before, was the "spiritual rabbi."

Since the Ministry of Education was directly responsible for the Jewish school system, its officials were most aware of its shortcomings. They detected the fatal flaw in the state's meddling in the religious life of Jewry: a religious curriculum for Jews was devised and overseen by Christians. The Minister of Education, E. Kovalevskii, wrote on 12 March 1859 that

> the spread of humane knowledge among the Jews by itself can shake and ultimately eradicate the moral-religious prejudices which are rooted in them. Therefore, it seems to me, every means should be used to encourage subjects necessary for a humane education, not only in state, but in private Jewish schools, and at the same time [we should] meddle as little as possible in the religious teaching of children, leaving that to the responsibility of their parents.[14]

These sentiments were echoed both by A. Golovnin, one of Kovalevskii's successors, and the overseers of a number of educational districts within the Pale.[15] This consensus produced the law of 6 September 1862, which authorized Jews to serve as headmasters of elementary and secondary state Jewish schools.[16]

Even broader changes were bruited, including imposition of mandatory education for Jews and the replacement of Jewish schools with Christian–Jewish public schools. Another Gintsburg petition, sent to Kovalevskii in September of 1858, called for "religion-free" education for Jews, as well as for privileges for the educated.[17] The government responded with a decree in 1859 which made education in state schools mandatory for the children of Jewish merchants and Honored Citizens. (This aspect of the decree remained no more than a statement of good intentions since this same law permitted the parents of students in the state Jewish schools the option of replacing the school religious curriculum with home instruction.)[18]

These issues were discussed in the pages of the fledgling Russian Jewish press. *Rassvet* was filled with articles on all aspects of education. Debates raged between advocates of mandatory attendance in the state Jewish schools, and those who argued that attendance could best be improved by reforming the schools to limit the religious curriculum. Rabinovich sided with those who favored reform, a reflection of his customary aversion to changes forced upon society from without.[19] *Sion*, in its turn, provided critiques of the rabbinical seminaries. Reflecting the desire to totally banish the religious element from the state Jewish schools, one correspondent called for the secondary schools to be transformed into *Realschulen*.[20]

The idea of reform for Jewish schools was clearly in the air, but contemporary events gave it special urgency. Russian education itself was in the throes of a transformation. In the wake of student disorders and professional restiveness, a new University Statute was promulgated on 18 June 1863. Debate over the nature and role of the universities expanded into a discussion of entry into the system, thus joining the on-going debate over classical or non-classical gymnasia. This struggle was momentarily stilled by a statute of 19 November 1864 which permitted district school authorities to decide whether local schools should be classical or non-classical gymnasia. This change had implications for the Jews because the statute further specified that students were to be admitted irrespective of their religion. Meanwhile, the rabbinical seminaries, with their gymnasium curriculum, still qualified graduates for the university.[21]

Equally significant was the transformation of the Russian primary school. Widespread social concern over the state of popular education in Russia culminated in the Sunday School movement of 1858–62, an attempt by students and other volunteers to spread popular literacy.[22] The government moved to reorganize its control of education. The Public School Statute of 14 July 1864 placed primary schooling under the supervision of district school boards, composed of representatives of the Ministry of Education, the Holy Synod, the zemstva, and an observer from the governor's office.

This set off a bureaucratic struggle between the Ministry of Education, headed by A. Golovnin, and the Holy Synod, led by Dmitrii Tolstoi, to annex as many school systems as possible. The Ministry of Education did not control all state institutions in Russia. The army, for example, retained control over military academies while the Holy Synod oversaw an extensive system of parish schools, including 3,800 institutions in the politically sensitive southwest. Under Golovnin, the Ministry of Education, which controlled the state Jewish school system, sought to extend its authority over the parish schools. This attempt by the ministry to capture a school system run by the Orthodox clergy was of obvious significance to the Jews, given calls to make state elementary schools out of the state Jewish schools, or proposals to make primary education mandatory for Jews. The issue became moot, however, when Golovnin's plans were defeated by Tolstoi.

The aftermath of the Polish revolt of 1863 raised a host of special problems in the Pale. Education, hitherto a prop of Polish cultural influence in the western provinces, was pressed into the service of Russification. General Muravev simply seized the state Jewish primary schools and turned them into "Russifying schools," designed to teach Russian grammar rather than Jewish subjects. In the Ukraine, the Governor-General's office used the new Russifying newspaper *Kievlianin* to solicit comments from the educated public on the Jewish school system.[23] In the decade between the Polish revolt and the abolition of the state Jewish school system in 1873, three themes dominated public discussion of Jewish education: the traditional Jewish school system, its state sponsored rival, and the role and relevance of the state rabbinate.

Jewish and gentile critics alike agreed on the unsatisfactory state of the traditional schools. This mood was apparent in both the general and specialist press. In *Severnaia pchela*, A. E. Landau, the future publisher of Jewish journals and newspapers, attacked the Jews of Kovno for the lamentable state of their Talmud-Tora. He described, in melodramatic terms, a wretched hovel with "over seventy-five half-starved children in two tiny rooms." Institutions like this, he complained, bore "the stamp of the outcast." Young, enlightened rabbis, who should be reforming the Talmud-Tora, directing students to the state schools and encouraging the Jewish Sabbath School movement, were inactive, paralyzed by their dependence on the conservative communities which had been forced to elect them (211:9/VIII/1863). The liberal St. Petersburg *Golos* warned that instruction by the *melamed* was dangerous to the physical as well as the intellectual health of students who were crammed into close, dirty rooms while heavy tomes cut off circulation in their legs (171:6/VII/1863). The pedagogical journal *Uchitel* was equally concerned. The mass of Jews who passed through the *heder*, it claimed, were weak and sickly, and still unable to read properly. The few who succeeded within this system became "scholars," and parasitic wards of the community (10: V 1864: 368–76).

In 1864, the Ministry of Education dispatched an inspector, F. Postels, to make a detailed examination of the Jewish school system, state and private. His long and thoughtful report was published in the ministry's *Journal* and attracted much attention in the press. Postels confirmed the low public image of the *heder*. He had been unable to find more than a few *hadarim* which satisfied elementary pedagogical requirements. "In *hadarim* belonging to the less satisfactory category, what strikes the eye is the close location, the general untidiness, the negligence of the proprietor himself; the children sit or stand, crowded at a small table in a room containing a bedstead and where the whole family of the proprietor is centered along with their domestic utensils." Postels' report was distinctive not for his negative description, but in his complete pessimism that anything could be done to rectify the situation. He noted that none of the numerous regulations applicable to the *hadarim* were being enforced. Rabbinical supervision was undercut by the state rabbi's dependence upon the community. The community was the crux of the problem. Parents were satisfied with the system and so defended and protected the *melamdim* and provided the funds for the continuation of their schools. Postels could do no more than recommend that state officials take their supervisory duties more seriously, even as he expressed his doubts as to the possibility of success.[24]

Other publicists, less well informed, were more sanguine on the possibility of significant changes. An editorial in the liberal *Kievskii telegraf* condemned the *hadarim* as the "source of evil" obstructing the progressive evolution of Jewish society by inculcating feelings of racial exclusivity and religious fanaticism in their pupils. The editor called for the abolition of the *hadarim* and their replacement with state Jewish schools (63:5/VI/1870). The following year an editorial in the rival *Kievlianin* rejoiced at a rumor that the state was planning to outlaw the *hadarim* or at least extend significant control over them. Some might view this plan as state interference in the religious affairs of a local group, conceded *Kievlianin*, but it was an urgent necessity to root out a body which harmed state interests by teaching Jewish youth to despise physical labor and exploit Christians (106:7/IX/1871). *Sanktpeterburgskie vedomosti*, mildly sympathetic to the Jews, offered a similar critique. The Jewish Question, it observed, was centered in the degradation and alienation of Russian Jewry, manifested in distrust and bitterness in Jewish–Christian relations. The Jews rationalized their merciless exploitation from the talmudic injunctions which they learned in the *hadarim*. The state had to struggle with this threat, motivated not by religious intolerance, but in the name of enlightenment. Some means must be found to bring the Jews into the state Jewish system (174:28/VI/1872).

Despite this universal criticism of the traditional schools, they were soon to lose their state rivals. The government wearied of the struggle to make the state Jewish system viable, and in a decree of 16 March

1873, announced the dismantling of the main elements of the system. The would-be reforms of past years fared no better. In 1875 *Kievlianin* gloated that the hour of reckoning for the *melamdim* had arrived at last: the twenty-year term, set by the law of 3 May 1855, in which all *melamdim* had to acquire an education in a state school, had expired.[25] In fact, the deadline came and went without effect. The government had come to recognize the futility of its attempt to control either the *hadarim* or their teachers.

While all commentators, Jew and gentile, agreed on the harmfulness of the *hadarim*, they parted company on the subject of the fate of the state Jewish system. Should the well-known shortcomings of the schools best be overcome by reform and modification, or was it better to abolish them outright and to encourage Jews to attend state schools? Not surprisingly, the chief partisans of the reform (and retention) of the state Jewish school system in the Russian press were its employees and graduates. Their energetic defense in the Jewish and Russian press ensured a wide public debate.

The battle was joined in 1863 when Lev Binshtok, a former teacher at the Zhitomir Rabbinical Seminary, wrote to *Golos* to defend the system from sniping in the press. He condemned the two parties within the Jewish community, the obscurantists and aristocrats, whom he accused of leading the drive for abolition. The fanatics condemned the schools because they taught secular subjects. The leaders of the obscurantists sought to undermine the position of the rabbis and teachers who graduated from the state schools precisely because their labors on behalf of enlightenment threatened the old ways. The wealthy community aristocrats, on the other hand, called for the abolition of the schools in order to expedite Russian–Jewish merging. These same magnates had stood by while *Rassvet* died from lack of resources. Were they now to judge what would best promote merger? If the state schools had flaws, claimed Binshtok, it was because the community had too much control over them and sabotaged them through malevolence or ignorance. Far from being abolished, the Jewish schools should be taken more closely under government control (246:19/IX/ 1863).

A writer in *Uchitel* agreed, seeing the key to reform in more control, not less. He recommended that the government extend the existing system by adding preparatory classes to replace the *hadarim* and prepare the young for admission to the state Jewish elementary schools (17: IX 1864). In 1864 *Vilenskii vestnik* carried a heated exchange between the overseers of two state Jewish schools.

O. Gurvich, of a Vilna state Jewish school, reflected the emphasis on Russification which dominated all the activities of Muravev's Governor-Generalship in Lithuania. Gurvich called for the russification of the curriculum through Russian-language instruction in all subjects (7:21/I/1864). M. Gurvich, overseer of a Novgorod-Volynsk state Jewish school, warned against a precipitous shift to Russian which he feared would decisively alienate the traditionalists who rejected the teaching of sacred subjects in the vernacular. Better to wait until 1875, he proposed, when all teachers in state or private schools would be obliged to have attended Russian language schools (26:7/II/1864).

In response to Postels' report an article in *Kievlianin* in 1865 proposed the elimination of the state Jewish system. A veritable flood of articles was dispatched to the editor by indignant Jews. A typical article tied a defense of Jewish education to the Polish menace, a theme sure to interest *Kievlianin* (55:13/V/1865). It was widely reported that Jews had been more active in the Polish uprising of 1863 than the movement of 1830, the author observed. Where had the Polonization of Jews taken place but in special Jewish schools where Jews studied apart from Poles but used the Polish language in the curriculum. Jewish books had been translated into Polish, so that with their first awareness of religion, Jewish youth imbibed Polish and a Polish political orientation. The focal point of Polish–Jewish merging had been the Warsaw Rabbinical School. In its thirty-five year existence, from 1827 to 1862, he claimed, it had failed to produce a single rabbi for a Jewish community. It had trained an entire generation of Jews in the language, customs and morals of Poland which they had carried to the masses. Exactly the same process was now taking place in the Vilna and Zhitomir seminaries whose graduates all spoke Russian, even as the graduates of gymnasia in the Northwest spoke Polish. The Russian spirit was also to be found in the primary school system, which the Russian state would abolish at its peril.

The Russian supplement to the Hebrew newspaper *Ha-Karmel* placed proposals to abolish separate Jewish institutions into the context of the struggle to achieve merger, "a word now found on the tongue of all the best Jews and gentiles; it is our moral and civil salvation; it is a goal which we have continually in mind, and which we should pursue in every way over which we have control" (23:9/IV/1865). The process of merging could not be accomplished instantaneously. Since the Jews had long been kept apart from gentile society by restrictive legislation, an attempt to merge the two peoples through casual contact in a common society was akin to attempting a chemical combination without a catalyst. Separate Jewish institutions, such as schools and the press, would provide the catalyst which could accomplish merger.

Golos offered its thoughts in the course of a detailed review of Postels' report (143:26/V/1865). In principle *Golos* favored a Jewish school curriculum similar to that of the state schools and had earlier advocated making the curriculum of the rabbinical seminaries identical to that of gymnasia. Yet the sensibilities of the conservative Jewish community had to be taken into consideration if schooling was to have any chance of acceptance. These concerns are apparent in *Golos'* critique of Postels' recommendations for the Jewish elementary schools. In order to attract more pupils he proposed that, where religious fanaticism was strong, non-Jewish subjects such as German which might be thought to compromise the faith, should be dropped. Where fanaticism was weaker, a few additional secular subjects such as geography and natural science might be added. *Golos* demurred. How were the authorities to gauge precisely the level of fanaticism in this or that community? Objections made against the teaching of German applied equally to Russian and dropping that language would defeat the whole purpose of the schools. *Golos* preferred a compromise. In areas inhabited primarily by Jews, the existing type of state Jewish school should be established. Where Jews were less numerous, they should be granted a stipend to study in Christian schools. If this measure encountered too much opposition, the government could return to the old method. *Golos* also followed a growing trend in advocating that religious subjects largely be dropped from the state Jewish school curriculum, especially since they were increasingly taught at home, as permitted by the law of 4 May 1859. The rabbinical seminaries should be left as the sole bastion of a state-sponsored curriculum of Jewish subjects. For the moment *Golos* was willing to accept separate Jewish institutions, but under the influence of Iakov Brafman, the editors soon moved in a very different direction.

No important issue, especially one touching on Russification, could escape the purview of M. N. Katkov's publications. In general, they supported the state Jewish schools. *Russkii vestnik* devoted almost fifty pages to a defense of the schools by Lev Binshtok in the wake of the Postels' report (LX:November 1865: 202–34, 574–91). Binshtok described the schools as an inexpensive vehicle for Russification of the Jews – the annual expense per student was only about one and a half silver rubles. The schools were constantly improving, especially now that Jews were serving as overseers. More students were enrolled, and the schools had already produced an enlightened contingent in the population. There still remained too high a level of mutual antipathy between Christians and Jews for the two to study successfully in school. Moreover, warned Binshtok, waving the bloody shirt, education in public schools in the borderlands, as they presently existed, would Polonize rather than Russify the Jews.

More change was still needed. The curriculum should be reduced to a simple Jewish catechism and the study of the Old Testament. All instruction should be in Russian. Education for Jews in the elementary state Jewish schools should be mandatory. The curriculum of the rabbinical seminaries, on the other hand, should be broadened to approximate that of a classical gymnasium. Graduates should have access to the university.

Katkov himself, in *Moskovskie vedomosti*, advocated the retention of the state Jewish schools, but for reasons which were far from flattering to the Jews. The state Jewish system had been a mistake from the beginning because it placed Christians in the incongruous position of prescribing a religious curriculum for Jews. These religious elements should all be stripped away, creating the equivalent of Russian primary schools. Why not simply educate Jews in Russian schools? asked Katkov. His answer, echoing Ivan Aksakov, was that general schools should have a Christian character, which would be missing if Christians and Jews shared the classroom (148:8/VII/1865). As Katkov became concerned that "Germanization" also posed a threat to russification, he proposed one final change: German and Yiddish should be barred from the schools, and replaced with Russian (149:16/VII/1866).

Other Russifiers also took up the cause of the state Jewish schools. The official *Varshavskii dnevnik*, little more than the publication of the army of occupation in Warsaw, monitored the Polish-language press and published statistics and imperial decrees. The paper was continually alert for new methods to undermine Polish dreams and promote Russification. In 1868 the paper defended state Jewish schools as agents for Russification, especially if Russian was the language of instruction. The paper argued that there was a natural antipathy between Poles and Jews, despite the evidence of 1863. Separate schooling could help to maintain the gap between them. The Jews in Poland, as in the border provinces, might be won to the Russian side (167:2/VIII; 218:10/X/1868).

The newspaper which occupied pride of place in the campaign to abolish the state Jewish schools was *Kievlianin*. The editor had shown an interest in Jewish education almost from the first issue, and it was appropriate that the Governor-General's office used *Kievlianin* to solicit recommendations for the improvement of Jewish schools.[26] In 1864 the paper published letters from Berdichev which proposed that the underattended Jewish secondary school be converted into a Russian pro-gymnasium which would be open to both Jews and gentiles.[27] A *Kievlianin* editorial took the proposal further by suggesting that Jews also be encouraged to enroll in general schools, which would be modified to respect Jewish sensibilities (24:25/VIII/1864).

Postels' report gave *Kievlianin* an opportunity to return to this theme through the pen of its resident authority on the Jewish Question, Vladimir Fedorov. Fedorov was the baptismal name of the Jewish convert Khaim Grinboim [Haim Grinbaum]. He was a graduate of St. Vladimir University in Kiev and served as the censor of Jewish books in the Kiev Educational District.[28] Fedorov put the question into the context of the politics of Russification in the Ukraine. The government had originally sought to expand Russian influence in the area by attracting Russian settlers with lands and privileges. This program was now seen to be slow and onerous, and it could not guarantee that the small influx of settlers might not be assimilated by the Poles. The key was for Russians, like the Poles before 1863, to recognize the significance of the Jewish population of the Ukraine. If Jews could be reeducated into Russian citizens, "Polonism would melt away like wax before the fire." This process could be expedited not just by imposing a knowledge of Russian language upon the Jews, but also by promoting love and respect between Russian and Jew. This goal could best be achieved by common schooling. The creation of a separate Jewish system had been a mistake. It could be rectified by opening a parish elementary school in every village and town and encouraging Jews to attend. Existing Jewish primary and secondary schools should be replaced by elementary schools which would offer a two-year curriculum of Russian language, arithmetic, geography and history, with an emphasis on the history of Russia. Enrollment in these schools should be made mandatory for Jews. Without a diploma they should be denied permission to marry, to enroll in the merchant estate, enter a family partnership or pursue various trades (44–45:17–20/IV/1865). *Kievlianin* published dissenting opinions (55:13/V/1865), but Fedorov's views became those of the editor.

Even newspapers that had supported the state system, such as *Sanktpeterburgskie vedomosti*, now began to waver. An editorial noted the concerns of the director of the Kiev state Jewish schools. These institutions had failed to win the confidence of the fanatical and ignorant masses. Jews who did attend drew no benefit from the curriculum since it satisfied neither their religious nor secular needs. Like Fedorov, the editor could see no better alternative than to close the Jewish schools and replace them with good general schools in the district towns. This proposal lacked the element of coercion. Rather, the new schools should adopt a vocational curriculum which would make them desirable to Jewish students in search of a livelihood. The process of merging could take place in these schools successfully and rationally (174:28/VI/1866).

Provincial echoes of the abolitionist debate were heard. In 1867, *Bessarabskie oblastnye vedomosti*, the official publication of the territory of Bessarabia, turned its attention to Jewish education. A correspondent, I. Truzson, denounced the existing system as an impediment to Russification since both the staff and students were Jews. He called instead for destruction of Jewish religious fanaticism and for "moral merging" through the combination of state Jewish and general schools, and the abolition of all private Jewish schooling. Education for Jews was to be made mandatory, reinforced by heavy fines on recalcitrant parents (50:9/XII/1867). The editor rejected this extreme position (51:16/XII/1867).

The debate was now joined by the highest levels of the government. In 1867 Count Dmitrii Tolstoi, the Minister of Education, inspected Jewish educational institutions. He was impressed with the accomplishments of Odessa Jews, where private initiative had helped make the system a success, and correspondingly disappointed with the schools elsewhere, which had only succeeded in building up large debts. Tolstoi believed that the schools had outlived their usefulness as more and more Jews attended gymnasiums and women's seminaries. Consequently, he recommended that the state system be closed and the resources used to improve the existing district schools, where Jews might study useful trades alongside Christians. He appointed a committee to explore the question.[29]

When an excerpt from Tolstoi's report was published by *Kievlianin* (50:1/V/1869), abolitionists rushed to agree. In an accompanying editorial, *Kievlianin* declared that the idea of a separate Jewish school system had long outlived its time. Christians and Jews must be educated together with the single proviso that, where Jews were a significant part of the student body, parents should have the option of requesting a class in Jewish catechism, taught by a Jew. *Kievskii telegraf* similarly applauded Tolstoi's observations. The principle of equality was being violated: why should the government expend more care on the education of Jews than on that of Christians? Jews hardly needed the advantages which education gave them over the peasantry (51:5/V/1869).

Although the handwriting was clearly on the wall, a small rear-guard action in defense of the Jewish school system was waged, largely by the Russian–Jewish *Den*. But even the adherents of the system were half-hearted, and the reorganization of Jewish state schooling in 1873 was greeted with neither surprise, disappointment nor glee, with the exception of an exuberant *Kievlianin* editorial (38:29/V/1873).

A Ministry of Education decree on 16 March 1873 amalgamated first and second form schools into Jewish primary schools while drastically reducing their number, and reorganized the state rabbinical seminaries as purely teacher training institutions. Tolstoi announced that the system was abolished because it was no longer needed. There was an impressive increase in the enrollment of Jews in public institutions which he credited to the intermediary role of the state Jewish school system. This was an intimation of subsequent official concern that too many Jews were flooding into Russian schools. In 1875 the program of school stipends for Jews was dropped when the Committee of Ministers expressed concern that Jews were denying gymnasium places to Christians. The situation grew more severe with an accelerated flow of Jews into higher education, prompted by the exemptions offered for education by the Military Statute of 1 January 1874.[30]

The rabbinical seminaries of Vilna and Zhitomir had always drawn the least criticism in the debate over Jewish education.[31] From the government's point of view they accomplished their task of training rabbis and teachers. The two schools produced over 244 graduates between 1847 and 1863.[32] These graduates were a decisive component in the emergent Russian Jewish intelligentsia, and they provided first-hand models of enlightened Jews. Yet their position was not immune from attention, especially because they were tied to the vexatious problem of the state rabbinate.

The latter problem came to a head with the 1857 decree that all persons elected as rabbis must have had instruction in the state schools. It proved easier to train enlightened rabbis than to secure their election. A number of scandalous incidents took place when local authorities were accused of using intimidation and force to secure the election of a suitable candidate. *Kolokol* published an account of such a coerced election in Vilna in 1860. The authorities refused to allow the

Jewish electors to leave the synagogue until the candidate they approved was chosen. The nasty incident provoked an international scandal when it was reported in the Polish and Austrian press (73/74:15/VI/1860).

The communities found effective ways to fight back. In Minsk province the electors chose an unqualified candidate as state rabbi. When the authorities refused to confirm their choice, they failed to conduct another election.[33] The struggle between the state and the communities became chronic, since the state rabbis were elected only for three-year terms. Reelection battles attracted the attention of the press, especially in Odessa, where a triennial struggle surrounded the election of the German rabbi Schwabacher from 1860 to 1888. Communal struggles served to keep the question of the state rabbis in the public eye, and prompted debates as to why the communities rejected the new rabbis and how the schools might best prepare candidates who could exert a good moral influence and also gain reelection.

What role was the state rabbi supposed to play in Jewish society? The government had charted a bureaucratic mission for the state rabbi, but was negligent in defining a social role, leaving this task to others. Press discussions developed three distinct conceptions of the state rabbinate, all of which had their vocal supporters. The state rabbi was variously seen as an active transformer of the Jewish community, as a passive enlightener, or as merely a government official.

The most ambitious vision was described in *Rassvet* by I. Gorvits (13:19/VIII/1860). Greater numbers of Jews were moving into the wider gentile society, only to find that their medieval customs and traditions were obsolete under contemporary conditions. Their frustration offered a splendid opportunity for the state rabbis to "bring religious regulations into correspondence with the spirit of the times, cleanse religious law of all its foreign, human admixtures, separate the essence of the seed from the husk which history had created." To undertake such a task the rabbi was required to be fully conversant with both Judaism and contemporary civilization. The rabbinical seminaries were incapable of producing persons who could pursue these dual goals, Gorvits complained. He recommended instead, that a post-gymnasium curriculum of "higher Jewish studies" be created for the training of rabbis in Odessa or some other progressive center.

Commenting on the question of whether or not communities should retain the right to elect state rabbis, O. A. Rabinovich offered his own model for an enlightened rabbi.

> He should lead an irreproachable life, with a complete understanding of his pastoral duties, and provide instruction in civil obligations, morality and love. He should not be a partisan of innovation for its own sake, but neither should he swim against the current of the times. He must have a positive influence upon the young generation and for this a systematic education is required. The rabbi should come out of the community. (17:16/IX/1860)

These sentiments were echoed by the energetic Jewish publicist M. Morgulis in *Kievskii telegraf* (18–19–20–21:12–19–20–21/III/1861). The survival of the Jewish people depended on the emergence of enlightened individuals who could work their transformation by "explaining to Jews young and old the difference between true religion and superstition, between sacred belief and obscure superstition." Enlightened rabbis would work this transformation in partnership with the Russian state.

These lofty prescriptions, the enthusiasm for *Wissenschaft des Judentums*, and the desire to imitate reformed Judaism in the West – exemplified by the Breslau Rabbinical Seminary – were not shared by traditionalist communities which were more inclined to consider the new-style rabbis "wild beasts not fit for co-existence with human beings" (*Rassvet* 30:16/XII/1860). The casual reader of the contemporary press would find sufficient material to suggest that state rabbis, far from working the moral transformation of society, were incapable even of carrying out the supervisory and bureaucratic side of their duties. A state rabbi, writing in *Vilenskii vestnik*, lamented that he and his fellows were viewed by their communities as an unnecessary burden. They could neither fulfill their official duties nor attack popular obscurantism lest they fail to be reelected. They were forced to juggle the census books, certify the marriage of minors, and save promising talmudic students from the military draft. Preaching sermons, a major responsibility of European rabbis, was discouraged. If permitted to speak on holidays, they were obliged to "praise the Jews to the skies." The only solution to this predicament, the young rabbi asserted, was to remove the communal right to elect the state rabbi (94:26/VIII/1869). *Kievskii telegraf* reported a similar lament from another state rabbi, who was so overwhelmed with petty bureaucratic duties that he was unable to spend the time necessary to teach and lead his community (125:31/X/1873).

Distinct from the enthusiasts for reform were publicists who envisioned a more limited role for the state rabbinate. An anonymous correspondent in *Rassvet* took issue with the optimistic assumptions of

I. Gorvits, dismissing his plans as an attempt to build a house from the rafters down. Foreign examples were inappropriate. In Europe enlightened communities demanded educated rabbis, while in Russia the situation was reversed. Any attempt of rabbis outside Odessa, Riga or Mitau to force the pace of change would provoke a catastrophic response. The efforts of the state rabbis should be confined to narrowing the deep abyss which separated Russian Jews from any form of contemporary learning. Under the best of circumstances this would be a long and tedious process (34:13/I/1861).

This view was widely shared. Writing in *Kievskii telegraf* in 1865, Kh. Slonimskii, the head of the Zhitomir Rabbinical Seminary, predicted that the spiritual rabbi would remain a presence in the traditional Jewish community despite the government's preventive measures. Consequently, young enlightened rabbis were a practical necessity lest the obscurantists totally block any aspiration for secular learning within the community. He admitted ruefully that the state rabbis were at best a countervailing force: not strong enough to spread enlightenment, they were at least able to check the spread of fanaticism, the first step in preparing enlightenment. The muted expectations of Slonimskii might be expected, coming from a man well aware of the fate of most of the graduates of his institution. In fact, the surest demonstration he could make that enlightenment was slowly spreading was to note that a few state rabbis had actually been elected to a second term (102:3/IX/1865).

Lev Binshtok, whose article in *Russkii vestnik* has already been cited, was a former faculty member at the Vilna Rabbinical Seminary, so it is understandable that he defended the schools and their graduates, although, like Slonimskii, he was cautious in his expectations. The state rabbinate could stand as a force against the spread of Hasidism, which Binshtok saw as the principal obstacle to Jewish enlightenment. They might also promote the gradual spread of Russian language among the Jews, a serious requirement for the success of Russification. Even these modest goals required modification of the rabbinical seminaries. They had to develop a truer Russian spirit, which could be accomplished by making Russian the language of instruction for every class. The secular knowledge of graduates should be increased by making the seminaries the equivalent of classical gymnasia, with an additional three-year curriculum of Jewish subjects. Perhaps reflecting his own experiences, Binshtok also called for higher salaries and pension rights for the faculty and administration of the Jewish school system. State rabbis too should receive higher salaries and should be spared triennial elections. The right to appoint rabbis should become the responsibility of the seminary administration and the governor's office.

Binshtok and others had argued the case against coeducation with the claim that Jews were afraid to study in institutions dominated by Christians. The Jewish school system played an important, albeit temporary, role as an intermediary, accustoming the Jews to the idea of secular schooling. If the separate system were to be abolished, "there would not be even a ray of light." Gentile commentators began to question this logic, especially when the goal of education was characterized as Russification. A. Novosilstev, writing in *Vilenskii vestnik*, called for immediate coeducation. If additional expertise were required in Jewish subjects, it could be obtained through a post-gymnasium course of studies, on the model of Catholic seminaries in the West (28–29:12–14/III/1870).

At the other extreme from those who wanted the state rabbis to do everything were those who sought to limit their powers, or to abolish the institution altogether. Typical for this camp were the views of Emmanuel Soloveichik (*Rassvet* 3:10/VI/1860). Soloveichik explained that in Judaism the rabbi did not serve as a priest or clergyman because there were no rites which required his presence. The rabbi was no more than a member of the community who was skilled in the nuances of Jewish religious life, to whom individuals repaired for guidance and advice. The rabbinical seminary students whom the government forced on the communities commanded no confidence, and could not be expected to serve as community leaders. The state rabbi was obliged to perform bureaucratic functions which had never been associated with the traditional rabbinate. If properly carried out, these functions would destroy any influence which the state rabbis might hope to exert on the community. If he refused to sanction the marriage of an underage child, the marriage would take place anyway in a neighboring town. If he denounced a visiting *tzaddik* to the police, he would be viewed as an enemy of the faith. Those who challenged society's values could never hope to secure election or reelection. In short, as presently constituted, the state rabbinate was of no value to either the Jews or the Russian state.

To make it in any way useful, the office required a complete transformation. The bureaucratic functions of the office should be withdrawn. The young educated rabbi might then have some influence: "They can and should serve as an example to society: they should, by the way they live, show society how it is possible to join true piety with strict fulfillment of their state obligations, and join love for their people with love for their fatherland. They should serve as the center for all the educated people of their community." Soloveichik's proposal was so far from the state's conception of the duties and functions of the rabbinate, that it might best be termed reform through abolition. Fedorov, writing in *Kievlianin*, agreed that, as it stood, the state rabbinate was incapable of working change. "A handful of people cannot transform a whole nation, especially when the rabbis do not possess the weapons with which one can overcome the fanaticism of the masses" (73:24/VI/1865).

The faculty and students of the rabbinical seminaries emphasized the external obstacles to progress, especially the traditionalism of the community. Other critics pointed to the failures of the rabbis and the teachers themselves. The editor of the Russian supplement to the Hebrew-language *Ha-Karmel* complained that the young rabbis were actually setting back reform by their impolitic enthusiasms. They were "vandal-reformers" engaged in jousts, like Don Quixote, far removed from the field of their actual responsibilities. While religious reform was necessary for Russian Jewry, it was apparent that the Jews would not be easily alienated from age-old beliefs. Those who sought to do so quickly lost the confidence of the masses, and confirmed their prejudice that education undermined religious faith.

> Yet these reformers naively hope, as their words reveal, that one fine morning the Jewish people will reject them [their religious beliefs], as if by magic. It never occurs to them that eloquence is not enough for a reformer, and that one ought to be a genius of such mind as to embrace all the spiritual experiences of his people, to plumb their souls, experience their history, feel their fate, in order to place them on the proper course.

The author warned of the dire consequences inherent in the beliefs of "provincial progressives" that "the repudiation of the dictates of faith is the first step toward reform, and that the total breaking of things that the people hold dear will serve for their complete victory" (73:24/VI/ 1865).

The popular view of the seminaries and their graduates is mirrored in the description of the system in P. Smolenskin's Hebrew novel, *The Joy of the Godless (Simhat Hanef)*, published in 1872.

> Whom, then, may we trust in the role of guardian of Israel's wisdom? The institutes which are called rabbinical seminaries? You would be hard put to find anyone who either knows the Torah or is interested in it there. Does anyone go there in search of knowledge? There the

attitude toward the years of study is like that of a hired worker waiting for his wages. They look forward eagerly to the time of their release; and as soon as a student has obtained his certificate of graduation, he abandons the study of Torah completely, henceforward despising both it and its admirers. For he regards it not as a crown of glory but merely as an instrument for earning a livelihood. And the teachers? Do they strive to implant a love of Torah and understanding in the minds of their pupils? Never! They, too, are more concerned with an elegant use of Russian than with knowledge, and with Greek lyrics than the Psalms of David.[34]

Just as they differed in their evaluation of the deficiencies of the rabbinical seminaries, so too did commentators disagree as to how they might be remedied. Writing in *Den* (20:27/IX/1869), Soloveichik recommended that all religious functions be taken away from the state rabbinate, and that they be formally appointed as government bureaucrats with well-defined official functions. An editorial in *Kievskii telegraf*, reflecting the paper's liberal program, proposed a similar solution. It was anachronistic for the Russian state to strive for oversight of Jewish religious life. This objective was not only inappropriate, but failed due to the popular view of the state rabbi as nothing but a policeman, not a religious leader. The position must be recognized as the official bureaucratic post which it was in reality (18:13/II/1874).

If the state was to strip the state rabbis of any pretense of religious leadership, than the religious curriculum of the seminaries, already maligned by critics, was completely superfluous. A common reform proposal, offered again in *Den* in 1871 (16, 17:16–23/IV/1871) was simply to convert the seminaries into gymnasiums for Jewish youth. Given the widespread criticism of a separate Jewish school system voiced by Russifiers, such proposals were not calculated to appeal to the Ministry of Education. With the wholesale transformation of the state Jewish system in 1873, the two seminaries were converted into institutes for the training of teachers for the few remaining Jewish elementary schools. Since these schools were slated for closure, the teacher's institutes were also living on borrowed time.

The drastic reduction of the state Jewish school system left one problem unaddressed and unresolved. Although the government withdrew from the business of providing training for state rabbis, it neither abolished the post nor changed it in ways recommended by its critics. The state rabbinate was left in place, causing problems as the supply of graduates began to dry up. This remained an anomaly which the state could not or would not resolve, another relic of the state's efforts at social engineering for the Jews.

11 Partisans of enlightenment: The OPE

The ideologues of rapprochement and merger assumed that these were mutual processes involving both Christians and Jews. In the optimistic years of the late 1850s and early 1860s, when Russian society appeared to be actively pursuing this joint goal, plans were made for an organization to assist the government in its struggle with "the forces of darkness and obscurantism." The Polish Uprising provided a setting in which Jews might prove their loyalty and utility in the struggle for Russification if only a suitable mechanism could be devised. The agency which came to play this role was the Society for the Spread of Enlightenment among the Jews in Russia, usually known under an acronym of its Russian name, the OPE.[1]

The prime movers in this endeavor were the prosperous merchant Jews gathered around Baron E. Gintsburg. (The official founders were Gintsburg and A. M. Brodskii, the sugar-beet magnate.) These men comprised the core of the *shtadlanim*, the elite go-betweens, who had long been accustomed to interceding with the government on behalf of Jewish causes. They were on close terms with high officials, and were ready to follow governmental hints and leads. As L. M. Rozental, one of the founding members of the OPE, recalled:

> Highly placed individuals, with whom we came in contact and to whom we turned with our petitions and reports about improving the welfare of our coreligionists, continually reproached us that the Jews were sunk in darkness and fanaticism, stood aloof from everything Russian, and were given to harmful and degrading pursuits. These high officials told us: 'How can you hope that we will open the country before the Jews in their present condition?' 'Why,' they asked, 'don't you undertake anything to help your people escape from their low moral condition?' ... Each time that we spoke about civil rights for the Jews, high officials demanded of us a practical demonstration that the Jews had changed for the better and deserved these rights.[2]

It was against this background that the Petersburg activists resolved on a society which would demonstrate the Jews' commitment to enlightenment.

Planning was one thing, accomplishing another. As was frequently the case in imperial Russia, a private initiative, even when called forth by the government itself, was viewed with suspicion. It took two years of difficult negotiations with the government before the Society was approved on 2 October 1863. The first meeting of the new Society took place on 8 December 1863. Additional difficulties attended efforts to open provincial branches of the Society, even though they were permitted in the original charter. The first branch, in Odessa, was not approved until 1867, and the second, in Riga, not until 1898.[3]

The leadership of the OPE was clearly in the hands of the Maecenases in the capital – how could it be otherwise when the annual membership fee was a hefty 25 rubles? For several years Baron Gintsburg provided over half of the funding for the OPE.[4] Energetic efforts were made to attract, as honorary members, Russian journalists of a liberal cast. Thus, the founding members included A. A. Kraevskii, publisher of *Golos* and *Otechestvennyi zapiski*, P. S. Usov, editor of *Severnaia pchela*, A. Skachkov, editor of *Birzhevye vedomosti*, I. V. Vernadskii, editor of *Ekonomist*, I. Balabin, editor of *Narodnoe bogatstvo*, V. F. Korsh, editor of *Sanktpeterburgskie vedomosti*, later joined by *Russkii invalid*'s P. Lebedev. (This may account for the excellent press which the Society received in its first years.) A number of prominent officials in the Ministry of Education, A. I. Georgievskii, A. F. Postels and A. M. Bogdanovich, were also recruited.[5] Specialists on aspects of Jewish life were made honorary members. These included Professor B. Utin, V. Fedorov (Grinbaum), the Kiev censor, and the best-known convert of his day, D. Kh. Khvolson, who was to play a prominent and controversial part in the Society's early activities.

The objectives of the Society were framed in the following terms:

> The Society has as a goal the spread of enlightenment among the Jews living in Russia, the encouragement of literature and the support of student youth. In these guises it assists the dissemination of Russian among the Jews, it publishes and assists others to publish useful collections, translations and periodical publications in the Russian and Jewish tongues [i.e., Hebrew] which also seek to spread enlightenment among the Jews, and it encourages the young to education by giving them stipends.[6]

The founders thus eschewed purely pedagogical endeavors, pursuing a variety of activities to bring Jewish culture closer to Russian culture.

In pursuit of this general goal, the OPE followed two paths, one external and one internal.

The external role entailed mediating between the Jewish population and the government, defending Jewish interests from outside forces, and offering a positive picture of Jews and Judaism to the outside world. A middleman role came easily to a society founded by veteran *shtadlanim*. What the OPE represented was the centralization of what had been random and frequently uncoordinated activities. In Lederhendler's characterization, the OPE became "a new center of gravity in Jewish state relations ... a central address in what had been an amorphous system."[7]

Since the Society was viewed in this way, petitions began to flood its offices. They ran the full gamut of community concerns: help in securing the abolition of the *korobochka* tax on kosher meat; assistance for agricultural colonists or craftsmen who wished to move to the interior; defense against over-zealous enforcement of the 50 verst *cordon sanitaire* restricting settlement near the frontiers; help in opening a school or removing a Judeophobic school overseer; intervention on behalf of merchants who wished to participate in municipal elections or hire Christian servants; support for a printer who sought permission to keep both Cyrillic and Hebrew type in his shop. The OPE was thus confronted with the great and small questions of Jewish life, originating across the social spectrum, and often bearing only a tenuous relationship to the "spread of enlightenment."[8]

The OPE accepted such petitions, even if it did not always act upon them. While sometimes offering only lukewarm support for various pedagogical endeavors, the Society could be roused to vigor when it was necessary to defend Jews from bureaucratic harassment or public attack. Thus, in 1869, OPE presumably arranged for the election of one of its members, Emmanuel Levin, as a delegate from Vilna to the Vilna Jewish Commission. He immediately claimed leadership of the Jewish delegation. The enthusiasms of Russian nationalists in the Northwest led to repeated attacks upon the Jews by the official *Vilenskii vestnik*. Prodded by letters from indignant Jews, the OPE protested to the Chief Department for Press Affairs and to Governor-General von Kaufman in 1866 against the articles published by editor A. I. Zabelin in *Vilenskii vestnik*. It requested a retraction and an apology. The censorship board rejected this intervention, advising the OPE that its charter did not extend to "questions relating to the civil position of the Jews."[9]

The Society attempted to present Russian Jewry in the best possible light to the outside world through the medium of the press. It subsidized Russian-language newspapers, although with indifferent success. A number of publications, including the St. Petersburg thick journal *Deiatelnost* and the Kiev-based *Kievskii telegraf*, offered to publish Judeophile articles in return for subsidies, but the Society rejected a formal connection. It did offer some subvention by purchasing subscriptions for distribution to the provinces, but this proved a wholly ineffective method of holding editors to a sympathetic line.[10]

Efforts were made to publish materials for a general audience, even a specifically gentile one. These efforts encountered endless difficulties with the censor. Typical was the fate which befell an attempt to publish a Russian contribution to the *Wissenschaft des Judentums*, in the form of a *Miscellany* (*Sbornik*). Authorization to publish was obtained from the Chief Office for Press Affairs, only to be further delayed by the censor for the Holy Synod, who had a few niggling objections which had to be satisfied.[11] Another publication of the OPE, *The World-View of the Talmudists*, was designed to show Christians that the Talmud was a work of elevated moral values. However, it appeared in the midst of a virulent press campaign against the Talmud in the 1870s and served as grist for the mill of Judeophobes, who used its appearance to substantiate their claim that even educated Jews were slaves to the anti-Christian dictates of the Talmud.[12] The very existence of the OPE offered support for Iakov Brafman's charge that the kahal still existed as an organized force in Russia. Taken as a whole, the external successes of the OPE were ambiguous at best.

The external mission of the OPE was at least characterized by uniform objectives. Such clarity was missing from its internal objectives. The founders of the OPE were united in their determination to illumine the dark corners of the Jewish milieu, and to raise the cultural level of Russian Jewry. This task clearly implied the spread of European culture and its Russian variant. For the Russian officials among whom the founders moved, this meant Russification, in the sense of acquiring and using the Russian language, assimilating Russian culture, and adhering to the Russian side in the political conflict in the western provinces. But the mission of Jewish enlightenment did not mesh easily with the task of Russification, for the vast majority of the Empire's Jews lacked any command of Russian. It had not even been the language of the early Russian Haskalah.[13] The inherent contradiction spawned a vigorous contest between the partisans of four different linguistic paths to enlightenment, German, Yiddish, Hebrew and Russian. The partisans of one language did not necessarily disparage the utility of the others or discourage their use, but they did insist that their choice must receive priority in the division of resources.

German was a candidate largely because of the efforts of German rabbis who had been brought to Russia by congregations seeking an "enlightened pastor." The two most prominent were Rabbi Avraam Neiman of St. Petersburg and the long-serving Odessa rabbi, Shimon Aryeh Schwabacher [Shvabakher]. They were joined by a Russian partisan, Kh. S. Slonimskii, the overseer of the Zhitomir Rabbinical Seminary. The preferences of the two German rabbis were self-evident: both spent decades in Russia and never mastered the language. Slonimskii's support may be explained by the lingering respect for Germany as the birthplace of Haskalah, and German as the language of its dissemination. It was appropriate for the head of a rabbinical seminary to hold such views, since the Russian government itself had originally employed German as a language of instruction within its halls.

The partisans of German were always a minority among the Russian–Jewish intelligentsia and frequently under attack. Well before the foundation of the OPE, O. A. Rabinovich directed an editorial salvo against the efforts of Germanizers "to displace our beautiful and rich Russian tongue" (*Rassvet*, 48:21/IV/1861). The use of German even became faintly unpatriotic after the onset of political Russification, the more so when conservatives like Mikhail Katkov discovered that Germanization, as well as Polonization, was a menace in the borderlands. In any event, the use of German received short shrift in the internal discussions of the OPE.

The use of Yiddish, as will be seen, was always considered a necessary evil by the OPE. The real battle for supremacy was waged between the partisans of Hebrew and Russian. As a group, the supporters of Hebrew were the first generation "Old Maskilim." They were fully grounded in Hebrew literature themselves, and they knew on the basis of experience the dangers of offending the religious sensibilities of the Orthodox Jewish masses. Until enlightenment itself was widespread, they argued, there was no possibility of spreading Russian language or culture. The complexities of enlightenment could best be resolved through the "sacred language" – Hebrew. A typical adherent to this position was L. M. Rozental, one of the most important founders of the OPE.[14]

The Russifiers within the OPE were characteristically second-generation, "Young Maskilim," as well as those in the Gintsburg Circle who were closest to the seats of power. Three of the strongest partisans of Russian were E. B. Levin, A. Ia. Garkavi (whose scholarly investigations sought to show that the earliest Jewish settlers in Slavic lands spoke a Slavic vernacular), and D. A. Khvolson. All three held degrees from Russian universities. Khvolson's conversion to Russian Orthodoxy was widely recognized to be only for the sake of his academic career. While conceding that Hebrew might be employed to publish a few works of popular literature, the Russifiers envisioned a full range of publications in Russian, including historical works, a Russo-Jewish newspaper, and – Khvolson's pet project – a Russian translation of the Old Testament.

An internal committee was appointed to resolve the issue, and the Russifiers won the day, an understandable triumph in the prevailing climate of Russification. The committee reported that:

> the government does not at present plan the gradual extension to Jews of the right to participate in public affairs with Christians on an equal basis, the most effective way to promote their merger in daily affairs, outlook, morals, customs, aspirations and hopes – and until such time it follows that the foremost people of our nation, with the Society as their representative, should call forth Jewish literature in the Russian tongue.

Past attempts to spread enlightenment, the report explained, failed when reformers directly attacked the prejudices and superstitions of the masses, causing them to reply in kind. "Would it not be better to turn to neutral ground, where there is no room for distrust and suspicion? Instead of the correction of beliefs and convictions ... we will give our people the greatest treasures of knowledge, which are everlasting, precious and, most of all, uncontroversial."[15] When the members of the Society met on 8 February 1864, they accepted this report as a guide for future operations.

Any traveler to the western regions could see the wishful thinking inherent in the new report. As *Vestnik russkikh evreev* noted editorially at the end of the decade, Jews in the Pale were more likely to know Belorussian or Ukrainian, to say nothing of Polish, before Russian. If the Society confined its activities to the Russian language, it ran the risk of having no influence at all upon the Jewish masses (9:28/II/1871). In the event, the rhetoric of ardent Russification notwithstanding, pragmatism prevailed and the Society offered support for the Hebrew-language Russian press, especially Aleksandr Tsederbaum's *Ha-Melits* as well as the purchase and distribution of large numbers of Hebrew books, especially in the field of popular science.

Hebrew, at least, was a language with a glorious past and a rich treasury of literature. The need to support and use Yiddish, on the other hand, was a painful embarrassment. To an age which has seen the foremost Yiddish writer of his day, I. B. Singer, win the Nobel Prize for Literature, and recognizes the rich tradition of Yiddish literature, the scorn of educated Russian Jews for Yiddish might seem paradoxical. For them it was "jargon" (*zhargon*), an unsystematic mish-mash of languages, symbol of the fate which had harried the Jews from land to land. The Russian supplement to *Ha-Karmel* condemned it as "not even a language at all, but only a mixture of various tongues which, having neither a literature nor a grammar, hinders any intellectual development" (29:1/VI/1865). A commentator in *Vilenskii vestnik* agreed: "The language of the Jews at present is a mess of languages and dialects of all nations with which they dealt in their great historical migrations, a mess without rules of grammar or logic, with no principle for growth or development" (14:6/II/1864). The Jewish educator O. Gurvich even denied that Yiddish had any real affinity to German (*Vilenskii vestnik*, 7:21/VIII/1864). D. Lazareo, writing in *Uchitel*, denied that Russification could ever take place as long as Jewish women used Yiddish as their daily language (15–16: VIII/1864). The Russian–Jewish newspaper *Den* took regular swipes at the publisher Aleksandr Tsederbaum whose Yiddish newspaper, *Kol Mevaser*, was published, it claimed, "in a wondrous jargon which not even Jews can understand" (47:20/XI/1870).

These condemnations dripped with frustration, and with good reason: Yiddish was the daily vernacular for the vast majority of Russian Jews. Translations and original works in Yiddish sold well, even as writers remained ambivalent about the necessity of employing Yiddish as a medium of enlightenment.[16] *Kol Mevaser*, despite the scorn heaped upon it, assisted the development of literary Yiddish by adopting a uniform system of spelling and choosing a specific dialect as normative for the paper, and by publishing great stylists like Mendele Mokher Sforim.[17] A large popular devotional literature, often of Hasidic orientation, also circulated. Reluctantly, and despite its own rhetoric, the OPE was forced to recognize reality and offer an occasional work in Yiddish, which inevitably provoked criticism from parties less sympathetic or realistic. Consequently, the work of the OPE was carried on in three languages, although in vastly different proportions.

Having resolved, or at least confronted, the issue of language, the OPE faced the task of producing educational materials. Efforts to publish materials under the Society's imprint were ill-starred from the beginning, given the censorship problems of the *Miscellany*, and the hostile reception given *The World-View of the Talmudists*. More contentious still was the Society's decision to sponsor a Russian translation of the Jewish Bible. It embroiled the Society in misadventures both secular and spiritual.

It was no accident that Daniel Khvolson was the principal advocate of a Russian Bible for the Jews. He was already engaged in producing a translation of the Old and New Testaments for the Russian Orthodox Church. At this time there did not yet exist a complete rendering of the Scriptures into modern Russian. A translation was available only in Old Church Slavonic, the archaic liturgical language of the church. The Russian branch of the British and Foreign Bible Society had almost completed a modern translation in the reign of Alexander I (1801–25) before politics intervened and prevented its circulation. It was this work which comprised the foundation for Khvolson's project. To complicate matters still further, a Russian translation of the Hebrew Bible had been completed by A. L. Mandelshtam in Germany, but was not allowed to circulate in Russia.

The main difficulty lay with the Russian Orthodox Church which did not have a tradition of independent Bible reading, and which was suspicious of any text which did not carry an approved commentary. Their fear was that a Jewish version might fall into peasant hands. Church authorities were especially concerned with Russian Orthodox sectarians. Judaizing tendencies among their ranks were sufficiently strong to provoke legal bans on Jewish proselytism throughout the nineteenth century. For these reasons, the Ecclesiastical Censorship of the Holy Synod repeatedly refused OPE requests for a translation throughout the 1860s, just as it rejected petitions for a Jewish prayer book in Russian. Khvolson was unwilling to abandon the idea, and proposed a compromise. The OPE should seek permission to publish a text identical to the one on which he was working for the Russian Orthodox Church. It would include, of course, only the books of the Old Testament considered canonical by Jews, and with a few minor translation changes and reordering of books to respect Jewish sensibilities. In May of 1869, the OPE petitioned for the right to print the Khvolson version, and in September permission was granted.[18] A spectacular furore erupted at this point, led by the Odessa-based Jewish newspaper, *Den*.

From its inception *Den* had belabored the OPE for its maladroit intervention in the deliberations of the Vilna Jewish Commission. This latest action added fuel to the fire. *Den* bitterly attacked the decision to publish a Jewish version of the Russian Orthodox text, arguing that public opinion unanimously recognized the justice of allowing the Jews to have their own translation (10:7/III/1870). Khvolson retorted that the Holy Synod would never permit an independent translation (14:4/IV/1870). He also defended his own role in the project, explaining that his only motive was to spread Russian among the Jews (18:1/V/1870). This was a touchy subject. Although Khvolson attained near-legendary status as a defender of the Jews, he was a convert to Russian Orthodoxy and a teacher in an Orthodox seminary. Everything of a religious nature which he touched was suspect. D. Slonimskii went so far, in a letter to *Novoe vremia*, as to accuse him of seeking to convert the Jews to Christianity (125:8/V/1870). The foreign Jewish press also began to criticize the OPE.[19] Chastised, the Society dropped its plans for a Russian Bible and shortly thereafter, in 1871, the Holy Synod gave permission for Mandelshtam's translation to be sold in Russia.

Ultimately the Society abandoned the task of dealing with the Russian censor, and confined itself largely to subsidizing or purchasing and distributing the works of others. Large numbers of textbooks for Jewish schools, published through private initiative, were disseminated by the OPE. Particular favorites for distribution to provincial Jewish libraries were the works of the great Russian Jewish legal historian and publicist Ilia Orshanskii. Numerous works in Hebrew on popular science were distributed. The Society attempted to spread Russian literacy by sending subscriptions for Russian newspapers to Jewish schools. This practice was stopped due to the protests of provincial administrators, apparently concerned by the liberal tendencies of some of these papers.[20] With the reorganization of the state Jewish school system, subscriptions went to local communities instead. It became more difficult to find satisfactory organs, as some of the most prominent publications in Russia grew hostile to the Jews, including *Golos* and *Novoe vremia*. In the 1870s, the Society began to provide subscriptions to the Jewish press instead, although this meant publications in Hebrew rather than Russian.[21]

Ironically, some of the most frustrating experiences of the OPE leadership came from its sponsorship of the Jewish press. The Society dreamed of acquiring a journalistic organ of its own and entered into a series of arrangements with the editor Aleksandr Tsederbaum. In 1864 the Society contracted to pay Tsederbaum a subsidy for his Hebrew-language *Ha-Melits*. In return, the paper was to add a section devoted to scholarship and education which would be edited by the educator and journalist Kh. Z. Slonimskii. The arrangement proved unsatisfactory, and broke down after only seventeen weeks. Slonimskii carried out his editorial duties in Zhitomir, and sent his materials to the Odessa-based printing press of Tsederbaum. The quality of printing and editing by Tsederbaum was quite poor, and upon occasion the section was simply dropped. In February of 1865 the special arrangement ended, although Tsederbaum continued to receive some financial assistance from the OPE, as did every other Hebrew publication printed in Russia.[22] A similar fate befell the subsidy given to Tsederbaum's Yiddish *Kol Mevaser*. The Society insisted, as the price of its support, that Tsederbaum elevate the language to bring it closer to colloquial German. When Tsederbaum proved unwilling or unable to meet this demand, he lost the subsidy in 1865.[23] This break came even though *Kol Mevaser* was playing a pivotal role in the evolution of Yiddish as a vigorous literary language. Moreover, the paper commanded a large and enthusiastic audience, primarily women and poorly educated men. In retrospect, *Kol Mevaser* was perhaps the most appropriate vehicle for spreading enlightenment on the Jewish street.

Support was also offered to the Russian-language Jewish press. The Russian supplement to the Hebrew *Ha-Karmel*, published in Vilna, received subsidies amounting to 900 rubles between 1865 and 1868. The results were not impressive, as the paper was of indifferent quality and was generally ignored by the rest of the Russian press.[24] More enthusiastic support was rendered to the highly regarded almanac, *Evreiskaia biblioteka*, published through the 1870s by A. E. Landau in St. Petersburg.[25] Similar support for the Odessa-based *Den*, on the other hand, proved most unsatisfactory to the Society.

With the failure of *Rassvet/Sion*, no Russian–Jewish newspaper appeared in Odessa for almost a decade. In 1869 the Odessa branch of the OPE attempted to revive *Rassvet*. It petitioned for an enlargement of the defunct paper's program. Using the still-valid franchise to publish – institutions in Russia could take as long to die as to be born – it revived the paper as *Den: Organ russkikh evreev*. Editorial duties were assigned to S. S. Ornshtein, who had been active in securing permission to publish. The paper was given an initial subsidy of 550 rubles. The Odessa OPE appointed a committee to vet all articles proposed for publication in *Den*, but the arrangement was stillborn. Ornshtein was independent from the very beginning.

The St. Petersburg OPE was wary of the Odessa project, and its worst fears were soon realized. The paper was rambunctious and contentious, eager to wade into polemical exchanges with the Russian press at every opportunity. The editors refused to know their place, espousing tactics most distasteful to the cautious and discreet activists of the capital. Worse still, the capital leadership became a favorite whipping boy for the editorialists of *Den*. With the fourth issue of the paper (8/VI/1869), *Den* made the leaders the epitome of communal apathy and ineffectiveness. To add insult to injury, *Den* also decried the secrecy of the central body. There was further criticism of Emmanuel Levin's role on the Vilna Jewish Commission and savaging of the plans for the Khvolson Bible project. The enraged Petersburgers demanded that the Odessa OPE rein in *Den*, only to be told that the paper was no longer under their effective control.[26] The attacks ended only when *Den*, together with the Odessa OPE, perished amidst the disillusionment which followed the Odessa pogrom of 1871. Meanwhile, the OPE offered a subsidy to Tsederbaum to publish a Russian newspaper in the capital, secure in the knowledge that "it will not, like *Den*, speak impertinently to the authorities."[27]

Although the OPE saw its mission as ranging far beyond the narrow field of education, it was inevitably drawn into debates on the state Jewish school system. In particular the Society responded to rumors of the impending closure of the schools with ardent appeals that they be kept open. The Society was far from satisfied with the state of the schools, but envisioned their reform, not their abolition. When the system was partially dismantled in 1873, the Society attempted to fill the gap. It provided stipends to send Russian Jews to study in the Breslau Rabbinical Academy so that communities could still recruit enlightened rabbis. The Society did not forget the laborers in the vineyard: it appealed to the government to provide pensions for the faculty members of the state Jewish schools.[28]

Through the 1870s the OPE remained a narrowly based institution whose membership never exceeded 500. Disturbingly, no more than half of these members were to be found scattered about the Pale. Thirty cities had only one member. Important Jewish centers like Vitebsk and Chernigov had no members at all. Typically, the provinces received more in largesse than they contributed to the enterprise. One commentator, not inaccurately, complained that the OPE resembled a charity fund, run out of the office of two or three benefactors, without any participation by the masses (*Rassvet* 29:28/VII/1880). Calls were made to democratize the Society by including membership categories of 5 and 2 rubles (*Rassvet* 16:28/XII/1879). While the old leadership never went that far, they did eventually reduce the minimum membership fee to 10 rubles.

Under these circumstances, the logical approach of the OPE might have been to recruit more members, or narrow its activities. Instead, the Society moved in a completely different direction. At its annual meeting in 1880, the Society accepted a proposal to radically expand its undertakings. Two new sections were to be founded, one devoted to the spread of agricultural expertise among the Jews, and the second to encourage Jewish artisan ventures. In keeping with this expanded mission, the Society petitioned the government to change its name to "The Society for the Spread of Useful Work Among the Jews."[29] Critics wondered how the Society could embark upon such a gigantic undertaking when its less ambitious projects had enjoyed only indifferent success (*Rassvet* 42:16/X/1880). Such complaints became moot, however, when the government refused to accept the expanded program, and the task of changing the economic profile of Russian Jewry was left to other initiatives.

The Society and its activities appeared increasingly irrelevant throughout the 1880s, especially after the outbreak of the pogroms of 1881 called into question all the old assumptions of the Russian Jewish intelligentsia. Other movements evolved within Russian Jewish culture and provided a ready alternative to Russification. The growth of Zionism and socialism directly challenged the underlying assumptions of the OPE, based as they were on the spread of Russian language and culture and absolute loyalty to the throne. Restricted to educational activities, the Society found even these obstructed by the state it professed to serve. In 1882, for example, the Society was forbidden to continue its program of stipends for Russian rabbinical students at Breslau.[30] The Society's past efforts to assist Jewish students who sought advanced degrees in Russian universities appeared to be repudiated by efforts at the local and national level to restrict Jewish access to higher education. At best the OPE could console itself with the thought that enlightenment had, after all, taken root among Russian Jews.

The fate of the OPE in the 1880s belied the gracious reception which it had received from the Russian press a quarter century earlier. Even before its first meeting, the liberal newspaper *Russkoe bogatstvo* hailed the charter, although it did find fault with the high dues scale, and the proviso that the directors be elected from the highest membership categories. These undemocratic features were more than balanced by the Society's openness to every class, gender and religion. In the light of the emergence of the Woman Question, the editor observed, it was especially gratifying to see equality of the sexes in the quest for enlightenment (257:26/XI/1863). The pedagogical journal *Uchitel* was happy to point out to the OPE features of domestic and state Jewish schooling which it recommended for reform (10: V 1864). *Birzhevye vedomosti* encouraged the founders to press ahead, especially in the light of the numerous obstacles which they faced (105:7/V/1866), although the editors later turned on the OPE for its support of Jewish primary schools, considering them an obstacle to the process of merging (193:16/VII/1875). *Sanktpeterburgskie vedomosti* habitually supported the Society and wished it well, especially in its attempts to spread the Russian language (45:25/II/1864). The Russifying outpost in Warsaw, through *Varshavskii dnevnik*, also welcomed the Society's efforts (135:24/VI/1869).

The Society proved adept at generating publicity for itself. It published an annual report of its activities, provoking comment in the Russian press. The Society's reports were frequently republished without comment even by publications of a decidedly Judeophobic bent, such as *Kievlianin, Novorossiiskii telegraf* and *Novoe vremia*.

Not all of the press was so approving. Some critics dismissed the Society as ineffective, such as the writer in the conservative, Russifying St. Petersburg newspaper *Narodnyi golos*, which cited the Society for its inability to command the financial support of the communal aristocrats and for its support of trivial projects (28:4/II/1867). The doyen of Russification, Katkov, was also slow to approve the Society's endeavors. He was initially displeased by the Society's provision of stipends for young Jews to study in Russian schools, fearing that this would skim off the Jewish intellectual elite, and alienate them from the masses (*Moskovskie vedomosti*, 148:8/VII/1865). Ironically, the Society's decision to support publication of the Khvolson translation of the Hebrew Bible, as well as Jewish prayer books in Russian – actions which caused dangerous divisions within the Jewish camp – won Katkov to its side. He had long been a proponent of just such activities in the Russification campaign, and offered warm approval of the Society's direction (143:9/VII/1866).

The OPE was very much the representative of the "old guard" Jewish communal leadership. Its founders were merchants and contractors, and the scholars and publicists upon whom they relied for direction and advice were largely the older generation of maskilim. While espousing the rhetoric of linguistic and cultural Russification, the merchants and the Old Maskilim were keenly aware of the religious and national sensibilities of the people. Thus, while the "Russians" had won the theoretical debates over language, the Society continued to support Hebrew and Yiddish publications. It was easy for outsiders to see the OPE as the well-publicized plaything of a few rich men, who conducted its affairs from the Olympian heights of St. Petersburg. In return for a small handout, they expected the new generation to be grateful and quiet.

The hostile response to the efforts of the OPE by many of the younger generation reveals a generational split within the Jewish intelligentsia, pitting those who were Russifiers first against those who were maskilim first. The former were impatient and intolerant of the old ways and the old sensibilities. Some remained within the community, secure in the rightness and inevitability of their course. Others, like Portugalov and Zelenskii, who were ready to reject the Talmud without knowing what it was, were in the process of breaking away from the Judaic milieu. They were eager to sacrifice their Jewishness on the altar of public utility, if only a suitable ceremony could be devised. The OPE offered this faction a suitable target upon which to vent their frustrations.

The critics found an appropriate vehicle for their criticisms in the St. Petersburg newspaper *Glasnyi sud*. The paper had begun in 1866 as a colorless liberal organ offering stenographic accounts of court cases. In the summer of 1867, eager to resuscitate the paper's failing fortunes, the editor invited the participation of journalists from the radical thick journal *Delo*. A number of well-known writers accepted, including N. A. Demert, N. S. Kurochkin and N. K. Mikhailovskii. The reorganized paper promptly issued an editorial call for the complete equalization of Jewish rights, warning that "slavery and semi-freedom are equally harmful." The Jews, if widely dispersed and given broader fields of endeavor, would no longer be forced to survive at the expense of their Christian neighbors (200:8/V/1867).

This editorial elicited a flood of letters from young Jews complaining of OPE's activities. *Glasnyi sud* published a series of three articles by an anonymous Jewish author, which bear eloquent witness to the generational split (252–259–264:6–13–18/VII/1867). While thanking the editors for their solicitude, he denied that the Jewish masses, in their present state, were capable of using freedom properly. Freedom, he asserted, should not be given to the Jews as a gift or an act of charity, but should be earned through the attainment of at least an elementary education and the adoption of occupations which would require freedom to be successful. He lamented that the Jewish intelligentsia was divided as to how this might best be done.

The younger generation "assumes that, by quitting everything Jewish except the name, and through the acquisition of a higher, true education, they can become Russians (i.e., Russian Citizens of the Mosaic Faith). By not mixing up nationality and religion, the young ... believe that every Jew, freed from the external fetters of his religion, may assimilate (*usvoit' sebe*) everything Russian, and become a useful member of the society of which he is a part." The older generation, while desiring mild reform, was paralyzed by the intimidating force of religion, with all of its demands on the individual. Having asserted a monopoly on educational endeavors, the older generation sought "through various palliative measures, to smooth out all those short-comings which so sharply catch the eye of any educated person."

In principle, the OPE could be a positive force if it combatted "the terrorism of Jewish religion and Jewish despot-fanatics." Such an organization might advise the government on the proper ways to influence the Jews, while itself struggling against "the miasma of Jewish scholasticism." It must destroy the old learning and support the new, "creating a modern synthesis and not just disguising old fail-ings." The OPE, dominated by a conservative old guard, failed com-pletely to accomplish these goals. Its attempts to spread Russian were confined to the publication of the *Miscellany*, which was too abstract and difficult for an educated person, still less the masses. Russian–Jewish writers supported by the Society were nothing but the clients and protégés of the leadership. For the spread of useful knowledge the Society employed Hebrew and Yiddish. In view of the organization's stated commitment to Russian, this was the most base hypocrisy. Even the Society's choice of "useful knowledge" was flawed: they distribu-ted texts on physics or zoology, which would do nothing to advance the fundamental religious changes that must take place in Jewish society. In short, the Society's efforts were hypocritical and inade-quate. Russian publications, filled with praise of the Society, might not understand this, the author observed sourly, but Jewish youth did.

While Jews squabbled among themselves, malevolent gentile critics followed hard upon the first flush of approval. One of a series of anti-Jewish articles carried by *Vilenskii vestnik* under the editor Zabelin not only attacked the OPE, but also the very premises of Jewish education. The author, Aleksandr Vladimirov, a provincial echo of Ivan Aksakov, voiced misgivings at the spread of modern education among the Jews.

> We hope that nobody will deny that all contemporary enlightenment is Christian, and that Christianity is the only door to contemporary civilization ... The Jews should create their own Jewish enlighten-ment or they will be forever parasites on Christian civilization or even

worse, as experience shows: in the field of science, or wherever a prominent mind of Jewish origin appears, they immediately turn with hostility against Christianity and as a consequence direct their activity to undermining the bases of civilization. Are we hard pressed to point out how many contemporary nihilists ... who decompose Russian and all civilized society have come from the kin of *enlightened* Jews? (116:3/VI/1866)

Vladimirov's attack could be dismissed by the partisans of the OPE as the rantings of a provincial bigot. Considerably more complex were the Society's dealings with the St. Petersburg *Golos*. *Golos*, which generally advanced classic liberal positions, was one of the most influential and highly regarded papers of its day, both at home and abroad. Its editor, A. A. Kraevskii, was one of the gentile founding members of the OPE. The paper's attitude toward the Society, nonetheless, ranged from the critical to the malicious, a reflection of the ambivalent attitude of Russian liberalism as a whole toward the Jews.

After a brief honeymoon, *Golos* restricted itself to mild criticism. In its review of the Society's report for 1868, for example, *Golos* condemned the OPE for printing even one book in Yiddish, since this ran counter to its professed goal of merging (152:3/VI/1868). A month later, a converted Jew, M. Gurvich, accused the Society of abandoning the Talmud, only to replace it with a Jewish nationalism which was incompatible with assimilation (152:3/VI/1868). The annual report for 1873 prompted extended criticism. *Golos* noted the paucity of members, only 278 after ten years, and the modest expenditure of funds, 5,454 rubles for 1872. The Society's support of students at the Universities of Derpt and Zurich, and at the rabbinical seminaries of Berlin and Breslau, called into question its support for the Russian language. Only one branch of the Society, in Odessa, was in existence, and its energies were directed toward improving primary school education, rather than spreading Russian. Only one Russian manuscript, a translation of the Pentateuch, was under consideration for publication by the Society. *Golos* complained that the Society's present goals were far removed from those of its charter. In Belostok, for example, the members of the Society wanted to create a "Society for the Promotion of Industry," with the aim of creating an exclusively Jewish craft school. When the local authorities refused the request, the Society appealed this decision to the Ministry of Internal Affairs, only to be told that such activities were not within its competence. It was noteworthy, *Golos* observed, that having failed to achieve its original objectives, the OPE now sought to expand its activities. Such a reorientation, the paper mocked, would transform the Society into a Russian version of the Alliance Israélite Universelle (164:15/VI/1873).

The identification of the OPE with the Alliance may have been a harmless jibe in 1873, although it did reflect official disquiet at Gintsburg's ties to the Alliance. By 1876 it had come to constitute a serious charge. *Golos*, by now the premier Judeophobic publication in Russia, opened its pages to Iakov Brafman, whose charges against the persistence of the kahal in the 1860s grew ever more exotic in the 1870s. Brafman had begun to link the Alliance to an international Jewish conspiracy against the Christian world, and it was a logical extension to assign the OPE a role as the Russian branch of this Alliance.

The occasion for this charge was the publication of *The World-View of the Talmudists* which Brafman reviewed for *Golos* (117:28/IV/1876). In the review, "The Jesuits of Jewry," Brafman denounced the book as an attempt to mislead the Russian public about the true nature of Jewish belief. Brafman asserted that, contrary to the claims of the book, the Talmud permitted Jews to harm their gentile neighbors in any way possible. Education would not make the Jews less fanatical as the OPE leaders pretended.

> The difference between Jews trained in the Talmud, and Jews receiving a general education lies only in the following: those trained in the Talmud wait for the restoration of the Judaic kingdom to occur suddenly, unexpectedly, without the participation of the Jews, by some miracle; educated Jews preach that the restoration of the Judaic kingdom will occur naturally, and that the Jews ought to prepare for it through education, which will give their nation good generals, engineers, lawyers and people required for the restoration and survival of the state, things for which the Talmud offers no preparation.

To support his claims, Brafman quoted an article in the Hebrew-language periodical *Ha-Shahar*, published in Vienna, in which the author exhorted the Jews of Russia to prepare themselves for a wide range of secular activities, lest the Messiah, when he came, found them unfit for worldly labors. The author was none other than L. O. Gordon [Judah Leib Gordon], the OPE secretary.[31] In a subsequent *Golos* editorial, obviously written by Brafman, the connection was made more specific: the OPE was the Russian branch of the dreaded Alliance (216:6/VIII/1876). This was the tone of *Golos* articles on the Jews until the end of the decade.

The OPE soldiered on. Despite the warnings and advice of Brafman, and many other publicists, the Russian government never sought to curtail its operations. By the 1880s the Russian press generally ceased to critique its annual report. From the perspective of the leadership, this might have seemed an improvement. The OPE had become a symbol for Jews of impotence and inactivity, and for Russians of an international, subversive institution, intent on the destruction of Christian Europe in general, and Christian Russia in particular.

12 "A state within a state"

"Our Russian Pfefferkorn" was the dismissive epithet coined for Iakov Brafman by one of his Jewish opponents (*Den* 29:29/XI/1869). This tag is simultaneously apt and misleading. Both Johannes Pfefferkorn and Brafman were apostates from Judaism, who did significant damage to their former coreligionists by denouncing them to the gentile authorities. Both posed as learned men, while offering tendentious and misleading interpretations of the Judaic tradition. But there was also one overriding difference between the two men. While Pfefferkorn in his denunciations to the imperial authorities of sixteenth-century Germany, located all the harmfulness of the Jews in the writings of the Talmud, Brafman discovered the pernicious center elsewhere, in the system of Jewish communal government known as the kahal. Brafman's career encapsulates the evolution of Russian attitudes toward the Jewish Question from vague distress at the perceived disorder of Jewish religious and economic life to paranoid obsession with international Jewish conspiracies. Brafman can justly be called the grandfather of *The Protocols of the Elders of Zion*. It was his – and Russian Judeophobia's – great contribution to the rise of modern Antisemitism.

Iakov Aleksandrovich Brafman was born in the shtetl of Ketsk, Minsk province, in 1824. He came from a poor family, was orphaned early, and was raised by distant relatives. There was little question of Brafman receiving an adequate traditional education, and his later claims to expertise on all things Jewish were clouded somewhat by his inability to translate even uncomplicated, contemporary Hebrew. His later patron, the director of the Northwest Educational District, I. P. Kornilov, had difficulty employing him, because he was unfit to teach general subjects.[1]

An obstreperous youth, Brafman clashed with representatives of the Ketsk community, especially after his young daughter died and the Burial Society (Hevra Kaddisha) demanded a payment beyond his resources. A member of the Society snatched a pillow from the bed of the dead child as a pledge for the debt.[2] (Brafman had his revenge through his description of the Hevra Kaddisha in his works, including a poignant description of its representatives intimidating a grief-stricken family, mirroring his own experiences.) Brafman's poverty and rebelliousness made him a prime candidate to be assigned by his community as an army recruit, and he took to the road until the age of thirty-four. He failed at a variety of professions, including a period as a photographer in Minsk. In 1858, he converted to Russian Orthodoxy in Minsk. In his entry on Brafman in *Evreiskaia entsiklopediia* (IV, 917), Iulii Gessen claims that there was evidence of an earlier conversion, to Lutheranism, in Kiev. If this claim is accurate, it is strong evidence of Brafman's cynicism, not only because of multiple changes of religions, but also because Lutheranism, decentralized and less liturgical, was notorious as the "religion of convenience" for insincere Jewish converts.

With his conversion to Orthodoxy, Brafman's life entered onto a new path. He became a missionary, unsuccessfully attempting to spread Christianity among Russian Jews. Brafman thus gained a toe-hold in the world of Russian officialdom through his clerical contacts, and he attempted to use them to the fullest. In 1858, Tsar Alexander II made a state visit to Minsk, and Brafman submitted a memorandum to him on the most effective means of converting Jews. He proposed formation of a missionary society which would carry on its work in Yiddish, and offered to translate the New Testament into Yiddish.[3] The memorandum was forwarded to the Holy Synod in St. Petersburg, and Brafman was summoned to the capital to give a fuller report on 29 October 1859. As an outcome of his visit, he was appointed to the post of teacher of Hebrew at the Minsk Russian Orthodox Seminary in 1860.[4]

Jewish folklore, and Brafman's own writings, depicted the position of *melamed*, the teacher of elementary subjects, including Hebrew, to young children as the last resort for the incompetent and unskilled. Now, ironically, Brafman became a *melamed* for Christian clerics. Brafman, whose character was marked in equal measure by vanity and ambition, did not rest content. He continued to approach higher authorities with projects to restructure Jewish life as preparation for expediting religious conversion. An attempt to interest the Russifying governor of the Northwest, Mikhail Muravev, failed in 1864, but Brafman remained undaunted.

In 1866 he took a leave of absence from his Minsk position, and decamped to Vilna where he received a polite if cautious reception from such Jewish Russifiers as L. O. Levenda. He then set to work to interest local authorities in his schemes. It is difficult to ascertain whether Brafman's journalistic endeavors first caught the attention of his future patron, I. P. Kornilov, or if they were the consequence of having already achieved favor. In any event, Brafman's initial contribution to Russian journalism was a series of articles, "The View of a Jewish Convert to Orthodoxy on the Jewish Question in Russia," which appeared in *Vilenskii vestnik* (149:13/VII; 151:15/VII, and 173:16/VIII/1866), the official publication of the Northwestern Educational District.

Brafman reported that his missionary efforts had resulted in only forty conversions in six months, but that this was an impressive achievement when measured against the difficulties faced by would-be neophytes anxious to escape Judaism. He rejected the claims of contemporary Jewish progressives that if Jews were emancipated, Judaism would embark on a progressive development and reform. History testified otherwise. All efforts to help or reform the Jews – the creation of agricultural colonies for a life of honest toil, the development of a primary school system to break down Jewish fanaticism, and efforts to train progressive rabbis in state rabbinical schools – were all obvious failures.

To this point, Brafman's attacks on the Jews differed little from similar articles printed by *Vilenskii vestnik* decrying the abuses of Jewish life in Russia.[5] In his article in number 173, Brafman announced a great discovery. Hitherto resistance to change and Jewish religious fanaticism were universally attributed to the influence of the Talmud. In reality, the strength of Judaism lay in its organization as a civil corporation, a phenomenon completely ignored by observers. Christian states unwittingly maintained this talmudic kingdom, by confirming the power of its rabbis, ratifying the selection of kahal leaders, and expediting a system of internal taxation. The talmudic bureaucracy, made up of a communal elite, was thus able to rule and dominate the Jewish masses. To prove his charge, Brafman appended documentary proof, "a Jewish document from the kahal book of one of the provincial centers," which revealed how Jews prevented outsiders from judging them by maintaining the integrity of the talmudic court, the *bet din*. This was the first incarnation of *The Book of the Kahal*, and it set forth in embryo all the themes which Brafman was to develop over the next decade.

Kornilov was much impressed. One day after the appearance of

Brafman's third article, he wrote to the Ministry of Education to lament the despotism of the kahal and to decry the bonds of Jewish corporatism.[6] He assisted Brafman in more tangible ways. Praising him as "unique, indispensable," he persuaded the Governor-General of the Northwest, K. P. von Kaufman, to appoint Brafman as Censor of Jewish books in Vilna, and secured him a stipend of 2,500 rubles to assist in the translation and editing of the documents which Brafman claimed cast valuable light on the internal workings of the Jewish community.[7] The reports which Brafman subsequently submitted to von Kaufman through Kornilov led to the creation of the Vilna Jewish Commission.

What were the documents which formed the basis of Brafman's *The Book of the Kahal*? In his *Vilenskii vestnik* articles, Brafman called them a "kahal book," preserved in the archive of the Vilna Educational District. Whatever the process by which he acquired them – Levitats claims that Brafman stole them, Zolotonsov that they were provided by Kornilov – the documents were apparently the communal record book, or *pinkas*, from the kahal of Minsk, covering the years from 1794 to 1833.[8] The sloppy translation, and even more the tendentious editing of Brafman, which characterized the documents published in 1867, 1868 and 1869, led some contemporaries to question their authenticity. With the publication of the expanded and corrected edition of 1875, doubts were stilled, the more so since the authenticity of some of the documents received independent confirmation. *The Book of the Kahal* is a genuine *pinkas*, one of a number of such documents which have proven essential for the study of the workings of Jewish autonomous institutions in Russia prior to the abolition of the kahal in 1844.[9]

Translation of the Minsk *pinkas*, to be financed by funds from the Jewish communal candle tax at the disposal of Kornilov's office, was undertaken by N. P. Guriev (Moisei Gurvich), a convert and teacher at the Vilna Rabbinical Academy, and three of his students, Ia. Bratin, G. L. Levin and one known only as Tiger, under Brafman's direction. This work was ultimately published, under Brafman's name and with his commentary, in the periodical press and in two books, *Jewish Brotherhoods, Local and International* (Vilna, 1868) and *The Book of the Kahal* (Vilna, 1869).[10] They were published with Kornilov's assistance, and reportedly dispatched to governmental offices around the Pale in order to acquaint Russian bureaucrats with the realities of Jewish life. This was the source of the oft-repeated but exaggerated depiction of the book as "an official publication of the Russian government."[11]

Brafman appeared before the Imperial Geographical Society in 1870 to defend his work from criticism, and was voted funds to continue his work.[12] An expanded and corrected version of *The Book of the Kahal* was published by the Society in 1875. Meanwhile, other versions also appeared, including one in Polish, published in Lwow in 1874, and a French edition in 1873. The 1875 Russian edition contained the complete Minsk *pinkas*, 1,055 documents in all, as compared with the 1869 edition, which included only 285. In 1882, Brafman's son published an expanded edition in two parts, the first containing an extended version of Brafman's earlier commentary on the *pinkas*, and the second, the 1,055 documents. The two parts were republished as a unified edition in 1888.

The Book of the Kahal, as it first appeared in Vilna, was actually three distinct entities, each of which was expanded in subsequent editions. First, there were the 285 protocols of the Minsk community, forming the bulk of the work entitled *The Book of the Kahal*. There was, in addition, Brafman's explication, without which, as even the book's admirers conceded, the protocols made no sense at all.[13] The main analysis, eighty-six pages in length, prefaced the protocols in *The Book of the Kahal*. A third book, *Jewish Brotherhoods* was in fact chapter 3 of this explication, published separately as a work of 171 pages. All these components were finally brought together in the two-part edition of 1882. While this edition is therefore the most complete, it is necessary to examine the earliest versions of *The Book of the Kahal* in order to understand, not only what it initially was, but what it grew to become.

The version of *The Book of the Kahal* produced in Brafman's Vilna period unfolded in a linear, logical fashion. Brafman began, in his *Vilenskii vestnik* articles, by discussing the difficulty of converting Jews to Christianity. This led him to expand on the problem of making any change whatsoever in the Jewish style of life. He then announced his key discovery, that the kahal made the Jews what they were, rather than the dictates of the Talmud. As Brafman's supporters recognized, this was a striking innovation in traditional Christian Judeophobia and necessitated forceful justification and proof. This was the task of Brafman's two books, which completed the cycle. Their theme was announced on the title page by a German expression attributed to the German playwright Schiller: "Die Juden bilden einen Staat im Staate."

In Brafman's explication of Jewish history, Jewish society prior to the Roman conquest was sharply differentiated between a patrician elite and a downtrodden plebeian mass. During the siege of Jerusalem, after the Jewish rebellion against Rome, members of a scholarly brotherhood led by Rabbi Johanan ben Zakkai, deserted the city and threw themselves on the mercy of the Romans. Vespesian, delighted to sow discord among his enemies, welcomed them, and settled them in the town of Javneh. Here, with Roman approval, Rabbi Johanan ben Zakkai took total control of the settlers' internal government, ultimately creating institutions which endured even when the Jews were driven from Palestine by the Romans. Thus was the kahal born (Brafman I, 11–14).

Practical problems remained for the framers of the new kahal institutions. With the destruction of the Temple of Jerusalem, Jewish religious law lost its force, leaving a significant gap in national life. This loss was rectified by Judaic scholars, who devised a system to discipline and control every aspect of the Jew's private and public life. A bewildering array of rules, born in the minds of scholars rather than in the text of the holy scriptures, took shape. These rules regulated the slaughter of cattle, the use of meat and other foods, the whole system of *tref* and *kosher*, rites concerning women, and the like. The written aggregation of these rules, and commentaries on them, comprised the Talmud (Brafman I, 15–18). Brafman emphasized two aspects of this history. First, the kahal antedated the Talmud, and was obviously not dependent upon it but quite the reverse. Second, the kahal system maintained the power of the communal aristocracy, an elite of learning and wealth, over the Jewish masses. "The Jewish upper class, having placed the masses into a position from which it might profit, a blind tool for its own goals, preserves a haughty pride, limitless ambition and scorn for its unhappy little brothers, whom it has sucked dry, exploited and despised" (Brafman I, 19). Brafman proceeded to demonstrate how the contemporary kahal functioned in an internal and international guise.

Religious rites were the most direct means to subordinate the individual Jew to the leadership. While nothing in Judaism prevented the solitary Jew in the diaspora from praying directly to God, without benefit of rite or clergy, the kahal leadership established the supremacy of the central prayer house, or synagogue, by requiring universal attendance during the High Holidays. These holidays, beginning with Yom Kippur and culminating in Rosh Hashanah, served to perpetuate base superstitions. A special device was inculcation of a fanatical belief in the eventual rebirth of the Jewish kingdom, exemplified by the Passover toast, "Next year in Jerusalem!" Having forced the Jewish people to perform public prayer, the kahal leadership devised ceremonies to reinforce its power and authority while stressing the insignificance of the masses, exemplified by the *aliyah* or call to prayer, whereby a privileged few were given the special honor of reading the Torah (Brafman II, xxxv–vi, xxiii–iv).

The kahal indoctrinated its adherents through a system of talmudic study for males. Filthy *hadarim* and wretched *yeshivot* produced young scholars so valued by the community that they were allowed to sit in idle study, while the toil of the honest working man was both exploited and scorned. Few young Jews became scholars, of course, but all received at least the rudiments of a traditional Jewish education. This schooling served only to engender and reinforce religious fanaticism (Brafman II, lxxv–lxxix).

Requirements governing prayer and schooling were only the tip of the iceberg, for talmudic injunctions intruded into the most intimate areas of the daily life of every Jew. A bewildering set of regulations, regarding *kosher* and *tref* (ritually pure or impure) ensured that the communal expert in the law, the rabbi, would continually be called upon to adjudicate ridiculous minutiae. The requirement of ritual slaughter of animals gave the kahal leaders control over the price of meat and the very diet of Jews. Regulations on the ritual cleanliness of women allowed the kahal to intrude into intimate conjugal relations (Brafman II, xv–xix, lxxxiii).

Kahal control was facilitated through a network of Jewish brotherhoods, devoted to some aspect of the "nationalist-talmudic banner." They were the arteries of Jewish society, the heart of which was the kahal. For example, educational brotherhoods helped to maintain talmudic fanaticism, behind the mask of religious piety and devotion (Brafman I, 22–30). Charitable brotherhoods were even more hypocritical. The Brotherhood for the Ransom of Prisoners had long since lost its original purpose, and now existed to help any Jew under arrest, no matter what the reason or degree of guilt (Brafman I, 33–7). Worst of all was the Burial Brotherhood (Hevra Kaddisha). Ostensibly it existed to ensure a proper burial for the poor. In fact, its members humiliated and exploited the poor in their darkest hours by intemperate demands, and even antagonized the rich through exorbitant funeral charges.

The Burial Brotherhood was used by the kahal leadership to maintain discipline and intimidation, by threatening a dishonorable place in (or outside) the Jewish cemetery for miscreants, "heretics," or opponents. The abuses of the Hevra Kaddisha were archetypal, for whenever one looked closely into the workings of any brotherhood, whatever its purpose, one found fanaticism, hypocrisy and vice (Brafman I, 38–70).

Those who opposed the kahal leadership did not necessarily have to die to receive retribution. The kahal also enjoyed the right of excommunication or the ban (*herem*) which expelled the victim from the community, and forbade any further contact. Extreme penalties could be used against a person under the ban, especially if they were viewed as a threat to the community. They could be falsely denounced to the gentile authorities or even, *in extremis*, murdered (Brafman II, xxx–xxxi).

Clearly the kahal exercised sufficient prerogatives, positive and negative, to maintain internal control over its members. Since Jews did not live in isolation, the kahal also faced the task of dealing with the external world of the gentiles, or *goyim*. The kahal sought to ensure, first of all, that gentiles never had a pretext for invading Jewry's internal world. All disputes between Jews had to be kept from their eyes, and far from gentile courts. This was accomplished through an internal court system, the *bet din*, administered by the rabbiniate on a foundation of talmudic law. The *bet din* adjudicated all disputes between Jews. Any Jew who had recourse to gentile courts ran the risk of being placed under the ban. If participation in gentile litigation was necessary, due to the involvement of non-Jews, the community spared no effort to assist the Jewish litigant. Perjury and deception were common expedients. According to Brafman, one of the features of the rituals accompanying the Jewish Day of Atonement liberated Jews from guilt for the sin of perjury.

Business competition between Jews posed another threat to Jewish solidarity. The kahal, in its thoroughness, resolved even this problem. It developed the concept of *hazakah*, a monopolistic right, administered by the kahal, given to a particular Jew to exploit a gentile's property. The right was assigned or sold by the kahal. Once a Jew had secured a *hazakah* for a specific enterprise or service, no other Jew could compete with him without risking the ban. Thus could Jews dictate economic terms to any gentile. Under the protection of the kahal, the Jews easily controlled the economy of any region where they lived, no matter how small their numbers (Brafman II, xxiv–xxviii, xxxiv).

Brafman recognized how offensive the concept of *hazakah* would be to non-Jews and emphasized it in his writings. He quoted talmudic authority to the effect that the possessions of *goyim* constituted an empty lake, upon which only Jews might cast their nets. He provocatively characterized gentiles and their property as "a sort of free territory, constituting the state property of the kahal." Thirty-seven of the originally published 285 documents dealt with some aspect of *hazakah*.

Nor was the influence of the kahal restricted to individual localities. Through five international brotherhoods, the kahal possessed national and international significance. These particular brotherhoods were a new phenomena, never before seen in Judaism, testimony both to the widening of Jewry's horizons and the changes brought about by rapid communication in the modern world. Although headquartered in one or another country, brotherhoods were international in composition, and many of the members were leaders of contemporary learning and science. Such leaders deluded European opinion by their exhortations to enlightenment of the Jews, to be followed by emancipation. They proclaimed themselves Frenchmen, Germans, Englishmen and Russians of the Mosaic Law. A careful observer, however, could observe that the brotherhoods had little to do with real enlightenment and Europeanization, and much to do with schooling the Jews in cultural isolationism while preparing them for citizenship in a future Jewish kingdom.

Thus, the Brotherhood for the Awakening of the Slumbering, founded in England in 1864 and numbering 1,700 of the most influential men in the world among its members, pursued its so-called enlightenment goals by publishing textbooks of talmudic wisdom in Hebrew. Its Russian branch, Brafman revealed, was the Society for the Spread of Enlightenment among the Jews of Russia (OPE). He could not easily accuse the OPE of the same objectives as the English Brotherhood, of seeking to reinforce the Jewish national spirit, Judaism and "the Jewish talmudic intelligentsia" by publishing Hebrew works. Rather, he claimed its mission to be "the revitalization of the organs of this prostrate (Jewish) kingdom by the infusion of living science." Supplementary roles were played by such bodies as the Brotherhood for the Settlement of the Jewish Land and the Brotherhood for the Assistance of Jewish Emigrants.

This left the Alliance Universelle Israélite, whose interventions on behalf of Jews throughout the world had already drawn the critical attention of Judeophobes outside Russia and Russian officials within.[14] Since the Alliance came to play a much greater role in Brafman's writings, it should be noted that in 1869 he presented an accurate, if critical, summary of its goals and objectives. Brafman complained that the Alliance was ready to intervene anywhere in defense of a Jew, no matter what the merits of the case. Moreover, the Alliance was prone to ignore the causes of Christian hostility to the Jews, namely the unacceptable style of Jewish life, and to focus only on "persecution," as in the recent cases of Romania and Russia (Brafman I, 96–157).

Brafman depicted the international Jewish brotherhoods as united to one end: "to prepare in Judaism everything necessary to attain its highest goals, the resurrection of an independent Jewish political life" (Brafman I, 127). This serious charge was directed squarely in opposition to the possibility and necessity of Jewish emancipation, and the readiness of the Jews to be good subjects in Russia. Yet the charge that the Jews desired a return to Palestine was neither new nor unbelievable. *The Book of the Kahal*, in its earliest form, lacked the fantastic and occult elements already emerging in modern European Antisemitism, and to be found in its own later versions.

Having described the "talmudic municipal republic" in detail for his readers, Brafman had one last sensation to present: kahal malfeasance rested on the support and collusion of Christian governments. Ever since the Roman government had foolishly permitted Rabbi Johanan ben Zakkai to establish a Jewish national center in Javneh, states which ruled over the Jews had granted them extensive powers of self-government. The Jewish leadership used these opportunities to keep the kahal structure in place, and maintain its despotism over the Jewish masses.

National governments might appear to gain from this arrangement, since the kahal served as a convenient channel for tax collection, and for carrying out decrees from the center. The cost was high, however. Part of it was paid by the Jewish masses who bore the brunt of unfairly allocated taxes and who remained sunk in fanaticism and ignorance. The gentile population also suffered the exploitative force of the kahal, exercised through the hapless Jewish masses. Moreover, the kahal was deceptive in its service to the state. It disguised the true size of the Jewish population in order to shortchange the government of taxes and military recruits. The Jewish masses were heavily taxed nonetheless, in order to pay for the secret schemes of the kahal leadership. This situation had profound implications for the contemporary debate in Russia on the desirability of some form of emancipation for the Jews. If the kahal was permitted to endure, the granting of greater rights to the Jewish population would make it no more enlightened nor less fanatical, would not expedite its merging with the native population and certainly would not transform Jews into good citizens. On the other hand, deprived of the protection of laws restricting the Jews, the native population would suffer still more from Jewish depredation.

No less an authority than Napoleon Bonaparte had demonstrated this lamentable fact. The French Revolution emancipated the Jews of France, but by the time of Napoleon the Jews still remained aloof and apart, a self-proclaimed chosen people. Napoleon determined to end this situation, and to force the Jews to reciprocate French assumptions that they were fellow citizens, willing to embark upon intermarriage and assimilation. He pursued this goal by convening a Paris Sanhedrin, composed of rabbis from all over the French Empire. He assumed that the decisions of such a body would have the force of talmudic law and he extracted from it various assurances about gentiles, including toleration of mixed marriages. Further state control was extended through the creation of consistories, with a disciplined hierarchy of rabbis. What was the outcome? The Jews remained as before, a hostile exploitative burden on the French population, while the kahal was unbroken. In 1808 Napoleon was forced, as a consequence, to rescind Jewish emancipation, by taking away many of the political rights of French Jews (Brafman II, lxv–lxvii).

Russia served as another example. Russia's Jews were acquired from Poland at a time when the power of the autonomous Jewish community was at its height. Unacquainted with the Jews, the Russian state was at first inclined to leave to the kahal all its accustomed prerogatives. The results were predictable. The agents of the kahal acted to block every change and reform prescribed by the Russian government for the Jews. They did not even quail at the prospect of bribing the members of a reform commission created by Alexander I in 1802 to deal with the economic disorders perpetrated by the Jews. The Russian state ultimately recognized its mistake and abolished the kahal in 1844. Lacking any other way of collecting taxes or recruits from the Jewish community, it created an independent system of Jewish tax collectors and recruitment officers. Unbeknown to the Russians, these officials became subordinate tools of the underground kahal leadership. Attendant reforms, such as creation of the state-run Jewish school system, or the attempt to impose enlightened rabbis as leaders of the Jewish community in order to reduce Jewish fanaticism, likewise foundered on the secret opposition of the kahal. In this way, the Russian government unwittingly supported the very elements which continued to give support to the Jewish "municipal talmudic republic" (Brafman II, lxxi–lxxiv).

If Iakov Brafman, through his book, really did set out to take revenge on those who had wronged him in the past, he was more than successful. His astute choice of targets allowed him to maintain a consistent pose as a friend of the Jews, rather than a renegade Judeophobe. Brafman emphasized that it was a small band of miscreants, the kahal leadership, who were to blame, not the Jewish masses. Indeed, one can see the poor young Brafman, victimized by the burial society and driven to vagrancy by the kahal leadership, in his description of how the leaders preyed on the Jewish plebs. In his public poses, such as his missionary activities and, even more, his efforts on the Vilna Jewish Commission, he claimed to pursue the best interests of the Jews themselves. He was intent on overthrowing a system which, according to him, exploited Christians and tyrannized Jews, even while making them an inevitable target of Christian hostility.[15] This is a point worth emphasizing: Brafman argued that Jewish hostility to Christianity antedated and provoked the phenomenon of Christian Jew-hatred.

Brafman's discoveries had great significance for another part of the Jewish community. Brafman himself was not at first badly received by the russified Jewish intelligentsia of Vilna, even when he appeared in their midst as a Christian missionary. (The circle of Jewish Russifiers included many converts to Christianity.) They were ill-paid in return. *The Book of the Kahal* was very ambivalent about enlightened Jews. True, they were not part of the old aristocracy of talmudic learning. Yet their consistent advocacy of some form of immediate emancipation for Russian Jews directly challenged Brafman's claim that such legal measures, without the prior destruction of the kahal, would have catastrophic consequences for the Christian population, while making no positive improvement for the Jewish masses. Likewise, by the very fact of being enlightened and freed from talmudic fanaticism, the Jewish Russifiers should have been Brafman's allies, ready to confirm his discoveries and support his claims and proposals. Quite the contrary, the Jewish Russifiers of Vilna helped to deflect the Vilna Commission from Brafman's proposals for the legal subordination of Jews to the peasant community. It was Jewish intellectuals who savaged Brafman's works in the Russian press. Indeed, if Jewish intellectuals were now to admit the existence of the kahal, as described by Brafman, they would have to explain why they had not earlier been more forthcoming on the subject. Emerging as Brafman's fiercest critics, the Russian–Jewish intelligentsia rapidly became Brafman's principal target.

The Russian press greeted the publication of *The Book of the Kahal* as a significant moment in the history of the Jewish Question in Russia. Over a dozen newspapers and thick journals reviewed it, including some of the Empire's most prestigious publications. A sympathetic review by Brafman's collaborator, Ia. Bratin, appeared first in *Vilenskii vestnik*, and was widely reprinted in such publications as *Kievlianin*, *Sovremennye izvestiia*, and *Sudebnyi vestnik*. For those newspapers which welcomed *The Book of the Kahal*, Brafman's revelations hardly come as a bolt from the blue. References to the kahal and its misdeeds had already began to percolate into articles and editorials. The newspaper *Syn otechestva*, for example, greeted *The Book of the Kahal* as vindication of an earlier series which it had carried in 1867, arguing against legal equality for the Jews while the kahal endured. Such a proposition, warned the author, P. Takolcha-Mokritskii, was equivalent to arming the Jews with a revolver and the peasants with a switch (236–7:11–12/X/1867).

G. Levin, one of Brafman's translators, also found a forum in *Syn otechestva* (286:17/XII/1868). His article attempted to reverse Brafman's thesis by characterizing the Talmud as the basis for the kahal and the brotherhoods, the "cause of causes." A similar caveat appeared in a review published in the Ministry of Education's *Journal*. The author, M. O. Koialovich, asked why the kahal system produced no party of internal opponents. The answer, he suggested, lay in the fact that the kahal and the Talmud were part of one unified whole. "Thus any Jew who speaks against the kahal naturally assumes that he speaks against the Talmud, against the faith; consequently, he either loses the wish to speak out, or abandons Judaism." In addition, however heavy the kahal structure might be, it was still supported by all Jews because of the protection it provided and the advantages which it gave (152: December 1870: 284–7). (This was an example of how Brafman's own differentiation between the kahal "patricians" and the communal "plebs" could easily break down into a uniform hostility, which ignored such distinctions.)

A similar reemphasis on the role of the Talmud appeared in *Vilenskii vestnik*'s favorable review by F. Vetlugin (25:5/III/1870). *Novorossiiskii telegraf*, a newly minted Odessa newspaper, and one of the first provincial publications in private hands, welcomed *The Book of the Kahal* for its exposé of the dark side of Russian Jewry. The paper offered its services to help confirm Brafman's contention that the kahal made the Jews a privileged group within the Russian state (204:13/IX/1870; 230:16/X/1870). In future years, the paper became celebrated for its coarse and vituperative Judeophobia. The paper's flirtation with Brafman certainly started it along this path.

With such fledgling Jew-baiting organs as *Novorossiiskii telegraf* only beginning to cut their teeth on the Jewish Question, pride of place among contemporary Judeophobes belonged to two influential and widely read newspapers, *Kievlianin* and *Golos*. Both greeted *The Book of the Kahal* with more than just sympathetic reviews. They were not converted by Brafman's work, but saw it as a vindication and explanation of their pre-existing Judeophobia. Here was proof positive, based upon documentary material, that the Jews were a harmful force for Russia.

Kievlianin in particular became the vigilant watchdog of the reputation of *The Book of the Kahal*. It reviewed and summarized Brafman's work copiously throughout 1870, and responded with indignation and scorn to the critics of Brafman, especially those who wrote in the Russian–Jewish press. The eagerness of the Jewish intelligentsia to savage Brafman also confirmed the editor of *Kievlianin* in his growing conviction that even enlightened Jews could not be trusted.[16] "At last the progressives, who accuse us of intolerance and bigotry when we talk about the realities of life in our area can see the facts of Jewish life," declared an editorial. "The publicists of *Rassvet*, *Den* and *Sion* could hardly have failed to know about these abuses, so why have they never said anything about them? Is it because they were more concerned with protecting their personal interests by speaking patriotic lies?" (48:23/IV/1870). At this juncture the paper was still willing to make Brafman's distinction between plebs and patricians, placing the guilt for the Jews' "hellish superstitions and fanaticism" exclusively on Jewish institutions and self-government (39:31/III/1870). However, as its circle of trustworthy Jews grew ever more narrow, *Kievlianin* was increasingly reluctant to assume the good intentions of *any* group of Russian Jews.

Golos, the prestigious liberal newspaper from the publishing stable of A. A. Kraevskii, was no stranger to the content or concerns of *The Book of the Kahal*. The paper had followed with approval the creation of the Vilna Jewish Commission, and had given space to correspondents like M. Gurvich, Brafman's translator, to defend its activities (289:19/X/ 1867; 152:3/VI/1868). The previous year, *Golos* had commented sourly on the activities of the Alliance Israélite Universelle upon the occasion of a visit by its president, Adolphe Crémieux to St. Petersburg (273:3/X/ 1869). *Golos* was therefore an appreciative audience for Brafman's charges and devoted five long editorials – although there was hardly such a thing as a short *Golos* editorial – to the kahal, describing and analyzing its actions in scrupulous detail.

The implications of the kahal disconcerted the *Golos* editorialist. While agreeing with commentators who warned that the Jews could not safely be emancipated in their existing condition, he went further by assuming that the kahal elite did not really desire emancipation. "The equalization of Jews with the surrounding population would demand an equalization of Jewish society regarding rights and limits of self-government; the patricians would be forced to surrender their dictatorial power, controlling even the petty details of domestic life. Some individuals might make this sacrifice, but not a whole party" (145:27/V/1870). Thus, the key to resolving the Jewish Question was to be found in the weakening of the kahal leadership, and its agents and allies. *Golos* took as its task in the following decade the unmasking of kahal institutions and their leaders, a feat which proved frustrating indeed. The paper availed itself of a good guide, however, taking on Brafman himself as a correspondent.

While the critics of Brafman did not have access to publications as prestigious as those of his supporters, they nonetheless showed themselves to be able and articulate in articles written for *Birzhevye vedomosti, Deiatelnost, Novoe vremia* and *Den*. Their chief disadvantage was that, as Jews, they could not pretend to be a disinterested party.

Den, the chief critic, was a specialized Russian Jewish newspaper. *Novoe vremia*, still a struggling liberal organ, was not yet the shaper of opinion which it became under the editorship of A. S. Suvorin. *Deiatelnost*, with a low circulation and censorship worries, failed early in 1872. Its credibility as a defender of the Jews would not have been helped had the public known that the editor frequently proposed to the OPE that it receive a subsidy as a reward for its Judeophile efforts.[17] Nor were matters simplified when among the critics appeared Brafman's erstwhile collaborators Levin and Bratin. *Kievlianin*, in particular, heaped scorn on these "repentant Mary Magdalenes" (104:1/IX/1870).

The Book of the Kahal was attacked from a variety of perspectives. The preferred tactic in the beginning was to launch *ad hominem* assaults on Brafman's intentions and abilities. The most revealing insights into Brafman's methods came from his erstwhile collaborators Levin and Bratin, in a sense the real authors of *The Book of the Kahal*. Both young men, archetypal Young Maskilim, displayed a self-assured confidence in their civilizing mission. Their collaboration with Brafman gave them prestige, money (although both complained that it was an insignificant amount) and inflated ambitions (Brafman promised Levin help in getting into a university). They published articles hostile to the Talmud and to the kahal in important periodicals. But suddenly they found themselves enveloped in a terrible scandal, and they assumed the role of naughty schoolboys being disciplined for some thoughtless prank which had produced serious if unforeseen consequences. Levin wrote a series of articles for *Novoe vremia*, questioning the veracity of Brafman's documents. He recalled his initial amazement that a baptized Jew could manage to secure so many "authentic" kahal documents. Doubts increased once his translation work began. Levin reported that a uniform hand had written all the documents, which ranged over thirty-nine years, and that not one carried the kahal seal. More important was the translation method which Brafman employed: the sense of a document was frequently changed to conform with Brafman's own interpretation. Levin lamented that "a feeling of delicacy and restraint" toward an older patron had kept him from objecting to distortions and additions made to the original text. These discrepancies could easily be confirmed by examining the differences in documents published first in *Vilenskii vestnik* and then in *The Book of the Kahal*. Levin's eyes were now opened to the true nature of his mentor: "There is no question of the good of the Jews or the good of our great fatherland. We understand that we were blind tools in the hands of a man who hates all his former coreligionists just because he once stood with them under the same banner, and he now wishes to ingratiate himself with the Russian public, foisting any untruth upon 'his brothers by blood'" (177:1/VII/1870).

Bratin's response was more abject still. He wrote to *Novoe vremia* to complain that Levin's articles left the impression that he had assisted the goals of Brafman consciously and through conviction, "which was untrue and for me extremely regrettable ... Coming to work for Mr. Brafman straight from the school bench, still unacquainted with the realities of life, I would never have decided to serve them, had I understood them." And so the man who admitted writing much of the text of *The Book of the Kahal* (as opposed to the commentaries), disavowed his work. "I now unwillingly shudder, remembering that no more than five months ago, I wrote a laudatory review, published this year [1870] in *Vilenskii vestnik* about things which now ... should be recognized as a lie and a slander."[18] In similar fashion, the publicist I. Zeiberling, writing in *Birzhevye Vedomosti*, warned his readers that "it is well known that people who change their faith are, for the most part, hostile to their former religious beliefs, and even act as the most ferocious persecutors of them; consequently Mr. Brafman, motivated by a wish to give greater zest to his book, and lacking a firm foundation for his knowledge of the Jewish language and talmudic literature, involuntarily misleads himself and confuses others." Brafman's great discoveries were "born in his hostile imagination" (263:26/VI/1870).

Should *The Book of the Kahal* be considered a forgery? The most extensive response to this problem came from the pen of the Jewish publicist I. I. Shershevskii, who wrote a long series of articles, published in *Novoe vremia* and *Den*, and in book form, on the subject.[19] Shershevskii advanced many arguments which called into question the authenticity of Brafman's documents. He pointed out that some protocols were dated on the Sabbath or holidays, when Jews were forbidden to write. There were numerous incorrect dates. The acts either were not signed and thus not official, or were signed by persons who had no right to do so. The documents were not in chronological order, as Brafman claimed, and there were suspicious gaps between meetings. Kahal elections were an annual event, but many years passed without elections being called. To this could be added Brafman's consistent mistranslation – such as *bene ha-ir* for "the local kahal" instead of "the residents of the town" – and tendentious editing. Finally, the work was historically inaccurate, recording oaths by Jewish judges to follow the dictates of the kahal in court at a time when Jews did not possess the right to serve as judges in Minsk.[20]

As even Shershevskii conceded, quoting Victor Hugo, "it is easier to disfigure than to kill" (*Novoe vremia* 267:29/IX/1870). Many of Brafman's critics were willing to accept the veracity of the original *pinkas*, however marred by Brafman's editing and translation. There was in fact nothing unusual or unexpected about the kahal acts – and certainly no hint of an anti-state "talmudic, municipal republic" – if they were placed in their proper historical context, a task undertaken by the veteran Jewish publicist, M. Morgulis, in a series entitled "The Kahal and the Institution of Magdeburg Law."

Morgulis simply reversed Brafman's interpretation of events. The exclusivity of the Jews in Central and Eastern Europe, which frequently made them a target of hatred, was nothing less than a response to external persecution. The creation of the kahal was in no way different, for example, from the growth of urban guilds in their struggle with feudalism. Jews were given more and more internal autonomy as the state itself proved unable or unwilling to protect them.

The same conditions of turmoil and anarchy which made the Magdeburg Law – commonly given to cities for self-administration by Polish kings – unworkable for Jews, gave rise to the kahal structure in Poland. Far from being a force hostile to gentile authority, however, it acted as a service agency for the state, by collecting taxes and administering justice in the community. Yet it was precisely these prerogatives which so horrified Brafman, and which he misunderstood in his depiction of the kahal. Even a phenomenon like the *hazakah* only existed for the innocent purpose of regulating the civil relations between Christians and Jews in ways which were neither forbidden nor unknown by Polish law.[21]

A Jewish convert to Christianity, O. Notovich, writing in *Deiatelnost*, likewise conceded the existence of the kahal, while denying that it was capable of doing any harm to the non-Jewish population. The government had tolerated the old Jewish kahal as a special administrative organism, to help in the governance of the country. In time, the kahal might become a useless communal burden. This was a special internal concern for the Jews themselves, however, and need not trouble the Christian population, who were in no way touched by other peoples' obsolete institutions.[22]

The editorialist of the Jewish newspaper *Den* conceded that the kahal had once existed, and that Brafman's protocols might be genuine. The paper was even ready to indulge *Golos'* hypothesis that *The Book of the Kahal* was the key to understanding the Jewish Question and explaining all the ills of Jewry. This perspective viewed emancipation as impossible until the kahal was abolished. But the Judeophobes of *Golos* neglected a key point. The kahal *had* been abolished in Russia in 1844. If Jewish separatism and isolation still existed, it must be due to external circumstances, and not some imaginary kahal.

The legislation of the Russian Empire constituted one set of external circumstances. Brafman accused the law of maintaining the kahal and thus promoting Jewish separation and social alienation. Rather, the law created Jewish separatism through restrictive decrees, which made the Jews separate and distinct from the rest of the population. The Jews were saddled with special taxes, which they paid through separate collectors. Their passport system was separate, as was their military recruitment. Jewish agricultural colonists were legally separated from Christian peasants. Jewish "solidarity" was more to be found in the principle of collective responsibility governing all the Jews' civic obligations, than in the kahal. The ill-fated Vilna Commission was a case in point. Its program, aimed at merging the Jewish and peasant population had failed because its framers wanted to subordinate the Jews to the peasant community without simultaneously giving them the full civil rights enjoyed by the peasants (19:9/V/1870; 21:23/V/1870).

Den used its criticisms of *The Book of the Kahal* to sound one of its favorite themes, that Jewish separatism, and all its negative features, were the fruits of ill-considered official policies. Only complete civil emancipation could remove the Jewish desire for a separate existence, and make them into loyal and conscientious citizens.

The winner of the war of words surrounding *The Book of the Kahal* is difficult to judge, although Brafman was certainly not the loser. The casual reader was undoubtedly put off by the meticulous but arcane arguments of his opponents. Despite the vilification heaped upon him, Brafman was never forced to produce the original *pinkas* documentation. Criticism of his methods and scholarship did not deter elite groups like the Imperial Geographical Society from giving him their patronage. Despite the controversy, his service career flourished. In 1870 he was called to St. Petersburg, and promoted to the post of Censor of Jewish Books, in the Chief Office for Press Affairs.[23] In 1872, he served on the committee drafting the military service law of 1874. He wrote for the prestigious newspaper *Golos*. He died of pneumonia in the capital, in 1879, although Judeophobes hinted darkly that the agents of the kahal had at last revenged themselves on the man who had done so much to torment them (*Novoe vremia*, 2186:1/IV/1882).

The Book of the Kahal was the most successful and influential work of Judeophobia in Russian history. By itself, *The Book of the Kahal* probably made few converts. The newspapers that accepted it were already Judeophobe in orientation, just as Brafman's foes were all Jews or Judeophiles. What *The Book of the Kahal* did do was to offer an apparently factual basis for accumulated prejudices, fears and resentments. The work was, after all, based upon reality, as Brafman's critics were generally forced to admit. What difference did it make if Brafman's transliterations from Hebrew to Russian were deficient, or if an occasional date was wrong? His work "proved" what a Judeophobe knew by commonsense observation, that the Jews were alien, non-Russian and separatist.

More importantly, Brafman's work served as a symbolic philosopher's stone for an understanding of the bewilderingly complex Jewish Question. At a stroke, the entire Jewish Question was elegantly oriented into a new frame of reference. Religious fanaticism, economic exploitation and social alienation, phenomena which heretofore had been disparate problems, could now all be viewed as deriving from the same first principle, the kahal. Simple problems admitted of simple answers, and this was another charm of Brafman's discovery. If the kahal impeded the resolution of the Jewish Question in Russia, it was only necessary to abolish the kahal. Protests that this had already been done, in 1844, were met by the claim that the secret kahal still existed. "The kahal" became a convenient catch-all phrase to characterize any aspect of Russian Jewry that opponents found inconvenient, offensive or undesirable. Unsurprisingly, in 1881, when the government established commissions in the provinces of the Pale to explain the anti-Jewish pogroms which were then wracking the country, the most common explanation was "the kahal," and the most frequently prescribed remedy was "the abolition of the kahal."

Another strength of *The Book of the Kahal* was a vitality which made the work capable of growth, evolution and elaboration. This was particularly evident in later editions of the book, especially that of 1882, which expanded to cover social problems scarcely hinted at in the 1860s. For example, when universal military service was introduced into the Russian Empire in 1874, it was widely believed that Jews were evading service. Brafman simply inserted a chapter in the new edition, which explained how the kahal expedited Jewish draft evasion (Brafman III, chapter XV, 161–7). As the Alliance Israélite Universelle increased its activities, Brafman expanded his exposition and condemnation of it, while linking it more firmly with the Russian OPE (Brafman III, chapter XXVII, 321–43). Indeed, Brafman's vehicle did not even require his inventiveness to keep it going – much of the 1882 edition was clearly the work of his son Alexander, producing, as a final irony, the fact that Brafman never composed, in its entirety, any edition of the book that made his name famous.[24]

The Book of the Kahal has often been connected with an even more infamous work, *The Protocols of the Elders of Zion*.[25] Some qualifications should be made, which will place Brafman's work more securely in its historical context and explain its success. Unlike *The Protocols*, there are no fantastic or occult elements in Brafman's work. To claim that Jews sought to preserve their national and religious particularities, or that they banded together against gentiles, may have led Brafman to exaggerated extremes, but they were a far cry from the utterly fantastic scene in a Prague cemetery, where the Elders met to plan the conquest of the Christian world. In fact, early versions of *The Protocols* were published in the early 1870s in Russia by the Judeophobe press, and nobody sought to connect them with Brafman.

Yet at the same time, the ambiguously true *Book of the Kahal* was a bridge over which writers could pass from fact to fiction. The evolution of Brafman's – or his son's – treatment of the Alliance Israélite Universelle offers a pertinent example. The 1868 book on Jewish brotherhoods devoted space to five international brotherhoods, two of which were the Alliance and the OPE. In the 1882 edition, the Alliance was clearly singled out as the most significant brotherhood – indeed, discussion of any others but the OPE was dropped – and its role exaggerated: "In the program of the Alliance *kol Israel haverim* appears the spirit, not of a private society, but of a whole nation, a spirit conscious of its strength to go forward to the realization of a grandiose political mission" (Brafman III, 331). A subtle shift was also introduced into Brafman's summary of the objectives of the Alliance, taken from its own protocols. In 1868, Brafman noted simply that the Alliance sought to "oppose the influence of Christian missionaries among the Jews" (Brafman I, 138). By 1882, this had become the defense of Jewry "from the fatal influence of Christian civilization," anticipating the *Protocols'* theme of the war to the death between Judaism and Christianity (Brafman III, 332). Moreover, the 1882 edition is studded with excerpts from leaders of the Alliance which clearly prefigure a whole host of fraudulent speeches, usually attributed to Adolphe Crémieux, published by the European antisemitic press in the 1880s. Such speeches revealed Jewry's intent to dominate the entire world, rather than just recover the Jewish kingdom. The first Russian publication to print an apocryphal Crémieux speech – a forerunner of the *Protocols of the Elders of Zion* – was Ivan Aksakov's *Rus* in 1883. Aksakov, the sloganeer of "the Jewish banner and the Christian banner" was clearly predisposed to accept such a manichean view of the world. Significantly, he was also one of the most ardent supporters of *The Book of the Kahal* when it was republished in 1882, and he excerpted parts of it in *Rus*.[26]

Brafman's success was not restricted to newspaper columns, since his theories enjoyed an instantaneous vogue among Russian officials. As noted above, Kornilov dispatched copies of *The Book of the Kahal* throughout the Pale. His superior in Vilna, A. L. Potapov, although generally well-disposed toward the Jews, alerted the central government to the illegal activities of the kahal. In 1871 the Governor of Kovno province, K. Obolenskii, wrote to the Governor-General of the Northwest to report the existence of a secret Jewish kahal in his province. When pressed for evidence, he cited *The Book of the Kahal*.[27]

Even more ominously, the first meeting of the new Committee for the Transformation of Jewish Life (KUBE) drew into question the reliability of the recommendations of the Vilna Jewish Commission since it paid insufficient attention to important aspects of Jewish life – such as the role of burial brotherhoods.[28] The myth of the Jewish kahal had securely entered the collective consciousness of Russian officialdom. Brafman was truly revenged on that official of the Ketsk Hevra Kaddisha who had long ago snatched a pillow from a dead child's bed.

PART 3

The era of social change and economic turmoil

The second half of the nineteenth century in the Russian Empire was dominated by the planning, implementation and consequences of the abolition of serfdom. The emancipation decree of 18 February, 1861 made the serfs into "free rural inhabitants," liberated from the control of the landowning nobility. This single act necessitated the wholesale transformation of all aspects of Russian life. The state took over responsibility for peasant taxation and military recruitment, heretofore the obligation of the gentry landlords. New courts, based upon Western models, were created, although in the villages the peasantry retained a system of customary law. A system of local self-government, the zemstvo, featuring all-class participation, was introduced in rural and urban variants. Urban centers received a new municipal charter. These reforms occurred against the background of a changing economy as capitalistic relationships penetrated the countryside and the pace of urban industrialization quickened.

As a partial consequence of economic changes, the half-century was marked by severe social instability. There were sharp tensions between the peasantry and the landowning nobility, arising from the emancipation settlement. The government's attempt to maintain the nobility as a viable economic and social entity convinced the peasantry that "their" land had been stolen by the lords. A demographic explosion amongst the peasantry exacerbated their relentless "land-hunger." Economic differentiation proceeded apace in the village. The nobility sought to survive economically and to define a new political role, even while driven by exaggerated fears of its own demise. Merchants, manufacturers and entrepreneurs in the Russian heartland saw themselves under siege by foreign and intra-imperial rivals, while the government remained highly ambivalent about the need to render them protection and support.

Social tensions were complicated by political and ethnic tensions,

285

Нарождающаяся новая аристократія въ Россіи.

Ицко: Что такое? домъ? Развѣ панъ забылъ, что вчера срокъ векселю; деньги неуплачены, слѣдовательно домъ мой.

Господ: Но домъ мой стоитъ 10,000 р., а по векселю я вамъ долженъ только двѣ тысячи.

Ицко: Какое мнѣ до этого дѣло; можетъ десять, а можетъ и тысячи не стоитъ. Я человѣкъ акуратный: въ условіи написано, если въ срокъ не уплатите, то домъ будетъ мой; срокъ прошелъ, деньги не уплачены, слѣдовательно домъ мой.

20 "The birth of a new aristocracy." Itsko the Jewish moneylender on his way to foreclose on the house of an insolvent debtor

exemplified by the intractable question of Poland. Dissatisfaction with the terms and consequences of the emancipation settlement, as well as the inadequacy of the accompanying political reforms, inspired political dissidence and activism among liberals and radicals. These discontents drove a wedge between the state and much of civil society. The growth of political opposition and a revolutionary movement in their turn inspired construction of a formal conservative ideology.

All of these post-emancipation phenomena touched on the Jewish Question to some degree. New forms of taxation and recruitment had to be devised for the Jews. The degree of their participation in zemstvo and municipal self-government was widely debated.[1] Jews were a significant demographic and economic force precisely in those western borderlands which attracted the reforming zeal of the government, driven on by public opinion, in the aftermath of the Polish uprising of 1863. It was the misfortune of the Jews to be closely linked to a landowning economy dominated by the untrustworthy Polish nobility. In the commercial realm, Jews, like Germans and Poles, were considered dangerous "foreign" competitors by mercantile rivals in the Muscovite heartland. Reformers in the capitals, goaded by initiatives from the provinces, could not escape the need to deal with the Jews. Public opinion, freed from heavy-handed restraints upon the press, was able and ready to offer advice and criticism.

The Jews themselves were victims of the economic changes unleashed by emancipation, since they were overconcentrated in a decrepit semi-feudal economy. Like the peasantry, the Jews underwent a demographic explosion in the second half of the century, which saw their numbers in the Empire rise to almost 5 million persons by century's end. Even though the Kingdom of Poland and the Pale of Settlement were areas of dynamic economic growth, the Jews as a whole were slow to benefit from new opportunities. Although the formal legal position of the Jews improved significantly during the Reform Era, areas of discrimination remained, not least of which were the over-arching residence restrictions of the Pale. Even within the Pale the Jews were forced to fight for their rights. A prime example of this struggle was the on-going effort of Jewish merchants to settle freely in the city of Kiev.[2]

The most immediate effect of emancipation was to loose an economic crisis upon Russian Jewry, observed in the growing pauperization of large numbers of Jews who resided in rural areas of the Empire. This phenomenon was noted by observers in the 1860s, and underscored at the end of that decade by a terrible famine among the Jews of Kovno province, following a local crop failure.

The pre-emancipation economy bound the Russian peasantry to the land and to the village. Even peasants whose duties to their masters had been converted to a money payment, or quitrent (*obrok*), and who left the village to seek employment elsewhere, were legally bound to the village of their origin. The pre-capitalist Russian economy did offer some factory labor, but the typical opportunity for the peasantry lay in seasonal, non-mechanized farm labor. Migratory labor (*otkhod*) drew peasant work-gangs (*artely*) into developing areas like Novorossiia, but nowhere did they have much opportunity to engage in trade or middleman activity. In the Pale and in Novorossiia, trade and artisan activity were dominated by Jews. Jews also served in many capacities on rural estates, as overseers, foremen and lease-agents of the numerous feudal prerogatives possessed by the landlord. Pride of place among these rights was production and sale of alcohol.

One of the best accounts of Jewish mercantile activity in the feudal economy was provided, ironically, by the man destined to become

Russia's leading Judeophobe, Ivan Aksakov. In 1853, financed by St. Petersburg merchants, Aksakov journeyed through the Ukraine in order to prepare a report on the region's fairs. In his classic study, *An Investigation of Trade in the Ukrainian Fairs*, Aksakov assigned a vital role to the Jews. "Jews are the most active purchasers, especially of Russian manufactured goods, which they then carry throughout the western region, even into Belorussia. They are active buyers of livestock for sale abroad. Almost all trade in foreign goods via non-maritime routes is carried by either Russian or Austrian Jews."[3] Aksakov observed the symbiotic relationship between small-scale Jewish traders and wealthier Russian merchants at fairs. So vital were the services of Jews that restrictive ordinances against them at the Korenn and Kharkov fairs were very loosely enforced. Despite the energy of Jewish tradesmen, Aksakov claimed that the Russian merchant had no difficulty competing with them within the Pale.[4]

Confirmation of Aksakov's claims can be gleaned from the province-wide surveys conducted by members of the Russian General Staff in the years shortly before and after the peasant emancipation. The description of Grodno province characterized Jews as "the indispensable middlemen" between landlord and peasant.[5] The Kovno study asserted that "all trade in the province is controlled by the Jews," who purchased agricultural commodities at fairs, market places and in the field. They shipped produce to Kovno, Riga, Libau and Prussia, returning to the countryside with necessities which were normally available only in urban areas.[6] An official survey conducted in 1851 revealed that in twelve of the fourteen provinces of the Pale, the Jews constituted more than 50 percent of members of the three merchant guilds, although the vast majority of these were in the least prosperous third guild.[7]

Prescient observers predicted hard times for the Jews as early as 1861,[8] but it took almost a decade, marked by the expiration of "temporarily obligated status," during which the allocation of land was negotiated, and the economic consequences of the Polish uprising were felt, before the impact of the peasant emancipation upon the Jews became fully obvious.[9] The best contemporary analysis of this process was provided by Ilia Orshanskii, at the end of the 1860s, in the Jewish newspaper *Den*.

Orshanskii recalled the pre-reform countryside: a powerful class of landowning nobles, a backward and dependent peasantry, a diminutive commercial class, a weak exchange system, and primitive methods of communication. He dismissed the szlachta of the western borderlands as lazy and unfit for agricultural pursuits, content to leave the actual management of their affairs to Jewish agents. The peasant was equally in thrall to the Jew, to whom he sold his surplus harvest, and from whom he purchased the few trade goods available. The Jews provided the sole source of credit in the countryside, and were patronized by master and serf alike.

Emancipation deprived the nobleman of his free labor and necessitated a more rational economy. The landlord was now constrained to live on his estate and manage it. Enterprizing members of the gentry organized the marketing of their own produce, and pooled resources to provide local agricultural credit. They were no longer so dependent upon the Jews. The peasantry also broke the bonds of dependency, becoming more self-reliant and knowledgeable about the marketplace.

Economic potential released by emancipation also served to harm the Jews. Many Jews had previously made a living by keeping inns and post houses. They were ubiquitous as coachmen and teamsters, professions rendered obsolete by the growing network of steamships and railroads. The interdependent Jewish trade network was rapidly decaying. Russia was improving her system of taxation and state finance, to the detriment of Jews who participated in the liquor tax farming system. The old practice of military contracting, which had enriched Jews before and after the Crimean War, was being reformed (although not rapidly enough to escape dependence upon the Jews during the Russo-Turkish War of 1877–78). Rich Jewish contractors provided a living for many of their poor coreligionists, but this was becoming a thing of the past. The introduction of local banking operations through the zemstva was part of this trend, and also harmful to Jewish interests. Finally, general phenomena like the tariffs of 1857 and 1868, which reduced the profitability of the Jewish-dominated import trade, also took their toll (14:15/VIII/1869).

The paradox of these changes, Orshanskii explained, was that the very forces which served to ruin the Jews were progressive and beneficial for Russia as a whole. The Jews were merely victims of an economy in transition, and they too would find their niche in the emergent new economy. "Thus, the impoverished situation of our coreligionists in Russia ... is a transitory phenomenon, a temporary one, and will be eliminated to the degree that Jewry adapts itself to the new structure of life, forgetting old trades and occupations which are now obsolete, and learning new ones" (15:22/VIII/1869).[10] These became accepted Judeophile arguments for the rest of the century, and were enshrined in the definitive economic analysis of Jewish life in

Russia presented by A. P. Subbotin to the Palen Commission in the 1880s, even as economic reality appeared to overtake the more optimistic predictions of Orshanskii's analysis.[11]

The standard proposal for the ultimate resolution of the Jewish Question, beloved of friends and foes of the Jews alike, was their transformation into peasants. This goal had been encouraged by Russian legislation as early as 1804. Recurrent efforts to settle large numbers of Jews on the land failed, blighted by bureaucratic blundering as much as by the absence of agricultural expertise among the Jews. The growing impoverishment of Jews in their customary occupations, and the unsettled state of the post-emancipation countryside, nonetheless encouraged some Jews to turn to agriculture.

Jews had always been forbidden to acquire serfs or peasant land, lest they "gain mastery over Christians." Large tracts of land without a work force were valueless, so Jews had avoided investment in land. The emancipation changed all this. Although Jews were forbidden by the emancipation statute to purchase outright peasant or gentry properties, land began to pass into their hands through indirect routes. Labor services now had to be hired, rather than secured through feudal obligations, and Jewish landowners proved quite capable of competing with gentry rivals for scarce workers. Some observers claimed that Jews with ready money were better equipped to negotiate labor contracts with the peasants. Gentry forays into the labor market were handicapped by bad feelings which followed the emancipation settlement. Peasant households insistently demanded additional land, but lacked capital or sources of credit to purchase it outright. Large rental tracts in the possession of a landowner or leaseholder could be profitably sub-leased to the peasantry. The Judeophobe press characterized the technique of sub-leasing as an especially "Jewish" practice, although it was routine practice among gentry landowners. During a brief experiment in 1862, when Jews were allowed to buy as well as lease estates in the western provinces, the Russian government sought to use Jews as a counterweight to the Poles and to draw Jewish investment capital into agriculture. This initiative was short-lived, falling victim to existing prejudices against the Jews as economic allies of the Poles or exploiters of the peasantry.

While most Jews had no capital to invest in agriculture or anything else, amidst the general destitution of the Jewish masses there emerged a Jewish elite enriched by military contracting and alcohol tax farming. A number of Jewish entrepreneurs seized the economic opportunities of nascent capitalism. E. G. Gintsburg distinguished himself as a banking magnate. S. S. Poliakov and A. M. Varshavskii became plutocrats through contracting to build the early network of Russian railroads.[12] Poliakov's sardonically named "Jew-roads" included the Kozlov–Voronezh–Rostov, Orlov–Griazsk and Kursk–Kharkov-Azov lines. Some of these magnates, like the Gintsburgs, retained their religious faith and their ties to the traditional community, playing prominent roles as *shtadlanim*. Poliakov, until late in his life, was less obviously a benefactor of the Jews, to the extent of endowing a student dormitory at the University of St. Petersburg which excluded Jewish students (*Volnoe slovo*, 48:1/XI/1882). In 1880, on the other hand, he was a prime mover behind the formation of the Society for the Promotion of Handicrafts and Agricultural Work among the Jews in Russia (ORT).[13] Perhaps most important, his rail-building enterprises provided employment for many Jews.

Jewish plutocrats became symbols of incipient capitalism for Russian radicals and conservatives alike. Recurrent denunciations of "the Gintsburgs, Poliakovs and Varshavskiis" symbolized a growing, albeit exaggerated, fear of the economic power of the Jews in the Russian Empire. Poliakov was the *bête-noire* of a group of patriotic Moscow entrepreneurs who dreamed of Russian railroads constructed and run without the assistance of foreigners and "aliens" (i.e., Jews). These prejudices were reinforced by the alleged shady financial aspects of Poliakov's lines, an indictment leveled against many non-Jewish operations as well. Particularly galling was Poliakov's ability to meet construction deadlines, which his opponents attributed to sloppy engineering and construction. He was also accused of giving most of the jobs on his railroads to Jews, and of using them as a virtual colonizing force in frontier areas along the Don river which were opened by his lines.[14] These accusations comprised a major part of the debate which led the Russian government in 1880 to move the territory of the Don Cossack Host outside the area permitted for Jewish settlement.[15]

It should be stressed that while Jewish plutocrats grew to become a symbol of capitalism for conservative Judeophobes, their main concern initially was the "exploitative" role of the Jewish tavern-keeper and usurer. Only after capitalism came to represent a negative and destructive force for gentry conservatives was its connection with the Jews made more overt. Ironically, this equation occurred before capitalism struck deep roots in Russia and despite the fact that, save for a few highly visible individuals, Jews were an insignificant force in the growth of Russian capitalism, particularly in the Russian heartland.

Nonetheless, Russian radical ideologues who painted capitalism as a harmful phenomenon for Russia were prone to tar all Jews with the reputation of the capitalist Gintsburgs and Poliakovs.[16]

Even while serving as scapegoats for the negative and economic consequences of Russian capitalism, Jews failed to benefit fully from the changes in their legal status spurred by the economic requirements of post-emancipation Russia. The cardinal example was a new law on Jewish residence, promulgated on 28 June 1865. The law laid down conditions under which Jewish artisans and distillers could settle outside of the Pale of Settlement. The law of 28 June was potentially the most significant piece of legislation enacted for the Jews in the entire reign of Alexander II. It opened a door for the largest single category of Jews ever to receive the right of empire-wide residence throughout the Empire. The law was widely seen as the decisive step in the forward march of Jewish emancipation. The bureaucratic debates surrounding the law clearly reveal economic motives at work, and the effectiveness of the new regulations was thus a major component in assessing how and if the Jewish Question might be resolved. This was a crucial factor since Tsar Alexander remained unresponsive to emancipationist arguments based on abstract, humanitarian principles. Public opinion, as expressed in the periodical press, also emphasized that further Jewish rights should be held hostage to a successful outcome of the new law.

It is difficult to estimate the precise number of Jews eligible for resettlement. Census records placed the Jews into three broad occupational categories: the merchantry (*kupechestvo*), subdivided into three guilds based upon declared capital; the urban trade-artisan class (*meshchanstvo*), and agricultural colonists. All Jewish artisans were enrolled in the *meshchanstvo*, but not all members of this estate were artisans – quite to the contrary, most were involved in some form of petty trade. The surveys of the Russian General Staff are too impressionistic to shed much light on the question. P. Bobrovskii, speaking of the estimated 100,490 Jews in Grodno province, asserted that Jewish artisans were few in number and always prone to abandon their craft and turn to trade.[17] V. Pavlovich observed of the roughly 2,500 Jews in Ekaterinoslav province that "many Jews who are of the *meshchanstvo* engage in crafts ... The district towns here would be no more than villages if they were not enlivened by the permanent activity of a few Jews."[18] More useful are the records of locales where the authorities conducted an "assortment" of Jews at the behest of Nicholas I: according to I. Zelenskii, the tabulation for Minsk province in 1851 revealed

20,367 craftsmen and their families out of a total Jewish population of 95,767, representing 22.8 percent of the whole.[19] This tallies closely with P. P. Chubinskii's estimate in 1872 that 21 percent of the approximately 750,000 Jews of Kiev, Volynia and Podolia provinces were artisans and their families.[20] If these figures are accurate, then approximately one-fifth of the Jewish population of the Pale (not including the privileged groups of first guild merchants and honored citizens who had the right to live permanently outside the Pale) were eligible for resettlement. Official figures placed the number of Jews resident in the Pale at 1,430,643 persons. Consequently, 286,128 persons were potentially affected.

Within a year of the new law, Lev Levanda, in *Vilenskii vestnik*, lamented the paucity of results from an initiative which had been greeted with prayers of thanksgiving in synagogues when it was first announced. "Amidst the class of Jewish craftsmen," Levanda complained, "one cannot detect the slightest movement toward resettlement, although the Jewish craftsman is literally suffocated in this region because of excessive competition and is absolutely convinced that inside Russia an incomparably better fate awaits him" (26:1/II/ 1866). There was no one to dispute Levanda. In the next fifteen years there was general agreement that resettlement had been a failure, at least in the medium term, but sharp disagreement as to the cause.[21]

The typical Judeophobe explanation was that Jewish artisans did not move because they were satisfied with a life within the Pale based upon the exploitation of the native population. Ironically, this viewpoint originated with Levanda's article wherein he attempted to demonstrate the Jews' capacity for patriotism by stressing their view of Lithuania as a "new Palestine" and of Vilna as a "new Jerusalem." Responses to Levanda in *Vilenskii vestnik* seized upon this sentence. The Jews love Lithuania, wrote one anonymous author, because it was here that Polish pans first gave them the opportunity to exploit the peasantry (101:14/V/1866). A writer from Smolensk agreed, noting that in the Russian interior the Jews would lack a monopoly and have to contend with real competitors (152:16/VII/1866). *Golos* also took up the theme from Levanda, characterizing the Pale as a "golden Russian Colchis" and Vilna as both the "Second Jerusalem" and the metropolitanate of Jewry (247:7/IX/1866). As late as 1880 this claim was implicit in a *Kievlianin* editorial which taunted Jewish publicists to explain the continuing failure of the Jews to move (45:24/II/1880).

Even while arguing that the Jews preferred to live a life of exploitation in the Pale, few writers claimed that they prospered as a result.

The obvious poverty of the Jewish masses, underlined by disasters like the Kovno famine of 1869–70, made this an impossible task. Consequently, other answers to Jewish persistence in the Pale had to be found. The answer favored by Judeophiles was at the other extreme from the "Golden Russian Colchis" argument. The Jews, they claimed, were too poor to afford a move from the Pale to the interior. Continually reiterated, this argument won credence even among Judeophobes (*Golos* 48:17/II/1880). In response, editorialists occasionally exhorted the Jews to organize craft schools to qualify Jews for resettlement, or to underwrite relocation expenses.

In the light of significant internal Jewish movement within the Pale and emigration abroad throughout the second half of the nineteenth century, an explanation restricted only to poverty is clearly inadequate. Poverty did not prevent unqualified Jews from leaving the Pale in significant numbers, as all commentators attested.[22] Some writers cited the character of the law itself, chiefly its failure to give settlers a permanent legal status. The ambiguity of their position left them at the mercy of numerous external forces, including the police and local administration, their home communities as well as subsequent government circulars, often incorrectly interpreted by local officials.

In order to move, artisans had to secure an internal passport from their local community, periodically renew it, and receive certification from the local police. Upon resettlement, they had to register with the police of their new home and join a local craft guild. They were also obliged to resign from their previous guild, a risky undertaking, given their indeterminate status. Since the principle of collective responsibility (*krugovaia poruka*) was used to collect taxes and recruits from the Jewish community, local Jewish authorities were reluctant to lose direct control over a well-to-do member who could be counted on to pay his taxes. Poor artisans who desired to leave the community were obvious candidates for military recruitment (*Kievlianin* 122 and 123:1865). As Brafman's theories of the kahal gained credence, editorialists took for granted the role of the Jewish community in hindering the mobility of its individual members (*Beseda* III:March, 1872:235–6; *Russkii mir* 313:25/XI/1873). The willingness of the local police to accept bribes meant that legitimate settlers were obstructed from making a move, while charlatans easily secured the necessary documentation (*SPb vedomosti* 68:10/III/1873).

Difficulties did not cease with resettlement. The police outside the Pale were notoriously capricious in interpreting the resettlement law, especially when they were held personally responsible for any irregularities within their jurisdiction. In the early days of resettlement, the Jewish *Den* frequently reported such episodes. A craftsman in Moscow or St. Petersburg would hand in his passport to the police for registration and be told that since the police had received no specific instructions as to the control of such passports, residence could not be allowed. "And if you don't want to resort to a well-known type of protection [i.e., bribery], you have to leave the capital" (8:4/VII/1869). An article in *Voskhod* complained that the authorities were refusing to transfer the certification of artisan master status from one province to another (4/5: IV–V 1882). Once in place, artisans were still subject to harassment. *Den* complained in 1870 that the Excise Tax Administration in Kaluga was forbidding Jewish brewers and distillers – whom the paper claimed constituted the majority of settlers outside the Pale – to trade in alcohol which they produced themselves, although they were permitted by law to do so. Local authorities sought to prohibit artisans from trading in goods of their own making until the courts were forced to intervene in the Jews' favor (22:29/V/1870).

A decade later, looking back over the experience of Jewish "pioneers," A. E. Kaufman in *Russkii evrei* cited the continuing irregularity of their position as a major factor in deterring others. He remarked on the experience of Jewish distillers, alternately admitted and expelled from the interior. "Who knows but that this wandering, gypsy-like life of Jewish distillers and their coreligionists, before whom the road to the interior was first opened and then closed, caused a lack of confidence in the law of 1865 among Jewish craftsmen?" (27:2/VII/1880). The modern equivalent of this unprotected, unsettled situation, Kaufman observed, were recent attempts to expel Jews under an old law which ordered their removal from any province where "Judaizing" religious sects appeared among the peasantry (35:29/VIII/1880). Various other plausible reasons were also advanced in the press, especially the claim that Jews were reluctant to resettle individually in an alien environment, cut off from all communal activity and support, bereft of the services of the traditional Jewish community (*Den* 25:1/XI/ 1869; *Russkii evrei* 43:22/X/1880; *Golos* 48:17/II/1880).

Despite the universal recognition of the failure of the law of 1865, most of the press, Judeophobe as well as Judeophile, continued to call for the abolition of the Pale until about 1878. The liberal press couched the call in abstract terms of "human justice," and predicted that, once removed from the closed Jewish world of the Pale, Jews would quickly be Russified. The notorious chicanery of the Jews would founder against the hard-headed business sense of the Russian peasant and craftsman in the interior. This perspective implied a negative view of the Ukrainian and Belorussian peasantry within the Pale. The liberal *Golos*, which also viewed the Russian peasant in a pessimistic light, and which fully accepted the fantasies of Brafman, was a prominent exception to the general rule. But even *Golos* turned against the Pale when its retention became a doctrine of conservative Judeophobia (48:17/II/ 1880).

Judeophobes viewed resettlement primarily in terms of the benefits that might accrue to the overburdened western provinces. *Kievlianin*, for example, sought to demonstrate that where the Jewish population was smaller and less concentrated, and less able to harm others, Jews lived better themselves, and were seen in a more positive light by the rest of the population (65–66:1–3/VI/1876). The most familiar Judeo-phobe analogy was that of a drop of poison which loses its lethal properties when distilled in the ocean.

With the rise of a distinct conservative ideology, in which Jews played a prominent role as an anti-Russian force, spokesmen of the Right became partisans of retaining the Pale, especially if they lived in the capitals and not in the provinces. Prince N. N. Golitsyn, writing in the reactionary *Grazhdanin*, shifted the metaphor. The Jews were not poison, but a parasite which enters a healthy organism (35:7:19/XII/ 1878). The conservative press viewed with alarm proposals emanating from ORT to train Jewish artisans and relocate them out of the Pale. This would do no more than relocate the kahal to the interior, warned *Novoe vremia* (1727:17/XII/1880). *Rossiia* noted ORT's connections with the exploiter Poliakov and the Alliance Israélite Universelle. They sought "to strengthen migration, to direct it to where it has not yet gone, to string up a net of Jewish exploitation where it still lacks sufficient representatives ... In the Yid nests of the western region a myriad of parasites has long waited ... to infect the Russian nation (95:20/XII/1880).

Public debates both recapitulated and inspired arguments which raged within chancellery walls. Within a decade of emancipation, reports critical of the Jewish role in the new economic and political life of the country began to stream into the capital from provincial officials. They were attentively read by Alexander II, whose characteristic notation on them was "I desire that this question be urgently resolved." In consequence, a new official body was created in 1872, the Commission for the Organization of Jewish Life (KUBE).[23] The Commission set to work on the backlog of reports, beginning with that of the Vilna Commission of 1870 which recommended the removal of the

Pale. The KUBE also considered a report from the Governor-General of the Southwest Region, A. M. Dondukov-Korsakov, warning against the danger of Jewish economic domination of the Ukraine. Despite his different perspective, he shared the view of the Vilna reformers that the Pale be abolished. It was unjust, he argued, that the Southwest alone be saddled with the Jewish burden. The particular harmfulness of the Jews derived from their concentration in areas where they were well-served by the kahal system and by their deep historical roots. If allowed to escape from this localized isolation, the Jews would be diluted in the larger population. Cut off from the support services of the kahal, the individual Jew would find competition with the Russian peasant difficult, to say nothing of the Russian kulak.[24]

The KUBE was not convinced by the arguments of the Vilna Commission. Commission member V. V. Grigorev, charged with preparing a report on relaxation of the Pale, rejected Dondukov-Korsakov's arguments. Proposals to scatter the Jews, he observed, came not from the Jews themselves but from local administrators. They did not seek to improve the life of the Jews but to relieve the Christian population from the burden of Jewish overcrowding. "The task of relieving the western region does not consist in diminishing the size of the Jewish population there," he wrote, "but of changing the conditions of their life, to transform them from parasites into producers. If the Jews do not want this, resettling them throughout Great Russia will only spread the harm which presently gnaws away at the western frontiers of the Empire."[25] Grigorev commented adversely on the experiment of 1865. He charged that Jewish distillers did nothing but deceive the treasury while "dubious people" were masquerading as craftsmen. Settlers increased the crime rate where they lived. Two or three Jewish families in a village increased the trade in stolen goods, decreased the amount of honest money in circulation, and increased the spread of counterfeit coins.[26]

Faced with strong disagreements of opinion on the abolition of the Pale, the members of the KUBE took a familiar bureaucratic path: they delayed any action pending a wholesale review of the Jewish Question.[27] This proved to be an inadequate solution, even in the short term. Bereft of leadership from St. Petersburg, provincial governors developed their own home-grown solutions to the Jewish Question.

Midway through the 1870s, municipal authorities began to expel Jews under a variety of pretexts. In Bessarabia province Jews were expelled from the town of Izmail and from territories located within 50 versts of the border, under the pretext of enforcing an anti-smuggling law of 1843.[28] This was despite the fact that the territory in question was acquired by the Empire under the Treaty of Berlin, negotiated three decades after promulgation of the original law. The annexation decree itself had guaranteed the existing rights of the Jews.[29]

In Orel, located outside the Pale, local authorities in 1878 began to expel Jewish artisans who failed to satisfy all the provisions of the law of 1865, despite complaints in the local press that an economically useful segment of the population was thus being lost (*Orlovskii vestnik* 75:21/VII/1878). The zeal of the Orel authorities, and of officials in other towns, was apparently in response to a routine inquiry from the MVD about the occupations of Jews living outside the Pale. Local administrators apparently assumed, in the current climate of Judeophobia, that this investigation was the prelude to a crackdown on the large numbers of illegally resident Jews, engaged in trade rather than handicrafts. Officials sought both to demonstrate their initiative and diligence, while reducing competition for local tradesmen. Whatever the motives, some imagination was occasionally displayed. Authorities in Voronezh and Tambov, both outside the Pale, expelled Jews on the basis of an old law, dating to the reign of Alexander I, stipulating that all Jews were to be removed from any internal province where "Judaizing" heresies appeared among the local Christians.[30]

The question of Jewish residence even appeared in Finland, which enjoyed considerable political autonomy. Although Jews constituted no more than a handful of the population, the Finnish Senate resolved to expel all those who lived in the capital of Helsingfors (Helsinki) in 1881 (*Golos* 21:21/I/1880; *Vseobshchaia gazeta* 5:2/II/1881). The year 1880 witnessed yet another of the periodic expulsions of Jews from Kiev, as well as the eviction of a German Jewish commercial agent from St. Petersburg, a reminder of the stringent regulations discouraging even temporary residence in the capitals by foreign Jews (*Rassvet* 22:28/V/1880).

The response of the central government to these diverse initiatives is revealing. It chose not to intervene in Finland, where the paucity of Jews in Helsingfors made the expulsion largely a moot point. The Bessarabian authorities were allowed to remove some Jews from the frontiers, although farmers, distillers and artisans, who had been exempt from the original ban, were not touched. Kiev was permitted, as in the past, to ban Jews from certain quarters of the city, although a lively debate persisted as to what areas were actually included. The expulsion of the German Jew provoked an outcry abroad which even the Russian Jewish press, reluctant to be seen as providing ammunition to the foreign enemies of Russia, declared to be unseemly (*Russkii evrei* 22:28/V/1880). As was usually the case in such incidents, the Ministry of Foreign Affairs made a great show of standing firm. The ministry was accustomed to providing justifications abroad for Russia's Jewish policies at home, as when Foreign Minister Gorchakov pointed to the low level of Russian Jewry during debates at the Congress of Berlin in 1879.[31]

The most significant response to these and similar episodes came from the Ministry of Internal Affairs, whose original request for information had prompted some of the expulsions. On 3 April 1880 the ministry issued a circular to local authorities under the name of the Minister for Internal Affairs L. S. Makov. Jews who had moved out of the Pale before this date, it announced, were to be permitted to stay where they now resided, even if their original settlement was illegal. The so-called "Makov Circular" constituted a virtual amnesty for Jews living in the interior (*Russkii evrei* 22:28/V/1880; *Rassvet* 19:8/V/1880). After the resettlement of Jews from areas of "Judaizing" became known in the West, where it provoked hostile comment, local authorities were apparently informed by the center that "Judaizing" was no longer to serve as a pretext for resettlement (*The Times* 29,878:11/V/1880).

By the end of Alexander II's reign, the state's Jewish policies remained in flux. One striking feature of the Jewish Question had become apparent: the ease with which it was fitted into the wider social, economic and political preoccupations of the day, however tenuous the links. For example, as the following section will reveal, Jews were associated with the spread of socialism well before the time when they played a prominent role in the movement. They became synonymous with capitalism before Jewish entrepreneurs attained their greatest – albeit still limited – successes. A prominent aspect of the debate over the decline of the Russian gentry involved the claim that Jews were buying up noble estates, a claim that was repeatedly shown, by the government's own statistics, to have no objective basis. Moreover, these phantom dangers elicited concrete responses from Russian officialdom, from the provinces to the capitals. Finally, the issue of the Jews loomed large in debates between conservatives, liberals and radicals, remaining an ideological *idée fixe* to the very end of tsarism itself.

13   The theme of "Jewish exploitation"

Jews and serfdom

On 19 February 1861, the statutory status of serfdom came to an end in the Russian Empire although the complex process of mandatory redemption was still not completed by the turn of the century. At that late date it was still unclear to many within the government whether emancipation should be counted a failure or a success, in the light of the social and economic forces which it had unleashed.

The complexity of the peasant reform was further complicated in much of the Pale by the Polish uprising of 1863. In the Kingdom of Poland, as well as in the northwestern and southwestern regions, the government attempted to punish the Polish landlords and reward the loyalty of the peasantry by providing the latter with more generous land allotments and by removing the landowners' ability to delay redemption. Russification policies sought the transfer of land to Russian owners, in a bid to weaken Polish (and Jewish) economic power.

The emancipation process was dominated from start to finish by a pessimistic concern with the peasantry. They were seen as the "dark" people, loyal and patriotic, yet capable of violence and rebellion. Good-hearted, but ignorant, they were easy prey for predators from within and without the village. The peasant character was flawed, prone to sloth and drunkenness if not properly restrained. In a peasant village left to its own devices, the strong would soon devour the weak, and the tavern would mark the grave of good husbandry.

These conservative prejudices dominated the peasant emancipation. The land was not given outright to the individual peasant, but to the juridically constituted peasant community, the *mir* or *obshchina*, of which he was a member. Lacking legal title to the land, the individual peasant was incapable of alienating his allotment except in exceptional

300

circumstances. The community was responsible for redeeming, through payments to the state, those lands which negotiations with the gentry awarded to the peasants. The community bore all financial obligations under a system of collective responsibility known as *krugovaia poruka*. The community also controlled temporary and permanent departure from the commune. In this way, individual rights and initiative were subordinated to the needs of the collective. Whatever else the peasant might do, he would not lose his land, and somebody would pay his taxes.

Since the annexation of Jewish communities by Russia in 1772, government officials had viewed, as a major component of the Jewish Question, the problem of "Jewish exploitation," especially as practiced upon the gullible peasant. Although the government had sponsored agricultural colonization schemes for the Jews since 1804, and granted Jews the right to own land which did not have peasants (i.e. serfs) settled on it through statutes in 1804 and 1835, the emancipation decree of 1861 specifically denied Jews the right to acquire lands which had comprised part of noble estates.[1] This ban reflected old concerns about the harmful economic role which Jews allegedly played in the countryside, a role which would be intensified if Jews gained a permanent foothold in the village.

This restriction on the free flow of capital did not pass unchallenged in the unsettled economic conditions which followed the peasant emancipation. Jews were permitted to lease gentry estates,[2] but this was not enough for a group of first and second guild Jewish merchants in the Ukraine, who petitioned the Governor-General, I. I. Vasilchikov, for the right to acquire unsettled estates. Vasilchikov, a firm believer in using the Jews as an anti-Polish force in the region, was the right man to approach. He argued to the Jewish Committee that sale of estates to Jews would have the beneficial effect of taking them out of Polish hands. A ban would be ineffective in any case, since once sold to non-gentry owners, former gentry land could legally be resold to Jews. Impressed by these arguments, the Committee petitioned the Tsar to permit the purchase by Jews of "unsettled" gentry land (i.e., lands where statutory relations between peasants and landlords had lapsed), and the request was granted. When the permission was promulgated by the Senate, interestingly enough, the summary of the debate was disguised in order to make it appear that the revision of the law was based purely on legal precedent.[3] It was impolitic to tell the Poles what the government really hoped would happen to their land.

Events soon conspired against this important concession. The Polish uprising was followed by a spate of laws designed to weaken the influence of the Polish landowning class in the Russian–Polish borderlands. The Jews were direct casualties of this campaign. Early in 1864 the Russian government promulgated a set of rules and regulations designed to reduce Polish landowning. Special privileges were given to all people "not of Polish or Jewish descent" to purchase state and private land in the Northwest and Southwest.[4] The inclusion of the Jews arose from the government's awareness of how completely Jews were enmeshed in the prereform economy and their traditional role as the financial agents of the szlachta. Permitting the transfer of estates to Jews would allow Jews to front for Poles threatened with loss of their estates. A similar motive led to a tightening of the law in 1865, which banned the Jews from holding mortgages on properties that had been secured under the privileged conditions of the Russification campaign.[5]

A second blow at the Polish landlords was the decision to force them to complete the redemption process, whereby money and work duties were replaced by a land settlement and redemption payments. Redemption was made mandatory in the northwestern and southwestern provinces (whereas the time allotted for a final settlement was open-ended elsewhere) as a means of reducing the influence of Polish landlords over the peasantry.[6] This quickly freed up large amounts of land for public trade, land which Jews were entitled to buy under the law of 26 April 1862. To the Russifying Governors-General of the area, M. N. Muravev in Vilna and N. N. Annenkov in Kiev, this was an unacceptable situation, and they were supported by the Minister of Internal Affairs, P. A. Valuev. He approached the Western Committee, charged with the fight against Polish influence in the borderlands, with the request that the Jews be bridled. The Committee found that its Russifying measures would be at cross-purposes with Jewish land-owning rights, "since the Jews, disposing of significant capital and constituting at this time the creditors of a large part of the local landlords, are dangerous competitors for the sale of properties, with whom Russians could compete only with great difficulty."[7] The Committee also expressed its concern that "the peasant population, hardly freed from the burdensome influence of the landlords and in need of income, will fall into a new dependence upon Jewish landowners, who control large financial resources, and are suspect as to their political loyalties."[8] Once again, the true intentions of the government were disguised in the public announcement of this new restriction. A decree of only a few lines noted that the right the Jews had received to secure estate lands in 1862, "was not extended to provinces where mandatory redemption has been carried out."[9] The act deprived the Jews of landholding rights in the provinces comprising the Governor-Generalships of the Northwest and Southwest, but not in the rest of the Pale.

However brief the decree, the discussion which preceded it reveals the recurrent preoccupation of the government that statutory serfdom would be replaced by Jewish economic serfdom.

This fear was officially expressed in the wake of emancipation in a series of reports on individual provinces of the Russian Empire, conducted under the auspices of the General Staff of the Russian Army.[10] A. Shmidt set the tone in his description of the post-emancipation village in Kherson province, where "one can truthfully say that the peasant only lives freely where there are no Jews" (514). Emancipation replaced an economy based on serf labor with one requiring hired labor, forcing employers to have ready money. The Jew alone had capital, and was the logical intermediary between land and labor. "Without exaggeration one may say that a Jew, settled in a village with ten rubles for each recorded soul, in a few years becomes the master of the village more firmly than the present pomeshchik, and the peasant will work for them not three but six days a week" (514). On the southern steppe where peasant ties to the land were newer and weaker, the ruined peasant might well leave the land, "due to the weakness of his character and the guile of the Jew" (515). Given the riotous instincts of the peasants, the state should consider intervention before these antagonisms took their natural course and erupted into violence (515).

A decade after the peasant emancipation, the economic changes which had been predicted had, in the eyes of some observers, come to pass. In 1872, the talented young Ukrainophile geographer and ethnographer, P. P. Chubinskii, published a series of works on the Ukraine under the sponsorship of the Imperial Russian Geographical Society. He devoted most of a volume to the Jews. On the basis of what he saw occurring in the Ukraine, the otherwise liberal Chubinskii argued against the immediate grant of legal equality to the Jews. "One can't neglect the interests of the Christian working population, exploited by the Jews. Given full rights in a set period of time, the Jews would dominate the peasant who, freed from judicial slavery, would fall into economic slavery."[11]

Behind the petty Jewish exploiter in the village stood a greater danger: Jewish capitalists. Thwarted in their desire to buy land in

Right-Bank Ukraine, they leased land instead, including 819 properties comprising 516,958 desiatins, in the provinces of Kiev, Podolia and Volynia. If illegal short-term leases were added, Chubinskii claimed, Jews controlled one-sixth of southwestern agricultural lands and almost one-tenth of land on noble estates.[12]

The Jews were adept at leaseholding because of the dearth of liquid capital and rural credit in the countryside. Prereform credit institutions had all closed, and private initiative was slow to respond to an urgent need. While the rental price for a desiatin of land ranged from 2.20 rubles to 3.29 rubles in the three provinces, Jews were often able to contract at a ruble a desiatin because of their ability to pay in advance. The Jews were also skillful at securing a workforce by placing the peasants in an economic kabal. The Jewish leaseholder advanced the peasants money to pay their taxes, and the debt was repaid through field work, often at severely undervalued rates.[13] Despite this, Chubinskii asserted that peasants preferred to work for Jews: the peasants considered themselves superior to the Jews, and for their part the Jews treated their workers with a skill and tact conspicuously missing from peasant–pomeshchik relationships.[14]

Chubinskii saw these phenomena, not as capital pursuing opportunity, but as an irrational economy made possible by insufficient credit. The Jews had no affinity for agriculture – as the fate of Jewish agricultural colonization revealed – but held leases only because they were profitable. (Chubinskii reckoned their total profits from leaseholding at 3,600,000 silver rubles.) Jews had no regard for upkeep of the land, as they sought the maximum return during the period of the lease. Chubinskii described how Jews acquired agricultural land in the Southwest, by giving landowners large "loans," equivalent to the value of the estate. A relaxation of the law against landholding would be followed by their formal claim of title, he predicted. Although exploitation of a personal estate would presumably be more rational than one held on lease, Chubinskii also viewed this as a negative phenomenon.[15]

Chubinskii's concerns were precisely mirrored in the annual report for 1872 of the Governor-General of the Southwest Region, Prince A.M. Dondukov-Korsakov. The Governor-General's concerns ranged far beyond leaseholding itself and encompassed the virtual economic domination of the world, aided and abetted by "the universal Jewish kahal."[16] Leaseholding was the focus of his concern because, after emancipation, it became the surest device for the Jews to keep the peasants in thrall: "The Jews feel that previous means of enslaving the peasants may slip from their hands; that is why in recent times there has appeared a universal desire of the Jews to lease land. Agriculture is so foreign to the Jew that in his hands it serves only to pursue commercial goals."[17] The Jews leased estates, and then sub-leased them to peasants, not for money but for labor services, "far in excess of the value of the land, constituting in its way a new form of serfdom."[18]

To deal with this problem, Dondukov-Korsakov sought to ban Jews from leasing land. His arguments were buttressed by a similar recommendation from the Governor-General of New Russia and Bessarabia, P.E. Kotsebu, in 1869. The fate of this campaign is most revealing. The Tsar himself noted on Kotsebu's recommendation, "I view this as very useful," yet nothing ever came of it. At the time the Tsar was palmed off with the explanation that such a measure was inextricably linked to matters of wider importance for the Empire. The Tsar acceded to the recommendation of the Minister of Interior that such a project await the final legal resolution of the Jewish Question.

Dondukov-Korsakov's specific recommendation was rejected by the Jewish Commission, on the grounds that such a restriction would violate property rights without sufficient cause, that it would unwisely weaken the political loyalty of both Polish landlords and Jewish leaseholders, and that Jewish leaseholding lacked the negative economic traits attributed to it by the Governor-General.[19]

Another body of official documents helps to place these accounts in perspective. In 1872, the Ministry of State Domains, under P. A. Valuev, conducted a massive investigation of the state of agriculture and rural productivity in Russia. The resulting report, published in seven volumes in 1873, ranged over the whole panoply of official concerns for rural Russia. According to George Yaney:

> the malign influence of Jews, for example, was an almost universal theme in the reports from the western provinces. It seems that the Jews ran many of the landed estates, either as stewards or as tenants. Moreover, they operated most of the taverns and monopolized the buying and selling of grain. According to all reports that mentioned Jews, they did only harm. They reaped their profits heedless of consequences, while gentry, peasantry and soil all went to ruin.[20]

Yet as is clear from N. M. Druzhinin's summary of the Valuev Commission's report, there was nothing uniquely "Jewish" in these charges. The problems they described were to be found in other provinces, far from the Pale; the economic relationships were free of national characteristics; and an agricultural crisis – real or imagined – was possible quite independently of Jews.[21] What is distinctive, rather, is the ease with which a Jewish perspective entered into wider concerns. The average leaseholder of an estate in the Russian Empire was *not* a Jew, as all objective evidence revealed, yet for Russian officialdom, this was very much an integral part of the Jewish Question.

Public opinion mirrored – in so far as it did not prompt – official concern at the emergence of a new, Jewish form of serfdom. Although a few other provincial papers expressed disquiet at the changing role of Jews in the post-emancipation economy, it was *Kievlianin*, as so often, which took the lead.[22] The campaign can be dated to the 1865 dispute of *Kievlianin* with M. Morgulis over Jewish leaseholding, discussed above.[23] Beginning in 1869, *Kievlianin* launched a campaign which helped to create a crisis atmosphere, apparently in an effort to acquaint the newly appointed Governor-General, A. M. Dondukov-Korsakov, with the obsessions of local Judeophobes. Dondukov-Korsakov was quickly convinced and wrote to the capital that "every intrigue, every aspiration of the Jews at present is concentrated on changing this law, and there is no form or guise under which they will not attempt to evade a situation which is so restrictive for them."[24] In the category of "forms and guises" Dondukov-Korsakov probably included the Jewish-Russian newspaper *Den*, published in Odessa. The paper sought to rebut the claims of *Kievlianin*, even printing the work of Shulgin's old adversary, M. Morgulis. The resulting squabble helped to place the issue before a wider audience.

Kievlianin couched the problem in simple terms: why were the Jews so adept at breaking the laws on ownership and leaseholding? It sought an answer in laws governing Jewish land ownership and leasing. Before the Polish uprising it had been hoped that the Jews might serve as a counterweight to the Poles in the west, and so they were given landholding rights. The process of merger had not, in retrospect, been facilitated by these concessions because the Jewish masses remained sunk in isolation and ignorance. Consequently, the local administration recognized that Russification was not served by the Jewish element, and the restrictions of 1864 were introduced (15:6/II/1869).

Balked in their attempts to buy land, the Jews flocked to leaseholding, using leases either to exploit and ruin the land, or to take *de facto* possession until that day when the law was changed. The only argument in favor of Jewish leaseholding was that it provided capital for agriculture that the pomeshchiki did not have. This claim was countered by the ruination of estates under Jewish lease, the danger that leases would lead to *de facto* possession, and the inability of incoming Russians to compete with Jews in pursuing leases (16:8/II/ 1869).

Kievlianin supported its general accusation with specific examples. F. Samokhin qualified a peasant's complaint that a Jew in the village was "a real vampire," by observing that a vampire drains the blood and leaves the body. But once established in a peasant village, the Jew never left. He identified a new and sinister aspect of Jewish leasehol-ding. While the peasant was unable to sell his land to a Jew in payment of debts, he could lease it at very favorable rates. The Jew made loans which could never be paid off and then took up residence on the peasant land until repayment. In Radomysl district alone, 98 Jews had built houses on peasant land held as collateral for loans (23:25/II/1869). Another series offered anecdotal evidence of the peasant claim that the Jews were clever demons who took human form to carry off Christian souls. It chronicled how the Jew Berka in the village of B. destroyed the simple, honest peasant Stephan through vodka. "Land, water, forest, factories and capital are all in the hands of the Jews. The strength is theirs, the law is theirs" (35:25/III/1869). In the village of Romanovka, a Jewish leaseholder enjoyed "feudal suzerainty" over the peasants (93:5/VIII/1872). *Kievlianin* applauded efforts of the local administration (i.e., Dondukov-Korsakov) for its efforts to correct these evils by secur-ing a ban on the lease of land by Jews (142:29/XI/1870).

Efforts of *Kievlianin* to alert both the state and society to the danger of Jewish leaseholding found an immediate response among papers of a conservative gentry orientation. *Peterburgskaia gazeta* warned against the extension of Jewish civil rights by pointing to their activities as leaseholders (59:27/IV/1869). *Vest* published an attack on the Jews that was little more than a resume of *Kievlianin's* anti-lease articles from earlier in the year (198:19/VII/1869). Another prominent conservative organ, *Russkii mir*, used the rumors circulating about Dondukov-Korsakov's anti-leasing initiative as a pretext for a lengthy series on the harmful economic significance of the Jews. The paper characterized the Jewish Question as "second only to the Polish Question in impor-tance." But while the Polish Question was disappearing due to official measures, the Jewish Question still demanded the greatest strength and labor from both state and society (293:5/XI/1873).[25]

The *Kievlianin* campaign coincided with the appearance of the new and argumentative "newspaper of Russian Jews," *Den*. The paper was quick to defend the Jews from any *Kievlianin* accusation, but more so in the case of the land question. Two of the most important of the paper's journalists, I. Orshanskii and M. Morgulis, took a special interest in economic-political questions of this type. Between them they published two major series devoted to Jewish control of land, accompanied by numerous short notices on various aspects of the problem. These articles were articulate and logically reasoned arguments, but they reveal how unattuned Jewish publicists were to the underlying public concerns represented by the *Kievlianin* campaign. Admissions that Jews did widely circumvent the law, or that Jewish capital really was a potent force in the Southwest, did little to dispel the vision of Jews displacing Russians. Evidence of Jewish influence upon the peasants offered little comfort to those who viewed the peasants as weak, pliable and easily controlled and the Jews as culturally, as well as religiously, alien. Yet this is precisely the direction that the articles in *Den* took. *Den's* basic error was to pretend that the debate over land leasing and ownership was an economic one, to be won or lost through purely economic arguments, bolstered by assurances of Jewish political loyalty.

Orshanskii argued that restrictions on the Jews in the marketplace created economic irregularities, given the large amount of capital which they controlled. Capital followed land, especially in an economy where the Jews and the Polish landlord had such traditionally close links (7:14/II/1870). Unable to purchase land with their capital, Jews loaned it to peasants and landlords, at rates sufficient to turn a good profit, or used it for harmful trade speculation (9:28/II/1870). The incapacity of the Polish pans and the unfamiliarity of Russian owners with the area, ensured that in the confusion of the post-emancipation economy, where peasant–noble relations were still embittered, many agriculturists failed. Jewish creditors were faced with the return of a few kopeks on the ruble after the public auction of an estate, in which they could not participate. Understandably, prudent creditors never let matters go this far: they arranged for the transfer of the estate to a third party, although they took effective control (6:6/II/1870). Since increasing amounts of land were passing surreptitiously to the Jews under the natural workings of the marketplace, the government should legitimize the process. Jews should be positively encouraged to acquire or rent land (26:8/XI/1869).

What of arguments that the Jews only exploited the land and the workforce, never farming themselves, or that the failure of Jewish agricultural colonies confirmed the Jews' inability to farm? What was transpiring, Orshanskii argued, was the movement of city people into agriculture. Leases and hired labor were a natural way for them to test the waters and gain experience. The colonization experiments, badly run and confused, really proved nothing. As far as the political side was concerned, the Jews could be counted upon to favor those who treated them well. Since Russians were not acquiring the land in any case – foreign Germans were flooding into the area – ownership might better be left to the Jews (9:28/II/1870).

Morgulis viewed the problem in the light of social relations after emancipation. The bitterness of the settlement deterred peasants from working for their former lords, while they felt no animosity at all toward the Jews. Russians, new to the area, found it more convenient to lease to Jews, rather than enter the perilous world of labor relations with the peasantry (18:1/V/1870). The Jews had a vested interest in maintaining good relations, and this ensured that they treated their peasant workforce well. Morgulis pointed to Russification efforts of Jewish landlords among their peasants, or their discouragement of peasant drunkenness because of its negative effect on their economy (20:15/V/1870). *Den* supported these major arguments with short notices of how Jewish leaseholders assisted the welfare of their peasant help, in some cases even helping them to build churches (26:27/VI/1870). Pride of place in this regard was the report from a village where 2,500 peasants had unanimously elected a Jewish landowner to be a church elder (42:16/X/1870).

Den's arguments merely played into the hands of Judeophobes. Its concessions on the economic role of the Jews allowed *Kievlianin* to accept Jewish evasion of the law as a given. Far from accepting this as a natural functioning of the economy, *Kievlianin* condemned the Jews for their criminality, and heaped shame on third parties who "sold their name" so that Jews could illegally acquire land.[26]

In 1876, a more direct attempt to promote Jewish economic interests triggered renewed debate. That year saw the appearance of a brochure entitled "Notes on the Question of the Restoration of the Rights of Jews to Acquire Estates in the Western Region." It was apparently not offered at public sale at all, but sent to administrators as an open letter advocating Jewish landownership in the name of the economic betterment of the area.[27] After being attacked by a *Kievlianin* editorial, it attracted the attention of the capital press, led by *Pravitelstvennye vedomosti*, official publication of the MVD, and a flagship liberal newspaper, *Birzhevye vedomosti*. *Pravitelstvennyi vestnik* offered numerous examples of Jewish exploitation and warned against placing land in their hands.[28] This point illustrated the weakness in *Den's* logic: once the Jews were considered exploiters and speculators in one area of the economy, their opponents assumed that they would bring those qualities to any other field which they entered.

Birzhevye vedomosti shared this concern with speculation, seeing it as "predominating at the present moment in the midst of rich Jewry." Reflecting its liberal principles, the paper took issue with the conservative *Vest* as to the right type of people who should be settled in the southwest. Not the motley collection of railway men, contractors, speculators and imported bureaucrats: they had no interest in local affairs. But Jews would not be satisfactory either: "We need local people, Russian people, zemstvo people who will regard local interests not as a distant, alien matter, but as their immediate concern; we need people in the area who are capable of bringing life to the zemstvos, and strengthening Russian power so that, under the Russian banner, the principles of *Vest* or *Moskovskie vedomosti* will not sneak in" (131:13/ V/1876). If the Jews were so keen to invest their money, the liberal paper advised, let them invest in industry.

No better illustration of the extent to which concern with Jews on the land pervaded all ideological tendencies can be found in an article in *Otechestvennye zapiski* by V. Varzer, entitled "Jewish-Leaseholders in Chernigov Province." The article offered nothing new on the subject. It condemned Jewish leases as harmful speculation, and dismissed the Jewish agriculturists as "accidental people, with no ties to or respect for the land" (10/1879, 176). The Jews were accused of exploiting the peasants, a charge made more serious by the claim that Jews controlled about 40 percent of the land, with the volume still growing.[29] The sting of these criticisms was drawn somewhat by the admission that the economic system, not the Jews themselves, was to blame. Let there be an ample supply of rural credit, and the peasants could rent or buy their own land. Nevertheless, Jews were guilty of abusing the shortcomings of the system, and taking them to their worst extremes (201).

Such charges, long in the air, acquired a special force through their appearance in *Otechestvennye zapiski*, the prestigious journal of M. E. Saltykov-Shchedrin and N. A. Nekrasov. The charges gained a cachet and an acceptability attainable nowhere else. The article was widely reprinted and summarized, placing the seal of approval on this particular charge.[30] Champions of Jewish leaseholding and landownership had always been rare, but now they disappeared from the field altogether.

Jews and vodka

The profession of tavernkeeper had little to recommend it. It was based upon the exploitation of human weakness, and it often placed its practioners in physical danger – the press frequently carried reports of the murder of tavernkeepers and their families by bandits. The pogrom wave of 1881 was triggered in Elizavetgrad by a brawl outside a Jewish tavern. Since tavernkeepers were forced to operate on the edge of criminality, they suffered from a degraded social position. Tax farmers paid too much for their franchises to recoup their invest-ment honestly, and to operate profitably a tavernkeeper had to violate a whole series of laws designed to protect the consumer. (Neither the Jew E. Gintsburg nor the Russian V. A. Kokorev ever entirely escaped the stigma attached to their early careers in the vodka business.) On the other hand, the trade in vodka was immensely profitable: it was the largest single item of the Russian state budget, it made millionaires of Gintsburg and Kokorev, and it provided a living for tens of thou-sands of tax farm officials, distillers and humble tavernkeepers.

By the middle of the eighteenth century, taxes on vodka surpassed those on salt, and thereafter the government experimented with a variety of systems designed to maximize income from the vodka trade. By the middle of the nineteenth century a dual system had evolved. In the Russian heartland, the sale of vodka was conducted by tax farmers. Through a state auction the farmers secured the right to purchase vodka, largely from private gentry distilleries, and to sell it through their own network of taverns.

A different system operated in the "Privileged Provinces," a region which corresponded exactly to the Pale of Jewish Settlement. Tax farmers conducted the vodka trade in the cities of the Privileged Provinces, in the style of Great Russia. In the countryside, production and sale were gentry monopolies. Gentry distillers paid an excise tax on the liquor which they produced, and a license fee for the taverns which they set up on their estates.[31]

Dissatisfaction with the corruption and wastefulness of tax farming gradually persuaded the government to reform and then to abolish it. A law of 4 July 1861 decreed that, beginning in 1863, the tax farms were to be replaced throughout the Empire by an excise tax on spirits. While the law ensured that tax farms disappeared, distillers and tavern-keepers endured.

Jews, the traditional agents of the gentry monopoly on the

production and trade in alcohol in the Polish–Lithuanian Common-wealth, played a prominent role in all aspects of the Russian imperial system. Jewish financiers, such as Gintsburg and the Poliakovs, were active in the conduct of the Great Russian tax farms. The Russian press commented sarcastically on the "Jewish heroes" who appeared in the capital for the quadrennial tax farm auctions.[32] Jews provided exper-tise for the distilling industry, and were sought after to run the large commercial distilleries on Great Russian estates, as well as the smaller-scale gentry enterprizes in the Pale. The Jewish tavern-keeper was such a familiar figure as to become an enduring cultural motif in Eastern Europe.[33]

This prominent position of the Jews allowed them easily to become a scapegoat for the Russian government's guilty conscience at its own involvement in the liquor trade. By mid-century, a third of state revenues came from taxes on vodka. But if drink was "the joy of the Rus," as an ancient chronicle put it, it also had a high social cost. Alcohol abuse was a recurrent problem in Russia, particularly identi-fied with the peasantry. Consequently, although a government–gentry alliance made possible the liquor trade in its pre-emancipation form, both agents salved their consciences by blaming the Jews for its worst abuses. As early as 1799 the government was willing to concur with a gentry analysis which blamed peasant destitution in the Pale on the Jewish tavern.[34] The Jewish Statute of 1804 initiated attempts of the Russian government to drive the Jewish tavern-keeper out of the peasant village. In 1845, Jews were banned from operating taverns in the Ukraine. The "assortment" of the Jews under Nicholas I was aimed largely at tavern-keepers.[35] Concern for the post-emancipation peasantry likewise took the form of attacks on the Jewish tavern. Yet, paradoxically, the government could not dispense with the Jews, because it needed them to make the system run.

This was especially the case after the implementation of the new system of 1863. Distillation was permitted only in factories approved and supervised by the government. The increase in private factories that followed created a severe demand for technical personnel with distilling and brewing skills, and forced numerous concessions from the central government on behalf of the Jews. The law of 1865 which opened the Pale to Jewish craftsmen, for example, specifically included Jewish distillers and brewers.[36] Moreover, the decrees forbidding the sale or lease to Jews of lands in the southwestern and northwestern provinces secured through the Russifying campaign exempted Jews who were distillers or who leased taverns.[37] The rationale for this exemption was provided by the Senate in 1868, when it noted that "in the western region manufacturing and trade rests almost exclusively in Jewish hands and outside these circles it is almost impossible to find people capable of managing a mill or factory, requiring a certain technical knowledge and skill."[38]

While the government was willing enough to permit the Jews to produce alcohol, it remained reluctant to permit them to sell it. The new regulations on the liquor trade, promulgated on 4 July 1861, initially permitted the Jews inside the Pale of Settlement to trade only in towns and shtetlakh, a clear indication of the state's continuing reluctance to give the Jews a free hand in the peasant village.[39] On 18 March 1863, the State Council, traditionally moderate on the question of the legal rights of Jews, reinterpreted the law to permit the Jews to trade on an equal basis with all other citizens.[40] Such indulgence lasted less than a decade. In 1874, new regulations provided that Jews could trade in alcohol only in their own homes.[41] The stated reason was the government's wish to diminish drunkenness, and much ambiguity surrounded the term "in their own homes." But as M. I. Mysh observes, no other nationality or group was singled out for such attention, and the interpretation of "in their own homes" was continually made more restrictive.[42]

The abolition of the tax farms was preceded by a vigorous public debate, made possible by relaxation of censorship rules which had previously prevented discussion of the vodka trade. In the context of the larger debate, it was inevitable that the role of the Jews should be raised. Publications which were hostile to the Jews, like *Illiustratsiia*, were quick to focus on the wiles and depredations of the Jewish tavern-keeper, "keen, like a hare, sharp, like a cat" (44:6/XI/1858).

Even friends of the Jews, such as *Ekonomicheskii ukazatel*, were hard pressed to defend the Jewish presence in the trade. Describing a countryside in thrall to the Jewish tavern – such as the village of thirty families surrounded by twelve taverns – the author could think of no better defense than to condemn the native Russian publican: "isn't there roguery in Rus as well?"(103:21/XII/1858). *Kievskii telegraf* argued for a new fiscal system which would free the Jews from their obsessive goal of "making money and seeking ways to circumvent the law" (6:20/I/1860).

Discussions of the new excise tax of 1863 focused on the role of the Jews in the system, especially the ban on Jewish trade outside the shtetlakh and towns. *Birzhevye vedomosti*, always keen to decry restraint of trade, published three articles in 1862 which dealt with the consequences of the new law. An article by K. Stankevich anticipated difficulties for the landowners, who were used to leasing out the liquor trade on their estates to Jews; for the exchequer, as the ban forced large numbers of skilled people from the trade; and for the Jews, who suddenly found themselves engaged in illegal activity. Attempts to enforce the restrictions on the Jews would waste the valuable time of excise officials, as well as contradicting the existing policy of extending Jewish civil rights (184:29/VIII/1862). K. Shukin, in a subsequent article, agreed. The law now made illegal many phenomena that had long since become customary and rooted in the normal order of things. The "crimes" of the Jewish tavern-keeper should be laid at the door of the noble landlord who permitted him to reside and trade in the village – indeed, who rented him the tavern in the first place. Now, in the post-emancipation era, the lords were no longer beyond the law. Volost courts, the justices of the peace, the provincial authorities, would all be expected to supervise the welfare of the peasants. Under these safeguards, Jews could safely be permitted into the villages (208:3/X/1862).

A dissenting voice was heard from P. Kulish, a leading Ukrainian intellectual, and author of the Ukrainian protest letter against *Illiustratsiia* in 1858. Kulish emphasized the ruinous effect on the simple Ukrainian peasantry of the Jewish-dominated liquor trade, and applauded measures taken to restrict them. He indicted the Jewish innkeeper for corrupting the young, and making the tavern a center of drunkenness and trade in stolen horses. Kulish's indictment was consistent with his expressed views on the Jewish Question, which emphasized the suffering of the Little Russian people at the hands of the Jews, while also recalling past persecution of the Jews which caused them to hate and exploit Christians. In a note of extenuation, he observed that the Jews engaged in the liquor trade "under burden of need," and left it at the first economic opportunity.[43]

These qualifications did not spare Kulish a bitter denunciation in *Sovremennoe slovo*, the unofficial supplement to the liberal and Judeophile *Russkii invalid*. An unsigned *feuilleton* illustrated again the peculiar antipathy that permeated discussions of the Jewish Question involving a Ukrainian author. The feuilletonist chastised Kulish for "sharing the sickness of Mr. Aksakov." Kulish asked for strict governmental regulations to prevent the Jews from breaking the law. But the real source of blame lay with the native Ukrainian landowners, represented by the educated Kulish, who leased out taverns to the Jews in the first place. "You are now asking the government, through stricter laws, to keep you from breaking the law ... It is not the Jews but you who are to blame for the unhappiness of the people" (140:21/XI/1862).

Once the excise tax began to function, it was an obvious focus for Judeophobe critics intent on a struggle with "Jewish exploitation." In 1865 *Kievlianin* maintained that "the peasants are worse off under a Jewish leaseholder [of a tavern] than they were under the feudal system of field labor (*barshchina*)." The new system, which permitted Jews to lease distilleries, ensured the flowering of an elaborate distribution system, all run by Jews, from the distillery itself to the countless small taverns, which it supplied. Even the supervisory personnel and the officials from the state treasury were Jews, the paper claimed. This new form of "Jewish *barshchina*" was unquestionably harmful for the rural economy of the entire area (23:23/II/1865). By 1868 an editorial entitled "Jews and Vodka," warned of the "Jewishization" (*ob"evreenie*) of the Southwest, and the domination of Jewish exploitation. It was not just the sale of alcohol that harmed the peasantry, but all the attendant activities of the Jewish tavern-keeper. The absence of petty cash in the region permitted the Jewish tavern-keeper to sell on credit, with all the related abuses. (Sale of alcohol on credit was against the law.) Paid in kind, the Jewish tavern keeper also engaged in petty trade and, invariably, in money-lending and usury, again in circumvention of the law. The Jew in the Ukrainian countryside, claimed *Kievlianin*, was nothing less than the local version of the Great Russian kulak (93:6/VIII/1868). Several times in 1867, the Judeophobe *Syn otchestva* called for a complete ban on leasing taverns to Jews, especially because they had proven more than a match for any Christian competitor, and their domination in this field left the peasants at their mercy.[44] *Vest*, the conservative organ of the landowning gentry, defended its own constituency, under the guise of an attack on the Jews in defense of peasant interests. An article in 1868 complained that the Jews were opening taverns in peasant huts, and even building inns and distilleries on peasant land. Since this was illegal, the Jews bribed the *volost* secretary. Contracts had to be ratified by the village assembly, but its meetings were dominated by drunks and troublemakers in the pay of the Jews. Opposition was countered with free drinks and gifts. Contracts concluded under these conditions were entirely in the Jews' favor, and their peasant agents were rewarded by a large percentage of the rental fee that was supposed to go to the community. These agents also prevailed upon the members of the village to patronize "their" local tavern. The Jewish tavern soon became a center for fencing stolen goods and horses. Of equal

Первое знакомство.

— Нѣтъ-ли старыхъ вещей? я все покупаю.
— Какой онъ бѣдный! не сдѣлать-ли его шинкаремъ въ нашемъ селѣ?

21a "First meeting: 'Poor chap! Let's make him the village tavern-keeper'"

consequence, these Jewish taverns easily competed with the "orderly and well-run" taverns set up by landowners on their estates (29:8/III/ 1868).

Amidst this chorus of disapproval, the Russian Jewish press was virtually the only defender of the Jews in the liquor trade. Orshanskii turned to the liquor trade in a discussion of the economic position of Russian Jewry which appeared in *Den*. Belief in the negative role of the Jews was universal, "confirmed by continual newspaper articles which relate how this or that Itsko ruins a peasant community." These exposés helped convince the government to maintain the Pale. Yet it was unrealistic and unfair to blame the Jews for alcohol abuse. The problem lay in the nature of society and the needs of the state.

> As long as the Russian people are doomed to a burdensome and disadvantageous struggle with harsh nature and unfortunate social conditions, and until in their leisure hours they can both find and appreciate more humane recreations [than drinking], and until such time as a third of the state budget does not depend on alcohol, restrictions on trade and tradesmen will not forestall or prevent popular drunkenness, but increase it.

Послѣднее прощаніе (20 лѣтъ спустя).

Ну, все мое, у пана ничего нѣтъ и панъ еще остается мнѣ долженъ, у меня тутъ все записано: сахару взяли въ долгъ 30 фунтовъ за 5 р. и не платили 15 лѣтъ. Теперь посчитаемъ по 10 процентовъ въ мѣсяцъ: процентовъ за первый годъ 6 р., да капитала 5 р., всего 11 р.; за второй годъ процентовъ 13 р., да капитала 11 р., всего 24 р.; за третій годъ потому же счету 53 р.; за 4-й годъ—116 р.; за 5-й годъ—255 р.; за 6-й годъ—560 р.; за 7-я годъ—1230 р.; за 8-й годъ—2710 р.; за 9-й годъ—5970 р.; за 10-й годъ 13135 р.; за 11-й годъ—28835 р.; за 12-й годъ—63,200 р.; за 13-й годъ—132,000 р.; за 14-й годъ—277,000 р.; за 15-й годъ—608,000 р. Ну, а имѣніе пана сколько стоитъ? не больше 100,000 р. Я честный еврей, обижать пана нехочу, нехай лучше мое пропадаетъ; за весь долгъ беру имѣніе, а остальное дарю пану за то, что панъ пожалѣлъ меня, когда я былъ еще бѣднымъ жидочкомъ.

21b "Last goodbye (20 years later)." The former peddler forecloses on his benefactor's homestead

Orshanskii cited figures to show that there was drunkenness where there were few or no Jews, especially in the Russian interior, where drunkenness exceeded that of the southern and western provinces. (This argument became the staple Judeophile defense against claims that the Jews intoxicated the peasantry.) Statistics which showed a larger number of taverns in the Pale should be used cautiously, since the peasant-consumer benefited from competition.

Orshanskii, as was typical of all his economic arguments, argued for the superiority of free trade over restrictions and monopolies. Whenever the government launched a concerted campaign to remove Jews from the liquor trade in the villages, consumption and price both went up. The true beneficiaries of monopolies directed against the Jews were the landowners, who disguised their own selfish interests behind altruistic masks. Landowners already owned most of the distilleries, and they alone profited when restrictions were placed on the

Jews. To be sure, associations of peasants organized to run the liquor trade, as some critics desired, would be beneficial in theory, but in practice were only a dream. A mercantile class was a necessity in the countryside, for alcohol and for anything else, and for the moment, Jews were its sole constituent (21:4/X/1869). *Vestnik russkikh evreev* also saw the drunkenness charge as a major impediment to the abolition of the Pale of Settlement, and addressed the issue in 1871. It repeated Orshanskii's argument that drunkenness was widespread where there were no Jews. Moreover, Jews were superior tavern-keepers because they were sober, unlike their Christian equivalents. It was not strange that the Jews attempted to derive the maximum advantage from the liquor trade. This was the natural goal of any nationality, and it hardly was fair to hold the Jews to a higher moral standard than the rest of mankind (15:21/IV/1871).

It is easy to see why these arguments, even when repeated in the Russian press, failed to convince the Russian authorities.[45] As Orshanskii noted, anecdotal evidence about "this or that Itsko," was virtually universal in the press. A staple of journalistic *belles-lettres* was the tale of a Jew who established himself in a peasant village and brought ruination and corruption in his path. Given the Jews' widespread involvement in the spirit trade, it was cold comfort to learn that they were only following economic laws. Moreover, statistics were a two-edged sword. Dondukov-Korsakov's memorandum of 1872 contradicted Orshanskii's claim that the landowners dominated distilling. Whether in possession or lease, Jews controlled 500 of the 564 distilleries in the governor-generalship of the Southwest, as well as 119 of 148 breweries. Jewish distilleries produced 288,000,000 *gradus*[46] of undiluted spirits, sold through their 19,000 taverns.[47] This represented a veritable flood of Jewish spirits inundating the Ukraine. It is not surprising therefore, that modifications in the excise statute aimed at controlling rather than enlarging Jewish participation. This was certainly the intent of the 1874 decree that Jews could trade in alcohol "only in their own homes."[48] Finally, the landowning nobility was the most successful social pressure group in prerevolutionary Russia, and arguments which pitted the interests of Jews against the gentry were always destined for failure.

When the restrictive regulations of 1874 were introduced, the reaction of *Kievlianin* was unexpectedly muted. The paper was convinced that Jews would ignore the law, an assumption which meshed neatly with *Kievlianin*'s other concern in 1874, Jewish evasion of the new military service act.

We can hardly believe that there won't be numerous attempts to get around the law, since we doubt that the mass of leaseholders [of taverns] will eagerly seek another profession. We can imagine, for example, that they will claim as their "own home" houses held as collateral, or that they will procure inns with the help of Christians, and so on. We can imagine the Jews attempting to buy small houses in the village, but this brings up the problem of the right of Jews to buy land. We can only await reports from our correspondents. (78:2/VII/1874)

Reports were not long in coming, and exposés of Jewish lawlessness in the vodka trade became a staple of *Kievlianin's* subsequent report-age. Already in 1876 the paper characterized the 1874 regulations as a "dead letter, despite the vigorous efforts of the Kiev administration to enforce them" (150:16/XII/1876). An article in 1878 took special alarm at the extent to which individuals – and not just peasants – were aiding the Jews to evade the law, analogous to those who "sold their good name" to enable Jews to lease or purchase privileged land (90:1/VIII/ 1878). By 1880, *Kievlianin* was appealing for the creation of a system of public taverns as a last effort to combat the Jews, who now owned the peasants' land *de facto*, if not *de jure*, thanks to the spirit trade (32:8/II/ 1880).

Kievlianin, given its aptitude and location, was well situated to act as the alarm-bell against Jewish malfeasance, but it was not alone. *Odes-skii vestnik* welcomed the new regulations in 1874. While they would mean little to urban centers like Odessa where the Jews already owned large numbers of houses, they would permit the village dwellers "to breathe more freely." Still, given the practical nature of the Jews, care had to be taken that they did not circumvent the law (151:7/VII/1874). Before the month was out, *Odesskii vestnik* reported from Bessarabia on Jewish preparations to ensure their undisturbed residence in the village (169:31/VII/1874). In the summer of 1875, *Novoe vremia* described the victory of Jews over peasant communities attempting to expel them from the village under the 1874 regulations.[49] In 1879, *Russkii vestnik* carried an article describing the operations of the Jewish inn-keeper in the village of Pitiuki, Vertsalishskii district. In a village of nine households, just to break even, the Jews had to sell 53 rubles' worth of vodka per household. Under such conditions, could emanci-pation really be said to have freed the peasants from Jewish exploita-tion? (142 [VIII 1879], 785–6).

The government could only agree, and concern for peasant sobriety remained firmly linked to the Jewish Question. In 1881, the government called a "convocation of knowledgeable people" to review the vodka trade, and the role of the Jews constituted a significant part of their deliberations. When, in the aftermath of the pogroms of that same year, the government became convinced of an urgent need to restrain "Jewish exploitation," the Jewish spirit trade in the village was again one of the prime targets.

The Jew as kulak

Few examples better illustrate the propensity of both Russian state and society to project onto the Jews the cares of the minute than the evolving equation of Jews with the *kulak*. Because of its subsequent use as a pseudo-scientific category by Russian Marxism, the precise meaning of the word kulak (literally, a fist) has become contentious and unclear. As a socioeconomic category it can be traced at least to the late eighteenth century. The Dictionary of the Russian Academy, compiled between 1806 and 1822, offered such definitions as second-hand dealer and petty trader (*perekupshchik, peretorgovshchik, pereboishchik*). Vladimir Dal's famous dictionary offered additional connotations of miser or skinflint, and these implications of tight-fistedness may well be the popular origin of the term. In Dal there is a popular connection to the Jews: one of the synonyms connoting miserliness given by Dal is "*zhidomor*" or "Jewish mug." *Zhidomor* was also a synonym for usurer (*likhoimets*), a traditional Jewish occupation, and not a term associated at this time with the kulak. Dal's picture of the kulak as a petty trader, scouring the countryside, buying up rags and bones, or a few bushels of grain, suggests some activities normally associated with Jews. Also present are connotations of a transient outsider, not a permanent member of a stable community.

As the meaning of kulak shifted, it was applied more consciously to the Jews. One of the first articles to appear in the reform-era press on the Jews contrasted them with kulaks. The author, defending free settlement of the Jews throughout Russia, predicted their beneficial effect on trade in the Great Russian provinces, where commodity prices at bazaars were set by the agents of two or three wealthy merchants "and kulaks" through price-fixing (*stachko*). While the Jew might be accused of using short weights and measures, the author claimed, his devious skills could not compete with the kulak (*Ekonomicheskii ukazatel'*, 103:21/XII/1858). *Odesskii vestnik*, defending the economic activity of the Jews in 1865, noted that they were feared by every middleman and kulak for their ability to lower prices (61:21/III/1865).

Kievlianin, not surprisingly, was the first periodical actually to equate the two, observing in 1868 that in their conduct of petty trade, "the Jews fully correspond to the Great Russian kulak" (93:6/VIII/1868). A year later, *Den*, *Kievlianin's* great adversary, concurred. At first glance this might appear a fatal admission, but it was entirely in keeping with *Den's* assertion – as usual, through the pen of I. Orshanskii – that the negative features of Jewish life did not derive from specifically Jewish national characteristics, but from general economic forces. *Den* noted that while "Jewish kulaks" might have exploited the pre-emancipation peasantry, they were stymied by new economic forces unleashed by emancipation (48:28/XI/1870). Orshanskii also considered the claim that Jewish kulaks would overwhelm and ruin the peasantry of the Great Russian provinces if the Pale were abolished. Mirroring his arguments on the spirit trade, Orshanskii noted that kulaks were to be found throughout Great Russia, where Jews were largely forbidden to live. They used the ignorance, poverty and helplessness of the peasantry in order to exploit them. He cited no less an authority than Ivan Turgenev's *Hunter's Notes*.[50] Kulakism could be stopped, not through repressive legislation, but through the spread of popular education, organization of rural credit and easing peasant taxes and obligations (23:18/X/1869). Liberal organs like *Kievskii telegraf* fully accepted Orshanskii's arguments (98:29/VIII/1873). Official circles were much less impressed. V. V. Grigoriev, writing a special memorandum on Jewish residence rights for the KUBE, took exception to efforts to equate both Jews and kulaks as products of impersonal economic forces.[51]

The changes unleashed in the countryside had numerous unanticipated consequences, including the economic differentiation of the peasantry, and strains on the traditional peasant community, the *mir*. In particular, Populist commentators chronicled the rise of the *miroed* ("*mir*-eater"), a peasant who exploited the rest of the village and parasitically destroyed the old community. The *miroed* was also branded a kulak, although he was far from being the old petty trades-man. The Populists, with their exaggerated respect for the community as the basis for a future revolutionary social order, held a special antipathy for the *miroed*-kulak, whose features they gradually discerned and defined. The first great endeavor of this kind was V. V. Bervi (Flerovskii's) magisterial *The Situation of the Working Class in Russia*, first published in 1869. This was a celebrated and influential

Гоните муху въ дверь, она влетитъ въ окно.

Избави насъ, Боже, отъ глада, мора, воды, огня и иноплеменнаго нашествія.

Дозволено Цензурою. Кіевъ. 29 Марта 1884 г.

Иванъ: Бѣда съ этими жидами! Не успѣлъ достроить хаты, обнести заборъ, развесити садъ, огородъ, глядишь, а жидовъ, kakъ kлоповъ, набралось полныя щели, таkъ что ни самому, ни дѣтямъ повернуться негдѣ. Просто, хоть убирайся съ хаты!..
Гершко сзади: Здраствуйте, Иване, якъ се маетесь?
Иванъ: А ты чего здѣсь! Убирайся вонъ! У меня работы и безъ васъ много.
Гершко: Когда намъ таkъ хорошо у Васъ; мы вамъ не мѣшаемъ работать, мы только разставимъ свои лавочки, заведемъ шиночки, будемъ деньги одолжать, вы сами зайдете—выпьете водочки, рабочему человѣку нужно подкрѣпиться; у насъ можно и безъ денегъ.... принесите мѣрку овса. или четвертъ жита, мы все принимаемъ

22 "Chase the fly out the door, it comes in the window"

portrait of the Russian working class crushed by economic forces and governmental policies.[52] The *miroed* was a principal beneficiary of this process. Bervi-Florovskii described a number of features of the *miroed*. First, and most importantly, he was a peasant himself, a member of the commune, who was visibly evolving into a sort of peasant aristocracy.[53] Bervi-Flerovskii treated the kulak as a sub-form of *miroed*. The "snooping kulak" (*shniriaiushchii kulak*) shared some of the main features of the *miroed*, such as the purchase of land. But he was often a grain speculator and buyer as well, so omnipresent and dominant in the marketplace that the peasant was forced to travel 100 versts to find a truly free market.[54] Manipulation of the grain trade was a sin traditionally laid at the door of the Jews, but Bervi-Flerovskii did not make this connection, perhaps because the travels which produced the research for his book did not penetrate the Pale of Settlement.

The evolving role of the new-style kulak can also be discerned in the work of the Populist writer, A. N. Engelgardt, who resided on a rural estate in Smolensk province (outside but adjoining the Pale) from 1871 to 1893. His observations on the changes occurring in the countryside were published in his annual "Letters from the Countryside," which appeared in *Otechestvennye zapiski* from 1872 to 1882. In his second letter, published in 1872, he described the local petty trader-kulak, Matov, "who sells and buys everything." The portrait was not really a negative one, as it recounted how Matov brought the local drunk and thief Kostik to justice without intervention of the new-fangled judicial structures so incompatible with peasant ideas of justice. Matov was described as owner of a farmstead, as well as a small tavern. Engelgardt's petty tradesman-kulak was not a Jew, although he conformed to several popular Jewish stereotypes: his relentless pursuit of all knowledge about the local economy and the actors in it, and his sale of spirits. In short, the kulak was a natural, and not particularly harmful, part of the rural order.[55]

By his tenth letter, published in 1881, after a decade in which Engelgardt had chronicled the decay of his beloved peasant commune, he was overtly hostile to the kulak.

> Every *muzhik* is to a certain degree a kulak, a pike which is in the sea so that the carp don't slumber ... More than once I have indicated the peasant's extreme development of individualism, egoism, a striving for exploitation. Envy, lack of trust in one another, undermining of one by another, abasement of the weak before the strong, hypocrisy of the powerful, deference to wealth – all this is strongly developed in the peasant milieu. The kulak ideal reigns in it, each aspires to be the pike and to devour the carp.[56]

The petty tradesman-kulak, Matov, had given way to the "real kulak," a much more sinister force. He owned land, and was part of the village commune, but did not farm himself since his attitude was that "work loves fools." He used the land as a base from which to deploy his capital to entrap the peasants in debt. He was a true mir-eater. Wishing the villagers to cut their ties to the land, fall into debt and yet have ready money, he praised the charms of the city to the peasants, and encouraged them to seek work there. This "real kulak" had lost those traits of Matov, petty trade and inn-keeping, that carried a Jewish flavor, but replaced them with others, such as usury, and exploitation of peasant labor, which the Judeophobe press was increasingly identifying with Jews. Yet, for Engelgardt, the "real kulak" was not a Jew, but a peasant.[57]

The definitive portrait of the kulak was sketched, not by the Russian political economists, but by the great satirist, M. E. Saltykov-Shchedrin. The main object of his attention was the degeneration and decline of the petty and middling gentry in the period after the emancipation, as they proved incapable of dealing with new economic and social forces. But the agency of their downfall, as often as not, was the kulak, who appeared frequently in Saltykov-Shchedrin's tales. Indeed, two such kulaks, Razuvaev ("strips your boots off") and Kolupaev ("plucker") served as personifications of the kulak. It was sufficient for any author to refer, in passing, to "the Razuvaevs and Kolupaevs" to invoke the image of the kulak.[58]

Razuvaev rented forest land, and shipped timber to the city. He also pursued other operations which usually involved the peasantry. Razuvaev and Kolupaev had an additional source of income: taverns. As prosperous owners (*kabatchiki*) they represented the new pillars of the community, as the local priest confided to the ruined gentryman in "The Retreat of Mon Repos."[59] The origins of these kulaks is less clear. Saltykov-Shchedrin frequently called them "merchants," suggesting urban roots. Generically, Saltykov-Shchedrin classed them as "the scum" (*chumazyi*), the residue of the newly forming Russian bourgeoisie, whose development ran from the primeval *gorlpany* who dominated the village assembly through their arrogance; to kulaks in the guise of petty tradesmen and cattle dealers; and finally to the *miroed*. A product of the village, the *miroed* exploited it through his tavern, which he used to place the peasants in cabal.[60] Taken together, "the scum" is "something in the manner of a bourgeoisie, that is, a new cultural stratum, consisting of the liquor patent holders, usurers, railroad people, bankers and other embezzlers and mir-eaters. In a short space of time this idle louse (*prazdnoshataiushchaiasia tlia*) succeeded in tying up all our Palestines; in every corner it sucks, gnaws, destroys and in addition is impudent."[61]

Saltykov-Shchedrin's contribution, then, was to enlarge the category of kulaks, subsuming all the previous definitions. A Populist writer R. Grozdev elaborated on this theme a decade later:

> Like a chameleon the kulak changes his shape, or even his economic activities, depending on the economic atmosphere in which he lives and acts. He appears as the leaser of private land, sub-leasing it in plots to the peasantry; at the head of production artels in southern Russia, the Volga or in the God-forsaken North; and he figures as the middle man of *kustar* [peasant craft] wares, of grain, cattle, peasant livestock, not even squeamish about trading in the tickets of wards of the Foundling Home, we see him as village usurer, directing the activities of credit associations, a shop-keeper, a seller on credit, etc.... In a word, the kulak-usurer is something collective, composed of all those exploiters who are scattered all over the face of the Russian land, and who go under the diverse names of kulaks, mir-

eaters, *kashtani*, village usurers, and so on, the names of which only God knows.[62]

Since the term kulak became a synonym for all exploiters, a Jewish connection takes on an added significance. Saltykov-Shchedrin pointed the direction in this regard. While no overt connection was made – indeed, Razumaev and Kolupaev were definitely *not* Jews – his scorn for the *kabatchiki*, a profession closely associated with the Jews, was manifest throughout. The curious turn of phrase "succeeding in tying up all our Palestines," recalled the recurrent Judeophobe charge that the Jews found a "promised land" in the Pale. The "distancing" of the story from the Jewish milieu by placing "Mon Repos" in the environs of St. Petersburg is negated somewhat by the information imparted by the narrator that the nearby former princely seat had gone through two owners in two years – one of whom was a Jew. This revelation immediately preceded a list of "alien people" (*prishlye liudi*) who were buying nearby properties.[63]

Some authors, even when writing critically of the Jews, made an effort to differentiate between Jews and kulaks. Thus, V. Varzer, in his condemnation of Jewish leaseholding mentioned above, recommended extending credit to the peasant population. He emphasized that loans were not to go to the kulaks who would use them to gain a foothold in the village where, "though baptized, they are worse than the Yid."[64] *Novorossiiskii telegraf*, on the other hand, published an article in 1880 on the grain trade in New Russia which treated the terms "Jew" and "kulak" virtually as synonyms (1614:5/VII/1880). In that same year an editorial in *Smolenskii vestnik* compared kulaks and Jews to demonstrate that the latter were worse. The writer took alarm at a recent influx of Jews, in the guise of artisans, into Smolensk province, which was outside the Pale. Once they appeared, Jewish craftsmen abandoned crafts to take up money-lending, petty trade, tavern-keeping, and dealing in stolen goods. The paper noted how Jewish intellectuals admitted the existence of kulak-exploiters, only to claim that kulakism, rather than the Jewish kulak, should be the target of action. The author disagreed. Kulaks of all nationalities were harmful, but because of the kahal structure, which gave the Jews internal unity and mutual support, the Jewish was more harmful. The kulaks at least were Russians, while Jewish exploiters were not bound to the native Russian soil by language, religious belief, or customs. They were transients in Smolensk province as they were in Russia as a whole: if the Jews' capital and commercial inventiveness offered them more scope in Italy tomorrow, they would be gone without a thought of Russia (69:20/VI/1880).

The technique of contrasting Jews and kulaks was employed by B. Lenskii in a much discussed article in the September 1881 number of the influential Populist thick journal *Delo*. Lenskii wrote against the backdrop of the anti-Jewish pogroms, which were being widely blamed in the Russian press on Jewish exploitation. If this were so, he queried, why had there not been a similar outbreak against Russian kulakism, "more severe and more dangerous." Lenskii's article was a defense of the Jews disguised as an attack on their "exploitation." While he accepted the reality of charges against the Jews, he neutralized them by a comparison with the activities of the Great Russian kulak. Jewish exploitation was actually less harmful that that of the kulaks because the Jews were more numerous, concentrated, and in competition with one another. Instead of the kulaks' huge pump, the Jews used tiny stingers. They resembled summer midges which got in one's throat, eyes and ears, rather than the poisonous fly (the kulak). Lenskii also cited the chameleon aspect of kulakism which Grozdev emphasized at the end of the decade: while the Jewish exploiter in the village was easily identified, there were countless invisible kulaks in villages and towns. The kulak money-lender controlled the village through usurous rates no better than the "Jewish percent." Unlike the Jewish exploiter, who actually labored with remarkable industry and fervor and promoted lower prices, the kulak worked through the hired labor of others. This was the essential contrast: the kulaks were prosperous and well-to-do, while the Jews were as poor as the peasants they exploited. This helped to explain and justify Jewish exploitation, although Lenskii denied that this was his intention.

The Jews were driven to exploit by economic necessity, the effects of the Pale, a "kind of administrative exile for Jews." The Jews did not act maliciously but only participated in this facet of the economic system through force of circumstances. Statistics refuted the claim that the Jews controlled vast wealth. Restricted by law, burdened with taxes and the illegal exactions of local officials, the Jews were forced into exploitation and deterred from honest labor. "Work alone is inadequate, and for this reason they must turn to dishonesty and exploitation" (41).

The well-off kulak had no such excuse, and this explained why they had a negative moral influence on the village. The Jew was openly motivated by commercial considerations. The Russian kulak, however, claimed moral capital from those he exploited by pretending to be honest. The Jews pursued prosperity through fervid and uninterrupted commercial transactions, even if the net result was to the peasants' advantage. The kulak engaged in cold, calculated and deliberate transactions. "He bites into profit like a bulldog into a piece of meat, and you can never take it away from him." There was always something left in a field harvested by a Jew, but the kulak blighted it to the roots (50).

Two could play at the game of contrasts, as A. I. Umissa revealed in an article written for the short-lived Odessa thick journal *Iug* in 1882. Umissa asked a question identical to Lenskii's: if both kulaks and Jews exploited the peasants, why was popular violence directed only at the latter? While Lenskii's answer was conditioned by a radical Populism, Umissa was a devotee of conservative "native soilism" (*pochuchestva*). Umissa characterized both the kulak and *miroed* as products of the peasant milieu, brought up in the same life, customs and morals. Like the common people the kulak was illiterate, feared judicial proceedings and, like any good peasant, was willing to get drunk. Most of all, the kulak acted alone. He remained a member of the community, except that he was the brightest and most stable, most likely to take advantage of the needs and weaknesses of his fellow peasants. "The Russian soil" – which for Umissa comprised the Orthodox religion, peasant daily life, customs and morals – kept the kulak within bounds, limited the full extent of predatory activity and indeed frequently drew him away from kulakism altogether (2: February 1882, 14–15).

The Jews, on the other hand, were a product of alien surroundings, brought up with different customs, morals, daily life and religion. The Jew was literate and welcomed judicial proceedings. He never celebrated with the peasants, never even ate or drank with them. The Jewish kulak did not act alone, but through an unbroken network of ties with other Jews. Cleverer, more literate and more intellectual than the kulaks or anyone else in the community, the Jew was at the same time completely alien to the village. With no ties to the peasant world, and thus no fear of sundering them or of village opinion, the Jew was devoid of any restraint upon his predatory instincts. That the Jew was an alien exploiter in the peasant midst explained the assaults of the population against the Jews, rather than against the kulak.

Umissa described only vaguely the activities of kulaks, specifying trade, leasing and sub-leasing of agricultural land to peasants and at one point even conceded that the activities of the kulak were at times felt more keenly than those of the Jews. The decisive consideration, however, was Jewish solidarity. This was an old theme, to be sure. As early as 1871, in a discussion of the Odessa pogrom of that year,

Sanktpeterburgskie vedomosti condemned the Jews as "an *artel* [workers' collective] of kulaks" (128:11/V/1871). The point is that, even when native Russian elements were viewed individually as more harmful to the economy of the nation, they could still be used as a comparison to place the alien Jews in a worse light. Simultaneously, "Razumaev" and "Kolupaev" became easily recognizable synonyms for "Jews" as well as for "kulaks."

It would be a thankless and probably impossible task to enumerate all the fields of economic endeavor where "Jewish exploitation" was thought to exercise an invidious influence. Suffice it to say that the Jewish angle could be found where the concern was for abuses in recruitment, treatment and payment of contract labor,[65] mismanagement of forests,[66] or mistreatment of workers in agriculture-related industrial enterprises,[67] as well as prostitution.[68] Each of these concerns was linked to the Jews at one time or another by Russian publicists no matter how tenuous the connection, and each was quickly designated a special area of Jewish exploitation.

Some accusations had not yet developed to full flavor, or existed only in embryo. Thus, concern for Jewish involvement in the purchase and lease of land, coupled with alarm at alleged Jewish control and manipulation of rural credit and constraint of trade in market commodities were joined to the charge of Jewish control of high finance, especially banking. This led to Jews being made a principal culprit in the alleged "decline of the nobility." The Palen Commission ordered a survey of all Jewish landholding in the western provinces. The Commission's alarm was out of all proportion to the actual evidence on the printed page.[69] This inagurated a fashion of blaming the problems of noble landowners on "Yid banks," and the nature of the accusations grew ever more verdant in the decade before the Revolution of 1905.[70]

Productive work

The only factor to cast doubt on the picture of the Jews as merciless exploiters was the observable poverty of the Jewish masses. If the Jews were exploiters, they were hard pressed to make a living at it. The basic Judeophile interpretation of this phenomenon was that the Jews were restricted by the Pale of Settlement, which created abnormal conditions of competition. In the struggle for survival, desperate Jews were forced to resort to anything to survive. Judeophobes, on the other hand, argued that Jews simply avoided productive work, especially agriculture. Under the conditions of the Pale, an overreliance upon trade and middle-man activity invariably produced poverty. But the problem lay, not so much in the Pale, but with Jewish occupations within the Pale. Some pessimists went further still, and denied that the Jews were capable of any productive work. An innate laziness, buttressed by religious prejudice against physical labor, ensured that Jews, however many, would always be poor, even as they ruined their Christian neighbors with their depredations.

Reflecting the mild Judeophilia of the early reform era, V. I. Veselovskii in *Vilenskii vestnik* attributed Jewish pauperism to the Pale and promised benefits to the economy if it were abolished (14/II; 24/II; 27/II; 18/III:1859). An immediate rebuttal came from A. Korev, a participant in the survey of the provinces conducted by the Russian General Staff. The crux of the Jewish Question, Korev argued, was that four-fifths of the Jewish population desired to live at the expense of the rest of the citizenry. There was no excuse for idleness in a region that had a chronic need for agricultural laborers. Young Jews had an aristocratic disdain for common labor. They stood in the market-place raising healthy hands to beg, but refused to touch the plow. Their only dream was to become "pseudo-merchants" (*Vilenskii vestnik* 20:8/III/1860). He repeated this claim in his survey of Vilna province, condemning one-twelfth of the population (the Jews) for attempting to live at the expense of others, a luxury that a poor province could not afford.[71]

The new Russian–Jewish press initially appeared to accept, at least partially, these charges. The notorious letter of Lev Levanda from Minsk province in the first issue of *Rassvet* painted a grim picture of Jewish destitution and poverty, which led to parasitism, cheating and crime. Private charity among Jews merely encouraged further sponging. Levanda implied that an overemphasis on Talmud study was partly to blame. The outcry this letter provoked in the Jewish world, and the eagerness of Russian publicists to misinterpret it as an admission of guilt, forced a restatement in a subsequent editorial. It could hardly be claimed that all the Jews of the western region were lazy and shiftless, asserted Rabinovich. Modern science, moreover, had shown that there were other ways to work productively besides following a plow. The source of Jewish idleness, simply put, was the Pale of Settlement, augmented by the tax and passport system (14:26/VIII/1869).

Vilenskii vestnik re-entered the fray, lamenting Rabinovich's editorial as a retreat from a good beginning. Residence restrictions did hamper the Jews, the paper admitted, but could not be blamed for the refusal of Jews within the Pale to work, if only to clean the filth which filled their neighborhoods. The editorial offered figures to support its case. It set the Jewish population of Vilna at 32,941 persons and assumed that 1,038 were merchants and their servants, 1,755 were stall-holders and their families, 2,125 guild members and their assistants with 3,324 family members. Rounding this figure off to 15,761 and adding 2,000 paupers produced exactly half the Jewish population. How were the other 17,180 employed? The answer could be found in the large number of Jewish contrabandists and criminals or wastrels (83:21/X/ 1860).

Such provocative assertions did not pass unchallenged by the embryonic Jewish press in Vilna, the Russian language supplement to I. Finn's Hebrew newspaper, *Ha-Karmel*. G. Verblovskii responded by offering his own impressionistic categorization of Vilna Jewry. The number of people supported by merchants, as set by *Vilenskii vestnik*, was too low since it failed to include stall-holder Jews in the market-place, as well as "inn-keepers, tavern-keepers, purveyors of candles and yeast, milk, tradesmen in grain, cattle, fish, brickmakers, foresters etc." Neither servants nor the Jewesses of Rudniskaia Street, who engaged in sewing, making flowers and women's sundries, deserved to be omitted from the tally. If they were included, they exceeded the *Vilenskii vestnik* total of idlers by 134 persons (21:18/XI/1860).

As can be seen, this debate, which involved walking down the street and guessing the total number of Jewish shops, was not particularly sophisticated, nor did it attract any attention beyond Vilna and the New Russian provinces. As the first such public debate, it may none-theless stand as a paradigm for many others yet to come. One of the principal objectives of Orshanskii's various articles in *Den*, for example, was to dispute the claim that the Jews were unproductive and their activities exploitative and harmful. He frequently attacked Judeophobes as economic illiterates unable to understand that the national wealth was augmented by non-agricultural activity.

A response of this kind was necessitated by the failure of the numerous colonization projects for Jews which had been sponsored by the Russian state – although paid for by Jewish communal taxes – since 1804. The failure of colonization was a telling argument to be thrown into the teeth of Judeophile publicists at every opportunity. In the absence of any agricultural success stories, Judeophiles adopted a defensive tone and explained in fulsome detail the numerous factors which discouraged Jewish agriculture. Clearly, though, it was a topic best ignored, if that were possible.

The task of categorizing Jews as productive or unproductive according to the writer's own prejudices, remained ever popular. Thus, Dragomanov's article on the Jews in *Vestnik Evropy*, and his subsequent underground publications, took the raw data of Chubinskii's statistics on the Ukraine, and interpreted them to stress Jewish unproductivity.[72] One of the special passions of *Kievlianin* was to attribute the poverty of Ukrainian Jewry to their unwillingness to engage in productive labor, thus denying that Pale restrictions were to blame. *Kievlianin* pioneered the technique of calculating "Jews per square hectare" ratios for the provinces of the Pale, and proving, for example, that Russian Jews were more dispersed geographically in the Pale than were the Jews of England or France. This relentless chorus of criticism, which was not entirely devoid of substance, for the Pale clearly could not provide a decent living for an oversupply of petty Jewish tradesmen picking over the remains of a decrepit feudal economy, had some interesting effects. Whatever they might argue publicly, the Jewish leadership accepted the validity of their critics' claims. They responded by founding trade schools, like "Trud" (Work) in Odessa, and sponsoring entities like the Society for the Spread of Productive Work among the Jews (ORT). Jewish reformers and sectarians included in their "professions of faith," a rejection of tavern-keeping and usury and pledged their members to earn an "honest living from the soil."

Thus, on the eve of the pogroms of 1881, Russian public opinion was willing to concede Jewish poverty, while attributing it to the character flaws of the Jews themselves, rather than external forces. As usual, the Judeophobes manning *Kievlianin* had it both ways, blaming Jews for their own poverty, while claiming that much of the wealth of the southwest lay in Jewish hands.

14 Dead souls: Jews and the military reform of 1874

In 1862, the Russian War Ministry drew up plans for the first military recruitment since the close of the Crimean War. Serious discussion was directed to the possibility of exempting Jews from military service. A strong and ultimately successful intervention in favor of Jewish service was launched by Baron Gintsburg.[1] At first glance this plea for the drafting of Jews might appear paradoxical, coming from their foremost defender in the capital. The single greatest burden borne by Jews in the reign of Nicholas I had been the imposition of military service in 1827. Its enforcement had hastened the disintegration of the moral authority and legendary solidarity of the traditional Jewish community. The harshness and length of the twenty-five year term of service was compounded for Jews by the drafting of underage recruits (the cantonists) and widespread efforts at forced conversion. The signal for Russian Jewry that better times lay ahead had been the abolition of the cantonist system by Alexander II in his coronation decree of 26 August 1856. While there was a chance to avoid it, why should Jews accept the return of military service?

The Gintsberg Circle correctly understood that a willingness of the Jews to bear all civil obligations would place great moral weight behind their claim to a greater measure of civil rights. Jewish participation in the Crimean War was already seen in this light, and great care was taken to emphasize it. The Jewish leadership spent an inordinate amount of time and effort to secure construction of a war memorial to the Jewish troops who had fallen in the battle for Sevastopol. A woodcut of the new memorial graced the first publication of the OPE.[2] The poignancy of O. A. Rabinovich's stories "The Penalty Recruit" and "The Inherited Candlestick" flowed from the contrast between the service of Jews in the Russian military and their denial of the most elemental human rights. Moreover, the connection was confirmed when the government began to extend the right of residence outside

23 Memorial to Jewish soldiers killed in the Crimean War

the Pale to categories of Jewish veterans. In welcoming the new mood of toleration toward the Jews in 1858, *Russkii invalid* declared in a *feuilleton*: "Can the military forget the Jews or say an insulting word about them when there are thousands of Jews in the ranks of the Russian army, honorably and truly fulfilling their debt to Ruler and Fatherland, and when Jewish blood mingles with Russian at Sevastopol, where they even die fighting their coreligionists" (39:19/II/1858).

Nor were the instincts of the leadership mistaken in this regard. The numerous discussions of Jewish military service among Russian officials inevitably considered it in the context of the straitened civil position of the Jewish community. Ultimately, the commitment of the framers of a new military statute to equality and justice ensured that the Jews would receive equal treatment in virtually all of its provisions. The willingness of the Jews to serve in the reformed army was considered the first great test of Jewish patriotism and good citizenship. It was to provide tangible evidence of the desire for merger continually voiced by Jewish publicists. The widespread perception that the Jews had ignominiously failed this great test played a significant role in making Russian Judeophobia respectable.

The introduction of universal military service, and the creation of a modern army based upon a reserve system, was the last of the great reforms. It was certainly among the most important, for upon its success rested the fate of Russia as a great power. The old army of Nicholas I had been discredited, not just by its brutality and harshness, but by its failure on the battlefields of the Crimean War. Fortunately, the War Ministry under the reformer D. A. Miliutin had time to reflect and plan before Russian troops were again required on a foreign battlefield. The call-up of 1863, in response to the Polish disorders, re-emphasized the unpopularity of military service, the government conceding that "the barbaric features of the old style military recruitment aggravates the burden of recruitment and degrades the very name of soldier."[3]

Throughout the 1860s, palliative measures were introduced to blunt the "barbarism" of recruitment. One such negative feature was the right of those liable for service to hire a replacement, for which they received a substitution ticket or *kvitantsiia*. This system generated a brisk trade in *kvitantsii* – still to be found advertised in classified newspaper advertisements in the 1890s – and created a breed of speculators called "hunters" (*okhotniki*) who specialized in finding people willing to sell themselves into the army. In 1868 new regulations attempted to eliminate the "hunters" by conducting the sale of *kvitantsii* through a special fund. More substantial measures were of course required, and in August of 1870 the War Ministry created a special drafting commission to develop a plan for new conditions of military service and recruitment. Special sub-committees were created for these two areas of concern, and the chairmen cast their net widely for information and expertise. Consultations were conducted with representatives of government departments, from the social classes, and from various groups within the population, including the Jews. Zaionchkovskii's definitive study lists as Jewish consultants only Iosif Zeiberling, Daniel Khvolson and Baron Gintsburg, but it is known that Iakov Brafman was also consulted, although he had little effect on the subsequent statute.[4]

The drafting commission required two years of painstaking discussion – which spilled over into the periodical press – before it finally produced a draft statute to submit to the State Council. The completed draft envisioned a system of universal military service for all social estates, a term of active duty followed by service in the reserves, and a three-tiered system of exemptions for family reasons as well as generous reductions in length of service for *any* level of education. The situation of the Jews, and to a lesser extent, of Moslems, proved a special problem. Lengthy debates considered whether Jews should be drafted at all, or allowed to serve as volunteers (which reduced the term of service) and officers. These debates are most revealing for their insight into official attitudes toward the Jews at the start of the 1870s.

Assuming that the Jews were to serve, how should they be recruited? In the past, the Jewish community had simply handed over the requisite number of recruits, only theoretically following official guidelines. The new army, it was argued, required a uniform system for Jews as well as Christians. However, the recruitment sub-committee argued that, given the Jews' propensity to evade service, a common pool of recruits would result in a disproportionate number of Christians serving in place of Jews. It was well known, the sub-committee declared, that

> given the ties which exist amidst the Jewish population, they represent a group alien to us, one which lives its own life. The separation of the Jews from the Christian population leads us [to the assumption] that the Jews do not consider themselves citizens of our state; consequently, they display the greatest zeal to escape common state obligations and taxes, military service most of all.[5]

When the full commission debated the findings of the sub-committee, it was decided unanimously that the Jews should be responsible for service, and that they should be recruited in ways identical to the Christian population. This did not mean a common pool of recruits, however, blind to religion. Despite the view of the minority (constituting one-third of the membership) that equal forms of recruitment would reduce Jewish draft dodging to the same level as that of Christians, special precautions were written in to discourage evasion. For the first five recruitments under the new law, local recruiting

24 Count D. A. Miliutin

offices were empowered to draft Jews up to the age of thirty (the usual cut-off being twenty-one), if there were insufficient Jews of draft age. Christians and Jews were to form a common pool for the assignment of numbers in the draft, and were to be listed according to the number they had drawn. However, a Jew who was exempted from the draft for family reasons was to be replaced by the next Jew on the list, not the next person. This would ensure that Jews would not benefit from a disproportionate number of exemptions.[6]

The sub-committee on conditions of service debated accepting Jews as volunteers and as officers. After some discussion, it was agreed that Jews could volunteer. There was more controversy over officer status, a question which had been examined earlier in the reform era. Although a quintessential liberal, War Minister Dmitrii Miliutin opposed, as in the past, Jewish officers. His reasoning is illustrative: in the 1860s he rejected such a proposal "for even if it is apparently possible to let them enter any civil service post without exception, a Christian soldier will regard a Jewish officer with scorn, and the strongest discipline will be powerless in a struggle with religious feelings and convictions."[7] In other words, the motive for exclusion lay not with the Jews themselves, but in the religious prejudices of the general population. The chairman of the drafting commission, and exactly half of its membership, saw another reason for preventing officer status, one directly tied to the civil rights of the Jews.

> The right to reach officer rank ... should be extended to the Jews no sooner than with their equalization in all other civil rights with the native population of the Empire ... Even while recognizing the utility and necessity of the most rapid merger of the Jew with other inhabitants, we recognize, nonetheless, that at the present time, before the resolution of the general question of the Jews, they cannot be given the right to attain officer status.[8]

The decision was stalemated when the other half voted to allow officer status to Jews who secured a higher education. A few members even wished to include Jews who had received a secondary education. A zemstvo deputy from Bessarabia directly challenged Miliutin's fears: "The Russian people, to their honor, deserve less than any other reproaches for fanaticism and hatred of other nationalities."[9] With a tie vote, the decision of the commission chairman, Chief of the General Staff, Count F. L. Heiden was decisive. He vetoed officer status for Jews. Thus, the completed draft statute contained special precautions for Jewish recruitment, and barred the Jews from officer rank. In this form, it was submitted to the State Council for final revision and approval on 19 January 1873.

The passage of the military service statute through the State Council was difficult, for the State Council served as the theater for a last-ditch attempt by conservatives to cripple or eliminate the extensive privileges offered for any level of education. For almost a year the draft was attacked by Chief of Gendarmes Peter Shuvalov, Minister of Education Dmitrii Tolstoi, and a host of influential generals.[10]

Even after all this, the final draft favored the Jews: it eliminated special regulations for Jewish recruitment and gave Jews the right to serve as officers, although the War Minister was authorized to exempt areas of the army where he thought that this might prove harmful.[11] The representatives of the Jewish community could only rejoice at this unexpectedly fortuitous outcome. At the same time, they were aware that the equality and uniformity of the new military recruitment system disguised a strong current of distrust in the War Ministry toward the civic reliability of Russian Jewry. On this occasion, optimism and good intentions had won a narrow victory. The triumph could be sustained only if the Jewish community now vindicated the trust placed in it.

There was no shortage of monitors to oversee the behavior of the Jews as well as the functioning of the statute itself. Military critics made extensive use of the press, led by *Moskovskie vedomosti*, *Vest* and *Russkii mir*, to publicly criticize many of Miliutin's proposals. The reformers relied upon friendly organs like *Golos* to reply. Leak and counter-leak ensured that all aspects of the reform were publicly debated.[12]

Concern with the Jews and military service in the press preceded the establishment of the drafting commission. *Kievlianin* had long shared the War Ministry's concern over abuses in the activities of the "hunters," and marshalled its fears into its growing attack on "Jewish exploitation," a transformation typical of Shulgin's ability to give a local slant to items of national interest. Early in 1867, *Kievlianin* voiced its concern that the trade in recruits mirrored the slave trade, with Christian peasants in the guise of Negroes, and Jews in the role of slave-traders (13:28/II/1867). The paper began to chronicle Jewish abuse of the "hunters," and loudly applauded the reform of the procedure in 1868 (44:11/IV/1867; 39:3/IV/1869). The paper also noted sardonically that if the Jews were so interested in merger with the rest of the population, they could begin by serving in the army, instead of mobilizing all their energies to escape it (13:28/II/1867).

Kievlianin's continuing interest in the twin problems of the Jews and of military recruitment guaranteed that it was one of the first to raise the issue of potential Jewish draft evasion. Ultimately this concern led *Kievlianin* to resurrect Brafman's plan – recently rejected by the Vilna Commission – to subordinate the Jews to the peasant *volost*, where they could be more easily supervised (141:27/XI/1873). At the very least, a new census should be conducted in an attempt to get closer to the true number of Jews in the Empire. Of the rest of the conservative press, only *Russkii mir*, the organ of the military conservatives intimately involved in opposing the Miliutin reforms, offered a few vague recommendations regarding the best way to organize the call-up of Jews.[13]

The liberal press, joined by the young Russian–Jewish press, saw the full implications of the reform, and supervised the treatment of the Jews at every stage. Liberal organs such as *Deiatelnost* (12:16/I/1872) and *Kievskii telegraf* (148:22/XII/1871) confidently predicted that equality of obligations could and should give rise to equality of rights. This being the case, both papers explicitly rejected proposals leaking from the commission sub-committees to ban Jewish officers or to create special safeguards to inhibit Jewish draft evasion. *Deiatelnost* pointedly observed that the proposal to draft Jews up to the age of thirty for the first five recruitments violated the principles of uniformity of obligation according to age and class which had been invoked by the tsar in establishing the reform commission (56:11/XII/1871). The paper also queried restrictions on officer status, invoking the example of the Jews in the Crimean War and in foreign armies. Moreover, the equal treatment of the Jews in this regard would be a valuable instrument for merger (59:15/XII/1871). *Kievskii telegraf* attempted to place past Jewish draft dodging in historical perspective, and to disprove the more extreme claims about the organized efforts of the entire community to assist evasion (131:14/XI/1873; 148:24/XII/1873).

The Russian–Jewish press took a more activist approach to the new decree, anticipating new phenomena which the Jewish community must be ready to exploit. Thus, *Den* predicted that the generous exemptions in service given for education were sure to trigger a vogue for learning among young Jews. Unfortunately, the writer observed, there did not as yet exist sufficient institutions to satisfy this demand. The paper also argued for a more satisfactory census of the Jewish population in order to expedite a proper recruitment (3:15/I/1871). Especially given its support of "natural assimilation," it is surprising that *Den* writers, and especially Orshanskii, made no effort to apply the rubric to military service. The guarded response of the paper to the new system reflected concern that it would not serve the best interests of the Jews. This, indeed, may have prompted Orshanskii's efforts to show that Jews in the past had provided more than their fair share of recruitment as a way of preempting charges of evasion (1:3/I/1871). *Vestnik russkikh evreev* demonstrated a more sanguine attitude, predicting that the new law, if it treated the Jews equally, would improve social relations between Jews and gentiles, as well as raise the moral level of the Jews by promoting education (8:21/II/1871; 18:2/V/1871; 22/II/1873).

When the new military statute was finally promulgated in 1874, the Russian–Jewish press had departed the field, and it was left to Russian periodicals to pass judgment on the significance of universal service for the Jews. In general, with the exception of *Golos*, the liberal press predicted good things for the Jews from military service. Liberals demonstrated that the Jews were welcoming recruitment by reprinting a letter from Baron Gintsburg which appeared in the Hebrew press calling on all Jews to do their duty. They also gave prominence to the speeches of local rabbis at the first induction of Jewish troops.[14] *Kievskii telegraf* editorialized that "we know that the Jews, especially educated Jews, await the military reform with impatience – they see it as the truest and most decisive step toward their merger with the ruling nationality" (18:13/II/1874). *Sanktpeterburgskie vedomosti* predicted that the new law would give a powerful boost to the activities of the OPE (209:1/VIII/1874). *Novoe vremia* predicted that, "given the humane objectives of the law," it would soon bring the rights of Jews into equilibrium with those of all other non-Christian groups in the Russian Empire (52:24/II/1874).

The rest of the Russian press took a more pessimistic view. A typical response was to chronicle the means by which Jews attempted to evade service. *Moskovskie vedomosti* detected a wholesale flight of eligible young Jews abroad to America. The only compensation was that, since so many of these refugees made a living from smuggling, tavernkeeping and perjuring themselves in court cases, their departure threatened no loss for the state (264:22/X/1874). *Nedelia* reported from Mozyr how Jews fled from recruitment like the plague, and went to amazing lengths to avoid inclusion in the latest census upon which the recruitment lists were based (51:22/XII/1874).

A number of leading papers, especially *Kievlianin* and *Golos*, were not content to merely detail Jewish evasion, but placed it in a wider ideological context. Iakov Brafman was probably the author of a *Golos* editorial, "The Jews and Military Service," which appeared in 279 (9/X/1874). The editorial followed closely the themes of *The Book of the Kahal*. The kahal elite had always escaped service, the editorial explained, because those who studied the Talmud were free from any civil obligations, and the Jewish commoners were surrendered up in their place. The new law threatened this arrangement and so the leadership sought escape by gaining oversight from the state over communal vital statistics, which they manipulated to their advantage. This explained why educated Jews on the drafting commission proposed that existing communal officials, the tax collectors, take on these functions. Organized evasion was also expedited by international Jewish bodies, such as the Alliance Universelle and the London Board of Deputies. To remedy these problems, the writer recommended that existing civil rights – the right to pursue education, own real estate, enter a merchant guild, conclude contracts or receive legacies – should be made contingent on proper registration for the draft, to be confirmed by special registration booklets which each Jew would have to carry. The problem of evasion through flight should be resolved through international agreement among the European Great Powers in order to supervise Jewish brotherhoods within their borders. "Brafmanism" could be detected in the provinces as well. *Vedomosti odesskogo gorodskogo obshchestvogo upravlenia* (68:1874) carried a letter from a Jew condemning the communal leadership for assisting draft evasion. *Odesskii vestnik* devoted an editorial to the letter, praising it as doing more for the cause of merger than all the exertions of Jewish publicists, with their defense of the "ancient national errors" of the Jewish masses. "The Jewish world outlook, which rests upon talmudic complexities and subtleties to divide it from all other nationalities and from common human interests and goals, as well as their love for parasitism and exploitation ... comprises the basic, vital foundation of our Jewry, making it impossible for it to merge with the character, general principles or direction of our national life" (285:29/XII/1874).

The specter of draft dodging by Jews was grist for *Kievlianin*'s mill. In mid-1874, an editorial ridiculed the "highfalutin'" speeches with which Jews had greeted the new recruitment law. Realities were something else, and the paper meticulously assembled the mechanics of evasion: the metric book for 1853 for Kamenets had been lost; the Jews abused family exemptions; and so on. While Shulgin was editor, the chronicle of Jewish abuses led to practical, specific recommendations. An editorial considered two recent proposals to deal with the situation. The first was the subordination of Jewish record-keeping to the peasant *volost* elders and the police. Age would be assigned to Jews, not on the basis of documentation, but by physical appearance. Shulgin was skeptical of success, for it would depend on the efforts of the notoriously undependable local authorities. More promising was a proposal to estimate the total number of Jews, and to draft a certain percentage, irrespective of age, thereby rendering ineffective any attempt to hide twenty-one year olds. Such a measure would only be temporary, and Shulgin proposed that the Jewish community retain the system of family exemptions. Nonetheless, this proposal reveals his estimate of the problem: draft evasion was not a crime committed by individuals, but a collective crime of the entire Jewish community for otherwise, collective restrictions of the kind proposed would be ineffective (123:15/X/1874). *Kievlianin* still exercised sufficient objectivity to allow a response to its charges. A few days later the paper printed a communiqué from a representative of the trading firm of M. D. Vainshtein, which had collected evidence by telegraph from recruiting districts around the Pale, and endeavored to show that there had been no evasion by Jews. *Kievlianin* remained skeptical and anxious to know how many of these "paper recruits" were real flesh and blood and would report for service (127:24/X/1874).

Objectivity was not the strong suit of *Russkii mir*, the organ of the conservative militarists. The paper had fought the essential elements of the Miliutin reform, and was no more pleased with the new statute's treatment of the Jews. An article in the paper doubted that even the sterner measures rejected in the drafting commission would have been effective, given the Jews' talent for evasion. Nor was it particularly desirable that a contingent of Jews serve since they were sure to be bad soldiers. In the past, at least, recruits came from the artisan class. Now these would be joined by physical wreckage from the prayer house, "an example of moral and physical originality from which the army will sooner lose than gain" (295:27/X/1874). In a perverse way, *Russkii mir* also viewed the recruitment of Jews as an emancipatory activity. Those who served would be emancipated from the "seclusion of a superstitious life," and acquire the values of the dominant nationality. There was, of course, no mention at all in *Russkii mir* of emancipation in a political or civil sense.

The War Ministry was soon disillusioned with its experiment in Jewish equality, and moved to implement the restrictions which the State Council had thrown out in 1876. The press and public opinion appear to have played no role in this decision. Of all the Russian press, only *Kievlianin* pursued the theme of Jewish evasion, and with a marked lack of enthusiasm. No more than a handful of articles on Jewish draft dodging appeared in 1875. On 3 February 1876, recruitment boards were ordered to place the Jews in a separate curia for recruitment purposes (i.e., the place of an exempted Jew was to be taken by another Jew on the recruitment lists). Only a few newspapers even bothered to note this measure in editorials (*Molva*, 12:21/III/1876; *Kievlianin*, 32:13/III/1876). The following year, *Kievlianin* stood virtually alone in voicing its concern over continued evasion (10:10/I/1877; 24:24/I/1877).

In 1878, the recruitment rules for Jews were tightened yet again. The State Council, heretofore sympathetic to the ideal of Jewish equality, passed a resolution undermining one of the central features of the exemption program of the military reform. In the event of a shortage of Jewish recruits without exemptions, or with the family exemptions of the second or third class, recruitment boards were given the option of drafting Jews with a first class exemption. "The measure so indicated remains in force," the resolution declared, "until such time as the necessity passes, as a consequence of a better fulfillment of their obligations to the state by the Jewish population."[15]

Even this draconian enactment, with its gratuitous attack on the civic responsibility of the entire Jewish population, failed to attract much editorial interest. Those who did bother to comment, however, reached conclusions which carried ominous repercussions for the Jews. *Kievlianin* put it most succinctly: by equal rights, the Jews see the taking on of rights, not obligations. Permit the Jews to live near the border, but don't place restrictions on smuggling, and the Jew becomes a smuggler; allow him unrestricted trade in alcohol, and he intoxicates the population; concede Jews the right to live everywhere without restraint, and they exploit the native population. The Jews might deny this premise, but the implementation of universal military service confirmed it. The government began with a law before which everybody was equal, and was obliged to modify it solely because of its abuse by the Jews (65:3/VI/1878). *Novoe vremia*, now well embarked upon a Judeophobe path, tendered similar regrets. It was unfortunate that the fruits of evasion were sure to cause much individual suffering, as those who should be exempt were called up. Sadder still that Jews continued to evade service, which would have the effect of freeing them from the clutches of the kahal, and exposing them to Russian grammar and the Russian way of life (807:29/V/1878).

The following year, however, the press began to discover serious Jewish evasion and its implications. The reason lay not so much in increased Jewish draft dodging, or in the implementation of new restrictive measures, but in the reappearance of the Jewish press. Two new weeklies appeared, *Russkii evrei* and *Rassvet*. It was their argumentative defense, as much as anything, that made Jewish military service a controversial issue of exactly the kind that editors loved to address. Restrictive measures continued to be directed at the Jews: in 1882 they were refused assignment to the fleet and to certain military units such as fortress artillery, border guards and quarantine guards. In that same year a norm of 5 percent of staff totals was set for Jewish military doctors and feldshers (medical attendants). In 1886 restrictions were placed on the movement of Jews from one recruitment district to another, and fines were levied on the families of those who failed to report for service. In 1887, Jewish volunteers were denied the right to take the examination for admission to officer rank. In 1888, Jewish pharmacists who were called up from the reserves were forbidden assignment to pharmaceutical duties in the service. Many of these regulations were implemented with a minimum of publicity, while others, such as the system of fines in 1886, were well publicized. All were widely discussed and debated in the press under the momentum of the on-going debate over Jewish service.[16]

The Russian–Jewish press found itself in a quandary. The charge that Jews evaded service was universally accepted, and an enormous catalogue of tricks and deceptions employed by the Jews was assembled over the years, reinforcing the claim that each new government control was undermined by some new ruse. The charge that the Jews manipulated or forged information in the metric books, the most common charge throughout the 1870s, was joined in the 1880s by the charge of self-mutilation to avoid service, an indictment seemingly confirmed by a number of criminal cases. Tales spread of year-long fasts, of punctured eardrums, missing eyes or paralyzed hands.[17] The date of the loss of finger by a potential recruit was carefully scrutinized, with criminal charges often following a dismemberment conveniently close to recruitment time. Accounts were published of "experts" who specialized in rendering young men unfit for service (*Novorossiiskii telegraf* 1644:4/VIII/1880). Judeophobes took satisfaction in reporting one case, where a specialist in such tactics, after fifty-seven successful operations, sent one hapless client "to the land where there is no military service"(*Russkii evrei* 16:16/IV/1880).

In general, however, the Russian press reacted to such tactics with amazement and disgust, unable to fathom a fear of military service so great that it led to self-mutilation. Indeed such practices were seen as illustrating the abysmally low moral and cultural standards of the Jewish masses. But what excuse could be given for educated Jews who assisted evasion? How could one justify an "enlightened" state rabbi who "cooked" the metric books? Or gangs of evaders which included respectable people including, *Novorossiiskii telegraf* reported from Berdichev, a member of the city council (2917:14/XI/1884). *Vilenskii vestnik* noted critically the refusal of Jewish intellectuals to admit the obvious irregularities in the census statistics of the Jewish population, seeing in these denials "the whole falsity of their assurances of love and obligation of their fatherland" (53:10/III/1884). There was widespread suspicion of Jewish military doctors, who allegedly dispensed a disproportionate number of medical exemptions to their coreligionists (*Novorossiiskii telegraf* 1830:27/II/1881). In response, Jewish military doctors in the Odessa military district disqualified themselves from examining Jewish recruits in 1881. Far from combating the charge, their action merely promoted a scandal, for it was erroneously reported in the press that the act was on the initiative of the Odessa military district medical inspector.[18]

Revelations of how Jews abused the existing system of exemptions led the military authorities to question their applicability for Jews. Thus, a number of newspapers complained that the unhealthy and unsanitary style of life of the Jews rendered an inordinate number of potential recruits unable to meet minimum standards of chest size. This produced a dilemma: should the physical norms be lowered for Jews? This would bring in more Jews, but at the same time, it would lower the physical standards of the recruits.[19] *Kievlianin* led the way in exposing alleged means of evasion, including fraudulent adoptions to gain "only son" exemptions, the commission of both petty and serious crimes to escape service through a "bad character" disqualification, and many others (59:17/III/1882; 60:18/III/1882; 82:13/IV/1884). One opponent was finally led to observe that *Kievlianin* had abandoned any attempt to base its accusations on actual cases, and was engaged in the purely intellectual exercise of devising as many theoretical ways to evade service as possible, providing a service which would be of use to the Jews (*Zaria* 83:14/IV/1884). In addition, the flight of many able-bodied young Jews abroad in the wake of the pogroms of 1881–82, provided another source of recorded evaders. *Vilenskii vestnik* quickly wearied of the task of pursuing Jewish evasion techniques and suggested that it might be better for the Russian army not to draft Jews at all (56:11/III/1883).

Faced with this plethora of evidence and recriminations, apparently confirmed by the implementation of the discriminatory measures by the War Ministry, only two Russian newspapers, *Golos*, newly converted to Judeophilia, and the liberal Kiev daily *Zaria*, closed by the government in 1886, dared to defend the Jews with any consistency and vigor. Both were paid for their efforts by the scorn of the rest of the press. The Russian–Jewish press was also handicapped by its initial assumption that there was objective evidence that the Jews did evade service. Their treatment of the subject was therefore apologetic, and characterized by attempts to mitigate confessed guilt. *Rassvet* dealt with the embarrassing problem by ignoring it editorially for its first year. *Rassvet*'s only treatment during this period was an internal survey, lamenting the reality of evasion and condemning those who assisted it (4:24/I/1880).

Russkii evrei was more forthright, broaching the subject in an early editorial. It would be nice to reject the claim as easily as other Judeophobe accusations, the paper explained, "but the figures are against us – they show that in every place where the Jews live their failure to appear for the call-up is three to four times greater, and in some

provinces ten times greater than for non-Jews. The non-Jewish population and the government cannot be expected to look with equilibrium at such a serious crime"(4:24/IX/1879). The editorialist offered
three conjectures to explain the problem. There was the possibility that
inadequate book-keeping was creating the apparent deficiencies;
evasion might flow from the exclusive position that Jews occupied in
the past, and to a certain extent, in the present; part of the guilt,
"perhaps the smallest," must rest with the Jewish community.

An article two months later, noting that Jewish evasion had fallen
dramatically in the last recruitment period (from 2,666 to 752), noted
the special burden borne by Jewish recruits. Unlike Russian recruits,
whose army service entailed no change in cultural surroundings,
language or religion, the Jew found himself in a totally alien environment. This situation was exacerbated by the Jewish custom of early
marriage, which ensured that many Jewish recruits must leave a family
behind them. The author suggested that in order to reduce evasion,
Jews should be given wider scope to practice their religion in the army,
while the government might also consider forbidding marriage to any
young Jew who had not been through the draft, thus eliminating the
social problem of twenty-year olds with families to support (13:28/XI/
1879).[20] Another mitigating circumstance was advanced a week later to
counter the complaints of the Russian press that a suspiciously large
number of Jews failed to meet the physical standards of the military.
The answer, an editorial explained, lay in the state-levied *korobochka*
("basket") tax on kosher meat, which drove up the price and weakened the diet of poor Jews (14:5/XII/1879). *Russkii evrei* also floated
various measures to combat evasion. Foremost was a demand for
better record-keeping, but a number of articles toyed with the idea of
offering a bonus for all Jews who reported for service as required
(16:16/IV/1880). Eventually the paper rejected such expedients, arguing
that Jews, like Russians, should serve for patriotic motives, and calling
for education and exhortation of the Jewish masses (7:11/II/1881).

The Jewish press was joined in defense of the Jews by *Golos*, which
began to call for equal rights for Jews in 1879. The paper's past
Judeophobe inclinations revealed themselves in a curious editorial in
defense of the Jews, which illustrated the maxim, "God save me from
my friends." The editorial, which announced itself ready to "stand in
defense of Jewish pretensions even in those not rare situations when
justice is not fully on their side," complained that "the general evasion
of Jews from military service, and the obligatory appearance of Jews
and Jewesses in every political trial, cannot expedite the extension of

Jewish rights" (46:15/II/1881). This editorial elicited a forceful rebuttal from an anonymous Jewish correspondent. He noted the success of Jewish participation in foreign armies and placed responsibility for evasion in Russia squarely on the discriminatory policies of the Russian government.

> To give the Jews a fatherland which they can defend one must give the Jews a fatherland they *want* to defend out of their human nature. Until such measures are taken there will remain that pitiful misunderstanding between the Jews and their fatherland; the country will view the Jews as a source of taxation and only tolerate them, and the Jews will evade service and ignore their country. The Jews must be given full equal rights – only then will they be true sons of the fatherland, only then can they understand their obligations. (66:7/III/ 1881)

Golos moved to support this position by carrying in the same issue a report from Revel, where imprecisions in the law prevented a decorated Jewish war veteran from living as a civilian in the city where he had once been stationed.

Not all the Russian–Jewish press adopted an apologetic stance on the problem of Jewish draft evasion, and those that initially pursued this approach, such as *Rassvet* and *Russkii evrei*, soon abandoned it as counter-productive. Once again, gestures of good faith – the acceptance of Jewish evasion and a search for internal remedies – was not matched by any reciprocal actions from the bulk of the Russian press. *Voskhod*, the new Jewish "thick journal," edited by A. E. Landau, quickly made a reputation for its aggressive and belligerent style in rejecting the gibes of Judeophobes. Its response to a *Golos* editorial on evasion was typical. It emphasized the claim that rights and obligations should be given simultaneously, citing the newspaper *Poriadok* that "a rightless person cannot be under obligation." It recalled the travails of Jewish life in the Nicholine army, as creating a natural reluctance for military service in the folk memory. It condemned the careless record-keeping of local administrations, which reflected on the good name of Russian Jewry. In fact, claimed an editorial, the Jews actually provided a comparatively greater number of conscripts. Even allowing for a higher evasion rate, Jews served at a rate one-and-a-half times greater than that of the gentile population (III: March 1881, 87–9).

After its initial silence, *Rassvet* also mounted a more vigorous defense. It complained in the fall of 1880 that newspapers were opening a temporary section called "Evasion of the Jews," to run through the recruitment period. The realities of evasion could at least partially be explained by faulty record-keeping of vital statistics. For Russians, it sufficed for a neighbor or relative of a deceased person to attest to their death, and an oral report was sufficient. The Jews, according to 1874 regulations for reporting dead recruits, required a police attestation in the metric books, and this was difficult to secure. The sizeable number of Jewish "evaders," argued *Rassvet*, were in large part drawn from the ranks of the unreported dead. The paper advised the Jewish community to make formal complaint to the First Department of the Senate (42: 1880).

Russkii evrei was the last Jewish publication to adopt an argumentative tone, but it did so with a vengeance in 1882. The co-editor of *Russkii evrei*, M. G. Rabinovich, could hardly write passable Russian, but he was a skilled mathematician and statistician. In a series of articles, bristling with statistics, he surveyed Jewish military recruitment since 1874.[21] His findings were summarized in an editorial devoted to the latest recruitment: the per capita recruitment norm for Jews was 67.5 percent higher than for non-Jews, the norm of evaders was 10 percent lower, and the number of volunteers 17 percent higher than non-Jews. He advanced explanations for the phenomenon of Jewish evasion, none of them laid to the fault of the Jews. The first was incorrect recording of mortalities in the Jewish population, which meant that many Jewish "no-shows" were in fact in "the land of the shadows." Secondly, there were delays in communicating information about Jews who were already serving in the army, making them appear to be evaders on preliminary lists. Thirdly, the straitened economic condition of the Jewish population ensured that many young Jews were in transit from place to place looking for employment, and were recorded in the draft registration books of several communities where they had at one time lived. The call-up made these multiple-enrollers appear to be evaders. Even with these difficulties, the metric and registration books had gradually been placed in better order, and the number of evaders was dropping each year. Then came the pogroms, and the panicked flight of Jews for safety, and the alleged government announcement that the western borders were open for emigration. "Evasion" began to increase once again, reflecting the departure abroad of young men of draft age. None of this could be laid at the door of the Jews (10:11/III/1883).

Such arguments were accepted by a few newspapers, directly or indirectly, but by and large it was a case of preaching to the converted (*Odesskii listok* 160:19/VII/1884; *Golos* 299:3/XI/1882). The Judeophobe press preferred to dismiss or mock learned arguments, especially those which blamed the apparent high rate of evasion on Jewish "dead souls." *Novoe vremia* tried its hand at statistics-mongering, arguing that since the Jews provided nineteen times fewer recruits than gentiles, they were only one-nineteenth as patriotic (cited in *Russkii evrei* 11:16/ III/1884). In 1884, when quotas for Jewish students were being introduced into Russian higher education, *Voskhod* complained that the authorities underestimated the size of the Jewish population when setting educational norms. *Kievlianin* observed that in the past, *Voskhod* had argued that the Jewish population was overestimated for purposes of setting recruitment norms. How typical, *Kievlianin* editorialized, that the Jews used one set of figures when arguing about rights and another when discussing obligations (169:29/VII/1884). The debate carried on into the 1890s, provoked by the figures from each new military recruitment, or by new government measures to ensure Jewish compliance.

The introduction of universal military service into the Russian army in 1874 had important consequences for Russian Jewry. Large numbers of Jews did in fact serve in the army, with all the consequences of Russification and assimilation noted in the case of other national minorities drafted at the same time. The apparent proclivity of the Jews for draft evasion soon became legendary, reinforcing a pre-existing prejudice that the Jews were by nature cowards. The myths of evasion and cowardice became a persistent part of popular Judeophobia in Russia into the Soviet period. Finally, the failure of the Jews to fulfill civil obligations became a convenient justification for denying the Jews civil rights. As *Sanktpeterburgskie vedomosti* put it in 1886, greeting a new set of restrictions designed to combat Jewish evasion, "Equal rights for Jews, evidently, are still not possible because the [Jewish] masses remain unconscious of obligations [shared] in common with the Russian people before the fatherland" (148:31/V/ 1886).

15 The dilemma of the Russian Jewish intelligentsia

In 1869, after a hiatus of eight years, Russian Jewry again found an articulate voice in the chorus of national public opinion. In Odessa a group of young Jewish journalists published *Den, organ russkikh evreev* for two years. In St. Petersburg, Aleksandr Tsederbaum, publisher of the Yiddish *Kol Mevaser* and the Hebrew *Ha-Melits*, brought out *Vestnik russkikh evreev* from 1871 to 1873.[1] Gone were the days when all Russian literature rallied to the defense of insulted Jews, as in the *Illiustratsiia* Affair of 1858. No longer could Jewish publications confidently turn to Russian journalism, as *Sion* had done in 1861, to seek vindication in the midst of a polemic. Literary Judeophobia had become not only widespread, but respectable as well. Rather than chronicling the Jewish march toward progress and civil rights, new Jewish publications were obliged to take up arms against an army of critics or, as a *Den* editorial put it, to play the cat to prevent the literary mice from having free play (2:9/I/1871).

As a consequence, the old debate surrounding depiction of Jewish faults, which had so bedeviled *Rassvet*, became moot. Rather, it was necessary actively to defend Jews and to explain why resolution of the Jewish Question appeared more remote than it had in 1858 or 1861. The new Jewish press bore the burden of the past, and was obliged to resolve the old ambiguities surrounding the processes of rapprochement and merger.

The first editor of *Den* was S. S. Ornshtein, but the character of the paper was largely shaped by a three-member editorial committee named by the Odessa branch of the OPE. All three had journalistic experience as well as law degrees. M. G. Morgulis and M. Kulisher were graduates of the University of St. Vladimir in Kiev, while I. G. Orshanskii was trained at the University of New Russia in Odessa. Of all the professions in Russia, none was transformed by the Reform

25 I. G. Orshanskii

Era so thoroughly as the Bar. The creation of a reformed court system in 1865 was, in many ways, the most enduring and successful of all the post-emancipation reforms. The Russian Bar developed a strong liberal ethos. The lawyer-dominated *Den* was pervaded by a respect for Western-style concepts of economic and political liberalism. This orientation was apparent in *Den*'s formulation of an agenda for the development of Russian–Jewish amity.

Early on *Den* was forced to justify its existence in a response to *Birzhevye vedomosti*'s query asking why the Jews needed a special newspaper if their interests were identical to those of the rest of the population. *Den* explained that the state itself made the Jews a special case through its program of restrictive legislation (31:1/VIII/1870). Responding to similar taunts from the Judeophobe *Novorossiiskii tele-graf*, the editors declared that the paper existed to discuss the Jewish Question and, since this task was totally neglected by the Russian press, to serve a Jewish readership with information about themselves (41:9/X/1870). To gain a broader sense of *Den*'s stand on rapprochement/

merger, however, it is necessary to review the paper's discussion of the status and role of the Jews in Russian society and the process which I. Sosis termed "natural assimilation."[2]

Responding to concerns generated by the Polish uprising, *Den* argued that division and enmity among the constituent elements of the Russian Empire could no longer be tolerated. Russians must play the dominant role in the task of uniting all peoples of the Empire into a harmonious whole. The task was to determine how best to do this, since Russification for its own sake, a purely mechanical process which had no real tie to the needs of the Jewish or gentile population, was clearly unsatisfactory (13:28/III/1870). At the same time, the existence of natural rights, such as the right to choose residence or profession, must not be forgotten (13:9/VIII/1869). In a major series entitled "On the Question of the Russification of the Jews," Orshanskii argued that some spheres of life, such as family affairs, religious belief, personal life, customs, morals and communal life, were best served by natural development and not by the intervention of the state. There were distinctive features of Jewish life that had been developed over the centuries of persecution and discrimination, but they should be condemned when and if they contradicted the spirit of the times, not just because they were different or unique. Thus, Orshanskii did not automatically disapprove of Jewish cultural distinctiveness. Perhaps their unique features might disappear in the future, but Orshanskii never said so directly. He left the reader with the impression that distinctive Jewish institutions, which so distressed Russifiers, should be left in place. This also applied to education where, Orshanskii reminded his readers, other groups besides the Jews, such as the Crimean Tatars, maintained a separate school system (15:10/IV/1870). In the future the separatist Jewish press would evolve into periodicals concerned only with religious issues, resembling Russian Orthodox diocesan newspapers, the *Eparkhialnye vedomosti*. Special newspapers existed only to defend those exclusive interests of Russian Jewry which arose from exclusive laws (31:1/VIII/1870). In a truly modern state special free institutions and associations, such as the Jewish brotherhoods "discovered by that chameleon, Brafman," were logical and harmless. Consider the United States: "Nobody there doubts that the free development of the collective activity of all levels of the population only strengthens national and governmental unity, while constraints on free association leads to fatal bureaucratism" (17:24/IV/1870). Orshanskii rejected the claim that spontaneous, natural assimilation was a failure. In Odessa a large, thoroughly Russified Jewish community had developed. This phenomenon was promoted, not by the restraints of legal Russification, but by the humanitarian impulse of local society which demanded that Jews be treated as true citizens (13:28/III/1870). For this process to be maintained society must continue to reach out to the Jews. Unfortunately, this was not happening. Vague Judeophilia had been replaced by public apathy or narrow class interests. Those in the press who spoke about Russification were hypocritically insincere. "This is the point, that gentlemen who comment on the Russification of the Jews in the spirit of *Golos* and its provincial hangers-on don't have in mind the goal of this or that kind of russification, but just want to be in a position to throw into the teeth of the Jews the present unsatisfactory state of affairs, and in this way delay the emancipation of the Jews" (44:31/X/1870). Moreover, the Russians themselves had shown no great talent for the absorption of other peoples. Putting aside the issue of the Poles and Germans, Crimean Tatar culture ruled supreme in the Crimea, while Armenian was the language for trade in the Caucasus.

These considerations led to the crux of the matter: the legal condition of the Jews was a sure index of the moral and cultural level of the people among whom they lived (16:18/IV/1870). The Russian press had recently focused attention on the savage beating of an adulteress in a Jewish community, but surely the Russian peasantry could match such outrages deed for deed. Every critic was ready to excuse peasant degradation as flowing, not from some inherent flaw, but from the domination of the individual peasant by a backward community with a weakly developed morality. Why should not the same excuses be made for the Jews? The path to true merger, *Den* continually asserted, lay through education and economic development (20:15/V/1870).

Den's comments on the topical educational debate enabled the editors to continue their insistence upon the need to indulge the unique circumstances of Jewish life. Plans to close the Jewish school system were widely discussed at the end of the 1870s. *Den* proposed reform rather than abolition. Christian administrators should be removed, and Jewish teachers should receive a decent living wage (36:4/IX/1870). Despite their many flaws, state Jewish schools had the positive facility of sending Jews along the road to further education. *Den* pridefully predicted, in words that would become a Judeophobe indictment within a decade, that

> only a shortage of means, or special family circumstances make Jews stop halfway and fail to get a university education, once they start on the path through the public educational institutions, which is the

only way to guarantee greater prosperity. If this continues, Jews both can and will become the largest percentage of the state's intellectual strength, and most professions which can be entered only with a university education will pass into Jewish hands. (19:8/V/1871)

As Judeophobe opinion gained a wider acceptance in the press, *Den* was forced to dwell extensively on the charge of Jewish "economic exploitation." *Den*'s counter-argument was easily summarized. "In the moral as well as the physical world we encounter precise consequences: a given cause produces a given effect. One can't escape the natural order of things: in a country which has railroads, freedom of the press, equality before the law, and where human slavery has been abolished out of principle, a system restricting individual classes (*soslovii*) cannot endure and must collapse" (21:4/X/1869). Jews had historically been forced into middleman activity because all other occupations were closed to them, while they always needed money to buy protection or flee quickly from persecution. The economic burden imposed by the Jews on the peasantry was a natural consequence of the deformed legal system that kept them in the Pale, which was too small to absorb them all. Inside the Pale the Jews were forced to become tavern-keepers or usurers. Open the Pale, and this unnatural system would vanish. Russia itself would benefit as Jews fanned out through the Russian interior to provide competition for Russian kulaks and monopolists (15:22/VIII/1869; 45:6/XI/ 1870; 43:24/X/1870; 48–50:28/XI, 5/XII, 12/XII/1870).

The positive economic influence of the Jews would be accompanied by positive political significance as a Russifying force in the western provinces. In article after article *Den* asserted that the Jews had steadfastly resisted Polonization. Jews recognized the ultimate futility of Polish aspirations and also displayed a basic loyalty to the Russian state. If the Jews acted in this way when they received no tangible reward, what would be their response if the government adopted a positive program of emancipation to win over the Jews? Let the Jews Russify and develop the western borderlands, a task to which Russia herself had not proved equal (1–3:2/I, 10/I, 16/I; 5:30/I; 49:5/XII and 50:12/XII/1870).

When *Vestnik russkikh evreev* first appeared, it too was challenged to justify its existence. *Vestnik*'s response lacked panache and style, since it had few contributors who were as comfortable in Russian as the lawyers who editorialized for *Den*. Tsederbaum, born in 1816, was an autodidact and a typical first-generation Russian maskil. The sentiments of *Vestnik*, therefore, are an important gauge of how the Old

Maskilim viewed the tasks of rapprochement and merger. *Vestnik*'s first editorial justified the new paper's existence in terms which recalled *Den*'s arguments. Jews would like to pursue rapprochement with Russians in civil and social relations, while retaining the religion of their forefathers. When this process was completed, a special newspaper just for Jews would indeed be superfluous. Unfortunately, that moment had not yet arrived, since Jews remained alienated from the Christian majority because of the special conditions of their civil, social and economic life. Judeophobes blamed these conditions on the Jews themselves. *Vestnik* disagreed: "Indeed, Jews do not wish of their own free will to be differentiated from Christians, but they are so out of necessity, most obviously due to their inferior legal status" (1:3/I/1871). It was the obligation of the Jewish publicists, who knew their people well, to direct the attention of the government and society to anti-Jewish prejudices which were vestiges of the "epoch of ignorance and religious fanaticism."

A subsequent *Vestnik* editorial devoted to this theme is of special interest because it attempted to differentiate between rapprochement and merger. The writer claimed that merger implied that the Jews should not exist in the form of a religious community, but should convert to the religion of the dominant Russian majority. As thus presented, the concept of merger was rejected by *Vestnik*. The paper welcomed the process of rapprochement, examples of which were plentiful. Jews were entering the civil service, and they were to be found employed as writers, businessmen and barristers. Tsederbaum's concept of rapprochement clearly placed emphasis upon fluency in Russian. The editorial also praised the adoption by Jews of "the conditions of Russian daily life, insofar as it does not conflict with their religious feeling." This latter implied the disappearance of traditional Jewish garb, but not the abandonment of special dietary rules, which the editorialist assured his readers would cause no more inconvenience in Jewish–Christian relations than the strict adherence of the latter to the fasts of the Russian Orthodox Church (20:16/V/1871).

The rubric of "respect for religious feeling" was a complicated one, as Tsederbaum demonstrated on more than one occasion, especially as Jews themselves differed over the essential components of Judaism. *Vestnik*, like *Den*, defended the separate state Jewish school system, while also calling for reform. The schools had been created to serve the false goal of "weakening religious fanaticism," while they would be more effective in promoting rapprochement through spreading a knowledge of Russian. Tsederbaum recommended a reformed system of Jewish confessional schools to serve as a bridge from the *heder* to the public school. He proposed that representatives of the three emergent trends in Russian Jewry, progressive, orthodox and hasidic, be called together to design a new program for the schools (16:18/IV/1871).

A certain theoretical air clung to abstract discussions of rapprochement and merger by all the Jewish press, especially as other people's theories were transformed into reality. The activities of the Vilna Commission, the growing journalistic acceptance of Iakov Brafman's ideas, and the 1871 pogrom in Odessa, were all specific events that affected the broader question of Jewish-gentile relations.

The ostensible purpose of the Vilna Commission, formed in 1867, was to reduce the alienation of Jews from Christian society. The centerpiece of the projected reform was the integration of Jews into the basic institution of peasant self-government, the *volost*. To oppose the project required tact, and a convincing explanation of why such a reform was more likely to block than expedite merger. The task was taken up by E. Soloveichik, for a short time a member of the OPE's editorial board, coeditor of *Sion*, and a future editor of *Den*.[3] Soloveichik applauded the prospect of merger, which he defined as the acquisition of the Russian language, and completely identical treatment of Christian and Jew, save for the retention of traditional religious and charitable institutions by the Jews. (This latter stipulation was controversial indeed in the light of official acceptance of Brafman's claims.) The new zemstvo institutions, which provided for the participation of all citizens without religious or national exceptions, provided an excellent model.

The Vilna initiative presented a serious challenge to Jewish spokesmen. It claimed to pursue the complete merger of Christians and Jews, but what did this mean in context? While merger might theoretically be possible in the urban centers of the Pale, it would result only in Polonization of the Jews, since Polish influence was concentrated in urban areas. Merger with the peasantry was not even possible on a theoretical basis, since Jews and peasants belonged to different estates and had sharply conflicting class interests. If the subordination of the Jews to the peasant *volost* actually took place, one of two outcomes was inevitable. The majority of Jews might attempt to escape this fate by fleeing to the cities, there to become Polonized. Left behind would be a few wealthy Jews who would swell the ranks of the *miroedy* and the kulaks, the two foes of a rational peasant agriculture and a stable and prosperous village. The other option was that most Jews would stay, be reduced to the status of peasants, and evolve into a new class of

Jewish *batraks*, or destitute landless peasants, since there was clearly not enough arable land for them. Whether Jews remained in the countryside in greater or lesser numbers, subordination to the peasant *volost* would have the negative effect of exposing them directly to the virulent religious hatred borne them by the Roman Catholic peasantry led by clergy, who even at that moment were fabricating a ritual murder charge at Shaviansk.

Soloveichik's arguments enabled *Den* to claim that it opposed the Vilna reforms in the name of Russification and in support of the welfare of both rural Christians and Jews. The articles played on the Russian government's fear of a landless rural proletariat, a concern reflected in the provisions of the peasant emancipation. His attack on Roman Catholic fanaticism permitted an ingratiating comparison with the alleged tolerance of the Russian people. *Den* had the pleasure of seeing its attacks on the Vilna Commission crowned with success and its arguments repeated by influential papers like *Sanktpeterburgskie vedomosti* and *Birzhevye vedomosti*.[4]

Discrediting the discoveries of Iakov Brafman, widely hailed by Russians in the administration and the press, was a more daunting task. *Den* established itself as the most assiduous opponent of Brafman in his guises as a moving spirit of the Vilna Commission and author of *The Book of the Kahal*. The paper carried recantations by Brafman's collaborators, a major series on the historical origins of the kahal by M. Morgulis, and continued I. I. Shershevskii's scholarly demolition of the book, begun in *Novoe vremia*. The paper continually sniped at Brafman's character, motives and expertise.[5]

This proved to be an isolated position, as Brafman found a welcome in the literary world. "According to that part of society represented by *Golos*," lamented the paper, "it is not external conditions which have made the Jews into a 'dark kingdom,' but the very nature of the Jews themselves" (19:9/V/1870). Unfortunately, "that part of society" comprised a growing component of liberal opinion. On this one subject liberal opinion was joined by Russifiers and Judeophobes. While *Den* could nonchalantly dismiss as incoherent and illiterate the attacks of the notoriously unprincipled *Novorossiiiskii telegraf* (40:2/X/1870), the sarcastic taunts of *Kievlianin* were more unsettling. A *Kievlianin* editorial, in defense of Brafman, was directed at *Den*, deriding it as "an orphanage for Mary Magdalenes," because of its support for the repentant Bratin and Levin, Brafman's youthful collaborators (104:1/IX/1870). A *Den* editorial in response was uncharacteristically restrained and defensive, perhaps because the attack had been aimed, not just at the Jews, but at the Russian Jewish intelligentsia itself (37:12/IX/1870). Such a charge called into question the underpinning of all theories of merger and rapprochement, supposedly the common bond and objective of all segments of educated Russian society. Within a year a pogrom in Odessa exercised an even more unsettling effect upon these assumptions.

In 1871, pogroms, or anti-Jewish riots, were not yet a common phenomenon in the Russian Empire except for Odessa where minor clashes, usually between Greeks and Jews, had become endemic. Indeed, *Den* editorials routinely warned its Jewish readers of the risk of violence in anticipation of Christian Holy Week.[6] Past pogroms, such as those of 1821, 1848 and 1859, had retained a local character and they were barely reported outside Odessa. National coverage was usually restricted to excerpts from *Odesskii vestnik*, which invariably attributed pogroms to local factors, such as the commercial and religious rivalries between Greeks and Jews.[7] The pogrom of 1871 was an exception to this rule. An event which left 8 people dead, 21 seriously hurt, as well as scores of policemen and soldiers with injuries, and which resulted in the arrest of 1,156 people and millions of rubles worth of damage, could not be ignored by the Russian press, especially when tied to the topical Jewish Question.[8] The pogrom began on 28 March 1871 and lasted until 1 April. Accounts of the pogrom varied widely. The local administration, led by the Governor-General of Novorossiia, P. E. Kotsebu, sought to avoid blame for the outbreak of the pogrom, its severity, or the way it was suppressed. The official line dominated accounts in the Odessa press, especially *Odesskii vestnik*, which was under the Governor-General's direct control. The press in the capitals, on the contrary, were far more severe in their judgments. *Moskovskie vedomosti* in particular, but also *Golos* and *Birzhevye vedomosti*, faulted the local administration for failing to control the disorders, and for subjecting randomly arrested groups to mass flogging on the city's squares, in violation of the legal reform guidelines which prohibited collective punishment.[9]

The official version of the pogrom was provided by Governor-General Kotsebu, whose reports to his superiors in St. Petersburg were published in the authoritative *Pravitelstvennyi vestnik*. Kotsebu's first report maintained that "the cause of the initial clash between Greeks and Jews is not known, but fights between them usually occur during the Easter season, and the Greeks were joined by Russians who were also inspired by religious emotion."[10] Newspapers prone to religious Judeophobia quickly accepted this interpretation, and shifted blame squarely onto the Jews themselves. *Sovremennye izvestiia*, edited by the devout N. P. Giliarov-Platonov, emphasized that Judaism itself kept the Jews from being "a brother to others." Jews could not show tolerance toward any other national group and they could never be good citizens, because they recognized no other state or law and were bound only by race and greed.[11] The conservative *Syn otchestva* offered a variant reading of this theme. Since the Jews were universally hated, an editorial noted, the fault must lie within the Jews themselves. It was not the religious beliefs of the Jews *per se* which made them outcasts, but the secrecy with which they surrounded their cult. Since Christians encountered Jews only in the guise of exploiters and monopolists, it was logical for them to attribute this behavior to the dictates of religion. The editorial offered a perverted version of merger. Jews should receive civil rights only after they had dismantled the wall which they had built around themselves. Until they ceased to be a scourge for Christians, society was warranted in protesting against them (an obvious reference to the pogroms) and in seeking the protection of the government (76:6/IV/1871).

The day after his initial report, Kotsebu sent another explanation of the pogrom to the Ministry of Internal Affairs, which bore a distinctly Judeophobe cast.

> The recent events showed that the [religious] antipathy of Christians, primarily from the lower classes, is reinforced by bitterness arising from the exploitation of their labor by the Jews, and the latter's ability to get rich and to dominate all commercial and mercantile operations. From the crowds of Christians were often heard the words, 'The Jews mock Christ, they get rich and they suck our blood.'[12]

Kievlianin and *Golos* welcomed this charge, bearing an official imprimatur. *Kievlianin* published a lengthy report from its Odessa correspondent who attributed the disorders to "Jewish exploitation" (42:10/IV/1871), while *Golos* reprinted articles which presented the Jews in a bad light.[13]

The response of the Russian Jewish press to the pogrom was strangely muted, in contrast to its usually argumentative style. This has been attributed by some observers to the influence of the censorship. One article by Orshanskii on the pogrom was in fact suppressed. However this article was not of great importance – it did little more than criticize Odessa society for its apathy toward the pogrom.[14] At no time, apparently, did the censorship hinder *Den* from responding to the popular charge that the Jews brought on their own difficulties through exploitation. Rather, the tameness of the Jewish press was an indication of the disillusionment and despair produced among Russian Jewish intellectuals by the pogrom and its consequences. Two weeks after the pogrom, *Den* declined to seek the immediate causes of the pogrom, "still recovering from the first impression made on us by these events" (16:16/IV/1871). The first reports of *Vestnik russkikh evreev* did no more than praise the high civilization of Odessa Jewry, and attribute the pogrom to the frustrations of unsuccessful economic rivals (14:4/IV/1871). The paper never dealt editorially with the pogrom, except in the most indirect ways.[15]

In one regard a vigorous response by the Jewish press was not required since prestigious liberal papers of the capitals and the provinces – as always, with the exception of *Golos* – stepped forward to dispute the charge of Jewish exploitation. Rejecting this charge, *Birzhevye vedomosti* heaped blame upon the municipal authorities, on the religious fanaticism of the Greeks, on the inactivity of the Orthodox clergy and the apathy of "polite society." It never presented the Jews as anything other than a victimized minority badly in need of the full protection of the law (99:13/IV/1871). The premier liberal thick journal, *Vestnik Evropy*, raised the charge of exploitation only to dismiss it as a ruse devised by the Odessa authorities to distract attention from their dereliction of duty. If by chance the Jews displayed a few disagreeable characteristics, this was a consequence of the artificial constraints of the Pale.

> We have had occasion to speak of the necessity of changing these conditions and letting the Jews settle all over Russia along with all other inhabitants, and also of engendering a sense of full religious sensibility, which would lead the Jews from their artificially-maintained isolation and merge them with Russians, as they merge with Frenchmen in France, Englishmen in England, and with Germans in Austria. (5:V/1871, 414–5)

In Kiev, *Kievskii telegraf*, rather than the Jewish press, served as the chief conduit for the Jewish opponents of *Kievlianin*. The paper published two editorials, identified as written by Jews, which attacked *Kievlianin* and Shulgin, its editor, by name. The first author presented numerous examples of Jewish industry and productive activity to defend them from the charge of exploitation (52:5/V/1871). The second defended the Talmud, rejecting the claim that talmudic strictures were the motive force for exploitation (58:21/V/1871).

Surprisingly, given its ties to the administration, *Odesskii vestnik* soon qualified its call for an end to Jewish exploitation. Editorials sharply distinguished between the Jewish upper classes and the

Jewish masses, just as it differentiated among the various levels of Christian society. The paper admitted that the Jewish intelligentsia, Jewish bankers and mercantile leaders, were free of the defects of the masses, and had fully and successfully merged with gentile society. The Jewish masses, on the other hand, were at a lower level of development. Under the pressures created by the Pale of Settlement, they pursued a "crooked path" due to their absence of moral feeling. "If it was explained to the dark masses of the Jewish people that trade is a productive undertaking, that its essence lies in industry, not life at the expense of producers and consumers; that it is dishonorable to use the weaknesses and shortcomings of one's neighbor; that it is barbaric to exploit the needy – then, in fact, reconciliation would be quite possible" (84:22/IV/1871). *Odesskii vestnik* conceded that Christian society displayed the same dichotomy, the lower orders being oppressed by "poverty, weakness and helplessness." Those who escaped the proletarian milieu lost their fear and hatred of the Jews since they could cope with them on equal terms. Interestingly enough, the editorialist assumed that it would be a greater task to raise the moral level of the Christian than the Jewish masses (69:3/IV/1871). *Odesskii vestnik* editorials continued to attribute the negative aspects of Jewish life to external circumstances.

> Our region is primarily agricultural, and it requires trade and commerce to make an economic whole. The Jews provide this. But economic laws demand balance, and this they do *not* display. In order to support themselves they must engage not only in trade but in all manner of speculation. *This, we feel, is the prime source of the evil, and thus we feel it is important to permit the Jews wholesale settlement throughout Russia.* (Italics in the original)

The Jews represented "two million commercial machines," which should be employed in the exploitation of the riches of Russia rather than in the exploitation of the hapless peasant (81:17/IV/1871). Sentiments such as these, from what had been a hostile opponent, required no rebuttal from the Jewish press. Instead, the attention of Jewish publicists was attracted by an attack from an unexpected quarter.

Sanktpeterburgskie vedomosti was Russia's oldest newspaper. Under the editorship of V. F. Korsh, it was *Golos'* rival for the role of premier liberal periodical. Unlike *Golos*, it was generally sympathetic to the Jews. In its reporting of the Odessa pogrom the paper restricted itself to physical descriptions drawn from other papers, to official accounts from *Pravitelstvennyi vestnik*, and to the dispatches of the Russian Telegraph Agency. The editors were apparently content to view the pogrom from the Olympian heights, because they offered no significant editorial judgments. Over a month after the pogrom, when agitation and polemic had dropped to a low level, *Sanktpeterburgskie vedomosti* unexpectedly published two editorials devoted to the Odessa disorders. They struck Jewish publicists like a slap in the face from an old friend.

An editorial on 11 May 1871 announced the need to reexamine the Odessa pogrom. Hatred and resentment of the Jews in the West and Southwest was so strong that violence might erupt again at any time. Unsatisfactory attempts had already been made to explain the pogrom. Jews claimed that the sole cause was the religious fanaticism of the Russian people which in turn arose from their backward condition. This view, the editorialist warned, was dangerously misleading.

> Let a person with theoretical sympathy for the Jews, based on consideration of their wretched historical fate, spend but two years living in New Russia or the western provinces and he will lose all these theoretical considerations and come to one conclusion: the Jews are harmful, the Jews cannot and ought not to be tolerated as they are now in those places where they live.

As for the alleged backwardness of the peasantry, "antipathy [to the Jews] in many cases serves as virtually the sole, albeit underdeveloped conception by the people of their moral strength."

However disconcerting these sentiments were, coming from a formerly sympathetic newspaper, worse was to come when a subsequent editorial explained the nature of Jewish economic exploitation (130:13/ V/1871). This editorial compared the Jews to Russian work gangs (*arteli*), but one bound together by national, as well as economic interests, and unconcerned with the consequences of its economic activities. The Jewish artel was one composed of kulaks, not workingmen, and bent on exploitation, not mutual assistance. In words redolent of Iakov Brafman the paper declared:

> What mercantile opportunities the Jews have, through their language, unknown to other people, through their secret communications, impenetrable even to the most attentive eye, and, finally, to the institution of the kahal, through which the Jews constitute a state within a state ... One can say without much exaggeration that where the Jews have the mass of the population in their hands, they are able to construct a many-sided instrument of exploitation, and the people feel themselves under an unbearable yoke, with which not even the serfdom of the past can compare.

Although the editorial included among its proposals for reform the resettlement of the Jews throughout Russia, it did so reluctantly and with obvious misgivings, conceding only that the Jews might prove useful "to a certain degree."

The Jewish press could not ignore the defection of a newspaper whose name was routinely invoked as a sympathizer with the Jewish cause.[16] *Den* asked whether *Sanktpeterburgskie vedomosti* was ready to tuck its tail between its legs and ask forgiveness from its old conservative enemies in the press. A *Den* editorial sarcastically observed that the recent editorials "do honor to the liberal press, because not even such skilled purveyors of blindness as Brafman surpassed it" (21:22/V/1871). The last three editorials which *Den* published were devoted to the attacks of *Sanktpeterburgskie vedomosti*, and they displayed a thoroughness usually reserved only for *Kievlianin*, in its role as leader of the "principled" Judeophobe press. *Vestnik russkikh evreev* also published a long refutation of the editorials, taking special exception to the claim that pogrom violence represented the peasantry's growing awareness of its moral strength (21:23/V/1871). This issue also carried a plaintive letter which suggested, with some acumen, that the editorials were so contrary to the usual spirit of the publication that they must be the work of an occasional contributor.[17]

The Odessa pogrom of 1871, and public reactions to it, had a decisive impact upon the Russian Jewish intelligentsia, putting in motion a process of reflection and reappraisal which anticipated and prefigured the communal crisis which followed the more serious pogroms of 1881–2.[18] A new ambivalence quickly manifested itself in the press. On 22 April 1871, a Jew named S. Aizberg wrote to *Odesskii vestnik* to dispute that paper's earlier call for the suppression of all separate Jewish institutions, such as schools and charitable institutions, as a means to expedite rapprochement. Aizberg noted that education had not protected Jews from the pogromshchiki. "This fact showed to every single Jew that they have not succeeded in being called the brothers of Russians, and that they have nothing in common with them in the Russian land." An Ekaterinoslav Jew, M. Stanislavskii, noted in a letter to *Vestnik russkikh evreev* the great hostility of local society toward the Jews. Under such circumstances there could be no talk of rapprochement of Jews with Christians (22:30/V/1871). Orshanskii's banned editorial on the pogrom attempted to characterize "the general moral condition of contemporary Russian society." He stressed that although the common people expressed their hatred for the Jews in a crude and visible way, this hatred was actually centered in the local intelligentsia and the well-to-do classes. Apropos of these Judeophobes, Orshanskii recalled the Russian proverb, "There's no family without freaks," but voiced his regret that so many of them were involved in the administration of education and justice in the region.[19]

The disillusionment voiced by the Jewish proponents of rapprochement and merger was echoed and amplified by many of their gentile counterparts. The appearance of doubts and second thoughts in the intelligentsia milieu was of special significance. The world of letters represented the "neutral society" *par excellence*, and it was here that the movement of Jews into Russian society, by the criteria of numbers and influence, was most successful. It has already been noted that Jews made ample use of the Russian press as a forum, and that some of them made at least a partial living from journalism. From the late fifties to the early seventies, it is possible to identify more than thirty Jews (including converts) who published more than one article on the Jewish Question in the Russian press. Jews served as editors and editorial staff on both official and unofficial publications.[20] Many more contributed to such publications as *Moskovskie vedomosti*, *Russkii vestnik*, *Golos*, *Domashniaia beseda*, *Vilenskii vestnik* and *Odesskii vestnik*, to say nothing of the Russian, Hebrew and Yiddish language Jewish press. A striking uniformity may be found among those whose biographies are known. With the exception of a handful of autodidacts from the old generation, such as Tarnopol and Tsederbaum, they were educated in Russian educational institutions, including the universities of Moscow, St. Petersburg, Kiev, Kharkov and Novorossiia (Odessa), most often studying in the legal or medical faculties. At some point, many had studied in the state Jewish school system. Those who did not attend university were usually graduates of the Vilna or Zhitomir Rabbinical Academies, and they frequently served as teachers, state rabbis and Jewish Experts. They were a group whose collective orientation, and often their livelihood, depended on the state Jewish school system. In their command of the Russian language, in their espousal of a "Russian" education, in their criticisms of the "dark corners" of the contemporary Jewish masses, they were living examples of what the process of rapprochement/merger was supposed to achieve.

This being so, it is understandable why the Russian Jewish intelligentsia had received such a warm welcome from educated Russian society, exemplified by the *Illiustratsiia* Affair. The pages of the press, liberal, conservative, Russifying alike, were open to them. Their opinions were solicited by the state on such topics as the state Jewish school system, or the task of Russification in the Northwest. The activities of the OPE were carried out in the public eye. The press habitually applauded the efforts of the Jewish intelligentsia and urged them on to greater feats. Educated Jews had the open support of educated Russian society.[21]

Yet there was always an underside to this support, a weak current of distrust or impatience for the final outcome of the process. As early as 1859, an article in an obscure provincial newspaper attacked the "smooth-tongued" Jewish publicists who wished to divert attention from the harmfulness of their coreligionists.[22] Ivan Aksakov derided as "moral amphibions" those Jews who wished to abandon a flawed Judaism but would not convert to Christianity.[23] The assurances of support by the Ukrainophiles had mutated into attacks on the "Foremost Yids" during the *Osnova* Affair.[24] *Kievlianin* abandoned its initial sympathy for the Jews with its attack on Morgulis and his alleged plan for Jewish economic domination of the Ukraine.[25] By 1866 *Vilenskii vestnik* was condemning Jews as "hard-hearted cosmopolitans" who had nothing in common with Russia. Educated Jews were a *magnum nihil*, neither Russian nor Jew (99:12/V/1866). The paper rejected the Jews as "nihilists at heart," and abandoned rapprochement as an "empty chimera" (144:7/VII/1866). Even more ominous than these attacks, which could be dismissed as religious obscurantism, was the ease with which Iakov Brafman's charges against the kahal were first accepted by educated Russian society, and then expanded to encompass the Russian Jewish intelligentsia, now depicted as the tools of the kahal aristocracy. Individual Jewish publicists were often condemned as "representing the kahal," while the OPE was transformed into the Russian branch of the invidious Alliance Israélite Universelle.[26] In the 1870s, as Judeophobia grew more widespread and virulent, an important transformation took place. Judeophobe charges increasingly neglected the "dark Jewish masses" and concentrated instead upon the erstwhile proponents of rapprochement, the Russian Jewish intelligentsia.

A number of factors expedited this transformation. An undercurrent of religious Judeophobia, while never in the forefront of debates on the Jewish Question, did surface in attacks like those of Aksakov, and became more and more fantastic and irrational. The theme that Jews would dominate state service or a particular profession or field of endeavor, almost invariably appeared first in the Pale, and may have represented real fears by the local intelligentsia at the growing economic and intellectual might of a modernized Jewish elite. Analogous concerns are detectable in the discomfort of Russian administrators in the Pale, faced with the task of Russification in areas where there were not enough Russians and too many Jews.

The Russian Jewish intelligentsia also played a role in this process. This elite was always a tiny minority, culturally distinct from the traditional Jewish community, Mitnagdim and Hasidim alike. They spoke a different language, literally and metaphorically. They commanded neither fear nor respect from the Jewish masses, who regarded them as no better than heretics. This sense of "otherness" had already been established by some Young Maskilim, who had gone out of their way to shock and offend. In so doing, they tended to discredit all educated Jews in the eyes of the religiously devout.

Their effective isolation did not prevent Jewish intellectuals from appearing before the Russian government and Russian public opinion in the guise of spokesmen for the best interests of the Jewish community, just as the intellectuals who comprised Russian "society" (*obshchestvo*) arrogated to themselves the moral leadership of all Russia. Alternative voices were never heard in public.[27] The Russian public received a steady stream of condemnations directed against the Hasidim, the Yiddish language, "uncivilized rites," and occasionally the Talmud, accompanied by glib assurances that all these negative features of Russian Jewry were being rapidly exterminated by the cleansing power of rapprochement. As evidence of this process at work, the authors offered themselves. In short, members of the Russian Jewish intelligentsia were prone to speak in the name of those whom they did not represent, and to make assurances to Russian society which they could not possibly fulfil.[28] The failure of these assurances, which soon became apparent, produced frustration and disillusionment with Russian society, weaned as it was on simplistic formulas for the resolution of the Jewish Question. The antidote for this frustration proved to be a new simplistic solution, a "golden key": Brafman's depiction of the kahal and its decisive influence on Jewish life. A new resolution for the Jewish Question was proposed: abolish the kahal, end state support for a system of fiscal malfeasance and communal coercion, and the terrible system which impoverished and degraded Christian and Jew alike would wither away.

The Russian Jewish intelligentsia had been asked to do much in the name of rapprochement. They were asked to illumine the dark corners of Jewish life and they had done so, at times to excess in a fervor of youth, inexperience and high expectations. Now educated Jews were

Составъ редакціи одной русской либеральной Кіевской газеты.

Дозволено Цензурою. Кіевъ. 29 Марта 1884 г.

Чѣмъ больше крадутъ и чѣмъ чаще оправдываютъ воровъ и мошенниковъ, тѣмъ для насъ лучше; но все-же совсѣмъ оправдывать уличеннаго и сознавшагося вора въ газетѣ нельзя, а нужно такъ деликатно..... назвать его расптрату «усиленной тратой» и тому подобное. При прежнихъ судахъ негласно, за взятки, втихомолку оправдывали воровъ, такъ что никто объ этомъ незналъ— это была несправедливость, нарушеніе законовъ и мы громко объ этомъ кричали; при теперешнихъ же открыто, гласно оправдываютъ воровъ и мошенниковъ—это прогрессъ, либерализмъ! и мы еще громче будемъ кричать объ этомъ.

26 "The editors of a certain Kiev newspaper." The cartoonist ridicules the liberal newspaper *Zaria* and its many Jewish correspondents. A Star of David hangs on the wall, while Talmud scrolls are heaped in the corner

asked to confirm the existence of something which they knew to be false. Symbolically, young Bratin and Levin repudiated Brafman when they saw the use to which he put their work. Not the traditionalists, but the Russian Jewish intelligentsia took the lead in discrediting Brafman and rejecting all the claims of *The Book of the Kahal*. These activities led editorialists to question the trustworthiness of the Russian Jewish intelligentsia: if they did not know the existence of the kahal, how could their prescriptions for resolving the Jewish Question be given any weight; if they knew of the kahal and would not admit it, were they not an especially devious and dangerous element of the Jewish conspiracy against Russian civilization?[29] Their activity in other areas was equally revealing. The Russian Jewish intelligentsia claimed to be avid supporters of merger, but they took the lead in undermining the efforts made in this direction by the Vilna Commission.[30] Seeing the use to which it was put by Judeophobes, Jewish publicists even began to back away from another golden key in whose existence they had heretofore voiced qualified acceptance, the idea of Jewish economic exploitation.

Judeophobe journalists began to identify a new Jewish enemy. *Kievlianin* observed in 1872:

> Society, the state and the Jews themselves would benefit from a change in the [economic] role of the Jews. It is a task which necessitates the cooperation of the Jews themselves. Not the masses, of course, but those enlightened Jews who appear in their midst and who should be able to rise above simple instinct, exclusivity, narrow national egoism, willfulness and the like ... Unfortunately, their efforts have been characterized by disdain for the facts, apologetics, and by attacks on anybody who views the subject without sentimentality. (111:16/IX/1872)

In 1874 the radical thick journal *Delo* declared:

> In taking up the defense of their nationality, Jewish publicists resort to absurdities and to outrageous falsehoods, denying even criticisms of the dark side of Jewish life which are fully justified ... At the very beginning of public discussion on the Jewish Question, public opinion was apparently quite favorable to the fate of the Jews, but by the end it completely rejects the assumptions of the silly defenses of Jewish publicists. (3:III/1874)

A *Golos* editorial of 1875 announced:

> Defending what are in effect illegal institutions, whenever the question concerns the Jews, Jewish publicists don't answer the question, but start to defend the Jewish religion, to speak about the great worth of talmudic study, about fanaticism of Christians and their medieval prejudices, about the talents and extraordinary abilities of the Jews, and conclude with speeches about humanity, liberalism and the other fruits of contemporary civilization which, however, will only mature when the Jews are granted full and universal rights. (94:4/IV/1875)

The Russian Jewish intelligentsia was painfully aware that they had become the focus of Judeophobe criticism, and that their traditional ways of defending the Jewish masses – accepting the negative impact of external forces over time while predicting an imminent period of education and reform – were no longer adequate. *Den* responded to the changing environment in its very early stages. The circumstance was an *Odesskii vestnik* editorial which conceded that educated Jews displayed none of the features of the fanatical masses. This being so, the editor declared himself at a loss "to explain the solidarity with which they ally themselves with the Jewish masses. They have nothing in common with the rabble. What, for example, does Rothschild have in common with a *factor* [middleman] and that sort?" (84:22/IV/1871).

Den's response was a symbolic death-knell for the assumptions of "natural assimilation." *Odesskii vestnik* had spoken of the need to "reconcile" Christian and Jew. This was impossible when the nature of the dialogue was confined to wild passions, bestial instincts, blind prejudices and crude hatred. The Jews were the barometer of civilization, and their treatment testified to the moral level of society. Clearly, it was Russian society which needed to extend its moral understanding. The Jews, for their part, were the most ready to engage in Russification, and the least likely to receive adequate response from society. Now Jewish publicists were being made the scapegoat of Christian–Jewish antipathy (19:8/V/1871).

Clearly the journalists of *Den* were already demoralized. Their efforts at defending the Jewish masses engendered only crude and violent polemics. Violence had passed from the press to the streets. Russian society, at best, was apathetic to the fate of the Jews. At worst, educated Russians linked all Jews, high and low, enlightened and traditionalist, into a fanciful anti-Christian conspiracy. A proposal by the *Den* editors, led by Orshanskii, that the Odessa Jewish community bring a lawsuit against the pogromshchiki to recover damages was rejected by cautious communal authorities. Isolated internally and externally, the editors surrendered, and the last issue of *Den* appeared on 8 June 1871.[31]

16   The riddle of liberal Judeophobia

Nineteenth-century European liberalism was virtually synonymous with the process of Jewish emancipation. Conversely, Peter Pulzer is only one of many contemporary scholars who characterize European Antisemitism as "the rejection of liberalism."[1] In recognition of this fact, Jews rallied to the cause of political liberalism, and graced liberal parties with their participation and their votes. Other scholarship has detected a worm in the apple, however. A fatal ambivalence, apparent within the broad liberal ideology, made some aspects of liberalism less than sympathetic – if not outrightly hostile – to Jews and Judaism. Arthur Herzberg discovered important Judeophobic elements at the very root of the European Enlightenment movement which was credited with creating the preconditions for Jewish political emancipation.[2] Jacob Katz demonstrated the ease with which representatives of mature liberalism were able to incorporate anti-Jewish prejudices into their ideological systems.[3]

A similar pattern is apparent in Russia. The very first public pronouncement of Russian liberalism espoused the cause of the Jews. In 1853, the great Russian socialist and publicist, Aleksandr Herzen, founded what became the "Free Russian Press" in London, devoted to publishing uncensored and oppositional material about contemporary Russia. Beginning in 1855 Herzen published an occasional series "Voices from Russia," featuring articles from a trio of self-proclaimed Russian liberals, K. D. Kavelin, B. N. Chicherin and N. A. Melgunov.[4] An article published in 1857, "The Contemporary Objectives of Russian Life," set forth the nascent liberal program. The initial item on a list of prerequisites for a liberal society was freedom of conscience, "the first and most sacred right of the citizen."[5] Calling for the end of discrimination against Russian Orthodox Old Believers, the author further noted: "Finally, justice demands that the Jews be relieved of those oppressive restrictions to which they are subjected at the present time, for freedom of conscience is a right from which not one subject of the Russian Empire should be excluded; nobody should suffer for his religious conviction."[6] In the *Illiustratsiia* Affair of 1858, the names of prominent liberals dominated the Literary Protest, which itself was organized by Katkov's *Russkii vestnik*, at the time a leader of liberal opinion. The rest of the liberal press, such as *Odesskii vestnik* in 1858, and *Nashe vremia* in 1862, could also be relied upon to view the Jews with sympathy and good will. By the next century, the party that exemplified political liberalism, the Constitutional Democrats, was willing to defend the Jews at least rhetorically.[7] Their political enemies scornfully derided them as the "Jew-Kadets."

However, another side of Russian liberalism was extremely hostile to the Jews. The leading liberal newspaper of the reign of Alexander II, *Golos*, was notorious for its Judeophobia. In 1872, Rabbi A. Neiman of St. Petersburg actually sent a formal denunciation of the newspaper to the MVD. He claimed that no less than twenty-five issues during that year contained articles about the Jews which violated provisions of the criminal code which forbade incitement against religious or ethnic groups.[8] Sympathetic liberal organs like *Sanktpeterburgskie vedomosti*, were not averse to turning on the Jews at such traumatic moments as the Odessa pogrom of 1871.[9] The key to understanding liberal Judeophobia may be found in the general perspectives of Russian liberalism, and in the specific preoccupations of *Golos*, as the foremost proponent of both liberalism and Judeophobia.

The historian of liberalism in Russia, V. V. Leontovich, summarized it as "a system of individualism, giving the human personality and its rights priority over all else."[10] In Russia, this ensured that liberalism was destructive rather than creative, struggling against anything that threatened the development of individual freedom.[11] This is clear from the program of Russian liberalism advanced in 1857: freedom of conscience, freedom from serfdom, freedom of public opinion, freedom of the press, freedom of education, publicity for all governmental actions and openness of all judicial proceedings.[12] Such a program aimed not only at the destruction of the whole system of tsarist safeguards and restraints on the population, but sought to undermine serfdom, the essential prop of the social and economic system. When the great reforms of the Alexandrine era fulfilled at least part of this agenda, Russian liberalism developed a dual program. On the one hand it sought to preserve what had already been won by safeguarding the reforms and implementing them fully. On the other, liberals endeavored to extend the limits of the permissable. The quintessential liberal hope was that the Tsar would "cap the edifice" of the reforms by granting some form of written constitution.

The first generation of Russian liberals, most of whom were gentry landowners, were keenly aware that one of the greatest obstacles to their dream of a functioning constitutional monarchy lay in the low cultural level of the peasantry. Freedom of the press, speech and assembly were of little use to a vast illiterate and uneducated rural population. Even the most liberal of the great reforms had recognized this reality: side by side with the new court system, fit to stand beside the most advanced Western models, the system of peasant common law endured. The liberal gentry who lived with the peasantry in the countryside did not romanticize them: they were the "dark" masses. As the first liberal publicists put it: "The Russian peasant is the most submissive being in the world; but carried to extremes, he emerges from his meekness and may, if you please, act like a wild beast."[13] Gentry disquiet was shared by the tsarist government, which structured the peasant reform so that the land belonged, not to the individual, but to the peasant commune, which continued to exert pervasive control over peasant life.

For this reason, early Russian liberalism was very peasant-centered, as gentry liberals embarked upon a mission to raise the cultural level of the peasantry. As the archetypal gentry liberal, Ivan Ilich Petrunkevich put it, massive change would be possible only "when the popular mass raised itself to the understanding that it was possible to be not the object, but the subject of state government."[14] A fundamental preoccupation of the liberal movement – widely pursued through the new system of local self-government (the zemstvo) – was the spread of primary education in Russia. Liberals hoped in addition to improve the material conditions of the peasantry and to provide the muzhik with greater access to the judicial system, with its principle of equality before the law. Any phenomena which appeared to retard these objectives was a target for liberal opposition.

When liberal publicists turned to the Jewish Question, they found many analogues to their problems with the peasantry.[15] Jews, like peasants, displayed many negative features, albeit attributed to centuries of persecution, as well as to legal disabilities under which they long had languished in Russia.[16] The most serious aberration in contemporary Jewish life was their irregular economic position, which forced them to engage in activities which were at best unproductive, and at worst represented ruthless exploitation of the local population. Liberal publicists characteristically saw Jewish shortcomings as the

natural result of constraints placed on the marketplace, and confidently predicted that the Jews would cease to be a problem – indeed,
would turn into useful and productive citizens – as soon as the Pale of
Settlement was abolished. With the exception of *Golos*, virtually every
liberal publication called for the immediate abolition of the Pale of
Settlement, on grounds both economic (violation of the free operation
of the marketplace) and humanitarian (violation of the principle of
equal justice before the law).[17] Although a few publications suggested
that abolition alone would suffice to promote the process of *sliianie*
whereby the Jewish Question would be resolved, most also emphasized the need to raise the moral level of the Jews. The Russian peasant
masses were ignorant and superstitious, so why should anyone
assume that the Jewish masses were different? There was some debate
as to whether Jewish fanaticism and isolation, and the Jews' propensity for exploitation, were inculcated through persecution, or whether
they were dogmas of Jewish religious belief, especially as exemplified
by the Talmud.[18] In either case, education would lift the Jews above
their superstitious milieu, and enable them to become good citizens,
and to use their undeniable talents for the good of their Russian
fatherland. All liberal publications, without exception, devoted attention to the problem of Jewish education, at times to the exclusion of all
else. Liberal concern for the enlightenment of the peasantry was
precisely mirrored in concern for the enlightenment of the Jews.

It is difficult to establish a liberal consensus beyond the belief that
the Jews were remediable, that the Pale must be abolished and that the
negative features of Jewish life must be combatted with education.
Few liberal newspapers established a consistent ideological approach
to the Jewish Question beyond these generalities. *Kievskii telegraf*, for
example, took a general editorial position in support of some form of
Jewish emancipation, and then opened its columns to diverse opinions
as to how this might be accomplished. *Birzhevye vedomosti* limited itself
almost entirely to the discussion of educational problems within the
Jewish community. Many liberal papers, like *Deiatelnost*, were too
short-lived to develop a consistent and long-range view of the Jewish
Question. *Sanktpeterburgskie vedomosti*, liberal and Judeophile under
the editorship of V.F. Korsh (1862–74), lost its ideological coloration in
1875. Even during its liberal years, the paper was capable of changes, of
course, as in its famous attack on "Jewish exploitation" as the cause for
the Odessa pogrom of 1871. This incident exemplified the fact that, in
the eyes of liberals, the well-being of the peasantry *always* took prece-
dence over the well-being of the Jews. Even more striking, when the

liberal daily *Novoe vremia* passed into the hands of the renegade liberal A. S. Suvorin in 1876, he transformed it into the foremost Judeophobe newspaper in Russia. Important liberal publications like *Vestnik Evropy* or *Novosti* were slow to discover the Jewish Question, and disinclined to devote much attention to it before the late 1870s, when Judeophobia emerged as a fundamental ingredient of Russian conservatism.[19] The one exception to all these generalizations was *Golos*.

Golos was published from 1863 to 1883/4 by A. A. Kraevskii, who earlier established *Otechestvennye zapiski* as one of the foremost thick journals in Russia. *Golos* was founded with the support of the Minister of Education, A. V. Golovnin. Its brand of moderate reformism, journalistic innovation and excellent sources of information made it exceedingly popular among the intelligentsia. Abroad, it was viewed as the Russian equivalent of *The Times* of London. After V. A. Bilbasov joined Kraevskii as coeditor in 1871, the paper became livelier, and gradually acquired an oppositionist character as the great reforms increasingly came under attack. Kraevskii himself was a founding member of the OPE, and *Golos* might have been expected to be broadly sympathetic to Jews.

It was not, instead passing from a vague neutrality to active Judeophobia. This evolution becomes more explicable in the light of the specific concerns which illuminated *Golos'* general liberal orientation. The guiding ideal for Russian society, as proclaimed in the first issue of *Golos* was *sliianie*, here used in the sense of the "integration" of Russian society. This process of integration encompassed Russia's sociojudicial classes (*soslovie*), joining them into a common community by breaking down traditional legal and social barriers. Thus, the all-class zemstvo, the all-class jury system, the all-class municipal duma, and military service based upon universal conscription were all applauded. An editorial in the inaugural issue (1/I/1863), explained: "The reforms do not deprive the higher classes of their rights; they take from them only their privileges which, by virtue of the very transformations that are leading to the integration of the estates and the equalization of their rights, lose all meaning and value. Precisely here begins the real activity of society."[20]

But *sliianie* had an additional aspect: just as Russia's estates were to be moulded into an integral society, so too the Empire's non-Russian nationalities should be blended into an integral nation. The culmination of this process would be an integrated social and national organism, the Russian civic body (*grazhdanstvo*). The mechanics of integration involved the removal of all legal barriers between estates, and of all privileges or disabilities which set off one nationality from another. As the group most bound by special regulations of this sort, the Jews were a regular target for the attention of *Golos* editorialists. *Golos* defined the problem in a lengthy series of eighteen articles, running from May to July of 1863, the first year of its publication. The author, in a detailed review of Russian legislation on the Jews, lamented an absence of consistency and order. The Jews were treated variously as an estate (*soslovie*), a religious community and an ethnic corporation. The resultant legal system gave rise to a situation that contradicted *Golos'* ideal of *sliianie* in two regards: the Jews were treated as a special ethnic group, distinct from Russian society as a whole, and as an estate within an estate (132:28/V/1863). The rules and regulations for the Jews lacked any uniformity, as they not only discriminated against the Jews but also granted them privileges in the form of communal autonomy, a further violation of *Golos'* view of a well-ordered state.

Golos' initial portrait of the Jews was far from sympathetic, characterizing them as backward, fanatical and exploitative. The only mitigating factor was the role played in this by persecution through the ages. Some of Judaism's negative elements, however, were seen as innate. As a moral system, Judaism was far inferior to Christianity. Even if the Talmud as a whole did not retard good relations between Jew and gentile, individual tracts "inspired hatred toward the followers of Christ and Mary." While Jews as a whole did not practice ritual murder, "it is no way unbelievable that among the followers of the Mosaic teaching are to be found their own kind of fanatics" (188:23/VII/1863).

While *Golos* did open its pages to the debate on reform of the Jewish school system, it remained cool to the liberal panacea that the Jewish Question could be resolved quickly and expeditiously through the spread of education and enlightenment among the Jewish masses (246:19/IX/1863). *Golos* was virtually the only liberal publication which rejected the immediate abolition of the Pale of Settlement, at a time when even conservative critics of Jewry were abolitionists. *Golos'* contribution to the debate was highly qualified: "Our view on the right of Jews to settle in this or that locale is that one must consider the condition of their domestic and public life, the possible advantages of their resettlement, and also the contemporary religious and judicial situation of Christian society" (149:14/VI/1863).

The Polish uprising, and attendant questions of Russification, caused *Golos* to become briefly more sympathetic to the Jews. As early as the summer of 1863 a *Golos* editorial noted, with apparent approval, that more humane treatment of the Jews by Polish society had caused the former to rally to the Polish side. This phenomenon had obvious implications for Jews outside the Kingdom of Poland (146:11/VI/1863). Following the August 1865 decree admitting Jewish artisans into the Russian interior, *Golos* editorials hailed the approaching end of the Jewish Question. The decree had taken the proper approach, permitting the departure of those who were engaged in productive work. Their emigration would create openings for Jews heretofore supported by unproductive petty trade, middleman activity or by no profession at all (199:2/VIII/1865). Even a small out-migration would make the Jews collectively more productive, since the Pale was insufficiently large to support a total population in which the Jews comprised more than 8 percent (228:19/VIII/1865). The Pale was not only too restrictive for the Jews, but it obstructed Russification. The outright abolition of the Pale was an inescapable prerequisite to "giving the cities of the western region a purely Russian character." Full civil rights for Jews, in short, would serve Russification (230:21/VIII/1865).

This was as close as *Golos* came for two decades in calling for the abolition of the Pale and it soon gave way to a mood of pessimism when the reform failed to produce immediate results. Why did the Jews not depart the western regions for the interior? a *Golos* editorial asked in 1866. Because it was a "golden Russian Colchis," "a second Palestine," in which they could happily be "leeches on the state organism." "The pursuit of one's personal interest at all costs can be tolerated when it is the activity of a single individual, but the matter takes on a different significance when this exploitation is conducted by a whole, isolated caste, the more so by an entire race, standing in isolation due to its religious, fanatical elements" (247:7/IX/1866). *Golos'* concern was not so much the lack of mobility of the Jews as the fear that they were dominating the economically weak and underdeveloped peasantry. As *Golos* claimed, not even Jewish publicists denied the reality of exploitation. What made the paper's criticism still more serious, however, was the new claim that the causes of exploitation should not be sought exclusively in external conditions, as the paper had previously accepted. "It is no less tactless, in our opinion, to seek the cause of the very unpleasant relations between the Jewish race and the inhabitants of the area exclusively in external conditions, and not to recognize the existence of many of these causes, and hardly the least important, in the very depths of the Jewish race" (258:18/IX/1866). Additional articles emphasized Jewish exploitation of the peasantry in post-Napoleonic Germany and in contemporary Galicia, making numerous analogies to Russian conditions (276–9:6–9/X/1866).

The reality of Jewish exploitation argued against the further extension of civil rights for Jews, especially given the unequal level of economic and moral development between peasants and Jews. As *Golos* editorialized in 1867:

> The Jews, of course, will be happy to use all the rights given them; they do not understand rapprochement with the Christian population in any other form; but there is still no evidence by which one could judge that they won't use these rights for bad purposes, or that they will be willing and able to bear equal state and social burdens, along with the native population. (26:26/I/1867)

This editorial demonstrated a growing tendency for *Golos* writers to place responsibility for abnormal relations between gentiles and Jews on the latter. The author specifically rejected religious intolerance, historical conditions or persecution as causal factors. Jewish exclusivity derived from the theocratic side of the primordial Jewish state, which had rejected any dealings with non-Jews in order to ensure its survival. "Where there are gathered several Jews, there is the Kingdom of Israel, there too reigns the talmudic kingdom, with all its harmful and ugly institutions, the *mikva, heder, klaus* and the like, completely removed from the spirit of the times and contemporary social conditions, remaining unchanged to the present day" (26:26/I/1867).

Golos was not yet entirely under the spell of Iakov Brafman. There was no hint of class division within the Jewish community and, more to the point, *Golos* was still ready to give credence to the views of the Russian Jewish intelligentsia. "Leading Jews are not only hostile to the dead decrees of Talmudism, but to the racial isolation of the Jews. They believe that the exclusion of the Jews from Christianity harms the brilliant role which the Jews might have been expected to play, given their past and the favor of God. Speaking as a neutral, these Jewish radicals are right" (273:3/X/1869). Sympathy for Jewish intellectuals in their struggle with obscurantism came naturally to *Golos*. Many of its correspondents on the Jewish Question were Jewish converts to Christianity or Jews active in the state-sponsored Jewish school system. Their lonely battle had obvious parallels with the struggle of the Russian intelligentsia against the "powers of darkness" in their own society.

On the other hand, there were numerous factors which predisposed *Golos* to embrace the doctrines of Brafman when they appeared. There was a deep fear and suspicion of the dark Jewish masses, and disdain for corporatism as an obstacle to integration. There was the paper's existing awareness of the kahal, noted above, as well as its willingness to listen to self-proclaimed specialists on the Jewish Question. *Golos* formally announced its conversion in 1870 in an article entitled ominously, "The Force of the Kahal" (110:22/IV/1870). The editorial asked why "relations of Jewish society, with or without rights, with the surrounding non-Jewish population are everywhere one and the same?" The answer, *Golos* announced, had been shown by Brafman, "on the basis of indisputable documents," to lie in the kahal, the municipal talmudic republic. On the strength of Brafman's evidence, the emancipation of the Jews without the prior abolition of the kahal was a deadly gamble.

Brafman's theories were irresistible to the ideologues of *Golos*. The newspaper had never been able to develop a satisfactory program toward the Jewish Question because of conflicting loyalties. Concern for the welfare of the peasant masses made *Golos* reluctant to grant full emancipation to the Jews, even though this clashed with the ideals of political and economic liberalism. The small number of Jewish publicists who appeared in *Golos* – to say nothing of the experience of the Jews in Western Europe – demonstrated the capability of Jews for enlightened civilization. Conversely, the still benighted masses demonstrated the failure of education to date, and the remoteness of a swift resolution of the Jewish Question on liberal principles. Now a new solution presented itself, even if it required a certain amount of ideological adjustment. Criticism was shifted from the "dark Jewish masses," now revealed as mere pawns in a grander scheme, to the small kahal elite.[21]

This editorial shift had a corollary. *Golos*' "enlightened" Jewish publicists were aghast at Brafman's charges, and publicly rejected them. They acknowledged the fanaticism and backwardness of Russian Jewry, but denied any idea of a world-wide conspiracy. As noted above, members of the Jewish intelligentsia were willing at times to denigrate Orthodox Judaism, but they could not share Brafman's fantasies, which they knew to be false. Enlightened Jews, the one group with the knowledge to do so, refused to provide the legitimizing imprimatur for *The Book of the Kahal*. As "kahalomania" gained ascendancy, typified by *Golos*' unsympathetic treatment of the Odessa pogrom of 1871, *Golos* became a newspaper to which no self-respecting Jew could contribute (115:27/IV/1871). *Golos*, for its part, now turned on the Jewish intelligentsia, complaining that their mission was obviously to denounce Russians for medieval fanaticism, while praising everything Jewish as touched with genius. "They [Jewish intellectuals] collect filth, not in order to clean up the hut, but in order to throw it in the face of the master" (216:6/VIII/1876).

There were compensations for breaking old alliances and contracting a new one with Iakov Brafman. Whereas the Jewish Question had previously appeared to be intractable, Brafman's theories provided a quick fix. According to Brafman, the Russian government need only remove legal sanction from the special privileges enjoyed by the kahal under the pretext of religious freedom. For example, the Russian government assisted the communal system of ritual slaughtering, a prerequisite for the restricting dietary rules of *kashrut*, by attaching it to the system of taxation. This self-same system allowed the kahal leadership to control the masses, isolated Jews from Christian society, and gave huge discretionary revenues to the kahal. The government-approved tax on kosher meat, the basket tax, while apparently an effective tax collection system, provided the kahal leadership with the means to undermine and circumvent the intentions of the government at every turn.

This was precisely a form of argument calculated to appeal to *Golos'* editors. Special forms of taxation for the Jews, as well as the vestigial elements of communal autonomy, were examples of *soslovie* exclusivity which *Golos* was sworn to combat. There was a remarkable symmetry between *Golos'* previous characterization of the Jews as a "*soslovie* in a *soslovie*" and Brafman's celebrated description of the kahal as a "*corpus in corpore.*" The crowning glory was the efficiency with which the whole problem might be remedied. It was not necessary to wait generations while education slowly worked its wonders, but only to abolish special Jewish institutions. With this simple legislative act, the Jewish Question would largely disappear. Such a proposal had the added advantage, in contrast to the proposed abolition of the Pale, of not threatening the underdeveloped peasant masses with exploitation from Jews freed from governmental oversight and control.

Identifying those elements of the "municipal talmudic republic" which had to be eliminated led *Golos* into repeated attacks on the Talmud, denouncing it as a "code of political teachings, directed against Christianity in general, and against any Christian social order in particular" (191:7/XI/1872). Such beliefs led to very illiberal extremes: "Religious toleration holds only so far as religious beliefs do not contradict the aspirations of the state. But when a religion preaches hate of everything Christian, the government may take it in hand, and control the propagandization of its laws" (191:7/XI/1872). *Golos* actually called for the prohibition of public worship by Jews, in parallel with a similar ban on Russian Orthodox sectarians, such as the *Molkane*, classified by the law as "pernicious." *Golos* denied for a time the fundamental tenet of liberal hopes for Jewish reform, that education could transform Jews into good and useful citizens of the Russian state. "We can declare it impossible, given the present state of the Jews, and we deny it even when they affirm that it can be accomplished through education. We are ready to agree that education, to a certain degree, can abolish the roughness of fanatical intolerance, but it cannot abolish religious belief, or the Jews would cease to be Jews" (212:28/XI/1872). This was a declaration which would have been fully accepted by Ivan Aksakov.

Golos' Judeophobia grew more articulate still when Brafman joined the paper as a regular contributor. His work was seldom signed and not until 1874 did an article appear that bore all of his distinctive touches, although a series of attacks on the OPE were almost certainly inspired by him, if they did not come from his own pen (164:15/VI/ 1873). His article surveyed attempts by Russian Jews to evade military service, a special concern of Brafman, who served as a consultant to the committee which drafted the military recruitment statute of 1874. Brafman noted that ablebodied Jews were fleeing abroad to escape service, with the assistance of Jewish groups abroad. The Alliance Universelle had even held a secret meeting in Berlin to plan its response to the new law. For Jews who remained, recruitment was complicated by the disorderly state of communal vital statistics (279:9/ X/1874).

This overt attack on the Alliance Universelle drew a protest from its president, Adolphe Crémieux. He denied that the Jewish religion encouraged Jews to avoid military service, quoting the Talmud that "the law of the state is the highest law." He pointed out that Jews had proven valiant and conscientious soldiers in Europe, where they were treated equally (i.e., where they could become officers). Crémieux hotly denied that the Alliance encouraged or assisted evasion of the law. The organization existed, he explained, to combat religious persecution, through legal involvement in court cases and through publicity, and to assist Jews in need, as during the Kovno famine in 1869 (94:4/IV/1875).

On the occasion of Crémieux's visit to St. Petersburg in 1869, as representative of the Alliance, *Golos* had published an ambivalent editorial, praising the Jewish "radicals" who rejected the "dead decrees of Talmudism," but suggesting that Russia was not Romania and Alliance meddling of a political nature was not welcome. None-theless, the editorial concluded, if Crémieux displayed tact and avoided politics, his visit could have a very useful effect (273:3/X/1869). Now, six years later, Crémieux's interjection gave Brafman the oppor-tunity to publish an editorial illustrating all of his favorite themes, with evidence readily at hand. Crémieux's letter was typical of Jewish publicists who

> as usual don't answer the question itself, but begin to defend the Jewish religion, speaking of the great worth of talmudic study, about Christian fanaticism and medieval prejudices, about the talents and extraordinary abilities of the Jews, before passing on to speeches about humaneness, liberalism, and the other fruits of contemporary civilization which will mature only with the grant to Jews of full and universal equal rights. (94:4/IV/1875)

Brafman rejected Crémieux's citations from the Talmud, reminding his readers that it was a chaotic mess, from which any opinion could be confirmed. As for Crémieux's claim that the Alliance was above poli-tics, and that the diversity of national groups within it prevented the emergence of a uniform program, Brafman offered evidence to the contrary. Could the Alliance's notes to the Great Powers in 1868 concerning the situation in Romania be considered anything but poli-tical intervention? Crémieux's trip to St. Petersburg in 1869 was not intended to help famine victims, but to sabotage the work of the Vilna Jewish Commission, and to "paralyze and repress the voice of a dangerous member of this Commission, a Jewish convert to Ortho-doxy, who was not deterred from exposing the dark side of Jewish life [i.e. Iakov Brafman]." This trip was followed by a campaign organized by the Alliance in America to convince American president U. S. Grant that Jews were being persecuted for their religion. This was followed by an Alliance meeting in Berlin in 1874 to deal with the threat posed to the Jews of Russia by the imposition of universal military service. As for the diversity of opinion within the Alliance, let Crémieux's own words, from a speech in 1869, serve as a refutation: "We are brothers, we are all children of one nation, we are not French, nor the divided Germans. We all have one heart – Israelite."

Having attacked the Alliance Universelle, Brafman assailed the body which he considered its Russian branch, the OPE. In an 1876 *feuilleton* entitled "The Jesuits of Jewry," he branded the Society's publication, *The World-Outlook of the Talmudists*, a whitewash of the true nature of the Talmud. This led to a condemnation of Jewish intellectuals in general:

The difference between Jews trained in the Talmud and Jews receiving a general education, lies only in the following: those trained in the Talmud await the restoration of the Judaic kingdom suddenly, unexpectedly, without Jewish participation, by some miracle; educated Jews preach that the restoration of the Judaic kingdom will occur naturally, and that Jews ought to prepare for it by means of education, which will give the nation good generals, engineers, lawyers and in general, people necessary for the restoration and fullest existence of the state. (117:28/IV/1876)

As a final coup, Brafman cited a speech given by the respected secretary of the OPE, L. O. Gordon.[22] Brafman's article was thus a contribution to two ongoing phenomena, a growing Talmudophobia in the Russian press, and an increased disenchantment with the Jewish intelligentsia. After 1876, Brafman's brief ascendancy began to wane. In 1877, only one article bore his mark, a description of Christian missionary activities among Russian Jews (75:16/III/1877).

Golos was beginning to turn away from its strident Judeophobia even before Brafman's death at the end of 1879. Gessen identifies this change with the addition of N. I. Bakst to the editorial board.[23] The turn began with a period of neglect, the Jewish Question virtually vanishing from the pages of Golos in 1878. When discussions resumed in 1879, many phenomena had emerged to make Judeophobia disreputable. The issue of Jewish emancipation was very much in the news, because articles of the Treaty of Berlin, which concluded the Russo-Turkish War of 1878–9, provided for the extension of civil rights in newly independent Romania. In Germany, on the other hand, the antisemitic movement, now given a name by Wilhelm Marr, appeared with a new assertiveness and aggressiveness. Golos increasingly found that its sympathies lay with the largely liberal opponents of German Antisemitism.

Events in Russia did still more to discourage liberal Judeophobia. The middle 1870s marked the rise of "occult Judeophobia," characterized by attacks on the Talmud by thoroughly disreputable publicists, and accusations of Jewish ritual murder (which years before Golos was willing to consider). The campaign culminated in a celebrated ritual murder trial in the Georgian town of Kutais. Golos covered the trial in detail, and warmly greeted the verdict of acquittal. Nor was Golos any longer alone as the chief Jew-baiter among the representatives of the "prestige" press. Under the direction of A. S. Suvorin, the St. Petersburg daily Novoe vremia made virulent Judeophobia a fundamental editorial principle, welcoming the Kutais ritual murder trial, and attributing the growing revolutionary movement to the Jews. In addition, *Novoe vremia* was a leading ideological opponent of *Golos*-style liberalism. Any discomfiture which *Golos* felt at finding itself in such strange company was reinforced when distinguished European publications, such as *The Times* of London, began a campaign to discredit Russia and the Russian press because of their "persecution of the Jews."[24]

With these incentives, from 1880 to 1884, when it ceased publication, *Golos* was more sympathetic to the Jews. The paper patched up its quarrel with the Jewish intelligentsia, symbolized by the welcome which *Golos* extended to the new Jewish newspaper, *Russkii evrei*, in 1879 (210:31/VII/1879). Editorials began at last to call for full civil rights for the Jews and the removal of the Pale of Settlement, ironically on the eve of the 1881 pogroms which caused other newspapers to rethink this prescription (48:17/II/1880; 76:16/III/1880).

Golos thus adopted a remedy just as it was being abandoned by others. This was a fittingly ironic end to the pre-pogrom relationship of Russian liberalism and the Jewish Question, as Russia entered a period when both liberalism and Judeophilia became discredited ideologies.

17 The crystallization of conservative Judeophobia

Although Russian conservatism was the philosophy which provided the ideological underpinning of the modern Russian Empire until 1917, it remains a comparatively unknown phenomenon. A precise enumeration of its distinguishing characteristics has proved especially elusive. Hans Rogger draws attention to "the diversity of Russian conservatism, the paralyzing tensions with which it was afflicted within itself and *vis-à-vis* the state" as perhaps its most distinctive features and the reason for its political and intellectual weakness.[1]

In an effort to identify the common foundation of Russian conservatism, Richard Pipes casts his net wide to characterize it as "an ideology which advocates for Russia an authoritarian government subject to restraints neither by formal law nor by an elected legislature, but only of such limitations as it sees fit to impose on itself."[2] In the second half of the nineteenth century, Pipes observes, conservatism was shaped by the post-emancipation debate over the future of Russia. Conservatism acquired a special orientation after the appearance of Russian Nihilism. "To Russian conservatives of the 1860s and 1870s the 'nihilist' is not merely a passing phenomenon but the symptom of all that is wrong with Western culture in general and with Russian Westernism in particular ... In the most general case, post-1860 Russian conservatism is a theory of anti-nihilism, an attempt to provide an alternative to the frightening specter that Chernyshevsky's 'new man' has raised before Russian society."[3] In this way conservatism became a theory of change, abandoning its past commitment to the status quo, embodied in gentry conservatism's ideal of harmony between autocracy and the nobility. Conservatism became anti-elitist, replacing the old ties with one linking the autocracy and the common people. This transformation was accompanied by the abandonment of conservative cosmopolitanism and its replacement with nationalist and xenophobic predilections.[4]

Pipes' paradigm of the new conservatism as a theory of "anti-nihilism" offers a convenient starting point to consider how Judeophobia became a constituent element of Russian conservatism. Early gentry conservatives, both in and out of the Pale, were largely indifferent to the Jewish Question. Intelligentsia conservatism, which represented the next stage of conservative development, was not automatically Judeophobic in its preliminary stage. Representatives like Ivan Aksakov and Fedor Dostoevskii both had a Judeophile phase, and the leading conservative spokesman M. N. Katkov never became a Judeophobe at all.[5] Yet there is no question that Judeophobia and Antisemitism became essential components of pre-revolutionary conservatism. What was the process by which Judeophobia became integrated into Russian conservative thought?

Slavophiles and Pan-Slavs

Slavophilism and Pan-Slavism were the most articulate and influential conservative ideologies of the second half of the nineteenth century in Russia.[6] Historians of both movements have addressed the problem of how they developed strains of chauvinism in general, and Judeophobia in particular. Vladimir Solovev detected a logical progression in this process: "The worship of one's own people as the preeminent bearer of universal truth; then the worship of this people as an elemental force, irrespective of universal truth; finally the worship of those national limitations and anomalies which separate the people from civilized mankind, that is, the worship of one's own people with a direct negation of the very idea of universal truth."[7] Stephen Lukashevich, biographer of Ivan Aksakov, takes as his starting point the observation of N. Berdyaev (Berdaev) that "the Russian people, because of its polarized nature and its messianic consciousness, shows certain similarities to the Jews."[8] Moving from Aksakov in particular to the Slavophiles as a whole, Lukashevich conjectures that

> Slavophilism was based on a belief in the particular virtues of the Slavic race; yet what race was more attached to the cultivation of its particular virtues than the Jews? The Slavophiles viewed the Russians as a chosen people with a mission to fulfill in the world – the Jews also believed that they were a chosen people and had a long tradition of messianic prophecies. For the Jews religion was the essence of their nationality – for the Slavophiles, the words Orthodox and Russian were interchangeable. The Slavophiles dreamed of a peasant commune based on Orthodox principles, but the Jews already had communities ruled by their religious leaders. Finally, the

Slavophiles preached Slavic solidarity at a time when Jewish solidarity was proverbial in Russia. From this brief comparison one can see that the Jewish way of life had a great deal in common with the Slavophiles' vision of the future Russian society. There is, however, not enough room for two in any fantasy, and this is why, perhaps, Slavophilism was potentially antisemitic. Besides, the similarity between the basic striving of Slavophilism and Judaism were conducive to antagonism and hatred.[9]

In his numerous examinations of Russian Antisemitism, Shmuel Ettinger also emphasized the role of the Slavophiles in introducing hatred for the Jews into Russian intellectual life. Ettinger sought to identify Judeophobic strains in the thought of the early Slavophiles, especially that of A. S. Khomiakov, one of the founding fathers of Slavophilism. This view conflicts with those of a number of specialists on Slavophilism. Nicholas Riasanovsky argues that

Khomiakov was not at all antisemitic. He believed that the Jews were an Iranian tribe,[10] as attested above all by their great religion, and that they had made at the time of the Old Testament a most important contribution to humanity, but he thought that by denying Christ they had denied their own tradition, and had thus terminated the creative period of their history ... Anti-Semitism acquired a definite place in the Slavophile ideology only after the death of the early Slavophiles.[11]

Similarly, Andrzej Walicki notes that, for Khomiakov, only Israel in the pre-Christian world remained faithful to pure Iranian principles. The religion of the Israelites – the first monotheistic faith – was a pure expression of the inspired spirit of freedom. For Walicki, "in classical Slavophilism antisemitism had no place."[12]

Ettinger's argument is based on a number of comments which Khomiakov made regarding the Jews. In notes unpublished in his lifetime he observed that "a Jew, after Christ's coming, is no more than a living contradiction, which has no reasonable excuse for existence; therefore he has no meaning in history."[13] (This statement was cited by Ivan Aksakov in his *Den* article discussed above.) In his article "On the Possibility of a Russian School of Art," published in the Slavophile periodical *Moskovskii sbornik* in 1847, Khomiakov said of Rothschild that

he is not obligated to chance circumstances or a lucky turn of mind for a family which contains a hundred millionaires or for his right to be considered a financial power: his financial power recalls the whole history and religion of his race. Here is a people, without a fatherland who hold in hereditary succession the mercantile spirit of ancient Palestine, especially with its love of earthly gain, which made it impossible for them to recognize the messiah in poverty and abasement.[14]

It was no accident that one of the greatest philosophers of all time, Spinoza, was a Jew. The logic that underlay Judaism, with its vague monotheism, ensured that once it rejected Christ, it must move in the direction of either anthropomorphism or Spinoza's pantheism.[15]

In excerpted form, Khomiakov's ideas appear far sharper than they do in context. Khomiakov was not concentrating on the Jews; rather he was illustrating how different national characters respond in different ways to external stimuli. Besides Rothschild, the symbol of Jewish financial prowess, and Spinoza, the flawed genius of modern pantheist philosophy, Khomiakov cited the plethora of Jewish musicians and writers (although they were all faulted for displaying "something false in feeling and sense"). In similar fashion, he attributed the lack of Jewish sculptors and painters to their lack of regard for the earthly form of man.[16] Khomiakov, as a devout Christian, considered his culture superior to that of the Jews. His discussion of them in his works, however, was less an attempt to condemn them than to use them as the most obvious demonstration of persistence of national character.

For Khomiakov and the other founders of Slavophilism, the Jews did not represent a contemporary social problem, but a philosophical construct, an abstraction in the clash of ideas. Khomiakov's conception of the Jews – or more properly, the Hebrews – as an Iranian people, or the inclination of Spinoza for Pantheism as a consequence of his Jewish forebears' rejection of the New Testament, had nothing to do with contemporary Jews as such, and still less with the Jewish Question. Insofar as the early Slavophiles had influence, it was through the second generation of the movement. Ettinger argues that "the antisemitic propaganda of the Slavophile circles wielded considerable influence" in the 1860s and after.[17] This statement, which can only refer to second-generation leaders such as Iurii Samarin and Ivan Aksakov, requires some qualification. Samarin's "influence" – he was in fact hardly ever cited by Judeophobe propagandists – was derived from German Antisemitism, and was hardly "Slavophile" in origin at all. Aksakov, who made use of Khomiakov's ruminations about the Jews in his own Judeophobe works, appears to constitute a more direct link, although his Judeophobe biases also suggest German influence. But any consideration of Aksakov must differentiate between the Slavophile and Pan-Slav phases of his career.

Pan-Slavism has also at times been blamed for the spread of Judeo-phobia in Russia. In contrast to the complex philosophizing which underlay the Slavophile movement – and which made it so inaccessible to the general public – Pan-Slavism was an ideology permeated by action and active politics. The closest Pan-Slavism had to a prophet was Nikolai Danilevskii, whose *Russia and Europe* first appeared in 1869. Like Khomiakov's *Notes*, it was an exercise in universal history, and Jews made frequent appearances in its pages. Danilevskii's central theory was that of "historico-cultural types," national peculiarities as distinct as different styles of painting or architecture. Progress occurred through the organic growth and development of individual types. To Danilevskii's day there had been ten varieties of civilization in history, and the Slavic peoples constituted the eleventh. Some civilizations were multifaceted, with achievements in a variety of cultural spheres, while others were mono-elemental. A prime example of the latter case was the Jews, whose genius lay in "vital religious consciousness and awareness," and whose political life was so weak that they "nowhere manifest the slightest impulse to join a specific political group."[18]

Danilevskii reserved a special place for the new, eleventh cultural type to be created by Slavdom under the leadership of Russia. Russia had already demonstrated the unique talent to be active in all aspects of human culture, especially the religious and social. The Slavs had a special ability to understand and assimilate the achievements of other historico-cultural types, and were close to the ideal of "universal humanity." Danilevskii's utopian vision might have portended a clash between the gifted Slavs and the Jews, who claimed the highest development of the religious idea. In fact, the construct of Danilevskii's thought ensured that this was not the case. The achievements of each historico-cultural type, although not the type itself, could be assimilated by any other historico-cultural type. Types in the decline of their organic cycle presented no rivalry or danger to an ascendent type. Thus the unique status of the Jews could easily be appropriated by the young, fresh and creative Slavs. Danilevskii, in fact, noted that the Slavs were the true inheritors of the status of a Chosen People.[19] As in the case of the Slavophiles, philosophical Pan-Slavism had little regard for the Jews as a living component of the Russian Empire, and was unconcerned with the contemporary Jewish Question. As with Slavo-philism, it is difficult to establish an inevitable conjunction of Pan-Slavism with Judeophobia: Ivan Aksakov, the most ardent Pan-Slav of all, was a leading Judeophobe; K. Pobedonostsev became a Judeophobe after he rejected Pan-Slavism, and the Pan-Slav publicist Katkov never became a Judeophobe at all.

Nevertheless, the heyday of Russian Pan-Slavism, the period of the Eastern Crisis of 1875–79, was also a period of growing conservative Judeophobia. Objective circumstances did not "cause" conservative Judeophobia, but provided fertile ground for the growth of native concerns and prejudices, with the addition of foreign elements. Conservative reactions to the economic changes which followed the peasant emancipation especially lent themselves to this process. In the village, the destruction of the mythical harmony of the peasant commune was attributed to the "Yid-kulak." Partisans devoted to the welfare of the Russian landholding nobility lamented the destructive economic role of "Yid-banks," and warned of the wholesale transfer of gentry land into "Yid hands." The transformation of the countryside was only a part of the advent of capitalism in Russia, and for some conservative ideologues the Jews were the very embodiment of the "disruptive modernity" of capitalism. Heinz-Dietrich Löwe has perceptively characterized conservative Judeophobia as a "reactionary utopia." He argues that the Jews served as a social class against which one could mobilize support for the conservative cause. The target was not "real" Jews – who were largely starvelings, harmed rather than helped by the advent of industrialization – but the image of the Jews as the outriders (*Vorreiter*) of a capitalist economic system destined to lead to political democratization and parliamentarianism. Löwe attributes this conservative perception of the Jews as the catalyst in the destruction of the old agrarian system to their distinctive social structure. Jewish overrepresentation in trade and crafts was in sharp contrast to the occupational pyramid of the gentile population.[20] Löwe is mistaken only in dating the emergence of this "reactionary utopia" to the very end of the nineteenth century. By this time conservative Judeophobia was certainly in full flower. Nonetheless, its integration into conservative thought was well under way at least a decade earlier, making it harder to tie Judeophobia directly to the actual, rather than the anticipated, consequences of vigorous capitalism. The peculiarities of conservative Judeophobia suggest a variety of sources. The obsession of Russian conservatives with the ritual murder accusation, which runs through conservative thought from Dostoevski, Giliarov-Platonov and Pobedonostsev to the Russian authors of the Beilis Affair from 1911 to 1913, is a case in point. Ritual murder had little to do with emergent capitalism, and much to do with the occult tradition of Judeophobia which flourished in Russia in the 1870s, and the popular superstition on which it was based. In other circumstances, the occult and the anti-capitalist themes could mesh, as in the myths of the "Golden International" and the international Jewish conspiracy directed toward world domination. Four general sets of events, divided between the foreign and the domestic, helped to bring about the crystallization of conservative Judeophobia in the 1870s. They were the "Eastern Question," the emergence of "Nihilism," the flood of Jews into Russian public education, and the rise of an articulate antisemitic movement in Central Europe.

The Eastern Question

"The Eastern Question" was shorthand for the complex involvement of the Great Powers in the Balkan Peninsula and the Ottoman Empire which culminated in the Russo-Turkish War of 1877–78 and the reorganization of the Balkan states at the Congress of Berlin in 1878. Russia had long been involved in this strategic region. Russia's geo-political interests were given ideological justification by the Pan-Slavs, who emphasized common cultural and religious links between Russia and the Balkan Slavs. Although the Pan-Slavs differed on many points, they usually shared the dream of a southeastern Europe liberated from Turkish influence and linked under the bene-volent hegemony of Russia. What had begun as a cultural movement attained political dimensions in the 1870s under the leadership of M. Katkov and I. Aksakov. They advocated a more aggressive Russian role in Balkan affairs. After a series of revolts against the Turks began in Bosnia-Herzegovenia and embroiled independent Serbia in war with the Ottoman Empire, the Pan-Slavs urged Russian intervention and organized a private supply of volunteers and war material. Under intense pressure from public opinion, itself influenced by Pan-Slav propaganda, Alexander II entered the war against the Turks in 1877. After an unexpectedly difficult campaign, beset by organizational and supply difficulties, a series of Russian victories forced the Turks to accept the harsh Treaty of San Stefano (31 January 1878). The treaty virtually drove the Turks from Europe and created a large indepen-dent Bulgaria, presumably to become a Russian protectorate. The San Stefano treaty was too great a threat to the regional balance of power to be tolerated by Russia's Balkan rivals. They forced Russia to agree to a European congress which met in Berlin in June and July of 1878, and considerably revised the peace treaty, to Russia's disadvantage.[21] The Pan-Slav leadership was outraged. Ivan Aksakov publicly denounced

27 A. E. Landau

the Berlin treaty as "nothing other than an open conspiracy against the Russian people, a conspiracy with the participation of the very representatives of Russia!" Aksakov was exiled from Moscow for his audacity, and the principal Pan-Slav agency, the Moscow Slavonic Benevolent Society was closed down.[22]

At first glance, there was nothing in these events which had a direct link with the Jews. Initially the Russian Jewish leadership, like Russian society in general, enthusiastically supported the Balkan Slavs and Russian intervention. Jews were not absent from the ranks of Pan-Slav journalists. *Russkii mir*, the fiercely nationalistic newspaper briefly edited by General M. G. Cherniaev, before he departed to command the Serbian army, counted three Jews on its staff. *Novoe vremia*, edited by A. S. Suvorin from 29 February 1876, became one of Russia's most successful and popular newspapers through its coverage of the Russo-Turkish War.[23] Before it made Judeophobia a journalistic staple, it counted on its staff some of the best known Jewish journalists of the day, including L. O. Levanda and A. E. Landau. According to the memoirist A. Kaufman, M. I. Kulisher wrote almost half of the daily articles in *Novoe vremia* in support of the Slavs.[24] The young Kaufman himself published a brochure in Odessa in 1876 in which he pledged the support of Russian Jewry for the Slavic cause.[25] The Russian volunteer force which fought in Serbia included a number of Jews. The heroics of one of them, D. A. Goldshtein, were well-publicized in the Russian press and were praised by Cherniaev himself.[26] The liberal newspaper *Novosti*, edited by the converted Jew, O. K. Notovich, continually emphasized the role of Jewish soldiers in the subsequent Russo-Turkish War. The press gave prominence to the charitable efforts of Jews in war relief. The state rabbi of Odessa, S. Schwabacher, collected 1,143 rubles for war relief, and expressed the hope that it would demonstrate that, outside the synagogue walls, "Jews are Russians and wish to be recognized as such" (*Novorossiiskii telegraf*, 474:29/VIII/1876). The columns of *Vilenskii vestnik* were filled with appeals from Jews to their brothers to support actively the Slavic cause (153:21/VII/1876; 168:11/VIII/1876; 179:25/VIII/1876).

Yet Simon Dubnov had a valid point when he wrote in 1891 that "the roots of contemporary Russian Antisemitism took hold in the epoch of the last Russo-Turkish War – a fact having not only a chronological significance, but including something deep, fatal, psychologically irresistible."[27] The mobilization of the Russian army for war with the Turks was roughly contemporary with the tightening of recruitment procedures for the Jews, a painful reminder of the apparent lack of patriotism on the part of Russian Jewry as a whole. It was partially in response to complaints about Jewish draft evasion that *Novosti* labored so energetically to emphasize the heroic role of Jewish troops in the war.[28]

The war itself began with a series of brilliant Russian successes – the crossing of the Danube and the capture of the strategic Shipka Pass – which presaged a rapid and complete Russian victory. The Russian advance halted dramatically before the Turkish fortress at Plevna. Three massive but unsuccessful assaults were made on the fortress between July and September 1876, "the first an oversight, the second an error, the third a crime."[29] Russian losses at Plevna were heavy, and the failure placed the entire Russian strategic position at risk. As casualties began to mount, so too did opposition to the war, now sarcastically renamed "The Grand Dukes' War," to place blame on the lackluster leadership of the imperial family. The dissatisfaction of the public was fully matched by second thoughts and doubts even within the royal family.[30] It was against this background that the press began to call into question the patriotism of "alien" elements within the army. The special targets were Muslims and Jews. After the third reverse at Plevna, it was reported that Jews and Tatars had taken cover or kept to the rear, helping to demoralize the beaten Russian forces.[31]

Much more important in discrediting Russian Jewry were those "score of bold plunderers" who, in Dubnov's words, "fell on the provisioning trade like a bird on carrion."[32] The outbreak of war found the post-reform Russian army as ill-prepared to equip and supply its forces as had been its predecessors. Units of the army were simply paid in grain which they used to feed themselves and to trade for equipment and other provisions. Supply deficiencies always multiplied when the army was on campaign. Indeed, failures of internal supply were a crucial factor in Russia's loss of the Crimean War. Supply problems multiplied as the Russian advance stalled before Plevna.

European wars in the seventeenth century witnessed the emergence of Jews as military contractors on a massive scale. A pan-European network of credit and an extensive system of Jewish sub-contractors ensured that Jews were well-placed to serve nations at war.[33] It was testimony to the backwardness of the Russian quartermaster command that similar arrangements were necessary for the campaign in the Balkans. The commissariat department was further dependent upon the financial assistance of the firms of Gintsburg and Poliakov.[34] Provisioning in the field was the responsibility of firms like Greger, Gorvits, Kogan and Company, two of whose directors were of Jewish descent. A principal supplier of livestock was A. M. Varshavskii, another Jew. The directors of such companies grew rich, while widespread corruption and malfeasance marked their dealings with subcontractors, many of whom were Jews, and the army. Failures of supply became legendary, and prompted a series of well-publicized legal proceedings after the war.[35] M. A. Suvorin, the editor of *Novoe vremia*, who reported from the front, led a crusade against Greger, Gorvits, Kogan and Company (although his enemies claimed that his zeal appeared only after the firm refused him a bribe of 60,000 rubles).[36] His attacks on the profiteers as "enemies worse than the Turks," boosted *Novoe vremia's* circulation and marked the paper's decisive turning to a Judeophobe course.[37]

Russia's great antagonist in her attempt to resolve the Eastern

28 A. S. Suvorin

Question on her own terms was Great Britain. Hostility to the British reached almost pathological dimensions in the Russian press, especially as Russian gains on the field of battle were lost at the conference tables of Berlin. The British leader who thwarted Russian aims most effectively, and who was best known for his Russophobia, was Benjamin Disraeli, Earl of Beaconsfield, who was of Jewish ancestry. His Russian opponents neither forgot nor forgave Disraeli's origins, citing them to explain his presumed propensity to favor the Turks. "The mind of Beaconsfield," wrote Suvorin in *Novoe vremia*, "is dimmed by a racial predisposition toward the Turks. For two thousand years the Jews have dreamed of the resurrection of a Jewish kingdom. Why shouldn't the Jews be inflamed by the rebirth of Turkey?"[38] Ivan Aksakov linked together the interests of Great Britain, for whom the subjugation of the Christian gospels to the Muslim Koran was an act of patriotism, and those of Austria-Hungary, that "freakish political combination of German-Yid culture and Magyar *bashi-bazouk* savagery."[39]

A key to Disraeli's actions was frequently sought in his alleged efforts to pressure Russia into better treatment of her Jewish minority. This claim was given credence by the campaign of various Jewish organizations, and especially the Alliance Israélite Universelle, to ensure that civil rights for Jews were guaranteed in the constitutions of the newly independent Balkan states. The press campaign grew to such heights that the Jewish community of Berdichev, apparently under the prodding of the local authorities, published an open letter in Katkov's *Moskovskii vedomosti* protesting the role that Britain presumed to play in support of Russian Jewry.

> We Russian Jews boldly declare before all the Russian people that we don't have and don't wish to have anything in common with the English Prime Minister, that we live quite well in Russia, and that throughout the reign of our adored monarch, the liberator of peoples, our rights have been more and more expanded, and that we have no grounds to complain to anyone, least of all a foreigner, no matter how high a position he might occupy. (10/IV/1878)

When the Congress of Berlin opened in June of 1878, the treatment of religious minorities was included on the agenda. Perhaps fearful that the legal status of Russian Jewry might be raised, the Russian Minister of Foreign Affairs, A. M. Gorchakov, delivered a preemptive speech on 28 June, in which he reminded the delegates that "in Serbia, Romania, as in Russia, the Jews represent a danger: they don't resemble the Jews of Paris, London, Berlin and Vienna, and therefore the equalization of their rights would have harmful consequences for these countries."[40] Despite Russian disapproval, Romania's independence from the Ottoman Empire was made contingent upon constitutional guarantees of civil equality for all religious groups, which essentially meant the Jews. In the years that followed, the Russian press carefully followed the attempt of successive Romanian governments to implement or evade this stipulation. Conservative organs consistently sympathized with efforts at evasion, pointing out to readers that Romanian Jews were just like Russian Jewry. Nor were readers allowed to forget that the outcome of the Congress of Berlin was very much the handiwork of Lord Beaconsfield.[41]

Thus, the unsuccessful resolution of the Eastern Question from the Russian point of view was tied to a rise in Judeophobia on many different levels. Internally, Jews were perceived as a disloyal, alien element within the patriotic Russian society. Externally they were linked to the foreign foes of Russian national interests.

Лернейскій змѣй въ Россіи.

29 Russia battles the dragon of nihilism, which is fed on Jewish gold

Judeophobia as anti-nihilism

The identification of Jews with revolutionary socialism, given justification by the apparent role played by Jews as Populists and Marxists, has long been accepted as one of the integral parts of conservative Judeophobia. This characterization melds easily with Pipes' conceptualization of conservatism as a theory of anti-nihilism. Nonetheless the equation of the Jews with socialism was a relatively late component in the development of Russian conservatism.

There were objective reasons for this. The Jewish community itself was an extremely conservative political entity. Centuries of self-preservation in the midst of potentially hostile gentiles had taught the Jewish leadership the virtues of loyalty and obedience. Jewish youth who turned to the revolutionary movement severed their links with the traditional Jewish community. The vehicle for Jewish alienation was secular Russian education, and the first Jewish revolutionary levies came from the gymnasium and university and the state rabbinic schools, especially Vilna. Since the total number of these students was relatively small, so was the smaller percentage engaged in political activity. With a few prominent exceptions, Jews were almost entirely

30 F. M. Dostoevskii

absent from the first organized revolutionary socialist groups.[42] They
played little role in the "going to the people" movement of the first
half of the 1870s, and were an insignificant percentage of the terrorist
movement until the 1880s.[43] Even if, as Erich Haberer convincingly
argues, Jews played a far more influential role in Russian Populism
than is generally assumed, they were nonetheless absent from the
public eye: there was not a single Jew involved in the big trials of
revolutionary youth in the first half of the 1870s.[44] The first event for
which Jews were punished – there is some question as to whether they
were mistaken victims or actual participants – was the famous demonstration in the square of the Church of Our Lady of Kazan on
6 December 1876, one of the first demonstrations by workers in the
history of the Russian revolutionary movement. Those arrested by the
police, and convicted by the courts in 1877, included three Jews. Before
1881, only one Jew was executed for an act of political terrorism: on

20 February 1880, I. O. Mlodetskii, a young "free-lance" terrorist, unsuccessfully attempted to assassinate Count M. T. Loris-Melikov, the leading figure in the government of national reconciliation known as "the dictatorship of the heart." The best known Jewish terrorist of this period was Gesia Gelfman, who assisted the assassination of Alexander II on 1 March 1881. Outside of Russia Jews were slow to organize revolutionary groups, in contrast to the plethora of other national groups in exile. Only in 1880 did a group of Jewish exiles in Geneva, with the assistance of M. P. Dragomanov, publish a manifesto in the name of "the group of Socialists-Jews."

Given the paucity of Jewish revolutionaries, the image of the "Jewish nihilist" was slow to develop. Dostoevskii was one of the first conservatives to note the participation of Jews in the Kazan Cathedral demonstration when he spoke in 1878 of "lots of nondescript Jews and Armenians" who helped to swell the crowd. In an uncirculated letter written a month later he went much further:

> Apropos: when will people finally realize how much the Yids (by my own observation) and perhaps the Poles are behind this nihilist business? What a collection of Yids were involved in the Kazan Square incident, and then the Yids throughout Odessa history. Odessa, the city of Yids, is the center of our rampant socialism. In Europe, the very same situation: the Yids are terribly active in the socialist movement, and I'm not speaking about the Lassalles and Karl Marxes. And understandably so: the Yids have everything to gain from every radical cataclysm and coup d'etat because it is he himself, *status in statu*, that constitutes his own community, which is unshakable and only gains from everything that undermines non-Yid society.[45]

The recipient of this letter was V. F. Putsykovich, the editor of the reactionary newspaper *Grazhdanin*. Through this conduit Dostoevski's ideas passed into print as an editorial interjection. Two months after the letter was written, *Grazhdanin* published a series of articles by N. N. Golitsyn on the need to reform Russian Jewry. In the midst of a passage where Golitsyn was discussing the corrosive effect of the Jewish presence on the national character of Germany, Putsykovich placed an interpolation:

> Editor: Recognized as the chief leader of all contemporary conspiracies which seek to destroy the entire political and social side of the Christian world, and of participants in attacks on the lives of Christian monarchs, is the Jew Karl Marx, sheltered in London under the protection of the government of Lord Beaconsfield, and whose chief precursor was the Jew Lassalle. (29–31:24/XI/1878)

In 1879 other conservative newspapers with official ties, such as *Sovremennye izvestiia* and *Russkii mir*, began to identify Jews with nihilism. In October, *Sovremennye izvestiia* carried an article entitled "Revolutionary Jewry" which pointed to a recent political trial in which eight of the twenty-eight defendants were Jews. This was the first trial where Jews constituted such a high proportion, the paper noted, and it was submitted as visible proof of the danger of educating Jews.[46] The paper returned to this theme in November, observing that "Kiev, Taganrog, Nikolaev, Odessa, Kharkov are revolutionary knots; these cities from of old have been centers of Jewry. The spread of political agitation in Russia has coincided with the extension of the rights of Russians of the Mosaic Confession."[47] *Russkii mir* joined the chorus in December, warning that the Jews were sacrificing their sons and daughters on the altar of a new Moloch – nihilism. The entire Jewish community was indicted: "The rich money-lenders and bankers give their money; the poor give their daughters."[48]

Neither *Sovremennye izvestiia* nor *Russkii mir* (soon to cease publication) were influential publications, and their references to the political unreliability of the Jews did not attract much attention. Quite a different response greeted an article published in *Novoe vremia* early in March of 1880.[49] By the end of the reform era *Novoe vremia* was one of the most influential newspapers in the Russian Empire and certainly the best-read conservative publication in St. Petersburg. The article, moreover, was by an occasional contributor to the paper, Professor V. P. Vasilev, a respected philologist, lexicographer and student of China. Clearly inspired by the recent capture and execution of the Jewish terrorist Mlodetskii, the article claimed that "the Yids are the firm allies of Nihilism" and "from times of old these Yids have been representatives of the revolutionary spirit."

Novoe vremia came under attack for this article not only by its domestic liberal adversary, *Golos*, but also by the prestigious *Times* of London. A reply was necessitated both because the paper itself had been criticized, and also the Russian government was accused, because of its repressive legislation, of encouraging a hatred of the Jews "which is a disgrace to our century" (29,830:16/III/1880). In a riposte entitled "By the Rivers of Babylon," *Novoe vremia* gave vent to its well-developed antipathy to the Jews through an indictment of the Jewish nihilist and the Jewish capitalist. Why should *Novoe vremia* be maligned by the *Times* for pointing out the anti-Russian proclivities of the Jews? the paper asked. *Novoe vremia* did not encourage the Jews to engage in revolutionary propaganda, give them pens to enable them to write revolutionary publications abroad, place revolvers, pamphlets and detonators for bombs in their hands, nor did the paper scribble passionate hymns for the Jews and Jewesses who had fallen as "martyrs for the Russian people." *Novoe vremia* had only shown how the Jews had a fatal influence on all strata of Russian society. At one extreme, they were the partisans of capital, which they manipulated so as to prevent the emergence of a native commercial class. In the lower ranks of society, the Jews were agents of revolutionary propaganda. *Novoe vremia* addressed the apparent paradox of modern Antisemitism: how could Jews be simultaneously partisans of socialism *and* capitalism? The answer for *Novoe vremia* lay in the essence of Judaism, the principle of cosmopolitanism. This meant that the entire world existed for them only as an object of exploitation, and capitalism and socialism were merely parallel paths to the same goal (1456:18/III/1880).

The reply of *Golos*, "In Defense of the Innocent," demonstrates how the liberal paper's role as a defender of the Jews was in part forced upon it by the belligerent Judeophobia of its principal conservative rivals. *Golos*, always happy to claim the brotherhood of the *Times* in the league of "progressive" newspapers, used the London paper's editorial as the starting point for an attack on *Novoe vremia*. It dismissed hostility to the Jews as an outpouring of religious prejudice. As such, it was easily remedied: "Only let the rights of the Jews be equalized with those of Russians and the enmity of the Russian people will disappear of itself" (76:16/III/1880). To equate Judaism with Nihilism and its anti-capitalist objectives was especially ludicrous, the paper claimed, given the Jews' ties to capital. If an occasional Jewish terrorist appeared, he should be seen, like revolutionaries of all other nationalities, as "the pathological excrescence of a state organism suffering from a common illness." To suggest otherwise was to play the dangerous game of sowing discord among people of different religions and nationalities. *Golos* did not need to remind its readers that this was a violation of the Russian criminal code.

The reborn and resurgent Russian Jewish press played a major role in this debate. *Russkii evrei* reminded the Judeophobes that the most striking feature of Jewish revolutionaries was their complete rejection of the Jewish world. They blushed with shame when reminded of their origins. "We boldly and directly declare that there is not a single Jew who, loving his country and concerned with its interests, has anything in common with those who wish to change the world by means of murder and robbery" (14:5/XII/1879). *Russkii evrei* dismissed the views of *Russkii mir* as a curiosity: "Other publications try to increase subscribers by promising a supplement or a bonus such as embroidered slippers, carpets or *festorchiki*, but *Russkii mir* promises something still more piquant: to nag the Yids in every possible way" (17:26/XII/1879). The prominent Professor Vasilev could not be dismissed so lightly. *Russkii evrei* posed a set of leading questions to the professor: Did he not think it dishonorable to indict an entire nation for treason without giving any proof? In the present confused political situation, did he think it proper to use his professorial authority to stir up national hatreds? Was he not aware that "the newspapers of doormen and teamsters" would use his words to incite their guileless readers against the Jews? These were questions, the paper solemnly declared, that no honorable man could leave unanswered, although Vasilev did precisely that (12:19/III/1880).

The rival Russian Jewish newspaper, *Rassvet*, disputed figures which *Novoe vremia* used to show that Jews, who constituted 3 percent of the population of the Empire, produced 7 percent of those tried for political crimes. The proper approach, *Rassvet* argued, was not to examine the percentage of Jews in the country as a whole, but their proportion in those segments of the population, overwhelmingly urban in location and mercantile by estate, which provided the greatest number of political criminals. Jews were concentrated in the urban population so that a figure of 7 percent, even if correct, was misleading. There was only one Jew, the baptized Mlodetskii, among the most prominent socialists and terrorists. The appeal of the revolutionary movement, moreover, was almost entirely directed toward the peasantry, and this effectively excluded the Jews. *Novoe vremia*'s attempt to condemn the Jews for both capitalism *and* socialism was unconvincing. "The Jews are a vital, living part of Russian society. All things that distress the Russian people distress Russian Jewry. Their joys and sorrows are one" (10:6/III/1880).

A further attack on the claims of *Novoe vremia* came from an unexpected quarter, the illegal newspaper of the terrorist group *Narodnaia volia*. The Populists themselves were ambivalent toward the Jews, and they clearly assumed that their cause was harmed by its association with non-Russian groups like the Poles or the Jews. Two articles, entitled "Regarding Statistics on State Crimes in Russia" addressed the issue (4:5/XII/1880 and 5:5/II/1881). Using public and private figures which categorized prisoners by religion, the author demonstrated that Orthodox Christians constituted 74 percent of the accused, Catholics (most of whom were presumably Poles) were 15 percent, while Jews numbered 4 percent. The percentage of Jewish political prisoners was slightly less than the percentage of Jews in the total population of the Empire. This refuted the claim of the conservative Katkov that nihilism was a "Polish intrigue" or Suvorin's Judeophobe assertion that the revolutionary movement was somehow Jewish.

Despite these and other rebuttals, Judeophiles, in subtle ways, began to accept the equation of Jews and revolution. This came in the course of attempts to explain why the Jews might be tempted by Nihilism. For example, the December 1880 issue of the prestigious liberal thick journal *Vestnik Evropy* carried a sketch entitled "In the Procurator's Office." The story recounted an elderly Jew's intervention with the authorities on behalf of his son, who had been arrested for revolutionary activity. He responds to the procurator's question of why Jews constitute such a large contingent of socialists by blaming the education they receive in the Christian milieu. This education alienates them from everything Jewish – faith, customs, outlook, even the love of money. Christian students had a fatherland, so that people and education was not an alienating experience. The educated Jew, by contrast, found himself bereft of a fatherland, and devoid of a people whom he could call his own. The simple expedient was to turn to the socialist movement whose ideals viewed everyone, Russians, Jews, Germans and Poles, as the same. To remedy this situation, Jews had to be given a homeland (i.e., made equal citizens of the Empire) and made to feel a real part of the Russian state.

This story was told from a Judeophile perspective, but it casually accepted almost all the Judeophobe arguments about Jews and revolution. It conceded Jewish participation in the socialist movement and accepted the claim that education merely made the Jews more harmful to the Russian state than they already were. The story's "moral," that the Jews should be given civil rights, stood refuted by the claim, generally accepted by Judeophobes, that Jews in their present condition could not safely be granted more rights and turned loose on the defenseless Christian population.

Similarly damaging concessions were made by the veteran Jewish writer and journalist G. Bogrov, writing in *Novoe vremia* itself. Bogrov was speaking on a different theme, arguing that Russian law should be modified to expedite mixed marriages involving Christians and Jews, since this was the surest means of Jewish assimilation. To illustrate his claim that it was the law, not the insularity of the Jews which was blocking assimilation, he pointed to the eager reception which Jewish youth gave to Nihilism as a "truth, mournful for the Jews." Inspired by its promise of brotherhood and its comradely sympathy toward all members, Jews joined the movement and sacrificed to it their careers, their future and their lives (2134:5/II/1882).[50]

With even Jews inclined to accept Jewish involvement in socialism as a special problem, it was no wonder that Russians, committed to combatting Judeophobia, were placed on the defensive. *Golos*, never comfortable in its role as a Judeophile newspaper, typified this predicament. By 1881 the editors were publicly committed to full civil equality for the Jews. At the same time, editorials complained that Jews were complicating the struggle by their failure to perform their existing obligations, such as military service. Revolutionary activity presented another problem. *Golos* asked the Jewish intelligentsia to explain the dark force that drove Jewish youth onto the field of political agitation. Why did so many political trials now feature Jews, often in a leading role? (46:15/II/1881).

The hyperbole of the friends of the Jews when dealing with Jewish revolutionaries demonstrates how successfully, and painfully, the cliché of the "Jewish Nihilist" had established itself in the midst of the debate on the Jewish Question. The accusation became even more troublesome as Jewish participation in the revolutionary movement increased in the 1880s and 1890s. Dostoevski's "discovery" of the Jewish role in 1878 became an actual fact within a few years. The existence of the cliché also explains why, after the assassination of Alexander II on 1 March 1881, only a veiled journalistic reference by *Novoe vremia* that one of the assassins was of "an asiatic type" created panic in the Jewish community, and helped create the myth that a press campaign against the "Jewish regicides" was a principal cause of the pogrom wave of 1881.

"The Yid Is Coming"

In his March 1880 attack on the Jews in the revolutionary movement, Professor Vasilev noted in passing that, among university students, Jews were "hardly the most conservative element." Shortly thereafter the paper returned to this theme, initiating another effective campaign against Russian Jewry. The article, and the crusade which it inspired, was of special importance, because it challenged one of the most deeply held assumptions of Judeophiles and Judeophobes alike, that the ultimate resolution of the Jewish Question lay through the schoolhouse door. The article was in the form of a letter to the editor, and the heading which the editor gave it – *"Zhid idet,"* "The Yid Is

Coming" – replaced Aksakov's slogan of "the Jewish banner" as the chief catchphrase of Russian Judeophobia.

The anonymous author drew attention to recent statistics from the Ministry of Education. Out of the total of 65,835 students enrolled in secondary education (*gimnazii* and *realschulen*), the Jews constituted 6,732. At first glance this was an insignificant number. A closer look revealed that while Jews were only one-twentieth of the total population of the Empire, their ration in the schools was 1:6. More alarming, while Jews were 9.9 percent of the total in 1876, they had risen to 10.7 percent in 1877. How long would it take for the Jewish contingent to double or triple? All agreed that education was better than ignorance, but what would be the effect on the moral health of the Russian people if Jews came to dominate the liberal professions? Moreover, the expenses of public education were taken from the meager funds of the peasantry, who were themselves greatly in need of education. "Each Ioshka and Gershka who attends the gymnasium displaces a Russian pauper, and this guarantees that every such Ioshka acquires the opportunity to mistreat many paupers for a long time to come, while he advances himself and his kin" (1461:23/III/1880). The author denied that he sought to close gymnasium doors to aliens; he asked only that the Russian intelligentsia ponder the significance of their dilution by foreign elements. This exhortation encouraged commentators to pass from the general to the specific, and to consider the impact of an influx of Jews into their own particular educational district.

Kievlianin took up the problem in editorials and articles. The issue had alarming implications for the Kiev Educational District, a writer warned, since Jews constituted not 10.4 percent but 12 percent of gymnasium and pregymnasium students, and this in a city that, except for two districts, was technically outside the Pale of Settlement. Over the last five years the student body of city secondary schools had increased by 40 percent, while the number of Jews increased by 140 percent. *Kievlianin* articles added a new concern to the analysis. *Novoe vremia* feared lest Jews displace Christians from the school benches and dilute the Russian element in the national intelligentsia. The Kiev newspaper warned that Jewish influence upon schools was a negative one. "Be convinced that neither study nor occupation can cleanse the hard, crusty bark [of the Jews] or direct the former Ioshka, Gerskh or Leib to activities which are pure and free from tradition, although twenty times over they rechristen themselves Iosif, Leon and German. *Gescheft* remains their eleventh commandment, their worship of Lassalle, Marx and the like notwithstanding" (93:25/IV/1880). The

Jewish pursuit of *Gescheft* – the Judeophobe code-word for Jewish exploitation – was further demonstrated by their tendency to flock to the most profitable areas of university study, especially the law.

Kievlianin presented the struggle in terms of a *Kulturkampf* but, interestingly enough, placed the onus on Russian society rather than on the Jews. Education, a writer warned, was capable of transforming alien groups into superficial Russians, but this was not the same thing as assimilation or the mixing of races, both of which required the considerable passage of time. Nor could it ever occur if an alien element began to dominate the Russian intelligentsia, obstructing national development, alienating educated society from the people and generating misunderstanding and discord. "We must take care that in the future there is always a compact majority of the native race in the educated ranks of Russian society, and not aliens, be they the Jerusalem nobility, Baltic barons or Georgian princes" (106:11/V/1880). One might understand the Jewish striving for education, for it freed them from military service, extended their civil rights and conformed to their traditional respect for learning. Jews might even reproach Russians because they failed to duplicate Jewish educational aspirations. The key to resisting the "Judaization" of the Russian intelligentsia did not lie in restrictions upon the Jews, but in strengthening popular education and encouraging literacy. At the most, school officials should give preference to Christians over Jews for vacancies at the Kiev municipal gymnasium.

Ivan Aksakov's *Rus* published a letter from an Orthodox priest who cited figures to demonstrate that the Jews were poised to overwhelm secondary education in Kovno and Vilna provinces. He painted a poignant picture of rural parents and their unsophisticated, rustic children turned away from schools dominated by urbanized Jews. "It is hard to live with the Jews now, and it will be still harder when they become the intelligentsia of our region, something that apparently cannot be avoided" (40:15/VIII/1881). *Novorossiiskii telegraf* commented darkly on the involvement of Jews in university disorders early in 1881. The Jews, a people devoid of scruples or moral foundations, constituted a disproportionately high number of students in the university, a contributor complained. This was the natural effect of the milieu from which they sprang, dominated as it was by stock exchange manipulation, swindling, usury, kulak activity, "venality of word and cynicism of deed" (1824:18/II/1881).

The Jewish press was slow to take the danger of this campaign seriously. Their negligence was understandable, because for years the predominant Judeophobe charge against the Jews was that they failed to attend Russian schools in sufficient number. *Rassvet* ignored the concerns raised by *Novoe vremia* by pointing with pride to the ever-increasing number of Jews in Russian schools (8:21/II/1880; 2:8/I/1881). *Russkii evrei* also pleaded guilty, in the name of Russian Jewry, to a "criminal passion for education." It derived in part from the traditional Jewish love of education and their pursuit of universal literacy. It was also a direct consequence of the numerous legal restrictions on the Jews, which could be overcome by recourse to higher education. *Russkii evrei* thus attempted to turn the fear of educated Jewry into a call for civil rights for Jews: if the abnormal legal position of the Jews were relaxed, the artificially motivated pursuit of higher education by Jewish youth would decrease (42:15/X/1880).

The moderation and limited scope of the initial debate over Jewish participation in public education is extremely deceptive. The concern took deep root, and reappeared in strengthened form once the outbreak of the pogroms raised the Jewish Question to the category of a national emergency. It is not difficult to explain the rapid spread of the fear that "the Yid is coming," even though it reversed, seemingly overnight, one of the most long-lived solutions to the Jewish Question. The official desire to attract Jews to Russian schools had persisted for so long precisely because it had not succeeded. Once Jews began to increase competition for school places in a system that was both overextended and underfunded for a nation of Russia's size, envy and hostility appeared. The Jews appeared to constitute a real threat to the integrity of the system. Mathematical acrobatics predicted rates of increase for Jewish students that would have overwhelmed resources. As Judeophobes came to distrust the Russian Jewish intelligentsia, and as fear of Judaism as a "revolutionary ferment" grew, Jews were assumed to be an agent of educational degradation. Rather than the schools enlightening the Jews, Jews would corrupt schools and the Christian students in them.

It should also be stressed that the campaign, although associated with *Novoe vremia* in St. Petersburg, had its genesis in the provinces.[51] The original warning against the Jews came from Odessa, and the first paper to explore its implications in depth was *Kievlianin*. When restrictive measures were first devised against the Jews, it was in the educational districts of the Pale. There was also a class element in the campaign. The rural priest from Lithuania who warned the readers of *Rus* about the Jewish influx, presented his statistics not only by religious confession, but also by social estate. They revealed that gymnasiums for both sexes in the region were dominated by two estates, the nobility (and the children of Russian state officials) and the urban estates. Out of a total enrollment of 1,352 gymnasium students cited in the letter, noble children constituted 585, while those of the urban estates numbered 601. In the cities of the Pale, of course, the members of these urban estates were likely to be Jews. In fact, the 554 Jews enrolled in the gymnasiums could only have come from the urban estates.

The nobility, rather than the peasantry, was the estate most directly threatened by Jewish competition. Russian conservatives in the post-emancipation era grew more and more concerned with the loss of gentry power and prerogatives and the alienation of noble land. Education provided one final bulwark for the survival of the *dvorian-stvo*. It was now threatened by the Jews as a destructive numerical and cultural force.

Russian conservatism provided ideological underpinning for gentry fears. Concern that Jews would introduce an alien element into the Russian intelligentsia was a logical outgrowth of Ivan Aksakov's juxta-position of the "Christian banner" and the "Jewish banner," and joined neatly with growing suspicion of the Russian Jewish intelli-gentsia. Jews in schools came to be seen not just as a negatively harmful force, keeping natives from the school benches, but a posi-tively dangerous carrier of cosmopolitan, nihilist ideas into these same schools.

Antisemitism

European Antisemitism, which emerged as a fully modern ideology and as an organized political movement in the 1870s, had an enormous impact upon Russian conservative thought. European Anti-semitism fulfilled a variety of functions for Russian Judeophobes. Perhaps most importantly, it served to make hatred of Jews respectable in Russian society. *Novorossiiskii telegraf*, itself under fire for its militant Judeophobia, greeted the submission of a so-called "Anti-Jewish Pet-ition" to Otto von Bismarck, the German chancellor: "And so, besides those well-known Russian barbarians who persecute the Jews, yet another nation, Prussia, heretofore considered an enlightened state, has appeared in Europe to rise up against the predominance of the Jews" (1655:17/VIII/1880). The conservative press greeted the outbreak of minor anti-Jewish violence in Germany and Austria with sentiments close to rapture: such events helped to relieve Russia of the shame of

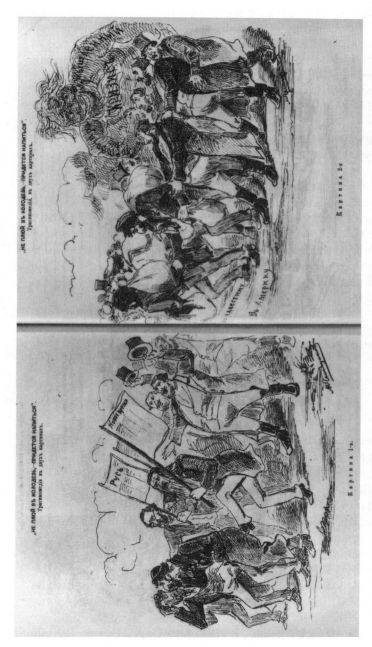

31 "Don't spit in the well you drink from." Jews are tormented by A. S. Suvorin and I. S. Aksakov, editors of *Novoe vremia* and *Rus*, cheered on by Russian merchants. In the economic crisis which follows, the same merchants beg the Jews to stay

the pogrom wave of 1881, which was harshly criticized in the foreign
press. The appearance of pogroms in "civilized" states, the conservative press explained, verified the Russian claim that the cause of the
pogroms was to be sought in the Jews themselves, rather than in the
savagery and barbarism of the Russian masses (*Kievlianin*, 212:25/IX/
1882; *Novoe vremia*, 2202:17/IV/1882).

European Antisemites also provided models which Russian conservatives could imitate or emulate. This helps to explain the rapid
spread in Russia of innovative antisemitic concepts that were still far
removed from objective Russian realities. Conservatives embraced
Western antisemitic clichés like the "Golden International" and the
"Judaized periodical press," long before there were Russian examples
to be cited. Marx and Lassalle had to do service for a long time as the
quintessential Jewish revolutionaries in the absence of homegrown
terrorists of sufficient stature. It was conservative thinkers who were
closest to the Germanic milieu – Ivan Aksakov, Fedor Dostoevskii,
Konstantin Pobedonostsev, V. P. Meshcherskii and N. N. Golitsyn –
who were the most assiduous developers of conservative Russian
Judeophobia of a foreign type. In contrast, the more home-grown
Kievlianin developed a more distinctly "Russian" brand of Judeophobia, which drew its examples from Russian realities, and was less
inclined to imitate foreign models.

This raises again the problem of the connection of Judeophobia to
Slavophilism. Despite the total lack of interest in the Jewish Question
by the early Slavophiles, a connection is usually made through the
writings of their epigones, Ivan Aksakov and Iurii Samarin. The origin
of Ivan Aksakov's Judeophobia is especially revealing. Initially it was
based on rather primitive Christian prejudices, which Aksakov himself
felt to be disreputable. As a young bureaucrat serving in the Pale of
Settlement, he found that Jews "leave a strange impression on me; I
can't get out of my head that every Jew continues to crucify Christ."[52]
At the same time he attempted to acquaint himself with Jewish beliefs
by holding theological discussions with Jews and even reading the
Jewish catechism used in the state Jewish schools. From these investigations he satisfied himself that there was not a single moral obligation
which Judaism did not share with other higher religions. A belief that
the true essence of a religion resided in its spirit kept him from
granting his complete approbation.

> The laws of Moses value material good, the structure of a worldly life
> which is national and exclusive, and they do not propagate the [idea
> of] the sacredness of every human soul – in a word, they bear a

> historical character, rooted to a particular time, and beside this there
> is much which the Talmud and the later rabbis destroyed ... I often
> argue with my Jewish acquaintances, telling them openly that I
> would oppose the full emancipation of the Jews.[53]

Yet simultaneously with these impressions, Aksakov gathered the
physical evidence which led him to reject the concept of "Jewish
exploitation" in his examination of the Ukrainian fairs.

Aksakov's first journalistic foray into the Jewish Question was his
famous discussion of the Jewish and Christian banners. His article was
prompted by a specific piece of Russian legislation, but it was analogous to a campaign of German conservatives against the entry of
Jews into the civil service in the 1840s. Aksakov may have taken
inspiration from Germany, although he made no reference to it in his
own work. As his Judeophobia grew more extreme, however, his debt
to western, and especially German models became more obvious. This
tie also revealed Aksakov's great talent as an Judeophobe publicist – he
was able with great success to give a distinctive Russian coloration to
the precepts of German Antisemitism.

Iurii Samarin served with Aksakov as one of the few generational
links of the Slavophile tradition. Samarin's Judeophobia is attested to
by exactly one lengthy quotation from his voluminous works and
correspondence, and should be quoted in full. In March of 1876 he
wrote to a friend and correspondent, Baroness de Rahden, to lament
that Germany was polarized between two parties. The conservatives
stood for "God and the Hohenzollern, revelation and the monarchy."
The other party was that of the Jews.

> You certainly know that today there is no longer any Berlin, but a
> new Jerusalem which speaks German. When it is a question of
> Judaism, which rules in the assembly which Bismarck *all at once* let
> assume the right to serve, which directs higher education, which
> insinuates itself near women, as the family doctor, the tutor, or simply
> as the initiator, replacing the confessors of the seventeenth and
> eighteenth centuries, which finances and inspires the majority of
> newspapers – it is not a question, of course, of the Old Testament nor
> of a nationality elevated to the heights of a chosen race. It is some-
> thing which, impalpable and imperceptible on the whole, is the most
> complete extract which has ever existed of all the elements which are
> completely hostile to a moral and social order based on Christianity.
> To be sure these elements are to be found everywhere, but to divine
> their presence, to extract them from the moral filth and from the most
> obscure corners of the conscience, to expose them in broad daylight,
> above all to study them unblushingly and finally to constitute them as

a body of doctrine and a political party, it is necessary only to see the Jews in action: an infallible perspicacity and an absolute ruthlessness in the negation of tradition. Only the Jews have this, or, at least, possess these attributes in an incomparably higher degree than anybody else, and also carry an ascendent historical tradition, uninterrupted since the beginning of the world and a high, almost completely other-than-Christian (say *other-than* rather than *Anti-*Christian) culture as an entire race. It is impossible not to admire the variety of forms and colors which this inclination has at its disposal, while never disrupting its unity. In politics – it is the worship of success and the cult of the golden calf; in philosophy – it is the material which develops complete self-awareness; in social matters – it is the harmony of all historical institutions to recover the ground of *pure* Manchesterism, which is the increase of productivity taken in the abstract, or as the highest goal in and of itself; in the areas of the family – it is the good of the individual as the only basis for profit; in matters of education – it is the development and the direction of the instincts; instinct and impulse – nothing more, and as a goal, the struggle of the destructive against the creative.[54]

This analysis, written from Berlin, drew entirely upon the contemporary German experience, described a German–Jewish community far different from the Jews of the Russian Empire, and owed more to antisemitic ideas which were popular in the German capital than to the traditions of the Russian Slavophile movement. Samarin made no reference whatsoever to Russia, not even to explore the implications of his observations. In fact, taken in context, the "Judaification" of Germany apparently had no repercussions for Russia except to weaken a rival great power. Moreover, the ability of other conservatives, who lacked Aksakov and Samarin's Slavophile orientation, to assimilate German antisemitic ideas calls into question the claim that Slavophile philosophy conditioned its adherents to accept Antisemitism.

Antisemitism in Russia was not an obscure ideology. Any well-read Russian was fully conversant with Western Antisemitism, since all segments of the press devoted space to the phenomenon throughout the 1870s. The arguments of Richard Wagner, August Rohling, Heinrich von Treitschke and Wilhelm Marr were fully summarized and discussed soon after their initial appearance in Germany. For example, N. N. Golitsyn wrote a series on the Jews for *Grazhdanin* in 1878, replete with accusations that Jewry had become the dominant power within Europe, especially in Germany and Austria, through its control of the stock exchange, the markets and the press. Most of the authorities which he cited were German.[55] Fulsome coverage was given to political Antisemitism, including Marr's Antisemitic League, Ernst Henrici's

Social Reich Party and Adolf Stöcker's Christian Social Workers' Party.[56]

While reporting the activities of foreign Antisemites, editors of all political persuasions in Russia were somewhat diffident toward the movement. Liberals were dismissive of German Antisemitism as a recrudescence of medieval fanaticism, but they were more concerned that the movement might serve as a stalking horse for attacks upon public freedom in Germany, represented for them by the opposition National Liberal Party, with its Jewish leader Eduard Lasker. Nor were anti-liberal Russian newspapers automatically supportive of the movement. It was, after all, foreign, "Teutonic," and located within the context of German internal politics. German politics inevitably revolved around Otto von Bismarck, and a writer's view of this towering figure often determined his attitude toward an antisemitic initiative. Ivan Aksakov, for example, persistently viewed the struggle as one between a pro-Bismarck "Christian German Party" and a "Progressive German Party."[57] As a whole, the conservative press remained ambivalent toward political Antisemitism until its decline in the late 1880s.

In private, German Antisemitism as a part of a conservative *Weltanschauung* found an approving reception within the circle of contributors and friends of Prince V. P. Meshcherskii's reactionary newspaper *Grazhdanin*. These included Dostoevskii and Pobedonostsev. David Goldstein, in his extensive study *Dostoyevsky and the Jews*, argues that the writer assimilated hatred of the Jews – which Goldstein painstakingly elaborates – from his environment, to which he added his own mystical and messianic hopes for the Russian people. In the 1870s, Dostoevskii's environment increasingly was "governmental circles and the most reactionary elements of Russian society for whom out-and-out Antisemitism was an article of faith."[58] Goldstein points to a variety of Russian sources that fueled Dostoevskii's Judeophobia: his hatred of European financiers, Lord Beaconsfield, Jewish war-profiteers, and the Jewish predator and parasite. By the mid-1870s Dostoevskii did not have to restrict himself to a conservative milieu to absorb these stereotypes, since they could be found across the Russian political spectrum. Very little of Dostoevskii's Judeophobia was original aside from his minor role in introducing some German antisemitic stereotypes into Russian conservatism. His writings helped spread the myths of the "Golden International" and Jewish domination of the press. By 1876 he was routinely placing opponents into the harmful categories of "Judaizers and Europeanizers." Nonetheless, Dostoevskii remained better known as a novelist – in whose work Judeophobia

32 K. P. Pobedonostsev

was absent or muted – than as a Judeophobe publicist. The slurs and asides against the Jews which punctuated his publicist work were indistinguishable from the daily Jew-baiting of publications like *Novoe vremia* or *Novorossiiskii telegraf*. Only one installment of his publicist *Diary of a Writer* (*Dnevnik pisatelia*) was devoted specifically to the Jewish Question, and it was a blend of irony and sham reconciliation.[59] Dostoevskii's antipathy to the Jews was real and evident, but it was not his chief defining characteristic as a public figure. He was a writer first, a publicist second, and a Judeophobe third.

Nonetheless, Dostoevskii was an important conduit for the private spread and reinforcement of Western Antisemitism among his friends.

This role is illustrated by Dostoevskii's relationship with K. P. Pobedonostsev. The latter's biographer, Robert Byrnes, claims that Antisemitism "was particularly strong among the Slavophile, Pan-slav, conservative nationalist circles in which he grew up and through which he passed, and it apparently became more prevalent and more powerful in Russia from the time of the Crimean War until the 1880s."[60] This unsupported statement is far too broad to permit a precise dating of Pobedonostsev's antisemitic proclivities, and even ignores the possibility that he absorbed some of the prejudices against the Jews which characterized the liberal milieu of which he was once briefly a part. As Byrnes also observes, it was the "Eastern Question," and especially foreign press opposition to the Bosnian uprising, which provided a critical impetus for the development of Pobedonostsev's Judeophobia. But this was at a time when Dostoevskii was already well advanced on his Judeophobe course, as indicated by his editorship of the Judeophobe newspaper *Grazhdanin* in 1873. Pobedonostsev, on the other hand, did not really discover the Jewish Question until May of 1876. He wrote to the Tsarevich Alexander to recommend to him the work of Prince N. N. Golitsyn on the Jews. He characterized the reform of the Jews as "very important for Russia."[61] Thereafter his Judeophobia became more pronounced. He substituted "Yid" (*zhid*) for "Jew" (*evrei*) in his vocabulary, a very significant and conscious transition. He used the adjective "Yid" (*zhidovskii*) as a synonym for "liberal" or "progressive," and became obsessed with the influence of "Yids" on the periodical press. These borrowings suggest a foreign provenance, perhaps reinforced by the intervention of European liberals against the "persecution of the Jews in Russia."[62] Pobedonostsev frequently followed Dostoevskii's lead, as revealed in their correspondence. Dostoevskii wrote to Pobedonostsev from Ems, in Germany, on 9/21 August 1879:

> While still in Berlin, I mentioned to Putsykovich that, in my view, Germany, Berlin at least, is being Judaized. And then here in *Moskovskie vedomosti* I read an excerpt from a pamphlet that has just appeared in Germany: "Where is the Yid There?" It is the answer of one Yid to a German who dared to write that Germany was becoming terribly Judaized in every regard. "There is no Yid," answers the pamphlet, and the German is everywhere, but if there is no Jew, there is a Jewish influence everywhere, for, it says, the Jewish spirit and nationality are superior to the German, and they have indeed infused into Germany *the spirit of speculative realism*, etc. etc. Thus my view turned out to be right: the Germans and the Yids testify to it.[63]

Pobedonostsev replied at once:

> What you write about the Yids is quite correct. They fill everything
> up, they undermine everything, and the spirit of the century is
> identical to them. They are at the root of the revolutionary-social
> movement and regicide. They control the periodical press, the finan-
> cial markets are in their hands, the popular masses fall into financial
> slavery to them, they guide the principles of present day science,
> seeking to place it outside Christianity. And beside this, hardly does
> any question about them come up when there goes up a chorus of
> voices for the Jews in the name of some sort of civilization or toler-
> ation (i.e., indifference to faith). As in Romania and Serbia, as with us
> – nobody dares say a word about the Jews filling everything up. Even
> our press is become Jewish. *Russkaia pravda*, *Moskva*, *Golos*, if you
> please – are all Jewish organs; and they even started up special
> journals: *Evrei* and *Vestnik evreev* and *Biblioteka evreiskaia*.[64]

Despite the attempt to "russify" these charges through reference to
the Judaizing Russian press, the Western pedigree of this tirade is
quite apparent. As Russian realities began to conform to these preconceptions – Jews became more widely represented in the terrorist
movement; concern grew over the percentage of Jews in the public
school system; and Russian liberalism identified itself more forcibly as
anti-antisemitic – they were comfortably integrated into the conservative world view.

While Judeophobia was not an integral component of modern
Russian conservatism from the very beginning, the inclusion of anti-
Jewish stereotypes was a natural process. A movement which
equated nationality with "Russian" and religion with "Russian
Orthodoxy," proved incapable of absorbing the concept of "Russians
of the Mosaic Faith." Ivan Aksakov demonstrated this fact in his
rejection of "moral amphibians" – Jews who rejected their natural
environment without converting to Christianity. Other conservative
thinkers shared his skepticism. Writing in 1864, Nikolai Strakhov
asserted that "Russian Germans, Russian Catholics, Russians of the
Mosaic Faith, and so forth – these are phenomena unsuited for any
rich and fruitful development but, on the contrary, represent the
possibility of an uninterrupted deviation from any healthy development."[65]

Under the best of circumstances Russian conservatism would have
been hard pressed to assimilate Jews and Judaism. Still less could
conservatives accept the options which were actually available: the
Jewish masses, resistant to change, and the Russian Jewish intelligentsia, offering a compromise which still preserved many of the
distinctive features of Russian Jewry. Once the amalgam of foreign

Antisemitism and domestic Judeophobia was planted in Russian soil, it quickly developed those pathological characteristics which appeared to later observers to be such a natural and organic part of Russian conservatism.

18 The occult element in Russian Judeophobia

Its malice and hostility notwithstanding, Russian Judeophobia until the 1870s was based largely on objective realities. Critics and polemicists might differ as to the threat posed to Christians by Jewish life, culture and economic activity, but they based their arguments upon observable evidence. Even Iakov Brafman's work derived from genuine physical evidence, the *pinkas* of the Minsk Jewish community. But Brafman initiated a new trend by going far beyond reality in his commentaries, in his portrayal of the kahal as a manifestation of a gigantic, united, international Jewish movement. Following Brafman's lead, other writers parted company with reality and drew a new, horrific picture of the Jews which had only a tenuous connection to reality. This vigorous, if not entirely new, element in Russian Judeophobia may be termed "occult," both in the sense of its exposure of allegedly secret Jewish activities and conspiracies, and because these charges were often fantastic, esoteric or even supernatural.[1] Occult elements emanating from the West had impinged upon official attitudes in the past. Now they received a domestic coloration, spread to a wider public, and provided topics for debate in serious publications. Occult Judeophobia acquired a familiarity and respectability never before enjoyed. Since occult phenomena are not susceptible to rational investigation, their widespread acceptance revealed a new psychological orientation as Russian society moved away from practical attempts to solve the Jewish Question.

Although the scope of occult Judeophobia was limited only by the imagination of its creators, several categories stand out for their endurance, acceptability and implausibility: indictments of the Jews for ritual murder, the Talmud as an anti-Christian document, and Jewish fanaticism. Each of these, not unique to Russia by any means, was encompassed by a more comprehensive accusation: a supposed conspiracy of world Jewry, aiming at world domination and the destruction of Christian civilization.

The Blood Libel

The claim that Jews kidnapped Christian children, ritually tortured and murdered them, and used their blood for various religious purposes, especially for the baking of Passover matzot, is usually assumed to be a striking example of "traditional Russian religious Antisemitism." Actually, the charge was virtually unknown in medieval Russia, and the Russian Orthodox Church played a minimal role in disseminating the idea. The Blood Libel originated in eleventh-century England, and gradually spread eastward across Europe. It became widespread in Poland at the time of the Catholic Counter-Reformation. Thereafter ritual murder charges and trials were a regular phenomenon in Poland. The legend spread to Russian Orthodoxy through the Uniate branch of the Catholic Church in areas of Poland acquired by the Muscovite and Russian Empires. Cases of ritual murder were treated as matters of criminal law, not religious belief, by Russian officials, and the Orthodox clergy played little role in instigating them.

The durability of the Blood Libel owed something to the fact that it was a convenient explanation for any unsolved murder, especially if the disappearance occurred near a Jewish settlement, or if a corpse displayed any evidence of mutilation. In old Poland, such discoveries offered grounds for the arrest of the leadership of the local Jewish community. Russian officials usually were skeptical of these charges.[2] Responding to complaints from Jewish representatives about a ritual murder claim made in Grodno in 1816, Alexander I forbade Russian courts to accept ritual murder as a criminal motive in the absence of physical proof.[3] Despite this injunction, ritual murder cases continued to appear and to be investigated. One of the most notorious cases occurred at Velizh, Vitebsk province, which dragged on through the pre-reform Russian courts for twelve years between 1823 and 1835. It ended with the acquittal of all the accused Jews, although some of them had died in prison in the meantime.[4]

The Velizh Affair concluded with the exile of the chief Christian accusers to Siberia, but aspects of the case continued to bother Nicholas I, who had monitored its progress. He feared that the acquitted Jews might indeed be guilty, since "numerous examples of similar murders ... go to show that among the Jews there probably exist fanatics or sectarians who consider Christian blood necessary for their rites."[5] Either in response to the Tsar's concerns, or on his own initiative, in the early 1840s the Minister of Internal Affairs, L. A. Perovskii, commissioned a full study of the question. Scholarly debate surrounds the identity of the author of this report, since it may have been written by the celebrated Russian lexicographer and folklorist V. I. Dal, who was serving in the ministry at that time.[6] Whoever the author (or, more likely, authors), the manuscript itself was a true scissors and paste job, a compendium of unlikely sources which were in the archives of the MVD as a result of the lengthy investigation of the Velizh Affair. The report drew upon some of the non-Russian classics of occult Judeophobia in the eighteenth century.[7] The literary merit of the work was nil and, since it was published in an edition of only ten copies for internal use, it became an instant bibliographical rarity. When the issue of ritual murder became a public topic, on the other hand, it provided a handy compendium of cases which could be used to substantiate the charge and give it historical background.

The Blood Libel appeared before the public owing to a case which bridged the reign of Nicholas I and the Reform Era.[8] An alleged ritual murder occurred at Saratov, thus making it the first in modern Russian history to appear outside the Pale. The conviction of the accused Jews in 1860 led the government to appoint a special commission to investigate the reality of the Blood Libel.[9] The commission included figures such as A. K. Giers and the nationalist Ukrainian historian, N. Kostomarov. Kostomarov, as a consequence of his service on the committee, accepted the ritual murder to the end of his life.[10] Among those who served on this commission was D. A. Khvolson, a converted Jew who was on the faculty of the Saint Petersburg Theological Seminary, and a leading authority on the Jewish Question in the MVD. Distressed by the convictions, despite his own efforts to debunk the allegations, Khvolson authored a detailed study of the Blood Libel for the commission and published it in the popular *Biblioteka dlia chteniia* in 1861.[11] The Russian press devoted little attention to the Saratov Affair, perhaps due to the censorship, but also because of the distance of the event from the capital, and because the administrative investigation of the case did not lend itself to newspaper coverage. Critical response to Khvolson's first articles and book on the subject was similarly muted.

The Russian Jewish press broke this customary silence. The Russian language supplement to *Ha-Karmel* defended Jews from a ritual murder charge in the Shavel district of Kovno province in 1861. This action prompted a favorable review from the influential *Russkii invalid* in St. Petersburg. Jewish journalists discovered that the timely publicizing and discrediting of blood libels, as was done by *Ha-Karmel*, *Rassvet* and *Ha-Melits* in 1861, made them heroes in the Jewish community.[12] Aggressive journalism posed dangers as well, since the government was not pleased with the negative publicity such campaigns gave Russia abroad. In 1879, when Aleksandr Tsederbaum's *Ha-Melits* published an inaccurate account of a ritual murder charge, it was temporarily closed by the Chief Department of Press Affairs as a punishment.[13]

Given the paucity of press coverage and commentary, it is difficult to estimate the extent to which the Blood Libel was accepted by Russian society when it first appeared. It is more difficult still to estimate the extent to which it infected popular culture, although the spread of the charge into the Russian interior is suggestive.[14] An assessment offered by *Golos* in 1863 may have been typical:

> All religions not yet cleansed from superstition show examples of [human sacrifice], and since all religions have their fanatics, it is in no way unbelievable that among the followers of the teachings of Moses are to be found their own brand of fanatics. It is likely that these people don't know the Talmud very well, but having heard of the superstition about Christian blood, resolved upon cruelty and murder. (188:23/VII/1863)

To fair-minded Russians who knew nothing of Jews or Judaism, this was a reasonable proposition. It exonerated all but a minuscule minority of Jews from guilt and, emphasizing that it arose from factors extraneous to Judaism, blamed fanatics who did not know their religion well. Nevertheless, it was a formulation which no honest Jew – not even a renegade like Brafman – was prepared to accept.[15] The absolute refusal of the Russian Jewish intelligentsia to accept any aspect of the Blood Libel was an ingredient in society's gradual disenchantment with them as a reliable source of information on the Jews. Russians became convinced that there was no smoke without fire.

In the absence of foreign or domestic cases, efforts to publicize the charge before 1870 enjoyed little success. In 1870, P. I. Bartenev, the publisher of the historical journal *Russkii arkhiv*, reprinted the ritual murder report produced by the MVD in 1844. He explained in a foreword that, in light of the Saratov Affair, the charge held contemporary as well as historical interest. Implying that ritual murder was the work of a few Jewish fanatics, he called for the investigation and eradication of the practice.[16] No response was forthcoming, and even the contentious Jewish *Den* declined to comment. Nor was there any

33 N. P. Giliarov-Platonov

public attention given to a report from *Trudy kievskoi dukhovnoi akademii* (July 1869) about an incident in 1833 in Volynia when Jews reportedly performed mutilations to secure blood, even though it was reprinted in *Kievskii telegraf.*

The first successful campaign against ritual murder was launched almost entirely by the Moscow daily *Sovremennye izvestiia*, for whose editor, N. P. Giliarov-Platonov, the Blood Libel constituted a mild obsession.[17] In official circles, Giliarov-Platonov was widely respected for his great, if somewhat eccentric, intellectual gifts. He was educated at the Moscow Theological Seminary, where he later held a chair as a specialist on the Orthodox Church schism. He pursued a service career as a censor for the Ministry of Education. In 1857 he traveled abroad to study Jewish educational institutions. He was close to Slavophile circles, especially the Aksakov family, and was a close friend of

Pobedonostsev.[18] His sponsorship of the Blood Libel did much to give it intellectual respectability.

An article by Giliarov-Platonov published in March 1873 (No. 67) was filled with insinuations. He reported a recent rumor that Jews had bought blood from a woman, as a way of recalling the Saratov and Velizh Affairs. The 1844 report of the MVD demonstrated that ritual murder accusations reoccurred in uncanny succession. He repeated a rumor that, when the report was being reprinted, a Jewish typographer absconded with the galleys. At first, only a few other periodicals were prepared to touch such an esoteric subject. *Kievlianin* published a lengthy article by K. Kozlovskii, later issued as a pamphlet, entitled "A Dark Question in Jewish History," based upon materials in the Kiev Central Archive. The author was skeptical of the charge in the modern era, although he speculated that, at some time in the past, Jews might have accidently murdered a Christian who was impersonating Haman during a drunken Purim celebration.[19]

Having tested the waters, Giliarov-Platonov published a report from Perm in 1875 that Jews had kidnapped a Christian child for ritual purposes (152:5/VI/1875). Enough public attention was attracted to this case that the governor of Perm province and the official *Permskie gubernskie vedomosti* published formal denials (*Sanktpeterburgskie vedomosti*, 177:8/VII/1875). *Sovremennye izvestiia* was not disciplined. Serious newspapers like *Sanktpeterburgskie vedomosti* and *Novoe vremia* (166:6/VII/1875) attacked both the charge and *Sovremennye izvestiia* for making it. The conservative *Russkii mir*, on the other hand, noted the strength of the tradition and printed a detailed account of the Saratov Affair (102:17/VII/1875). *Gazeta A. Gattsuka* treated the accusation as a proven fact (32:15/VIII/1875). Most of the press carried excerpts from the *Sovremennye izvestiia* story and some, like the prestigious *Sudebnyi vestnik*, without comment (120: 1875).

The result of this publicity was predictable. Incidents multiplied, as Christian parents became more vigilant for the safety of their children during the season of Jewish Passover. In 1876 the popular St. Petersburg newspaper *Molva*, citing the *Sovremennye izvestiia* precedent, carried two reports. The first was the claim that Jews had kidnapped a Christian child in Vilna province to slaughter at Passover. A parallel report from Tula recounted that a Christian woman, offered 300 rubles by the Jews to procure them a child, had kidnapped a young girl from the waiting room of a local doctor (14:4/IV/1876). The report from Tula was especially ominous, as an indication that the Blood Libel was spreading outside the Pale.

Growing public interest in the topic provided opportunities for the unscrupulous, especially in the person of one of the most incredible representatives of literary Judeophobia, Ippolit Liutostanskii. Liutostanskii's venality, opportunism, complete lack of scruples and his theatrical ability to play the buffoon, kept most ideological allies from embracing him too closely, even as they dipped into his polluted reservoirs of wisdom. Nonetheless, Liutostanskii was unquestionably the most versatile, successful and obstinate purveyor of the Blood Libel.

It is extremely difficult to reconstruct Liutostanskii's biography, both because he was a pathological liar, and because his contemporary opponents were intent on depicting him in the worst possible light. His frequent involvement in lawsuits did ensure that some confirmable details came to light. Ippolit Liutostanskii was Polish-born and baptized a Roman Catholic in 1835. Ordained a Catholic priest in 1864, he was defrocked in 1867 for sexual misconduct, contracting syphilis in the process. He was tried, but apparently not convicted of perjury and rape.[20] He converted to Russian Orthodoxy in 1868 and briefly was an Orthodox monk. In 1911 Liutostanskii claimed that, while a student at the Moscow Theological Seminary (where Giliarov-Platonov was on the faculty) he was assigned the topic of ritual murder for a candidate degree thesis. When Jewish friends learned of his work, they arranged – at Liutostanskii's suggestion! – to persuade the state rabbi of Moscow, Z. Minor, to collect a bribe of 500 rubles for Liutostanskii to have a new thesis written, a necessity since his Russian was so poor.[21] (It is entirely characteristic of Liutostanskii that he would tell this improbable story, which hardly redounds to his credit, about himself.) Sometime in the 1870s, Liutostanskii appeared in Moscow and revealed his overwhelming vice – graphomania. He published three books in 1875 alone: *An Explanation of the Roman Catholic Mass or Liturgy and an Analysis of its Dogmatic Side*, *On the Necessity of the Incarnation of the Son of God for the Salvation of the Human Race*, and *Teaching about the Holy Spirit at the Last Supper of Jesus Christ and His Disciples*.

Straightforward books of a theological nature did not bring Liutostanskii the recognition or income which he thought his due, and by the end of 1876 he had left the Orthodox clergy. He turned to literary Jew-baiting and in 1876 he published in Moscow *The Question of the Use by Jewish-Sectarians of Christian Blood for Religious Purposes, in Connection with Questions of the General Attitudes of Jewry to Christianity*. This book, while a *succès de scandale*, failed to bring Liutostanskii monetary rewards. In 1880 he surfaced in St. Petersburg as a raconteur of "Jewish sketches" at a local tavern. In the capital he made the acquaintance of the publisher M. A. Aleksandrov and entered negotiations with him to bring out a second edition of the ritual murder book, plus a new work devoted to the Talmud. In the midst of these negotiations Aleksandrov began to have strange visitors. A mysterious woman – subsequently identified as Liutostanskii's landlady – appeared at his flat and offered him 100,000 rubles for the publication rights to all of Liutostanskii's works. A baptized Jew made a similar offer of 50,000 rubles. A letter arrived from Moscow assuring him that the local kahal had raised 100,000 rubles to pay Liutostanskii not to publish his books. Excited at such interest in material which had not yet appeared, Aleksandrov agreed to publish both books and to give an advance of 400 rubles. Once published, the books sold neither at the publisher's outlet nor at bookshops around the capital, even when Liutostanskii placed pictures of himself wearing *tellis* in the windows. (This was the apparent source of the rumor that Liutostanskii had once been a rabbi.) Liutostanskii purchased 1,600 copies of his books at 40 kopecks a pood, but when these failed to sell he was unable to repay his debt to Aleksandrov. When the publisher refused to give Liutostanskii more books on credit, the latter sent him a letter calling him a "thief, swindler and a robber." Aleksandrov brought suit for defamation of character, while Liutostanskii launched a counter-suit claiming that the publisher had stolen his books. The ensuing court cases, which titillated the Petersburg reading public for months, ended with Liutostanskii sentenced to two weeks in prison.[22] Liutostanskii was unlucky at law. In 1880 he also lost a defamation suit against the Jewish publisher Aleksandr Tsederbaum, who had challenged him to a public disputation in order to demonstrate his complete ignorance of Judaism.[23]

Another bizarre turn occurred in 1882. In the midst of the anti-Jewish pogroms of that year, Liutostanskii published *A Contemporary View of the Jewish Question* in Moscow. He denounced the pogroms as the result of "the secret intrigues of the enemies of Russia," and dramatically repudiated his past claims that the Jews used Christian blood. This work was in turn repudiated in 1902 in the second edition of *The Talmud and the Jews*. Liutostanskii explained that five attempts had been made on his life after the Blood Libel book was published, and that he had withdrawn his claims in fear for his life. Venality may also have played a role. In 1882 Liutostanskii approached Baron Gintsburg for "assistance" in printing his collections in a naked attempt to solicit a bribe and even sought a subsidy for a series of his lectures.[24] In the period before the First World War, Liutostanskii resurfaced periodically to fire further broadsides at the Jews.

34 I. Liutostanskii demonstrating the Jewish prayer shawl and phalacteries. The caption confuses the Jewish festival of Purim and the play ("Purim-Shpil") which celebrates it

Critics of Liutostanskii faulted him for being a compiler rather than an author of books. There is truth to this claim. Liutostanskii's books were typified by multi-page quotes from works such as *The Book of the Kahal* and extracts from the periodical press. When *The Question of the Use of Christian Blood* was reissued in Petersburg in 1880, it had grown to two volumes in length, augmented by attacks upon scholarly rivals in the investigation of the Blood Libel.[25] Liutostanskii always made a great show of his academic skills, and his works do follow academic methodology, with bibliographical citations in Latin, German, French and Polish, some of them dating to the sixteenth century. Unsurprisingly, some citations, such as that of "Rambam" (i.e. Maimonides) are clearly fraudulent.[26] What seems likely is that Liutostanskii relied upon little-known works like those of Pikulski, Chiarini and Skripitsyn, extrapolating citations from them which he pretended to cite from the original.[27]

To be fair, Liutostanskii's books did present their arguments in an ordered and logical way, and they were not as incoherent as much occult Judeophobe literature. (They were certainly more readable than *The Book of the Kahal*.) If Liutostanskii was not a learned man, he could certainly imitate one. He presented his arguments in a racy, vigorous style, which could be quite entertaining with its blend of scholarship and buffoonery.

Liutostanskii's starting point was always the Talmud, which he depicted as a font of anti-Christian propaganda and hatred. This hatred in the past inspired anti-Christian acts of sacrilege and desecration. This is what had provoked the persecution of Jews by Christians. Liutostanskii never claimed that the Talmud directly advocated ritual murder, but that small groups of fanatics or sectarians took the anti-Christian prejudices of the Talmud to extremes. As he piously announced: "Jews who acquire only the external trappings of European – and consequently, of Christian – civilization, sitting down at the table of humane enlightenment, not only are blameless of this custom, but don't even know about it. At present . . . the popularity of this custom, which arose amidst the gloom of the Middle Ages, has passed and is perhaps already on the direct road to eradication."[28]

The duplicity of this statement is manifest. It allowed Liutostanskii to pose as objective and fair for not branding all Jews with the accusation, while at the same time insisting upon its reality. If educated Jews had no knowledge of the practice, then their claims and defense of the Jewish masses were uninformed and valueless. Liutostanskii's attacks upon a small band of sectarian fanatics could easily be read another way. Judeophobes customarily singled out the Hasidim as the most ignorant, backward and fanatical of Jews. They thus became a convenient target for the Blood Libel. But the Hasidim were not in fact a small sect, but a branch of East European Jewry which numbered millions of Jews, and much of the Jewish population of the Ukraine and Poland. Singling out the Hasidim, consequently, did not restrict the charge but universalized it. If the practice was so widespread, then it was questionable that it could be hidden from educated, russified Jews like Khvolson, who had studied the charge in detail. Liutostanskii and his successors followed the direction of their own logic. They denounced the Russian Jewish intelligentsia for knowingly suppressing criminal evidence.[29]

The centerpiece of Liutostanskii's work was a series of accounts of

modern ritual murder cases. The persistence of the charge, he maintained, demonstrated that there must be a kernel of truth. He summarized the Damascus Affair of 1840, and devoted almost half the book to
the Velizh and Saratov Affairs within the Russian Empire.

It is curious that Liutostanskii's books were apparently unprofitable,
for they created an enormous stir in the Russian press, generating
scores of reviews and – greater praise still – imitators. Whether
reviewers were friendly or hostile, they all treated the books as serious
works of scholarship, deserving of a conscientious critique. The
popular *Peterburgskii listok* offered a detailed synopsis, emphasizing
that the charge was directed only against the Hasidim, and used it to
explain the reported kidnapping of a Christian child in Tula (68:8/IV/
1876). *Grazhdanin* welcomed the book as the first scholarly attempt to
study the problem. Noting that blame should only be placed on
fanatical sectarians, the author found it disquieting "how many fanatical sectarians we have in our midst" (4:25/I/1876). In 1878 the editors
retracted from their earlier praise when they published their own
series on the Blood Libel. They promised their readers information
superior to "the confused account of Liutostanskii." In fact, the series
was nothing more than the MVD report of the 1840s, which *Grazhdanin*
attributed to Skripitsyn rather than Dal. The original report was
updated to 1871 with material that may well have come from Liutostanskii's book.[30]

Not all publications were so indulgent of the Blood Libel. An Orthodox Church publication, *Strannik*, not known for sympathy toward the
Jews, published a lengthy review written by its editor, Father S. V.
Protopopov (II: II/1877:259–85).[31] Protopopov criticized the onesided-
ness of Liutostanskii's sources, offered a negative but more balanced
assessment of the Talmud, and bade Christians to be charitable in
rejecting false accusations.

Liutostanskii's works provoked a spate of other books. N. D. Shigarin published two books denying the charge in 1877 and 1880, at least
partly in an effort to secure a subsidy from the OPE, although the
organization remained true to its commitment not to fund polemical
works.[32] Prince N. N. Golitsyn, an indefatigable commentator on the
Jewish Question and the new editor of *Varshavskii dnevnik*, published a
rather confused study of the Blood Libel which failed to reach any
precise conclusion.[33] Rabbi Z. Minor, the state rabbi of the Moscow
Jewish community, and Professor D. A. Khvolson, published short
pamphlets in 1879.

The literary debate was suddenly overtaken by events: on 5 March

1879 the Kutais District Court indicted nine Georgian Jews for the murder of Sarra Iosifova Modebadze. The indictment made no overt reference to ritual murder, but few commentators missed the point. The disappearance of young Sarra occurred the day before the feast of Passover, a detail included in the indictment and noted by the defense when it introduced the issue of Blood Libel into the trial. The evidence against the accused was circumstantial: they had passed along the road near Sarra's house about the time that she disappeared. When her corpse was discovered two days later, the body bore marks of mutilation. Georgia, in the Caucasus, had been the site of an earlier ritual murder accusation, at Suram in 1847.

The leadership of the Jewish community in St. Petersburg recognized the significance of the accusation, and procured two outstanding attorneys, P. Ia. Aleksandrov, who had defended the terrorist Vera Zasulich in a celebrated political trial, and L. Kupernik.[34] Kutais was the first Blood Libel trial in Russia to be heard in the post-reform courts, in the new confrontational style, before a jury. Full publicity was permitted. The trial ended on 13 March 1879 with the full acquittal of all the defendants. Under Russian legal procedure, the prosecution was permitted to appeal the verdict. The appeal was heard by the higher court in Tiflis in April of 1880. Again, acquittals were handed down.

This case, with its public procedures, the ample opportunities to comment on the workings of Russian justice, and the sensational nature of the accusation, made the matter a *cause célèbre*. The Russian Jewish press, represented now by two weeklies and an almanac, gave the case maximum publicity. They carried full transcripts of the trial, and published them in book form. Most Russian papers also devoted their "judicial chronicle" sections to the trial.

There was much to provoke comment, especially the ambiguous nature of the forensic evidence presented by the prosecution. The medical inspector originally ruled that Sarra had drowned in a driving rain, a claim that was dismissed with ridicule by those who suspected a ritual element. The defenders of the Jews, in their turn, pointed to the "mutilations" on the girl's body as the work of birds and small animals. Under the spell of the ritual accusation, initial dispositions were revised. Local peasants testified that what they had previously identified as the bleating of a goat in a sack carried by one of the Jews they belatedly knew to be cries from the hapless girl.

The trial itself was a godsend to periodicals which had been pressing the Blood Libel claim, and which had been attacked for "medieval fanaticism." *Grazhdanin* recalled that its previous year's series on ritual murder had been ignored by other editors, either because they were afraid of being branded "illiberal" or because they were dominated by liberal Jews. "Yet in February, in Kutais District Court, there will be tried the 149th such case, by our reckoning, involving the activities of Jewish fanatics" (4:6/II/1879). *Grazhdanin* feared that justice might not be done since there were rumors that the Jews had collected 25,000 rubles for bribes.

In *Sovremennye izvestiia*, Giliarov-Platonov explained that only Christian fanatics believed that most Jews used children's blood for ritual purposes. Since Christian society produced fanatics, it was logical to assume that the rude, unenlightened mass of Jewry did so as well. "Isn't it possible that this hatred [of Christians] has led to inhuman extremes; could it not have turned into a rule, an obligation, a tradition, formalized, for example, into a certain specific command to torture children"? (67:9/III/1879). Since only a small group of Jewish fanatics were involved, Giliarov-Platonov urged enlightened Jews, for their own security, to admit the reality of the charge and to extirpate it among their fellows. He was ruefully skeptical, however, that the Jewish intelligentsia would ever stop calling the charge "medieval fanaticism" or equating the Kutais court with the Inquisition.

The liberal press greeted the acquittals with jubilation. *Golos*, ready to accept the possibility of ritual murder by Jewish sectarians in 1863, greeted the end of a drama "which has weighed already on the conscience of Christians for seven centuries" (74:15/III/1879). The paper was in retreat from its militant Judeophobia of the previous two decades, and the trial provided an excellent opportunity for reconciliation. "From our very soul we greet, in the Kutais trial, the first *local* verdict on this absurd accusation, which has taken the lives and honor of hundreds of thousands of innocent persons, and to this day casts a shadow over assumptions about the religious life of our Jews." *Otechestvennye zapiski* denounced the "superfluous and inflammatory affairs of this sort," and urged prison terms for those guilty of criminal incitement in such cases (6/VI/1879:199–210). Commenting on the Appeal Court's confirmation of the acquittal, *Russkii evrei* expressed its dismay not at the Blood Libel itself, which was a product of medieval credulity like belief in witchcraft, but at the thought that modern, intelligent persons were ready to entertain it. Surely the case should have been dropped after the initial investigation, given the numerous contradictions in the testimony of witnesses (19:7/V/1880). *Sanktpeterburgskie vedomosti* agreed. It was understandable that "children of nature," the half-wild mountain people of Georgia, attuned to the legends and superstitions of their forefathers, should believe the Blood Libel but it was inexplicable that the Caucasian state prosecutor should accept this fantasy. In the past, criminal charges of this type evaporated as soon as they reached the last court of appeal, the Senate. The prosecutor should have been aware of these historical precedents, because now there was the risk that the charge, given publicity, would spread all over the Pale (74:16/III/1879). A correspondent in *Odesskii vestnik* focused on the claim that ritual murder was practiced by sectarians such as the Hasidim. The author noted that the Blood Libel was older than the hasidic movement. Besides there were no essential religious differences between Hasidim and Mitnagdim. Belief in bloodthirsty sectarians was nothing more than the "fruit of an ignorant mind" (78:11/IV/1879).

The innocent verdict produced a mournful post-mortem from Giliarov-Platonov.

> A crime has occurred against an innocent child and, despite the fact that the voice of the child cried out for vengeance, the crime now appears to be, for some reason, not a crime, not a punishable act at all; all of those who were indicted for the murder of Sarra were acquitted; acquitted although, as is obvious to a reader of the transcript, the legal process did not provide a satisfactory explanation of what, other than murder, might have produced the death of the unhappy Sarra. (112:25/IV/1879)

Giliarov-Platonov refused to concede victory to the "anarchist-liberal press." *Golos* was jubilant at the verdict, he grumbled, because the editors had assumed that the case was lost. *Golos'* claims notwithstanding, the trial was not a public refutation of the Blood Libel since the Kutais case was an ordinary murder trial without religious overtones. This contention directly contradicted the accusatory *Sovremennye izvestiia* editorial of 9 March 1879.

A number of papers avoided the rejoicing of *Golos* or the spleen of *Sovremennye izvestiia*. A third approach, one marked by diffidence or ambivalence, was typified by *Kavkaz*, a daily published in the Georgian capital of Tiflis and one of the region's oldest Russian publications. The paper lamented that the real outcome of the trial was that nothing was resolved: "the spirit of contradiction infected it from start to finish." There had been three medical examinations of the corpse, and each had reached different conclusions. The testimony of the witnesses was contradictory, and some of them admitted to lying in their initial dispositions. There were contradictions in the criminal indictment, and even in the speeches of the three defense attorneys (83:15/IV and 88:22/IV/1879). The Judeophobe but opportunistic *Novorossiiskii telegraf* of Odessa was clearly uncertain of how to play the story, alternating critical and credulous articles (1209:16/III; 1223:1/IV; 1249:5/V/1879). The populist *Nedelia* found the Kutais Affair "imprecise, puzzling and contradictory." It had not resolved one way or the other the question of the Blood Libel but had shown the grain of truth in the popular belief. In the present case, the accused Jews had been acquitted only after a mass of evidence against them was refuted by the exertions of very prominent attorneys. Even then, their acquittal rested on the rubric of the reformed law that provided that every doubt was to be resolved in favor of the accused. The paper reviewed recent ritual murder literature, and found much in Liutostanskii's work to recommend it (6:6/V/1879).

While *Golos* made the transition from Judeophobia to Judeophilia, *Novoe vremia* moved in the opposite direction. This transition was still in progress – *Sovremennye izvestiia* still assumed that *Novoe vremia* would automatically side with the Jews on the Blood Libel issue and attacked the paper as "filled up with Jews" – but the paper's treatment of the Kutais Affair helped to complete the shift. The paper pursued what had become the middle course: belief in the Blood Libel while attributing it to a small group of "extreme fanatics" (1169:2/VI/1879). *Novoe vremia*'s own reporter in the courtroom asserted that neither those who sat through all the testimony nor those who lived in the area were satisfied with the verdict. The witnesses were poor peasants, confused by legal proceedings conducted in a bewildering mix of Russian and Georgian, and easily tripped up by the skilled attorneys who led them over the fine points of dispositions which they had given over a year previously. (These same attorneys were rumored to have suborned some of the witnesses.) This report attributed the acquittal to the defense team's ability to convince the court that there was no dogma of the Jewish religion which required the use of Christian blood at Passover. But this begged the question, for the charge was not being made against Orthodox Jews, but against sectarians like the Hasidim. The home village of the accused murderers was populated by Hasids. Moreover, the chief prosecutor had been ill and failed to argue a convincing case. The whole affair was highly unsatisfactory (1106:28/III/1879).

The debate did not end with the acquittal. New editions of the work of Khvolson and Liutostanskii kept the issue alive in the review sections of the press. The contemporary affair also helped to stir up memories of the past. *Sanktpeterburgskie vedomosti,* in faulting the local prosecutor for bringing the case, claimed that the highest authority, the Senate, invariably dismissed ritual murder cases. This was not entirely true. The Senate had in fact upheld the conviction of the Jews accused in the Saratov Affair of 1852–60. The pardon subsequently given the surviving defendants – given, it could be argued, in deference to the intervention of influential foreign Jews – did not invalidate the original verdict. A voice from the Saratov investigation now spoke out. It was not the voice of a provincial prosecutor or a credulous peasant, but a distinguished man of letters, N. Kostomarov.

During a period of internal exile after the breakup of the Society of Saints Kyril and Methodius, the young Kostomarov served in the chancellery of Saratov province.[35] One of his duties during this time was to assist in the investigation of the Saratov Affair. He was convinced of the guilt of the accused. He considered it a provocation when Khvolson, who had also served on the investigating committee, published a pamphlet which specifically defended the innocence of the accused Jews of Saratov, and faulted the Russian officials who had been involved for their confusion and ignorance. Kostomarov, now a professor at the University of St. Petersburg, responded to a favorable review of Khvolson's book in *Novoe vremia* with a defense of the original proceedings. He insisted that there was ample evidence to implicate Jewish sectarians in the practice of ritual murder. Seeking authority to support this charge, he invoked Liutostanskii, thus giving considerable academic cachet to the Polish adventurer.[36] Khvolson replied to Kostomarov in a long article in *Novoe vremia* which recapitulated all the Saratov evidence. Khvolson warned Kostomarov of the danger of continuing to spread the Blood Libel among the public. Besides the Kutais Affair, ritual murder charges had recently been raised in Berdichev, Dunaburg, Trentelberg near Riga, Mikhailovka near Belostok and elsewhere. In Kovno province a crowd of peasants, led by a Catholic priest, had recently attacked local Jews when a peasant from the village disappeared. Khvolson asked Kostomarov if Jews must be placed in danger every time a drunken peasant spent too much time away from his village (1192:25/VI/1879).

This was not an idle fear, especially when respectable, widely circulated newspapers like *Novoe vremia* spread Blood Libel news at every opportunity. In October of 1879, for example, the paper published a rumor making the rounds in St. Petersburg that a child had been kidnapped, "somewhat like the Kutais Affair" (1292:3/X/1879). The kidnapper was said to be a Jewish doctor, thus spreading the charge against educated Jews, not just hasidic fanatics, a point that a number of newspapers immediately pointed out.[37] On the eve of Christian Holy Week in 1881, when religious feeling ran high against the Jews, *Novoe vremia* and other papers reported the kidnapping of a Christian child. Rival papers, especially after the outbreak of pogroms in 1881, attacked these stories as the height of irresponsibility.[38]

Ritual murder charges were only a minor feature in early pogroms, such as those in Odessa in 1859 and 1871. A few contemporary accounts of the pogroms of 1881 suggest that the Blood Libel was bruited about in some pogrom locations, and *Novoe vremia* was widely condemned for publishing an inaccurate account that a Jew had kidnapped a Christian child on the eve of Passover (1841:15/IV/1881). On the whole the charge was always subordinate to broader Judeophobe attacks. There was only one significant exception, but it is worth a brief note because it involved the first pogrom, in Elizavetgrad, which triggered the "southern storms."

The most common account of what happened in Elizavetgrad on the evening of 15 April 1881 is that a Jewish publican roughly evicted from his tavern a Christian simpleton who had broken a glass. A crowd gathered to the cry of "they are beating Christians," and the ensuing street fight escalated into the pogrom (*Elizavetgradskii vestnik*, 42:19/IV/1881). A totally different account, appearing nowhere else, was published in 1881. The correspondent reported that a group of tradesmen found, near a market stall, a crate containing glass jars filled with human anatomical remains. The jars were subsequently found to be those of two children who had been poisoned and whose internal organs were being sent for medical examination. The discovery of the remains, according to this account, triggered a ritual murder rumor and this grew into the pogrom. This account is curious – it is buttressed by names and specific details – but was reprinted nowhere else.[39]

In contrast to these shadowy reports, the Blood Libel was more directly responsible for the last major pogrom of the nineteenth century in Russia, the massacre of the small Jewish population of Nizhnii Novgorod in 1884. The event made a very strong impression upon public opinion in Russia. Not only did it occur outside of the Pale or Poland, but its victims were educated Jews, presumably well-integrated into the community. Ten Jews were barbarously murdered with axes by a mob which was inflamed by the report that a missing child had been kidnapped by the Jews for her blood (*Moskovskii vedomosti*, 160–3:11–13/VI/1884).

Despite the controversy which surrounded it, the Kutais trial was not the most celebrated ritual murder affair to be reported in the Russian press. That dubious distinction goes to the Tisza-Eszlar Affair in 1883 in Hungary. Unlike the Kutais trial, where there were no direct witnesses and the Jews protested their innocence, the Tisza-Eszlar Affair was based on testimony of the most spectacular kind, the accusations of the five and fourteen-year-old sons of the chief defendent, Josef Sharf. They claimed that their father had assisted in the torture and murder of fourteen-year-old Esther Solimosi, who disappeared without a trace on the eve of Passover in 1882. Although there was no forensic evidence, the case was taken up by prominent members of the political antisemitic movement in Hungary, especially by the parliamentary deputies Gyozo Istoczy and Geza von Onody. Their pressure and influence helped to force the indictment of fifteen Jews from Tisza-Eszlar. When the body of a drowning victim, dressed in Esther's clothes, was pulled from a nearby river, Antisemites insisted that the Jews had substituted another body, and called for the case to be brought to court. The ensuing trial, which featured a confrontation between the older Sharf and his teenage son Moritz, was lurid and dramatic. The state prosecutor, Zeifert, created a sensation when his summary speech lamented that an indictment had ever been handed down. The acquittal of all the defendants in 1883 touched off anti-Jewish rioting in rural Hungary and an anti-Jewish pogrom in Pressburg. Esther Solimosi was canonized by Antisemites as the symbol of Christian Europe under attack by Jews, and her portrait was hung on the podium of the Second World Antisemitic Congress in Dresden.

While the Tisza-Eszlar affair captured the fancy of the Russian reading public, the Judeophobe press did not lead the way. Perhaps it was a case of "once bitten, twice shy" or the growing realization that the conflicting testimony in the case would probably lead to an acquittal, but the Judeophobes had little to say for the record. *Novoe vremia*, which accepted the Blood Libel, and *Kievlianin*, which did not, carried complete transcripts of the trial, but provided no editorial comment. Ivan Aksakov's *Rus*, in the midst of a vitriolic campaign against "international Jewry," failed to discuss the case at all. Only one Russian publication embraced the Blood Libel on this occasion, the idiosyncratic magazine *Gazeta A. Gattsuka*, an illustrated periodical of dubious moral principles. It published a portrait of Esther Solimosi and an interior view of the synagogue, complete with instruments of torture, where the murder was supposed to have occurred.[40]

In contrast, the liberal and moderate press seized on the trial. Russia had been under continual attack from the European press for its "barbarism" after the outbreak of the 1881 pogroms. (Indeed, another serious pogrom broke out in Ekaterinoslav at almost the same time as the Tisza-Eszlar Affair was being reported.) That part of the Russian press which refused to justify pogroms had to suffer and be still in the face of foreign gibes. This convenient opportunity enabled the liberal press to demonstrate its patriotism by attacking the critics of Russia, and to do so in the name of liberal principles. The Antisemites involved in the Tisza-Eszlar Affair, were abused as fanatics and anti-liberals.

Zaria, a liberal Kiev publication, characterized the trial as "something that seems to have stepped out of a medieval archive." It observed disdainfully that torture had been used to secure testimony – one of the jailers had made reference to thumbscrews – and condemned the "scandals and outrages of the Antisemites" (133:21/VI/ 1883). *Russkii kurer* assumed that the government had permitted the trial to go ahead purely in order to discomfit the radical political opposition, some of whom were prominent Antisemites. The results of "this tendentious case were absolutely harmful" (113:9/VII/1883). *Odesskii vestnik* reported that the Pressburg pogrom had been prepared by the Antisemites well in advance once they realized that they would lose the criminal case. Their actions were devoid of enlightenment or morality (164:27/VII/1883). The radical thick journal *Delo* called upon Hungary to decide whether or not it wished to be a civilized nation (8:VIII/1883, 108–9). *Odesskii vestnik* was most comprehensive in its condemnations of this "monstrous case." What could one expect from polite Magyar society, it queried, when it already persecuted Slavs, Romanians and Germans in the name of Magyarization, while at the same time doing nothing for the Magyar peasantry, which now revealed its backwardness and obscurantism (136:22/VI/1882).

The failure of the Judeophobe press to capitalize on the Tisza-Eszlar Affair as a vehicle to attack Russian Jewry should not be misconstrued. The Blood Libel had acquired credence and intellectual respectability within conservative ranks, and was capable of reappearing at any moment. An interesting aspect of the spread of the charge was the insignificant role played by the Russian Orthodox clergy. The main carriers were laymen, like Giliarov-Platonov, who was educated in the Moscow Theological Seminary and taught there. It was Konstantin Pobedonostsev, the lay Ober-Procurator of the Holy Synod, who sponsored the cults of ritual murder victims like Blessed Gavriil Zablu-dovskii. Church officials were far more reluctant to admit this cult, perhaps because it was of Uniate provenance.[41]

Russian believers in the Blood Libel argued that it was not born of religious fanaticism, which they professed to eschew. Rather, they maintained that the persistent reappearance of the charge demonstrated its kernel of truth. As Giliarov-Platonov declared, "there must be something there, some kind of reality, and not just an opinion" (67:9/III/1879). They legitimized the charge with a peculiar appeal to ecumenism. They were willing to concede that there were fanatical Christian sects which might even practice ritual murder. Why did Jewish intellectuals obstinately refuse to even entertain the possibility that obscure Jewish sects might do the same? Why must all Jews be invested with a moral superiority denied to all Christians? Jewish denials merely reinforced their belief. As members of a secure, dominant religion, they were unable to understand the significance of the charge for Jews, a symbol of Jewish insecurity in the midst of Christian society. Thus, conservatives were always receptive to the search for the physical evidence that would acquit them of the charge of religious fanaticism, and confound hostile European opinion. These facts help to explain the notorious Beilis Affair of 1911–12, which is usually presented as the fruit of popular fanaticism and cynical opportunism by unscrupulous officials. These elements were certainly present, but so was the predisposition to accept the Blood Libel which led Russian conservatives down the slippery slope of the Beilis prosecution. There were Russians of good mind and character who could accept the claim of ritual murder with a clean conscience.

Once accepted, the charge spread, often trickling down from intellectuals to the common people. It penetrated to the Russian interior, to Perm, Nizhnii Novgorod, Tula and even St. Petersburg. In 1884, the newspaper *Ekho* reported from Tambov that Jewish travelers attracted great attention from crowds of people who were convinced that they drank blood and had an extra eye (1218:21/VI/1884).[42]

Victims of fanaticism

Once the principle was accepted that the Jews slew young children, it was a short step to the belief that they routinely murdered Christian adults and recalcitrant members of the Jewish community. A common motive provided the link – religious fanaticism. The stubborn adherence of the Jews to their ancestral religion, their alleged hostility to converts and renegades, the reality of the occasional murder of individual reformers deemed dangerous to the survival of the community, was long an integral feature of Judeophobe lore. In 1867 a crowd of Jews outside the Staryi Pochaev monastery staged a near riot to prevent the baptism of a young Jewess. Ivan Aksakov used this event as a starting point for his claim that "Jewish privileges" were so great that they could effectively delay or prevent the baptism of would-be converts (*Moskva*, 84:15/VII/1867). *Vilenskii vestnik* reported another attack in 1867 on a Jew seeking baptism (83:20/VII/1867), while *Kievlianin* claimed in 1869 that a would-be convert had been murdered at the instigation of the local rabbi (105:6/IX/1869). It was to counter such intimidation and threats that a number of refuges were organized for Jewish converts in St. Petersburg, under the sponsorship of members of the royal family.[43]

With the public's discovery of the kahal, the charge was transferred from a few obscure fanatics to this organized, illegal Jewish community. Brafman emphasized that the kahal did not stop at murder to achieve its ends. Taking this cue, the press was filled throughout the 1870s with reports of the murder of those who had opposed the kahal's will: a tavernkeeper who resisted the kahal's monopoly; an informer who denounced kahal misdeeds to the authorities; an informer who helped to break up a draft-dodging ring.[44] Most popular of all were combinations of these motifs which described the murder or abduction of would-be converts by the kahal.

This theme was sounded by Giliarov-Platonov in the midst of *Sovremennye izvestiia*'s campaign against ritual murder, and represented a logical extension of his accusations against the Jews (167:20/VI/1875). The charge was enthusiastically taken up in the 1880s by both the boulevard and the serious press.[45] When a rumor was floated in 1885 that the Kishinev reformer, Josif Rabinovich, had been murdered on the street by a mob of Jewish fanatics, it was reprinted and believed at home and abroad, and still cited as evidence of Jewish conduct in a thick journal two years after it was shown to be false.[46] The death of Iakov Brafman was widely believed to be the work of the kahal.[47]

Nor were Christians safe. There were recurrent tales of violence directed against those who assisted the conversion of Jews. Even more frequent were stories of the elimination of lovers who threatened to draw a Jewish son or daughter away from the faith. The most notorious of these cases was the criminal trial of Zimel and Ester Lotsov, accused of murdering their young Christian servant girl, Maria Drich. The prosecutor established as the motive of the homicide the couples' fear that Maria had seduced their son and was trying to convert him to Christianity. After an acquittal in a lower court, the couple was convicted, to the raucous delight of the Judeophobe press. Here at last was a criminal case where the Jews had not been able to slip the bonds of justice. *Novoe vremia*, one of many papers to carry a complete trial transcript, hailed the verdict as legal proof that the Jews were capable of committing the most heinous crimes "entirely from religious motives" (3490:14/XI/1885). The sensationalizing *Golos Moskvy*, like many such papers, assigned the ultimate blame for such outrages to fanaticism generated by the Talmud (198:29/IX/1885).

The Talmud and the Jews

Surveying the debate generated by Aleksandrov's articles in 1862 on the Talmud, V. Fedorov (Grinbaum), the Jewish convert who served as censor of Jewish books for the Kiev Educational District, lamented to a friend that "neither *Ha-Melits* nor *Ha-Karmel*, nor the two rabbinical seminaries – all these institutions which could come forward with magnificent citations from the Talmud – don't say a word. We are poor in people!"[48] In fact a variety of Jewish voices were heard in the debates on the Talmud which occupied the late 1860s. Fedorov's lament is justified by the failure to present a united or coherent view of the Talmud. For every Jew willing to give an apologetic or balanced view of the Talmud,[49] there were others, like Brafman's young collaborator, G. Levin, who condemned it as "the chief obstacle to the progressive development of Russian Jewry" (*Syn otechestva*, 286 and 287: 17–18/XII/1868).

For the conservative and publicity-conscious Jewish leadership in St. Petersburg, an articulate and unified defense was needed. If the game was to be played with talmudic citations, Jews could also participate. The OPE resolved to sponsor a work which would reveal the Talmud's high moral tone, and silence the malicious interpretations of ignorant publicists. Significantly, the project was suggested by D. Khvolson, the scholar-convert who bridged the Jewish and gentile worlds. Ostensibly designed to promote the use of Russian among Jews, the resultant work, *The World-View of the Talmudists*, was actually an apologetic work which sought to acquaint Russians with Jewish learning. The first volume appeared in 1874, the second and third in 1876.[50]

The moment appeared propitious, as the ferocity of the original debates on the Talmud in the 1860s had died down. In a perverse way, Brafman's brand of Judeophobia, which centered the negative features of Jewish life in the kahal rather than in the Talmud, redirected the debate.[51] But this proved to be merely the calm before the storm, because Judeophobes were not prepared to let a defense of the Talmud pass unchallenged. The publication of the first volume of *The World-*

View, for example, prompted an entire book in reply from Ippolit Liutostanskii, *The Talmud and the Jews*.[52] Liutostanskii had already voiced his opinion of the Talmud in his book on ritual murder as "nothing more than the historical demonstration of that hatred which Jewry has nourished toward Christianity from the first moment of its appearance in the world, nothing more than a deliberate, malevolent perversion, the corruption of the Old Testament in one exclusive direction – blind, boundless hostility toward Christ and His followers."[53] There may also have been external circumstances which helped to popularize hatred of the Talmud in Russia. In 1871 a respected Catholic scholar, August Rohling of Prague, published *Der Talmudjude*, an attack on the Talmud and the moral foundations of contemporary Judaism. The work ultimately provoked a sensational lawsuit in which Rohling's ignorance of the Talmud was demonstrated.[54] Both before and after Rohling's fall, his book was widely publicized. In 1875 it was published in Polish translation in Lwow, making it more accessible to the Slavic world. Rohling's name began to appear alongside Eisenmenger's in the bibliographies of the Judeophobe movement (and as a mine of misquotations).[55]

All the negative features of Jewry, real and imagined, were linked to the Talmud. They ranged from ritual murder to efforts at world domination. The Jewish publicist G. Bogrov drew the obvious conclusion in *Novoe vremia* in 1875. If Jewish interpretations of the Bible and the Talmud were as the Judeophobes claimed, then the Jews were "some sort of anachronism among the civilized states of Europe, some sort of ruthless barbaric Mongolism, some sort of systematically-raised and trained vampires." In short, the Jews would have to be considered "moral *skoptsy*" (166:6/VII/1875). By the end of the decade the transformed *Novoe vremia* placed the center of the Jewish Question in the Talmud, "the alpha and omega ... the fundamental law of Jewish civilization and citizenship" (1371:21/XII/1879). This being the case, measures should be taken. In 1883 and 1884, *Rus* and *Varshavskii dnevnik* both recommended the convocation of a government committee to censor the Talmud of its anti-social and anti-Christian elements.[56] Until reform of this sort took place, opined *Novoe vremia*, resolution of the Jewish Question was impossible: "in the Talmud lies the foundation of Judaism as a closed world with those cultural, domestic and moral characteristics which, whenever Jews meet adherents of another religion, invariably and universally gives birth to the Jewish Question" (2991:27/VI/1884).

The international kahal

Since Russian Judeophobes were the fabricators of *The Protocols of the Elders of Zion*, the most notorious "proof" of the Jewish world conspiracy, it is ironic that the motif was somewhat delayed in entering Russia. The organized enmity of the Jews toward Christian Europe was a recurrent theme in European religious Jew-hatred. In the absence of a similarly articulated religious Judeophobia in Russia, the charge was imported. It is true that Russians, most particularly Iakov Brafman, made significant contributions to the myth. It was not a component of Brafman's original indictment of the Jews, however, and was only added after Brafman became more acquainted with Western conspiracy theories. Once the concept was generated, it did find ready soil in Russia, where paranoid fears grew and flourished, nourished and legitimized by new infusions from the West.

Occult themes from Western Jew-hatred appeared in Russia in the 1870s. The first was a forerunner of *The Protocols*, a short document usually called "The Rabbi's Speech." It was actually a chapter entitled "The Jewish Cemetery in Prague," taken from the novel *Biarritz*. It was published in Berlin in 1868 under the name "Sir John Retcliffe," the pen name of Hermann Goedsche. The hero of the novel spies on the centennial meeting of representatives of the Twelve Tribes of Israel who have come to report to the devil on their success in undermining and subjugating the Christian world. The elders are encouraged by a speech of the chief rabbi who assures them that soon all the world's gold – and thus its power – will be in their hands. The kings of the world are already their debtors, while the Christian Church is increasingly demoralized.

The chapter was published as a pamphlet in a cheap edition of 6,000 copies in St. Petersburg in 1872. The following year it was reprinted in *Kievlianin*, clearly labeled as fiction (45–48:17–24/IV/1873). The next year demonstrated the ease with which it could be linked to Brafman's work when it was published in a Polish "reworking" of *The Book of the Kahal*.[57] The material now was treated as a factual event. From this source it was picked up by Liutostanskii for his *Talmud i Evrei*, illustrating the proclivity of Judeophobes for plundering each other's works for the choicest morsels.[58] Although it should have been familiar due to frequent reprintings, "The Rabbi's Speech" attracted considerable attention when it appeared in K. Volskii's *Evrei v Rossii*, perhaps because it was translated from a French edition.[59] The public had a short memory: the reviewer for *Russkaia mysl* found "The Rabbi's

Speech" to be the only novelty in the book (11: November 1887), while *Sanktpeterburgskie vedomosti* and *Novoe vremia* seriously treated the speech as the latest factual evidence of the Jewish world conspiracy.[60]

A less enthusiastic welcome greeted an anti-Jewish tract which had enjoyed some success in the West, *The Subjugation of the World by the Jews*, by "Maior Osman Bei."[61] The book described the Jews' master plan to achieve world domination through the accumulation of all the world's wealth. "We will gather into our hands," they thought, "the gold of our enemies; we will exploit their work and leave to them their fields and vineyards which they will work for our benefit. We will become the masters, they the slaves."[62] In the modern age, Osman Bei claimed, the Jews had almost completed this task. Cosmopolitan ideas and religious toleration had allowed them to pretend to assimilate. The unification of the world market let them gain control of all the capital in the world. On the last two pages of his book, almost as an afterthought, he identified the agency which served as a central bureau for the coordination of all these activities: the Alliance Israélite Universelle. In contrast to Osman Bei's later works, few details were given of the Alliance's activities.[63]

Russian reviewers were unimpressed. *Delo* marvelled at the author and his work, "which seems to have dropped from heaven," and which presumed in forty-eight pages to encompass the entire history of the Jewish race (4:IV/1874, 79–81). *Kievlianin* sarcastically juxtaposed the alleged "subjectors of the world" to the hapless Kiev tavern-keeper, whose livelihood was threatened by new laws regulating the spirit trade (80:6/VII/1874). *Odesskii vestnik* provided two reviews. The first simply dismissed his premises, predicting that the Jewish Question would disappear with the spread of enlightenment (176:9/VIII/1874). A second accepted his claim of Jewish internationalism and called upon Jews to sever their foreign links (204:17/IX/1874). Significantly, none of these reviews paid any attention to the Alliance, or even mentioned its name.

Iakov Brafman was the first to alert Russian society to the dangers of the Alliance, as he gradually integrated western motifs into his homegrown theories. Brafman had done no more than name the Alliance as one of many "Jewish brotherhoods, local and international," in his 1868 book of that name. Nor was the Alliance overtly connected with the Russian OPE. The Alliance and the OPE were treated as non-occult, human institutions, whose greatest crime was the attempt to recreate an independent Jewish political life. In 1874 Brafman either wrote or consulted on a *Golos* editorial which complained that the kahal was helping Jews to avoid military service, and condemned foreign Jewish groups for sheltering Jewish draft dodgers. The editorial noted that the Alliance had met in closed session in Berlin to discuss the problem of military recruitment in Russia (279:9/X/1874). This claim drew a response from the chairman of the Alliance, Adolphe Crémieux. He cited the Talmud to prove that Jews were religiously bound to follow the laws of the state of which they were citizens. He denied that the Alliance assisted draft evasion, or that it pursued any political objectives beyond that of combatting Jewish persecution (94:4/IV/1875).

Crémieux's letter provided Brafman with a pretext to launch an extended attack upon the Alliance, and to view it in a far different light than he had done in 1868. Brafman rejected the claim that the Alliance lacked a political agenda by pointing to its multiple interventions on behalf of "persecuted Jews" in a number of countries, its sabotage of the work of the Vilna Jewish Commission, and its endeavors to embroil Russia and the United States in a diplomatic squabble over the Jews. Crémieux responded in his letter that the Alliance was composed of English, German, Italian, American and Austrian members, each expressing the disparate views of their respective countries. Brafman rejected this assertion with a quote from a Crémieux speech of 1869: "We are brothers, we are all children of one nation, we are not French, nor the divided Germans. We all have one heart – Israelite" (94:4/IV/1875).[64] In 1876, *Golos*, under Brafman's influence, made the connection between the Alliance and its "Russian branch," the OPE. The OPE's publication of books in Hebrew and its subsidies to the Hebrew press were seen as an attempt "to keep alive the linguistic bonds tying together all the Jews of the world (which constitute their national banner) and keeps alive the talmudic and doctrinaire beliefs of the Jews" (216:6/VIII/1876). Heretofore Brafman had described the objectives of the kahal and its agencies as the preservation of the national Jewish spirit, which was a passive, defensive goal. Now he portrayed Jewish aims as active, designed to degrade and undermine the Christian Russian state and ultimately to dominate it. By 1882 the Alliance and the OPE had become thoroughly mythologized into a joint institution pursuing a "grandiose political mission" against the Christian world.[65]

The extreme Judeophobe press followed Brafman's lead. In 1878, Prince N. N. Golitsyn, the former editor of *Varshavskii dnevnik* and a recognized expert on the Jewish Question, characterized the Alliance as a unique institution, "with agents everywhere who dare, without middlemen, to intercede with governments, including that of Russia" (*Grazhdanin*, 29–31:24/XI/1878). When a revised edition of *Kniga kagala* was published in 1881, Aksakov's *Rus* excerpted much of its new material, including the book's call for the Russian government to close the "local branch" of the Alliance, the OPE, and to prevent the parent branch from meddling further in Russian national affairs (46–47:26/IX–3/X/1881). The excerpts were said to show the great discrepancy which existed between the public goals of the Alliance and the OPE, as stated in their charters and protocols, and their real objectives. "Contraband is almost always hidden under legal goods. It is well known that secret protocols exist in Russia, different from those submitted to the government" (47:3/X/1881). Given this assertion, the excitement of Ivan Aksakov may well be imagined when he succeeded in laying his hands upon one of these "secret protocols."

The document in question, which was reprinted from the French newspaper *L'Antisemitique*, purported to be the real speech that Crémieux delivered upon the foundation of the Alliance in 1860. Crémieux was quoted as saying that "the union which we wish to found is neither French, English nor Swiss, but an *international* Jewish union ... We have no fellow-citizens, but only coreligionists; our nationality is the religion of our fathers". Christianity was in decline, and the world would soon be converted to Judaism, the only religious and political truth. The Judaization of the world would not mean universal equality and unity, however. Power and dominion in the world would belong to the Jews alone. *L'Antisemitique*'s editor observed how far the Jews were along the path to world domination. They were able to expend enormous funds to place spies in every government and on the stock exchange. They had captured and funded Freemasonry. They had proven able to cope with unexpected emergencies such as the Tisza-Eszlar Affair.

The Crémieux Manifesto was, like The Rabbi's Speech, a crude forgery, and one directed more to the concerns of French Antisemites than Russian Judeophobes. Thus, the area of Christianity under most direct attack in the speech was the Roman Catholic Church in France. The concern with Freemasonry was peculiarly Western, as pioneered by Gougenot des Mousseaux' *Le Juif, Le Judaisme et La Judaisation des Peuples Chretiens*, published in Paris in 1869.[66] Yet in other ways the Crémieux Manifesto was effective propaganda. While essentially an occult theme, it was superficially less absurd since it lacked the magical elements found in The Rabbi's Speech. From the Russian point of view, the choice of Crémieux as the speechmaker was a stroke of genius.

First of all, he was dead and unable to defend himself. Until his death in 1880, he was one of the most visible Jews in Europe, a member of the revolutionary government of 1848 and a leading public figure in the French Second Empire. He was one of the founders and a familiar spokesman for the Alliance. Well-informed Russians could recall his interventions with the Russian government, including his trip to the capital in 1869, and his letters to the Russian press. The protocols published at the foundation of the Alliance, as well as a speech given by Crémieux at the time, had been integrated into an early version of *The Book of the Kahal*, and the tendentious interpretations given them by Brafman were not strikingly different from the new version.

The Crémieux Manifesto easily lent itself to exegesis, and Ivan Aksakov, as so often in the past, led the way, inspired by attacks upon his paper for reprinting the document. Aksakov could not resist a dig at the Russian Jewish intelligentsia, and their Russian supporters. The author of the speech was Crémieux, "the same one to whom our intelligentsia of a certain stripe love to point and say, 'there's France, a truly enlightened nation; they are not afraid to entrust their jurisprudence to an enlightened Jew, because in the sphere of higher culture, all are equal ...' Do our intelligentsia now recognize the identity of their ideals with those of the Jews?" (*Rus* 21:1/XI/1883).

Even closer to Aksakov's heart, and fully consistent with the positions which he had developed twenty years earlier, was the religious aspect, encompassed in the juxtaposition of Judaism and Christianity. Aksakov was particularly sensitive to this issue because the Jewish *Nedelnaia khronika Voskhoda* had recently argued that there was nothing in Christianity which was not to be found in the Mosaic Pentateuch. The Manifesto, on the contrary, revealed the real essence of Judaism.

> The majesty of religious truth for the Jews is not a kingdom of truth and of the spirit, nor an internal moral enlightenment of human nature, but a conception of a powerful *temporal* kingdom of Jewry, ruling over the entire earth and holding in its hands all the wealth of the world as a privilege given by God to His "Chosen People" ... Rejecting Christ, failing to recognize God in His person, Jewish monotheism limited God Himself, restricting His attributes to external force and external truth, and serving Him through the external fulfillment of the Law – they confused and materialized the truth, and changed the eternal into the temporal and transitory. For the Jews, God has come to represent nothing more than the silver and gold of the entire world. (*Rus* 21:1/XI/1883)

Christian Europe was threatened by a relentless attack, aided by Jewish control of the press and the stock exchange. The fate of Catholicism in France, which was now drowning in a sea of secularism, was a graphic illustration of the danger against which Aksakov had first warned in his article on the Christian banner and the Jewish banner.

Jews and Judeophobes attacked the manifesto in ways that virtually forced Aksakov to reply. *Russkii evrei* printed excerpts from Crémieux's actual speech at the foundation of the Alliance (43:11/XI/1883), while *Nedelnaia khronika Voskhoda* offered the actual foundation protocols (45:13/XI/1883). *Russkii kurer* challenged Aksakov to prove that he had not been duped into printing an obvious forgery with no other goal than to spread antipathy between Christians and Jews (246:19/XI/1883). Aksakov was highly regarded in Russian society as an honest and upright man, no matter how eccentric his views might sometimes be. His opponents seized on his reputation for probity. *Russkii evrei* sarcastically attacked the "honest Moscow *Rus*" and declared it "hard to find a name for this disgraceful deed of a Moscow chauvinist" who printed a tendentious document which he could not verify (43:11/XI/1883). The veteran Jewish publicist Lev Binshtok published an open letter to Aksakov in *Russkii kurer* in which he challenged him as a man who, "although he hates the Jews, is still honest and guided by moral principles," to reject the Manifesto whose false words "would dishonor the rudest *tzaddik*." He urged Aksakov to recall the heroes of Russian folk tales who never touched the weak lest they accidentally hurt them (251:24/XI/1883).

Discomfited by criticism of this kind, Aksakov offered an uncharacteristically weak defense, arguing that, if the document were false, Jewish publicists in Europe should have disproved it when it first appeared (*Rus* 23:1/XII/1883). He asked why the Jews did not sue *L'Antisemitique* for libel, even as he printed a formal denial of the authenticity of the Manifesto from the Alliance itself (24:8/XII/1883). But there was one obvious reply to his critics that Aksakov did not fail to use. Why had he not immediately recognized the Manifesto as a forgery? – Because there was nothing in it that contradicted the contemporary attitudes or activities of European Jewry. As proof, Aksakov went through the Manifesto point by point. It was demonstrably true, he argued, that the Alliance was an international union, as confirmed by its Hebrew motto, "One for all and all for one." The Alliance had intervened repeatedly in Russia on behalf of Russian Jewry, thus providing them with an alternative government. Aksakov compared this to a theoretical declaration by all the world's Muslims of their solidarity with the Russian Tatars in Kazan and the Crimea, or an imaginary attempt by Russia's Baltic Germans to group themselves around a unified German state.

Also confirmed by events was the Manifesto's claim that Jewish nationalism was tied with their religious beliefs. The Jews had neither a common language nor a common territory – religion alone was their unifying force. Only their anticipation of the imminent arrival of their messiah kept them from disappearing into the surrounding milieu. For Jews, "the faith of their fathers" was not a personal, mystical union with God, but a national union. Consequently, as even *Russkii evrei* was forced to admit: "We Jews wish to remain Jews, for if one does not want this, then all the misery and suffering of the Jewish people must be considered a crying stupidity" (*Rus* 23:1/XII/1883). Jewry was inextricably tied up with the political implications of its teachings about the "Chosen People." It lacked any affinity with the Christian ideal of equality and brotherhood of Christ, of which St. Paul wrote that "we are neither Hellene nor Jew." "The idea of a 'Chosen People' leads directly to the idea of a privileged people," Aksakov wrote in the same article. "What will be the extent of this privilege when Jerusalem itself is the house of prayer for all nations? Dominion will pass to the Jews and, logically, all the riches of the earth, for the kingdom of the Jewish Messiah is a *temporal kingdom*." Aksakov closed with one final challenge to his tormentors, the Russian Jewish intelligentsia. Could they really be ignorant of the true nature of Jewish national aspirations, or were they hypocrites, intent on defending a regressive, unchristian, anachronistic Judaism?

This episode shows Aksakov in his characteristic guise as the leading intellectual Judeophobe in Russia. He demonstrated again his genius for blending his own unique religious-philosophical conceptions and elements of Western Antisemitism into systems which managed to strike receptive chords in important segments of Russian society, especially on the Right. His slogans – "The Christian Banner and the Jewish Banner," "Privileged Jewry," "International Jewry" – provided some of the most persistent themes in Russian Judeophobia. His philosophical ideas were inevitably vulgarized, but this did not negate his central achievement in making religious Judeophobia respectable, and joining it to Western concepts to help create a specifically Russian, occult form of Judeophobia.[67]

Other prominent newspapers which reprinted the Crémieux Manifesto followed similar lines of defense. *Novoe vremia* and *Sankt-peterburgskie vedomosti* argued that, real or not, the document provided an accurate picture of Jewish attitudes toward the Christian world.[68]

Novoe vremia equated the religious and political attitudes of Jewry. The Jews, like adherents of all other religions, viewed unbelievers unsympathetically. Because faith and nationality were synonymous for them, they also placed all gentiles in a lower political category. Under the circumstances, merger with the rest of the population was clearly impossible. "Every Jew, educated and uneducated, lives by this ideal, which comprises the tightest link of Judaism and is also the battlement upon which these foes of the Christian world stand now and will always stand" (2770:13/XI/1883). *Sanktpeterburgskie vedomosti*'s editors announced that they had no qualms in publishing the Manifesto, despite its dubious origins, because it represented nothing new or unprecedented in Jewry. Anyone who disagreed was invited to peruse *The Book of the Kahal*, which revealed a Judaic tradition which stretched back to the time of Moses (308:14/XI/1883). These comments were relatively restrained when compared to the sentiments expressed in *Tserkovnyi vestnik*, the official publication of the Holy Synod. It illustrates the inroads of occult Judeophobia into the world of Russian Orthodoxy. The paper observed that

> the idea has been expressed more than once that amidst the terrible contemporary events in Western Europe and Russia, one can see a devilish design, directed by skillful hands. The question remains as to whose hands they are. In seeking a criminal, they say, it is important to seek the person who would benefit from the crime. Applying this rule we naturally come to the conclusion that the contemporary decline of Christianity, along with the entire external and internal side of Christian society, is useful to an anti-Christian power. And Jewry appears as such a force in the midst of Christianity. (2770:13/XI/1883)

Perhaps because it was so thoroughly compromised in 1883 – Judeophiles emphasized its origins in the Parisian "gutter press" – or because it was too much oriented to the concerns of French Antisemites, the Crémieux Manifesto never enjoyed the popularity of The Rabbi's Speech in Russia. What did endure, however, was the motif of Jewry as a vast, coordinated anti-Christian force, a force which could be blamed for all the world's problems. In 1887, *Novoe vremia* offered the following definition of a "Yid":

> he directs all his strength toward disturbing that foundation of religious, political and civil life, upon which are based the contemporary states which give him equal rights ... The Jew remains the same enemy of the rest of the world that he has been from the time of the exodus from Egypt. With political and civil rights, he possesses

> additional means and resources to harm his enemy, to trample on
> him and to seek his destruction. (4127:26/VIII/1887)

As Prince Meshcherskii described the Jewish Question in 1889: "Everything is hidden in it, its satanic goals, with its genuinely satanic
attributes, flies under a false flag in order to hide its main intention
which is, sooner or later, to destroy the Orthodox Church, the autocracy, and the integrity of the people (*narod*) – in a word, Russia"
(268:27/IX/1889).

Generalized fears of Jewry as an abstract, malevolent force did not
preclude continued concern at the activities of the Alliance and other
Jewish groups. *Novoe vremia* emerged as the trendsetter in this regard,
predicting that the Alliance would transfer its headquarters from Paris
to Berlin to reflect the growing role of Jewry as an instrument of
"Germanization" (3604:12/III/1886). Greater alarm still was raised by
the rumor that the Alliance was planning to open an office in St.
Petersburg itself, where it could carry on its activities behind a mask of
philanthropic rhetoric (3911:18/I/1887). A chilly reception was given to
the offer of the French Jewish philanthropist, Baron Moritz Hirsch, to
provide over a million francs for a fund to assist Russian Jews to
pursue more productive work. While this might seem a goal which
even Judeophobes could applaud, they instead recalled the Baron's
past involvement with projects of the Alliance Israélite. *Varshavskii
dnevnik* observed darkly that "the sixth great power – world Jewry – is
mobilizing its power, the power of capital" (245:10/XI/1887). *Novorossiiskii telegraf*, described the gift in apocalyptic terms in 1889, demonstrating that occult Judeophobia was now thoroughly in the public
domain.

> The Jewish Question is near resolution, and in this hour the accumu-
> lated strength not just of Russian but of world Jewry is brought into
> play. Baron Hirsch is only the representative of these thieves, and
> even his millions are nothing more than a down payment. For the
> Russian people "the charitable gift of Baron Hirsch" is truly a "Greek
> gift," a new Trojan Horse, as one may call it, in which the hero of
> international Jewry hopes safely to penetrate the stronghold of the
> state and ... ultimately to open its gates to an invasion of the Russian
> land ... from all the ends of the earth. (4376:30/III/1889)

Occult Judeophobia had come of age in Russia by the era of the
Counter-Reforms and it was quickly assimilated by Russian conservatives, in and out of state service. The unprincipled Judeophobe press
embraced its bizarre and exotic fantasies, which appealed to a credu-

lous, sensation-seeking readership. Surprisingly, perhaps, occult Judeophobia was not immediately accepted by the principled Judeophobe press, which still based their criticisms of the Jews on objective realities, however misinterpreted and misunderstood. *Kievlianin*, always a leader in the Judeophobe movement, was slow to assimilate occult variations. Yet occult Judeophobia proved to be highly infective. Those who were accustomed to view Jews as fanatics and exploiters found that it was not such a great step to consider them a "dark, satanic force."

For liberals and moderates, on the other hand, the spread of occult Judeophobia, and its obvious irrationalism, effectively ended any inclination to play with Judeophobia. This was even more the case because liberals were routinely pilloried as agents of international Jewry, dupes in its attempt to subvert Russia and rule the world.

Conclusion

At the onset of the Reform Era, the Jewish Question scarcely existed as a matter of public concern in the Russian Empire. By the end of the reign of Tsar Alexander II in 1881, it was one of the most contentious issues of contemporary debate, the focus of hundreds of books and pamphlets, and a popular editorial theme for some of the Empire's most influential and widely read newspapers. Any knowledgeable reader would have reckoned it among the most significant problems facing the Empire.

How did this striking transformation in the status of the Jewish Question come about?

At the start of Alexander II's reign, the Jews were a minor concern to the imperial authorities, who had dealt with them only for the three-quarters of a century since the first partition of Poland in 1772. The Russian conceptualization of what constituted the Jewish Question rested very much on Western models, and relied upon Western-style solutions, despite their dubious efficacy in a Russian setting.

Russian bureaucrats, following the lead of Western economic theorists, dismissed most Jewish economic activity as "exploitation," despite the fact that Jews were an integral part of the neo-feudal economy of Poland, which the Russian state accepted and utilized. Jews were faulted for dominating trade and crafts, although serfdom obstructed the rise of non-Jewish artisans and the residence restrictions of the Jewish Pale of Settlement ensured an oversupply of Jewish middlemen. Jews were condemned for "intoxicating the peasantry," even as the state sold the right to produce and sell alcoholic beverages to wealthy Jewish entrepreneurs.

This confused understanding of economic realities produced muddled responses. The state sponsored agricultural colonization of Jews – as though the Russian state suffered a shortage of peasants –

forced resettlement from rural areas, and attempted to drive the Jews into different, often inappropriate, social categories.

Also borrowed from the West was the assumption that Jewish "religious fanaticism" underlay the abnormal relations said to exist between Christians and Jews. Russian policy makers accepted these claims even in the absence of any real understanding of Judaism or Jewish culture. As late as the 1840s, Russian officials did not understand the issues dividing the Hasidim and the Mitnagdim. They knew little of the Talmud except that it was "a bad thing." Criminal cases were seriously investigated for evidence of Jewish ritual murder.

Efforts to eradicate "religious fanaticism" employed devices popularized in the West by the Haskalah, the Jewish version of the general European Enlightenment movement. The Russian government sponsored a Jewish school system based on the assumptions of the Haskalah. The state sought to train a generation of "progressive" rabbis and to establish them as government agents in the midst of the Jewish community. Laws sought to rip caftans off the backs of Jewish males, and wigs off the heads of their wives.

These official endeavors were carried out with the assistance of a small band of Russian maskilim, totally at odds with the values of the majority traditionalist community. Consequently, these would-be reformers were seen as renegades, heretics and informers. Only the protection of the state allowed the maskilim to propagandize their ideas and to emerge as a genuine movement. Whatever good intentions might be voiced by bureaucrats and maskilim, their plans for Russian Jewry demanded coercion and constraint. All facets of the state's Jewish policy took place in silence, since the censor specifically banned from the press any discussion of official initiatives toward the Jews.

The Reform Era, spawned by defeat in the Crimean War, witnessed the critical reevaluation of all aspects of Russian life, but especially serfdom, the socioeconomic prop of the Russian *ancien régime*. The abolition of serfdom in 1861 necessitated reforms in all areas of life, including local government, the judicial system, taxation and military recruitment. Everything came under the reformers' gaze. Nor did bureaucrats operate in isolation: under a rubric known as "publicity" (glasnost), educated society (*obshchestvo*) received an unprecedented invitation to offer its own critiques and suggestions and to provide support for the reform process.

The Jewish Question was one of a number of secondary concerns to emerge into the light of publicity, inspired by the many obvious analogies between the liberation of the serfs and the emancipation of the Jews. The issue of economic utility was also an important consideration. The coercive measures of the past were relaxed, and efforts were centered more on rewarding "good Jews" with greater rights than in punishing "bad Jews" by restrictions. A major role in encouraging this process was played by a small group of wealthy Jewish bankers and businessmen in St. Petersburg, centered on the Barons E. and H. Gintsburg, who followed the Jewish tradition of *shtadlanut*, or high-level intercession.

Reformers also found ready and useful allies among a band of acculturated Jews, most of whom had emerged from the world of the state Jewish school system. A number of them advanced beyond the optimistic simplicities of the Russian Haskalah to confront the challenges posed by the greater integration of Jews into Russian society. They were highly visible because of their connections with the emergent Russian press, where they played a leading role in creating and leading public debate on the Jewish Question. These representatives of a new Russian Jewish intelligentsia rivaled the Petersburg *shtadlanim* in their claim to speak for the entire Jewish community. In their spokesman role they, like the maskilim before them, accepted many of the government's critical assessments of Jewish life, including "exploitation" and "fanaticism," although they attributed them to factors external to the Jews. As a remedy they pointed to on-going phenomena variously characterized as *sblizhenie* (rapprochement) and *sliianie* (merger) which they claimed were transforming the Russian Jewish community in a positive way.

It is obvious in retrospect that no consensus existed as to the exact nature of *sblizhenie/sliianie*. The acquisition of Russian language was accepted as a given, but there was less agreement as to what aspects, if any, of Jewish identity and culture should be retained. Early in the Reform Era the Russian public was content to accept the assurances of Jews and their Judeophile allies that *sblizhenie/sliianie* were moving briskly forward, and would soon eradicate the Jewish Question in the Russian Empire. Publicists who dissented from this consensus, whether motivated by old-fashioned religious prejudices or new-style racialist arguments, were decisively rejected by public opinion.

Vague benevolence toward the Jews was eroded by two pivotal events in the reign of Alexander II: the short-term political considerations provoked by the Polish uprising of 1863, and the long-term socioeconomic consequences of the emancipation of the serfs in 1861.

The Polish uprising directed official attention to the western borderlands of the Empire – the Ukraine, Belorussia and the Baltic region – which were strongholds of Polish economic and cultural influence. To win these areas from the Poles, and urged on by influential journalists like M. N. Katkov, different ministries introduced a variety of uncoordinated, anti-Polish measures known collectively as "Russification." Jews were an important part of the regional economy in their guise as middlemen, artisans and agents for Polish-owned estates, so any discussion of economic measures had to weigh their role as potential allies or obstacles to Russification. After some initial wavering, the most ardent local Russifiers, led by the newspaper *Kievlianin*, identified the Jews as a major obstacle to the spread of Russian influence. Efforts of the Russian Jewish intelligentsia to establish good russifying credentials failed to convince their opponents, while serving to alienate partisans of other national movements, especially the nascent Ukrainophiles.

The questions raised about the reliability of Jews as a russifying force brought into question the speed and inevitability of *sblizhenie/sliianie*. This was even more the case when Russian publicists ceased to view Jews as a theoretical ideal, but dealt with the real and complex problems raised by Jewish economic life within the Pale of Settlement, where their activities were seen as detrimental to the "native" peasant population. These were problems which admitted no easy answers.

Public disenchantment with the promises of the Russian Jewish intelligentsia facilitated the rise of charlatans like the Jewish renegade Iakov Brafman, discovered and patronized by regional Russifiers. Brafman's *Book of the Kahal* had such a great appeal because it simultaneously explained why the processes of *sblizhenie/sliianie* had apparently failed among Jews, while proposing, as a simplistic alternative, the abolition of the kahal. When the Russian Jewish intelligentsia repudiated Brafman's claims, denying even the existence of the kahal, critics questioned their credentials as spokesmen for the Jewish community, or as honest mediators between Russians and Jews. Judeophobes soon identified the Russian Jewish intelligentsia as members of a vast Jewish conspiracy, led by the international kahal, and directed against the foundations of Christian civilization.

The forces of incipient modernization unleashed by the emancipation of the serfs affected every social class in the Empire. For Jews, economic change offered splendid opportunities to a small elite of Jewish financiers, even while impoverishing the Jewish masses. The Jewish population in Eastern Europe underwent a demographic explosion while trapped in the ruins of a decrepit semi-feudal economy. Russian society was more concerned with the effects of modernization on the countryside, especially the economic differentiation of the peasantry, and expressed in the rise of the kulak and *mir*-eater within the village.

The longstanding paradigm of "Jewish exploitation" had already established Jews, in their various guises as inn-keepers, petty tradesmen, and usurers, as the archetypal enemies of peasant prosperity. This image was easily extended to encompass the phenomenon of kulakism. However, the Jewish kulak was seen as even more pernicious than his Christian equivalent, because he was defended by the full force of the "solidarity of the kahal." Concern for the welfare of the peasantry was a central concern for Russian liberal thinkers and fear of a destructive role played by Jews in the post-reform village dominated liberal thought. Consequently, those who were partisans of emancipation and civil equality in theory questioned the logic of granting full civil rights to Jews as long as they remained mired in their unreformed, fanatical mode of life.

The government, less liberal in its inclinations, was equally concerned by the Jewish presence in the countryside, especially the spreading influence of Jewish capital, represented by purchase and lease of gentry land. Joined to these fears were complaints from economic rivals of the Jews, exemplified by the Moscow merchantry, who juxtaposed images of "natives" and "aliens" on the marketplace. The symbol of the Jew as exploiter proved capable of infinite extension, and ranged from the beggarly shtetl Jew to the wealthy plutocrats in St. Petersburg. It ensured that Jews were occasionally blamed for the disruptions of capitalism even at a time when they played a minimal role in Russia's economic development.

The Great Reforms set off a struggle to define the nature and limits of Russia's new civil society, a struggle which served to formulate both revolutionary and conservative ideologies. Through a complex, evolutionary process, in which foreign, especially German, antisemitic doctrines played a role, Jews were linked in the mind of conservatives to "Nihilism," a movement which threatened the very foundations of old Russia. Jews were defined as a corrosive and degenerative force which ate away at the foundations of Christian society. Mature conservative ideology rejected the liberal expedient of education as the surest way of resolving the Jewish Question, having concluded that Jews corrupted their Christian schoolmates. These arguments paved the path for norms on Jewish students in the reign of Tsar Alexander III. Ironically, some negative views of the Jews inspired proposals which could have worked in the Jews' favor. Provincial Judeophobes argued that it was unfair that the western provinces had to bear the full weight of the "Jewish yoke," and advocated abolition of the Pale of Settlement.

As Jews came to encapsulate all manner of conservative fears, a new strand of Judeophobia emerged, based on fantasies and paranoia. Occult Judeophobia became obsessed with fears of a world-wide Jewish conspiracy to dominate the Christian world, or the reality of Jewish ritual murder in Russia. While foreign influences played a role, Russian Judeophobes made their own contribution to antisemitic fantasies, chiefly through the theme of the international kahal, pioneered by Iakov Brafman. Occult Judeophobia proved highly infectious, and easily corrupted the world-view of more rational, objective Judeophobes. The most salient characteristic of Russian Judeophobia was its ability to incorporate literally all of the fears and obsessions of a society in the midst of traumatic social change. The seriousness of the Jewish Question had not changed over the twenty-five years of the Reform Era, but public perceptions of it had.

By the end of the Reform Era, in 1881, the Jews of the Russian Empire occupied an extremely ambivalent position. Their legal situation had improved over the period, but at the cost of a public backlash. The earlier, vague public consensus that the Jews were in need of reform and were reformable broke down. There was no longer agreement even within ideological camps. Most conservatives and Russifiers were Judeophobes, but the foremost representative of both camps, M. N. Katkov, was not. Many provincial conservatives opposed the Pale of Settlement, while many liberal spokesmen argued for its retention. Revolutionaries were interested in the Jews only as a "bourgeois" element to be opposed. The Russian Orthodox Church took almost no interest in the Jews at all.

At best, Jews were viewed as a social problem which proved more resistant to solution than had been assumed, and confidence waned in traditional expedients of educational and economic reform. At worst, Jews were demonized as the very spirit of Nihilism, as active foes of Russian Christian culture, as bloody vampires ready to feast on Russia's children. They were an international, malevolent, exploiting force which threatened rich and poor alike. Public opinion, at one time mildly sympathetic to the plight of the Jews, grew hostile and skeptical of any solution to the Jewish Question. It was a lethal mix. If official policy did not yet follow the lead of public opinion, it required only the crisis triggered by the pogroms of 1881 to transform public prejudice into official policy.

Abbreviations in text, notes and bibliography

Archives

GPB	Rossiiskaia Natsional'naia Biblioteka
RGIA	Rossiiskii Gosudarstvennyi Istoricheskii Arkhiv
TsDIA	Tsentral'nyi Gosudarstvennyi Istoricheskii Arkhiv Ukrainy
TsGAOR	Gosudarstvennyi Arkhiv Rossiiskoi Federatsii

Places and institutions

KOME	Committee for the Transformation of the Jews (1840–63)
KUBE	Commission for the Reorganization of Jewish Life (1872–81)
M	Moscow
MNP	Ministry of Education
MVD	Ministry of Internal Affairs
OPE	Society for the Spread of Enlightenment among the Jews of Russia
SPb	St. Petersburg

Publications

BZIH	*Biuletyn Żydowskiego Instytutu Historycznego*
CMRS	*Cahiers du Monde russe et soviétique*
EB	*Evreiskaia biblioteka*
EE	*Evreiskaia entsiklopediia*
ES	*Evreiskaia starina*
JGO	*Jahrbucher für Geschichte Osteuropas*
NkhV	*Nedel'naia khronika Voskhoda*
JSS	*Jewish Social Studies*
PPSZ	*Polnoe sobranie zakonov* (first series)
RBS	*Russkii biograficheskii slovar'*
SEER	*Slavonic and East European Review*
SR	*Slavic Review*
VPSZ	*Polnoe sobranie zakonov* (second series)

Notes

Preface

1 See Jeffrey Brooks, *When Russia Learned to Read* (Princeton, 1985).
2 Louise McReynolds, *The News under Russia's Old Regime* (Princeton, 1991), Table 6. The rare exception was *Syn otechestva* which sold 20,000 copies empire-wide. The prestigious and influential *Golos*, on the other hand, sold only 10,000.
3 A. Reitblat, *Ot Bovy k Bal'montu* (M, 1991), 8–15.
4 Bruce Lincoln, *The Great Reforms* (DeKalb, IL, 1990), 123, 161–2.
5 *RGIA*, f. 821, op. 8, ed. khr. 257 (1858–9), l. 13.
6 *Materialy komissi po ustroistvu byta evreev (po Imperii)*, I (SPb, 1879), 3. Hereafter *Materialy KUBE*.
7 *RGIA.*, f. 821, op. 8, ed. khr. 232 (22/XI/64), ll. 1–2.
8 I. V. Gessen, *Nakanune probuzhdeniia* (SPb, 1906), 161.
9 See *TsDIA*, f. 442, op. 47, d. 308, ll. 2–8o (1868), and f. 442, op. 831, d. 283, ll. 1–51o (1881) for official investigations triggered by reports in *Golos* and *Rus'* respectively.
10 *Polnoe sobranie zakonov rossiiskii imperii. Sobranie pervoe*, 45 vols. (SPb, 1830) cited as *PPSZ. Sobranie vtoroe*, 55 vols. (SPb, 1830–84), cited as *VPSZ*.
11 John D. Klier, "1855–1894 Censorship of the Press in Russian and the Jewish Question," *Jewish Social Studies*, 45, 3–4 (1986), 257–68.

Introduction

1 The Committee's name in Russian was Komitet dlia opredeleniia mer korennogo preobrazovaniia evreev v Rossii, and it functioned from 1840 to 1863.
2 Iu. I. Gessen, *Istoriia evreiskogo naroda v Rossii*, 2 vols. (SPb–Leningrad, 1925–7), II, 142. See *RGIA*, f. 1149, op. 5, ed. khr. 7 (1858–9), l. 2.
3 The development of this official consensus is the topic of my book *Russia Gathers Her Jews* (DeKalb, IL, 1986).
4 A principal conduit for anti-Talmudic feeling into Russia was the priest, L. A. Chiarini, who was Professor of Oriental Languages at the University of Warsaw. With the assistance of the Russian state he published a two volume work entitled *Théorie du Judaïsme, appliquée a la réforme des Israélites*

in Paris in 1830. His work clearly derived from J. A. Eisenmenger's famous anti-Talmudic tract *Entdechtes Judenthum*.

5 There is an enormous literature on the subject of the cantonists. See especially the work of S. M. Ginsburg in *Historishe verk [Historical Work]*, 3 vols. (New York, 1934), and "Mucheniki-deti (iz istorii kantonistov-Evreev)," *ES*, 13 (1930), 50–79. See also Michael Stanislawski, *Tsar Nicholas I and the Jews* (Philadelphia, 1983), 13–34.

6 *VPSZ*, XI:9226 (27/V/1836); XI:12,486 (29/VII/1839).

7 *VPSZ*, X:8054 (13/IV/1835).

8 *TsDIA*, f. 442, op. 1, d. 4026 (1841–4), ll. 19–22.

9 *VPSZ*, XXV:24,127 (1/V/1850).

10 S. M. Dubnov, "Istoricheskie soobshcheniia," *Knizhki Voskhoda*, 21, 5 (1901), 8–9.

11 *Ibid.*, 16–20.

12 S. M. Dubnow, *History of the Jews in Russia and Poland* II (Philadelphia, 1918), 143.

13 Stanislawski, *Tsar Nicholas I*, 124.

14 *Ibid.*, 124.

15 *VPSZ*, XIX:18,559 (23/XII/1844).

16 A. Beletskii, *Vopros ob obrazovanii russkikh evreev v tsarstvovanii Imperatora Nikolaia I* (SPb, 1894), 66; Julius Hessen (Iu. I. Gessen), "Die russische Regierung und die westeuropaischen Juden," *Monatsschrift für Geschichte und Wissenschaft des Judentums*, 57, 5/6 (1913), 257–71; 7/8 (1913), 482–500.

17 *VPSZ*, XIX:18,420 (13/XI/1844).

18 I. M. Cherikover, *Istoriia obshchestva dlia rasprostraneniia prosveshcheniia mezhdu evreiami v Rossii, 1863–1913 gg.* (SPb, 1913), 3. See Stanislawski's enlightening discussion of the oft-made charge that Uvarov viewed the school system as a device for converting the Jews to Christianity, *Tsar Nicholas*, 59–69.

19 Beletskii, *Vopros*, 90, 147.

20 For the definitive examination of the crown rabbinate, see the study of Azriel Shochat, *Mossad ha-rabanut mita'am be-Rusia* (Haifa, 1975).

21 *VPSZ*, XXV:24,298 (3/VII/1850). See also my "Russkaia voina protiv 'khevra kadisha'," in D. A. El'iashevich, ed., *Istoriia evreev v Rossii: problemy istochnikovedeniia i istoriografii* (SPb, 1993), 109–14.

22 Gessen, *Istoriia*, II, 102.

23 Petr Keppen (Koeppen), *Deviataia reviziia. Issledovanie o chisle zhitelei v Rossii v 1851 godu* (SPb, 1857). According to statistics provided by the Ministry of Internal Affairs in 1865, there were 1,430,643 Jews in the Pale of Settlement, out of a total population of 18,222,538. Thus, they constituted 7.85 percent of the population of the Pale. *VPSZ*, XL:42,264 (28/VI/1865).

24 *VPSZ*, X:8,054 (13/IV/1835). Most of these areas had been secured from Poland, and comprised the historical areas of Lithuania, Malorossia (Little Russia or the Ukraine), Belorussia (White Russia), and the Baltic provinces of Kurland and Estland.

25 *VPSZ*, XVIII, 16,767 (20/IV/1843).

26 For the Kingdom of Poland, see the extensive works of Artur Eisenbach, especially "Materiały do struktury i działalności gospodarczej ludności żydowskiej w Królestwie Polskim w latach osiemdziesiatych XIX wieku," *Biuletyn Zydowskiego Instytutu Historycznego*, 29 (1959), 72–111; "La Mobilité territoriale de la population juive du Royaume de Pologne," *Revue des études juives/Historia judaica*, 126, 1 (1967), 55–111; 4 (1967), 435–71; 77, 1 (1968), 39–95.

27 See reprint of N. Leskov's apologetic work, *Evrei v Rossii* (SPb, 1920), which depicts the widespread collusion of local authorities with itinerant Jewish craftsmen, 39–41.

Part 1   The era of the Great Reforms

1 Beginning in 1850, the government instituted stringent demands on the Jewish community. Three recruits were demanded for every recruit missing from the community's levy. Recruits were demanded as a punishment for tax arrears. Community leaders were drafted to make up shortfalls. Communities received the right to hand over as a recruit any Jew found without a passport. Jews were assessed at a rate of 10 per 1,000, far in excess of the rate for most of the rest of the population. For these measures, and for their impact upon the Jewish community, see Stanislawski, *Tsar Nicholas I*, 184–88.

2 Gessen, *Istoriia*, II, 140–1.

3 Subsequent legislation permitted some of the victims of the old system, but not cantonists who had converted to Christianity, to return to their families. *Ibid.*, 141.

4 Terence Emmons, *The Russian Landed Gentry and the Peasant Emancipation of 1861* (Cambridge, 1968), 51.

5 See Alfred Rieber, ed., *The Politics of Autocracy. Letters of Alexander II to Prince A. I. Bariatinskii, 1855–1864* (Paris–The Hague, 1966); Lincoln, *The Great Reforms*, 24–60; David Saunders, *Russia in the Age of Reaction and Reform, 1801–1881* (London and New York, 1992), 204–77.

6 Gessen, *Istoriia*, II, 142.

7 *VPSZ*, XL:42,264 (28/VI/1865).

8 *Ibid.*

9 *Ibid.*

10 V. N., "Istoricheskie dokumenty. 'Proekt ob ustroistve evreev' podannyi v 1856 g. grodnenskim gubernskim striapchim I. K. Kozakovskim," *Voskhod*, 1, 5 (May 1881), 131–3.

11 *Ibid.*, 136–7.

12 Iu. I. Gessen, "Popytka emansipatsii evreev v Rossii," *Perezhitoe*, I (SPb, 1909), 158–62.

13 *Ibid.*, 162.

14 Gessen, *Istoriia*, II, 148.

15 Iu. I. Gessen, *Zakon i zhizn'* (SPb, 1911), 130–1.

16 Gessen, *Istoriia*, II, 158–50.

17 For English treatments of the emancipation debates, see Emmons and Field; for the classic Soviet study, see P. A. Zaionchkovskii, *Otmena krepostnogo prava v Rossii*, 3d ed. (Moscow, 1968).

18 *RGIA*, f. 1282, op. 2, ed. khr. 64 (1860–1), 60-7.

19 Gessen, *Zakon i zhizn'*, 128–9.

20 "Aleksandr II, Russkii Imperator," *EE*, I, 811–12.

21 *VPSZ*, XL:42,264 (28/VI/1865).

22 See the discussion of this phenomenon in Eli Lederhendler, *The Road to Modern Jewish Politics* (New York and Oxford, 1989), 19–21, 52–7.

23 B. V. Anan'ich, *Bankirskie doma v Rossii, 1860–1914 gg.* (Leningrad, 1991), 37–71.

24 The term "Gintsburg Circle" was not used by contemporaries, but this seems an appropriate description of the group centered around the two barons.

25 *RGIA*, f. 1149, op. 5, ed. khr. 7 (1858–9), 3–3o.

26 Gessen, *Zakon i zhizn'*, 113.

27 Dubnow, *History*, II, 160–1.

28 *RGIA*, f. 1149, op. 5, ed. khr. 7 (1858–9), 11–18.

29 *RGIA*, f. 796, op. 144, ed. khr. 159 (1863–5), 1–18o.

30 See the numerous drafts of petitions to the government contained in the archives of YIVO, in the Elias Tcherikower Archives, file 775, fos. 63204–63217 et seq.

31 Cherikover, *Istoriia obshchestva dlia rasprostraneniia prosveshcheniia mezhdu Evreiami v Rossii* 16. *VPSZ*, XXXIV:34,461 (4/V/1859). For evidence that local authorities took note of this new law, even if they did not enforce it vigorously, see TsDIA, f. 707, op. 87, d. 3690, ll. 180–1, where the administrator of the Kiev Educational District cited this law in refusing to permit first guild merchants to educate their children at home, outside the state school system.

32 There is a voluminous historical literature devoted to efforts to differentiate the various groups within the Jewish intelligentsia. To choose only the most representative examples of those whose work is fully cited in the bibliography: the pioneering works of I. Sosis offered a nuanced description of Jewish intellectuals, based primarily on a reading of the Jewish press; Israel Zinberg's (Tsinburg) magisterial study of Jewish literature is especially good for the rise of the Russian Haskalah. P. S. Merek examined the contrast between the various generations of Russian maskilim. Elyohu Cherikover explored the ideology of Jewish revolutionaries, while the works of S. M. Ginsburg examine, among others, the group whom I term the Total Assimilationists.

Contemporary scholars whose work touches on this problem include Jonathan Frankel, who chronicles the ideological crisis of the Jewish intelligentsia; Michael Stanislawski, who explores the rise of the maskilim, and the careers of some of its most representative figures, as well as the typology of conversion, which has a bearing on the Total Assimilations; Eli Lederhendler examines the politics of the maskilim, while Yehuda Slutsky,

Alexander Orbach and Dan Miron consider the role of the press and literature, and debates over language use; recent work by Yosef Salmon divides the maskilim into categories of secular, observant and radical. Azriel Shochat has provided an important study of the politics surrounding the state rabbinate. Finally, Steven Zipperstein has employed Odessa as a test case for the ideological struggles within Russian Jewry prior to 1881.

33 For Levinson, see Stanislawski, *Tsar Nicholas I*, 52–6; for Stern, *EE*, XVI, 111–12; for Grosman, *TsDIA*, f. 442, op. 67, d. 43, ll. 1–57.

34 S. M. Ginsburg, *Meshumodim in tsarishn Rusland* (New York, 1946), 119–56.

35 YIVO, Elias Tcherikower Archives, file 755, fos. 63218–9.

36 Gessen, *Istoriia*, II, 147–8.

37 *VPSZ*, XXXVI:37,684 (27/XI/1861).

38 *VPSZ*, XXXVI:36,659 (19/II/1861).

39 *VPSZ*, XXXVI:36,674 (19/II/1861).

40 *VPSZ*, XXXVII:38,214 (26/IV/1861). This right did not outlive the Polish uprising of 1863. See the discussion below, pp. 302–3.

41 *VPSZ*, XXXVI:37,080 (4/VI/1861); 37,738 (11/XII/1861).

42 *VPSZ*, XXXVII:38,444 (3/VI/1862); Gessen, *Istoriia*, II, 144.

43 *VPSZ*, XL:42,268 (28/VI/1865).

1 Moshkas and Ioshkas

1 Iu. I. Gessen, "Smena obshchestvennykh techenii. II. 'Pervyi russko-evreiskii organ'", *Perezhitoe*, III (SPb, 1911), 37.

2 See "Evreiskie religioznye sekty v Rossii", *Zhurnal Ministerstva Vnutrennikh Del*, 15 (September 1846), 3–49; (August), 282–309; (November), 211–73; (December), 500–80. On the other hand, see the valuable *Ustroistvo i sostoianie evreiskikh obshchestv* by B. Miliutin, published in SPb in 1849–50 and also in the *Zhurnal* of the MVD.

3 See the standard study by Joshua Kunitz, *Russian Literature and the Jew* (New York, 1929), 1–57.

4 Iu. I. Gerasimova, *Iz istorii russkoi pechati v period revoliutsionnoi situatsii kontsa 1850-kh – nachala 1860-kh gg.* (M, 1974), 15.

5 *Ibid.*, 35–7. For guidelines and a number of famous scandals that ensued see A. Egorov (Konsparov), *Stranitsy iz prozhitogo*, 2 vols. (Odessa, 1913), II, 36–40; and N., "Moskovskii obed 28–go dekabria 1857 g. i ego posledstviia," *Russkaia starina* (January 1898), 62–72; 297–302.

6 Gessen, *Istoriia*, II, 150–1. *Russkii invalid* was the official journal of the Ministry of War, and followed a reformist line during the debates over social issues in the 1850s and 1860s.

7 In the case of the Peasant Question very few periodicals supported the government's own plans for emancipation as contained in the so-called Nazimov Rescript. Gerasimova, 51–2.

8 N., "Moskovskii obed," 66–71.

9 See John D. Klier, "*Odesskii vestnik*'s Annus Mirabilis of 1858," *Canadian Slavonic Papers*, 23, 1 (1981), 41–55.

10 *Ibid.*, 49–53.

11 Iu. I. Gessen, *Gallereia evreiskikh deiatelei* (SPb, 1898), 7–15.

12 Reprinted in *Sochineniia O. A. Rabinovicha*, III, 373–80.

13 This was a different publication from that of the same name which was the focus of the famous protest discussed in chapter 2.

14 *Sochineniia*, III, 101–07.

15 *Ibid*, III, 49–62.

16 *Severnaia pchela*, edited by N. I. Grech and the Polish renegade F. V. Bulgarin (Tadeusz Bulharyn), was the outstanding example of the so-called "reptile press" in Russia, suborned by the government. *Severnaia pchela*, for example, was virtually the only paper in Russia to wholeheartedly support the government's initial guidelines for peasant emancipation. Gerasimova, *Iz istorii russkoi pechati*, 51–2.

17 *RGIA*, f. 772, op. 7, d. 4370, ll. 42–3, 50–1 (1858). See Klier, "1855–1894 Censorship of the Press," 258–9.

18 *RBS*, no vol. (1916), 86–9. Rabinovich was not impressed with the general. He wrote to an associate that "I know this bird well; he's as stupid in fact (*na dele*) as in his literary articles." Iu. I. Gessen, "Pis'ma O. A. Rabinovicha," *ES*, III, 1 (1911), 74.

19 Alexandre Moreau de Jonnès, *Statistique des peuples de l'antiquité* (Paris, 1851), I, 151.

20 See Leon Poliakov, *The Aryan Myth: A History of Racist and Nationalist Ideas in Europe* (London, 1974).

21 See B. P. Koz'min, *Zhurnal "Sovremennik" – organ revoliutsionnoi demokratii* (M, 1957) and V. E. Evgen'ev–Maksimov, *"Sovremennik" pri Chernyshevskom i Dobroliubove* (Leningrad, 1936).

2   The *Illiustratsiia* Affair of 1858

1 The seating of Lionel Nathan Rothschild as a member of Parliament in 1858 was widely reported and discussed across Europe. Rothschild had been elected in 1847 but refused to take the parliamentary oath in its Christian form. In 1858, after a long battle and the passage of the Jews Disabilities Bill, he was allowed to take his seat. See Cecil Roth, *A History of the Jews in England*, 3rd ed. (Oxford, 1964), 259–66.

2 The Russian word *zhid* was derived from the Latin *Judaeus* and was the standard usage in the Muscovite and early imperial period, although occasionally replaced by the synonym *evrei*. It began to acquire a faintly pejorative connotation due to its use by Russian literateurs. The literary work most often blamed for encouraging this process was Faddei Bulgarin's picaresque novel *Ivan Vyzhigin* (SPb, 1829). In chapter 6, entitled "A Rich Jew (*Zhid*). The Sources of His Wealth," Ivan falls in with a tavernkeeper, Movsha, and witnesses his exploitation of the peasants, smuggling operations, and other criminal acts. See my article "*Zhid*: The Biography of a Russian Pejorative," *SEER*, 60, 1 (1982), 1–15.

3 I attribute this entry of the Diary to Zotov on the basis of internal evidence

and because it was his regular column. This assumption is supported by Soviet scholars. See A. G. Dement'ev, et al., *Russkaia periodicheskaia pechat'* (M, 1959), I, 362. In the course of the ensuing controversy Zotov pretended that he was not in fact the author.

4 These latter articles were occasionally confused with Zotov's Diary as the cause for the protest which now erupted. Similarly, the legend sprang up that the protest had been inspired by Zotov's use of the word Yid. For one example see *NkhV* (22:29 May 1888).

5 K. D. Kavelin was the editor of *Ethnograficheskii sbornik*, the publication of the Imperial Russian Geographical Society; V. D. Spasovich was a legal specialist who was later involved in the publication of *Zhurnal grazhdanskogo i torgovogo prava* and *Sudebnaia gazeta*; V. I. Bezobrazov was the editor of the *Zhurnal* of the Ministry of State Domains; A. D. Galakhov was a prominent writer and contributor to *Sovremennik* and *Otechestvennye zapiski*; N. Chernyshevskii was the celebrated revolutionary publicist and at this time the coeditor of *Voennyi sbornik*; P. V. Annenkov was the acclaimed literary memoirist; Ivan Turgenev was the famous novelist, who had most recently published *Rudin*; N. S. Tikhonravov was a historian and contributor to *Russkii vestnik*; A. A. Kraevskii was the former coeditor of *Sovremennik*, the coeditor of *Sanktpeterburgskie vedomosti*, the editor–publisher of *Otechestvennye zapiski*, and the future editor–publisher of *Golos*.

6 S. M. Gintsburg, "Zabytaia epokha," *Voskhod*, 16, 5–6 (1896), 133.

7 *Ibid.*

8 V. Evgen'ev-Maksimov, "*Sovremennik*", 256.

9 A. V. Nikitenko, *Zapiski i dnevnik* (SPb, 1904), 536–7.

10 S. S. Gromyka, a former gendarme official, published articles on the police in *Russkii vestnik*. He had acquired a reputation as a liberal for leading a petition campaign of St. Petersburg writers protesting the arrest of M. I. Mikhailov. He had served in the town of Berdichev, which had a significant Jewish population.

11 I. K. Babst, *Ot Moskvy do Leiptsiga* (Moscow, 1859), 3–11. Babst was professor of political economy at Moscow University from 1857 to 1874, and at the time of the Protest served as assistant editor of the economic monthly *Vestnik promyshlennosti*.

12 *Ibid.*, 7.

13 Roman Serbyn, "Ukrainian Writers on the Jewish Question: In the Wake of the *Illiustratsiia* Affair of 1858," *Nationalities Papers*, 9, 1 (Spring 1981), 101.

14 See below, chapter 5.

15 These qualifications aside, the impact of the polemic should not be underestimated. The concern for the insulted feelings of Jews was so strong at the end of 1858 that one correspondent of *Kolokol*, Alexander Herzen's progressive newspaper in exile, chided the editor, surely no proponent of religious or national intolerance, merely for identifying somebody as a Jew (*Evrei*), as though this alone were insulting. *Kolokol* promptly denied any such intent (30–31:15/XII/1858).

3 Defining terms

1 Gessen, *Gallereia*, 38–9.
2 1:1/VII; 2:4/VII; 15:19/VIII; 17 26/VIII; 18:29/VIII/1859.
3 14:17/II; 16:24/II; 17:27/II; 18:3/III/1859.
4 I. Sosis, "Obshchestvennye nastroeniia 'epokhi velikikh reform'," *ES*, 6, 1 (1914), 34–5.
5 See Patricia Herlihy, *Odessa: A History, 1794–1914* (Cambridge, MA, 1986), 95.
6 See J. D. Klier, "The Pogrom Paradigm in Russian History," in J. D. Klier and S. Lambroza, *Pogroms: Anti-Jewish Violence in Modern Russian History* (Cambridge, 1991), 13–38.
7 Iu. I. Gessen, ed., "Pis'ma O. A. Rabinovicha," *ES*, 3, 1 (1911), 74–5.
8 Gessen, ed., "Pis'ma," 71; Gessen, "Pervyi russko-evreiskii organ," 38–9.
9 L. Levanda, "K istorii vozniknoveniia pervogo organa russkikh evreev," *Voskhod*, 1, 6 (1881), 138–9.
10 Gessen, "Pervyi russko-evreiskii organ," 40–1.
11 *RGIA*, f. 821, op. 8, ed. khr. 256 (1857), l. 3o.
12 *Ibid.*, 38–9.
13 *Ibid.*, 45. In general the government was quite sympathetic to the efforts of maskilim to publish "progressive" newspapers in a Jewish language. For example, see the favorable assessments of S. Finn's *Ha-Karmel* in *RGIA*, f. 821, op. 8, ed. khr. 255 (1856–9); of A. Tsederbaum's *Ha-Melits, ibid.*, ed. khr. 258 (1859), ll. 1–6; and of a proposal to publish a Hebrew-language journal at the Zhitomir Rabbinical Institute, *ibid.*, ed. khr. 260 (1859–60).
14 *Ibid.*, 46.
15 Levanda, "K istorii," 140. Y. Slutsky suggests that it was the pogrom which led to the resubmission of the original project. *Ha-itonut ha-yehudit-rusit ba-me'ah ha-tesha-esreh* (Jerusalem, 1970), 41–2.
16 *Ibid.*, 48–50.
17 Jacob Katz, "The Term 'Jewish Emancipation': Its Origin and Historical Impact," in *Emancipation and Assimilation* (Westmead, England, 1972), 21–46.
18 See Gregory L. Freeze, "The *Soslovie* (Estate) Paradigm and Russian Social History," *American Historical Review*, 91, 1 (1986), 11–36.
19 J. D. Klier, "The Concept of 'Jewish Emancipation' in a Russian Context," in Olga Crisp and Linda Edmundson, eds., *Civil Rights in Imperial Russia* (Oxford, 1989), 121–44.
20 Vladimir Dal', *Tolkovyi slovar' zhivogo velikorusskogo iazyka*, 4th ed. (SPb–M, 1912), I, 67.
21 By the twentieth century modern connotations are clearly present. Compare the definition of *assimiliatsiia* in *Evreiskaia entsiklopedia*: "protsess sliianiia rasseiannykh v razlichnykh strankakh chastei evreiskogo naroda s okruzhaiushcheiu sredoiu," 3, 311.
22 *Dal'*, IV, 41–42.
23 *Ibid.*, IV, 252.
24 *Vopl' dshcheri iudeiskoi* (SPb, 1803). This rare work was reprinted in *Budushch-*

nost', 3 (1902), 118–31. A Hebrew translation (or perhaps the original) was published in Shklov in 1804, reprinted in *He-avar*, 2 (1918).

25 *Ibid.*, 131.

26 *TsDIA*, f. 442, op. 1, d. 4026, ll. 19–23; Also reprinted in Dubnov, "Istoricheskie soobshcheniia", 25–40; 3–21.

27 *Ibid.*, 39o.

28 Stanislawski, *Tsar Nicholas I*, 83.

29 For a striking analogue, see the words of Uvarov to Nicholas I in 1843, where he reminded the Tsar that "you commanded me quickly to study all measures that would lead ... to a rapprochement between these two hostile elements [Russians and Poles]," and to end "the long mutual hatred of one language toward the other, of the Roman church to the Orthodox, of Western Civilization to the Eastern." Quoted in Cynthia H. Whittaker, *The Origins of Modern Russian Education* (DeKalb, IL, 1984), 191.

30 I employ the admittedly clumsy term "merger" to translate *sliianie* because it is more neutral and less ideologically charged than "assimilation," a word which carries a whole set of assumptions and preconceptions to the modern reader. A central objective of this study is to define exactly the context and meaning of words like *sliianie* and *sblizhenie*. Interpretation of these terms is further complicated due to their use in contemporary Soviet writing on nationality questions.

31 See Part 1, p. 15.

32 "Aleksandr II," *ES*, I, 814.

33 *Ibid.*, 814.

34 The title of "Honored Citizen" (*pochtennyi grazhdanin*) was a high social rank awarded by the Russian government to members of the urban estate.

35 *EE*, VII, 375–6.

36 I. Tarnopol, *Opyt sovremennoi i osmotritel'noi reformy v oblasti iudaizma v Rossii* (Odessa, 1868). A chapter was published in *Odesskii vestnik* (37:5/IV/1858).

37 Tarnopol, *Opyt*, 264.

38 *Ibid.*, 35, XIII.

39 *Ibid.*, 36–42.

40 *Russkii invalid* (47:3/III/1859).

41 *Ibid.*, 205–9.

42 *Ibid.*, 12–13.

43 *Ibid.*, 25–32.

44 For the history of synagogue reform in Odessa, see Steven Zipperstein, *The Jews of Odessa* (Stanford, 1985), 56–64.

45 In an 1860 letter in French to the *Archives Israélites* of Paris, Tarnopol used the term "emancipation" to describe his objective for Russian Jews in the future. Moshe Perlmann, "Notes on *Razsvet* 1860–61," *Proceedings of the American Academy for Jewish Research*, 33 (1965), 31, 36.

46 *Ibid.*, 270–4. The establishment of this quid pro quo differentiated Tarnopol's proposals from those of his coeditor, O. A. Rabinovich, who argued that civil rights should not be tied to the moral condition of the Jews. See below, chapter 4, pp. 96–7.

47 *Ibid.*, 19.
48 *Ibid.*, 86–7.
49 Perlman, "Notes," 36.
50 Tarnopol, *Opyt*, 267.

4 *Rassvet* and the future of Judaism

1 A substantial literature exists on *Rassvet* and the role which it played in Russian and Jewish society. See S. L. Tsinberg (I. Zinberg), *Istoriia evreiskoi pechati v Rossii v sviazi s obshchestvennymi techeniiami*, (SPb, 1915), 40–62; Yehuda Slutsky, *Ha-itonut ha-yehudit-rusit ba-me'ah ha-tesha-ereh*, (Jerusalem, 1970), 37–55; Alexander Orbach, *New Voices of Russian Jewry* (Leiden, 1980), 22–53; B. Shohetman, "Ha-Rassvet ha-rishon," *He-avar*, 2 (1954), 61–72.
2 Jacob Katz, *Out of the Ghetto* (Cambridge, MA, 1973), 42 et seq.
3 Tarnopol, *Opyt*, 84–90. See above, pp. 71.
4 Levanda, "K istorii", 141–4.
5 See Eli Lederhendler's suggestive study of the role played by informing in the development of Jewish politics in the Russian Empire, and his specific comments in this regard on the role of *Rassvet*, in *Road*, 12–14, 88–100, 119–33.
6 Orbach, *New Voices*, 38; Lederhendler, *Road*, 126.
7 Rabinovich, "Pis'ma O. A. Rabinovich," 80.
8 Gessen, "Smena obshchestvennykh techenii. II. 'Pervyi russko evreiskii organ,'" 56–7.
9 "Pis'ma O. A. Rabinovicha," 85–7. Rabinovich's editorial was discussed by the Committee for the Transformation of the Jews in St. Petersburg, and its negative evaluation was confirmed by the Tsar. The Committee complained that "the author, failing to consider the measures already taken by the government to gradually equalize the rights of Jews with the other subjects of the Empire, portrays the present position of the Jews ... in the most gloomy and realistic guise, calculated to arouse in the reader doubts about the intentions of the government in regard to the Jews". *TsDIA*, f. 293, op. 1, d. 717, ll. 14o (14 July 1861).
10 Gessen, "Pervyi," 59.
11 *Ibid.*, 59.
12 *Ibid.*, 57.
13 L. G. Zakharova, "Samoderzhavie, biurokratiia i reformy 60kh XIX v. v Rossii," *Voprosy istorii*, 10 (1989), 4.
14 *Ibid.*, 58–9.
15 O. M. Lerner, *Evrei v novorossiiskom krae* (Odessa, 1901), 197.
16 Perlmann, "*Rassvet*," 179.
17 These included Dr. S. Stern, *Geschichte des Judentums von Mendelssohn bis auf die Gegenwart* (Frankfurt am Main, 1857); Heinrich Graetz, *Geschichte des Juden von der altesten Zeit bis auf die Gegenwart* (Berlin, 1853); Marcus Jost, *Geschichte des Judentums und seiner Sekten* (Leipzig, 1859).
18 1:1/VII; 2:4/VII; 15:19/VIII; 17:26/VIII; 18:29/VIII/1859. This sympathetic series, which Roman Serbyn plausibly attributes to the liberal historian at

St. Vladimir University in Kiev, P. V. Pavlov, began in the inaugural issue of *Kievskii telegraf*, initiating the Judeophile line which the paper pursued until its closing by the government in 1876 for alleged Ukrainophile sympathies. Roman Serbyn, "The *Sion–Osnova* Controversy of 1861–1862," in P. J. Potichnyi, H. Aster, eds., *Ukrainian–Jewish Relations in Historical Perspective* (Edmonton, 1988), 86.

19 It was typical of this milieu that any energetic defender of the Jews was routinely accused of being suborned by Jewish money, or of being a Jew himself. G. B. Sliozberg claims in *Dela minuvshikh dnei* (Paris, 1933) that Georgievskii was born a Jew and converted to Christianity in his youth, II, 86. In fact, see the biography by Friedhelm Berthold Kaiser, *Hochschulpolitik und studentischer Widerstand in Der Zarenzeit* (Wiesbaden, 1983), 7, for Georgievskii's thoroughly Russian pedigree.

20 For David Friedlander's proposal to Pastor Teller, see Michael A. Meyer, *The Origins of the Modern Jew* (Detroit, 1967), 70–8.

21 Zacharias Frankel, together with Heinrich Graetz and Manuel Joel, were the chief exponents of the Positive-Historical School, which viewed the development of Judaism as "a process carefully nurtured within a popular religion and rooted in custom and ideas, behind which a living people stood." Heinz Moshe Graupe, *The Rise of Modern Judaism* (Huntington, NY, 1978), 154.

22 The "barometer" expression was coined by the writer Berthold Auerbach in his novel *Dichter und Kaufman* in 1840. Simon Markish, "Osip Rabinovich," *CMRS*, 21, 1 (1980), 12–13. There is a direct analogue to the Russian debate over the priority of self-improvement or emancipation in the prior German Jewish experience. See Meyer, *Origins*, 62–3.

23 Compare the critique of the "adepts of European knowledge" appearing in a sketch in 31:23/XII/1860: "These people, of course, have a complete right to our respect for their contemporary education; on the other hand, where they advance as reformers, ignorant of their own people, they are more likely to promote complete reaction rather than achieve anything significantly good."

24 *Rassvet* did not completely reject the notion of Jewish periodicals in other languages, but was very lukewarm in its endorsement of the announced appearance of the Hebrew–German *Ha-Melits*, published by A. Tsederbaum and A. I. Goldenblium (10:29/VII/1860).

25 This open attack on the Pale demonstrates the ineffectiveness of the Russian censorship and shows how, as Rabinovich reported to Levanda, "the case was often won." It also casts doubt on Rabinovich's complaint to Rozental about his inability to wring concessions from the Chief Office of Press Affairs and secure permission to print an editorial openly attacking the Pale. Gessen, "Pervyi," 85–7.

26 (5:24/VI/1860); (16:9/IX/1860); (21:14/X/1860).

27 It should be noted that maskilic debates took on a different flavor in publications published in Hebrew, Yiddish or German, and intended only for a Jewish audience. The Hebrew language section of *Ha-Melits* offered readers undemanding articles which argued for the compatibility of faith

and reason. The German text presented more sophisticated treatments on the need for religious reform, taken wholesale from the German Jewish press. I. Sosis, "Natsional'nyi vopros v literature kontsa 60kh i nachala 70kh godov," *ES*, 7, 2 (1915), 89.

5 *Sion* and the problem of nationality

1 For Tsederbaum and his publishing efforts, see Orbach, *New Voices*, 54–155.
2 For a biography of Portugalov, see Serbyn, "The *Sion-Osnova* Controversy," 85–7.
3 *Ibid.*, 88.
4 A. Gattsuk, "Evrei v russkoi istorii i poezii" (1:1/VI/1861).
5 Serbyn, "The *Sion-Osnova* Controversy," 85.
6 Kostomarov's semi-fictional article "Zhidotrepanie v nachale XVIII v.," *Kievskaia starina*, 1, 3 (1883), was widely criticized as an endorsement of anti-Jewish pogroms. His willingness to lend his public support to the ritual murder accusation is demonstrated by his article published in *Novoe vremia*, 1172: 5 June 1879. Kostomarov, as a young bureaucrat, had been involved in the investigation of a notorious Russian ritual murder case, the Saratov Affair (1852–55).
7 Serbyn, "The *Sion-Osnova* Controversy," 96.
8 *Den'*, 8:4/VI/1869.
9 Slutsky, *Ha-itonut*, 47.
10 A Russian supplement accompanied the Vilna-based Hebrew publication *Ha-Karmel* until 1865.
11 Michael A. Meyer, *Response to Modernity: A History of the Reform Movement in Judaism* (New York and Oxford, 1988), 59. There were, of course, elements of semi- or proto-nationalism in the works of Z. Frankel and H. Graetz.

6 The religious element in Russian Judeophobia

1 See S. Ettinger, "Ha-hashpa'ah ha-yehudit al ha-tesisah ha-datit ve-mizrahah shel Europa be-sof ha-me'ah ha-tet-zayin," in *Yitzhak F. Baer Jubilee Volume*, S. W. Baron, ed. (Jerusalem, 1960): 228–47; and "Medinat Moskva be-yahasah el ha-yehudim," *Zion*, XVIII (1953): 136–68.
2 Klier, *Russia Gathers*, xiv–xv.
3 *Domashniaia beseda* was linked to the higher Orthodox clergy by the well-informed *Russkii vestnik* in 1861 (33: May 1861, 9–10).
4 The *Russkii vestnik* article quoted in note 3 merely reminded *Domashniaia beseda* that its attacks on Poles and Jews were not in the Christian spirit, 9–13.
5 Ivan's father, S. T. Aksakov, was the author of *A Family Chronicle*, which offers a famous portrait of the gentry "nests" which produced so many of the Slavophiles. Ivan's brother Konstantin (1817–60) was an important Slavophile theoretician.
6 For a broader discussion of Slavophilism and Panslavism and the Jewish Question, see chapter 17.

7 Much of the third volume of Aksakov's collected works is devoted to the Jewish Question, and even this omits material from his publications which was probably written by him. I. S. Aksakov, *Polnoe sobranie sochinenii* (M-SPb, 1886–7).

8 I. S. Aksakov, *Ivan Sergeevich Aksakov v ego pis'makh* (M, 1888–92), II, 18–19, 27–8, 35–7, 80, 92–3.

9 I. Aksakov, *Issledovanie o torgovle na ukrainskikh iarmarkhakh* (SPb, 1858).

10 Meyer, *Response to Modernity*, 66–7.

11 The slogan of the "Christian state" was popularized by the writings of Friedrich Julius Stahl in 1847, but it also contained echoes of the debate on the subject of Jewish emancipation between Bruno Bauer and Karl Marx. For Stahl see Jacob Katz, *From Prejudice to Destruction* (Cambridge, MA, 1980), 198–202. For the religious context of the Bauer–Marx debate in 1843–4, see Julius Carlebach, *Karl Marx and the Radical Critique of Judaism* (London, 1978), 125–84.

12 Goldstein, 39–46. It might be noted, however, that *Sovremennik* was not a journal strongly interested in the Jewish Question.

13 Emmons, *Russian Landed Gentry*, 359–60.

14 Charles Ruud, *Fighting Words: Imperial Censorship and the Russian Press, 1804–1906* (Toronto, 1982), 127–8.

15 A. Aleksandrov was the pseudonym of A. N. Aksakov, a relative of I. S. Aksakov. His identity was unknown to Aksakov when he received the article, and he published it under the misapprehension that it was a legitimate "voice from the provinces." A. N. Aksakov became a well-known philosopher and theologian, and Russia's foremost expert on Spiritualism. N. I. Tsimbaev, *I. S. Aksakov v obshchestvennoi zhizni poreformennoi Rossii* (M, 1978), 82. To avoid confusion, A. N. Aksakov's pseudonym will be used in the discussion of his article.

16 Jewish publicists were sensitive even to oblique criticisms of the Talmud. Early in 1862 A. Gordon published an article critical of a historical piece which had appeared in *Otechestvennyi zapiski* describing an estate-management project devised by an advisor to Alexander I as a "Talmud for his peasants." *Severnaia pchela* (17:18/I/1862).

17 Stanislawski, *Tsar Nicholas I*, 110–11.

18 S. M. Ginsburg, *Meshumodim in tsarishn rusland* (New York, 1946), 256.

19 Reprinted in *Kievskie eparkhal'nye vedomosti* (2:15/I/1863).

Part 2 The era of Russification

1 Artur Eisenbach, *Kwestia równouprawnienia Żydów w Królestwie Polskim* (Warsaw, 1972), 114. Chapter 1 of this important study enumerates the various disabilities borne by Polish Jewry.

2 *Ibid.*, 260–2.

3 *Ibid.*, 272–7. See also Kazimierz Bartoszewicz, *Wojna Żydowska w roku 1859* (Warsaw–Krakow, 1913).

4 R. F. Leslie, *Reform and Insurrection in Russian Poland, 1856–1865* (London, 1963), 52.

5 Artur Eisenbach, "La problème des Juifs polonais en 1861 et les projects de réforme du Marquis Aleksander Wielopolski," *Acta Poloniae Historica*, 20 (1969), 149. For police investigations of Polish agitation among Jews, see *TsDIA*, f. 442, op. 812, d. 4 (1862), ll. 56–7; 83–4; op. 811, d. 249 (1861–2), ll. 1–10.

6 Eisenbach, *Kwestia*, 419.

7 *Ibid.*, 422–5.

8 N. M. Gelber, *Die Juden und der polnische Aufstand 1863* (Vienna, 1923), 94.

9 Eisenbach *Kwestia*, 507–8.

10 Gessen, *Istoriia*, II, 186.

11 *Ibid.*, II, 195.

12 *Ibid.*, II 194–5. The improvement of the legal position of Polish Jewry continued even after the outbreak of the Polish revolt. They were permitted into state service (perhaps as a subtle jab at the Poles), and free passage from Kongresowka into the Pale, and Polish Jews were brought under the regulations which extended the right to some categories of Jews to reside in the Russian interior. For a detailed examination of the fate of the Jews in Poland after the revolt, see Michael J. Ochs, "St. Petersburg and the Jews of Russian Poland, 1862–1905," unpublished doctoral dissertation, Harvard University, 1986. See also Artur Eisenbach, *Emancypacja Żydów na ziemiach polskich 1785–1870 na tle europejskim* (Warsaw, 1988), 468–513. (Translated in English as *The Emancipation of the Jews in Poland, 1780–1870* [Oxford, 1991].)

13 Ochs, "Jews of Russian Poland," 240–1.

14 *Sion*'s correspondent in Warsaw did not hide his enthusiasm for Polish–Jewish rapprochement. He praised Warsaw rabbis who offered sermons in Polish, and welcomed the appearance of a Polish prayer book for Jewish women (3:21/VII/1861). An October report described Jewish participation in local elections and praised the activities of Rabbi Meisels (14:22/IX/1861). In November an article noted that the Polish State Council was discussing Jewish rights. The author stressed the need to end the isolation of the Jews and make them part of the "national whole" (19:10/XI/1861).

15 By the twentieth century the role of Jews in the Polish uprising of 1863 had acquired a certain respectability. The historical journal *Evreiskaia starina* carried a number of enthusiastic articles by Polish–Jewish scholars detailing Jewish participation in a national, democratic movement. A typical article of this sort is cited in note 24. A petition of the Gintsburg Circle to the government in 1862 did note in passing the Polish reforms, seeing in them a favorable omen of better treatment for Russian Jews. *RGIA*, f. 796, op. 144, ed. khr. 159 (1863–5), l. 6o.

16 *Ha-Tsefirah*, edited by Hayyim Zelig Slonimski, future director of the Zhitomir Rabbinical Seminary, was published for a brief six months from February to August 1862, and was thus spared the need to comment on the Polish Revolt itself.

17 Mark Baker, "The Reassessment of Haskala Ideology in the Aftermath of the 1863 Polish Revolt," *Polin*, V (1990): 221–49.

18 *Ibid.*, 239.

19 S. S. Tatischev, *Imperator Aleksandr II, ego zhizn' i tsarstvovanie*, 2 vols. (SPb, 1903), 1, 511–12, 526–7.

20 See Martin Katz, *Mikhail N. Katkov: A Political Biography, 1818–1887* (The Hague and Paris, 1966), 118–31 and Stephen Lukashevich, *Ivan Aksakov, 1823–1886* (Cambridge, MA, 1965), 76–95.

21 *VPSZ*, XXXVII:38,214 (26/IV/1862).

22 I argue this point at length in "The Polish Revolt of 1863 and the Birth of Russification: Bad for the Jews?," *Polin*, I (1986), 95–110.

23 Sliozberg, *Dela*, II, 147.

24 Ia. Shatskin, "K istorii uchastiia evreev v pol'skom vosstanii 1863 g.," *ES*, I (1915), 29–30.

25 Michael B. Petrovich, "Russian Pan-Slavists and the Polish Uprising of 1863," *Harvard Slavic Studies*, I (1953), 246–7.

26 My discussion of publications edited by Katkov assumes that editorials were either written by Katkov or directly approved by him.

27 143:9/VII/1866; 149:16/VII/1866. But see the dissenting opinion of *Birzhevye vedomosti* (61:19/III/1866) which reminded Katkov that Jewish religious tradition discouraged the use of the vernacular by the Jews for religious purposes.

28 See editorials in nos. 110, 115, et seq. for 1870.

29 269:30/IX/1869 and 273:4/X/1869. For the Vilna Jewish Commission, see chapter 7.

7   Russification in the Northwest

1 While Nazimov saw the Jews of the Northwest as badly in need of reform (see p. 21), in November of 1861 he wrote to the capital recommending that the government deal more leniently with the local Jews, "who are ... the only inhabitants loyal to the government." *Żydzi a powstanie styczniowe* (Warsaw, 1963), 49.

2 Mikhail Zolotonosov, "U istokov russkogo antisemitizma," forthcoming in vol. 5 of *Vestnik Moskovskogo Evreiskogo Universiteta*.

3 Leslie, *Reform*, 224–6.

4 B. Nadel, "O stosunku Żydow na wilenszczyznie do powstania styczniowego," *BZIH*, 28 (1958), 41.

5 Liverant, "Prikliucheniia evreia vo vremia pol'skogo vosstaniia 1863 goda," *ES*, 3 (1910), 378–90. Studies which emphasize the participation of Jews in the Polish national movement are: B. Rozenshtadt, "Evreiskie zhertvy v pol'skom vosstanii 1863 goda," *ES*, 4 (1913), 485–92; Shatskin, "K istorii," *ES*, 1 (1915), 29–37. In October, 1863, Muravev restricted the issuance of passports for Jews traveling abroad for business purposes since he distrusted their ties to Poles in emigration. *Żydzi a powstanie styczniowe*, 185–6. A number of Jews were exiled to Siberia for assisting Polish insurgents. See *RGIA*, f. 821, op. 9, ed. khr. 207 (1883–7).

6 Cherikover, *Istoriia*, 72.

7 *Ibid.*

8 Tsinberg, *Istoriia evreiskoi pechati*, 129–30.

9 *Istoricheskie svedeniia o vilenskom ravvinskom uchilishche* (Vilna, 1873), 36–7.
10 *Ibid.*, 49.
11 Stanislawski, *Tsar Nicholas I*, 138–41, 72.
12 Dubnov, *History*, II, 133–5.
13 Nadel, "O stosunku Żydow," 45–8.
14 Levanda's picture of Russian officialdom on the eve of the January uprising depicts them as completely cut off from the realities of the region and hostile to any thought of cooperation with the Jews. See *Goriachee vremia*, *EB*, 1–3 (1871–3), 1–71; 1–160; 8–93.
15 I. Kornilov, *Russkoe delo v severo-zapadnom krae* (SPb, 1908), xi-xii.
16 *Ibid.*, 36.
17 *Ibid.*, 230–2, 223–4.
18 Orbach, *New Voices*, 57–8; Alkoshi, "Ha-itonut ha-ivrit be-vilnah ba-me'ah ha 19," *He-Avar*, 13 (1966): 59–97; 14 (1967): 105–53. For the Russian supplement, see Slutsky, *Ha-itonut*, 52–55.
19 A. E. Landau, ed., "Iz perepiski L. O. Levandy," *EB*, 9 (1901), 14.
20 A. Druianov, "Iz perepiski L. O. Levanda," *ES*, 5, 2 (1913), 280–1.
21 164:3/VIII; 166:5/VIII; 171:12/VIII; 174:17/VIII and 192:12/IX/1866.
22 Cherikover, *Istoriia*, 253.
23 Kornilov, *Russkoe delo*, 249.
24 Landau, "Iz perepiski," 61.
25 *Ibid.*, 61–2.
26 16:7/II and 42:11/IV/1867. Wohl was an exponent of the use of German in the state Jewish schools. For the debate, see Nadel, "O stosunku Żydow," 45–6.
27 Landau, "Iz perepiski," 61–2.
28 Iu. Gessen, "Iz letopisi minuvshogo: vilenskaia komissiia po ustroistvu byta evreev (1866–1869 gg.)," *Perezhitoe*, 2 (SPb, 1910), 306–7. *RGIA*, f. 821, op. 9, ed. khr. 164 (1881–2), ll. 63, 76.
29 Landau, "Iz perepiski," 61.
30 Published in *Vilenskii vestnik*, 92: 1867 and Iakov Brafman, *Kniga kagala* (Vilna, 1869), I, 156–7.
31 *Ibid.*
32 *Ibid.*
33 *TsDIA*, f. 442, op. 47, d. 308 (1868), l. 11.
34 *RGIA*, f. 821, op. 9, ed. khr. 165 (1872–81), ll. 78–87o.
35 *RGIA*, f. 1282, op. 2, ed. khr. 73 (1868), ll. 1–23.
36 Lederhendler, *Road*, 144.
37 Lederhendler sees the work of the Vilna commission as playing an important role in the modernization of the traditional efforts of the shtadlanim, 144.
38 Ex-deputat, "O deiatel'nosti byvshei vilenskoi delegatsii," *Den'*, 2:10/I/1870. The anonymous author was in fact M. L. Knorozovskii of Grodno. He complained that Levin, "the self-appointed head of the delegation" had neglected his promise to publicize the activities of the Jewish delegation.
39 For the operation of the Rabbinical Commissions, see Lederhendler, *Road*, 73–4, 150–2.
40 *Den'*, 2:10/I; 3:16/I; 7:14/II; 8:21/II/1870.

41 S. An—ski [S. Z. Rapoport], "Evreiskaia delegatsiia v vilenskoi komissii 1869 goda," *ES*, 4, 2 (1912), 189–90; *Den'*, 2:10/I/1870.

42 The justification presented to the deputies for this proposal clearly bore the stamp of Brafman: "The Jewish religion lacks a real foundation; it appeared accidently through the medium of learned Talmudists and their followers. The Talmud in turn is nothing but an ulcer; it ruins the Jewish people and harms all humanity," *Den'*, 11:13/III/ 1870.

43 *Den'*, 4:23/I/1870.

44 *Materialy KUBE*, I, 5–6.

45 *Den'*, 4:23/I/1870.

46 *Den'*, 21:23/V/1870.

47 *Materialy KUBE*, I, 7.

48 An—skii, "Evreiskaia delegatsiia," 201.

49 *RGIA*, f. 821, op. 9, ed. khr. 91 (1872–5), ll. 1–4o. A similar petition was presented unsuccessfully to the KUBE in 1875.

50 *Materialy KUBE*, I, 8.

51 Lederhendler, *Road*, 144–5.

8 "Kiev is Russian"

1 A. F. Smirnov, *Vosstanie 1863 goda v Litve i Belorussii* (M, 1963), 301.

2 Edward C. Thaden and Marianna Forster Thaden, *Russia's Western Borderlands, 1710–1870* (Princeton, 1984), 132–3.

3 *Ibid.*, 53. For the attack upon the Polish nobility in the Ukraine under Nicholas I see Daniel Beauvois, *Le Noble, le serf, et le révizor: la noblesse polonaise entre le tsarisme et les masses ukrainiennes (1831–1863)* (Paris, 1985).

4 Edward C. Thaden, *Conservative Nationalism in Nineteenth-Century Russia* (Seattle, 1964), 47.

5 Peasants were under "temporarily obligated status," which required them to continue to provide money and/or labor duties to the landowners, until the final allotment of land was agreed upon. It was the duty of the land arbitrators to oversee peasant–landlord negotiations. Land in dispute, obviously, could not be allocated. For the details of the emancipation settlement in Right-Bank Ukraine, see Zaionchkovskii, *Otmena*, 225–31.

6 See the complaints on this score by Governor-General N. N. Annenkov to the Western Committee early in 1864, in *TsDIA*, f. 442, op. 815, d. 118, ll. 16–30o.

7 Official figures for 1865 counted 602,754 Jews in Right-Bank Ukraine. *VPSZ*, XL:42,264 (28 June 1865).

8 *EE*, V, 344–5. Vasilchikov was responsible for relaxing residence restrictions on Jewish residence in Kiev, which soon brought a flood of settlers into the city.

9 Gessen, *Istoriia*, II, 157.

10 Hans Rogger, *Jewish Policies and Right-Wing Politics in Imperial Russia* (London, 1986), 125.

11 *VPSZ*, XXXVII, 38,214:26/IV/1862.

12 Katz, *Mikhail N. Katkov*, 100. See *Russkaia starina* (October 1915), 92–4. In an

editorial in number 153 of *Moskovskie vedomosti* for 1865, Katkov emphasized the need to settle the western provinces with Russian landowners, since "alien" (*inorodtsy*) elements, like the Jews, could easily pass to the side of the Poles if events warranted.

13 *VPSZ*, XXXIX, 40,656:5/III/1864.

14 *VPSZ*, XXXIX, 41,039:10/VII/1864.

15 *VPSZ*, XL, 42,328:23/VII/1865.

16 *TsDIA*, f. 442, op. 815, d. 440 (1864–5), ll. 30–13o.

17 *Ibid.*, 320.

18 *RBS*, XV, 515–17.

19 *Entsiklopedicheskii slovar'* (SPb, 1895), XV, 252.

20 Shulgin offered a less than positive view of Ukrainian Jewry in his book *Iugozapadnyi krai v poslednee dvadtsatipiatiletie, 1838–1863* (Kiev, 1864). He described the Jews as loyal neither to Russia nor to Poland, "but for money ready to help both and sell both" (20). He appeared to agree with the attitude which he attributed to Prince Vasilchikov that the Jews were parasites, but that it was unfair to attribute their negative characteristics to the whole people. Moreover, the negative features of the Jews had been caused by persecution, and the surest way to raise their moral and material level was to end legal discrimination against them (240–1).

21 See numbers 6:14/VII/1864; 8:18/VII/1864; 21:15/VIII/1864; 22:18/VIII/1864.

22 See chapter 10.

23 *RGIA*, f. 821, op. 8, ed. khr. 232 (22/XI/64), ll. 1–2.

24 This discussion of *Kievlianin* assumes that all editorials were written by Shulgin, unless there is specific internal evidence to the contrary.

25 For Morgulis, see *EE*, 11, 298–302. Morgulis' memoirs were serialized in *Voskhod* from 1895 to 1897, and concluded in *Evreiskii mir* in 1909.

26 The local administration shared Shulgin's sense of outrage at Morgulis' proposals. A brochure reprinting his article was confiscated by the authorities, *EE*, XI, 300.

27 A series of articles by the converted Jew V. Fedotov appeared in nos. 44, 45, 73, 122, 123, 130, 131 and 132 for 1865.

28 Alfred J. Rieber, "The Moscow Entrepreneurial Group: The Emergence of a New Form in Autocratic Politics," *JGO*, 25, 2 (1977), 176.

29 This terminology was redolent of Marx's notorious essay "Zur Judenfrage," published in 1844. Many of Aksakov's slogans suggested a German provenance, but he rarely cited his sources, and always put foreign terminology to his own idiosyncratic uses.

30 See 21:18/II/1865: "Such solidarity of action, endeavoring to weaken the impact of the demands of officials, to whom the Jews always have access due to their money, makes these people an autonomous corporation in western Russia, rarely bound by the law of the land, and aware only of their law, their court system and their punishments."

31 See numbers 15, 16, 23, 35, 37 and 130, all for 1869.

32 See numbers 35, 47, 39 and 104 for 1870.

33 Numbers 45, 46, 47 and 48 for 1873.

34 Numbers 96 and 97 for 1873.

35 Published as Maior Osman-Bei, *Pokorenie mira evreiami* (SPb, 1874), and reviewed in 80:6/VII/1874.

36 For a contemporary description of the *oblava*, see the report submitted to Governor-General M. I. Chertkov by I. B. Grinshtein in 1879. *TsDIA*, f. 442, op. 829, d. 51 (1879), ll. 1–4.

37 Rogger, *Jewish Policies*, 127.

38 *Materialy KUBE*, 4.

39 *Ibid.*, 11–12.

40 Dubnow, *History*, II, 196–8.

9 "Kiev is Ukrainian"

1 Consider the formulation of Ukrainian aspirations voiced by Kostomarov in a letter in Herzen's *Kolokol* in 1860. "Let neither Russians nor Poles call theirs the lands populated by our people," he declared. At the same time he welcomed a prospective unification of all Slavic peoples under the Russian Tsar, if he would become the "sovereign of free peoples," rather than the "autocrat of an all-devouring Tatar–German Muscovy," Dmytro Doroshenko, *A Survey of Ukrainian History* (Winnipeg, 1975), 542–3.

2 See P. A. Zaionchkovskii, *Kirillo-Mefodievskoe obshchestvo, 1846–1847* (M, 1959).

3 Doroshenko, *Survey*, 535–8.

4 M. D. Bernshtein, *Zhurnal "Osnova" i ukrains'kyi literaturnyi protses kintsia 50–60kh rokiv XIX st.* (Kiev, 1959), 65–70.

5 Katz, *Mikhail N. Katkov*, 131–3.

6 *Den'*, 4:25/I/1864.

7 Mikhail Lemke, *Epokha tsenzurnykh reform, 1859–1865 godov* (SPb, 1904), 302.

8 V. Antonovich and M. Dragomanov, *Istoricheskie pesni malorusskogo naroda* (Kiev, 1875); P. P. Chubinskii, *Trudy etnografichesko-statisticheskoi ekspeditsii v zapadno-russkii krai*, 7 vols. (SPb, 1872–8) Jews are treated in volume 7 (1872).

9 See Fedir Savchenko, *The Suppression of the Ukrainian Activities in 1876* (Munich, 1970), 1–114.

10 M. P. Dragomanov, *Rozvidki Mykhaila Drahomanova pro ukrains'ku narodniu slovesnist' i pys'menstvo* (Lwow, 1899), I, 22. The "Union" was the Union of Brest of 1596, by which the Orthodox Church in Poland–Lithuania recognized the authority of Rome.

11 Antonovich, Dragomanov, *Istoricheskie pesni malorusskogo naroda*, II, 1, 20–32.

12 Zaionchkovskii, *Kirillo-Mefodievskoe obshchestvo*, 157.

13 N. I. Kostomarov, *Literaturnoe nasledie* (SPb, 1890), 74.

14 George Luckyj, *Panteleimon Kulish: A Sketch of His Life and Times* (Boulder, CO, 1983), 97–8.

15 See chapter 2, pp. 61–4.

16 Doroshenko, *Survey*, 544.

17 Serbyn, "Ukrainian Writers," 100.

18 *Osnova*, 6 (June 1861), 134–5.

19 *Ibid.*, 140–1.

20 *Ibid.*, 142.

21 *Osnova*, 9 (1861), 135–8.
22 *Osnova*, 1 (1862), 42–6.
23 Moshe Mishkinsky, "The Attitudes of the Ukrainian Socialists to Jewish Problems in the 1870s," in Peter J. Potichnyi and Howard Aster, eds., *Ukrainian–Jewish Relations in Historical Perspective* (Edmonton, 1988), 60–1.
24 Efforts to defend Dragomanov against the charge of Antisemitism are found in Elizbieta Horn, "Problem Żydowski w Twórczości Dragomanova," *BZIH*, 69, 1–3 (1966), 3–37 and Ivan Rudnytsky, "Mykhailo Drahomanov and the Problem of Ukrainian Jewish Relations," *Canadian Slavonic Papers*, XI (Summer 1969), 182–98, reprinted in Ivan Rudnytsky, *Essays in Modern Ukrainian History* (Cambridge, MA, 1987), 283–97. Hereafter cited as Rudnytsky, *Essays*.

A recent effort to re-emphasize Dragomanov's alleged Antisemitism is found in Shmuel Galai, "Early Russian Constitutionalism, 'Vol'noe Slovo' and the 'Zemstvo Union': A Study in Deception," *JGO*, 22, 1 (1974), 35–55. Galai finds Dragomanov's views particularly reprehensible because they were publicized at a time of mass persecution of the Jews. See also M. Mishkinsky, "Al emdata shel ha-tenu'ah ha-mahpekhanit ha-rusit le-gabe ha-yehudim bi-shnot ha-70 shel ha-me'ah ha-19," *He-avar*, IX (1962):38–66, especially 48–54 and 63–5. Finally there are the important reminiscences of a Jewish contributor to Dragomanov's *Vol'noe slovo* in Ben-Ami, "Moi snosheniia s M. Dragomanovym i rabota v 'Vol'nom slove,'" *ES*, 8, 3–4 (1915), 346–66; 7, 1 (1916), 75–101. While the author regretfully emphasized Dragmanov's Judeophobia, the editor of *ES*, commenting on this passage, accepted its validity only in the "widest possible sense," 360.
25 See the biographical sketch by B. A. Kistiakovskii in M. P. Dragomanov, *Sobranie politicheskikh sochinenii*, 2 vols. (Paris, 1906), ix–lix. All citations from Dragomanov's Russian-language work in exile will be cited from this edition. M. Mishkinsky argues that the complexity of the situation in Galicia was an important element in making Dragomanov a pioneer of the radical camp "which tried to deal with all aspects of the Jewish question theoretically and programatically." Mishkinsky, "Ukrainian socialists," 66–7.
26 See "Drahomanov as Political Theorist," in Ivan L. Rudnytsky, *Mykhaylo Drahomanov, A Symposium and Selected Writings* (New York, 1952), 112–15.
27 Specialists, such as Ivan Rudnytsky, argue that Dragomanov's thinking on the Jewish Question had "developed and matured" when he began to write on the Jewish Question in earnest while settled in Geneva, "Mikhailo Drahomanov," 186. I am struck, rather, by the consistency of thought on the subject: the major leitmotifs are set out in his first article on the Jewish Question which appeared in *Kievskii telegraf* in 1875, expanded in his review in *Vestnik Evropy* a few months later, and serve as the starting point for all subsequent comments. The *Kievskii telegraf* article, as far as I know, has never been attributed to Dragomanov. Its organization and even some of the wording are identical to the *Vestnik Evropy* essay. Dragomanov was at this time the de facto editor of *Kievskii telegraf*.
28 Compare this statement in *Kievskii telegraf* with M. Dragomanov, "Evrei i Poliaki v iugo-zapadnom krae," *Vestnik Evropy*, 7 (1875), 137–41.

29 *Ibid.*, 137–9.
30 "Evreisksii vopros v slavianskom kruzhke v Londone," *Vol'noe slovo*, 28:13/25 February 1882, in *Sobranie*, II, 541–2.
31 "Istoricheskaia Pol'sha i velikorusskaia demokratiia," in *Sobranie*, I, 236. Published in *Vol'noe slovo* in 1881 and as a separate brochure in Geneva in the same year.
32 Ben-Ami, "Moi snosheniia," 96. Ben-Ami was the pen-name of the Jewish socialist M. I. Rabinovich.
33 M. Drahomanov, "Ukrajins'ki sel'ane v mespokojni roki, 1880–1882," *Hromada*, V (Geneva, 1882), 251–7.
34 "Given the present relationship between the Ukrainian people and the Jews one can expect that any movement against this order of things will be accompanied by bloody scenes of Jewish massacre [which would be] much more unjust than the scenes of the seventeenth and eighteenth centuries." Dragomanov's afterword to the brochure *Ot gruppy sotsialistov-evreev* (Geneva, 1880) and in *Sobranie*, II, 327.
35 "Evreiskii vopros v Ukraine," *Sobranie*, II, 527.
36 "Istoricheskaia Pol'sha," *Sobranie*, I, 236–7.
37 "Evreiskii vopros v Ukraine," *Sobranie*, II, 534.
38 "Evrei i Poliaki," 137–8.
39 "The Program of the Review *Hramada*," in Rudnytsky, *Mykhaylo Drahomanov*, 206.
40 "Evreiskii vopros v Ukraine," *Sobranie*, II, 536–7.
41 "Evrei i Poliaki," 138–9.
42 "Ot gruppy," *Sobranie*, II, 327.
43 "Evreiskii vopros v Ukraine," *Sobranie*, II, 538–40.
44 Ben-Ami, "Moi snosheniia," 364. Dragomanov on several occasions offered a positive appraisal of Jewish sectarian movements, which seemed to offer a greater chance of assimilation with the Ukrainian people, "Ukrajins'ki selane," *Sobranie*, I, 258 and "Istoricheskaia Pol'sha," 233. Such sentiments reveal the fatal flaw which poisoned Dragomanov's relations with the Jews. He carried many prejudices against Jewish culture and customs, even accepting the possibility of the blood libel, which were components of Ukrainian folk Judeophobia. In his view these negative features of Jewry would presumably vanish with assimilation.
45 Ben-Ami related that Dragomanov, despite his own strong opinions, was always deferential to his expertise, "Moi snoshenie," 364.
46 "Evrei i Poliaki," 138–9.
47 "Ot gruppy," *Sobranie*, II, 327–8.
48 Frankel, 101–2.
49 "Slavianskom kruzhke," 541–2. This was a feature which Dragomanov also faulted in Russian socialists of Ukrainian descent. See "The Centralization of the Revolutionary Struggle in Russia," *Dragomanov Symposium*, 181–92, especially 190.
50 "Evreiskii vopros v Ukraine," *Sobranie*, II, 532.
51 One might contrast Dragomanov's regret at the pogroms with the response of the former Ukrainophile Kostomarov. In *Kievskaia starina*, a journal

devoted to the organic work of recapturing the Ukrainian past, he published a sympathetic fictionalized account of a Jewish ritual murder accusation in seventeenth-century Ukraine which led to a pogrom. The analogy with the present was noted by commentators. See "Zhidotrepanie v nachale XVIII v.," *Kievskaia starina* 1, 3 (1883).
52 Galai, "Early Russian Constitutionalism," 47–8.
53 The series on the World Antisemitic Congress appeared in two forms. Five articles, entitled "The First International Antisemitic Congress" are essentially objective reportage. (*Vol'noe slovo*, 45, 46, 47, 48 and 49 for 1882). Two interpretative pieces by the same author, "The Essence of the Antisemitic Movement" (nos. 50 and 51) fully deserve Galai's characterization.
54 "Evreiskii vopros v Ukraine," *Sobranie*, II, 530.

10   Education and Russification

1 *Vilenskii vestnik*, 67:1865.
2 Patrick L. Alston, *Education and the State in Tsarist Russia* (Stanford, 1969), 93 et seq.
3 *VPSZ*, XXXII:31,831 (13/V/1857).
4 *VPSZ*, XXX:29,276 (3/V/1855). As noted above, the pace was forced still further by the decree of 1857 which established criteria for the election of state rabbis effective immediately.
5 *VPSZ*, XXXI:31,104 (5/XI/1856).
6 *VPSZ*, XXXII:31,831 (13/V/1857).
7 Beletskii, *Vopros*, 90, 147.
8 Cherikover, *Istoriia*, 15–16.
9 Gessen, *Zakon i zhizn'*, 113.
10 See the attacks on this petition in *Den'* in chapter 15.
11 Cherikover, *Istoriia*, 12–18.
12 Beletskii, *Vopros*, 104.
13 See files in *TsDIA*, f. 707, op. 87, d. 3690 (1859–61), ll. 46–59, for examples of how *melamdim* evaded the regulations, in some cases by securing medical certifications of poor health to excuse their failure to meet the required deadlines.
14 Cherikover, *Istoriia*, 14.
15 *Ibid.*
16 *VPSZ*, XXXVIII:38,641 (6/IX/1862).
17 Cherikover, *Istoriia*, 33–4.
18 *VPSZ*, XXXIV:34,461 (4/V/1859). For implementation, see *TsDIA*, f. 707, op. 87, d. 3690 (1859), ll. 180–1, and the ease with which provisions were evaded in Berdichev.
19 For the debate on mandatory schooling, see nos. 29 (9/XII/1860), 33 (6/II/1861) and 36 (27/I/1861). Rabinovich's comments appeared in no. 29.
20 See nos. 20 (17/XI/1861) and 35 (2/III/1862).
21 The government inspector Postel's (see note 24) credited the law of 27 November 1861, opening the civil service to the Jews, for an influx of students into the rabbinical schools, 46–7.

22 Reginald Zelnik, "The Sunday School Movement in Russia, 1859–62," *Journal of Modern History*, 2 (1965):151–70.

23 See above, chapter 8, p. 188.

24 "Otchet chlena soveta ministra narodnogo prosveshcheniia Postel'sa, po obozreniiu evreiskikh uchilishch s 7 maia po 7 sentiabria 1864 goda," *Zhurnal MNP*, 125 (SPb, 1865). Prilozhenie, 1–116. Cited as Postel's. The description of *hadarim* is found on pp. 82–6.

25 84:17/VII/1875.

26 This initiative was considered significant enough to merit a report from the Governor-General, A. Annenkov, to the Ministry of Education. See *RGIA*, f. 821, op. 8, d. 232 (1864), ll. 1–2.

27 Nos. 6:14/VII/; 8:18/VII/; 20:15/VIII/1864.

28 For a short biography of Grinboim, and his motives for converting to Christianity, see Stanislawski, *Tsar Nicholas I*, 144, 146; see also *EE*, XVI, 423–5.

29 Erich Haberer argues that the rise of student radicalism was a major factor in the decision to close the rabbinical seminaries. The expressions of official concern which he cites date to 1850 and 1861 and were not part of a sustained campaign. Erich E. Haberer, "The Role of Jews in Russian Revolutionary Populism, 1868–1887" (Doctoral Dissertation, University of Toronto, 1986), 155–6. Tsarist officials were not reticent in explaining their policies and there was no reason for Tolstoi to dissemble if radical politics in the seminaries were indeed his true motive. In 1888, when the government was debating educational norms for Jews in schools, Tolstoi presented the Tsar with a long memorandum on the subject. While fully in accord with limitations, nowhere did he attribute their need to Jewish revolutionary activity, then a very popular theme in the government. *RGIA*, f. 821, op. 8, ed. khr. 246 (16 November 1888), ll. 117–29.

30 *Ibid.*, l. 122o; M. I. Mysh, *Rukovodstvo k russkim zakonam o evreiakh*, 433.

31 See the favorable report on their activities in Postel's, 10–16.

32 *EE*, XIII, 259.

33 *Rassvet*, 6:1/VII/1860.

34 Patterson, *The Hebrew Novel in Czarist Russia* (Edinburgh, 1964), 180.

11   Partisans of enlightenment: the OPE

1 In Russian, Obshchestvo dlia rasprostraneniia prosveshcheniia mezhdu evreiami v Rossii.

2 Cherikover, *Istoriia*, 30–1.

3 *Ibid.*, 40–4, for preliminary drafts of the Society's charter, and for problems with the government. The Society had to lobby until 1867 to secure minor changes in the original charter, 49.

4 *Ibid.*, 47–8. Disappointed with the paucity of its annual income, the Society instituted a new category of members in 1866, with a membership fee of 10 rubles.

5 Postel's would author the Ministry's report on the Jewish school system; Georgievskii was the editor of *Odesskii vestnik* under Pirogov. Georgievskii,

an important contributor to *Rassvet*, rose to become Deputy Minister of Education.

6 Cherikover, *Istoriia*, 41.

7 Lederhendler, *Road*, 112.

8 *Ibid.*, 55–8. For the discussion of these, and other questions confronting the OPE, see the protocols of meetings, published as L. M. Rozental, ed., *Toledot hevrat marbei be-yisrael be-eretz Rusia*, 2 vols. (SPb, 1885–90). Cited as *Toledot*.

9 Cherikover, *Istoriia*, 253; Kornilov, *Russkoe delo*, 230–3; *Toledot*, I, 38.

10 Cherikover, *Istoriia*, 223.

11 John D. Klier, "1855–1894 Censorship of the Press in Russian and the Jewish Question," *Jewish Social Studies*, 48, 3–4 (1986), 260. This work was finally published as *Sbornik statei po evreiskoi istorii i literature* (SPb, 1866).

12 *Mirovozzrenie Talmudistov*, 3 vols. (SPb, 1874–6). Cherikover, *Istoriia*, 91–3. For the politics of the preparation of these volumes, and their ultimate objectives, see Moshe Perlmann, ed., "L. O. Levanda and J. L. Gordon: Levanda's Letters to Gordon, 1873–5," *Proceedings of the American Academy for Jewish Research*, 35 (1967), 139–85.

13 See P. Marek, "Iz istorii evreiskoi intelligentsii," *Evreiskii vestnik* (Leningrad, 1928):124–42.

14 See Yosef Salmon, "The Emergence of a Jewish Nationalist Consciousness in Eastern Europe during the 1860s and 1870s," *AJS Review*, 16, 1–2 (1991): 107–32, for a characterization of the succeeding generations of maskilim, whom Salmon terms "observant maskilim" and "secular maskilim," 109.

15 Cherikover, *Istoriia*, 64.

16 See Ellen S. Cannon, "The Political Culture of Russian Jewry During the Second Half of the Nineteenth Century," unpublished doctoral dissertation, University of Massachusetts, 1974. For the strong current of ambivalence, see Dan Miron, *A Traveler Disguised* (New York, 1973), 1–33.

17 Orbach, *New Voices*, 116.

18 Cherikover, *Istoriia*, 95–8.

19 *Ibid.*, 99.

20 *Ibid.*, 225–6.

21 *Ibid.*, 226–7.

22 Orbach, *New Voices*, 100–1.

23 Cherikover, *Istoriia*, 121.

24 *Ibid.*, 91.

25 *Ibid.*, 87.

26 *Ibid.*, 243–6.

27 *Ibid.*, 90.

28 *Ibid.*, 216.

29 The protocols of this meeting were widely reprinted, including *Rassvet*, 36–37:4–11/IX/1880.

30 *Nedel'naia khronika Voskhoda* (52:30/XII/1882).

31 For this episode see Michael Stanislawski, *For Whom Do I Toil?* (New York and Oxford, 1988), 118–19.

12 "A state within a state"

1 Kornilov, *Russkoe delo*, 249. A biographical sketch appearing in *Russkii biograficheskii slovar'*, XII (SPb, 1908), 334–5, based on material provided by Brafman's son Alexander, claimed that Brafman was proficient in Hebrew, Chaldean, Arabic, German, Polish and French. This claim is more a tribute to filial devotion than to the real state of Brafman's skills. Nonetheless, Brafman was a crafty intriguer, and contemporaries warned against underestimating him. See M. L. Knorozovskii, "Eshche o vilenskoi evreiskoi komissii 1869g.," *Perezhitoe*, 3 (SPb, 1911), 389–90. Ginsburg reprints the famous story that Brafman once asked the Imperial Public Library for help in locating the much-cited compendium *"Ibidem,"* in Ginsburg, *Meshumodim*. N. N. Golitsyn, the Judeophobe journalist and historian, declared in a session of the Palen Commission that he had seen the reader's slip from Brafman requesting this item. M. G. Morgulis, "Iz moikh vospominanii," *Evreiskii mir*, 1, 6 (1909), 28.

2 Ginsburg, *Meshumodim*, 66. Ginsburg provides most of the accepted details of Brafman's life and career, unfortunately without citations. The pillow story comes from L. O. Gordon, "Otryvki vospominanii," *Evreiskii vestnik* (Leningrad, 1928), 46.

3 *RGIA*, f. 821, op. 8, ed. khr. 184 (1858), ll. 1–5.

4 These details are taken from the first edition of *Kniga kagala* (Vil'na, 1869), iii.

5 See the series by Brafman's erstwhile collaborator N. P. Gur'ev, condemning the Talmud as the underlying cause for the bad citizenship of Russian Jews, published as Solomon Pravdin, "Evreiskii vopros v ego deistvitel'nom vide," in numbers 164:3/VIII, 166:5/VIII, 171:12/VIII, 174:17/VIII, 192:12/IX/1866. The removal of A. Zabelin as editor after number 230 of the newspaper put a temporary halt to such articles.

6 Kornilov, *Russkoe delo*, 230.

7 *Ibid.*, 249–51; *EE*, IV, 918.

8 Isaac Levitats, *The Jewish Community in Russia, 1844–1917* (Jerusalem, 1981), 191; Zolotonosov, "U istokov."

9 Isaac Levitats, "Le-vikoret 'Sefer Ha-Kahal' shel Brafman," *Zion*, 3 (1938), 170–8. One of the protocols in Brafman's collection is found in another source which reliably quotes from the Minsk *pinkas*, 175.

10 Hereafter cited in the text as Brafman I (*Brotherhoods*) and Brafman II (*Book*). The 1882 edition, as combined and reprinted in 1888, will be cited as Brafman III. Part of Brafman's work was first published in *Vilenskii vestnik*, in numbers 62–5, 67–8, 70–1, 74–5 and 83, in 1868. A virtual precis of *Brotherhoods* was published in *Vilenskii vestnik*, 135:21/XI/1867 by "G. V." This was a pseudonym which Brafman never used elsewhere, so the author's identity must be considered unknown. M. Gurvich, having earlier broken with Brafman, attempted to steal some of his thunder with his own series on Jewish brotherhoods, published in *Vilenskii vestnik*, 56/57/58:21/23/25/V/1868.

11 L. O. Gordon, "Moi vstrechi s Konstantinom Petrovichem Kaufmanom," *EB*, 9 (1901), 130.

12 For Brafman's presentation to the Imperial Geographical Society, see "Sochinenie g. Brafmana," *Varshavskii dnevnik*, 133:23/VI/1870.

13 See the review to this effect in *Kievlianin*, 47:21/IV/1870.

14 For a few examples from many of official concern at the activities of the Alliance, see *RGIA*, f. 821, op. 9, ed. khr. 167 (1881–2) and f. 821, op. 9, ed. khr. 202 (20/I/84).

15 There are examples that Brafman was motivated by sentiments other than altruism. In his memoirs L. O. Gordon, himself a target of Brafman's attacks, reports that Brafman sought to solicit a huge bribe from Baron Gintsburg in return for a relaxation of his attacks on the Jews. "Otryvki vospominanii," 46–7.

16 Articles on Brafman appeared in numbers 35, 39, 47, 48, 54, 57, 65, 94, 104, 121 and 132 for 1970.

17 Cherikover, *Istoriia ORPME*, 225.

18 Reprinted in *Den'*, 31:1/VIII/1870.

19 See *Novoe vremia*, 246:8/IX/1870, 248:10/IX/1870, 266:28/IX/1870 and 267:29/IX/1870; *Den'*, 10:5/III/1871, 17:23/III/1871 and 18:29/IV/1871; and I. I. Shershevskii, *O knige kagala* (SPb, 1872).

20 Shershevskii's technical arguments are conveniently summarized in *O knige kagala*, 173–83. Levitats dismissed them all in his article cited above.

21 See *Den'*, numbers 4, 6, 11, 13, 14, 19 and 22.

22 See *Deiatel'nost'*, numbers 128, 133, 138, 167, 172, 174, 110 and 119 for 1870.

23 Gordon reports many stories in his memoirs of Brafman's activities as censor, which were characterized by mendacity and ineptitude. Gordon, "Otryvki vospominanii," 43–7. There are some suggestions in the literature that Brafman's service career was harmed by some egregious errors of judgment as a censor.

24 Gurvich, Bratin, Levin and Tiger were, in many respects, the "authors" of the first edition, and not even Brafman himself ever claimed to have translated the Minsk *pinkas*. While some new material written by Brafman was included in the 1882 edition, there are many entries that refer to events which took place after Brafman's death, such as the pogroms. The 1882 edition, in fact, is virtually a new book as distinct from the first edition, to say nothing of the improved and completed translation of the *pinkas* text, first published in 1875 and republished in 1888 with the explication of 1882.

25 See Norman Kohn, *Warrant for Genocide* (New York, 1969), 53–5.

26 For another example, see the eclectic Russo-French creation by K. Vol'skii, *Evrei v Rossii* (SPb, 1887). It is a pastiche of *The Book of the Kahal*, "The Rabbi's Speech," and Alphonse de Toussenel, *Les Juifs rois de l'époque*, with a hint of German racism added for good measure.

27 For Potapov, see chapter 7, pp. 172–80; *RGIA*, f. 821, op. 9, ed. khr. 95 (1872), ll. 3–5.

28 *Materialy KUBE*, I, 8.

Part 3   The era of social change and economic turmoil

1 For the lengthy debates surrounding Jewish participation in municipal self-government, see *EE*, VI, 711–16.

2 See *TsDIA*, f. 442, op. 45, d. 564 (1864–76), ll. 1–327; f. 442, op. 532, d. 304 (1879 et seq.), ll. 1–222.

3 *Issledovanie o torgovle na ukrainskikh iarmarkhakh* (SPb, 1858), 36.

4 *Ibid.*

5 P. Bobrovskii, *Grodnenskaia guberniia* (SPb, 1863), 764.

6 D. Afanas'ev, *Kovenskaia guberniia* (SPb, 1861), 475.

7 Rieber, *Merchants and Entrepreneurs*, 58–9.

8 In an editorial dated 21 June 1861, the Russian supplement of *Ha-Karmel* predicted dire consequences for the Jewish masses with the completion of the St. Petersburg–Warsaw railroad, as well as changes forthcoming in the alcohol tax-farming system, which supported many Jews.

9 "Temporarily obligated status" referred to the period during which arrangements were negotiated between landlords and peasants over the final division of the land. Peasants were supposed to continue payment of customary dues, either in money or labor, during this period.

10 These articles were published in a collection of Orshanskii's essays, *Evrei v Rossii* (SPB, 1877).

11 See *Vestnik russkikh evreev*, 36:16/IX/1871; *Russkii evrei*, 23:4/VI/1880; A. P. Subbotin, *Obshchaia zapiska po evreiskomu voprosu* (SPb, 1905), 131–2.

12 Anan'ich, *Bankirskie doma* (Leningrad, 1991), 37–110.

13 Leon Shapiro, *The History of ORT* (New York, 1980), 13–38. See also *RGIA*, f. 821, op. 9, ed. khr. 212 (1884–90), ll. 1–41.

14 *Novoe vremia* published a sensationalist exposé of Poliakov in 1879 (nos. 1340–1, –45, 1353, –59, –64, –69, –81). Judeophobe concern with Russian–Jewish entrepreneurs was anticipated by attacks upon foreign Jewish entrepreneurs, who helped to build the first Russian rail network. A group, identified by A. J. Rieber as "Slavophile entrepreneurs," protested as early as 1856 against the construction of Russian rail lines by "Yids and foreigners." In 1860, *Vestnik promyshlennosti* denounced the Jews of the French-based Grande Société des Chemins de Fer Russes as "those clever Jews – les rois de L'Europe," an obvious play on the title of A. Roussenel's notorious anti-Jewish tract of 1845, *Les Juifs les rois de l'époch.* Alfred J. Rieber, "The Formation of La Grande Société des Chemins de Fer russes," *JGO*, 21, 3 (1973), 387–8.

15 Gessen, *Zakon i zhizn'*, 151–2.

16 Heinz-Dietrich Löwe, *Antisemitismus und reaktionäre Utopie* (Hamburg, 1978), 11–12.

17 P. Bobrovskii, *Grodnenskaia guberniia* (SPb, 1863), 856.

18 V. Pavlovich, *Ekaterinoslavskii guberniia* (SPb, 1862), 263.

19 I. Zelenskii, *Minskaia guberniia* (SPb, 1864), II, 276–7. Zelenskii further noted that almost 50 percent of the Jews classified as "settled meshchane" were also engaged in crafts.

20 Chubinskii, *Trudy*, VII, *Evrei*, 210.

21 The available statistics confirm this general impression. At the inception of the law, the Governor-General of the Southwest required his subordinate governors to submit annual reports on the number of resettling Jewish artisans. Records exist for a total of thirteen years covering the three

provinces of Kiev, Volynia and Podolia. No more than five resettlers were recorded. *TsDIA*, f. 442, op. 44, d. 436 (1865–76), ll. 1–22. Out-migration did increase in later years, as indicated by the large number of Jews expelled from Moscow in 1892 for not conforming to all the provisions of the law. Nor did the Kiev statistics record those Jews who had not completed reregistration.

22 Dubnow, *History*, 2, 171.

23 *Materialy kommisii po ustroistvu byta Evreev (po Imperii)*, I, 2–9. Separate pagination throughout.

24 *Ibid.*, 1–12.

25 Doklad V. V. Grigov'eva, *ibid.*, 12.

26 *Ibid.*, 12.

27 Session of 4 December 1872, *ibid.*, 1–9.

28 *VPSZ*, XVIII, 16,767 (20/IV/1843). This law dated to regulations in the reign of Alexander I, in 1812.

29 *Odesskii vestnik*, 270:29/XI/1880; *Russkii evrei*, 45:5/XI/1880; *Rassvet*, 3–4–5:15–22–29/I/1881.

30 *PPSZ*, XL:30,436 (29/VII/1825).

31 Dubnow, *History*, II, 202.

13   The theme of "Jewish exploitation"

1 Restrictions appeared in two places in the enabling legislation. The statute governing redemption of land by peasants provided that peasants who fell seriously in arrears with their redemption payments could have their land confiscated and sold at public auction. Jews were singled out as ineligible to bid for such properties. Jews, as non-nobles, had always been barred from acquiring "settled" properties (i.e., properties with serfs living on them). A new regulation extended this prohibition to estate lands without peasants living on them. *VPSZ*, XXXVI, 36,659 (19/II/1861), st. 135, no. 4; st. 136, no. 4; st. 137, no. 3; Gl. I, st. 3, 4.

2 *Ibid.*, chapter 2, st. 1. This regulation stated that land could be leased to "people of every *soslovie*."

3 *VPSZ*, XXXVII, 38,214 (26/IV/1862).

4 *VPSZ*, XXXIX, 40,656 (5/III/1864).

5 *VPSZ*, XL, 42,328 (23/VII/1865). See the comments to this effect in reports of the governors of Kiev, Podolia and Volynia in *TsDIA*, f. 442, op. 815, d. 440 (1865), ll. 5–15, even while they conceded that less than a handful of Jews had actually purchased property in any one province.

6 Zaionchkovskii, *Otmena*, 183–231.

7 *Materialy KUBE*, I, 82–3.

8 *Ibid.*

9 *VPSZ*, XXXIX, 41,039 (10/VII/1864).

10 *Materialy dlia geografii i statistiki Rossii sobrannye ofitserami general'nogo shtaba*. D. Afanas'ev, *Kovenskaia guberniia* (SPb, 1861). A. Korev, *Vilenskaia guberniia* (SPb, 1861). A. Zashchuk, *Bessarabskaia oblast'* (SPb, 1862). V. Pavlovich, *Ekaterinoslavskaia guberniia* (SPb, 1862). P. Bobrovskii, *Grodnenskaia guberniia*,

3 vols. (SPb, 1863). A. Shmidt, *Khersonskaia guberniia*, 2 vols. (SPb, 1863). I. Zelenskii, *Minskaia guberniia*, 2 vols. (SPb, 1864). M. Domontovich, *Chernigovskaia guberniia* (SPb, 1865). As appropriate, volume and page numbers are cited in the text.

11 P. P. Chubinskii, *Materialy i issledovaniia*, VII (SPb, 1872), 6.

12 *Ibid.*, 182–4.

13 *Ibid.*, 184.

14 *Ibid.*, 185.

15 *Ibid.*, 185–6. Chubinskii identified eleven estates illegally owned by Jews in the Ukraine, totalling 17,903 desiatins, a negligible total.

16 "Vypiska," *Materialy KUBE*, I, 4. As Rogger observes, this memorandum was rather a novelty for its negative view of Jewish industrialists and manufacturers, "Government," 127.

17 *Ibid.*, 2.

18 *Ibid.*

19 "Zhurnal zasedaniia 4 dekabria 1872," *ibid.*, I, 1–9.

20 George Yaney, *The Urge to Mobilize: Agrarian Reform in Russia, 1861–1930* (Urbana, 1982), 42.

21 N. M. Druzhinin, "Pomeshchich'e khoziaistvo posle reformy 1861 g.," *Istoricheskie zapiski*, 89 (Moscow, 1972), 187–230.

22 See *Odesskii vestnik*, 123:6/VI/1964; *Kievskii vestnik*, 18:11/II/1866; *Podolskie eparkhal'nye vedomosti*, 2:15/I/1967; *Golos*, 281:11/X/1968.

23 See chapter 9, 191–2.

24 "Vypiska," *Materialy KUBE*, 2.

25 This was an introduction to a lengthy series, "Evrei v iuzhnoi Rossii," in part based upon statistics from the office of the Governor-General as published in *Kievlianin*.

26 See *Kievlianin*, nos. 69:13/VI, 87:25/VII, 144:3/XII for 1878, no. 68:9/VI/1879 and 52:4/III/1880.

27 *Kievlianin*, 51:29/IV/1876.

28 Quoted in *Kievlianin*, 51:29/IV/1876.

29 Journalists displayed a tendency to adopt an impressionistic approach to statistics. See the claim in *Vilenskii vestnik* in 1879 that three-quarters of the land in Grodno was being leased by Jews. Since the quality of land in the Northwest was poor, renting was not popular, and Jewish leaseholding was not commonly perceived as a problem.

30 Reprints in *Kievlianin*, 143:1878; *Russkaia pravda*, 34:1878; *Svet*, 1:1878; *Nedelia*, 44 (1878); *Syn otechestva*, 254, 256 (1878); *NT*, 1134: 1878.

31 David Christian, *Living Water: Vodka and Russian Society on the Eve of Emancipation* (Oxford, 1990), 117–54.

32 *Ibid.*, 276.

33 See Magdalena Opalski, *The Jewish Tavern-Keeper and His Tavern in Nineteenth-Century Polish Literature* (Jerusalem, 1986).

34 Klier, *Russia Gathers*, 81–115, 116–43.

35 Mysh, *Rukovodstvo*, 389, and "Bor'ba pravitel'stva s piteinym promyslom Evreev v selakh i derevniakh," *Voskhod*, I, 8, 9 (1881):14–47; 1–21.

36 *VPSZ*, XL, 42,264 (28/VI/1865).

37 *VPSZ*, XL, 42,328 (23/VII/1865).
38 "Otnoshenie," *Materialy KUBE*, 5.
39 *VPSZ*, XXXVI, 37,197 (4/VII/1861).
40 *VPSZ*, XXXVIII, 39,386 (18/III/1863).
41 *VPSZ*, XLIX, 53,524 (14/V/1874).
42 Mysh, *Rukovodstvo*, 390–5.
43 No. 239, reconstructed from the *Sovremennoe slovo* article.
44 See nos. 102, 104 and 105: 6, 9 and 10/V/1867, and 236–237: 11–12/X/1867. The
    latter series complained that the "neat and friendly" Cossack-run taverns
    in Poltava had passed into Jewish hands.
45 In an editorial dispute with *Kievlianin* in 1872, *Kievskii telegraf* repeated
    almost verbatim Orshanskii's claim that it was not the Jews who were the
    cause of drunkenness, but the intellectual level of the masses, and the
    organization of the spirit trade (63:2/VI/1872).
46 *Gradus* or degree; a measure of alcoholic strength or proportion of pure
    alcohol. Christian, *Living Water*, 421.
47 "Vypiska," *Materialy KUBE*, 4.
48 In theory these regulations, which revised the 1861 excise law, were
    designed to control the abuse of the spirit trade among all social classes.
    Greater leeway was given to peasant communities to shut down unwanted
    taverns.
49 Reprinted in *Vilenskii vestnik*, 96:6/V/1875.
50 In the first sketch in his collection, "Khor and Kalinych," written in 1847,
    Turgenev described the trade in scythes, marketed in the village by
    "knavish townsmen," charging almost three times more for a few weeks'
    credit before the harvest, and the "eagles" who buy up rags and cloth from
    peasant women. *Polnoe sobranie sochinenii*, IV (M–SPb, 1903), 15–16.
51 "Grigor'ev," *Materialy KUBE*, 12.
52 See the analysis of Bervi-Flerovskii's work in Franco Venturi, *Roots of
    Revolution* (London, 1952), 487–94; and D. Offord, "The Contribution of
    V. V. Bervi-Flerovsky to Russian Populism," *SEER*, 66 (1988):236–51.
53 V. V. Bervi-Flerovskii, *Polozhenie rabochego klassa v Rossii* in *Izbrannye ekono-
    micheskie proizvedeniia v dvukh tomakh* (M, 1958), I, 326. This is a reprint of the
    second edition, published in 1872.
54 *Ibid.*, 328.
55 A. N. Engel'gardt, *Iz derevni* (M, 1960), 34–59.
56 *Ibid.*, 415.
57 *Ibid.*
58 "The Razumaevs and Kolupaevs" figure frequently in the work of
    V. I. Lenin. M. E. Saltykov-Shchedrin, *Sobranie sochinenii* (M, 1972), XIII, 706.
59 M. E. Saltykov-Shchedrin, "Ubezhishche Monrepo" in *Sobranie sochinenii*,
    XIII, 296.
60 M. S. Ol'minskii, *Shchedrinskii slovar'* (M, 1937), 389, 702. See also Nikander
    Strelsky, *Saltykov and the Russian Squire* (New York, 1940, reprinted AMS
    Press, 1966), 14, 55.
61 "Ubezhishche Monrepo," 349.
62 R. Grozdev, *Kulachestvo-Rostovshchichestvo* (SPb, 1899), 1.

63 "Ubezhishche Monrepo," 270. Saltykov-Shchedrin was not considered a Judeophobe by contemporaries. See the critical analysis of his work from a Judeophobe perspective in P. Pokov [P. K. Liubimov], *Po povodu vzgliada M. E. Saltykova na evreiskii vopros* (Kiev, 1883).

64 Varzer, "Evrei-arendatory," 200–5.

65 *Kievlianin*, 37:29/III/1869; *Kievskii telegraf*, 17:9/II/1866; *NT*, 1065:14/IX/1878.

66 *Bereg*, 100:3/VII/1880; *Kievlianin*, 64:30/V/1874.

67 *Golos*, 81:2/III/1876; *Kievlianin*, 1:1/I/1876.

68 *Kievlianin*, 140:23/XI/1867; 145:9/XII/1869; 64:30/V/1874; *Volynskie gubernskie vedomosti*, 34:21/III/1867; *Vseobshchaia gazeta*, 6:9/II/1881.

69 V. D. Alenitsin, *Evreiskoe naselenie i zemlevladenie v iugo-zapadnykh guberniiakh evropeiskoi Rossii* (SPb, 1884). See pages ix-xvi for the alarmist conclusions. S. Becker's evidence on land transfers emphasizes the mythological aspects of this alarm by indicating that Jews were concentrated precisely where gentry landholding was *most* stable. See *Nobility and Privilege in Later Imperial Russia* (DeKalb, 1985), 40–3.

70 For recent views on the "decline of the nobility," see G. M. Hamburg, *Politics of the Russian Nobility, 1881–1905* (New Brunswick, 1984) and Becker, *Nobility*. The reference to complaints against "Yid banks" is found in the latter, page 80, dating to 1896. The works of Saltykov-Shchedrin are permeated by the crisis motif.

71 A. Korev, *Vilenskaia Guberniia* (SPb, 1861), 422.

72 See chapter 8, pp. 216–17.

14 Dead souls: Jews and the military reform of 1874

1 Sliozberg, *Dela*, I, 93.

2 When *Sion* failed, subscribers were urged to contribute the cost of their unfilled subscriptions to the construction of the Sevastopol monument. See *SPb vedomosti*, 14:14/I/1863.

3 P. A. Zaionchkovskii, *Voennye reformy 1860–1870 godov v Rossii* (Moscow, 1952), 82.

4 Zaionchkovskii, *Voennye reformy*, 307. Iosif Zeiberling was a long-serving censor of Jewish books for the Ministry of Education. Ironically, he was the author of a book attacking Brafman's *The Book of the Kahal*. In 1872 *Vestnik russkikh evreev* reprinted a memorandum, said to have been submitted to the drafting commission, addressing the problem of Jewish draft evasion. It gives every indication, by style and content, of having been written by Brafman, 4:26/VII/1872.

5 Zaionchkovskii, *Voennye reformy*, 312–13.

6 *Ibid.*, 313–14.

7 *Evreiskaia entsiklopediia*, III, 164.

8 Zaionchkovskii, *Voennye reformy*, 309.

9 *Ibid.*

10 Forrestt A. Miller, *Dmitrii Miliutin and the Reform Era in Russia* (Nashville, 1968), 218–25.

11 Zaionchkovskii, *Voennye reformy*, 323–4.

12 Miller, *Dmitrii Miliutin*, 200–6.
13 Reported in *Kievlianin*, 147:11/XII/1871.
14 *SPb vedomosti*, 314:14/XI/1874; the Gintsburg letter appeared in *Ha-Magid*, 44 for 1874, and specifically tied military service to increased civil rights; *Kievskii telegraf*, 93:16/VIII/1874.
15 Mysh, *Rukovodstvo*, 505–6.
16 For an overview of this legislation, see Mysh, *Rukovodstvo*, 491–513.
17 *Kievlianin*, 40:19/I/1881; *Novorossiiskii telegraf*, 1991:11/IX/1881; *Varshavskii dnevnik*, 19:26/I/1881; *Kievskii listok*, 97:8/XII/1879.
18 See *Odesskii listok*, 199:25/XI/1881 for the initial, erroneous report and 208:5/XII/1881 and 211:9/XII/1881 for a corrected account of the episode.
19 *Kievlianin*, 280:28/XII/1883; *Novoe vremia*, 2669:4/VIII/1883; *Novorossiiskii telegraf*, 2778:23/V/1884.
20 These arguments, if not convincing, would certainly have been understandable to the Russian authorities. The drafting commission had seriously considered placing all recruits with an education in special units based in large towns, so that they would not suffer overly much from mixing with the rude peasant masses, nor suffer the proverbial boredom of life in a garrison town, Zaionchkovskii, *Voennye reformy*, 323. The problem of early marriage among Jews is one which exercised the Russian government as early as the eighteenth century.
21 See 46:19/XI/1882; 6:11/II/1883; 7:18/II/1883; 9:4/III/1883; 11:16/III/1884; 12:23/III/1884.

15   The dilemma of the Russian Jewish intelligentsia

1 Technically *Vestnik russkikh evreev* appeared from 1873 to 1879, but only in the form of an annual issue which Tsederbaum published in order to retain his publishing franchise. The early years of this publication were bedeviled by unsatisfactory collaborators and the irregular appearance of the paper. It was reconstituted on a more stable basis after 1879, and renamed *Rassvet*.
2 Sosis, "Obshchestvennyia nastroeniia," 136. This concept was particularly associated with the publicist I. Orshanskii.
3 See *Den'*, 16:29/VIII/1869; 8:4/VII/1869; and 18:12/IX/1869. Only the last article is signed by Soloveichik, but I would attribute the other two to him on the basis of their style and content.
4 See chapter 7.
5 For recantations, 31:1/VIII/1870; Morgulis appeared in nos. 4:22/I, 5:30/I, 11:12/III, 13:26/III, 14:6/IV and 22:29/V/1871; Shershevskii appeared in nos. 10:5/III and 18: 29/IV/1871; for Brafman's motives, nos. 29:29/XI/1869, 29:17/VII/1870 and 32:8/VIII/1870.
6 See, for example, the *Den'* editorial in 17:7/IX/1869.
7 Klier and Lambroza, *Pogroms*, 13–38.
8 The number of fatalities (six of whom drank themselves to death on plundered alcohol), injuries and arrests comes from the tally of the Odessa police chief, M. Stenbok, carried in *Odesskii vestnik*, 68:2/IV/1871. The Odessa Chief of Gendarmes, K. G. Knop, received a reprimand because the capital

press carried pogrom accounts before his official reports reached St. Petersburg. *TsDIA*, f. 385, op. 1, d. 53 (1871), ll. 64–65o.

9 *Moskovskie vedomosti*, nos. 70:4/IV/1871, 71:6/IV/ and 73:8/IV/1871, faulted the
conduct of the authorities and the explanations of *Odesskii vestnik*, the
organ of the higher administration. *Birzhevye vedomosti* criticized the
authorities' conduct, nos. 96:10/IV/ and 97:11/IV/1871. The paper also condemned collective punishments (99:13/IV/1871), and was joined in this
criticism by *Golos* (98:10/IV/1871) and *Vestnik Evropy* (5:1871).

10 Reprinted in *Sanktpeterburgskie vedomosti*, 90:3/IV/1871. The report was in
the form of a telegram to the Ministry of Internal Affairs, dated 30 March
1871.

11 Quoted in *Kievskii telegraf*, 58:21/V/1871.

12 Quoted in V. A. Ia., "Demonstratsii protiv evreev v g. Odesse", *Iug*,
1:I,1881:218.

13 *Kievlianin* offered editorial support for the thesis in 47:22/IV/1871. *Golos*
reporting of the pogrom was weak and derivative. Clearly the paper was
uncomfortable in dealing with the attendant issues of popular unrest, and
the excesses employed by the authorities to quash the pogrom.

14 By the vagaries of the censorship, materials banned in the periodical press
occasionally appeared in books. Orshanskii's banned article, "K kharakter-
istike odesskogo pogroma" was published in his *Evrei v Rossii* (SPb, 1877),
157–74.

15 For example, in editorials exploring religious antagonisms between gentiles and Jews (18:2/V/1871), with the alleged alienation of Jews from
Christian society (19:9/V/1871), or with the problem of merging (20:16/V/
1871). Only the first of these editorials even mentioned the pogrom. Likewise, an editorial in response to the charges raised by *Sanktpeterburgskie
vedomosti*, discussed below, omitted any reference to the pogrom (21:23/V/
1871).

16 See the Jewish editorialist in *Kievskii telegraf* who justified the Jews' refusal
to polemicize with *Kievlianin*'s Shul'gin because "if his pen does not fear
Sanktpeterburgskie vedomosti, he won't be deterred by some Jewish *Den'''*
(52:5/V/1871).

17 In fact, the tone of these editorials did vanish completely from the columns
of *Sanktpeterburgskie vedomosti*, and the ideas of Brafman did not gain
general acceptance there.

18 See Zipperstein, *Jews of Odessa*, 114–28.

19 Orshanskii, *Evrei v Rossii*, 157–9.

20 A. Dumashevskii was editor of *Sudebnyi vestnik*, and the convert O. K.
Notovich edited both *Novoe vremia* and *Novosti*. Lev Binshtok was associate
editor of *Volynskie gubernskie vedomosti* and L. O. Levanda was de facto
editor of *Vilenskie gubernskie vedomosti* as well as an associate editor of
Vilenskii vestnik.

21 For a cross-section of appeals to the Russian Jewish intelligentsia, see
Kievskii telegraf (1:1/VII/1859), which spoke of the "sacred obligation" of
educated Jews to raise the cultural level of their coreligionists; *Moskovskie
vedomosti*'s favorable comments on the commitment of Jewish youth to the

process of merger (32:12/II/1866); *Narodnaia gazeta*'s invitation to Jews to come forward and reform the local Talmud-Tora (41:19/X/1866); *Vilenskii vestnik*'s exhortation to educated Jews to fight fanaticism; *Varshavskii dnevnik*'s applause for the willingness of Jews to merge (135:24/VI/1869), and so on.

22 Mikhailo Serebriakov, "Dobryi sovet evreiam", *Vitebskie gubernskie vedomosti*, 14:4/IV/1859.

23 See chapter 6, pp. 142–3.

24 See chapter 5, pp. 110–11.

25 See chapter 8, pp. 191–2.

26 *Syn otechestva*, 295/6:21/XII/1867.

27 Of the thousands of articles which appeared in the Russian language press, I have not found a single one that could be attributed to a Jewish traditionalist, mitnagdim or hasidim. State rabbis appear in force, but spiritual rabbis or *tzaddikim*, never. The Judeophobe *Novoe vremia*, in fact, created a sensation when a correspondent fabricated an "interview" with a prominent *tzaddik* in the 1880s.

28 Russian journalists were well aware that the Jewish Question was more complex than the Russian Jewish intelligentsia tended to present it. A common theme in press reports was that of a conflict between "fathers and sons" in the Jewish community. See *Russkii invalid*, 251:12/XI/1861; *Sanktpeterburgskie vedomosti*, 160:1869; *Glasnyi sud*, 1867; *Peterburgskaia gazeta*, 108:1874.

29 *Kievlianin*, 94:8/VIII/1870 and 121:10/X/1870.

30 *Vilenskii vestnik*, 129:7/XI/1867.

31 Gessen, *Gallereia*, 145.

16   The riddle of liberal Judeophobia

1 Peter G. J. Pulzer, *The Rise of Political Anti-Semitism in Germany and Austria* (New York, 1964), 29–32.

2 Arthur Herzberg, *The French Enlightenment and the Jews* (New York, 1970), 268–313.

3 Katz, *From Prejudice* 129–38.

4 V. N. Rozental', "Pervoe otkrytoe vystuplenie russkikh liberalov v 1855–1856 gg.," *Istoriia SSSR*, 2 (1958), 115–118. Rozental' attributes the "Contemporary Objectives" article to Chicherin, 120.

5 "Sovremennye zadachi russkoi zhizni," *Golosa iz Rossii*, IV (London, 1857), 112.

6 *Ibid.*, 114.

7 Michael F. Hamm, "Liberalism and the Jewish Question: The Progressive Bloc," *The Russian Review*, 31, 2 (1972):163–72.

8 *YIVO Institute for Jewish Research* (New York), Elias Tcherikower Archives, File 757, p. 63,557.

9 See chapter 15, pp. 362–3.

10 V. V. Leontovich, *Istoriia liberalizma v Rossii, 1762–1914* (Paris, 1980), 3.

11 *Ibid.*, 1.
12 "Sovremennye zadachi," *Golosa iz Rossii*, IV, 112–25.
13 Rozental', "Pervoe," 121. See this page for other examples of liberal disdain for the peasantry.
14 Charles E. Timberlake, "Ivan Il'ich Petrunkevich: Russian Liberalism in Microcosm," in Charles E. Timberlake, ed., *Essays on Russian Liberalism* (Columbia, MO, 1972), 21.
15 This analogy was made overtly on a number of occasions in *Kievskii telegraf*, 117:16/X/1864 and 105:10/IX/1871.
16 *Kievskii telegraf*, 15:19/VIII/1859; *SPb vedomosti*, 169:23/VI/1868.
17 *Kievskii telegraf*, 6:20/I/1860; *SPb vedomosti*, 16:16/I/1869; *SPb vedomosti*, 68:10/III/1873; 93:4/IV/1873; *Birzhevye vedomosti*, 226:25/X/1862; *Vestnik Evropy*, 5 (1869):370–92 and 3 (1878):353–81.
18 See *Kievskii telegraf*, 2:2/VII/1859; *SPb vedomosti*, 174:28/VI/1872; *Birzhevye vedomosti*, 211:29/VI/1863.
19 In the case of *Novosti*, this reluctance was accentuated by the fact that the editor, O. K. Notovich, was a converted Jew. He was quite sensitive about his origins, and asked not to be mentioned in the obituary of his father, a celebrated talmudic scholar. *Novosti* did become a principal defender of the Jews after 1878.
20 This quotation, and the discussion of *sliianie* in *Golos* in general, is taken from Paul Anthony Russo, "*Golos*, 1878–1883: Profile of a Russian News-paper" (unpublished doctoral dissertation, Columbia University, 1974), 354–60.
21 This process of accepting and legitimizing Brafman's theories occurred in a series of articles published throughout 1870: 120:2/V; 126:3/V; 145:27/V; 185:7/VII.
22 Gordon's words, quoted accurately from the Hebrew-language *Ha-Shahar* were: "Let the son of David (the Messiah) appear, and then our reformist brothers in one minute will turn to him saying, we sinned, but now we are your slaves. And he will take them and make useful and helpful people of them, for all his aims. But what can he say to you and how can you offer help? ... Can he take ministers of finance, war, educated state bureaucrats, capable of being representatives to foreign governments, engineers, farmers and people necessary for his kingdom?" Gordon wrote *Golos* to protest that his words had been taken out of their context, a debate with traditionalist conservatives over the need to reform the *heder* (156:7/VI/1876). This merely provided Brafman with the pretext for a much longer attack on the OPE as the Russian section of the Alliance (216: 6 August 1876). It must have become apparent to Jewish publicists that it was self-defeating to engage in polemics with Brafman while he enjoyed the support of the editorial board of *Golos*. For this episode, see Stanislawski, *For Whom*, 118–22.
23 *EE*, III, 699.
24 John D. Klier, "*The Times* of London, the Russian Press and the Pogroms of 1881–1882," *The Carl Beck Papers*, 308:1–26.

17 The crystallization of conservative Judeophobia

1 Hans Rogger, "Reflections on Russian Conservatism, 1861–1905," *JGO*, 14 (1966), 196. Rogger identifies three major forms of Russian conservatism in this period: gentry conservatism, bureaucratic conservatism and Pan-Slavist conservatism.

2 Richard Pipes, "Russian Conservatism in the Second Half of the Nineteenth Century," *Slavic Review*, 30, 1 (1971), 120. Pipes sees Russian conservatism evolving through four main forms in Russian history, each identified with a specific social group: the clergy, the gentry, the intelligentsia and the bureaucracy.

3 *Ibid.*, 123–4.

4 *Ibid.*

5 Pipes identifies the principal theorists of anti-nihilist conservatism as Aksakov, Dostoevskii, K. Pobedonostsev, N. Danilevskii, Apollon Grigor'ev, M. Katkov, K. Leont'ev and Iu. Samarin, 124. Only the first three of these made Judeophobia an important part of their *Weltanschauung*.

6 Judged by their origins, forms and objectives, Slavophilism and Pan-Slavism were two separate and distinct ideologies. In particular, it is not helpful to consider Pan-Slavism as a later, "degenerate" form of Slavophilism, as it is sometimes described. The two ideologies have certain affinities which cannot be ignored, however. See Andrzej Walicki, *The Slavophile Controversy* (Oxford, 1975), especially chapters 12 and 13. To give one example, Walicki notes the complete absence of messianism in Slavophilism, while it became an essential aspect of Pan-Slavism, 149–50.

7 Nicholas Riasanovsky, *Russia and the West in the Teaching of the Slavophiles* (Cambridge, MA, 1952), 197. Quoted from "Slavianofil'stvo i ego vyrozhdenie," *Sobranie sochinenii*, V (SPb, nd), 228.

8 Quoted from *Christianity and Anti-Semitism* (New York, 1954), 5.

9 Lukashevich, *Ivan Aksakov*, 167–8.

10 In his *Notes on Universal History*, Khomiakov identified two antagonistic principles in history, the positive principle of freedom (which he termed Iranian) and the negative principle of necessity (which he called Kushite).

11 Riasanovsky, *Russia and the West*, 115.

12 Walicki, *The Slavophile Controversy*, 212, 502, n. 2.

13 Shmuel Ettinger, "Ha-reka ha-idiologi le-hofa'ata shel ha-sifrut ha-antishemit he-hadashah be-Rusia," *Zion*, 35, 1–4 (1970), 194.

14 *Ibid.*

15 *Ibid.*, 195.

16 A. S. Khomiakov, *Polnoe sobranie sochinenii* (M 1878–90), I, 88–90.

17 S. Ettinger, "The Modern Period," in H. H. Ben-Sasson, ed., *A History of the Jewish People* (London, 1977), 821. Compare the comments of the prominent conservative thinker N. Strakhov, written in the 1890s: "Every Slavophile is accused of sympathizing with despotism and hating foreigners ... I myself, whatever my sins, am free from these ... I have never written an anti-liberal page, and I have no hatred for Jews and Catholics," quoted in Linda

Gerstein, *Nikolai Strakhov* (Cambridge, MA, 1971), 136. See the discussion of Strakhov below.

18 See Walicki, *Slavophile Controversy*, 514–17; N. Ia. Danilevskii, *Rossiia i Evropa* (SPb, 1871), 236, and Robert E. MacMaster, *Danilevsky: A Russian Totalitarian Philosopher* (Cambridge, MA, 1967).
19 Danilevskii, *Rossiia i Evropa*, 511.
20 Heinz-Dietrich Löwe, *Antisemitismus und reaktionäre Utopie* (Hamburg, 1978), 11, 23, 29.
21 The definitive study of these events is B. H. Sumner, *Russia and the Balkans* (Oxford, 1937).
22 Lukashevich, *Ivan Aksakov*, 141.
23 Effie Ambler, *Russian Journalism and Politics: The Career of Aleksei S. Suvorin, 1861–1881* (Detroit, 1972), 141–63.
24 A. Kaufman, "Evrei v russko-turetskoi voine 1877 g.," *ES*, 8 (1915), 58–60.
25 A. G. Kaufman, *K vostochnomu voprosu* (Odessa, 1876).
26 Kaufman, "Russko-turetsoi voine," 61.
27 Kritikus [S. M. Dubnov], "Literaturnaia letopis,'" *Voskhod*, 9, I (January 1891), 39.
28 Kaufman, "Russko-turetskoi voine," 63.
29 Sumner, *Russia*, 324.
30 See *Pis'ma Pobedonostseva k Aleksandru III* (Moscow, 1925–6), I, 45 et seq.
31 Kaufman, "Russko-turetskoi voine," 64–5. A. N. Kuropatkin, the Chief-of-Staff of the commanding general, M. D. Skobelev, offered a special defense of the Tatars and Jews in refutation of these rumors in his memoirs of the Plevna battle published in *Voennyi sbornik* (July 1883).
32 Kritikus, "Literaturnaia letopis'," 39.
33 Jonathan I. Israel, *European Jewry in the Age of Mercantilism, 1550–1750* (Oxford, 1985), 132–3.
34 Sumner, *Russia*, 335. As part of his reward, Poliakov received Russian diplomatic assistance in his bid to build a Bulgarian railroad from Rustchuk to Sofia to Kustendil, 568.
35 K. F., "Tovarishchestvo Gregera, Gorvitsa i Kogana," *Rossiia*, 71:25/XI/1880. For a description of the chaos and irregularities that accompanied the company's operations, from the perspective of a participant, see N. N., "Iz vpechatlenii minuvshogo veka," *ES*, 8 (1915):185–200.
36 N. N., "Iz vpechatlenii," 187.
37 *Novoe vremia*, 2680:15/VIII/1883. The first attack on Jewish profiteers appeared in the paper on 4 July 1878.
38 Kaufman "Russko-turetskoi voine," 65.
39 I. S. Aksakov, *Slavianskii vopros, 1860–1886* (M, 1886), 275. The bashi-bazouks were the savage irregular troops who accompanied the Ottoman forces.
40 A. L., "Zametki: Berlinskii kongres," *EB*, 6 (1878):139–52. *EE*, 4, 246. This was the first public airing of what was to become the official line of the Russian Foreign Office when encountering foreign criticism of the legal condition of Russian Jews.
41 For representative articles, see *Novoe vremia*, 1226:29/VII/1879 and 1255:27/

VIII/1879: *Vostok*, 11:8/VII; 15:5/VIII and 19:3/X/1879; *Vecherniaia gazeta*, 210:2/ VIII/1879; *Novosti*, 23:5/VIII/1879.

42 Among the members of the first "Zemlia i Volia" group was Nikolai Utin, a baptized Jew. Mark Natanson, the first important Jewish revolutionary, was a member of the Chaikovskii group at the end of the 1860s.

43 See the most recent study of this problem in Erich E. Haberer, "The Role of Jews." Haberer assigns a greater role to Jews in the Populist movement than is generally admitted in the secondary literature, especially in Chaikovskii Circles of 1870–74 and in the politicization of the apolitical Populist movement between 1875 and 1879.

44 Lev Deich, *Rol' evreev v russkom revoliutsionnom dvizhenii* (Berlin, 1923), 37–8, 40, 50–7.

45 David I. Goldstein, *Dostoyevsky and the Jews* (Austin and London, 1981), 151–2.

46 Summarized in *Novorossiiskii telegraf*, 1386:28/X/1879.

47 Summarized in *Russkii evrei*, 14:5/XII/1879.

48 Summarized in *Russkii evrei*, 17:26/XII/1879.

49 Summarized in *Russkii evrei*, 12:19/III/1880.

50 Ironically, Bogrov's grandson, Dmitrii Bogrov, was the assassin of P. A. Stolypin in 1911.

51 The central government was aware of the increase of Jewish students, and in 1874 queried the overseers of the Vilna, Kiev, Odessa and Derpt educational districts about ending the special stipends which had been created to attract Jewish students. There is no evidence to suggest that the central government was alarmed at the increase of Jews in schools. See A. I. Georgievskii, *Po voprosu o merakh otnositel'no obrazovaniia evreev* (SPb, 1886), 191–205.

52 Aksakov, *Pis'makh*, II, 36.

53 *Ibid.*, 92–3.

54 D. Samarin, ed., *Correspondance de G. Samarine avec La Baronne de Rahden, 1861–1876* (M, 1894), 241–3.

55 The series appeared in the seven issues of *Grazhdanin* published between 10 November 1878 and 6 February 1879.

56 See John D. Klier, "Russian Judeophobes and German Antisemites: Strangers and Brothers," *Jahrbucher für Geschichte Osteuropas*, 37, 4 (1989):524–40.

57 *Rus'*, 44:12/IX/1881.

58 Goldstein, *Dostoyevsky and the Jews*, 162.

59 "Evreiskii vopros," in *Dnevnik pisatelia*, March, 1877. Reprinted in *Polnoe sobranie sochinenii*, 12, 82–97.

60 Byrnes, *Pobedonostsev*, 203.

61 *Pis'ma Pobedonostseva k Aleksandru III*, I (M, 1925), 44.

62 The evolution of Pobedonostsev's Judeophobe obsessions is easily traced in his personal correspondence. See R. M. Kantor, ed., "Pis'ma K. P. Pobedonostseva k grafu N. P. Ignat'evu," *Byloe*, 27–8 (1924), 71; *Pis'ma Pobedonostseva k Aleksandru III*, II (Moscow, 1926), 191, 320; B. Gorev, I. Aizenshtok, eds., "Pis'ma K. P. Pobedonostseva k E. M. Feoktistovu," *Literaturnoe nasledstvo*, 22–24 (1935), 539, 543, 544.

63 N. F. Bel'chikov, ed., "Dostoevskii i Pobedonostsev," *Krasnyi arkhiv*, 2 (1922), 244–5.

64 Leonid Grossman, "Dostoevskii i pravitel'stvennye krugi 70–kh godov," *Literaturnoe nasledstvo*, 15 (Moscow, 1934), 142.

65 Nikolai Strakhov, *Iz istorii literaturnogo nigilizma, 1861–1865* (SPb, 1890), 561.

18   The occult element in Russian Judeophobia

1 Compare Gavin Langmuir's characterization of Antisemitism as *chimerical*, in that it ascribes to the Jews attributes which have never been empirically observed. *Toward a Definition of Antisemitism* (Berkeley, 1990), 336.

2 See Klier, *Russia Gathers*, 98; and "The Origins of the 'Blood Libel' in Russia," *Newsletter of the Study Group on Eighteenth Century Russia*, 14 (1986):12–22.

3 Dubnow, *History*, 2, 74.

4 *Ibid.*, 75–82.

5 *Ibid.*, 83.

6 The three prime candidates for authorship are Dal', I. V. Kamenskii, an official in the ministry, and Skripitsyn, the director of the Department of Religious Affairs for Foreign Confessions. Iulii Gessen concedes that Dal' may have edited the work, but offers a strong argument that he was not the author. See Iu. Gessen, M. Vishnitser, A. Karlin, "*Zapiska o ritual'nykh ubiistvakh*" *(pripisyvaemaia V. I. Daliu) i eia istochniki* (SPb, 1914). A number of other bibliographers argued with equal intensity for the Dal' attribution. I.O. Kuz'min, *Materialy k voprosu ob obvineniiakh evreev v ritual'nykh prestupleniiakh* (SPb, 1913), 271–6. When the newspaper *Grazhdanin* reprinted the work in 1878, it was attributed to Skripitsyn. When the Judeophobe printing house of A. Suvorin reissued the book in 1914, in the aftermath of the Beilis Affair, as *Zapiska o ritual'nykh ubiistvakh*, 2nd ed. (SPb, 1914), it employed the more prestigious Dal' attribution.

7 These included such Polish works as J. Szarafinowicz, *Wyjawienie przd Bogiem i Swiatem obrzedow Żydowskich*, G. Pikulski, *Złość Żydowska* and *Błędy talmudowe*. For precise bibliographical citations of these often obscure works, see Kuz'min, *Materialy*, 264–71; for a characterization of their contents, see Gessen, "Zapiska," 31 et seq.

8 There was also a ritual murder accusation made by Poles living in the village of Suram in the Caucasus in 1847. Although it provoked an intervention from Sir Moses Montefiore, it was unpublicized in Russia itself, and specific details are hard to come by.

9 Dubnow, *History*, II, 150–3.

10 Kostomarov, *Literaturnoe nasledie*, 74. In 1883, in the aftermath of the pogroms in the Ukraine, Kostomarov published a fictionalized account of a pogrom in the eighteenth century, which arose from a ritual murder. See "Zhidotrepenie v nachale XVIII v.," *Kievskaia starina*, I, 3 (1883).

11 D. A. Khvol'son, "O nekotorykh srednevekovykh obvineniiakh protiv Evreev," *Biblioteka dlia chteniia*, nos. 164 and 165. The work was also issued in book form in 1861, and a second edition was produced in 1880, in the

aftermath of the Kutais Affair. A shorter version appeared in 1879 as a pamphlet, *Upotrebliaiut li Evreev khristiianskuiu krov'?* (SPb, 1879).

12 This was certainly the case with L. O. Gordon, who sent an early report of the Shavli Affair to *Rassvet*, and L. O. Levanda, who helped the authorities to investigate the Affair. See Gordon, "Otryvki vospominanii," 39–40; Stanislawski, *For Whom*, 42–4.

13 The erroneous material was sent to Tsederbaum by a personal enemy, the assistant rabbi of Odessa, S. Mandel'kern. See "Sudebnaia khronika," *Russkii evrei*, 2:9/I/1880.

14 To give two random examples: During his governor-generalship in Lithuania, M. N. Murav'ev reportedly attempted to include the cult of Gavrill Zabludovskii, a ritual murder victim venerated in the Uniate Church, into the calendar of saints of the Russian Orthodox Church. *Moskovskie tserkovnie vedomosti*, 16 for 1881. The Nizhny-Novgorod pogrom of 1884, deep in the Russian interior, was triggered by rumor of a ritual murder.

15 Brafman never conceded the possibility of ritual murder, even while condemning the Jewish community for other criminal practices, such as the murder of informers. Another convert, A. Alekseev, whose numerous books on Jews and Judaism received wide publicity, also publicly rejected the Blood Libel.

16 Kuz'min, *Materialy*, 275–6. Kuz'min claims that the report was published in *Russkii arkhiv* in 1870 and quotes from the introduction. I have been unable to locate this material in *Russkii arkhiv*.

17 Judging from his public comments, Giliarov-Platonov's fascination with ritual murder grew out of his interest in the *Skoptsy* ("Castrators"), a Christian sect in Russia. This group had long been targeted by the government as a "pernicious sect" which practiced self-mutilation and ritual murder. In 1869 Giliarov-Platonov noted that he had "read a manuscript about this fanatical cannibalism, but decided not to believe it." He noted that similar charges had been made against the Jews, and offered a compromise: "Why does [the Blood Libel] appear in all ages and in countries with no connection with one another? And you reach this conclusion: there is something. Certainly, there is no dogma of the Jewish religion, but rather a beastly superstition of the masses, a mark of blind hatred. We recognize fanaticism among those who persecute people for their religious beliefs – why can't it appear, with all its bestiality, among those who are persecuted for their faith?" *Sovremennye izvestiia*, 141:25/V/1869.

18 *RBS*, V, 208–16.

19 K. Kozlovskii, "Temnyi vopros v istorii Evreev," *Kievlianin*, nos. 96 and 97 for 1873. A reviewer of the pamphlet for *Sanktpeterburgskie vedomosti* argued that, whatever the reality of the charge itself, no credence could be given to judicial investigations which employed torture (269:30/IX/1873). In this same year *Golos* carried a letter from Voronezh which, in reference to the construction of a local railroad by Poliakov's company, reported that Jews were "drinking Christian blood in the literal as well as the figurative sense." The writer claimed to have spoken to a peasant who had sold his blood to Jews for a ruble a drop (114:26/IV/1873).

20 Fil. Borisov, *Ippolit Liutostanskii. Ego zhizn' i deiatel'nost'* (Kiev, 1912), 9–11.
21 *Rech'*, 185:9/VI/1911.
22 See the court record in *Peterburgskaia gazeta*, 34:10/II; 36:12/II; 38:14/II and 39:15/II/1881.
23 For this see *Novoe vremia*, 1619:31/VIII; 1629:10/IX/1880; *Russkii evrei*, nos. 39, 47, 48, 50 and 52: 1880 and *Rassvet*, nos. 40, 41, 47–51: 1880.
24 YIVO Institute for Jewish Research (New York), Elias Tcherikower Archives, File 757, p. 63,595 (10 May 1882).
25 The two editions of the work bore slightly different titles. They were *Vopros ob upotreblenii evreiami-sektatorami khristianskoi krovi dlia religioznykh tselei, v sviazi s voprosami ob otnosheniiakh evreistva k kristianstvu voobshche* (M, 1876); and *Ob upotreblenii evreiami (talmudistskimi sektatorami) khristianskoi krovi dlia religioznykh tselei v sviazi s voprosom ob otnosheniiakh evreistva k khristianstvu voobshche*, 2 vols. (SPb, 1880). Typical of Liutostanskii's inconsistency was his attack upon Khvol'son and N. N. Golitsyn. He pilloried Golitsyn for his ignorance of Hebrew or the Talmud and mocked him for "presuming to teach Khvol'son." In turn, he questioned Khvol'son's qualifications as a teacher of Hebrew. *Ob upotreblenii*, viii–xv.
26 For further examples, see Khvol'son, *O nekotorykh*, 2nd ed., 118–20; Z. Minor, *Rabbi Ippolit Liutostanskii* (M, 1879), 9–10.
27 See Liutostanskii, *Vopros*, 105–6.
28 *Ibid.*, vi.
29 Liutostanskii, *Ob upotreblenii*, x–xvii.
30 *Grazhdanin*, 23–25:10/X; 26:26/X; 27–28:10/XI; 38–40:31/XII/1878.
31 The book was published as a pamphlet in 1877. Liutostanskii accused Fr. Protopopov of being a "renegade, a wolf in sheep's clothing" who had published his work with a title identical to Liutostanskii's (published three years *later*!) in order to confuse the public. *Ob upotreblenii*, xii–xvi. The priest's articles were also republished with approval by *Vilenskii vestnik*, nos. 202, 207, 216 and 226 for 1878.
32 *Ob upotreblenii Evreiami khristianskoi krovi i neskol'ko slov o nashikh otnosheniiakh k Evreiam voobshche* (SPb, 1877) and *Poslednie vyvody iz skazannogo ob upotreblenii Evreiami v Rossii khristiianskoi krovi* (SPb, 1880). In the latter work Shigarin offered his services to the Jews as a literary agent to refute the Blood Libel, 227–8.
33 *Upotrebliaiut li Evrei khristianskuiu krov'? Po povodu sovremennogo spora* (Warsaw, 1879).
34 For the role of A. Tsederbaum, who recognized the importance of full publicity, see Orbach, *New Voices*, 68.
35 See chapter 9, p. 208.
36 *Pravda*, an Odessa newspaper, noted in its discussion of the Kutais trial that even "highly intelligent people, like N. I. Kostomarov," were convinced that the Jews used Christian blood (53:10/III/1879). A converted Jew, A. A. Alekseev, who also served on the Saratov Commission, noted in a later memoir that Kostomarov was convinced of the Blood Libel from the very first meeting of the commission. *Upotrebliaiut-li evrei khristianskuiu krov' sreligioznoi tseliu?* (Nizhnii Novgorod, 1887), 12.

37 *Russkii evrei*, 6:10/X/1879. *Novoe vremia* attempted to exonerate itself by claiming that the charge against a doctor was the result of a misprint (*miedic* for *medik*).

38 *Novoe vremia*, 1841:15/IV/1881.

39 *Zemstvo*, 24:13/V/1881.

40 Reported in *Russkii evrei*, 28:22/VII/1883. As *Russkii evrei* observed, Gattsuk, apparently from a Jewish family, had once been a contributor to *Sion* of Odessa. Another Russian paper, *Ekho*, noted in passing that the Alliance Israélite Universelle had "covered up" the events at Tisza-Eszlar.

41 S. M. Dubnov, "Tserkovnye legendy ob otroke Gavriile Zabludovskom," *ES*, 8, 4–8 (1916), 309–16.

42 So deeply rooted did this prejudice become, that it appeared unexpectedly on the streets of Moscow in Soviet Russia in 1921. A crowd attacked a Jewish hospital orderly who was escorting a corpse to the cemetery. The crowd suspected a ritual murder, and the Moscow police actually conducted an investigation. An article in *Pravda* (85:5/V/1993) accused Hasidim in Russia of the ritual murder of Christian clergymen.

43 *Den'* encountered many difficulties with the censor in its attempt to comment negatively on these refuges because of the court connection. See 42:16/X/1870.

44 *Kievlianin*, 58:16/V/1874; *Golos*, 68:8/III/1876; *Odesskii vestnik*, 90 and 91:25–26/IV/1881).

45 For example in *Elizavetgradskii vestnik*, *Novoe vremia*, *Odesskii vestnik*, *Sankt-peterburgskie vedomosti*, *Volyn*, and *Golos Moskvy*. In 1885 *Kievlianin* printed an entire catalogue of recent cases involving the murder of converts or Christian proselytizers (256:23/XI/1885).

46 *Zaria*, 14:17/I/1885; *Pravoslavnoe obozrenie*, 1: 1887.

47 Death of Brafman, see p. 281.

48 Cherikover, *Istoriia*, 93.

49 See, for example, the anonymous author in *Kievskii telegraf*, 58:21/V/1871, or the articles (and subsequent pamphlet) of M. P. Shafir in *Vestnik russkikh evreev*, nos. 6–13: 1871.

50 Cherikover, *Istoriia*, 92–3; for the preparation of the volume, see Perlmann, "Levanda's Letters to Gordon," 142–85.

51 This was Brafman's characterization of the Talmud on the eve of the publication of *World-View*: "The Talmud is ... the historical consciousness of the resentful mind and restless fantasy, cultivated on Jewish soil after the fall of the kingdom ... There is to be found a multitude of the most diverse statements, views, opinions and conceptions about God, man, nature, religion, government, society, etc. In this chaotic mess it is not difficult to find confirmation of any opinion. More: the Talmud is entirely set forth in the ancient Jewish–Chaldean tongue, long forgotten by the Jews and now quite dead, written without vowels, without punctuation marks, thus presenting the very widest field for diverse commentaries and interpretations. As a result of this purely external circumstance, two diametrically opposed opinions regarding one and the same object can always be

defended by the same place in the Talmud, which each person, it is understood, interprets and explains as it suits him." *Golos*, 94:4/IV/1875.

52 In the expanded version of his 1879 work, *Talmud i evrei*, Liutostanskii explained that the original work was inspired by the publication of *The World-View*. See p. ix.

53 Liutostanskii, *Ob upotreblenii*, I, 11–12.

54 George L. Mosse, *The Crisis of German Ideology* (London, 1964), 129–30; Katz, *From Prejudice*, 285–6.

55 See "Moral i pravo s tochki zreniia Talmuda po Rolingu," *Varshavskie gubernskie vedomosti*, 33, 36, 38, 39 (1878).

56 *Rus'*, 20:15/X/1883; *Varshavskii dnevnik*, 115:4/VII/1884.

57 K. Wzdulski, ed., *Żydzi i kahaly* (Lwow, 1874), 8–14. The author was identified as Sir John Readclef.

58 I. Liutostanskii, *Talmud i evrei*, 1st ed. 3 vols. (M., 1879), I, 183–8.

59 Vol'skii, *Evrei v Rossii*. The book is a crude pastiche of Brafman, "The Rabbi's Speech" and Alphonse Toussenel's *Les Juifs rois de l'époque* (Paris, 1845).

60 See *SPb vedomosti*, 113:26/IV/1887; *Vera i Razum* (1888) reprints *Novoe vremia*.

61 *Pokorenie mira Evreiami* (Odessa, 1874). The works of this author are usually ascribed to an apostate Romanian Jew named F. Millingen or Milliner.

62 *Ibid.*, 8.

63 *Ibid.*, 30–1, 47–8. In 1886, Osman Bei published *Révélations sur l'assassinat d'Alexandre II* (Geneva [Bern], 1886), which Walter Laqueur has called "one of the most remarkable books ever written outside a lunatic asylum," *Russia and Germany: A Century of Conflict* (London, 1965), 96. There was never any question of this book being published in Russia, for it maligned almost every contemporary Russian statesman (with the exception of Osman Bei's alleged employer, V. Pleve). The activities of the Alliance had grown exotically by the time this book was published: Adolphe Crémieux, through the Alliance, was credited with the assassination of Alexander II. *Revelations*, 103.

64 This quotation was cited from the Hebrew language *Ha-Magid*, thus demonstrating that the editor or a collaborator read the language. On *Golos* at the time, this could only be Brafman. See chapter 16, p. 380.

65 *Kniga kagala*, II, 331.

66 Liutostanskii, in his encyclopedic way, had included the concept of Masons and Jews in his work. Despite the important role that this motif played in twentieth-century Russian Judeophobia, it was not at first a popular concept in Russia. For the equation of Jews and Masons, see Jacob Katz, *Jews and Freemasons in Europe, 1723–1939* (Cambridge, MA, 1970).

67 Aksakov also had a special talent for differentiating between elements which were plausible and "respectable," and those which were not. He rejected the ritual murder charge in 1878, preferring to concentrate on the harmfulness of the Talmud. In 1880 he asked his Berlin correspondent to report in his dispatches on "the socialist and Jewish movement, only not scandals about Yids and without abuse, which always casts doubt on the

truth under discussion." See S. O. Iakobson, ed., "Pis'ma Iv. Aksakova k Putsykovichu," *Na chuzhoi storone*, V (1924), 154.

68 Among the other newspapers which reprinted the Manifesto were *Rizhskii vestnik*, *Varshavskii dnevnik* and *Ekho*.

Bibliography

I Archives

Kiev
Tsentral'nyi Gosudarstvennyi Istoricheskii Arkhiv Ukrainy (Cited as *TsDIA*)
Fund 293 Kiev Censorship Committee
Fund 294 Chancellery of the Kiev Censorship
Fund 274 Kiev Provincial Gendarme Administration, Secret Section
Fund 385 Odessa Municipal Gendarme Administration
Fund 442 Chancellery of the Kiev, Podolia and Volynia General-Governor
Fund 533 Kiev Military Governor
Fund 707 Office of the Overseer of the Kiev Educational District
Fund 1164 Kiev Rabbinate
Fund 1423 Archives of the Jewish Historical-Ethnographical Commission

Leningrad/St. Petersburg
Rossiiskaia Natsional'naia Biblioteka
(Formerly *Gosudarstvennaia Publichnaia Biblioteka imeni M. E. Saltykova-Shchedrina*) Manuscript Division (Cited as *GPB*)
Fund 183 D. G. Gintsburg
Fund 833 V. A. Tsee
Rossiiskii Gosudarstvennyi Istoricheskii Arkhiv
(Formerly *Tsentral'nyi Gosudarstvennyi Istoricheskii Arkhiv SSR v Leningrade*) (Cited as *RGIA*)
Fund 776 Chief Department of Press Affairs
Fund 796 Holy Synod
Fund 821 Department of Spiritual Affairs for Foreign Confessions
Fund 970 I. P. Kornilov
Fund 1149 The State Council
Fund 1263 Committee of Ministers
Fund 1269 Jewish Committees, 1840–65
Fund 1282 Chancellery of the Ministry of Internal Affairs
Fund 1405 Chancellery of the Ministry of Justice. Legislative Division

Moscow
Gosudarstvennyi Arkhiv Rossiiskoi Federatsii (GARF) (Formerly Tsentral'nyi
    Gosudarstvennyi Arkhiv Oktiabr'skoi Revoliutsii (Cited as TsGAOR)
Fund 102 Department of Police
Fund 586 V. K. Pleve
Fund 677 Aleksandr Aleksandrovich (Emperor Alexander III)
Fund 730 N. P. Ignat'ev

New York
YIVO Institute for Jewish Research
Elias Tcherikower Archive
File 755–57: Gintsburg Collection

II   Newspapers, periodicals and annuals

Atenei (M) 1858–9
Azovskii vestnik (Taganrog) 1871–8
Bereg (SPb) 1880
Beseda (SPb) 1871–2
Bessarabskie gubernskie vedomosti (Kishinev) 1854–1917
    (*Bessarabskie oblastnye vedomosti*)
Biblioteka dlia chteniia (SPb) 1834–65
Biblioteka zapadnoi polosy Rossii (Kiev) 1879–80
Birzha (SPb) 1872–7
    (*Nash vek*)
Birzhevye vedomosti (SPb) 1861–1879
    (*Molva*)
Birzhevye vedomosti (SPb) 1880–1917
    (*Birzheveye vestnik* and *Russkii mir*)
Chernigovskie gubernskie vedomosti (Chernigov) 1838–1917
Chernigovskii listok (Chernigov) 1861–3
Chteniia v obshchestve istorii i drevnostei rossiiskikh pri imperatorskom moskovskom
    universitete (M) 1858–1918
Deiatel'nost' (SPb) 1868–72
Delo (SPb) 1866–88
Den' (M) 1861–5
Den,' organ russkikh evreev (Odessa) 1869–71
Dnevnik pisatelia F. M. Dostoevskogo (SPb) 1876–7, 1880–1
Domashnaia beseda dlia narodnogo chteniia (SPb) 1858–77
Donskaia gazeta (Novocherkassk) 1873–79
Dukhovnaia beseda (SPb) 1858–76
Ekho (SPb) 1882–5
Ekho gazet (SPb) 1881
Ekonomicheskii ukazatel' (SPb) 1857–58
Ekonomicheskii zhurnal (SPb) 1885–93
Ekonomist (SPb) 1858–65
Golos Moskvy (M) 1885–6

Gusli (Tiflis) 1881–2
Elizavetgradskii vestnik (Elizavetgrad) 1876–94
Evreiskaia biblioteka (SPb) 1871–80
Evreiskie zapiski (Riga) 1881
Gazeta A. Gattsuka (M) 1875–90
Glasnost' (SPb) 1881–82
Glasnyi sud (SPb) 1866–7
Golos (SPb) 1863–84
Grazhdanin (SPb) 1872–77; 1882–1914
Ha-Karmel [Prilozhenie k Gakarmeliu] (Vil'na) 1860–9
Hromada (Geneva) 1878–82
Illiustratsiia (SPb) 1858–63
Istoricheskii vestnik (SPb) 1880–1917
Iug (Odessa) 1882
Iuzhnyi krai (Khar'kov) 1880–1919
Kavkaz (Tiflis) 1846–1918
Kievlianin (K) 1864–1918
Kievskaia starina (K) 1882–1906
Kievskie eparkhial'nye vedomosti (K) 1861–1917
Kievskie gubernskie vedomosti (K) 1838–1917
Kievskii kur'er (K) 1862
Kievskii listok (K) 1878–81
Kievskii listok ob"iavlenii (K) 1872–7
Kievskii telegraf (K) 1859–76
Kievskoe slovo (K) 1887–1905
Kolokol (London, Geneva) 1857–67
Kovenskie gubernskie vedomosti (Kovno) 1843–1915
Listok "Narodnoi voli" (1880, 1881, 1883, 1886)
Minskie gubernskie vedomosti (Minsk) 1838–1917
Minskii listok (Minsk) 1886–1902
Mogilevskie gubernskie vedomosti (Mogilev) 1838–1917
Molva (SPb) 1876
Moskva (M) 1867–8
Moskovskaia nedelia (M) 1881–4
Moskovskie tserkovnie vedomosti (M) 1880–1918
(*Moskovskie eparkhial'nye vedomosti*)
Moskovskie vedomosti (M) 1756–1917
Moskovskii telegraf (M) 1881–3
Moskovskii vestnik (M) 1859–61
Moskvich (M) 1867–8
Mysl' (SPb) 1880–2
Nabliudatel' (SPb) 1882–1904
Narodnaia gazeta (SPb, M) 1863–9
Narodnoe bogatstvo (SPb) 1862–5
Narodnyi golos (SPb) 1867
Narodnaia volia (SPb) 1879–85
Nash vek (SPb) 1877

Nashe vremia (M) 1860–3
Nedelia (SPb) 1866–1901
Nedel'naia khronika Voskhod (SPb) 1882–1906
Nov' (SPb) 1884–98
Novoe obozrenie (Tiflis) 1884–1906
Novoe vremia (SPb) 1868–1917
Novgorodskie gubernskie vedomosti (Novgorod) 1838–1917
Novorossiiskii telegraf (Odessa) 1869–1903
Novorossiiskie vedomosti (Odessa) 1869–72
Novosti (SPb) 1871–1906
(*Novosti i birzhevaia gazeta*)
Odesskie novosti (Odessa) 1884–1917
Odesskii listok ob"iavlenii (Odessa) 1872–1917
(*Odesskii listok*)
Odesskii vestnik (Odessa) 1828–93
Orlovskii vestnik (Orel') 1876–1918
Osnova (SPb) 1861–2
Otechestvennye zapiski (SPb) 1839–84
Peterburgskaia gazeta (SPb) 1867–1917
Peterburgskii listok (SPb) 1864–1917
Podol'skie eparkhial'nye vedomosti (Kamenets-Podolsk) 1862–1905
Podol'skie gubernskie vedomosti (Kamenets-Podolsk) 1838–1917
Pravda (Odessa) 1877–80
Pravoslavnoe obozrenie (M) 1860–91
Pskovskii gorodsoi listok (Pskov) 1881–1906
Podol'skie gubernskie vedomosti (Podol'sk) 1838–1917
Poltavskie gubernskie vedomosti (Poltava) 1838–1917
Poriadok (SPb) 1881–2
Pravitel'stvennyi vestnik (SPb) 1869–1917
Rassvet (Odessa) 1860–1
Rassvet (SPb) 1879–84
Rizhskii vestnik (Riga) 1869–1914
Rossiia (SPb) 1880
Rukhovodstvo dlia sel'skikh pastyrei (K) 1860–1917
Rus' (M) 1880–86
Russkaia mysl' (M) 1880–1918
Russkaia pravda (SPb) 1878–80
Russkaia rech' (M) 1861–62
Russkaia starina (SPb) 1870–1918
Russkie vedomosti (M) 1863–1918
Russkii arkhiv (M) 1863–1917
Russkii evrei (SPb) 1879–84
Russkii invalid (SPb) 1813–1917
Russkii kur'er (M) 1879–89, 1891
Russkii mir (SPb) 1859–63
Russkii pedagogicheskii vestnik (SPb) 1857–61
Russkii vestnik (M) 1856–1906

Russkoe bogatstvo (SPb) 1859–66
Russkoe delo (M) 1886–1910
Russkoe slovo (SPb) 1859–66
Sanktpeterburgskie vedomosti (SPb) 1728–1917
Sel'skii vestnik (SPb) 1881–1916
Severnaia pchela (SPb) 1825–64
Severnaia pochta (SPb) 1862–8
Severnyi vestnik (SPb) 1877–8
Sibir' (Irkutsk) 1873–77
Shkol'noe obozrenie (Odessa) 1889–92
Sion (Odessa) 1861–62
Slovo (SPb) 1878–81
Smolenskii vestnik (Smolensk) 1878–1917
Sovremennoe slovo (SPb) 1862–3
Sovremennost' (SPb) 1871–81
Sovremennye izvestiia (M) 1868–87
Sovremennyi listok (SPb) 1863–71
Strana (SPb) 1880–3
Strannik (SPb) 1860–1917
Sudebnaia gazeta (SPb) 1882–1905
Svetoch (SPb) 1882–5
Syn otechestva (SPb) 1856–61
Syn otechestva (SPb) 1862–1901
Tavricheskie gubernskie vedomosti (Simferopol') 1838–1917
Tiflisskii vestnik (Tiflis) 1873–82
Trudy kievskoi dukhovnoi akademii (K) 1860–1917
Tserkovno-Obshchestvennyi vestnik (SPb) 1874–86
Tserkovnyi vestnik (SPb) 1875–1916
Turkestanskie vedomosti (Tashkent) 1870–1917
Tverskie gubernskie vedomosti (Tver) 1839–1917
Uchitel' (SPb) 1861–70
Ukazatel' po delam pechati (SPb) 1872–8
Varshavskii dnevnik (Warsaw) 1864–1915
Vechernaia gazeta (SPb) 1865–81
Vek (SPb) 1882–4
Vera i Razum (Khar'kov) 1884–1917
Vremia (SPb) 1861–3
Vseobshchaia gazeta (SPb) 1880–6
Vest' (SPb) 1863–70
Vestnik Evropy (SPb) 1866–1918
Vestnik iugo-zapadnoi i zapadnoi Rossii (Kiev–Vil'na) 1862–8
Vestnik zapadnoi Rossii
Vestnik russkikh evreev (SPb) 1871–3
Vilenskii vestnik (Vil'na) 1841–1915
Vitebskie gubernskie vedomosti (Vitebsk) 1838–1917
Vol'noe slovo (Geneva) 1881–3
Volyn' (Zhitomir) 1882–1917

Volynskie gubernskie vedomosti (Zhitomir) 1838–1917
Voskhod (SPb) 1881–1906
Vostok (M) 1879–86
Zapadnorusets (K) 1881
Zaria (K) 1880–6
Zemstvo (M) 1880–2
Zhivopisnoe obozrenie (SPb) 1868
Zhurnal grazhdanskogo i ugolovnogo prava (SPb) 1871–1906
Zhurnal ministerstva iustitsii (SPb) 1859–68
Zhurnal ministerstva narodnogo prosveshcheniia (SPb) 1834–1917
Zhurnal ministerstva vnutrennikh del (SPb) 1829–61
Zhurnal obshchepoleznykh svedenii (SPb) 1847–59

Variant titles are listed in parentheses.

III   Pre-revolutionary published sources

Aksakov, I. S. *Issledovanie o torgovle na ukrainskikh iarmarkhakh.* SPb, 1858.
   Ivan Sergeevich Aksakov v ego pis'makh, 3 vols. Moscow, 1888–92.
   "Pis'ma Iv. Aksakova k Putsykovichu," S. O. Iakobson, ed., *Na chuzhoi
      storone*, 5 (1924): 129–58.
   Polnoe sobranie sochinenii, 3 vols. M–SPb, 1886–7.
Aksel'rod, P. B. *Perezhitoe i peredumannoe.* Berlin, 1923.
Alekseev, A. A. *Obshchestvennaia zhizn' evreev, ikh nravy, obychai i predrazsudki.*
   Novgorod, 1868.
   *Ocherki domashnoi i obshchestvennoi zhizni evreev, ikh verovaniia, prazdniki,
      obriady, talmud i kagal.* Novgorod, 1882.
   Upotrebliaiut-li evrei kristianskuiu krov' s religioznoi tseliu? Novgorod, 1886.
Alenitsin, V. D. *Evreiskoe naselenie i zemlevladenie v iugo-zapadnykh guberniiakh
   evropeiskoi Rossii.* SPb, 1884.
Amvrosi. *Istoriia rossiiskoi ierarkhii*, VI. Moscow, 1815.
An-skii, S. (Rapoport, S. Z.) "Evreiskaia delegatsiia v vilenskoi komissii 1869
   goda," *ES*, 4, 2 (1912): 187–201.
Antonovich [Antonovych], V., Dragomanov [Drahomanov], M. *Istoricheskie
   pesni malorusskogo naroda.* Kiev, 1875.
Babst, I. *Ot Moskvy do Leiptsiga.* Moscow, 1859.
Batiushkov, P. N. *Pamiatniki russkoi stariny v zapadnykh guberniiakh.* Part VII.
   (*Kholmskaia Rus'*). SPb, 1885.
   Belorussia i Litva: Istoricheskie sud'by severo-zapadnogo kraia. SPb, 1890.
Beletskii, A. *Vopros ob obrazovanii russkikh evreev v tsarstvovanii Imperatora Niko-
   laia I.* SPb, 1894.
Beliaev, A. D. *Sovremennoe sostoianie voprosa o znachenii rasovykh osobennostei
   semitov, khamitov i iafetitov dlia religioznogo razvitiia etikh grupp narodov.*
   Moscow, 1881.
Ben-Ami [M. Rabinovich], "Moi snosheniia s M. Dragomanovym i rabota v
   'Vol'nom slove,'" *ES*, 7, 3–4 (1915): 346–66; 8, 1 (1916): 75–101.

Berlin, I. *Istoricheskie sud'ba evreiskogo naroda na territorii russkogo gosudarstva.* Petrograd, 1919.

Bershadskii, S. A. *Litovskii evrei.* SPb, 1883.

Bervi-Flerovskii, V. V. *Polozhenie rabochego klassa v Rossii.* Moscow, 1958. (Reprint of 1872 2nd ed.)

Bikkerman, I. *Cherta evreiskoi osedlosti.* SPb, 1911.

Bogucharskii, V. Ia. *Iz istorii politicheskoi bor'by v 70–kh i 80–kh gg. XIX veka.* Moscow, 1912.

Borisov, F. *Ippolit Liutostanskii. Ego zhizn' i deiatel'nost'.* Kiev, 1912.

Brafman, Iakov. *Evreiskie bratstva, mestnye i vsemirnye.* Vil'na, 1868.
Kniga kagala, 1st ed. Vil'na, 1869.
Kniga kagala, 2nd ed. SPb, 1875.
Kniga kagala. (Vsemirnyi evreiskii vopros), 3rd ed., 2 parts. SPb, 1882–8.
Żydzi i kahaly. K. Wzdulski, ed. Lwow, 1874.

Brutskus, B. D. *Professional'nyi sostav evreiskogo naseleniia Rossii.* SPb, 1908.

Bulgarin, F. *Ivan Vyzhigin.* SPb, 1829.

Chem spasti korennoi russkii pravoslavnyi narod zapadnogo kraia Rossii ot nravstvennoi i material'noi zavisimosti ot evreev. Moscow, 1873.

Cherikover, I. M. *Istoriia obshchestva dlia rasprostraneniia prosveshcheniia mezhdu evreiami v Rossii, 1863–1913 gg.* SPb, 1913.

Chiarini, L. A. Abbé. *Théorie du Judaïsme appliquée a la réforme des Israélites,* 2 vols. Paris, 1830.

Chubinskii, P. P. *Trudy etnografichesko-statisticheskoi ekspeditsii v zapadno-russkii krai sniriazhennoi imperatorskim russkim geograficheskim obshchestvom. Iugo-zapadnyi otdel. Materialy i issledovaniia.* VII. *O evreiskom voprose.* SPb, 1872.

Dal', V. I. *Rozyskanie o ubienii evreiami khristianskikh mladentsev i upotreblenii krovi ikh.* SPb, 1844. (Reprinted as *Zapiska o ritual'nykh ubiistvakh.* SPb, 1914.)
Tolkovyi slovar' zhivogo velikorusskogo iazyka, 4th ed., 4 vols. SPb–M, 1912.

Danilevskii, N. Ia. *Rossiia i Evropa.* SPb, 1871.

Demidov San-Donato, P. *Evreiskii vopros v Rossii.* SPb, 1883.

Dostoevskii, F. M. *Polnoe sobranie F. M. Dostoevskogo.* Vol. XII. *Dnevnik pisatelia.* SPb, 1883.

Dragomanov [Drahomanov], M. P. *Rozvidki Mykhaila Drahomanova pro ukrains'ku narodniu slovesnist' i pys'menstvo,* 4 vols. Lwow/Lvov, 1899–1906.
Sobranie politicheskikh sochinenii, 2 vols. Paris, 1905–6.

Dubnov [Dubnov], S. M. *History of the Jews in Russia and Poland.* 3 vols. Philadelphia, 1916–20.
"Istoricheskie soobshcheniia," *Knizhki Voskhoda,* 21 (1901): 25–40; 5 (1901): 3–21.
"Iz istorii vos'midesiatykh godov," *ES,* 9, 1 (1916): 1–30; 4 (1916): 353–79.
[Kritikus]. "Literaturnaia letopis'," *Voskhod,* 9, 1 (1891): 22–41.

Efrimov, Sergii. *Evreis'ka sprava na Ukraini.* Kiev, 1909.

Egorov, A. [Konsparov]. *Stranitsy iz prozhitogo* II. *(1881–1906 gg.)* Odessa, 1913.

Eisenmenger, Johann Andreas. *Entdechtes Judentum.* 2 vols. Koenigsburg, 1711.

Emi. *Chto delat' evreiam?* 2nd ed. SPb, 1892.

Engel'gardt, A. N. *Iz derevni. 12 pisem, 1872–1887.* Moscow, 1960.

Entsiklopedicheskii slovar', 82 vols. SPb, 1890–1904.

Evrei. *Mysli i fakty k evreiskomu voprosu*. Odessa, 1895.

Evreiskaia entsiklopediia, 16 vols. SPb, 1906–13.

Evreiskoe naselenie Rossii po dannym perepisi 1897 g. i po noveishim istochnikom. Petrograd, 1914.

Evrei v privislianskom krae. Kharakteristika ikh deiatel'nosti sredi khristianskogo naseleniia etogo kraia. SPb, 1892.

Evrei v Rossii. Moscow, 1906.

Evrei v Varshave vo vremia poslednego pol'skogo miatezha. Vil'na, 1869.

"Evreiskie religioznye sekty v Rossii," *Zhurnal Ministerstva Vnutrennogo Dela*, 15, 8, 9, 11, 12 (1846): 3–49, 282–309, 211–73, 500–80.

Evreiskoe Statisticheskoe Obshchestvo. *Evreiskoe naselenie Rossii*. Petrograd, 1917.

Evreistvo pered sudom kritiki i zdravogo smysla. Moscow, 1880.

Feoktistov, E. M. *Vospominaniia za kulisami politiki i literatury*. Leningrad, 1929. Reprint Oriental Research Partners, Cambridge, MA, 1975. Introduction by Hans J. Torke.

Filippov, M. M. *Russko-evreiskii vopros*. Odessa, 1882.

Flisfeder, D. I. *Evrei i ikh uchenie ob inovertsakh*. SPb, 1874.

Evreiskii vopros, pred sudom istorii. SPb, 1882.

Frumkin, B. "Iz istorii revoliutsionnogo dvizheniia sredi evreev v 1870–kh godakh," *ES*, 4, 2, 4 (1911): 221–48, 513–40.

Garkavi [Harkavy], A. Ia. *Istoricheskie ocherki karaimstva*, 2 vols. SPb, 1897–1902.

Ob iazyke evreev zhivshikh v drevnee vremia na Rusi. SPb, 1866.

Sbornik statei po evreiskoi istorii i literature. SPb, 1867.

Georgievskii, A. I. *Doklad v Vysshuiu Komissiiu 1886 g. po voprosu o merakh otnositel'no obrazovaniia evreev*. SPb, 1886.

Gertsberg-Frenkel,' A. *Pol'skie evrei*. SPb, 1868.

Gessen I. V., Ratner, M. B., Shternberg, L. Ia. *Nakanune probuzhdeniia. Sbornik statei po evreiskomu voprosu*. SPb, 1906.

Gessen, Iu. I. *Gallereia evreiskikh deiatelei*. SPb, 1898.

Istoriia evreiskogo naroda v Rossii. 2 vols. 2nd ed. Leningrad, 1925–27.

"Iz letopisi minuvshego: vilenskaia komissiia po ustroistvu byta evreev (1866–1869 gg.)," *Perezhitoe*, II (SPb, 1910): 306–11.

K istorii korobochnogo sbora v Rossii. SPb, 1911.

"Na arene krovavogo naveta v Rossii. Proiskhozhdenie ritual'noi literatury na russkom iazyke," *Evreiskaia letopis'*, 1 (1923): 3–17.

"Popytka emansipatsii evreev v Rossii," *Perezhitoe*, 1 (SPb, 1909): 144–63.

"Ritual'nye protsessy 1816 goda," *ES*, 4, 2 (1912): 144–63.

"Die russische Regierung und die westeuropaischen Juden," *Monatsschift für Geschichte und Wissenschaft des Judentums*, 57, 5–6 (1913): 257–71; 482–500.

"Smena obshchestvennykh techenii. II. 'Pervyi russko-evreiskii organ,'" *Perezhitoe*, 3 (SPb, 1911): 37–59.

Zakon i zhizn'. SPb, 1911.

Gessen, Iu. I., M. Vishnitser, A. Karlin. *"Zapiska o ritual'nykh ubiistvakh" (pripisyvaemaia V. I. Daliu) i eia istochniki*. SPb, 1914.

Gets, F. B. *Slovo podsudimomu!* SPb, 1891.

Ginsburg [Gintsburg], S. M. "Iz obshchestvennykh nastroennii 60–kh godov," *Evreiskaia mysl'* (Leningrad, 1926): 246–61.

"Zabytaia epokha," *Voskhod*, 16, 1–6, 10–12 (1896): 87–104; 3–21; 69–87; 130–59; 130–43; 115–34; 71–98; 48–61.

Gol'dberg, B. A. L. O. *Levanda kak publitsist.* Vil'na, 1900.

Golitsyn, N. N. *Upotrebliaiut li evrei khristianskuiu krov'? Po povodu sovremennogo spora.* Warsaw, 1879.

Golosa iz Rossii. 9 vols. London, 1856–60.

Gordon, L. O. "Moi vstrechi s Konstantinom Petrovichem Kaufmanom," *Evreiskaia biblioteka*, 9 (1901): 124–34.

"Otryvki vospominanii," *Evreiskii vestnik* (Leningrad, 1928): 38–51.

Gradovskii, N. D. *Otnosheniia k evreiam v drevnei i sovremennoi Rusi.* SPb, 1891.

Torgovye i drugie prava evreev v Rossii, v istoricheskom khodie zakonodatel'nykh mer. SPb, 1885.

Grau, R. F. *Taina evreiskogo voprosa.* Odessa, 1889.

Grave, N. S. "K istorii evreistva," *Russkii arkhiv*, 10–12 (1910): 313–36; 449–92; 611–75.

Greene, F. V. *The Russian Army and its Campaigns in Turkey in 1877–1878.* London, 1880.

Grigor'ev, V. *Evreiskie religioznye sekty v Rossii.* SPb, 1847.

Grinevich, M. I. *O tletvornom vlianii evreev na ekonomicheskii byt Rossii i o sisteme evreiskoi eksploatsii.* SPb, 1876.

Grozdev, R. *Kulachestvo-Rostovshchichestvo.* SPb, 1899.

I., P. *Evrei v privislainskom krae: kharakteristika ikh deiatel'nosti sredi khristianskogo naseleniia etogo kraia.* SPb, 1892.

Iakushkin, P. I. *Sochineniia.* SPb, 1884.

Il'ish, R. *Evreiskie melodii.* SPb, 1864.

Istoricheskie svedeniia o vilenskom ravvinskom uchilishche. Vil'na, 1873.

Istoriia evreev v Rossii. 2 vols. Moscow, 1914–21.

Kanai, I. *Pol'sko-evreiskie otnosheniia (34–aia voina): sbornik statei.* Petrograd, 1915.

Kantor, R., ed. "Aleksandr III o evreiskikh pogromakh 1881–1883 gg.," *Evreiskaia letopis'*, 1 (Petrograd, 1923): 149–58.

Karnovich, E. *Evreiskii vopros v Rossii.* SPb, 1864.

Kaufman, A. E. "Evrei v russko-turetskoi voine 1877 g.," *ES*, 8 (1915): 57–72; 176–82.

K vostochnomu voprosu. Kharakteristika otnoshenii russkikh evreev k slavianskomu dvizheniiu i vzgliad ikh na nego. Odessa, 1876.

"Za mnogo let. Otryvki vospominanii starogo zhurnalista," *ES*, 5, 2–3 (1913): 201–20; 333–50.

Keppen [Koeppen], P. *Deviataia reviziia. Issledovanie o chisle zhitelei v Rossii v 1851 godu.* SPb, 1857.

Keppen [Koeppen], P. compiler. *Khronologicheskii ukazetel' materialov dlia istorii inorodtsev evropeiskoi Rossii.* SPb, 1861.

Khasim, E. *Evrei k evreiam.* London, 1892.

Khomiakov, A. S. *Polnoe sobranie sochinenii,* 2nd ed., 2 vols. Moscow, 1878–80.

Khvol'son, D. A. *O nekotorykh srednevekovykh obvineniiakh protiv evreev.* SPb, 1861, 2nd ed. SPb, 1880.

Upotrebliaiut-li evrei khristianskuiu krov'? 2nd rev. ed. SPb, 1879.

Kislinskii, N. A. *Nasha zheleznodorozhnaia politika po dokumentam arkhiva komiteta ministrov,* 2 vols. SPb, 1902.

Kleinman, I. A. "Evoliutsiia pol'sko-evreiskikh otnoshenii (1850–1906 g.)," *Golos minuvshogo,* 3 (1913): 90–111.

Knorozovskii, M. L. "Eshche o vilenskoi evreiskoi komissii 1869 g.," *Perezhitoe,* III (SPb, 1911): 385–92.

Kogan, D. "Pervye desiatiletiia evreiskoi obshchiny v Odesse i pogrom 1821 goda," *ES,* 3, 2 (1911): 260–7.

Kornilov, I. *Russkoe delo v severo-zapadnom krae.* SPb, 1908.

Korolenko, V. G. *Vospominaniia o pisateliakh.* M, 1934.

Kostomarov, N. I. *Literaturnoe nasledie.* SPb, 1890.

"Zhidotrepanie v nachale XVIII v.," *Kievskaia starina,* 1, 3 (1883).

Kraeva, S. M. *"Novorossiiskii Telegraf" i ego spodvizhniki.* Odessa, 1881.

Kutaisskii protsess. Delo o pokhishchenii i umershchvlenii evreiami krest'ianskoi devochki Sarry Iosifovoi Madebadze. SPb, 1879.

Kuz'min, I. O. *Materialy k voprosu ob obvineniiakh evreev v ritual'nykh prestupleniiakh.* SPb, 1913.

L., A. [A. E. Landau]. "Zametki: Berlinskii kongres," *Evreiskaia biblioteka,* 6 (1878): 139–52.

Lemke, M. *Epokha tsenzurnykh reform, 1859–1865 godov.* SPb, 1904.

Leontovich, F. I. *Istoricheskoe issledovanie o pravakh litovsko-russkikh evreev.* Kiev, 1864.

Lerner, O. M. *Evrei v novorossiiskom krae.* Odessa, 1901.

Tatarbunarskaia lozh' i kutaisskaia deistvitel'nost'. Odessa, 1880.

Leskov, N. S. *Evrei v Rossii. Neskol'ko zamechanii po evreiskomu voprosu.* SPb, 1884; reprinted Petrograd, 1920.

Levanda, L. O. "Goriachee vremia," *Evreiskaia biblioteka,* 1–3 (1871–3): 1–71; 1–160; 8–93.

"Iz perepiski L. O. Levandy," A. Druianov, ed., *ES,* 5, 2 (1913): 279–81.

"Iz perepiski L. O. Levandy," A. E. Landau, ed., *EB,* 9 (1901): 1–64.

"Iz zhizni L. O. Levandy: Pis'ma L. O. Levandy k M. F. de-Pule," N. A. Bukhbinder, ed., *Evreiskii vestnik.* Leningrad, 1925: 52–68.

"K istorii vozniknoveniia pervogo organa russkikh evreev," *Voskhod,* 1, 6 (1881): 132–52.

K voprosu o evreiakh v zapadnom krae. Vil'na, 1866.

"L. O. Levanda and J. L. Gordon: Levanda's Letters to Gordon, 1873–5," Moshe Perlmann, ed. *Proceedings of the American Academy for Jewish Research,* 25 (1967): 139–85.

Levanda, V. O. *Polnyi khronologicheskii sbornik zakonov i polozhenii, kasaiushchiksia evreev.* SPb, 1874.

Levinzon, I. B. *Damoklov mech'.* Tr. I. N. Sorkin. SPb, 1883.

Lion, A. *Khronika umstvennogo i nravstvennogo razvitiia kishinevskikh evreev (1773*

g. po 1890 g.) i obzor evreiskikh blagotvoritel'nykh uchrezhdenii v bessarabskoi gubernii, 2 vols. Kishinev, 1891.

Lisovskii, N. M. Russkaia periodicheskaia pechat' 1703–1900 gg. Petrograd, 1915.

Liutostanskii, I. Sovremennyi vzgliad na evreiskii vopros. Moscow, 1882.

Talmud i evrei, 1st ed. 3 vols. Moscow, 1879; 2nd ed. SPb, 1902.

Vopros ob upotreblenii evreiami-sektatorami khristianskoi krovi dlia religioznykh tselei, v sviazi s voprosami ob otnosheniiakh evreistva k khristianstvu voobshche. Moscow, 1876.

Ob upotreblenii evreiami (talmudistskimi sektatorami) khristianskoi krovi dlia religioznykh tselei v sviazi voprosami ob otnosheniiakh evreistva k khristianstvu voobshche, 2nd ed. 2 vols. SPb, 1880.

Liutsinskoe delo po obvineniiu Lotsovykh Gurevicha i Maikh v ubiistve Marii Drich: stenograficheskii otchet. SPb, 1885.

Liverant. "Prikliucheniia evrei vo vremia pol'skogo vosstaniia 1863 goda," ES, 2, 3 (1910): 378–90.

M—v, L. Russkii narod i evrei. SPb, 1908.

Maior Osman-Bei [Kibrizli-Zadé]. Pokorenie mira evreiami. SPb, 1874.

Révélations sur L'Assassinat d'Alexandre II. Geneva, 1886.

Mandal'shtam, L. I. V zashchitu evreev. SPb, 1859.

Marek, P. "Bor'ba dvukh vospitanii: iz istorii prosveshcheniia evreev v Rossii (1864–1873)," Perezhitoe, I (SPb, 1909): 105–43.

"Iz istorii evreiskoi intelligentsii," Evreiskii vestnik (Leningrad, 1928): 124–42.

Ocherki po istorii prosveshcheniia evreev v Rossii. Moscow, 1909.

Materialy po statistike dvizheniia zemlevladeniia v Rossii. SPb, 1901.

M—n [Miliutin], B. Ustroistvo i sostoianie evreiskikh obshchestv. SPb, 1849–50.

Minor, Z. Rabbi Ippolit Liutostanskii: ego sochinenie "Talmud i evrei". Moscow, 1879.

Moreau de Jonnès, Alexandre. Statistique des peuples de l'antiquité. 2 vols. Paris, 1851.

Morgulis, M. G. "Besporiadki 1871 goda v Odesse (po dokumentam i lichnym vospominaniiam," Evreiskii mir, no. 12 (1910): 42–66.

"Iz moikh vospominanii," Evreiskii mir, 1, 6 (1909): 22–43.

Sbornik statei po evreiskomu voprosu iz raznykh periodicheskikh izdanii. Kremenchug, 1869.

Voprosy evreiskoi zhizni. Sobranie statie. SPb, 1889.

Murav'ev, M. N. "Zapiski ego upravlenii severo-zapadnym kraem i ob usmirenii v nem miatezha, 1863–1866," Russkaia starina, 13, 11–12 (1882): 387–432, 623–46, 14, 1 (1883): 131–66.

Mysh, M. I. Rukovodstvo k russkim zakonam o evreiakh, 4th ed. SPb, 1914.

N. "Moskovskii obed 28–go dekabria 1857 g. i ego posledstviia," Russkaia starina, 1 (1898): 49–72; 2 (1898): 297–326.

N., N. "Iz vpechatlenii minuvshogo veka," ES, 8, 2 (1915): 186–200.

N., V. "Istoricheskie dokumenty. 'Proekt ob ustroistve evreev' podannyi v 1856 g. grodenskim gubernskim striapchim I. K. Kozakovskim," Voskhod, 1, 5 (1881): 131–9.

"Nekotorye rezoliutsii Imperatora Aleksandra II po evreiskomu voprosu (1861)," ES, 4, 4 (1912): 472–4.

Nemirovich-Danchenko, V. I. *Personal Reminiscences of General Skobeleff.* London, 1884.

Voinstvuiushchii Izrail'. SPb, 1880.

Nevakhovich, Leiba. *Vopl' dshcheri iudeiskoi.* SPb, 1803.

Nevedenskii, S. [Tatishchev, S. S.]. *Katkov i ego vremia.* SPb, 1888.

Nikitenko, A. V. *Zapiski i dnevnik,* 2 vols. SPb, 1904.

Nikitin, V. N. *Evrei zemledel'tsy.* SPb, 1887.

Mnogostradal'nye. Ocherki byta kantonistov. SPb, 1872.

Nikotin, I. *Stoletnyi period (1772–1872) russkogo zakonodatel'stva v vozsoedinennykh ot Pol'shi guberniiakh i zakonodatel'stvo o evreiakh (1649–1876).* 2 vols. Vil'na, 1886.

Notovich, N. *Pravda o evreiakh.* Moscow, 1889.

Obshchestvo dlia rasprostraneniia prosveshcheniia mezhdu evreiami v Rossii. *Mirovozzrenie Talmudistov.* 3 vols. SPb, 1874–6.

Sbornik statei po evreiskoi istorii i literature. vol. I. SPb, 1866.

Sbornik v pol'zu nachal'nykh evreiskikh shkol. SPb, 1896.

Obzor nyne deistvuiushchikh iskliuchitel'nykh zakonov o evreiakh. SPb, 1883.

Ocherki iz istoricheskogo i iuridicheskogo byta evreev. Kiev, 1866.

Orshanskii, I. G. *Evrei v Rossii. Ocherki ekonomicheskogo i obshchestvennogo byta russkikh evreev.* SPb, 1877.

Pasmanik, D. S. *Sud'by evreiskogo naroda.* Moscow, 1917.

Pereferkovich, N. "Klassicheskie pisateli o evreistve," *Voskhod,* 9 (1896): 49–74.

Peretts, E. A. *Dnevnik E. A. Perettsa (1880–1883).* A. A. Sergeev, ed. Moscow-Leningrad, 1927.

Peskovskii, M. L. *Rokovoe nedorazumenie. Evreiskii vopros, ego mirovaia istoriia i estestvennyi put' k razresheniiu.* SPb, 1891.

Pobedonostsev, K. P. *K. P. Pobedonostsev i ego korrespondenty: Pis'ma i zapiski.* 1 vol. in 2 pts. Moscow, 1923.

Moskovskii sbornik. Moscow, 1896.

"Pis'ma K. P. Pobedonostseva k E. M. Feoktistovu," B. Gorev, I. Aizenshtok, eds., *Literaturnoe nasledstvo,* 22–24 (1935): 497–560.

"Pis'ma K. P. Pobedonostseva k grafu N. P. Ignat'evu," R. M. Kantor, ed., *Byloe,* 22–28 (1924): 50–89.

Pis'ma Pobedonostseva k Aleksandru III. 2 vols. Moscow, 1925–6.

Pokov, P. [P. K. Liubimov]. *Po povodu vzgliada M. E. Saltykova na evreiskii vopros.* Kiev, 1883.

Polkovnik Vedi Izhe On [Vashkov, I. A.]. *Vyshe znamia nashe, Vyshe!* Moscow, 1882.

"Povest' o Feodore Zhidovine," *Letopisi russkoi literatury i drevnosti,* II, pt. 3. (Moscow, 1859): 69–71.

Pozner, S. V. *Evrei v obshchei shkole.* SPb, 1914.

Protopopov, Sviashchenik. *Ob upotreblenii evreiami khristiianskoi krovi dlia religioznykh tselei.* SPb, 1877.

Rabinovich, O. A., "Pis'ma O. A. Rabinovicha," Iu. I. Gessen, ed., *ES,* 3, 1 (1911): 71–88.

Sochineniia. 3 vols. Odessa, 1888.

Recueil de matériaux sur la situation économique des Israélites de Russie. 2 vols. Paris, 1906–8.

Registy i nadpisi. Svod materialov dlia istorii evreev v Rossii (80g. – 1800g.). I (SPb, 1899).

Rohling, August. *Der Talmudjude.* Munster, 1872.
Zgubne zasady Talmudyzmu do serecznei rozwagi Żydom i Chrześcianom. Lwow, 1875.

Rozenberg, V., Iakushkin, V. *Russkaia pechat' i tsenzura v proshlom i nastoiash-chem.* Moscow, 1905.

Rozenshtadt, B., "Evreiskie zhertvy v pol'skom vosstanii 1863 goda," *ES*, 4 (1913): 485–92.

Rozenson, M. *Uchenie evreev ob inovertsakh sostavleno po Biblii, Talmudu i rav-vinskoi pis'mennosti.* Warsaw, 1892.

Rozental', L. M. ed. *Toledot hevrat marbei haskalah be-yisrael be-eretz Rusia.* [Proto-cols of the Society for the Spread of Enlightenment among the Jews of Russia.] 2 vols. SPb, 1885–90.

Russia. General'nyi shtab. *Materialy dlia geografii i statistiki Rossii, sobrannye ofitserami general'nogo shtaba.*
Afanas'ev, D. *Kovenskaia guberniia.* SPb, 1861.
Bobrovskii, P. *Grodnenskaia guberniia.* 3 vols. SPb, 1863.
Domontovich, M. *Chernigovskaia guberniia.* SPb, 1865.
Korev, A. *Vilenskaia guberniia.* SPb, 1861.
Pavlovich, V. *Ekaterinoslavskaia guberniia.* SPb, 1862.
Shmidt, A. *Khersonskaia guberniia.* 2 vols. SPb, 1863.
Zashchuk, A. *Bessarabskaia oblast'.* SPb, 1862.
Zelenskii, I. *Minskaia guberniia.* 2 vols. SPb, 1864.

Russia. Komissiia po ustroistvu byta evreev. *Materialy komissii po ustroistvu byta evreev.* 3 vols. SPb, 1879.

Russia. Komitet ministrov. *Istoricheskii obzor deiatel'nosti Komiteta Ministrov.* 5 vols. SPb, 1902.

Russia. Kommissiia dlia issledovaniia nyneshnego polozheniia sel'skogo khoz-iaistva i sel'skoi proizvoditel'nosti v Rossii. *Doklad.* SPb, 1873.
Prilozheniia. I–VII. SPb, 1873.

Russia. Kommissiia dlia peresmotra deistvuiushchikh o evreiakh v Imperii zakonov. *Obshchaia zapiska vysshei komissii dlia peresmotra deistvuiushchikh o evreiakh v Imperii zakonov (1883–1888).* SPb, 1888.
Prilozhenie k "obshchei zapiske" vysshei komissii. SPb, 1888.

Russia. Ministerstvo Narodnogo Prosveshcheniia. *Materialy otnosiashchiesia k obrazovaniiu evreev v Rossii.* SPb, 1865.

Russia. Ministerstvo Vnutrennikh Del. *Sbornik ukazonenii, kasaiushchikhsia evreev, sostavlen po rasporiazheniiu ministra vnutrennikh del, v departamente politsii ispolnitel'noi.* SPb, 1872.

Russkie liudi o evreiakh. SPb, 1891.

Russkii biograficheskii slovar'. 25 vols. SPb, 1896–1918.

Saltykov-Shchedrin, M. E. *Sobranie Sochinenii.* 20 vols. Moscow, 1965–77.

Samarin, G. *Correspondance de G. Samarine avec La Baronne de Rahden, 1861–1876.*
D. Samarine, ed. Moscow, 1894.

Samoderzhavie i pechat' v Rossii. SPb, 1906.

Sapunov, A. *Pol'sko-litovskoe i russkoe zakonodatel'stvo o evreiakh.* Vitebsk, 1884.

Sbornik materialov ob ekonomicheskom polozhenii evreev v Rossii. Vol. I. SPb, 1904.

Sbornik postanovlenii i rasporiazhenii po tsenzure s 1720 po 1862 god. SPb, 1862.

Sbornik statei po istorii i statistike russkoi periodicheskoi pechati, 1703–1903. SPb, 1903.

Sementkovskii, R. I. *Evrei i zhidy.* SPb, 1890.

Seredonin, S. M. *Istoricheskii obzor deiatel'nosti Komiteta Ministrov.* 5 vols. in 7 parts. SPb, 1902.

Shatskin, Ia. "K istorii uchastiia evreev v pol'skom vosstanii 1863 g.," *ES*, 7, 1 (1915): 29–37.

Shershevskii, I. I. *O knige kagala.* SPb, 1872.

Shigarin, N. D. *Ob upotreblenii evreiami khristianskoi krovi i neskol'ko slov o nashikh otnosheniiakh k evreiam voobshche.* SPb, 1877.

Poslednie vyvody iz skazannogo ob upotrebkenii Evreiami v Rossii khristianskoi krovi. SPb, 1880.

Shul'gin, V. Ia. *Iugozapadnyi krai v poslednee dvadtsatipiatiletie (1838–1863).* Kiev, 1864.

Shul'gina, M. K., ed. *"Kievlianin" pod redaktsiei Vitaliia Iakovlevicha Shul'gina (1864–1878).* Kiev, 1880.

Shvartz, N. Sh. "Materialy k istorii evreiskoi pechati," *ES*, 13 (1930): 135–44.

Sistematicheskii ukazatel' literatury o evreiakh na russkom iazyke. SPb, 1892.

Sliozberg, G. B. "Baron G. O. Gintsburg i pravovoe polozhenie evreev," *Perezhitoe*, 2 (1910): 94–115.

Compiler. *Sbornik deistviushchikh zakonov o evreiakh.* SPb, 1909.

Zakony o evreiakh i praktika ikh primeniia. SPb, 1907.

Slovar' Akademii Rossiiskoi. 6 vols. SPb, 1806–22. (Reprint by Odense University Press, Odense, Denmark, 1970.)

Solov'ev, V. S. *Evreiskii vopros – khristianskii vopros.* SPb, 1906.

Natsional'nyi vopros v Rossii. Moscow, 1888.

Sorkin, O. *Nedobrozhelateliam evreev.* SPb, 1869.

Sosis, I. "Natsional'nyi vopros v literature kontsa 60kh i nachala 70kh godov," *ES*, 7, 2 (1915): 38–56, 129–46, 324–37.

"Obshchestvennye nastroeniia 'epokhi velikikh reform,'" *ES*, 6, 2–4 (1914): 21–41, 182–97, 341–64.

"Period krizisa. Obshchestvennye techeniia v literature 80kh godov," *ES*, 8, 1–6 (1916): 46–60, 194–209.

Sotsialisty-Evrei. Ot gruppy sotsialistov-evreev. Geneva, 1880.

Stahl, Friedrich Julius. *Der christliche Staat und sein Verhältniss zu Deismus und Judentum.* Berlin, 1847.

Stepniak [S. M. Kravchinskii]. *The Russian Peasantry: Their Agrarian Condition, Social Life, and Religion.* London, 1888.

Stepnin, I. *Evreistvo pered sudom kritiki i zdravogo smysla.* Moscow, 1880.

Strakhov, N. *Iz istorii literaturnogo nigilizma, 1861–1865.* SPb, 1890.

Subbotin, A. P. *Evreiskii vopros v ego pravil'nom osveshchenii (v sviazi s trudami I. S. Bliokha).* SPb, 1903.

Obshchaia zapiska po evreiskomu voprosu. SPb, 1905.

V cherte evreiskoi osedlosti. 2 vols. SPb, 1888.

Tarnopol,' I. *Notices historiques et caractèristiques sur les Israélites d'Odessa.* Odessa, 1855.

Opyt sovremennoi i osmotritel'noi reformy v oblasti iudaizma v Rossii. Odessa, 1868.

Tatishchev, S. S. *Imperator Aleksandr II: ego zhizn' i tsarstvovanie.* 2 vols. SPb, 1903.

Trivus, M., "Ritual'nye protsessy doreformennogo russkogo suda," *ES*, 3 (1912): 246–67.

Tsinberg, S. L. [I. Zinberg]. *A History of Jewish Literature.* 12 vols. Tr. and ed. by Bernard Martin. Cleveland and New York, 1972–8.

Istoriia evreiskoi pechati v Rossii v sviazi s obshchestvennymi techeniiami. Petrograd, 1915.

"Pervye sotsilisticheskie organy v evreiskoi literature," *Perezhitoe*, 1, (SPb, 1910): 233–63.

Usov, P. S. "Iz moikh vospominanii," *Istoricheskii vestnik*, 11, 1 (1883): 330–59.

Varadinov, A. N. *Istoriia ministerstva vnutrennikh del.* 8 vols. SPb, 1853–63.

Vol'skii, K. *Evrei v Rossii.* SPb, 1887.

IV Secondary sources

Alkoshi, "Ha-itonut ha-ivrit be-vilnah be-me'ah ha 19" [The Hebrew Press in Vilna in the 19th Century], *He-avar*, 13 (1966): 59–97; 14 (1967): 105–53.

Alston, Patrick L. *Education and the State in Tsarist Russia.* Stanford, 1969.

Ambler, Effie. *Russian Journalism and Politics: The Career of Aleksei S. Suvorin, 1861–1881.* Detroit, 1972.

Anan'ich, B. V. *Bankirskie doma v Rossii, 1860–1914 gg.: Ocherki istorii chastnogo predprinimatel'stva.* Leningrad, 1991.

Aronson, I. Michael, "The Attitudes of Russian Officials in the 1880s toward Jewish Assimilation and Emigration," *SR*, 34, 1 (1975): 1–18.

"The Prospects for the Emancipation of Russian Jewry during the 1880s," *SEER*, 55, 3 (1977): 348–69.

Baddeley, John F. *Russia in the 'Eighties'.* London, 1921.

Baker, Mark, "The Reassessment of *Haskala* Ideology in the Aftermath of the 1863 Polish Revolt," *Polin*, 5 (1990): 221–49.

Balmuth, Daniel. *Censorship in Russia, 1865–1905.* Washington, DC, 1979.

Bartoszewicz, Kazimierz. *Wojna Żydowska w roku 1859. (Poczatki asymilacyi i antisemityzmu).* Warsaw–Cracow, 1913.

Batiushkov, P. N. *Pamiatniki russkoi stariny v zapadnykh guberniiakh.* Part VII. *(Kholmskaia Rus').* SPb, 1885.

Beauvois, Daniel. *Le Noble, le serf, et le révizor: la noblesse polonaise entre le tsarisme et les masses ukrainiennes (1831–1863).* Paris, 1985.

Becker, Seymour. *Nobility and Privilege in Late Imperial Russia.* DeKalb, IL, 1985.

Bel'chikov, N. F., ed., "Dostoevskii i Pobedonostsev," *Krasnyi arkhiv.* 2 (1922): 240–55.

Ben-Sasson, H. H., ed. *A History of the Jewish People.* London, 1977.

Berezina, V. G. *Russkaia zhurnalistika vtoroi chetverti XIX veka (1826–1839 gody).* Leningrad, 1965.

Russkaia zhurnalistika vtoroi chetverti XIX veka (1840–e gody). Leningrad, 1969.

Berezina, V. G., et al. *Ocherki po istorii russkoi zhurnalistiki i kritiki*, II. Leningrad, 1965.

Bernshtein, M. D. *Ukrain'ska literatura kritika 50–70-kh rokiv XIX st.* Kiev, 1959. *Zhurnal "Osnova" i ukrain'skii literaturnii protses kintsia 50–60-kh. rokiv XIX st.* Kiev, 1959.

Blackwell, William L. *The Beginnings of Russian Industrialization, 1800–1860.* Princeton, NJ, 1968.

Bloch, Bronislaw, "Vital Events among the Jews in European Russia towards the End of the XIXth Century," in U. O. Schmalz, P. Glikson and S. Della Pergola, eds., *Papers in Jewish Demography, 1977*. Jerusalem, 1980: 69–81.

Bokhanov, A. N. *Burzhuaznaia pressa Rossii i krupnyi kapital, konets XIX v.-1914 g.* Moscow, 1984.

Borovoi, S. Ia. *Evreiskaia zemledel'cheskaia kolonizatsiia v staroi Rossii*. Moscow, 1928.

"Evreiskie gazety pred sudom 'uchenykh evreev,'" *Evreiskaia mysl'*. Leningrad, 1926: 282–93.

Brant, Evgenii. *Ritual'noe ubeistvo i evreev*. Belgrad, 1926.

Brik, Oleksander S. *Ukrains'ko-evreiski vzaemovidrosini*. Winnipeg, 1961.

Brooks, Jeffrey. *When Russia Learned to Read*. Princeton, NJ, 1985.

Cannon, Ellen S. "The Political Culture of Russian Jewry during the Second Half of the Nineteenth Century." Unpublished doctoral dissertation, University of Massachusetts, 1974.

Carlebach, Julius. *Karl Marx and the Radical Critique of Judaism*. London, 1978.

Carr, E. H. "Liberalism in Alien Soil," in *From Napoleon to Stalin and Other Essays*. London, 1980: 60–7.

Cherikover, Elyohu [Elias Tcherikower]. *Geshikhte fun der yidisher arbeter bavegung in di Fareynikte Shtatn*. 2 vols. New York, 1943–5. Tr. and ed. by Aaron Antonovsky as *The Early Jewish Labor Movement in the United States*. New York, 1961

"Peter Lavrov and the Jewish Socialist Émigrés," *YIVO Annual of Jewish Social Science*, 7 (1952): 132–45.

"Yidn revolutsionern in Rusland in di 60er un 70er yorn," *Historishe shriften*, 3 (Paris–Wilno, 1939): 60–172.

Christian, David. *Living Water: Vodka and Russian Society on the Eve of Emancipation*. Oxford, 1990.

Cohn, Norman. *Warrant for Genocide*. London, 1967.

Corrsin, Stephen D. "Language Use in Cultural and Political Change in Pre-1914 Warsaw: Poles, Jews and Russification," *SEER*, 68, 1 (1990): 69–90.

Deich, L. *Rol' evreev v russkom revoliutsionnom dvizhenii*. Berlin, 1923.

Delmaire, Jean-Marie, "La Haskalah et la Russification," *Slovo*, 5 (1984): 77–96.

Dement'ev, A. G., A. V. Zapagov and M. S. Cherepakhov, *Russkaia periodicheskaia pechat' (1702–1894): Spravochnik*. Moscow, 1959.

Dobrovol'skii, L. M. *Zapreshchennaia kniga v Rossii, 1825–1904*. Moscow, 1962.

Doroshenko, Dmytro. *A Survey of Ukrainian History*. Edited and updated by Oleh W. Gerus. Winnipeg, 1975.

Dowler, Wayne. *Dostoevsky, Grigor'ev, and Native Soil Conservatism*. Toronto, 1982.
"The 'Young Editors' of *Moskvityanin* and the Origins of Intelligentsia Conservatism in Russia," *SEER*, 60, 3 (1977): 310–27.

Drahomanov, Mykhaylo. *Mykhaylo Drahomanov: A Symposium and Selected Writings* in *Annals of the Ukrainian Academy of Arts and Sciences in the US*. New York, 1952.

Dreizin, Felix. *The Russian Soul and the Jew: Essays in Literary Ethnocriticism*. Lantham, ML, 1990.

Druzhinin, N. M. "Pomeshchich'e khoziaistvo posle reformy 1861 g.," *Istoricheskie zapiski*, 89 (Moscow, 1972): 187–230.

Russkaia derevnia na perelome, 1861–1880 gg. Moscow, 1978.

Dubnova-Erlikh, Sofia. *Zhizn' i tvorchestvo S. M. Dubnova*. New York, 1950.

Duin, Edgar C. *Lutheranism under the Tsars and Soviets*. Ann Arbor, MI, 1975.

Eisenbach, Artur. *Emancypacja Żydów na ziemiach polskich 1785–1870*. Warsaw. 1988. English translation as *The Emancipation of the Jews in Poland, 1780–1870*. Oxford, 1991.

Kwestia równouprawnienia Żydów w Królestwie Polskim. Warsaw, 1972.

"Materiały do struktury i dzialalności gospodarczej ludności Żydowskiej w Królestwie Polskim w latach osiemdziesiatych XIX wieku," *BZIH*, 29 (1959): 72–111.

"La Mobilité territoriale de la population juive du Royaume de Pologne," *Revue des études juives/Historia judaica*, 126, 1 (1967): 55–111; 4: 435–71; 127, 1 (1968): 39–95.

"La Problème des Juifs polonais en 1861 et les projets de réforme du marquis Aleksandr Wielopolski," *Acta Poloniae Historica*, 20 (1969): 138–62.

Eisenbach, A., Fajnhaus, D., Wein, A. *Żydzi a powstanie styczniowe: Materiały i dokumenty*. Warsaw, 1963.

Emmons, Terence. *The Russian Landed Gentry and the Peasant Emancipation of 1861*. Cambridge, 1968.

Endelman, Todd M., ed. *Jewish Apostasy in the Modern World*. New York and London, 1987.

Ettinger, Shmuel. *Ha-antishemiyut ba-et ha-hadasha: pirke mekhar ve-iyun* [*Antisemitism in the Modern Age: Research and Investigations*]. Tel-Aviv, 1978.

"Ha-hashpa'ah ha-yehudit al ha-tesisah ha-datit be-mizrahah shel Europa be-sof ha-me'ah ha-tet-vav" [Jewish Influence on the Religious Ferment in Eastern Europe at the End of the Fifteenth Century], *Yitzhak F. Baer Jubilee Volume*. S. W. Baron, ed. Jerusalem, 1960: 228–47.

"Medinat Moskva be-yahasah el la-yehudim" [The Muscovite State and its Attitude toward the Jews], *Zion*, 18 (1953): 136–68.

"Ha-reka ha-idiologi le-hofa'ata shel ha-sifrut ha-antishemit ha-hadasha be-Rusia" [The Ideological Background of the Appearance of Modern Antisemitic Literature in Russia], *Zion*, 35 (1970): 193–225.

Evgen'ev-Maksimov, V. *"Sovremennik" pri Chernyshevskom i Dobroliubove*. Leningrad, 1936.

Fajnhauz, D. "Ludność żydowska na Litwie i Białorusi a powstanie styczniowe," *BZIH*, 37 (1961): 3–34.

Fischer, George, "The Russian Intelligentsia and Liberalism," *Harvard Slavic Studies*, 4 ('s-Gravenhage, 1957): 317–36.

Flynn, James T. "Uvarov and the 'Western Provinces': A Study of Russia's Polish Problem," *SEER*, 64, 2 (1986): 212–36.

Frankel, Jonathan. *Prophecy and Politics: Socialism, Nationalism, and the Russian Jews, 1862–1917*. Cambridge, 1981.

Freeze, Gregory L. "The *Soslovie* (Estate) Paradigm and Russian Social History," *American Historical Review*, 91, 1 (1986): 11–36.

Galai, Shmuel. "Early Russian Constitutionalism, 'Vol'noe slovo' and the 'Zemstvo Union': A Study in Deception," *JGO*, 22, 1 (1974): 35–55.

Gatrell, Peter. *The Tsarist Economy, 1850–1917*. London, 1986.

Geilikman, T. B. *Istoriia obshchestvennogo dvizheniia evreev v Pol'she i Rossii*. Moscow–Leningrad, 1930.

Gelber, N. M. *Die Juden und der polnische Aufstand 1863*. Vienna and Leipzig, 1923.

Gerasimova, Iu. I. *Iz istorii russkoi pechati v period revoliutsionnoi situatsii kontsa 1850–kh – nachala 1860–kh gg*. Moscow, 1974.

Gerstein, Linda. *Nikolai Strakhov*. Cambridge, MA, 1971.

Ginsburg, Saul M. *Historishe verk*. 3 vols. New York, 1937.

  Meshumodim in tsarishn Rusland [Apostates in Tsarist Russia]. New York, 1946.

  "Mucheniki-deti (iz istorii kantonistov-evreev)," *ES*, 13 (1930): 50–79.

Gleason, Abbot. *Young Russia: The Genesis of Russian Radicalism in the 1860s*. Chicago and London.

Goldstein, David I. *Dostoyevsky and the Jews*. Austin, TX and London, 1981.

Graupe, Heinz M. *The Rise of Modern Judaism*. Huntington, NY, 1978.

Greenberg, Louis. *The Jews in Russia: The Struggle for Emancipation*. 2 Vols. New Haven, 1944–51.

Grossman, L. "Dostoevskii i pravitel'stvennye krugi 70–kh godov," *Literaturnoe nasledstvo*, 15 (Moscow, 1934): 83–162.

Haberer, Erich E. "The Role of Jews in Russian Revolutionary Populism, 1868–1887." Unpublished doctoral dissertation. University of Toronto, 1986.

Ha-Cohen, Mordekhay ben Hillel. *Olami [Memoirs]*. 5 vols. Jerusalem, 1927–9.

Hamburg, Gary M. *Politics of the Russian Nobility, 1881–1905*. New Brunswick, NJ, 1984.

Hamm, Michael F. "Liberalism and the Jewish Question: The Progressive Bloc," *The Russian Review*, 31, 2 (1972): 163–72.

Herlihy, Patricia. *Odessa: A History, 1794–1914*. Cambridge, MA, 1986.

Herzberg, Arthur. *The French Enlightenment and the Jews*. New York, 1970.

Hildermeier, Manfred. "Die judische Frage im Zarenreich," *JGO*, 32, 3 (1984): 321–57.

Horn, Elizbieta. "Problem Żydowski w Twórczosci Dragomanova," *BZIH*, 62, 1–3 (1966): 3–37.

Hrushevsky, Michael. *A History of Ukraine*. New York, 1970.

Israel, Jonathan I. *European Jewry in the Age of Mercantilism, 1550–1750*. Oxford, 1985.

Iukhneva, N. V. "Evrei Peterburga v period reform 1860–kh godov: sotsial'no-demograficheskaia kharakteristika," in *Peterburg i guberniia*. Leningrad, 1989.

Kahan, Arcadius. *Essays in Jewish Social and Economic History.* Roger Weiss, ed. Chicago, 1986.

Kaiser, Friedhelm Berthold. *Hochschulpolitik und studentischer Widerstand in der Zarenzeit. A. I. Georgievskij und sein "Kurzer historischer Abriss der Massnahmen und Plane der Regierung gegen die Studentenunruhen" (1890).* Wiesbaden, 1983.

Katz, Jacob. *Emancipation and Assimilation.* Westmead, England, 1972.

    From Prejudice to Destruction: Anti-Semitism, 1700–1933. Cambridge, MA, 1980.

    Jews and Freemasons in Europe, 1723–1939. Cambridge, MA, 1970.

    Out of the Ghetto. Cambridge, MA, 1973.

Katz, Jacob, ed. *Toward Modernity: The European Jewish Model.* New Brunswick, NJ and London, 1986.

Katz, Martin. *Mikhail N. Katkov: A Political Biography, 1818–1887.* The Hague–Paris, 1966.

Klier, John D. "The Concept of 'Jewish Emancipation' in a Russian Context," in Olga Crisp and Linda Edmundson, eds. *Civil Rights in Imperial Russia.* Oxford, 1989: 121–44.

    "1855–1894 Censorship of the Press in Russian and the Jewish Question," *JSS,* 45, 3–4 (1986): 257–68.

    "German Antisemitism and Russian Judeophobia in the 1880's: Brothers and Strangers," *JGO,* 37 (1989): 524–40.

    "The Jewish *Den'* and the Literary Mice, 1869–71," *Russian History,* 10, 1 (1983): 31–49.

    "*Odesskii vestnik's* Annus Mirabilis of 1858," *Canadian Slavonic Papers,* 23, 1 (1981): 41–55.

    Russia Gathers Her Jews: The Origins of the Jewish Question in Russia, 1772–1825. DeKalb, IL, 1985.

    "The Polish Revolt of 1863 and the Birth of Russification: Bad for the Jews?" *Polin,* I (1986): 91–106.

    "Russkaia voina protiv 'khevra kadisha,'" in D. A. El'iashevich, ed. *Istoriia evreev v Rossii: problemy istochnikovedeniia i istoriografii.* SPb, 1993: 109–14.

    "*The Times* of London, the Russian Press and the Pogroms of 1881–1882," *The Carl Beck Papers,* 308 (nd): 1–26.

    "*Zhid*: The Biography of a Russian Pejorative," *SEER,* 60, 1 (1982) 1–15.

Klier, John D. Lambroza, Shlomo, eds. *Pogroms: Anti-Jewish Violence in Modern Russian History.* Cambridge, 1991.

Kohn, Hans. *Pan-Slavism: Its History and Ideology.* Notre Dame, IN, 1953.

Koz'min, B. P. *Zhurnal "Sovremennik" – organ revoliutsionnoi demokratii.* Moscow, 1957.

Kucherov, Samuel. *Courts, Lawyers and Trials under the Last Three Tsars.* Westport, CN, 1974.

Kunitz, Joshua. *Russian Literature and the Jew.* New York, 1929.

Langmuir, Gavin I. *Toward a Definition of Antisemitism.* Berkeley, 1990.

Laqueur, Walter. *Russia and Germany: A Century of Conflict.* London, 1965.

Lederhendler, Eli. *The Road to Modern Jewish Politics.* New York and Oxford, 1989.

Leontovich, V. V. *Istoriia liberalizma v Rossii 1762–1914.* Paris, 1980.

Leslie, R. F. *Reform and Insurrection in Russian Poland, 1856–1865.* London, 1963.

Levitats, Isaac, "Le-vikoret 'Sefer Ha-Kahal' shel Brafman," [The Authenticity of Brafman's Book of the Kahal], *Zion*, 3 (1938): 170–8.
   The Jewish Community in Russia, 1772–1844. New York, 1943.
   The Jewish Community in Russia, 1844–1917. Jerusalem, 1981.
Lincoln, W. Bruce. *The Great Reforms: Autocracy, Bureaucracy and the Politics of Change in Imperial Russia*. DeKalb, IL, 1990.
Longworth, Philip. *The Cossacks*. New York, Chicago and San Francisco, 1969.
Löwe, Heinz-Dietrich. *Antisemitismus und reaktionäre Utopie*. Hamburg, 1978.
Lozinskii, S. G. *Kazennye evreiskie uchilishcha*. Petrograd, 1920.
Lukashevich, Stephen. *Ivan Aksakov, 1823–1886: A Study in Russian Thought and Politics*. Cambridge, MA, 1965.
Luckyj, George. *Panteleimon Kulish: A Sketch of His Life and Times*. Boulder, CO, 1983.
Lvov-Rogachevsky, V. L. *A History of Russian Jewish Literature*. Arthur Levin, ed. and tr. Ann Arbor, 1976.
McLean, Hugh. *Nikolai Leskov: The Man and His Art*. Cambridge, MA, 1977.
   "Theodore the Christian Looks at Abraham the Hebrew: Leskov and the Jews," *California Slavic Studies*, 7 (Berkeley, Los Angeles, London, 1973): 65–98.
MacMaster, Robert E. *Danilevsky: A Russian Totalitarian Philosopher*. Cambridge, MA, 1967.
McReynolds, Louise. *The News under Russia's Old Regime: The Development of a Mass-Circulation Press*. Princeton, 1991.
Maor, Yitshak, "Ha-kruz ha-antishemi shel 'narodnaya volya'" [The Antisemitic Pronouncement of 'Narodnaia volia'"], *Zion*, 15 (1950): 150–5.
   She'elat ha-yehudim be-tenu'ah-liberalit ve-ha-mahapkhanit be-Rusia [The Jewish Question in the Liberal and Revolutionary Movement in Russia]. Jerusalem, 1979.
Markish, Simon. "Osip Rabinovic," *CMRS*, 21, 1–2 (1980): 5–30; 135–58.
   "*Voskhod* – Glavnyi zhurnal russkogo evreistva," *CMRS*, 28, 2 (1987): 173–81.
Mashkova, M. V., Sokurova, M. V. *Obshchie bibliografii russkikh periodicheskikh izdanii, 1703–1954*. Leningrad, 1956.
Mathes, William. "N. I. Pirogov and the Reform of University Government, 1856–1866," *SR*, 31, 1 (1972): 29–51.
Meyer, Michael A. *The Origins of the Modern Jew*. Detroit, 1967.
   Response to Modernity: A History of the Reform Movement in Judaism. New York and Oxford, 1988.
Mijakovs'kyi, Vlodymyr. *Unpublished and Forgotten Writings*. New York, 1984.
Miller, Forrestt A. *Dmitrii Miliutin and the Reform Era in Russia*. Nashville, TN, 1968.
Miron, Dan. *A Traveler Disguised: A Study in the Rise of Modern Yiddish Fiction in the Nineteenth Century*. New York, 1973.
Mishkinsky, Moshe. "Al emdata shel ha-tenu'ah ha-mahpekhanit ha-rusit le-gabei ha-yehudim bi-shnot ha-70 shel ha-me'ah ha-19" [The Attitude of the Russian Revolutionary Movement to the Jews in the 1870s], *He-avar*, 9 (1962): 38–66.

Morison, Gary Saul. "Dostoevsky's Anti-Semitism and the Critics: A Review Article," *Slavic and East European Journal*, 27, 3 (1983): 302–17.

Moronov, Boris. "The Russian Peasant Commune after the Reforms of the 1860s," *SR*, 44, 3 (1985): 438–67.

Mosse, George L. *The Crisis of German Ideology: Intellectual Origins of the Third Reich*. London, 1964.

Mosse, W. E., "Imperial Favorite: V. P. Meshchersky and the Grazhdanin," *SEER*, 59, 4 (1981): 529–47.

Nadel, B. "O stosunku Żydow na wilenszczyznie do powstania styczniowego," *BZIH*, 28 (1958): 39–63.

Nardova, V. A. *Gorodskoe samoupravlenie v Rossii v 60–kh – nachale 90–kh godov XIX veka. Pravitel'stvennaia politika*. Leningrad, 1984.

Nol'de, B. E. *Iurii Samarin i ego vremia*. Paris, 1926.

Ochs, Michael. "St Petersburg and the Jews of Russian Poland, 1862–1905." Unpublished doctoral dissertation, Harvard University, 1986.

Offord, D., "The Contribution of V. V. Bervi-Flerovsky to Russian Populism," *SEER*, 66 (1988): 236–51.

Ol'minskii, M. S. *Shchedrinskii slovar'*. Moscow, 1937.

Opalski, Magdalena. *The Jewish Tavern-Keeper and His Tavern in Nineteenth-Century Polish Literature*. Jerusalem, 1986.

Orbach, Alexander. *New Voices of Russian Jewry: A Study of the Russian-Jewish Press of Odessa in the Era of the Great Reforms, 1860–1871*. Leiden, 1980.

Owen, Thomas C. *Capitalism and Politics in Russia: A Social History of the Moscow Merchants, 1855–1905*. Cambridge, 1981.

"The Moscow Merchants and the Public Press, 1858–1868," *JGO*, 23, 1 (1975): 26–38.

Patterson, David, "A Growing Awareness of Self: Some Reflections on the Role of Nineteenth Century Hebrew Fiction," *Modern Judaism*, 3, 1 (1983): 23–37.

The Hebrew Novel in Czarist Russia. Edinburgh, 1964.

"Some Linguistic Aspects of the Nineteenth-Century Hebrew Novel," *Journal of Semitic Studies*, 7, 2 (1962): 307–24.

Perlmann, Moshe, "Notes on Razsvet, 1860–61," *Proceedings of the American Academy for Jewish Research*, 33 (1965): 21–50.

"Razsvet 1860–61, the Origins of the Russian-Jewish Press," *Jewish Social Studies*, 24 (1962): 162–82.

Petrovich, Michael B., "Russian Pan-Slavists and the Polish Uprising of 1863," *Harvard Slavic Studies*, 1 (1953): 219–47.

Pipes, Richard, "Russian Conservatism in the Second Half of the Nineteenth Century," *SR*, 30, 1 (1971): 121–8.

Poliakov, Leon. *The Aryan Myth: A History of Racist and Nationalist Ideas in Europe*. London, 1974.

Pomper, Philip. *Peter Lavrov and the Russian Revolutionary Movement*. Chicago, 1972.

Potichnyi, P. J., Aster, H. eds. *Ukrainian–Jewish Relations in Historical Perspective*. Edmonton, 1988.

Proskuriakova, N. A., "Razmeshchenie i struktura dvorianskogo zemlevladeniia evropeiskoi Rossii v kontse XIX – nachale XX veka," *Istoriia SSSR*, 1 (1973): 55–75.

Pulzer, Peter G. J. *The Rise of Political Antisemitism in Germany and Austria*. New York, 1964.

Raisin, Jacob S. *The Haskalah Movement in Russia*. Philadelphia, 1913.

Reitblat, A. I. *Ot Bovy k Bal'montu: Ocherki po istorii chteniia v Rossii vo vtoroi polovine XIX veka*. Moscow, 1991.

Riasanovsky, Nicholas V. *Russia and the West in the Teaching of the Slavophiles*, Cambridge, MA, 1952.

Rieber, Alfred. "The Formation of La Grande Société des Chemins de Fer Russes," *JGO*, 21, 3 (1973): 375–91.

Merchants and Entrepreneurs in Imperial Russia. Chapel Hill, NC, 1982.

"The Moscow Entrepreneurial Group: The Emergence of a New Form in Autocratic Politics," *JGO*, 25, 1–2 (1977): 1–20; 174–99.

Rieber, Alfred, ed. *The Politics of Autocracy: Letters of Alexander II to Prince A. I. Bariatinskii, 1855–1864*. Paris–The Hague, 1966.

Rogger, Hans J. *Jewish Policies and Right-Wing Politics In Imperial Russia*. London, 1986.

"Reflections on Russian Conservatism, 1861–1905," *JGO*, 14 (1966): 195–212.

Rossiia i evrei. Berlin, 1923.

Roth, Cecil. *A History of the Jews in England*. 3rd ed. Oxford, 1964.

Rozental,' V. N. "Pervoe otkrytoe vystuplenie russkikh liberalov v 1855–1856 gg.," *Istoriia SSSR*, 2 (1958): 113–30.

Ruckman, Jo Ann. *The Moscow Business Elite: A Social and Cultural Portrait of Two Generations, 1840–1905*. DeKalb, IL, 1984.

Rudnytsky, Ivan L. *Mykhaylo Drahomanov: A Symposium and Selected Writings*. New York, 1952.

Essays in Modern Ukrainian History. Ed. by Peter L. Rudnytsky. Cambridge, MA, 1987.

Russo, Paul A. "*Golos*, 1878–1883: Profile of a Russian Newspaper." Unpublished doctoral dissertation. Columbia University, 1974.

Ruud, Charles. *Fighting Words: Imperial Censorship and the Russian Press, 1804–1906*. Toronto, 1982.

Salmon, Josef. "The Emergence of a Jewish Nationalist Consciousness in Eastern Europe during the 1860s and 1870s," *AJS Review*, 16, 1–2 (1991): 107–32.

Sapir, Boris. "Jewish Socialists around 'Vpered'," *International Review of Social History*, 10 (1965): 365–84.

"Liberman et le socialisme russe," *International Review of Social History*, III (1938): 25–88.

Sapir, Boris, ed and introduction. "*Vpered!: 1873–1877: From the Archives of Valerian Nikolaevich Smirnov*. 2 vols. Dordrecht, 1970.

Saunders, David. *The Ukrainian Impact on Russian Culture, 1750–1850*. Edmonton, 1985.

Savchenko, Fedir. *Zaborona Ukrainstva 1876 r*. Kiev, 1930. Reprinted as *The Suppression of the Ukrainian Activities in 1876*. Munich, 1970.

Schiper, I. *Dzieje handlu żydowskiego na ziemiach polskich*. Warsaw, 1937.

Serbyn, Roman. "The *Sion-Osnova* Controversy of 1861–1862," in P. J. Potichnyi, H. Aster, eds. *Ukrainian–Jewish Relations in Historical Perspective*. Edmonton, 1988: 85–110.

"Ukrainian Writers on the Jewish Question: In the Wake of the *Illiustratsiia* Affair of 1858," *Nationalities Papers*, 9, 1 (1981): 99–104.

Shanin, Teodor. *Russia as a "Developing Society"*. London, 1985.

Shapiro, Leon. *The History of ORT*. New York, 1980.

Shatilov, T., "Vilenskii evreiskii uchitel'skii institut," *Evreiskaia letopis'*, 3 (1925): 106–09.

Shavit, David, "The Emergence of Jewish Public Libraries in Tsarist Russia," *The Journal of Library History*, 20, 3 (1985): 239–52.

Shochat, Azriel. *Mossad ha-rabanut mita'am be-Rusia* [*"The Crown Rabbinate" in Russia: A Chapter in the Cultural Struggle between Orthodox Jews and Maskilim*]. Haifa, 1975.

Shohetman, B., "Ha-rassvet ha-rishon" [The First Rassvet], *He-avar*, 2 (1954): 61–72.

Silber, Jacques, "Some Demographic Characteristics of the Jewish Population in Russia at the End of the Nineteenth Century," *JSS*, 42 (1980): 269–80.

Silberner, Edmund. *Sozialisten zur Judenfrage*. Berlin, 1962.

Sliozberg, G. B. *Dorevoliutsionnyi stroi Rossii*. Paris, 1933.

Dela minuvshikh dnei. 3 vols. Paris, 1933.

Baron G. O. Gintsburg, ego zhizn' i deiatel'nost'. Paris, 1933.

Slutsky, Yehuda. *Ha-itonut ha-yehudit-rusit ba-me'ah ha-tesha-esreh* [*The Russian Jewish Press in the Nineteenth Century*]. Jerusalem, 1970.

Smirnov, A. F. *Vosstanie 1863 goda v Litve i Belorussii*. Moscow, 1963.

Smith, Anthony D. *The Ethnic Origins of Nations*. Oxford, 1986.

Stanislawski, Michael. *For Whom Do I Toil? Judah Leib Gordon and the Crisis of Russian Jewry*. Oxford, 1988.

"Jewish Apostasy in Russia: A Tentative Typology," in Todd M. Endelman, ed. *Jewish Apostasy in the Modern World*. New York and London, 1987: 189–205.

Tsar Nicholas I and the Jews: The Transformation of Jewish Society in Russia, 1825–1855. Philadelphia, 1983.

Steinberg, Aaron, ed. *Simon Dubnow: The Man and His Work*. Paris, 1963.

Strelsky, Nikander. *Saltykov and the Russian Squire*. New York, 1940. (Reprint: New York, 1966).

Sumner, B. H. *Russia and the Balkans*. Oxford, 1937.

Thaden, Edward C. *Conservative Nationalism in Nineteenth-Century Russia*. Seattle, WA, 1964.

Thaden, Marianna Forster. *Russia's Western Borderlands, 1710–1870*. Princeton, 1984.

Timberlake, Charles E., ed. *Essays on Russian Liberalism*. Columbia, MO, 1972.

Tsimbaev, N. I. *I. S. Aksakov v obshchestvennoi zhizni poreformennoi Rossii*. Moscow, 1978.

Venturi, Franco. *Roots of Revolution*. London, 1952.

Walicki, Andrzej. *A History of Russian Thought from the Enlightenment to Marxism*. Oxford, 1980.

Whittaker, Cynthia H. *The Origins of Modern Russian Education: An Intellectual Biography of Count Sergei Uvarov, 1786–1855*. DeKalb, IL, 1984.

Yaney, George. *The Urge to Mobilize: Agrarian Reform in Russia, 1861–1930*. Urbana, IL, 1982.

Zaionchkovskii, P. A. *Kirillo-Mefodievskoe obshchestvo*. Moscow, 1959.
Otmena krepostnogo prava v Rossii. 3rd rev. ed. Moscow, 1968.
Rossiiskoe samoderzhavie v kontse XIX stoletiia (politicheskaia reaktsiia 80–kh – nachala 90–kh godov). Moscow, 1970. [*The Russian Autocracy under Alexander III*. David R. Jones, tr. and ed. Gulf Breeze, FL, 1976.]
Voennye reformy 1860–1870 godov v Rossii. Moscow, 1952.
Zakharova, L. G. "Samoderzhavie, biurokratiia i reformy 60kh XIX v. v Rossii," *Voprosy istorii*, 10 (October 1989): 3–24.
Zaslavskii, D., "Evrei v russkoi literature," *Evreiskaia letopis'*, 1 (1923): 59–86.
Zelnik, Reginald. "The Sunday School Movement in Russia, 1859–62," *Journal of Modern History*, 2 (1965): 151–70.
Zipperstein, Steven J. "Haskalah, Cultural Change, and Nineteenth-Century Russian Jewry: A Reassessment," *Journal of Jewish Studies*, 34, 2 (1983): 191–207.
    "Jewish Enlightenment in Odessa: Cultural Characteristics, 1794–1871," *Jewish Social Studies*, 44, 1 (1982): 19–36.
    The Jews of Odessa: A Cultural History, 1794–1881. Stanford, 1985.
    "Transforming the Heder: Maskilic Politics in Imperial Russia," in Ada Rapoport-Albert and Steven J. Zipperstein, eds., *Jewish History: Essays in Honour of Chimen Abramsky*. London, 1988: 87–111.
Zitron, Shmuel Leib. *Shtadlonim*. Warsaw, 1926.
Zolotonosov, Mikhail. "U istokov russkogo antisemitizma," forthcoming in *Vestnik Moskovskogo Evreiskogo Universiteta*.
Żydzi a powstanie styczniowe. Warsaw, 1963.

Index

Cambridge Russian, Soviet and Post-Soviet Studies